THE
"LOST" PENSIONS

Settled Accounts of the Act of 6 April 1838

Craig R. Scott, C.G.R.S.

Willow Bend Books
Lovettsville, Va.
1996

Willow Bend Books
39475 Tollhouse Road
Route 1, Box 15A
Lovettsville, Virginia 22080-9703

Visit our bookstore at:

http://www.mediasoft.net/ScottC

or e-mail us at willowbend@mediasoft.net

ISBN Number: 1-888265-03-5

Library of Congress Catalog Card Number: 95-62145

Introduction

This book is a finding aid to 144 boxes of payment records found in the series entitled "Settled Accounts for Payment of Accrued Pensions (Final Payments)" found in the Records of the Third Auditor, Records of the Accounting Officers of the Department of the Treasury, Record Group 217, at the National Archives in Washington, D.C. They represent accounts from the Revolutionary War, War of 1812, various Indian Wars before 1860, and the Mexican War. Many of the individuals identified in this list are not found in the various pension indexes that cover the period. This volume is designed to make access to these records possible.

They are arranged by account number for 105 boxes and in a variety of methods for 39 more boxes. They are settled accounts for pensions claimed under various acts prior to and including the provisions of the U.S. Congressional Act of April 6, 1838. This act permitted persons to claim from the Treasury of the United States pensions that had accrued to a pensioner and had not been claimed for over eight months. Prior to this act claims were made at the field pension office that served the pensioner. That is why these claims exist in a separate series of Treasury records. The accounts frequently show the pensioner's date and place of death and names of heirs and include supporting documents, such as proof of identity of claimant, pension certificates, power of attorney, and related correspondence. In some cases, where the payments were a result of Congressional action a copy of the bill is included in the file. Other types of claims are also included in this series. There are also some claims of special contractors for rations and forage.

The title "Lost Pensions" is a misnomer, these records were never lost. With a little digging anyone could have found them and at least two archivists in the National Archives knew exactly where they were when I first asked about them three years ago. But the records were so infrequently used that the dust on the top of the boxes had turned to that oily grime that sticks to everything, especially clothes. Moreover, the term pensions itself misleading and causes some researchers to expect the file to offer other types of records. To some, a "pension" is the pension application file. However, experienced researchers recognize that there are at least three types of available types of records relating to pension benefits: applications, ledgers and payments. These so-called "Lost" pension files, for the most part, are payments to pensioners or their heirs.

These payment records are not part of the collection of "Selected Final Payment Vouchers" that were the result of a five year project by the National Archives to extract genealogical material from the Revolutionary War payment vouchers. That project resulted in about 55,000 vouchers being separated from the pension accounts. It was while working in these records that I frequently found reference to the Act of 6 April 1838. I became intrigued because the payments under this Act were usually made years after the Revolutionary War soldier had died.

Not all of the records identified in this volume are final payments, some are five year half pay pensions. Widows of soldiers who died in the War of 1812, Indian Wars, and the Mexican War, in some cases, were entitled to payments every six months at half-pay, for a period of five years, if they did not remarry. Orphans under the age of sixteen collected, if the mother remarried. War of 1812 widow pensions have been located in another series of records in the National Archives and are currently being cataloged.

Craig R. Scott, C.G.R.S.
39475 Tollhouse Rd.
Route 1, Box 15A
Lovettsville, VA 22080

Acknowledgments

This book would not have been possible without the support of several different groups of people. First the National Archives staff, especially the members of the Military Reference Branch, without whose support this work would not have been possible. They were Michael E. Pilgrim, DeAnne Blanton, and Michael T. Meier. Bill Lind helped me start the project in the Revolutionary War pension payment records that brought these 1838 account records to my attention. In the final days of checking and rechecking John Vandereedt of the Civil Reference Branch, was most helpful. Second, the technicians on the National Archives staff who pulled the records for my use; especially Mary E. Linné. Third, James Pylant, editor of *American Genealogy Magazine*, who published a series of box lists of this material and provided national exposure to its availability. Fourth, and probably most important, those three people who continually seem to prod me on into creating these types of materials: Marty Hiatt, C.G.R.S.; Marie Varrellman Melchiori, C.G.R.S., C.G.L.; and Elizabeth Shown Mills, C.G., C.G.L.

Craig R. Scott, C.G.R.S.

How to use this book

Each entry contains the name of the individual, the pension office, the box at the National Archives in which the payment is contained, and the account number. In the case of some boxes from Connecticut, the files are in alphabetical order; in some boxes from Virginia, the boxes are arranged by year. However, once you have the box in hand, the numbering system is obvious.

The use of the words "card" and "slip" indicates that the pension payment voucher itself is not located in this series. Usually these placeholders indicate that the records were checked out and never returned. Efforts are on-going by the compiler to determine the disposition of these missing records. These entries are included in this book in order to establish that, at one time, there were records concerning the pensions of these individuals. Cards may have information about dates of death and other summary information. Slips rarely have any information on them, except the name of the individual.

There are multiple entries for many pensioners. This is especially true for widows pensions that are included in this series. It is important to examine all of the documents associated with each pensioner.

How to obtain copies of records

Copies of the records listed in this volume may be obtained from the compiler for a fee. At the time of publication the cost is $10.00 for the first pension and $5.00 for each additional pension. A self-addressed stamped envelope (SASE) with sufficient postage to cover 2 ounces is required for each pension request. Payment is in U.S. funds and is due in advance. This pricing is subject to change without notice.

A portion of the research fee and royalties from this book will be donated to the Malcolm H. Stern–NARA Gift Fund for microfilming of these records so that they can be made available to a wider audience. Readers are invited to contact the Federation of Genealogical Societies for information on this invaluable program.

Abbreviations

—	information not provided
a/o	administrator of
AGO	Adjutant General's Office
Arty	Artillery
Cav.	Cavalry
c/o	children of
comm/o	committee of
e/o	executor of
est/o	estate of
g/o	guardian of
h/o	heir of
Inf.	Infantry
lr/o	legal representative of
O.T.	Oregon Territory
over/o	overseer of
PA	Pension Agent
s/o	sister of
SpC	Special Contractor
w/o	widow of
W.T.	Washington Territory
V#	voucher number
#	account number
QMC	Quartermaster Corps
#F	folder number

The Act of 6 April 1838

Chap. LVI. — *An Act directing the transfer of money remaining unclaimed by certain pensioners, and authorizing the payment of the same at the Treasury of the United States.*

Be it enacted by the Senate and House of Representatives of the United States of America in Congress assembled, That all money which has been, or may hereafter be, transmitted to the agents for paying pensions, which may have remained, or may hereafter remain, in the hands of said agents unclaimed by any pensioner or pensioners for the term of eight months after the same may have or may become due and payable shall be transferred to the Treasury of the United States; and that all pensions unclaimed, as aforesaid, shall be thereafter payable only at the Treasury of the United States, and out of any money not otherwise appropriated.

—The Public Statutes at Large of the United States of America, From the Organizations of the Government in 1789, to March 3, 1845, Volume 5.

This book is dedicated to the Staff of the National Archives, who kept these records safe, and never lost them; not once.

A

Abbey, Horace B., Albany, N.Y., 73, #12872

Abbey, Horace B., Albany, N.Y., 76, #13951

Abbey, Horace B., Pittsburgh, Pa., 95, #1254

Abbey, Horace B., w/o, Pittsburgh, Pa., 109, #10411

Abbott, Andrew, w/o, Mich., 125, #1607

Abbott, Caleb, c/o, Mass., 50, #5613

Abbott, Elias, c/o, Boston, Mass., 122, #8672

Abbott, Elias, c/o, Concord, N.H., 105, #8142

Abbott, Ezra, w/o, Concord, N.H., 97, #2377

Abbott, John, w/o, N.J., 76, #13799

Abbott, Moses, a/o, Concord, N.H., 113, #1394

Abbott, William, Miss., 88, #17928

Abel, Eliza, a/o, Rutland, Vt., 141, #2061

Abel, Elizabeth, a/o, Morganton, N.C., 125, #2056

Abercrombie, James, c/o, Mass., 47, #5000

Abney, Lemon, g/o c/o, N.C., 127, #4310

Abney, William, a/o, Ill., 71, #12288

Abrams, Hetty, New York City, 140, #1088

Abrey, Rhody, Ill., 120, #6169

Abshine, Abraham, Va., 74, #13133

Abshire, Abraham, Va., 1, #17881

Ackaberget (or Eiklberger), David, Philadelphia, Pa., 70, #12148

Acker, Mary, N.Y., 80, #14845

Acker, Mary, a/o, Nashville, Tenn., 120, #6333

Acker, Peter, c/o, New York City, 116, #3172

Ackerman, Christopher, w/o, Pittsburgh, Pa., 119, #5422

Ackerman, John, Ohio, 80, #14901

Ackerson, Cornelius, Albany, N.Y., 71, #12443

Ackerson, Mary, Albany, N.Y., 127, #4882

Ackley, Mehitable, c/o, Conn., 30, #13231

Ackley, Mehitable, c/o, Conn., 63, #8914

Ackley, Simeon, w/o, Mass., 50, #5513

Acock, Robert, a/o, Ky., 133, #212

Acton, Smallwood, w/o, Ky., 91, #19099

Adams, Anna, c/o, Albany, N.Y., 134, #716

Adams, Asa, w/o, Boston, Mass., 66, #10164

Adams, David, Miss., 55, #6944

Adams, David, Miss., 62, #8803

Adams, David, Ohio, 89, #18378

Adams, Elijah, w/o, Albany, N.Y., 78, #14397

Adams, Hannah, Albany, N.Y., 106, #8759

Adams, Hannah, a/o, New York City, 130, #7350

Adams, Pvt. Henry, w/o, N.C. Militia, 112, #1001

Adams, Jesse, w/o, Nashville, Tenn., 73, #12899

Adams, Joseph, Maine, 96, #1537

Adams, Joseph, a/o, E. Fla., 70, #12090

Adams, Levi, Albany, N.Y., 63, #9044

Adams, Lydia, a/o, New York City, 110, #281

Adams, Mary, a/o, Albany, N.Y., 122, #8566

Adams, Mary, c/o, Mass., 109, #10415

Adams, Molly, a/o, Concord, N.H., 123, #9239

Adams, Patty, Vt., 63, #9058

Adams, Rebecca, a/o, Richmond, Va., 100, #4281

Adams, Sarah, e/o, S.C., 117, #4232

Adams, Unicy, Nashville, Tenn., 108, #10308

Adams, William, Pittsburgh, Pa., 45, #4622

Adams, William, c/o, Albany, N.Y., 134, #717

Adams, William, c/o, Pittsburgh, Pa., 116, #3087

Adams, William, g/o, Pittsburgh, Pa., 80, #14912

Adcock, Joseph, c/o, Ky., 132, #9580

Adcock, Joseph, g/o c/o, Ky., 128, #5051

Adcock, Joshua, N.C., 67, #10545

Adcock, Thomas, c/o, E. Tenn., 58, #7765

Addington, William, Ga., 100, #4422, card

Addington, William, w/o, Ga., 1, #4422

Addis, Richard, c/o, S.C., 122, #8614

Addison, Jacob, Ohio, 46, #4811

Addoms, Jonas, c/o, New York City, 80, #14938

Aderson, Leonard, w/o, Ky., 80, #14791

Adington, William, Ga., 65, #9749

Adkins, Azubak, a/o, Mass., 124, #777

Adkins, Stephen, c/o, D.C., 91, #19328

Adlurn, John, D.C., 83, #15706, card

Agee, Jacob, —, 124, #480, card

Aiken, Dyce, Mo., 136, #3009

Aiken, Hannah, S.C., 113, #1710, card

Aiken, Hannah, a/o, S.C., 1, #1710

Aiken, Susannah, Bellows Falls, Vt., 75, #13647

Aiken, William, w/o, Charleston, S.C., 1, #7684

Aikens, Nathaniel, w/o, Albany, N.Y., 49, #5413

Aikins, Mary, Albany, N.Y., 78, #14251

Ailling, Phebe, a/o c/o, Conn., 54, #6700

Akerd, Andrew, Richmond, Va., 56, #7424

Akerd, Andrew, Va., 83, #15852

Akers, Andrew, Richmond, Va.,
69, #10855
Akin, James, Ga., 46, #4743
Akin (or Aiken), William, S.C.,
105, #7684, card
Akin, William, S.C., 81,
#15137
Albee, Asa, w/o, Mass., 122,
#8925, card
Albertson, Early, Nashville,
Tenn., 77, #14188
Albertson, Early, Nashville,
Tenn., 80, #14894
Albertson, Early, Nashville,
Tenn., 90, #18598
Albertson, Early, w/o,
Nashville, Tenn., 96,
#1849
Alburtis, Capt. William, c/o, 2nd
Inf., 110, #11160
Alburtis, Capt. William, w/o,
2nd Inf., 105, #8130
Alburtis, Capt. William, w/o,
2nd Inf., 107, #8957
Alburtis, Capt. William, c/o, 2nd
Inf., 111, #653
Alburtis, Capt. William, w/o,
2nd Inf., 103, #6485
Alburtis, Capt. William, w/o,
2nd Inf., 104, #7291
Alburtius, Capt. William, w/o,
2nd Inf., 101, #5381
Alburtius, Capt. William, w/o,
2nd Inf., 101, #4991
Alchich, Noah, Bellows Falls,
Vt., 63, #8967
Alden, Elijah, Mass., 63, #9062
Alden, Roger, N.Y., 39, #3003
Alder, James L., e/o, Md., 121,
#8007
Aldrich, Cable, w/o, Concord,
N.H., 115, #2754

Aldrich, Oliver, R.I., 54, #6661
Aldrich, Polly, a/o, Albany,
N.Y., 134, #1491
Aldridge, John, a/o, Ind., 91,
#19132
Aleschite, John C., Richmond,
Va., 57, #7503
Alexander, Dan, Jackson, Tenn.,
43, #3926
Alexander, Dan, Jackson, Tenn.,
92, #187
Alexander, Elijah, w/o, Artillery,
72, #12658
Alexander, Eliphaz, c/o, Albany,
N.Y., 115, #2992
Alexander (now Cox), Eliza,
Cincinnati, Ohio, 121,
#7600
Alexander, Elizabeth,
Philadelphia, Pa., 84,
#16121
Alexander, Elizabeth,
Philadelphia, Pa., 102,
#5573
Alexander, George, Mobile,
Ala., 60, #8286
Alexander, George, Mobile,
Ala., 76, #13826
Alexander, George, Mobile,
Ala., 84, #15942
Alexander, Ian, Jackson, Tenn.,
55, #6973
Alexander, Isaac, Ky., 39, #3050
Alexander, Isaac, w/o, Ky., 103,
#6896
Alexander, Jeremiah, Huntsville,
Ala., 64, #9681
Alexander, Jeremiah,
Tuscaloosa, Ala., 73,
#12756
Alexander, John, Ind., 48,
#5046

Alexander, John, Ky., 41, #3461

Alexander, Jonathan S., Albany, N.Y., 44, #4407

Alexander, Martha, Albany, N.Y., 106, #8652

Alexander, Nathan, —, 123, #9951, slip

Alexander, Rhoda, c/o, N.C., 106, #8426

Alexander, Robert, New York City, 129, #6485

Alexander, Robert, Wheeling, Va., 39, #3136

Alexander, Samuel, w/o, Fayetteville, N.C., 108, #10382

Alexander, Sarah, a/o, Pittsburgh, Pa., 134, #1343

Alexander, Silas, Albany, N.Y., 43, #4010

Alexander, William, —, 78, #14488, card

Alexander, William, c/o, N.C., 1, #14488

Alexander, William, c/o, Tenn., 1, #9951

Alexander, Rebecca, Jackson, Miss., 130, between #8038 and #8046]

Alford, Asahel, a/o, Albany, N.Y., 125, #2433

Alfred, John, e/o, Nashville, Tenn., 86, #17258

Alfred, Matilda, Ga., 121, #7014

Algar Sr., Conrad, —, 40, #3200, card

Alger, Elijah, a/o, Albany, N.Y., 70, #12103

Alinger, Catharine, Indianapolis, Ind., 125, #2189

Alinger, Catharine, Indianapolis, Ind., 124, #1301

Allen, Alathea, Pulaski, Tenn., 124, #504

Allen, Alathea, Pulaski, Tenn., 126, #3921

Allen, Benjamin, a/o, Albany, N.Y., 94, #284

Allen, Catherine, Va., 78, #14354

Allen, Charles, —, 99, #3212, slip

Allen, Charles, —, 97, #2341, slip

Allen, Charles, Va., 1, #2341

Allen, Cyrus, Montpelier, Vt., 101, #5006 V#5

Allen, David, w/o, Albany, N.Y., 69, #10825

Allen, David H., c/o, Mo., 125, #1626

Allen, Elihsa, w/o, Pittsburgh, Pa., 85, #16457

Allen, Elijah, Albany, N.Y., 57, #7471

Allen, Elijah, Albany, N.Y., 46, #4842

Allen, Fannie, a/o, Richmond, Va., 135, #2411

Allen, Hannah, N.J., 44, #4416

Allen, Ira, Mich., 118, #4599

Allen, Israel, c/o, Mass., 61, #8394

Allen, Jacob, Mass., 42, #3689

Allen, Jacob, c/o, Mass., 82, #15349

Allen, Jane, Richmond, Va., 36A, #F3 V1

Allen, Joel, c/o, Albany, N.Y., 131, #8290

Allen, John, a/o, Ohio, 100, #3891

Allen, John, w/o, Maine, 64, #9158

Allen, Lydia, a/o, Vt., 1, #10603

Allen, Moses, c/o, Richmond, Va., 133, #537

Allen, Moses, w/o, N.J., 1, #13050

Allen, Peter T., Richmond, Va., 138, #4841

Allen, Philip, Albany, N.Y., 107, #9275

Allen, R., —, 118, #4710, slip

Allen, Rasmus D., Cleveland, Ohio, 130, #7741

Allen, Richard, —, 92, #19840, card

Allen, Richard, N.J., 55, #7220

Allen, Richard, c/o, —, 92, #19567, card

Allen, Richard, c/o, —, 92, #19688, card

Allen, Richard, c/o, —, 92, #215, card

Allen, Richard, c/o, N.C., 1, #19840

Allen, Richard, c/o, N.C., 1, #215

Allen, Richard, c/o, N.C., 1, #19688

Allen, Richard, c/o, N.C., 1, #19567

Allen, William, —, 92, #19840, card

Allen, William, Indianapolis, Ind., 143, #6519

Allex, Isiah, W. Tenn., 83, #15751, card

Alley, Isaiah, a/o, Nashville, Tenn., 1, #15751

Alley, Samuel, Ind., 46, #4764

Alley, Samuel, Ind., 66, #10181

Alley, Samuel, w/o, Ind., 121, #7139

Allis, Stephen, Mass., 39, #3095

Allison, George, c/o, Wheeling, Va., 64, #9182

Allison, James, N.C., 74, #13293, card

Allison, James, w/o, N.C., 1, #13293

Allison, Mary, a/o, Cincinnati, Ohio, 130, #7273

Allmond, Winefred, Fayetteville, N.C., 100, #3962

Allred Sr., Elias, Ga., 46, #4673

Allyn, Timothy, lr/o, Boston, Mass., 64, #9125

Almon, Thomas, Indianapolis, Ind., 142, #3593

Almond, John, a/o, Richmond, Va., 135, #1849

Almond, William, c/o, Ohio, 64, #9497

Alsebrook, Jesse, Mobile, Ala., 51, #6048

Alspack, Michael, w/o, Cincinnati, Ohio, 118, #4882

Alstoll, John, w/o, Ind., 60, #8303

Alton, Sarah, Charleston, S.C., 105, #8025

Alton, Sylvester, Fort Gibson, Ark., 113, #1693

Alton, Sylvester, Mo., 105, #8351

Altorn, Sarah, c/o, S.C., 136, #2829

Alvis, John, w/o, Ky., 104, #7339

Alvord, Nancy, Cleveland, Ohio, 134, #1314
Alvord, Phineas, Windsor, Vt., 60, #8225, card
Alvord, Phineas, w/o, Vt., 1, #8225
Alwood, Abraham, D.C., 114, #1937
Alworth, James, Pittsburgh, Pa., 80, #14863
Ambler, Abigail, Poultney, Vt., 98, #2550
Ames, Margaret, Ohio, 79, #14658
Ames, Milo, Pittsburgh, Pa., 121, #7960
Ames, Milo, Pittsburgh, Pa., 129, #6138
Ames, Milo, Pittsburgh, Pa., 136, #2850
Ames, Nathaniel, Wisc., 127, #4789
Amet, Anthony, Ky., 39, #3149
Amet, Anthony, Ky., 61, #8584
Amicks, Matthew, c/o, Ky., 1, #4362
Ammerman, Albert, Ill., 58, #7854
Ammin, Samuel, c/o, N.J., 117, #3919
Ammon, Christopher, Richmond, Va., 56, #7405
Ammon, Christopher, Richmond, Va., 62, #8744
Ammon, Christopher, Richmond, Va., 39, #3027
Ammon, Christopher, Va., 74, #13398
Ammon, Christopher, e/o, Va., 86, #16935
Ammonet, Phebe, Richmond, Va., 137, #4327

Ammonett, Phebe, Richmond, Va., 131, #8118
Ammons, Jane, Pittsburgh, Pa., 123, #9621
Amos, John, g/o c/o, Knoxville, Tenn., 131, #8897
Amos, Martin, Ohio, 41, #3469
Amoss, Martin, Ohio, 46, #4657
Amsden, Noah, e/o, Albany, N.Y., 122, #8671
Amy, William, c/o, Burlington, Vt., 105, #8173
Amy, William, c/o, Poultney, Vt., 98, #2851
Amy, William, c/o, Portsmouth, Vt., 103, #6575
Anderman, Maria, New York City, 115, #2873
Andermann, Maria, D.C., 125, #1987
Andermann, Maria, D.C., 131, #8779
Andermann, Maria, D.C., 135, #2350
Anders, James, N.C., 54, #6846
Anderson, Alexander, Nashville, Tenn., 64, #9309
Anderson, Bailey, —, 110, #11084, card
Anderson, Bailey, —, 126, #3143, card
Anderson, Bailey, c/o, La., 1, #3143
Anderson, Charles, a/o, New York City, 92, #19716
Anderson, Daniel, c/o, Va., 73, #12991
Anderson, David, Mass., 39, #3096
Anderson, Elizabeth, Richmond, Va., 131, #8283

Anderson, Enoch, Ga., 136,
#2921
Anderson, Isaac, w/o, Ohio, 67,
#10332
Anderson, James, c/o, Ky., 55,
#7089
Anderson, James, w/o, Mass.,
40, #3238
Anderson, James, w/o,
Philadelphia, Pa., 97,
#1896
Anderson, Capt. James, w/o, 2nd
Inf., 103, #6371
Anderson, Capt. James W., w/o,
2nd Inf., 115, #2510
Anderson, Capt. James W., w/o,
2nd Inf., 104, #7260
Anderson, Capt. James W., w/o,
2nd Inf., 106, #8526
Anderson, Capt. James W., w/o,
2nd Inf., 107, #9351
Anderson, Capt. James W., w/o,
2nd Inf., 111, #730
Anderson, Capt. James W., w/o,
3rd Inf., 108, #9896
Anderson, John, Pittsburgh, Pa.,
45, #4560
Anderson, John, e/o, N.C., 1,
#5004
Anderson, John, w/o, Ky., 49,
#5441
Anderson, Jordan, c/o,
Richmond, Va., 112, #833
Anderson, Joseph, w/o, Albany,
N.Y., 90, #18625
Anderson, Joseph, w/o, D.C.,
85, #16463
Anderson, Lucy, Richmond, Va.,
63, #9057
Anderson, Margery, a/o,
Wheeling, Va., 140, #801

Anderson, Maria, D.C., 121,
#7395
Anderson, Martha, Va., 74,
#13093
Anderson, Pinckney, Little
Rock, Ark., 136, #3548
Anderson, Pinkney, Ark., 119,
#5375
Anderson, Ruth, e/o, R.I., 110,
#288
Anderson, Thomas, S.C., 51,
#5950
Anderson, William, D.C., 143,
#7517
Anderson, William, Mo., 140,
#19
Anderson, William, Mo., 141,
#2467
Anderson, William C., PA, St.
Louis, Mo., 118, #5086
Andness, Evin, Tallahassee,
Fla., 53, #6437
Andreas, Cynthia, c/o, Conn.,
136, #2513
Andress, Even, Fla., 88, #18093
Andress, Evin, E. Fla., 90,
#18652
Andress, Evin, St. Augustine,
Fla., 94, #332
Andrew, John, Philadelphia, Pa.,
143, #6458
Andrew, Varney, Va., 84,
#16113
Andrews (or Andruss), Abner,
e/o, Conn., 38, #F1826
Andrews, Athelstan, Jackson,
Tenn., 45, #4563
Andrews, Betty, a/o, Albany,
N.Y., 69, #10980
Andrews, Chester G., g/o c/o,
Mich., 126, #3436

Andrews, Chester G., g/o c/o, Mich., 126, #3443

Andrews, Ebenezer, a/o, Vt., 88, #17743

Andrews, Elkanah, Richmond, Va., 63, #9089

Andrews, Elkanah, c/o, Va., 121, #7592

Andrews, Ephraim, Maine, 41, #3420

Andrews, Ephriam, Maine, 92, #19890

Andrews, Lt. George T., 3rd Artillery, 120, #6596, Special

Andrews, Hugh, N.C., 109, #10799

Andrews, Isaac, N.J., 119, #5639

Andrews, Isham, Va., 71, #12384

Andrews, Nathaniel, w/o, Pittsburgh, Pa., 122, #8446

Andrews, Phineas, a/o, Philadelphia, Pa., 119, #5392

Andrews, Samuel, Albany, N.Y., 127, #4520

Andrews, Samuel, w/o, Albany, N.Y., 85, #16608

Andrews, Samuel, w/o, Albany, N.Y., 123, #9585

Andrews, Stephen, w/o, Albany, N.Y., 120, #6255

Andrews, Thomas, Richmond, Va., 62, #8730

Andrews, Thomas, Richmond, Va., 41, #3510

Andrews, Thomas, Va., 80, #14847

Andrews, Varney, Va., 66, #10108

Andrews, Varney, Va., 90, #18575

Andrews, William, Mass., 86, #16872

Andrews, William, a/o, Va., 77, #14102

Andrus, Nathan, Pa., 66, #10078

Angel, Daniel, Albany, N.Y., 89, #18480

Angel, Daniel, c/o, Albany, N.Y., 90, #18557

Anger, Esther, a/o, Albany, N.Y., 114, #2411

Angevine, Stephen, Albany, N.Y., 41, #3439

Angling, John, w/o, Nashville, Tenn., 87, #17443

Annabel, Edward, c/o, Albany, N.Y., 115, #2542

Annable, Edward, c/o, Albany, N.Y., 116, #3314

Annable, Edward, c/o, Albany, N.Y., 116, #3618

Annable, Edward, c/o, Albany, N.Y., 116, #3690

Annis, Michael, c/o, Concord, N.H., 51, #6061

Annis, Peggy, c/o, Va., 1, #3530

Ansltd, Henry, N.Y., 54, #6691, card

Anson, Surgeon W. H. I., Va. Vols., 120, #6598B, Special

Anspack, Philip, —, 102, #6087, slip

Ansted, Thomas, Mo., 105, #8047

Anthony, John, c/o, Albany, N.Y., 89, #18514

Anthony, Margaret, c/o, R.I., 108, #10275

Anthony, Mary, S.C., 64, #9311

Anthony, Philip, w/o, Jackson, Tenn., 51, #6052

Antress, George, New York City, 140, #326

Anucks, Matthew, Ky., 117, #4364, card

Apgar, Conrad, N.J., 1, #3200

Apple, Barthalomew, N.J., 52, #6124

Apple, Daniel, N.C., 39, #2991

Apple, Henry, a/o, Albany, N.Y., 124, #1563

Apple, Henry, c/o, Albany, N.Y., 125, #1715

Applegate, Garrett, Ind., 121, #6925, card

Applegate, Garrett, a/o, Ind., 1, #6925

Applegate, Rhoda, c/o, N.J., 130, #7607

Applegate (now Ayers), Mary, Mo., 112, #1026

Arbogast, Adam, Richmond, Va., 57, #7575

Arbogast, Adam, Richmond, Va., 103, #6763

Arbogast, Adam, Richmond, Va., 96, #1667

Arbogast, Adam, Va., 66, #10152

Arbogast, Adam, Va., 76, #13757

Arbogast, Adam, Va., 86, #16780

Arbogest, Adam, Richmond, Va., 63, #8984

Archer, Edwin C., c/o, Richmond, Va., 115, #2504

Archer, Moses, Ky., 54, #6695

Archer, Moses, Mo., 81, #15124

Ard, Abigail, Fla., 90, #18864

Armans, Charity, c/o, Ky., 129, #6180

Armbruster, Matthias, g/o c/o, D.C., 139, #7123

Armitage, William, D.C., 94, #337

Armstead, Col. W. K., 3rd Inf., 120, #6641, card

Armstrong, Abel, Ohio, 62, #8868, card

Armstrong, Abel, c/o, Ohio, 1, #8868

Armstrong, Benjamin, N.Y., 82, #15345

Armstrong, Dyer, g/o c/o, Conn., 37, #F1820

Armstrong, George, e/o, N.J., 114, #2258

Armstrong, J. S., Cincinnati, Ohio, 85, #16697, Agent

Armstrong, John, Albany, N.Y., 51, #5915

Armstrong, John, Albany, N.Y., 62, #8849

Armstrong, John, New York City, 71, #12357

Armstrong, John, a/o, Richmond, Va., 103, #6562

Armstrong, John, e/o, New York City, 100, #3974

Armstrong, Joseph, c/o, Philadelphia, Pa., 137, #4082

Armstrong, Mathew, w/o, Fayetteville, N.C., 1, #4147

Armstrong, Nanthan, Albany, N.Y., 46, #4767

Armstrong, Sarah, a/o, Ky., 135, #1676

Armstrong, William, Mo., 58, #7916

Armstrong, William, Richmond,
Va., 1, #2712
Armstrong, William, Richmond,
Va., 63, #8905
Armstrong, William, Richmond,
Va., 102, #5400
Armstrong, William, Richmond,
Va., 52, #6254
Armstrong, William, a/o,
Richmond, Va., 1, #2002
Arnell, William, e/o, Del., 134,
#970
Arno, Miriam, c/o, Maine, 138,
#4809
Arnold, Abraham, c/o,
Philadelphia, Pa., 64,
#9262
Arnold, Anna, c/o, R.I., 52,
#6128
Arnold, Benedict, g/o c/o,
Conn., 37, #F1820
Arnold, Edward, w/o, Albany,
N.Y., 95, #837
Arnold, Hezekiah, N.C., 49,
#5283
Arnold, Israel, w/o, R.I., 80,
#14766
Arnold, James, Ky., 41, #3363
Arnold, James, Ky., 54, #6740
Arnold, Joseph, Philadelphia,
Pa., 125, #1804
Arnold, Lindsey, a/o, N.C., 111,
#610
Arnold, Matthew, N.C., 43,
#4147, card
Arnold, Remington, R.I., 63,
#9037
Arnold, Remington, c/o, R.I.,
76, #13876
Arnold, Sarah, Conn., 30, #3576
Arnold, Solomon, w/o, N.C., 96,
#1543

Arnold, Sylrania, Hartford,
Conn., 131, #8543
Arnold, Sylvania, Conn., 131,
#8255
Arnold, Thomas, Mobile, Ala.,
64, #9296
Arnold, William, e/o, R.I., 70,
#12130
Arnold, Ziba, Ky., 42, #3561
Arnold, Ziba, Ky., 72, #12649
Arnold, Ziba, Ky., 80, #14815
Arrant, Peter, Charleston, S.C.,
76, #13909
Arrington, Adler, Richmond,
Va., 76, #13907
Arrington, Adler, Richmond,
Va., 43, #4084
Arrington, Samuel, Richmond,
Va., 102, #5715
Arrowsmith, Levina, Va., 46,
#4670
Arter, Levi, Mo., 131, #8334
Arterburn, James P., Jonesboro,
Tenn., 134, #827
Arthur, James, —, 134, #1440,
card
Arthur, James, c/o, Cincinnati,
Ohio, 1, #1140
Arthur, Richard, w/o, N.C., 45,
#4516
Arthur, Sally, Richmond, Va.,
95, #1059
Arthur, Sally, Richmond, Va.,
100, #3803
Arthur, William, Richmond, Va.,
123, #136
Arthur (now Manor), Nancy M.,
Ind., 109, #10618
Asbury, Henry, Ky., 78, #14490
Ashbrook, Thomas, Ind., 48,
#5076

Ashburn, Luke, w/o, Richmond, Va., 49, #5261

Ashcroft, Daniel, Ill., 88, #17905

Ashlock, Jesse, Nashville, Tenn., 84, #16120

Ashlock, Jesse, Nashville, Tenn., 87, #17648

Ashlock, Jesse, Nashville, Tenn., 43, #3834

Ashlock, Jesse, W. Tenn., 55, #7148

Ashlock, Jesse, W. Tenn., 61, #8416

Ashmore, David, Ky., 124, #547

Ashmore, David, Ky., 130, #7815

Ashton, John, Albany, N.Y., 105, #7687

Ashworth, Dixon, Mo., 108, #10263

Ashworth, Lucy, Richmond, Va., 129, #6439

Ashworth, Lucy, Richmond, Va., 134, #1408

Askew, William, N.C., 40, #3327

Askew, William, N.C., 46, #4742

Aslin, Martha, Tenn., 123, #9165

Atchison, James, Conn., 122, #8070

Atchison, James, Conn., 122, #8402

Atherton, Peter, Ill., 133, #628

Atherton, Thomas, a/o, Mass., 123, #9649

Atilla, Francis, Ky., 141, #3427

Atkins, David, e/o, Conn., 38, #F1845

Atkinson, Daniel, w/o, Va., 83, #15771

Atkinson, John, Mass., 43, #4086

Atkinson, Mary, Nashville, Tenn., 72, #12625

Atkinson, Reuben, Richmond, Va., 47, #4875

Atkinson, Reuben, a/o, Richmond, Va., 99, #3733

Atkinson, Richard, Wheeling, Va., 138, #5290

Atwater, Hannah, e/o, Albany, N.Y., 79, #14549

Atwater, Ichabod, w/o, Mass., 107, #8965

Atwell, Charles, Richmond, Va., 107, #9463

Atwell, Samuel, w/o, Conn., 116, #3600

Atwood, Elizabeth, Vt., 132, #8995, card

Atwood, Elizabeth, a/o, Burlington, Vt., 1, #8995

Atwood, Jabez, New York City, 44, #4349

Atwood, Jesse, w/o, Albany, N.Y., 51, #6031

Atwood, Ruth, a/o c/o, Mass., 129, #6287

Atwood, Ruth, c/o, Mass., 128, #5987

Augun, Felix, w/o, Albany, N.Y., 64, #9252

Aukerman, Susannah, Pittsburgh, Pa., 115, #2692

Aull, Aquilla B., Calif., 121, #7861

Aument, Amos, Philadelphia, Pa., 143, #7288

Austin, Abrather, Burlington, Vt., 43, #4055

Austin, Anne, Richmond, Va.,
103, #6706
Austin, Benjamin, N.C., 76,
#13778
Austin, Eusebius, c/o, Albany,
N.Y., 58, #7802
Austin, Horace, Chicago, Ill.,
142, #4522
Austin, Isaiah, a/o, Richmond,
Va., 109, #10675
Austin, James G., Ga., 135,
#2104
Austin, Jeremiah, Burlington,
Vt., 104, #7490
Austin, Noah, Albany, N.Y.,
112, #890
Austin, Noah, Albany, N.Y.,
117, #4557
Austin, Priscilla, Philadelphia,
Pa., 72, #12715
Austin, Stephen, Philadelphia,
Pa., 64, #9217
Austin, Susannah, a/o, Conn.,
113, #1865
Averill, Ebenezer, Albany, N.Y.,
45, #4576
Averill, Thomas, Albany, N.Y.,
64, #9201
Avery, Abel, Conn., 53, #6489
Avery, Benjamin, a/o, Albany,
N.Y., 95, #1276
Avery, Ebenezer, e/o, Conn., 38,
#F1828
Avery, Ezekiel, Philadelphia,
Pa., 75, #13712
Avery, Jacob, w/o, Albany,
N.Y., 139, #7099
Avery, Mary, Conn., 63, #8972
Avery, Mary, a/o, Conn., 119,
#5636
Axington, Adler, Richmond,
Va., 60, #8270

Aycock, Sarah, N.C., 77,
#14109
Ayers, Elizabeth, Baltimore,
Md., 129, #6523
Ayers, Thomas J., S.C., 129,
#6678
Aylor, Jacob, Richmond, Va.,
47, #5030
Ayres, Elihu, w/o, Richmond,
Va., 94, #661
Ayres, Hiram, Mo., 114, #2001
Ayres, Hiram, Mo., 117, #4029
Ayres, Hiram, Mo., 117, #4373
Ayres, Julia, New York City,
102, #6052 V

B

Babb, Lemuel, w/o, Va. Milita,
94, #693
Babb Sr., Seth, w/o, Jonesboro,
Tenn., 108, #10018
Babbit, Joy, Albany, N.Y., 111,
#446, card
Babbitt, Joy, Albany, N.Y., 1,
#446
Babcock, Beriah, Conn., 30,
#85
Babcock, Jesse, e/o, R.I., 67,
#10326
Babcock, Primus, Conn., 30, #1
Babel (formerly Dorn),
Margaretta, D.C., 129,
#6154
Baber, Milley, c/o, Ga., 100,
#3802
Bachelor, Mary, Mass., 113,
#1706
Backus, Josiah, Ohio, 53, #6374
Backus, Samuel, Pittsburgh, Pa.,
113, #1384

Backus, Samuel, c/o, Cleveland, Ohio, 127, #4410

Bacon, Eleanor, c/o, Conn., 30, #679

Bacon, Elijah, c/o, Albany, N.Y., 118, #4576

Bacon, Samuel, w/o, Albany, N.Y., 84, #16264

Bada, Rosina, c/o, D.C., 131, #8094

Bader, Rosine, D.C., 122, #8308

Badget, William, N.C., 111, #485

Badget, William, N.C., 98, #3027

Badget, William, Fayetteville, N.C., 105, #7762 V#1

Badgett, William, N.C., 122, #8703

Baggett, James, c/o, Nashville, Tenn., 73, #12992

Bagley, Asher, Ark., 65, #10037

Bagley, Azor, w/o, Ohio, 45, #4487

Bagley, Olive, a/o, Vt., 65, #9726

Bagwell, Frederick, Mobile, Ala., 59, #7965

Bagwell, Frederick, Tuscaloosa, Ala., 64, #9647

Bagwell, Frederick, Tuscaloosa, Ala., 88, #17826

Bagwell, Isaiah, c/o, Richmond, Va., 61, #8496

Bagwell, John, S.C., 61, #8525

Bagwell, John, e/o, S.C., 126, #3920

Bagwell, William, S.C., 1, #5655

Bailey, Eliphalet, a/o, Maine, 114, #2181

Bailey, George, a/o, Philadelphia, Pa., 91, #19529

Bailey, Hannah, Maine, 74, #13039

Bailey, Ichabod, w/o, Conn., 54, #6716

Bailey, James, Conn., 30, #241

Bailey, John, Concord, N.H., 73, #12814

Bailey, Joseph, Md., 1, #8890

Bailey, Joseph, Md., 131, #8890, card

Bailey, Meshack S., Knoxville, Tenn., 118, #4795

Bailey, Nancy, Va., 67, #10374

Bailey, Noah, a/o, N.C., 114, #2151

Bailey, Philip, Richmond, Va., 56, #7335

Bailey, Robert, Ill., 87, #17306

Bailey, Sally, a/o, Concord, N.H., 105, #8216

Bailey, William, N.C., 99, #3333

Bainbridge, Eaphan C., Mo., 140, #613

Baird, Mary, a/o, Ky., 134, #952

Baitsell, Joseph, Philadelphia, Pa., 129, #6551

Baitsell, Joseph, Philadelphia, Pa., 135, #2410

Baker, Abigail, c/o, Mass., 110, #11001

Baker, Abigal, a/o, Mass., 83, #15815

Baker (formerly Kauffman), Ann Eliza, Philadelphia, Pa., 138, #6474

Baker, Beal, w/o, Ga., 89, #18308

Baker, Charles, Ga., 56, #7377

Baker, Charles, Ga., 75, #13583
Baker, Daniel, e/o, New York
   City, 55, #7182
Baker, Lt. David, e/o w/o, Mass.
   Militia, 72, #12516
Baker, Elias, a/o, Ga., 135,
   #2179
Baker (formerly Van Meter),
   Elizabeth, Indianapolis,
   Ind., 136, #2593
Baker, Elizabeth D., Richmond,
   Va., 64, #9437
Baker, Elizabeth Dorothy,
   Richmond, Va., 67, #10391
Baker, George, e/o, Nashville,
   Tenn., 77, #14216
Baker, John, Albany, N.Y., 1,
   #5183
Baker, John, Albany, N.Y., 70,
   #12178
Baker, John, Albany, N.Y., 119,
   #5183, card
Baker, John, c/o, Ind., 92,
   #19560
Baker, Joshua, Albany, N.Y.,
   98, #2867
Baker, Mary, Nashville, Tenn.,
   111, #678
Baker (formerly Reed), Mary B.,
   N.C., 117, #3944
Baker, Nathaniel Y., c/o, Sea
   Fencibles, 64, #9611
Baker, Nathaniel Y., w/o, Sea
   Fencibles, 64, #9610
Baker, Richard Bohan, c/o,
   Charleston, S.C., 49,
   #5417
Baker, Sarah, a/o, Ga., 133,
   #268
Baker, Stephen, g/o c/o, Conn.,
   37, #F1826

Baker, Thomas, c/o, Ky., 64,
   #9498
Baker, Lt. Thomas M., S.C.
   Vols, 120, #6597, Special
Balakeney, John, S.C., 63,
   #9106
Balch, Thomas, w/o, Albany,
   N.Y., 70, #12071
Balckmore, Timothy,
   Pittsburgh, Pa., 95, #1056
Baldwin, Azel, Albany, N.Y.,
   61, #8572
Baldwin, Azel, Albany, N.Y.,
   69, #11025
Baldwin, Azel, Albany, N.Y.,
   47, #4952
Baldwin, Benjamin, a/o, Ohio,
   122, #8451
Baldwin, Brewer, a/o, Conn., 81,
   #15133
Baldwin, David, Boston, Mass.,
   1, #8068
Baldwin, David, Mass., 59,
   #8068, card
Baldwin, Edward, w/o, Ky., 81,
   #15178
Baldwin, Isaiah, New Albany,
   Ind., 1, #13452
Baldwin, John, Ohio, 65, #9921
Baldwin, Jonathan, Conn., 30,
   #31
Baldwin, Josiah, Albany, N.Y.,
   75, #13452, card
Baldwin, Pollard, Madison, Ind.,
   48, #5209
Baldwin, Rhonda, c/o, Albany,
   N.Y., 99, #3458
Baldwin, Samuel, Md., 50,
   #5790
Baldwin, Samuel, Md., 71,
   #12366

Baldwin, Samuel, Md., 89,
#18320

Baldwin, Samuel, c/o, Mass., 92,
#19604

Baldwin, Stephen, c/o, Albany,
N.Y., 2, #8899

Baldwin, Stephen, c/o, Albany,
N.Y., 134, #719

Baldwin, Submit, c/o, Cleveland,
Ohio, 129, #6580

Baldwin, William T., c/o,
Cincinnati, Ohio, 124,
#1003

Baley, David, w/o, Albany,
N.Y., 65, #9893

Baley, William, w/o, New York
City, 58, #7874

Ball, Aaron, c/o, N.Y., 122,
#8991

Ball, Eli, c/o, Mich., 133, #662

Ball, Elizabeth, c/o, Richmond,
Va., 136, #3089

Ball, James, Ind., 131, #8110,
card

Ball, James, a/o, Ind., 2, #8110

Ball, Letitia, Richmond, Va.,
36A, #F6, card

Ball, Thomas, Ky., 84, #16018,
card

Ball, Thomas, Ky., 84, #16019,
card

Ballard, Ann, c/o, Philadelphia,
Pa., 104, #7413

Ballard, Catherine, Ind., 41,
#3476

Ballard, Catherine, New Albany,
Ind., 63, #9020

Ballard, William, S.C., 130,
#7576

Ballard, William, S.C., 133,
#647

Ballard (now Dishon), Nancy A.,
Ky., 122, #8561

Ballerson, William, c/o, Md.,
116, #3560

Ballew, Joseph, Jackson, Tenn.,
43, #3926

Ballew, Joseph, Jackson, Tenn.,
78, #14469

Ballew, Richard, Ky., 68,
#10778

Ballew, Richard, Ky., 84,
#16154

Ballinger, Pleasant, a/o, S.C.,
136, #2643

Baltes, William, New York City,
139, #7449

Balthorp, Augustine, N.C., 54,
#6596

Balthrop, Holly, Richmond, Va.,
124, #485

Balthroph, Holly, a/o,
Richmond, Va., 136, #3404

Bancker, James, Albany, N.Y.,
54, #6761

Bancroft, John, c/o, Pittsburgh,
Pa., 53, #6461

Bancroft, Jonathan, c/o,
Concord, N.H., 103, #6689

Bander, Harriet, Ill., 133, #682

Bandy, Nancy, —, 117, #4403,
card

Bandy, Nancy, Nashville, Tenn.,
70, #11154

Bane, Ellis, c/o, Philadelphia,
Pa., 2, #6130

Banks, Jacob, c/o, Richmond,
Va., 112, #948

Banks, John, Richmond, Va.,
62, #8676

Banks, John, Richmond, Va.,
76, #13823

Banks, Mabel, e/o, Conn., 103,
#6715
Banks, Robert, Ky., 76, #13834
Banks, Sally, c/o, Richmond,
Va., 36A, #F1 V2
Banks, William, w/o, Madison,
Ind., 134, #1342
Banner, Benjamin, N.C., 47,
#4853
Bannerman, George, —, 90,
#18653, card
Bannerman, George, N.C., 96,
#177-, card
Bannerman, George, N.C., 71,
#12382
Barbee, Paulina, Mo., 116,
#3468
Barbee, Paulina, Mo., 132,
#9076
Barbee, Pauline, Mo., 129,
#6179
Barber, Dorcas, c/o, Maine, 2,
#10804
Barber, Jane, La., 126, #3509
Barber, Jane, New Orleans, La.,
131, #8264
Barber, Job, Poultney, Vt., 102,
#5426
Barber, Moses, w/o, R.I., 70,
#12159
Barber, Reuben, w/o, Albany,
N.Y., 110, #11073
Barber, William, c/o, Albany,
N.Y., 137, #4527
Barberdu, Stephen, Conn., 30,
#172
Barbour, Debroah, Maine, 78,
#14445
Barbour, Mordicai, c/o,
Richmond, Va., 100, #4266
Barbour, Major Philip N., w/o,
3rd Inf., 111, #426

Barbour, Major Philip N., w/o,
3rd Inf., 100, #4582
Barbour, Major Philip N., w/o,
3rd Inf., 102, #5477
Barbour, Major Philip N., w/o,
3rd Inf., 103, #6603
Barbour, Major Philip N., w/o,
3rd Inf., 104, #7336
Barbour, Major Philip N., w/o,
3rd Inf., 105, #8240
Barbour, Major Philip N., w/o,
3rd Inf., 107, #9099
Barbour, Major Philip N., w/o,
3rd Inf., 108, #10303
Barbour, Major Philip N., w/o,
3rd Inf., 109, #10862
Bard, Josiah, Albany, N.Y., 79,
#14711
Bardley, Frankey, Richmond,
Va., 109, #10513
Bardley, Samuel, e/o, Boston,
Mass., 64, #9257
Bargdon, Elijah, c/o, 34th Inf.,
105, #8214
Barham, James, Ky., 45, #4492
Barham, James, Mo., 140, #416
Barker, Benjamin, c/o, Concord,
N.H., 46, #4654
Barker, Dorcas, —, 109,
#10804, card
Barker, Ephraim, N.Y., 48,
#5055
Barker, Ethan, Conn., 30, #21
Barker, James, w/o, Savannah,
Ga., 92, #7
Barker, John, Ky., 53, #6527,
card
Barker, John, w/o, Lexington,
Ky., 91, #19367
Barker, John, w/o, Mass., 86,
#17046

Barker, John S., Mass., 116, #3391

Barker, Lydia, Conn., 30, #25

Barker, Nathaiel, w/o, D.C., 64, #9240

Barker, Oliver, a/o, Albany, N.Y., 111, #489

Barker, Stephen, Ky., 52, #6238

Barker, Timothy, Conn., 30, #101

Barker, William, w/o, Albany, N.Y., 114, #1997

Barkley, Sarah, a/o, Nashville, Tenn., 110, #11042

Barlow, Abner, Albany, N.Y., 72, #12671

Barlow, Eunice, Wisc., 84, #15984

Barlow, Eunice, Wisc., 99, #3292

Barlow, Joseph, Ky., 74, #13283

Barlow, Obed, w/o, Boston, Mass., 61, #8615

Barlow, Rebecca, Conn., 30, #15

Barnaby, Henery, w/o, Indianapolis, Ind., 139, #7372

Barnard, John, Albany, N.Y., 79, #14547

Barnard, Lucy, Vt., 81, #15088

Barnard, Phebe, a/o, Albany, N.Y., 114, #2207

Barnes, Barbara J., Nashville, Tenn., 116, #3157

Barnes, Barbara J., Pulaski, Tenn., 127, #4087

Barnes, Chesley, Fayetteville, N.C., 50, #5633

Barnes, Chesley, w/o, N.C., 70, #12015

Barnes, Ebenezer, w/o, Ill., 86, #16852

Barnes, Elijah, Ind., 44, #4368

Barnes, Elijah, Ind., 62, #8714

Barnes, Elizabeth, Jackson, Tenn., 127, #4120

Barnes, George, Cananadaigua, N.Y., 142, #4962

Barnes, James, Knoxville, Tenn., 66, #10266

Barnes, Jared, Conn., 30, #32

Barnes, John, N.Y., 2, #19257

Barnes, John, New York City, 91, #19257, card

Barnes, Joseph, Maine, 56, #7330

Barnes, Nehemiah, a/o, Philadelphia, Pa., 124, #1388

Barnes, Ruth, c/o, Albany, N.Y., 133, #281

Barnes, Shadrack, Ky., 42, #3608

Barnes, Shadrack, Ky., 101, #5011

Barnes, Silence, Hartford, Conn., 72, #12493

Barnes, William, Fort Gibson, Ark., 111, #477

Barnes, Isaac O., PA, Boston, Mass., 118, #5040

Barnet, Joseph, Wheeling, Va., 43, #3837

Barnett, Benjamin, Albany, N.Y., 54, #6894

Barnett, Charles, Va., 69, #11024

Barnett, David, a/o, S.C., 98, #2926

Barnett, Elizabeth, c/o, Madison, Ind., 102, #6160

Barnett, Elizabeth, c/o,
Madison, Ind., 100, #4495
Barnett, Moses, a/o, Vt., 2,
#1152
Barnett, Sally, a/o, Ky., 125,
#2034
Barnett, William D., Mo., 116,
#3776
Barnett, William D., Mo., 131,
#8401
Barney, Mabel, c/o, Vt., 61,
#8503
Barney, Mary, a/o, R.I., 130,
#7690
Barngrover, George, Ohio, 56,
#7296
Barnham, John, —, 42, #3566,
card
Barnhart, Mary Sophia,
Philadelphia, Pa., 96,
#1710
Barnhill, John, Ga., 51, #5944
Barnhill, John, Ga., 68, #10772
Barnthisel, Christopher, w/o,
D.C., 111, #326
Barr, John C., Ill., 131, #8723
Barr, John D., Richmond, Va.,
76, #13888
Barr, John, PA, Cleveland, Ohio,
115, #2461
Barrack, John, c/o, N.C., 113,
#1316
Barrett, Baxter, Conn., 82,
#15411
Barrett, Benjamin, —, 106,
#8841, slip
Barrett, Bethuel, New York City,
42, #3664
Barrett, Bethuel, c/o, New York
City, 45, #4458

Barrett, Henry, c/o,
Philadelphia, Pa., 130,
#7465
Barrett, Henry, c/o,
Philadelphia, Pa., 130,
#7565
Barrett, James, Philadelphia,
Pa., 2, #17446
Barrett, James, a/o, —, 87,
#17446, card
Barrett, Samuel, c/o, New York
City, 96, #1872
Barrett, Solomon, Md., 80,
#14764
Barrett, Walter, w/o,
Philadelphia, Pa., 2,
#13793
Barrick, Henry, —, 79, #14557,
card
Barron, James, w/o,
Philadelphia, Pa., 117,
#3856
Barron, Joseph, w/o, Albany,
N.Y., 105, #8134
Barrow, John J., Philadelphia,
Pa., 125, #2374
Barrow, John J., Philadelphia,
Pa., 134, #821
Barrow, John J., Philadelphia,
Pa., 140, #1107
Barrow, John James,
Philadelphia, Pa., 137,
#4613
Barrow, Phebe, c/o, Albany,
N.Y., 108, #9842
Barrows, N. D., PA, Jackson,
Miss., 118, #5047
Barry, Andrew, N.C., 80,
#14754
Barry, Eleanor, Albany, N.Y.,
81, #15172

Barry, William, Philadelphia,
Pa., 62, #8759
Barry, William B., Cincinnati,
Ohio, 121, #7871
Barsto, Ebenezer, Burlington,
Vt., 2, #4553
Barsto, Ebenezer, Burlington,
Vt., 45, #4553
Barstow, Mary, Maine, 124,
#428
Bartee, David, Richmond, Va.,
58, #7834
Bartee, David, Va., 79, #14740
Bartee, David, Va., 88, #18023
Barter, David, Richmond, Va.,
98, #2696
Bartholomew, Daniel, c/o,
Albany, N.Y., 118, #4892
Bartholomew, Joseph, New
Albany, Ind., 56, #7390
Bartholomew, Luther, Bellows
Falls, Vt., 63, #8967
Bartlett, Abraham, Albany,
N.Y., 44, #4259
Bartlett, Andrew, Bellows Falls,
Vt., 63, #8967
Bartlett, Asa, R.I., 52, #6086
Bartlett, Benjamin, Albany,
N.Y., 41, #3480
Bartlett, Ebenezer, c/o, Ill., 72,
#12672
Bartlett, Elizabeth, c/o, Maine,
74, #13230
Bartlett, Hannah, c/o, Maine,
136, #2624
Bartlett, Haynes, e/o, Albany,
N.Y., 120, #6536
Bartlett, Joanna, Albany, N.Y.,
2, #6006
Bartlett, Joanna, Albany, N.Y.,
102, #6006, card

Bartlett, Moses, a/o, Albany,
N.Y., 64, #9202
Bartlett, Nathaniel, a/o, Albany,
N.Y., 132, #9131
Bartlett, William, Calif., 126,
#3165
Bartlett, William, Ill., 122,
#8327
Barto, Reuben, Albany, N.Y., 2,
#3105
Barton, Aaron, Concord, N.H.,
48, #5188
Bartore, Morris, c/o, N.J., 56,
#7427
Bartram, Isaac, Conn., 112,
#834
Basell, John, S.C., 49, #5250
Basham, James, Lexington, Ky.,
44, #4299
Basinger, Frances K., —, 42,
#3666
Basinger, W. E., w/o, 2nd
Artillery, 46, #4820
Baskett, Frances, Ky., 98,
#3000
Baskirk, Catherine,
Indianapolis, Ind., 142,
#3509
Bass, Joseph, Richmond, Va.,
57, #7509
Bass, Joseph, Va., 45, #4595
Bass, Sarah, Richmond, Va., 98,
#2942
Bassett, David, c/o, Maine, 44,
#4182
Bassett, Henry, w/o, N.Y., 63,
#9072
Bassett, Nathaniel, c/o,
Knoxville, Tenn., 2, #3134
Bassett, National, Knoxville,
Tenn., 116, #3134, card

Bastine, Jacob, Milwaukee,
Wisc., 142, #5579
Baston, Jonathan, a/o, Maine,
119, #5654
Batchelder, John, Concord,
N.H., 73, #12719
Batchelder, Stephen, Maine, 54,
#6893
Batchelder, William, w/o,
Maine, 116, #3785
Bates, Benjamin, N.J., 56,
#7258
Bates, David, w/o, 37th Inf.,
111, #667
Bates, Humphreys, Ky., 48,
#5084
Bates, Isaac, c/o, Conn., 123,
#9563
Bates, Isaac, c/o, Conn., 131,
#8731
Bates, Jacob, a/o, Mass., 84,
#16073
Bates, James, Va., 80, #14763
Bates, Lavina F., Va., 121,
#7699
Bates, Phinehas, Philadelphia,
Pa., 73, #12742
Bates, Phinehus, Philadelphia,
Pa., 52, #6098
Bates, Rufus, c/o, Albany, N.Y.,
68, #10766
Bates, Rufus, c/o, Albany, N.Y.,
70, #11123
Batton, Henry, Madison, Ind.,
49, #5429
Baughan, Richard, c/o,
Richmond, Va., 111, #572
Baughart, William, g/o c/o,
Philadelphia, Pa., 131,
#8129
Baughman, Jeremiah, S.C., 114,
#1945

Baughman, Jeremiah, S.C., 125,
#2375
Baushee, Philip, Philadelphia,
Pa., 76, #13744
Baxter, John, Ga., 44, #4357
Baxter, John, Ga., 57, #7591
Baxter, John, Ga., 70, #11163
Baxter, John, Ga., 81, #15026
Baxter, John, a/o, Albany, N.Y.,
121, #7243
Baxter, John, c/o, Albany, N.Y.,
122, #8329
Bayles, James M., New York
City, 140, #178
Bayley, Zadock, a/o, Va., 68,
#10579
Baylis, Rebecca, Albany, N.Y.,
72, #12602
Bazwell, David, w/o, W. Tenn.,
64, #9496
Beach, Jedediah, Albany, N.Y.,
82, #15285
Beach, John, Albany, N.Y., 78,
#14325
Beach, John, Albany, N.Y., 42,
#3782
Beach, Nathan, w/o,
Philadelphia, Pa., 128,
#4889
Beach, Nathaniel, w/o, New York
City, 51, #6067
Beach, Obel, Ohio, 77, #14110
Beach, Obil, Ohio, 80, #14969
Beach, Obil, Ohio, 87, #17384
Beach, Obil, Ohio, 88, #17814
Beach, Obil, Ohio, 91, #18996
Beach, Obil, a/o, Ohio, 101,
#5301
Beach, Zenas, Mo., 108, #9893
Beal, Barsheba, Albany, N.Y.,
47, #4888

Beal, Julia, Richmond, Va., 36A,
#F6, card
Beale, E. F., —, 131, #8230,
card
Beall, Christopher, c/o, Md., 48,
#5094
Beall, Samuel L., Jackson,
Tenn., 130, #7841
Beall, Samuel L., Tenn., 120,
#6495
Bealmear, Daniel V., Ky., 119,
#5711
Beals, Bathsheba, Philadelphia,
Pa., 74, #13289
Beals, Bathsheba, c/o,
Philadelphia, Pa., 134,
#1270
Beals, Joshua, c/o, Mass., 124,
#408
Beam, John, w/o, Trenton, N.J.,
143, #7292
Beaman, Lemuel, a/o, Conn.,
103, #6429
Bean, Conrad, w/o, Ky., 118,
#4830
Bean, Daniel, w/o, Iowa, 75,
#13492
Bean, Leonard, Ky., 2, #5314
Bean, Leonard, Ky., 119, #5314,
card
Bean, Richard, Mich., 79,
#14581
Bean, Richard, Mich., 80,
#14924
Beanse, Prince, c/o, Boston,
Mass., 57, #7641
Beard, David, Conn., 30, #4996
Beard, Frederick, Philadelphia,
Pa., 64, #9687
Beard, Frederick, Philadelphia,
Pa., 51, #5999

Beard, Jacob, w/o, Ohio, 75,
#13643
Beard, Jonathan, Mass., 63,
#8973
Beard, Magdaline, a/o,
Philadelphia, Pa., 107,
#9362
Beard, Mary, a/o, Rutland, Vt.,
94, #701
Beard, Robert, Ga., 40, #3302,
card
Beard, Robert, Ga., 2, #3302
Beard, William, c/o, Pulaski,
Tenn., 109, #10574
Beardin, Hannah, Mo., 135,
#1887
Beardman, Jehiel, w/o, Albany,
N.Y., 69, #10822
Beardsley, Benjamin, w/o,
Albany, N.Y., 89, #18165
Beardsley, Icabod, a/o, Albany,
N.Y., 113, #1842
Beasley, Benj, Richmond, Va.,
51, #6058
Beasley, Benjamin, Richmond,
Va., 42, #3703
Beasley, Leonard, S.C., 66,
#10300
Beaston, William, w/o, N.J., 65,
#9971
Beatey, David, N.C., 42, #3619
Beatty, Arthur, w/o, Albany,
N.Y., 45, #4551
Beatty, John, w/o, Ky., 66,
#10284
Beatty, John, w/o, Philadelphia,
Pa., 78, #14516
Beatty, William, c/o, New York
City, 100, #4400
Beatty (formerly Edmonds),
Lavina, Richmond, Va.,
36A, #F5 V2

Beaty, David, N.C., 59, #8146
Beaty, David, N.C., 62, #8734
Beaver, Adam, Philadelphia, Pa.,
    57, #7608
Beavers, Jane, Ohio, 106, #8607
Beavers, Samuel, Ohio, 61,
    #8440
Beavers, Samuel, w/o,
    Cincinnati, Ohio, 135,
    #2241
Beazle, Adolph, Philadelphia,
    Pa., 102, #5995
Beazley, Anney, c/o, Richmond,
    Va., 36A, #F1 V8
Bebbard, Lydia, Albany, N.Y.,
    104, #7356
Bechtel, Philip, a/o,
    Philadelphia, Pa., 82,
    #15344
Beck, Rebecca, a/o, Wheeling,
    Va., 121, #6776
Beck, Samuel, Ga. Militia, 84,
    #16103 subsistence claim
Becker, John P., Albany, N.Y.,
    72, #12608
Becker, Philip Peter, w/o,
    Richmond, Va., 41, #3406
Beckett, John, Ohio, 2, #7465
Beckett, John, Ohio, 2, #5201
Beckham, James, c/o, Va., 61,
    #8507
Becknel, Thomas, Ky., 126,
    #3645
Becktel, Borick, Pa., 122,
    #8771, card
Becktel, Boyck, alias Beagle,
    c/o, Philadelphia, Pa., 2,
    #8771
Beckwith, Ann, e/o, Md., 135,
    #1937
Beddie, John, Huntsville, Ala.,
    53, #6498

Beddo, Thomas, w/o, Cincinnati,
    Ohio, 118, #4857
Bedford, Elias, w/o, Ind., 88,
    #18088
Bedlam, Elizabeth, c/o, Albany,
    N.Y., 55, #7225
Bedle, Francis, c/o, Cincinnati,
    Ohio, 135, #2175
Bedwell, Robert, Ind., 123,
    #9793, card
Bedwell, Robert, c/o, Ind., 2,
    #9793
Beebe, Asa, a/o, Albany, N.Y.,
    108, #9772
Beebe, David, Albany, N.Y.,
    106, #8599
Beebe, Richard, Albany, N.Y.,
    44, #4320
Beecher, Charles, D.C., 143,
    #6819
Beek, Nancy, Fairfield, Ill., 143,
    #6426
Beekman, Ann, Mobile, Ala.,
    62, #8796
Beel, Henry, New York City,
    115, #2594
Beeman, —, N.Y., 81, #15120,
    card
Beeman, Friend, Vt., 2, #15120
Beeman, William, w/o, Ill., 58,
    #7847
Beer, James, Pittsburgh, Pa., 80,
    #14874
Beer, James, Pittsburgh, Pa., 90,
    #18895
Beers, Gershom, Conn., 30, #36
Beers, James, Conn., 30, #150
Beers, John, Pittsburgh, Pa.,
    139, #6913
Beers, Zachariah, Pittsburgh,
    Pa., 78, #14252
Beesley, William, Ky., 2, #6111

Beesley, William, Ky., 102,
#6111, card
Behney, Ann M., Philadelphia,
Pa., 99, #3649
Beiderman, John, Philadelphia,
Pa., 141, #3146
Belcher, Robert, c/o, S.C., 133,
#136
Belcher, Robt., S.C., 53, #6446
Belden, Christian, Conn., 45,
#4623
Belknap, Francis, Conn., 30,
#27
Belknap, Josiah, Bellows Falls,
Vt., 48, #5085
Bell, Abraham, Conn., 30, #179
Bell, Andrew, a/o, Albany, N.Y.,
112, #807
Bell, Benjamin, N.C., 62, #8852
Bell, Benjamin, N.C., 71,
#12426
Bell, Benjamin, a/o, Vt., 123,
#9022
Bell, Daniel, Ky., 2, #3699
Bell, John, Richmond, Va., 86,
#17270
Bell, John, Richmond, Va., 51,
#5945
Bell, John, Va., 67, #10389
Bell, John, Va., 76, #13760
Bell, Margaret, —, 122, #8724,
slip
Bell, Margaret, Louisville, Ky.,
2, #8724
Bell, Maria C., D.C., 143,
#7489
Bell, Oliver, —, 56, #7255, card
Bell, Oliver, Albany, N.Y., 2,
#7255
Bell Sr., Robert, Va., 73,
#12757

Bell, Samuel, w/o, La., 122,
#8510
Bell, Samuel M., Pittsburgh, Pa.,
143, #6556
Bell, Thaddeus, Conn., 30,
#3259
Bell, Thomas, w/o, Ky., 2,
#16018
Bell, Thomas, w/o, Ky., 2,
#16019
Bell, William, Ky., 40, #3192
Bellesfelt, Peter, Pittsburgh, Pa.,
59, #8147
Bellinger, William L., c/o,
Cincinnati, Ohio, 117,
#3972
Bellos, Adam, N.J., 67, #10546
Belnap, Jesse, Pittsburgh, Pa.,
125, #1747, card
Belnap, Jesse, e/o, Philadelphia,
Pa., 2, #1747
Belsbury, Lyles, Richmond, Va.,
51, #6080
Beman, Moses, w/o, Wheeling,
Va., 91, #18962
Beman, Nathan, Albany, N.Y.,
105, #7768
Bement, Consider, Albany,
N.Y., 55, #7224
Bemis, Chauncey, Conn., 119,
#5736
Bemont, Consider, Albany,
N.Y., 67, #10364
Bemus, Asenath, Albany, N.Y.,
103, #6869
Benedict, Elizabeth, New York
City, 103, #7073
Benedict, Isaac, Conn., 30, #7
Benedict, Joseph, c/o, N.Y., 80,
#14781
Benedict, Lewis, Albany, N.Y.,
41, #3419, card

Benedict, Nathaniel, Conn., 30,
#236
Benedict, Thomas, w/o, Albany,
N.Y., 77, #13992
Benham, H. W., —, 107, #9165,
card
Benham, H. W., —, 114, #2024,
card
Benham, Margarett, c/o, Conn.,
30, #3229
Benham, W. K., —, 96, #1440,
card
Benhom, Thomas, Pittsburgh,
Pa., 82, #15286
Benjamin, Asa, Conn., 30, #116
Benjamin, Darius, c/o, Albany,
N.Y., 2, #594
Benjamin, Jonathan, c/o, Ohio,
81, #15023
Benjamin, Joseph, c/o, Md.,
137, #4172
Benjamin, Salah B., w/o,
Albany, N.Y., 91, #19519
Benjinger, John, Mo., 133,
#229
Bennent, John, e/o,
Philadelphia, Pa., 98,
#2964
Bennet, Catharine, a/o, Ohio,
108, #9701
Bennet, Delatiah F., Madison,
Wisc., 143, #6872
Bennet, Henry, w/o, Albany,
N.Y., 76, #13930
Bennet, Samuel, c/o, Windsor,
Vt., 2, #6789
Bennett, Abraham, Pittsburgh,
Pa., 105, #8218
Bennett, Abraham, c/o,
Cleveland, Ohio, 123,
#9574

Bennett, Abraham, c/o,
Cleveland, Ohio, 123,
#9778
Bennett, Andrew, c/o, Maine,
85, #16604
Bennett, Benjamin, c/o, Albany,
N.Y., 124, #1300
Bennett, Benjamin B., Ky., 112,
#1009
Bennett, Daniel, w/o, Albany,
N.Y., 73, #12846
Bennett, Elizabeth, Albany,
N.Y., 121, #7993
Bennett, Ephraim, Albany, N.Y.,
67, #10358
Bennett, Esther, Mass., 129,
#6263
Bennett, George, w/o, Md., 132,
#9278
Bennett, Joseph, a/o, Vt., 77,
#14063
Bennett, Joshua, w/o, Ind., 119,
#5670
Bennett, Phebe, a/o, Albany,
N.Y., 107, #9277
Bennett, Samuel, Windsor, Vt.,
54, #6789, card
Bennett, William, Wheeling,
Va., 130, #7868
Bennett 2nd, Stephen, c/o,
Burlington, Vt., 130,
#7925
Bensinger, Ferdinand, g/o c/o,
Cincinnati, Ohio, 140,
#9692
Benson, Jeptha, w/o,
Portsmouth, Maine, 135,
#1880
Benson, Joel, c/o, Albany, N.Y.,
44, #4219
Benson, John, c/o, Albany,
N.Y., 134, #1404

Benson, John, c/o, N.C., 60,
#8348
Benson, Sarah, Savannah, Ga.,
123, #9548
Benson, Travers, c/o, Md., 64,
#9365
Bent, Nathan, c/o, Portsmouth,
N.H., 49, #5346
Bentley, James, Ga., 20, #4963
Bently, Anna, Conn., 98, #2831
Benton, Joel, a/o w/o, Vt., 64,
#9702
Benton, Tamar, a/o, Burlington,
Vt., 138, #4784
Bercaw, Elizabeth, Cincinnati,
Ohio, 129, #6780
Bergh, Abraham, w/o, Albany,
N.Y., 44, #4386
Berkley, George, w/o,
Richmond, Va., 76, #13825
Berlin, Jacob, Richmond, Va.,
56, #7352
Berlin, Jacob, Richmond, Va.,
71, #12247
Berlin, Jacob, Va., 75, #13597
Berry, Bethia, c/o, Mass., 118,
#4884
Berry, Bethiah, c/o, Mass., 118,
#4653
Berry, Betty, c/o, Boston,
Mass., 102, #5569
Berry, Elizabeth, Richmond,
Va., 94, #457
Berry, Enoch, Nashville, Tenn.,
41, #3386
Berry, Enoch, w/o, Nashville,
Tenn., 106, #8753
Berry, Joel, Ky., 92, #19780,
card
Berry, Joel, Ky., 52, #6229
Berry, John, w/o, Knoxville,
Tenn., 89, #18445

Berry, John, w/o, Ky., 2,
#19368
Berry, Robert, N.C., 44, #4251,
card
Berry, Robert, w/o, N.C., 2,
#4251
Berry, Samuel, Poultney, Vt.,
94, #371
Berry, Samuel, Vt., 57, #7497
Berry, Samuel, Vt., 120, #6520
Berry, Thomas, Ky., 77, #14137
Berry, William, c/o, S.C., 2,
#8554
Berry, William, c/o, S.C., 2,
#5653
Berry, William, w/o, Va., 69,
#10973
Berryhill, Alexander, w/o,
Huntsville, Ala., 54, #6689
Berryman, Stephen, c/o, Va., 65,
#9707
Bert, Levi, w/o, Mass., 88,
#17985
Berting, Peter, a/o, Wheeling,
Va., 87, #17510
Bertris, Peter, Wheeling, Va.,
49, #5278
Bessee, Pvt. Isaac, w/o,
Birdsall's Co., U.S.
Volunteers, 131, #8681
Bessell, Noadiah, w/o, Concord,
N.H., 48, #5167
Bessent, John, E. Fla., 71,
#12299
Bessent, John, St. Augustine,
Fla., 54, #6710
Best, John J., w/o, Albany,
N.Y., 84, #16133
Betterson, Joseph, w/o, Albany,
N.Y., 55, #6911
Betterton, Joshua, S.C., 39,
#3101

Betterton, Joshua, S.C., 61,
#8589
Betts, Phebe, c/o, Conn., 54,
#6721
Beuzinger, John, St. Louis, Mo.,
118, #5017
Bever, Pvt. Peter, w/o, Va.
Milita, 113, #1575
Beveridge, Matthew, Maine, 41,
#3413
Bevier, Jacob J., Albany, N.Y.,
67, #10441
Bevier, Jacob J., Albany, N.Y.,
42, #3604
Bevill, Edward, Huntsville, Ala.,
60, #8180
Bevins, John, w/o, Pittsburgh,
Pa., 53, #6513
Bibber, James, c/o, Maine, 99,
#3511
Bibbie, Solomon, N.C., 87,
#17485
Bicker, Adam, w/o, Ohio, 100,
#3765
Bickers, Henry C., Tenn., 122,
#8130
Bickford, Jean, a/o, Albany,
N.Y., 95, #1090
Bickley, Charles, Richmond,
Va., 49, #5344
Bickley, Charles, Va., 39,
#3010
Bickley, Charles, c/o,
Richmond, Va., 61, #8389
Biddecomb, Ruth, Madison, Ind.,
102, #5792
Biddie, John, Huntsville, Ala.,
71, #12284
Biddie, John, Huntsville, Ala.,
56, #7239
Biddie, John, Huntsville, Ala.,
62, #8726

Biddies, John, Huntsville, Ala.,
64, #9604
Bieganski, Edward, La., 65,
#9923
Biegauskie, Edward, N.Y., 83,
#15727
Biffle, Jacob, w/o, Nashville,
Tenn., 2, #557
Bigbee, James N., Miss., 104,
#7342
Bigbie, James N., Miss., 107,
#8907
Bigbie, William, Va., 66,
#10145
Bigelow, Humphrey, w/o,
Boston, Mass., 89, #18346
Bigelow, Israel B., La., 134,
#1365
Bigelow, Jabez, c/o, Albany,
N.Y., 57, #7642
Bigelow, John, g/o c/o, Conn.,
37, #F1820
Bigelow, Jonas, w/o, Mass., 91,
#19271
Biggs, Henry, g/o c/o, Ill., 134,
#1333
Biggs, John, a/o, Richmond,
Va., 134, #738
Biggs, Joshua, w/o, Albany,
N.Y., 81, #15136
Biggs, Pvt. Willis, w/o, 24th
Inf., 131, #8412
Bigham, Joseph, a/o, N.C., 77,
#14147
Bigler, Jacob, g/o c/o, Mich.,
134, #1617
Biglow, Barna, w/o, Vt., 77,
#14107
Biles, Thomas, N.C., 45, #4528
Biles, Thomas, w/o, N.C., 97,
#2487

Biles, John D., PA, Vancouver, W.T., 139, #8828
Biles, John D., PA, Vancouver, W.T., 140, #9930
Bill, George, Mich., 111, #349, card
Bill, George, Wisc., 2, #3086
Bill, George, Wisc., 141, #3086, card
Bill, Phineas, w/o, Albany, N.Y., 70, #11041
Billings, Olive, Bellows Falls, Vt., 63, #8967
Billings, Thomas, Philadelphia, Pa., 113, #1340
Billings, Thomas, Philadelphia, Pa., 128, #5562
Billings, Thomas, Philadelphia, Pa., 140, #903
Bills, Elisha, Albany, N.Y., 105, #7865
Bills, John E., Va., 87, #17493
Bills, William, c/o, N.J., 45, #4471
Biner, George, c/o, Wheeling, Va., 108, #10226
Bingham, Abel, Mich., 81, #15202
Bingham, Elizabeth, Ohio, 71, #12453
Binham Sr., Thomas, c/o, Pittsburgh, Pa., 116, #3435
Birch, Jane, Ky., 109, #10777
Bird, Bonner, a/o, N.C., 101, #4641
Bird, Ebe, Albany, N.Y., 51, #6070
Bird, John, a/o, S.C., 94, #251
Bird, John, c/o, Philadelphia, Pa., 57, #7449
Bird, Samuel, —, 64, #9164

Bird, Susannah, Richmond, Va., 36A, #F1 V3
Bird, Susannah, c/o, Richmond, Va., 129, #6716
Bird, Thomas, Ill., 122, #8232
Bird, William, Ill., 122, #8404
Bird, William, Ill., 122, #8975
Bird, William, Ill., 123, #325
Birdle, John, Ga., 57, #7460
Birdwell, Benjamin, w/o, Jonesboro, Tenn., 71, #12230
Birmingham, Richard, New York City, 123, #63
Bisbee, Ebenezer, c/o, Mass., 136, #3418
Bisbee, Noah, a/o, Concord, N.H., 88, #17912
Bishop, Benoni, Albany, N.Y., 116, #3685
Bishop, Charity, e/o, Albany, N.Y., 142, #3510
Bishop, David H., Jonesboro, Tenn., 135, #2418
Bishop, Eli, Ky., 43, #4019
Bishop, Fanny, Richmond, Va., 92, #223
Bishop, Golden, c/o, —, 43, #3855
Bishop, Henry, Richmond, Va., 47, #5025
Bishop, Henry, w/o, Va., 58, #7846
Bishop, John, S.C., 47, #4946
Bishop, Levi, Vt., 89, #18166, card
Bishop, Levi, Vt., 3, #18166
Bishop, Mary, Conn., 30, #100
Bishop, Mary, Philadelphia, Pa., 64, #9312
Bishop, Mary, Philadelphia, Pa., 75, #13641

Bishop, Nancy, c/o,
Fayetteville, N.C., 108,
#9978
Bishop, Nicholas, S.C., 98,
#2816, card
Bishop, Nicholas, a/o, S.C., 3,
#2816
Bishop, Robert, h/o,
Montpelier, Vt., 104,
#7424
Bishop, Sarah, c/o, Albany,
N.Y., 116, #3562
Bishop, Simon, a/o, Conn., 38,
#F1826
Bishop, William, Mo., 140,
#385
Bissell, George, Conn., 30,
#165
Bissell, Jerijah, e/o, Conn., 84,
#16159
Bissell, Theodo, Albany, N.Y.,
76, #13931
Biteley, John, Albany, N.Y., 70,
#11144
Bitner, Margaret, c/o, Ill., 134,
#1260
Bixby, Samson, a/o, N.Y., 107,
#8959
Bizzel, Amy, N.C., 120, #6671
Black, David, Mobile, Ala., 56,
#7410
Black, David, Tuscaloosa, Ala.,
88, #17867
Black, David, Tuscaloosa, Ala.,
65, #9723
Black, Jacob, S.C., 79, #14681
Black, James, Philadelphia, Pa.,
90, #18863
Black, James, Philadelphia, Pa.,
43, #3883
Black, Leanora, S.C., 131,
#8909

Black, Lenorah, S.C., 117,
#4510
Black, Samuel, c/o, Mich., 125,
#2084
Black, Sarah, c/o, Philadelphia,
Pa., 98, #2999
Black, Willam, Ark., 88,
#17866
Black, William, Ga., 40, #3258
Black (now Bostick), Mary F.,
c/o, Ill., 117, #4558
Blackburn, James, Ohio, 54,
#6656
Blackburn, James, Ohio, 71,
#12399
Blackburn, William, Ky., 123,
#9642, card
Blackburn, William, c/o, Ky., 3,
#9642
Blackford, Jacob, Philadelphia,
Pa., 80, #14775
Blackman, Abigail, Mass., 105,
#7753
Blackman, Mary, c/o, Albany,
N.Y., 118, #4799
Blackman, Sarah, Pulaski,
Tenn., 114, #2136
Blackman, Timothy, Pittsburgh,
Pa., 89, #18452
Blackmore, Timothy,
Pittsburgh, Pa., 65, #9706
Blackwadder, Charles, N.C., 45,
#4511
Blackwelder, Isaac, N.C., 54,
#6619
Blackwell, Hugh, Ohio, 105,
#7766
Blackwell, John, W. Tenn., 87,
#17307, card
Blackwell, Robert, a/o, Mo., 77,
#14115

Blades, Delpha, Richmond, Va.,
127, #4793

Blair, Abraham, Ohio, 83,
#15786

Blair, James, e/o, Ind., 71,
#12375

Blair, Jane, Nashville, Tenn.,
100, #4294

Blair, Josiah R., a/o, Jackson,
Tenn., 113, #1770

Blair, Mary Ann, Richmond,
Va., 56, #7317

Blair, Mary Ann, Richmond,
Va., 61, #8640

Blair, Mary Ann, a/o, Richmond,
Va., 121, #7582

Blair, Mercy, g/o, Boston,
Mass., 63, #9085

Blair, Thomas, w/o, W. Tenn.,
63, #9076

Blair, William B., —, 138,
#5253, card

Blaisdell, Dorothy, Mich., 131,
#8185

Blake, Dorcas, c/o, Mass., 88,
#17763

Blake, Elijah, Albany, N.Y., 60,
#8384

Blake, Joseph, c/o, Madison,
Ind., 115, #2945

Blake, Reuben, Conn., 30, #2

Blake, Sarah, Albany, N.Y.,
113, #1809

Blakeley, Obed, a/o, Albany,
N.Y., 103, #6430

Blakely, Aquila, Decatur, Ala.,
45, #4629

Blakely, William, S.C., 62,
#8866

Blakemore, George, a/o,
Richmond, Va., 105, #8217

Blakeney, John, w/o,
Charleston, S.C., 108,
#10379

Blakeney, Nancy, S.C., 120,
#5874

Blalock, Daniel, —, 129,
#6954, card

Blalock, David, Jackson, Tenn.,
64, #9380

Blalock, David, Jackson, Tenn.,
43, #3907

Blalock, David, Jackson, Tenn.,
73, #12869

Blalock, Jeremiah, w/o, —, 75,
#13708, card

Blan, Jesse, Richmond, Va., 79,
#14578, card

Blanchard, Ama, Albany, N.Y.,
115, #2925

Blanchard, Jeremiah, w/o,
Mass., 116, #3559

Blanchard, Josiah, w/o, Mass.,
62, #8846

Blanchard, Sarah, c/o, Vt., 60,
#8202

Blanchard, Sarah, c/o, Vt., 72,
#12540

Blanchard, William, c/o, Vt., 61,
#8483

Blanchard, William, c/o, Vt., 72,
#12541

Blancher, Tamer, New York City,
104, #7343

Blancit, Joel, Richmond, Va.,
52, #6109

Blancit, Joel, c/o, Richmond,
Va., 99, #3161

Bland, John, w/o, Miss. Militia,
109, #10504

Blanden, Lamach, Ill., 46,
#4671

Blankenship, Reuben, Mobile, Ala., 95, #1188
Blankenship, Reuben, Tuscaloosa, Ala., 73, #12926
Blasdell, Ezra, a/o, Vt., 66, #10114
Blass, Joseph, e/o, Albany, N.Y., 84, #16300
Bledsoe, Sarah, c/o, Nashville, Tenn., 117, #4155
Blevens, James, Ind., 86, #16917
Blevins, Daniel, c/o, Madison, Ind., 115, #2972
Blevins, Hannah O., Ky., 115, #2829
Blevins, Hannah O., Ky., 143, #6690
Blevins, James, w/o, Ky., 98, #2842
Blevins, Lydia, Cincinnati, Ohio, 125, #1770
Blewer, James, Md., 90, #18791
Blick, James, c/o, Richmond, Va., 48, #5199
Blick, John, Ky., 80, #14929
Blimby, William, a/o, Albany, N.Y., 132, #8953
Blin, Simeon, a/o, N.Y., 106, #8771
Bliss, Jane, Pittsburgh, Pa., 105, #8172
Bliss, John, Philadelphia, Pa., 111, #411
Bliss, Joshua, a/o, Vt., 89, #18266
Bliss, Lucinda, a/o, Ohio, 114, #1931
Bliss, Timothy, g/o c/o, Conn., 37, #F1820

Bliss, Zenes, Albany, N.Y., 56, #7431
Blizzard, Burton, w/o, Va., 65, #9802
Blocken (now Crosby), Mary, S.C., 79, #14641
Blocker, Elizabeth Levina, g/o, S.C., 73, #12980
Blocker, Timothy B., w/o, S.C., 49, #5301
Blockers, Timothy B., g/o c/o, S.C., 82, #15395
Blodget, Abigal, Conn., 71, #12396
Blodget, Joshua, —, 83, #15813, card
Blodget, Joshua, c/o, Vt., 3, #15813
Blodgett, Samuel, w/o, Cincinnati, Ohio, 136, #2614
Blood, George, g/o, Boston, Mass., 101, #5271
Blood, Isaac, w/o, Albany, N.Y., 89, #18143
Blood, Israel M., a/o, Albany, N.Y., 117, #4122
Bloodgood, Sarah Jane, New York City, 122, #8729
Bloom, William, N.Y., 143, #7495
Bloom, William, New York City, 129, #6415
Bloomfield, James, a/o, N.J., 120, #6477
Bloxom, Leah, c/o, Richmond, Va., 125, #1735
Bloxsom, Scarborough, w/o, Richmond, Va., 43, #3857
Blue, Hannah, a/o, Maine, 71, #12360

Bluechard, Aaron, Montpelier,
Vt., 101, #5006 V#3

Blum, Anna Eva, a/o, Albany,
N.Y., 112, #1063

Board, Adam, Md., 61, #8497,
card

Boardman, Mary Ann, Hartford,
Conn., 104, #7642

Boas, Henry, a/o, Madison, Ind.,
129, #6908

Boatman, William, Ohio, 53,
#6380

Boatwright, Benjamin, w/o,
S.C., 49, #5336

Boatwright, Rebecca, S.C., 58,
#7892

Boawers, Balaam, Richmond,
Va., 48, #5073

Bobbitt, William, S.C., 48,
#5195

Bockius, George, Albany, N.Y.,
52, #6123

Bodley, William, a/o,
Pittsburgh, Pa., 127, #4948

Boger, Christain, w/o,
Philadelphia, Pa., 107,
#9477

Bogle, William, w/o, Mass., 85,
#16530

Boldman, John, Albany, N.Y.,
58, #7681

Boldman, John, w/o, Albany,
N.Y., 126, #3142

Bole, James, Nashville, Tenn.,
59, #8085

Bolener, Adam, Richmond, Va.,
72, #12662

Boles, Sarah, a/o, Knoxville,
Tenn., 128, #5685

Boley, Prestley, w/o, Richmond,
Va., 45, #4523

Bolin, Thomas, Ind., 48, #5044

Boling, Jarret, Richmond, Va.,
45, #4524

Boling, Jarret, Va., 40, #3333

Boll, Patterson, c/o,
Philadelphia, Pa., 103,
#7022

Bolt, James, New York City,
136, #3290

Bolton, Huldah, c/o, Ill., 97,
#2231

Bolton, John, w/o, Ill., 61,
#8624

Bond, Adonijah, Albany, N.Y.,
65, #10038

Bond, Bethnel, Albany, N.Y.,
68, #10755

Bond, Joseph, N.Y., 97, #1927,
card

Bond, Patsey, a/o, Richmond,
Va., 126, #3148

Bonds, Joseph, w/o, Albany,
N.Y., 3, #1927

Bondy, John, w/o, N.C., 92,
#19806

Bone, George, S.C., 54, #6646

Boner, Charles, Richmond, Va.,
55, #7124

Boner, Charles, Richmond, Va.,
60, #8310

Bonhonnon, Olive, Concord,
N.H., 91, #18995

Bonnel, John, Philadelphia, Pa.,
76, #13953

Bonnell, Abner, c/o, Cincinnati,
Ohio, 135, #1922

Bonner, Jane, Philadelphia, Pa.,
63, #9105

Bonner, John, w/o, Nashville,
Tenn., 91, #18975

Bonner, William, Richmond,
Va., 105, #7866

Bonner, William, Va., 46,
#4677
Bonnett, Roger, w/o, Albany,
N.Y., 55, #7155
Bonney, Silence, Mass., 117,
#3943
Booker, Isaac, Ohio, 53, #6541
Booker, John, S.C., 51, #6057
Booker, Samuel, Ky., 40, #3304
Booker, Samuel, Ky., 70,
#12014
Booker, Samuel, w/o, Ky., 119,
#5363
Booker, Sarah, Maine, 67,
#10351
Boon, Polly, N.C., 103, #6844
Boon, Polly, a/o, N.C., 117,
#4233
Boos, Jacob, g/o c/o,
Cincinnati, Ohio, 128,
#5934
Booth, Isaac, c/o, Albany, N.Y.,
89, #18525
Boothby, Elizabeth, c/o,
Portland, Maine, 107,
#9194
Boothe, Anne, c/o, Mass., 111,
#717
Borden, Job, c/o, Ohio, 82,
#15529
Borders, Christopher, Ohio, 68,
#10757
Borders, Christopher, Ohio, 80,
#14851
Borders, Esther, Ky., 134, #709
Boren, William, Mo., 61, #8429
Boren, William, Mo., 62, #8722
Boroughs, Daniel, Pittsburgh,
Pa., 64, #9624
Borrett, Elizabeth, Ohio, 58,
#7813

Boston, Jacob, e/o, N.C., 100,
#3898
Bostwick, Doctor, c/o,
Cleveland, Ohio, 121,
#7959
Boswell, Charles, Hartford,
Conn., 114, #2430
Boswell, George W., g/o c/o,
Ill., 137, #4436
Boswell, George W., g/o c/o,
Indianapolis, Ind., 129,
#6783
Bosworth, Cyrus, Augusta,
Maine, 143, #6873
Bosworth, Elizabeth, c/o, La.,
120, #6673
Bosworth, Felix G., c/o, La.,
131, #8265
Bothman, Barnhart, w/o,
Pittsburgh, Pa., 90, #18623
Botkin, Margaret, Richmond,
Va., 103, #7082
Bott, Frederick, Va., 80, #14817
Botts (formerly Stewart), Maria
L., Ky., 137, #4302
Botts, Moses, —, 108, #10274,
card
Botts, Moses, a/o, Ky., 3,
#10274
Bottsley, Purch, Bellows Falls,
Vt., 63, #8967
Bourland, Hampton H., g/o c/o,
Ill., 130, #7689
Bourland, John D., Ill., 116,
#3178
Bourn, Ebenezer, a/o, Ill., 92,
#208
Bourn, William, a/o,
Philadelphia, Pa., 79,
#14724
Bousher, Philip, Philadelphia,
Pa., 66, #10171

Boutard, Joseph, Philadelphia,
Pa., 43, #3879

Boutwell, John, Albany, N.Y.,
41, #3546

Bovee, Philip, Pittsburgh, Pa.,
40, #3202

Bowden, Arthur, Boston, Mass.,
120, #5835

Bowden, Elias, a/o, Jackson,
Tenn., 120, #6096

Bowels, Samuel, w/o, Mo., 121,
#7016

Bowen, Benjamin, w/o, S.C.,
51, #5875

Bowen, Consider, Vt., 58,
#7853, card

Bowen, Consider, w/o, Vt., 3,
#7853

Bowen, Elizabeth, Md., 84,
#16314

Bowen, Innocent, Pittsburgh,
Pa., 104, #7476

Bowen, Innocent, Pittsburgh,
Pa., 98, #3013

Bowen, John, Ga., 62, #8684

Bowen, John, Ga., 75, #13432

Bowen, John, Ga., 106, #8564

Bowen, John, c/o, Ga., 119,
#5389

Bowen, Micajah, Richmond,
Va., 119, #5642

Bowen, Nancy, a/o, Ga., 136,
#2917

Bowen, Samuel, Albany, N.Y.,
64, #9553

Bowen, Samuel, Maine, 115,
#2710, card

Bowen, Samuel, c/o, Maine, 3,
#2710

Bowen, Samuel, w/o, Ga., 96,
#1628

Bowen, Sarow, a/o, Maine, 102,
#6031

Bowen, Stephen, w/o, Ga., 72,
#12549

Bowen, William, Md., 42,
#3762

Bowen, William, e/o, R.I., 135,
#1905

Bowen, William F., Nashville,
Tenn., 137, #4445

Bowens, Balaam, Richmond,
Va., 54, #6807

Bowens, Michael, w/o, Conn.,
68, #10660

Bowers, Anna, a/o, Pittsburgh,
Pa., 105, #8015

Bowers, Balaam, c/o, Richmond,
Va., 73, #12950

Bowers, Benajah, g/o c/o,
Conn., 37, #F1831

Bowers, George, c/o,
Philadelphia, Pa., 110,
#104

Bowers, Leonard, w/o,
Jonesboro, Tenn., 84,
#16177

Bowers, Sally, c/o, Poultney,
Vt., 97, #2177

Bowers, William, g/o,
Philadelphia, Pa., 135,
#2046

Bowers, Lloyd, late PA, Mobile,
Ala., 135, #1810

Bowes, Emeline, D.C., 125,
#2051

Bowes, Emeline, D.C., 138,
#6519

Bowke, William, La., 132,
#9299

Bowles, Chesterfield, Richmond,
Va., 143, #6862

Bowles, Samuel, Mo., 58, #7711

Bowles, Thomas, Va., 71,
#12431

Bowley, Grace, Md., 137, #4039

Bowling, Letty M., Va., 65,
#10023

Bowling, Martha, Indianapolis,
Ind., 140, #1190

Bowling, William, Ohio, 43,
#3900

Bowman, Daniel, Nashville,
Tenn., 81, #15040

Bowman, David, g/o c/o, Md.,
129, #6655

Bowman, Elisha, Philadelphia,
Pa., 119, #5643

Bowman, John, Richmond, Va.,
62, #8685

Bowman, John, e/o, Richmond,
Va., 96, #1841

Bowman, William, New Albany,
Ind., 90, #18952, card

Bowman, O. P., SpC, (Rations),
100, #4426

Boyce, Abby, c/o, Albany, N.Y.,
67, #10520

Boyd, Ann, Richmond, Va., 96,
#1618

Boyd, Henry, e/o, Jonesboro,
Tenn., 72, #12646

Boyd, James, Mobile, Ala., 70,
#12060

Boyd, James, Mobile, Ala., 102,
#5471

Boyd, James, Richmond, Va.,
71, #12364

Boyd, James, e/o, Richmond,
Va., 101, #5248

Boyd, John, Mo., 143, #7273

Boyd, William, Va., 80, #14943

Boyd, William, w/o, Ky., 108,
#10204

Boyden, Josiah, Mass., 79,
#14644

Boyden, Susan B., g/o, Mass.,
140, #1087

Boydston, Samuel, Jackson,
Miss., 94, #625

Boydston, Samuel, Miss., 83,
#15641

Boydston, Samuel, Miss., 91,
#19384

Boydston, Samuel, Natchez,
Miss., 81, #15121

Boydston (or Poyston), Samuel,
Miss., 72, #12693

Boyer, John, e/o, Ind., 76,
#13840

Boyer, Peter, Ind., 63, #9074

Boylan, Sarah, Philadelphia,
Pa., 64, #9152

Boyle, James, Albany, N.Y.,
143, #6773

Boyle, Margaret, Knoxville,
Tenn., 107, #9537

Boylston, William, a/o, Boston,
Mass., 119, #5129

Boynton, Betty, Concord, N.H.,
99, #3536

Boynton, Eunice, Albany, N.Y.,
122, #8328

Boynton, Moses, N.H., 64,
#9282

Boyt, Sally, a/o, Va., 109,
#10880

Boyt, William, w/o, Richmond,
Va., 107, #9539

Brace, Joseph, Mich., 108,
#9811

Bracket, John, w/o, Albany,
N.Y., 67, #10521

Brackett, Betsy, c/o, Mass.,
125, #2502

Brackett, Rebecca, Boston,
Mass., 102, #5428

Bradaman, John, N.Y., 81,
#15046

Bradford, David, e/o, Boston,
Mass., 86, #17114

Bradford, James, N.C., 45,
#4527

Bradford, Lucy, a/o, Montpelier,
Vt., 105, #7853

Bradford, Lucy, c/o, Albany,
N.Y., 133, #228

Bradford, Margaret, e/o, N.J.,
128, #6010

Bradford, Sam K., w/o, Va., 101,
#5182, card

Bradford, William S., La., 128,
#4990

Bradick, Gideon, —, 62, #8745,
card

Bradley, Albert, c/o, Cincinnati,
Ohio, 117, #3954

Bradley, Aner, e/o, Conn., 38,
#F1824

Bradley, Benjamin, e/o,
Concord, N.H., 73, #12724

Bradley, Franky, Richmond, Va.,
104, #7525

Bradley, Franky, Va., 67,
#10347

Bradley, James, Richmond, Va.,
3, #12254

Bradley, James, Richmond, Va.,
64, #9159

Bradley, James, Richmond, Va.,
47, #5036

Bradley, James, Va., 71,
#12254, card

Bradley, Lois, Conn., 30, #28

Bradley, Parnel, Pittsburgh, Pa.,
100, #3835

Bradley, Simeon, Indianapolis,
Ind., 132, #9546

Bradshaw, Elizabeth, a/o, Ky.,
97, #2444

Bradshaw, Larner, a/o, Ky., 85,
#16394

Brady, Benjamin, Md., 40,
#3233

Brady, Benjamin, Md., 45,
#4453

Brady, Bernard S., Spingfield,
Ill., 142, #5065

Brady, Thomas, D.C., 143,
#7367

Brag, William, w/o, Albany,
N.Y., 89, #18460

Bragdon, Elijah, c/o, 34th Inf.,
105, #8213

Bragdon, Elijah, w/o, 34th Inf.,
95, #819

Bragg, William, w/o, Knoxville,
Tenn., 91, #19091

Brainard, Amos, w/o, Pittsburgh,
Pa., 116, #3069

Brainard, Ansel, Pittsburgh, Pa.,
96, #1631

Brainard, Asahel, D.C., 107,
#9664

Brainard, Asahel, D.C., 113,
#1406

Brainard, Elijah, c/o, N.C., 44,
#4195

Brainard, Jabez, Concord, N.H.,
46, #4703

Brainard, Jabez, Concord, N.H.,
50, #5837

Brainard, Jerusha, a/o,
Cleveland, Ohio, 132,
#9105

Brainard, Rachel, c/o, Conn.,
30, #12993

Brainerd, Rachel, c/o, Conn.,
63, #9096
Bramble, Robert, w/o, Conn.,
100, #3936
Brammall, George G., SpC,
(Rations), 101, #5081
Branard, Ansel, Pittsburgh, Pa.,
86, #17237
Branard, Jebez, Concord, N.H.,
54, #6615
Branch, Lucy, c/o, Albany, N.Y.,
75, #13576
Branch, Olive, Richmond, Va.,
61, #8653
Brandon, Benjamin, Ohio, 106,
#8800
Brandon, Margaret, Richmond,
Va., 97, #2230
Brandon, Thomas, w/o, Va., 84,
#16057
Braneman, Christian, Ind., 48,
#5053
Branham, Richard, Ga., 74,
#13372
Branham, Richard, Ga., 77,
#13985
Brank, Robert, Ky., 3, #7052
Brasfield, James, w/o, Ky., 74,
#13142
Brashears, Margaret, g/o, Ky.,
125, #1860
Brasher, John, c/o, Cincinnati,
Ohio, 122, #8437
Brasington, Samuel, w/o,
Albany, N.Y., 61, #8467
Brass, Caroline, D.C., 127,
#4637
Brass, Garrett, w/o, Pittsburgh,
Pa., 42, #3562
Brass, Lucy, Philadelphia, Pa.,
83, #15621

Brasswell, Herny, S.C., 46,
#4765
Braswell, Penelope, c/o, N.C.,
101, #4930
Braxton, Mary, N.C., 119,
#5144
Bray, Elisha, Oregon Territory,
125, #2011
Bray, Sampson, e/o, Albany,
N.Y., 71, #12436
Brazier, Richard, Mo., 126,
#3590
Brearley, Rachel, c/o, N.J., 64,
#9255
Breck, Daniel, w/o, Boston,
Mass., 83, #15897
Breden, Charles, W. Tenn., 64,
#9669
Breecher, William, e/o,
Nashville, Tenn., 124,
#1369
Breed, Esther, c/o, Albany, N.Y.,
56, #7339
Breed, Stephen, w/o, Albany,
N.Y., 57, #7554
Breedd, Polly, Concord, N.H.,
135, #1673
Breedd, Polly, Concord, N.H.,
141, #1505
Breeden, Enoch, a/o, Nashville,
Tenn., 83, #15918
Breeding, William, Mo., 116,
#3090
Breeding, William, w/o, Oregon
Territory, 128, #5687
Breedlove, William, Ky., 138,
#6184, card
Brees, Timothy, Ohio, 71,
#12457
Breese (formerly Hampton),
Clarissa, Spingfield, Ill.,
140, #9889

Breeze, Henry, c/o, N.J., 119,
#5215
Bregauski, Edward, New York
City, 91, #19335
Brend, William, Ga., 56, #7302
Brennah, James A., w/o,
Philadelphia, Pa., 97,
#2094
Brenneman, Abram M.,
Pittsburgh, Pa., 142, #5051
Brennin, Dennis, Ore., 140,
#783
Brentlinger (formerly Main),
Sohpronia, Evansville,
Ind., 137, #3800
Brenton, William, w/o, Ind., 3,
#6673
Brevard, Robert, Mo., 62, #8765
Brevard, Robert, Mo., 81,
#14996
Brevard, Robert, Mo., 90,
#18549
Brewer, Barnett, Mobile, Ala.,
59, #7964
Brewer, Isaac, Mass., 46, #4823
Brewer, Peter, a/o, Albany, N.Y.,
127, #4731
Brewer, Rebecca, Ky., 72,
#12484
Brewer, William M., c/o, Ind.,
118, #5116
Brewster, Eleanor, c/o, Concord,
N.H., 92, #19600
Brewster, Fredk, Albany, N.Y.,
62, #8665
Brewster, Hugh, Ga., 113, #1315
Brewster, Joanna, Mass., 130,
#7790
Brewster, Joshua, c/o, Mass.,
113, #1547
Brewster, Nathan, Ohio, 62,
#8702

Brewster, Nathan, Ohio, 67,
#10510
Brewster, Nathan, w/o, Ohio, 88,
#17778
Brewster, William, S.C., 60,
#8288
Brewster, William, S.C., 72,
#12560
Brewster, William, S.C., 81,
#15007
Brewster, William, S.C., 95,
#1077
Brewton, William, —, 54,
#6673, card
Bridgeman, Elisha, w/o,
Pittsburgh, Pa., 61, #8498
Brierly, Mary, Ky., 117, #3978
Briesler, Esther, Mass., 70,
#11048
Briggs, Abner, w/o, Maine, 58,
#7872
Briggs, Anderson, w/o, R.I., 57,
#7531
Briggs, Deborah, Mass., 84,
#15991
Briggs, Ephriam, w/o, Albany,
N.Y., 90, #18679
Briggs, John, Ill., 67, #10409
Briggs, Margaret, Ky., 122,
#8113
Briggs, Nancy, a/o, Albany,
N.Y., 123, #9159
Briggs, Phineas, Albany, N.Y.,
53, #6447
Briggs, Phineas, c/o, Albany,
N.Y., 117, #4548
Brigham, Elizabeth, Mass., 62,
#8680
Brigham, Elizabeth, Mass., 71,
#12343
Brigham, Eunice, Boston,
Mass., 71, #12342

Brigham, Jesse, w/o, Mass., 44,
#4269
Brigham, Lydia, Vt., 85, #16372
Brightwell (formerly Bowhan),
Susannah, Md., 113, #1295
Brimmer, Elizabeth, Knoxville,
Tenn., 104, #7456
Brink, Aaron, Mich., 105,
#7910
Brinkerhoff, Cornelia, N.J.,
112, #1109
Brinkerhoff, James J., w/o, N.J.,
92, #19811
Brinks (or Brank), Robert, Ky.,
103, #7052, slip
Brinzee, Wynson, Albany, N.Y.,
90, #18807
Briscoe, Henry, —, 70, #11059,
card
Briscoe, Henry, Ill., 3, #11059
Briscoe, Philip, Miss., 52,
#6091
Briscoe, Philip, Miss., 53,
#6479
Brisette, Louis, La., 99, #3318
Bristol, Samuel, N.Y., 54,
#6802, card
Bristol, Samuel, c/o, Albany,
N.Y., 3, #6802
Briton, Michael, N.C., 56,
#7283
Britt, Charles, S.C., 50, #5549,
card
Britt, Phinles, c/o, Charleston,
S.C., 3, #5549
Britten, Gershom H., Albany,
N.Y., 46, #4752
Britten, John, Albany, N.Y., 90,
#18827
Britton, Abigal, Albany, N.Y.,
75, #13702

Britton, Ebenezer N., Albany,
N.Y., 133, #230
Britton, Samuel, c/o, Albany,
N.Y., 133, #405
Britton, William, Ohio, 48,
#5202
Britton, William, Ohio, 55,
#7116
Britton, William, c/o, N.J., 116,
#3447
Britton, William, c/o, Ohio, 3,
#15097
Brittow, William, c/o, Ohio, 81,
#15097, card
Brizee, Wynsen, Albany, N.Y.,
63, #8931
Brizendine, Bartlett, w/o,
Richmond, Va., 91, #19329
Brizendine, R., c/o, Richmond,
Va., 102, #5686
Brizendine, Reuben, Va., 83,
#15760
Broaddus, Pryor, c/o, Va., 91,
#19001
Broaddus, Pryor, c/o, Va., 91,
#19221
Broaddus, William T.,
Richmond, Va., 138, #4810
Broadhead, Affy, e/o,
Philadelphia, Pa., 71,
#12347
Broadrick, John, c/o, Mass., 68,
#10665
Broadshaw, John, Va., 64,
#9614
Brock, Jesse, Ky., 53, #6578
Brock, Jesse, Ky., 85, #16555
Brock, Reuben, S.C., 69,
#10974
Brock, Reuben, S.C., 72,
#12691

Brock, Sarah, Maine, 72,
#12530
Brockenridge (formerly
Avilson), Dicey, Nashville,
Tenn., 128, #5006
Brockett, Asenath, Albany,
N.Y., 143, #7368
Brockingham, John, S.C., 68,
#10573
Brockway, Benjamin, Conn.,
38, #F1825
Brockway, Ephraim, w/o,
Albany, N.Y., 50, #5641
Brogles, Daniel, Knoxville,
Tenn., 78, #14432
Bromagen, Jarvis, Ky., 80,
#14879
Bromlet, Reuben, Ill., 82,
#15382
Bronson, Anna, Hartford, Conn.,
140, #9349
Bronson, Asahel, Conn., 44,
#4402
Bronson, Ashael, Conn., 58,
#7683
Bronson, Huldah, c/o, Hartford,
Conn., 30, #8799
Bronson, Isaac, w/o, New York
City, 60, #8308
Bronson, Phineas, Ill., 58,
#7878
Bronson, William, N.C., 59,
#8145
Brooghton, Mary, Jackson,
Tenn., 125, #1767, card
Brook, Henry, N.Y., 81, #15078
Brooke, Charles, Ohio, 59,
#8139
Brooke, Edmund, D.C., 64,
#9494
Brooke, Edmund, c/o, D.C., 99,
#3214

Brooker, Samuel, w/o, Boston,
Mass., 113, #1719
Brookes, Oliver, c/o, Pa., 3,
#2699
Brooks, A. S., w/o, 4th
Artillery, 46, #4740
Brooks, Lt. Col., w/o, —, 72,
#12569
Brooks, Lt. Col. A., w/o, —, 63,
#9110
Brooks, Lt. Col. A. S., w/o, —,
41, #3401
Brooks, Lt. Col. A. S., w/o, —,
57, #7596
Brooks, Lt. Col. A. S., w/o, —,
67, #10463
Brooks, Lt. Col. A. S., w/o, —,
76, #13929
Brooks, Alex. S., w/o, —, 52,
#6280
Brooks, Austin, c/o, Ill., 100,
#4112
Brooks, Barsheba, a/o,
Richmond, Va., 132, #9314
Brooks, Benjamin E., Ind., 122,
#8114
Brooks, Benjamin E., La., 124,
#878
Brooks, Daniel, c/o, Knoxville,
Tenn., 129, #7052, card
Brooks, Deborah, a/o, Boston,
Mass., 100, #3770
Brooks, Francis, Richmond, Va.,
62, #8728
Brooks, Francis, Richmond, Va.,
71, #12362
Brooks, George, c/o, Ga., 128,
#5688
Brooks, Guy, w/o, Albany, N.Y.,
141, #3144
Brooks, Jonas, w/o, Concord,
N.H., 113, #1382

Brooks, Littleton, Jonesboro, Tenn., 66, #10299

Brooks, Nancy, Richmond, Va., 104, #7582

Brooks, Nathaniel, a/o, Fayetteville, N.C., 133, #82

Brooks, Oliver, Pittsburgh, Pa., 115, #2799, card

Brooks, Richard, a/o, Md., 125, #1951

Brooks, Robert, Ga., 43, #3978

Brooks, Robert, Ga., 55, #7117

Brooks, Samuel C., La., 126, #3401

Brooks (formerly Williamson), Sarah, c/o, Richmond, Va., 36A, #F5 V4

Brooks, Surviah, a/o, Albany, N.Y., 118, #5058

Brooks, Wililam, N.C., 96, #1384, card

Brooks, William, Richmond, Va., 45, #4522

Brooks, William, Richmond, Va., 52, #6209

Brooks, William, Va., 40, #3331

Brooks, William, a/o, N.C., 112, #843, card

Brooks, William, a/o, N.C., 3, #843

Brooks, William, c/o, N.C., 3, #1384

Brooks, William, w/o, Va., 74, #13354

Brooks, Zachariah, S.C., 96, #1576

Brooks, Zachariah S., Charleston, S.C., 50, #5778

Brooks, Zachariah S., S.C., 39, #3080

Brooks, George, see Isum Peacock, 3, #4963, card

Broom, John, S.C., 55, #7096

Broom, John, c/o, S.C., 113, #1850

Brophy, Michael, Calif., 131, #8732

Brophy, Michael, Iowa, 105, #7798

Brophy, Michael, Iowa, 106, #8661

Brothers, Cyrus C., c/o, Ohio, 121, #6828

Brothers, Cyrus C., g/o c/o, Cincinnati, Ohio, 126, #3350

Brothers (now Pittman), Mary, Ohio, 120, #6593

Brotherton, William, w/o, Jonesboro, Tenn., 42, #3667

Brougham, Margaret, Albany, N.Y., 60, #8325

Broughten, Mary, a/o, Jackson, Tenn., 3, #1767

Brouse, Michael, Ohio, 77, #14138

Brouse, Michael, Pittsburgh, Pa., 54, #6688

Brower, Jacob, Philadelphia, Pa., 52, #6138

Brown, Adonijah, w/o, Albany, N.Y., 115, #2648

Brown, Amos, N.C., 105, #8051

Brown, Amos, N.C., 65, #9728

Brown, Amos, N.C., 79, #14726

Brown, Ann, N.C., 121, #6918

Brown, Benjamin, —, 128, #5782, slip

Brown, Benjamin, Ga., 61,
#8593
Brown, Benjamin, Ga., 85,
#16459
Brown, Benjamin, Ga., 128,
#5319
Brown, Benjamin, Ga., 128,
#5408
Brown, Benjamin, e/o, Ga., 129,
#6840
Brown, Caroline, g/o, Chicago,
Ill., 141, #1484
Brown, Charles F., Albany,
N.Y., 112, #1067
Brown, Christopher, w/o, R.I.,
95, #959
Brown, Clarissa, Nashville,
Tenn., 98, #3069
Brown, Cyrus, c/o, Albany,
N.Y., 123, #9499
Brown, David, c/o, Albany,
N.Y., 114, #2111
Brown, Ebenezer, Mich., 49,
#5461
Brown, Ebenezer M., Ill., 128,
#5005
Brown, Eliada, Burlington, Vt.,
47, #4913
Brown, Elias, Vt., 57, #7655
Brown, Elijah, w/o, Ga., 43,
#3979
Brown, Elizabeth, Morganton,
N.C., 121, #7636
Brown, Elizabeth, c/o,
Pittsburgh, Pa., 63, #9120
Brown, Elizabeth, c/o, Va., 47,
#4889
Brown (formerly Wildor), Emily,
S.C., 119, #5635
Brown, Enos, Philadelphia, Pa.,
56, #7331
Brown, Ephraim, Ga., 47, #5034

Brown, Ephraim, Ga., 68,
#10655
Brown, Ephriam, Ga., 57, #7648
Brown, Ezakiel, c/o, Ohio, 78,
#14463
Brown, George, Jonesboro,
Tenn., 66, #10076
Brown, George, Jonesboro,
Tenn., 71, #12300
Brown, George, Jonesboro,
Tenn., 79, #14583
Brown, George, Jonesboro,
Tenn., 85, #16431
Brown, George, Jonesboro,
Tenn., 87, #17588
Brown, George, e/o, Ill., 90,
#18788
Brown, George, w/o, Jonesboro,
Tenn., 99, #3442
Brown, Hannah, Conn., 30, #12
Brown (formerly Hatton),
Hannah, Ill., 136, #3090
Brown, Henry, D.C., 139, #8352
Brown, Henry, Richmond, Va.,
57, #7517
Brown, Henry, Richmond, Va.,
62, #8729
Brown, Henry, Richmond, Va.,
47, #4850
Brown, Henry, Va., 41, #3365
Brown, Henry, Va., 75, #13627
Brown, Isaac, Philadelphia, Pa.,
3, #87
Brown, Isaac, Philadelphia, Pa.,
110, #87, card
Brown, Isaac, c/o, R.I., 45,
#4609
Brown, Isham, g/o c/o, Ga., 123,
#9712
Brown, Isham, g/o c/o, Ga., 128,
#5910

Brown, Jacob, w/o, Jonesboro, Tenn., 44, #4355

Brown, Jacob, w/o, Jonesboro, Tenn., 56, #7298

Brown, Jacob, w/o, Philadelphia, Pa., 78, #14517

Brown, Major Jacob, w/o, 7th Inf., 110, #11161

Brown, Major Jacob, w/o, 7th Inf., 102, #5648

Brown, Major Jacob, w/o, 7th Inf., 103, #6657

Brown, Major Jacob, w/o, 7th Inf., 104, #7499

Brown, Major Jacob, w/o, 7th Inf., 106, #8409

Brown, Major Jacob, w/o, 7th Inf., 107, #9421

Brown, Major Jacob, w/o, 7th Inf., 108, #10238

Brown, Major Jacob, w/o, 7th Inf., 101, #5110

Brown, James, N.C., 50, #5579

Brown, James, c/o, Philadelphia, Pa., 103, #6840

Brown, James H., c/o, Mo., 125, #2115

Brown, John, Miss., 60, #8201

Brown, John, Miss., 80, #14827

Brown, John, Philadelphia, Pa., 64, #9213

Brown, John, Philadelphia, Pa., 41, #3537

Brown, John, Richmond, Va., 43, #4030

Brown, John, S.C., 48, #5121

Brown, John, Vt., 73, #12818

Brown, John, w/o, D.C., 115, #2971

Brown, John F., c/o, Mo., 117, #3864

Brown, Jonathan, c/o, Pittsburgh, Pa., 81, #15195

Brown, Jonathan, c/o, Pittsburgh, Pa., 84, #15943

Brown, Joseph, w/o, Knoxville, Tenn., 90, #18548

Brown, Josiah, Philadelphia, Pa., 89, #18375

Brown, Lucy, e/o, N.C., 92, #19915

Brown, Martha, Va., 75, #13638

Brown, Martha, a/o, Richmond, Va., 108, #10180

Brown, Martin, Mo., 125, #1723

Brown, Martin, Mo., 131, #8796

Brown, Mary, Knoxville, Tenn., 131, #8863

Brown, Mary, R.I., 101, #4811

Brown, Mary, c/o, Conn., 58, #7682

Brown, Mathias, w/o, Albany, N.Y., 127, #4147

Brown, Michael, Ohio, 57, #7478

Brown, Milly, Nashville, Tenn., 113, #1873

Brown, Morgan, Nashville, Tenn., 110, #11078

Brown, Morgan, c/o, Nashville, Tenn., 3, #11078

Brown, Morgan, c/o, Nashville, Tenn., 3, #10800

Brown, Nancy, Cincinnati, Ohio, 134, #1401

Brown, Nancy, Iowa, 139, #8132

Brown, Nathan, Ill., 72, #12582

Brown, Nathan, c/o, Ill., 114, #2268

Brown, Nathan, c/o, Ill., 134, #1275

Brown, Nathan, w/o, Ill., 90, #18797

Brown, Nehemiah, c/o, Albany, N.Y., 123, #9117

Brown, Phineas, Mich., 92, #19582

Brown, Pollard, Ga., 110, #11090

Brown, Pollard, S.C., 59, #8013

Brown, Pollard, S.C., 78, #14227

Brown, Pollard, S.C., 88, #18073

Brown, Pollard, S.C., 95, #1078

Brown, Pollard, S.C., 100, #3749

Brown, Priscilla, Albany, N.Y., 116, #3631

Brown, Lt. R. T., Special, Mo. Vols., 120, #6598

Brown, Rachel, c/o, Maine, 97, #2095

Brown, Rebecca, c/o, N.J., 123, #9227

Brown, Robert, Nashville, Tenn., 88, #17869

Brown, Robert C., g/o c/o, Savannah, Ga., 129, #6519

Brown, Samuel, Maine, 40, #3230

Brown, Samuel, New York City, 136, #3466

Brown, Samuel, New York City, 139, #9129

Brown, Sarah, c/o, R.I., 83, #15734

Brown, Sgt. David, w/o, 22nd Inf., 109, #10671

Brown, Solomon, w/o, Albany, N.Y., 55, #7058

Brown, Sophronia, Philadelphia, Pa., 134, #966

Brown, Stark, c/o, Ga., 72, #12547

Brown, Stark, c/o, Ga., 98, #2910

Brown, Stephen, c/o, Detroit, Mich., 129, #6531

Brown, Stephen, c/o, Knoxville, Tenn., 67, #10548

Brown, Tarlton, S.C., 49, #5351

Brown, Thomas, Va., 75, #13617

Brown, Thomas, Wheeling, Va., 75, #13559

Brown, Thomas, Wheeling, Va., 45, #4468

Brown, Thomas, Wheeling, W. Va., 40, #3164

Brown, Thomas, c/o, Ky., 58, #7849

Brown, Thomas, c/o, Ky., 134, #953

Brown, Wiliam, c/o, S.C., 119, #5373

Brown, William, Albany, N.Y., 70, #12125

Brown, William, Mo., 55, #7045

Brown, William, Mo., 76, #13795

Brown, William, N.C., 42, #3620

Brown, William, N.C., 62, #8735

Brown, William, Ohio, 41, #3422

Brown, William, Ohio, 58, #7718

Brown, William, Ohio, 62, #8686

Brown, William, Ohio, 102, #6138

Brown, William, Ohio, 108, #10167

Brown, William, Ohio, 97, #2486

Brown, William, Richmond, Va., 57, #7496

Brown, William, Va., 66, #10282

Brown, William, c/o, N.C., 97, #2376

Brown, William, e/o, Fayetteville, N.C., 104, #7309

Brownell, Delia, R.I., 127, #4542

Brownell, Delia, R.I., 128, #5003

Brownell, Juddith, a/o, Albany, N.Y., 128, #5173

Browning, Franceis, Richmond, Va., 48, #5181

Browning, Francis, Richmond, Va., 56, #7333

Browning, Francis, Richmond, Va., 62, #8717

Browning, Francis, Richmond, Va., 66, #10287

Browning, Francis, Richmond, Va., 77, #13981

Browning, Francis, Va., 71, #12415

Broyles, Daniel, Knoxville, Tenn., 95, #1166

Broyles, Daniel, c/o, Knoxville, Tenn., 117, #4454

Bruce, Benjamin, Albany, N.Y., 3, #13901

Bruce, Louisa, Mass., 130, #7691

Bruce, Silas, w/o, Mass., 118, #4725

Bruce, d. 13 Sep 1839, #-, New York City, 76, #13901

Bruette, Lucy, Mich., 143, #6568

Brumback, Peter, Ky., 52, #6232

Brumfield, John, c/o, La., 131, #8743

Brumfield, Pvt. Samuel H., c/o, Rangers, 111, #774

Brumley, Amos, g/o c/o, Conn., 37, #F1820

Brummal, Benjamin, w/o, Ky., 94, #456

Bruner, Alley, Richmond, Va., 36A, #F3 V2

Brunnell, Samuel, Vt., 59, #8095

Brunner, Valentine, w/o, Md., 86, #16748

Brunson, William R., S.C., 56, #7370

Brunson, William R., c/o, S.C., 118, #4943

Brush, Gilbert R., Calif., 126, #3558

Brush, Gilbert R., La., 119, #5772

Brusick, Abraham, St. Louis, Mo., 128, #5912

Brusus, Jacob, Philadelphia, Pa., 48, #5248

Bryan, Catherine, Philadelphia, Pa., 85, #16723

Bryan, Charles, c/o, Philadelphia, Pa., 136, #2733

Bryan, Elijah, c/o, Pittsburgh, Pa., 96, #1385

Bryan, James, Philadelphia, Pa., 52, #6088

Bryan, John, w/o, N.C., 96,
#1383
Bryan, Lucy, Conn., 30, #35
Bryan, Thomas, Ga., 47, #4925
Bryant, Alexander P., Albany,
N.Y., 143, #7290
Bryant, Ephraim, c/o, Va., 121,
#8034
Bryant, James, E. Tenn., 64,
#9473, card
Bryant, James, w/o, Knoxville,
Tenn., 3, #9473
Bryant, Johannah, c/o,
Portsmouth, N.H., 69,
#10856
Bryant, Martha, c/o, Maine,
132, #8955
Bryant, Mary, Ky., 97, #1946
Bryant, Mary, Mass., 66,
#10165
Bryant, Mary, c/o, N.J., 115,
#2563
Bryant, Robert, c/o, N.C., 94,
#558
Bryant, Robert, c/o, N.C., 100,
#3909
Bryant, Sally, Ky., 95, #878
Bryant, Sally, a/o, Ky., 104,
#7198
Bryant, William B., Ind., 55,
#7181
Bryant, William B., Ind., 58,
#7870
Bryant, William G., W. Tenn.,
65, #9902
Bryant, William G., e/o,
Nashville, Tenn., 89,
#18526
Bryant, Zenas, c/o, Mass., 139,
#8175
Bryon, Thomas, Ga., 64, #9661

Bryson, Daniel, w/o,
Fayetteville, N.C., 131,
#8198
Bubier, Hannah, Mass., 76,
#13904
Bubler, John C., D.C., 142,
#4899
Buchanan, Elijah, Albany, N.Y.,
143, #6758
Buchanan, George, Ga., 42,
#3602
Buchanan, George, Ga., 56,
#7303
Buchanan, George, Ga., 134,
#1398, card
Buchanan, Henry, a/o,
Richmond, Va., 125, #2116
Buchanan, Richard, Va., 120,
#6525
Buchanan, William, c/o, N.Y.,
90, #18771
Buchannon, George, c/o, Ga., 3,
#1398
Buchanon, William, c/o, N.Y.,
89, #18533
Buck, Aaron, Albany, N.Y., 90,
#18580
Buck, Aaron, Albany, N.Y., 53,
#6535
Buck, Isaac, w/o, Albany, N.Y.,
81, #15095
Buck, Johnathan, Pittsburgh,
Pa., 40, #3308
Buck, Sybil, a/o, Philadelphia,
Pa., 134, #1534
Buck, Thomas, w/o, Va., 106,
#8594
Bucken, Philip Peter, Richmond,
Va., 44, #4289
Bucker, Philip Peter, Richmond,
Va., 49, #5389

Buckland, Joshua, c/o, Conn.,
122, #8773
Bucklew, Peter, w/o,
Philadelphia, Pa., 122,
#8569
Buckman, George, Cleveland,
Ohio, 127, #4186
Buckman, George, Cleveland,
Ohio, 128, #5026
Bucknam, Naby, Va., 68,
#10713
Buckner, Jesse, Mo., 131,
#8188
Budd, John, Pa., 124, #1264,
card
Budd, John, c/o, Philadelphia,
Pa., 3, #1262
Budd, Ruth, lr/o, Pittsburgh, Pa.,
96, #1775
Buell, Timothy, c/o, Albany,
N.Y., 122, #8656
Buff, James, Md., 137, #3910,
card
Buff, James, c/o, Md., 3, #3910
Buffington, Margeret, c/o,
Cincinnati, Ohio, 130,
#7593
Buffington, Preserved, a/o,
Philadelphia, Pa., 92, #133
Buford, John, Ky., 42, #3771
Buford, John, Ky., 56, #7353
Bugbee, Methitable, Bellows
Falls, Vt., 63, #8967
Bugby, Ansel J., Milwaukee,
Wisc., 143, #7289
Buker, Israel, w/o, Cincinnati,
Ohio, 3, #8046
Bulasky, Simeon, Mo., 125,
#1794
Buley, George, w/o, Md., 62,
#8791

Bulkeley, John, Conn., 30,
#267
Bull, Reuben, Conn., 30, #133
Bull, Thomas, Ill., 51, #6002
Bulland, John, Boston, Mass.,
52, #6345
Bullock, Capt E. B., accounting,
49, #5368
Bullock, Catherine W., e/o,
Richmond, Va., 125, #1688
Bullock, David, Va., 61, #8466
Bullock, James P., Ky., 40,
#3305
Bullock, James P., Ky., 61,
#8591
Bullock, John, Philadelphia,
Pa., 56, #7364
Bullock, John, Philadelphia,
Pa., 77, #14139
Bultez, Eleonice P., New York
City, 136, #3387
Bumgarner, Catharine, Va., 122,
#8408
Bumill, Joseph, c/o, Boston,
Mass., 55, #7199
Bummer, Anna, a/o, Ky., 121,
#7461
Bumpass, William, c/o,
Richmond, Va., 112, #1233
Bumpus, Lydia, Mass., 125,
#2240
Bundy, Abigail, Albany, N.Y.,
92, #69
Bundy, Betsey, Conn., 37,
#F1820
Bundy, Nancy, Nashville, Tenn.,
3, #4403
Bunnell, Enos, Conn., 30, #51
Bunner, Henry P., g/o c/o,
Louisville, Ky., 126, #3024
Buntin, William, Jackson,
Tenn., 45, #4571

Buntin, William, Richmond,
Va., 42, #3773
Burbank, Mary, a/o, Maine, 123,
#9674
Burbeck, William, Albany, N.Y.,
57, #7659
Burbidge, Elizabeth, Conn., 38,
#F1829
Burbridge, Lincefield, Ky., 88,
#17779, card
Burbridge, Lincefield, c/o, Ky.,
3, #17779
Burch, Edy, Ohio, 46, #4828
Burch, Edy, Ohio, 78, #14476
Burch, Gustavus, g/o c/o, Ill.,
136, #3621
Burch, Jane, Ky., 102, #5804
Burch, Thomas, w/o, Albany,
N.Y., 3, #3370
Burch, Tomas, Albany, N.Y., 41,
#3370, card
Burchard, Jonathan, w/o,
Albany, N.Y., 69, #10890
Burchell, Daniel, c/o, Va., 119,
#5360
Burchett, John, Ky., 87,
#17632, card
Burchett, John, a/o, Ky., 3,
#17632
Burcktoorf, Jacob, w/o, Albany,
N.Y., 135, #1930
Burdett, Javis, c/o, Va., 47,
#4904
Burdick, Gideon, Pittsburgh, Pa.,
3, #8745
Burdick, John, Ohio, 60, #8192
Burdick, John, Ohio, 67,
#10373
Burdick, John, Ohio, 79,
#14636
Burdick, John, Ohio, 81,
#15149

Burdin, John, a/o, Wheeling,
Va., 99, #3363
Burdsall, Burnett, w/o, N.J.,
110, #11114
Burdwin, Lois, a/o, Albany,
N.Y., 99, #3346
Burgdoff, Conrad, w/o, Albany,
N.Y., 85, #16366
Burgess, Elizabeth, Albany,
N.Y., 70, #11176
Burgess, John, c/o, Va., 46,
#4747
Burget, Lambert, w/o, Albany,
N.Y., 108, #10079
Burgin, John, c/o, Mich., 115,
#2816
Burham, James, Ky., 96, #1588
Burham, Leah, c/o, New York
City, 107, #9103
Burk, Abigail, a/o, Bradford, Vt.,
135, #1875
Burk, Catharine, c/o,
Philadelphia, Pa., 119,
#5520
Burk, Malchijah, Md., 55,
#7227
Burk, Polly, Ky., 138, #6676
Burke, Elihu, w/o, Knoxville,
Tenn., 110, #86
Burkes, Samuel, Mo., 66,
#10236
Burkhard, Frederick, —, 83,
#15747
Burkhart, Henry, Va., 52,
#6134, card
Burkhart, Henry, c/o, Richmond,
Va., 3, #6134
Burley, Joseph, Vt., 63, #8955
Burley, Joseph, e/o, N.H., 67,
#10421
Burlingame, Christopher, e/o,
Ohio, 84, #16207

Burlison, John, Albany, N.Y.,
125, #2135
Burner, Mary, c/o, Va., 66,
#10064
Burner, Mary, c/o, Va., 75,
#13434
Burnett, John H., Ga., 132,
#9207
Burnett, Joshua, Ind., 54, #6852
Burnett, Joshua, c/o, Ind., 101,
#5186
Burnham, Elizabeth, c/o,
Concord, N.H., 135, #2238
Burnham, John, Conn., 30, #62
Burnham, John, w/o, Albany,
N.Y., 3, #3566
Burnham (or Burham), Jeremiah,
w/o, Ohio, 63, #8935
Burns, Elizabeth, Ky., 123, #62
Burns, James, N.C., 90, #18610
Burns, John, Mo., 60, #8257
Burns, John, Mo., 97, #2011
Burns, Matilda, Mo., 111, #672
Burns, Matilda, Mo., 114,
#1943
Burns, Matilda, Mo., 121,
#7631
Burns, Matilda, Mo., 127,
#4305
Burns, Matilda, Mo., 128,
#5732
Burns, Matilda, Mo., 135,
#2173
Burns, Matilda, Mo., 140,
#1025
Burns, Proctor M., Mo., 143,
#6520
Burns, Samuel, w/o, S.C., 98,
#2843
Burns, Williams, w/o, Ga., 117,
#4078

Burns, statement, Capt. J. A.,
7th Conn. Vols., 142,
#5398
Burnsides, Andrew, S.C., 58,
#7902
Burnsides, Andrew, S.C., 64,
#9631
Burr, Jane, c/o, Burlington, Vt.,
132, #9344
Burret, Charles, N.Y., 108,
#9812
Burris, Martin, c/o, Ill., 57,
#7573
Burris, Nathaniel, Ky., 43,
#4054
Burris, Nathaniel, Ky., 112,
#805
Burris, Nathaniel, e/o, Ky., 123,
#229
Burris, Solomon, w/o, N.C.,
100, #3867
Burroughs, Hannah, a/o,
Bradford, Vt., 138, #4665
Burroughs, Joanna, Richmond,
Va., 36A, #F4 V1
Burroughs, Joanna, Va., 124,
#617
Burroughs, Sarah, c/o, Albany,
N.Y., 64, #9670
Burroughs, Stephen, a/o,
Pittsburgh, Pa., 62, #8725
Burrow, Dobson, N.C., 66,
#10048
Burrows, Nathaniel, e/o,
Philadelphia, Pa., 82,
#15254
Burrows, Paul, Conn., 30, #29
Burt, Abner, Albany, N.Y., 82,
#15263
Burt, Joel, c/o, Boston, Mass.,
86, #17039

Burt, Thomas, —, 89, #18409,
    card
Burt, Thomas, Albany, N.Y., 78,
    #14437
Burton, John, c/o, Ill., 3, #9657
Burton, Malinda, Mo., 139,
    #8704
Burton, Malinda, Mo., 142,
    #3973
Burton, Marshall, c/o,
    Richmond, Va., 136, #3565
Burton, Robert, N.C., 78,
    #14454
Burton, Samuel, a/o, Va., 75,
    #13542
Burton, William, est/o, Capt.
    Brokens Co., 86, #16818
Busby, Nedom, S.C., 40, #3187
Bush, Abraham B., New York
    City, 117, #4143
Bush, Abraham B., New York
    City, 132, #9614
Bush, Benjamin, Conn., 105,
    #8103
Bush, Conrad, e/o, Albany,
    N.Y., 125, #1680
Bush, Elizabeth, Ky., 3, #8754
Bush, Elizabeth, Ky., 106,
    #8754, card
Bush, Hannah, Albany, N.Y.,
    133, #602
Bush, James, Ky., 96, #1711
Bush, James, a/o, Ky., 106,
    #8798
Bush, John, w/o, Albany, N.Y.,
    69, #10871
Bush, William, Ky., 92,
    #19659, card
Bush, William, Ky., 64, #9620
Bush, William, g/o c/o, Ky.,
    136, #3088

Bush, William, g/o c/o,
    Louisville, Ky., 142, #4523
Bushee, Patience, Fayetteville,
    N.C., 130, #7424, slip
Bushee, Samuel, Albany, N.Y.,
    41, #3512
Bushee, Samuel, w/o, Albany,
    N.Y., 69, #10917
Bushnell, Daniel, Conn., 30, #7
Buskirk, John, Madison, Ind.,
    44, #4370
Buskirk, John, a/o, Ind., 92,
    #19709
Buskirk, John V., Ind., 57,
    #7612
Bussey, Herman, Wisc., 133,
    #9948
Bussey, Judith, Boston, Mass.,
    101, #5371
Buster, Eleann, Richmond, Va.,
    133, #658
Buster, Eleanor, Richmond, Va.,
    36A, #F6, card
Buswell, Anna, Concord, N.H.,
    101, #4854
Butcher, Benjamin, w/o, Albany,
    N.Y., 110, #11172
Butler, Benjamin, W. Tenn., 60,
    #8362
Butler, David, c/o, Albany, N.Y.,
    117, #4407
Butler, Edward, Cananadaigua,
    N.Y., 143, #7086
Butler, Elizabeth, Nashville,
    Tenn., 119, #5644
Butler, Elizabeth, Nashville,
    Tenn., 121, #7768
Butler, Ezra, a/o, Burlington,
    Vt., 92, #19766
Butler, Frances, Richmond, Va.,
    110, #11047

Butler, Frances, a/o, Richmond, Va., 123, #254

Butler, GabriellaM., Philadelphia, Pa., 139, #9340

Butler, Ira, Albany, N.Y., 101, #5275

Butler, Isreal, Albany, N.Y., 3, #10281

Butler, Jane, Ill., 66, #10238

Butler, Jane, Ill., 109, #10464

Butler, Jane, a/o, Ill., 133, #137

Butler, Jethro, —, 121, #7876, card

Butler, John, N.C., 46, #4825

Butler, John, N.C., 59, #8107

Butler, John, N.C., 91, #19258

Butler, John, S.C., 97, #2022

Butler, John, a/o, Ky., 106, #8785

Butler, John, w/o, Albany, N.Y., 50, #5466

Butler, Jonathan, Concord, N.H., 46, #4751

Butler, Joseph, Richmond, Va., 59, #8055

Butler, Joseph, Richmond, Va., 98, #2972

Butler, Joseph, Va., 41, #3460

Butler, Mehitable, c/o, Conn., 120, #6237

Butler, Thomas, Ky., 3, #5002

Butler, Thomas, w/o, Ky., 58, #7766

Butler, William, Ky., 113, #1427

Butler, William, Mo., 76, #13885

Butler, William, a/o, Ky., 121, #6750

Butler, William, g/o c/o, Conn., 37, #F1826

Butler, William, w/o, Nashville, Tenn., 123, #9953

Butler, William, w/o, Philadelphia, Pa., 59, #8162

Butram, William, Ky., 98, #2923

Butrick, Oliver, c/o, Albany, N.Y., 119, #5771

Butt, Jacob, a/o, Richmond, Va., 51, #5951

Butter, Israel, —, 108, between #10280 & #10286, slip

Butterfeld, Rachel, Albany, N.Y., 71, #12439

Butterfield, Elijah, Albany, N.Y., 81, #15093

Butterfield, Elizah, Albany, N.Y., 98, #3142

Butterfield, Isaac, w/o, Albany, N.Y., 51, #5948

Butterfield, Orpha, a/o, Albany, N.Y., 95, #786

Butterfield, Sarah, c/o, Boston, Mass., 71, #12232

Butterworth, Alice, Philadelphia, Pa., 116, #3047

Butterworth, Alice, Philadelphia, Pa., 127, #4911

Buttle, Samuel W., N.J., 141, #2279

Button, Joseph, Philadelphia, Pa., 100, #4293

Butts, Eunice, c/o, Conn., 64, #9193

Butts, Eunice, c/o, Conn., 64, #9579

Buzzell, James, c/o, Maine, 58, #7820

Byant, Joseph, e/o, Maine, 109, #10624

Byer, Mary, Ga., 117, #4001

Byers, Mary, Ga., 113, #1311

Byers, William, c/o, Md., 62, #8792

Byington, Isaac, w/o, Albany, N.Y., 104, #7316

Bynum, Henry L., c/o, Richmond, Va., 112, #1054

Bynum, Henry L., c/o, Richmond, Va., 114, #2097

Byrd, Alexander, c/o, Tenn. Militia, 63, #9107

Byrd, Andrew, Richmond, Va., 44, #4379

Byrd, Anna, Richmond, Va., 95, #875

Byrd, Henry, Jonesboro, Tenn., 102, #6252

Byrd, Henry, Jonesboro, Tenn., 97, #1914

Byrd, Nancy, Mo., 141, #3293

Byrd, William, a/o, Va., 121, #7906

Byrn, Nancy, Nashville, Tenn., 132, #9720

Byrod, Frederick, e/o, Philadelphia, Pa., 124, #892

Byron, Standerd, Madison, Ind., 128, #5053

Byrum, Jacob, N.C., 46, #4784

Byter, Margaret, c/o, Nashville, Tenn., 132, #9348

C

Cackenbough, John, c/o, Pa., 89, #18224

Cacker, Margaret, c/o, Albany, N.Y., 75, #13701

Cady, Hannah, a/o, Albany, N.Y., 69, #11033

Cady, Jonas, g/o c/o, Conn., 37, #F1825

Cady, Mannapeh, w/o, Bellows Falls, Vt., 48, #5097

Cahill, James, Ohio, 114, #2131, card

Cahill, James, a/o, Ohio, 3, #2031

Cahoon, Naomi, a/o, Ky., 114, #2266

Cain, Patrick, w/o, Ky., 47, #4866

Cain, Robert, w/o, Pittsburgh, Pa., 122, #8239

Caldwell, Alexander, w/o, Indianapolis, Ind., 140, #235

Caldwell, Elizabeth, Fayetteville, N.C., 137, #4340

Caldwell, Isaac, PA, Louisville, Ky., 118, #5112

Caldwell, James, S.C., 39, #3100

Caldwell, James, S.C., 61, #8590

Caldwell, James, S.C., 80, #14756

Caldwell, James, S.C., 118, #4937, card

Caldwell, John T., w/o, Albany, N.Y., 64, #9688

Caldwell, Mary, c/o, Pittsburgh, Pa., 96, #1852

Caldwell, Meek, Mo., 129, #6703, card

Caldwell, Philip, Albany, N.Y., 43, #4110

Caldwell, Samuel, Ill., 88, #17967

Caldwell, Samuel, w/o, N.C., 67, #10497

Caldwell, Will, —, 61, #8585,
    card
Caldwell, William, Nashville,
    Tenn., 69, #10889
Caldwell, William, Nashville,
    Tenn., 72, #12573
Calewell, Samuel, Ill., 57,
    #7483
Calhoon, James, w/o, Albany,
    N.Y., 108, #10080
Calhoun, John, w/o, Richmond,
    Va., 36A, #F1 V4
Calhoun, John, w/o, S.C., 61,
    #8472
Calkin, Nathaniel, Albany,
    N.Y., 68, #10619
Calkins, Durkee, w/o, Poultney,
    Vt., 103, #6942
Calkins, Eli, Vt., 3, #14019
Calkins, Joel, Ind., 50, #5472
Callahan, David, Richmond, Va.,
    62, #8677
Callahan, David, Richmond, Va.,
    51, #5924
Callahan, Patrick, Boston,
    Mass., 143, #6970
Calvert, Willis, Ky., 60, #8300
Calvert, Willis, w/o, Ky., 109,
    #10646
Calvin, James, w/o, Ind., 52,
    #6315
Cameron, Alexander,
    Philadelphia, Pa., 65,
    #10021
Cameron, Alexander,
    Philadelphia, Pa., 45,
    #4503
Cameron, Duncan, New York
    City, 105, #7953
Cameron, Duncan, New York
    City, 117, #4405

Cameron, Duncan, New York
    City, 97, #2404
Cameron, Hugh B., Huntsville,
    Ala., 98, #2968
Cameron, Rachel, Richmond,
    Va., 36A, #F4 V3
Cameron (formerly Toler), Mary,
    Richmond, Va., 36A, #F5
    V3
Camp, Hosea, Ga., 127, #4050
Camp, John, c/o, Cincinnati,
    Ohio, 116, #3601
Camp, John, c/o, Cincinnati,
    Ohio, 117, #4354
Camp, John, c/o, Cincinnati,
    Ohio, 118, #4654
Campbell, Andrew, c/o, 19th
    Inf., 87, #17620
Campbell, Andrew, w/o, 19th
    Inf., 86, #16908
Campbell, Ann, Concord, N.H.,
    118, #4942
Campbell, Archibald, Albany,
    N.Y., 77, #14093
Campbell, Archibald, Richmond,
    Va., 47, #5019
Campbell, Archibald, w/o,
    Richmond, Va., 36A, #F2
    V1
Campbell, Archibald, w/o,
    Richmond, Va., 129, #6870
Campbell, Betsey, c/o,
    Philadelphia, Pa., 127,
    #4380
Campbell, Daniel, Indianapolis,
    Ind., 143, #7342
Campbell, David, Ala., 90,
    #18879
Campbell, David, Mobile, Ala.,
    41, #3535
Campbell, David, Tuscaloosa,
    Ala., 86, #17261

Campbell, David, Tuscaloosa,
Ala., 63, #9111
Campbell, David, c/o,
Philadelphia, Pa., 121,
#6720
Campbell, George, w/o,
Fayetteville, N.C., 108,
#9902
Campbell, James, Cincinnati,
Ohio, 143, #6073
Campbell, James, Knoxville,
Tenn., 3, #10644
Campbell, James, Knoxville,
Tenn., 39, #3091
Campbell, James, Ohio, 66,
#10293
Campbell, James, S.C., 40,
#3278
Campbell, James, S.C., 92,
#19676
Campbell, James, S.C., 109,
#10644
Campbell, Jane, a/o, Albany,
N.Y., 113, #1479
Campbell, Jemima, c/o,
Richmond, Va., 101, #4867
Campbell, Jeremiah, E. Tenn.,
92, #19855, card
Campbell, Jeremiah, Knoxville,
Tenn., 3, #19855
Campbell, John, N.J., 143,
#6257
Campbell, John, Ohio, 43,
#3970
Campbell, John, Richmond, Va.,
51, #6025
Campbell, John, a/o, Ky., 136,
#2577
Campbell, John, c/o, Albany,
N.Y., 116, #3276
Campbell, John, c/o, Ind., 91,
#18977

Campbell, Joseph, E. Tenn., 59,
#7939
Campbell, Joseph, Knoxville,
Tenn., 79, #14555, card
Campbell, Joseph, Knoxville,
Tenn., 48, #5204
Campbell, Joseph, Knoxville,
Tenn., 51, #6042
Campbell, Mary, Philadelphia,
Pa., 71, #12378
Campbell, Nancy, Ky., 141,
#2542
Campbell, Owen, w/o,
Richmond, Va., 73, #12898
Campbell, Richard, Nashville,
Tenn., 75, #13635
Campbell, Richard, Nashville,
Tenn., 86, #17074
Campbell, Richard, Nashville,
Tenn., 106, #8535
Campbell, Richard, Nashville,
Tenn., 43, #3844
Campbell, Richard, Nashville,
Tenn., 48, #5091
Campbell, Sabra, a/o,
Montpelier, Vt., 98, #2758
Campbell, Sarah, a/o,
Montpelier, Vt., 103,
#6887
Campbell, William, Ill., 52,
#6276
Campbell, William P.,
Wheeling, Va., 138, #4744
Campell, William P.,
Cincinnati, Ohio, 109,
#10514
Canada, Lakes, a/o, Pulaski,
Tenn., 133, #135
Canfield, Capt A., claim for
survey expenses, 46, #4688
Canfield, Ebenezer, Albany,
N.Y., 45, #4581

Canfield, Ithamar, Conn., 105,
#7746
Canfield, Ithamer, Conn., 76,
#13877
Canfield, Philo C., e/o, Conn.,
38, #F1827
Cannady, John, e/o, Richmond,
Va., 110, #254
Cannady, Molly, Albany, N.Y.,
126, #3351
Canning, Letitia, Philadelphia,
Pa., 136, #3013
Cannon, Abigail, e/o, Albany,
N.Y., 124, #1203
Cannon, Ira, w/o, Mass., 64,
#9417
Cannon, Israel, Ky., 142, #3831
Cannon, Nathaniel, Ga., 69,
#11012
Cannon, Nathaniel, Ga., 87,
#17539
Cannon, Nathl, Ga., 51, #6035
Cannon, Olive, Mass., 71,
#12468
Cannon, Pugh, Jackson, Tenn.,
47, #4924
Canny, John, w/o, Portsmouth,
N.H., 58, #7791
Canter, John, Ohio, 72, #12561
Canton (or Cantine), Mary, e/o,
New York City, 137, #3797
Cantrell, John, g/o c/o,
Nashville, Tenn., 126,
#3505
Capley, Benj, Boston, Mass.,
51, #6071
Capps, Dempsey, w/o, Ohio, 86,
#16853
Capps, Greenberry, a/o, S.C., 3,
#10317
Capps, Greenberry, S.C., 73,
#12718

Capps, Greenberry, S.C., 109,
#10579, slip
Capps, Greenbery, S.C., 60,
#8375
Capps, William, c/o, S.C., 126,
#3192
Capron, Capt. E. A., c/o, 1st
Artillery, 112, #882
Capron, Capt. Erastus A., 1st
Artillery, 100, #4223, slip
Capron, Capt. Erastus A., w/o,
1st Artillery, 104, #7159
Capron, Capt. Erastus A., w/o,
1st Artillery, 105, #7983
Capron, Capt. Erastus A., w/o,
1st Artillery, 109, #10670
Capron, Capt. Erastus A., w/o,
1st Artillery, 110, #207
Capron, Capt. Erastus A., w/o,
1st Artillery, 101, #5164
Capron, Capt. Erastus A., w/o,
1st Artillery, 103, #6521
Capron, Capt. Erastus A., w/o,
1st Artillery, 108, #9816
Capron, Capt. Erastus A., w/o,
4th Inf., 106, #8806
Capron, Capt. Erasutus A., c/o,
1st Inf., 113, #1621
Capwell, William, Albany, N.Y.,
81, #15092
Car, Esther, c/o, New York City,
70, #12120
Car, James C., —, 55, #7137,
card
Caradine, Elizabeth, S.C., 111,
#389
Card, Thomas, c/o, Albany,
N.Y., 133, #695
Carden, Sanford, Ohio, 79,
#14678
Cardwele, Wiltshire, w/o, Va.,
47, #4896

Cardwell, Mary, Richmond, Va.,
71, #12277
Cardwell, Robert, Va., 81,
#15187
Cardwell, Sally, Ky., 98, #2862
Cardwell, Wiltshire, w/o,
Richmond, Va., 62, #8688
Carey, John, a/o, Philadelphia,
Pa., 88, #18056
Carhartt, Hannah, Albany, N.Y.,
66, #10229
Carick, Adam, Charleston, S.C.,
50, #5600
Carick, Adam, S.C., 41, #3444
Caries, Peter, w/o, Albany, N.Y.,
49, #5307
Carlan, Elizabeth, Richmond,
Va., 135, #2480
Carleton, John, w/o, Md., 64,
#9642
Carlew, Edward, a/o, Vt., 66,
#10113
Carley, William, Jackson,
Tenn., 120, #6557
Carley, William, Jackson,
Tenn., 123, #285
Carley, william, Jackson, Tenn.,
126, #3439
Carley, William, Jackson,
Tenn., 133, #681
Carley, William, Jackson,
Tenn., 136, #2907
Carlin, John, Mass., 118, #4796
Carlisle, Margaret, S.C., 116,
#3523
Carlisle, Margaret, S.C., 126,
#3191
Carlton, Benoni, Va., 84,
#16160
Carlton, David, —, 101, #5090,
card
Carlton, David, N.C., 3, #5090

Carlton, Jane, Richmond, Va.,
71, #12242
Carmack, William, e/o,
Richmond, Va., 4, #6135
Carman, Mary, e/o, Mass., 114,
#2329
Carmical, Duncan, c/o, N.C., 80,
#14765
Carmine, Peter, Ky., 90,
#18706, card
Carmmet, Martha, Concord,
N.H., 82, #15422
Carnahan, Sarah, a/o, Nashville,
Tenn., 136, #3216
Carnal, Patrick, Richmond, Va.,
61, #8639
Carnell, William, Mo., 74,
#13092
Carnell, William L., Ark., 64,
#9222
Carner, Auth, w/o, Pa., 51,
#5843
Carney, John, Madison, Ind.,
69, #10824
Carney, Patrick, Pittsburgh, Pa.,
42, #3698
Carnine, Peter, w/o, Ky., 4,
#18706
Caroline, John, Fla., 47, #5015
Carothers, James, a/o, Ky., 4,
#16129
Carpenter, Benjamin, Ill., 42,
#3750
Carpenter, Ebenezer, a/o, N.H.,
87, #17326
Carpenter, Hope, Albany, N.Y.,
40, #3213
Carpenter, Hope, Albany, N.Y.,
55, #7039
Carpenter, Isaac, N.C., 82,
#15444

Carpenter, Jerusha, Albany,
N.Y., 112, #975

Carpenter, Jerusha, c/o, Albany,
N.Y., 113, #1263

Carpenter, Lewis, w/o, Albany,
N.Y., 90, #18579

Carpenter, Margaret, New York
City, 106, #8675

Carpenter, Martha, a/o, Albany,
N.Y., 128, #5157

Carpenter, Peggy, Richmond,
Va., 129, #6515

Carpenter, Peggy, a/o,
Richmond, Va., 36A, #F5
V3

Carpenter, Peggy, a/o,
Richmond, Va., 137, #4353

Carpenter, Rufus, w/o, Boston,
Mass., 55, #7060

Carpenter, Shubal, w/o, Ohio,
98, #2742

Carper, John, e/o, Richmond,
Va., 96, #1865

Carr, Benjamin, w/o, Albany,
N.Y., 91, #19330

Carr, Daniel, w/o, S.C., 70,
#12191

Carr, Ebenezer, a/o, Albany,
N.Y., 105, #7808

Carr, Edward, New York City,
142, #6027

Carr, Esther, c/o, New York City,
73, #12861

Carr, Gideon, Nashville, Tenn.,
41, #3436

Carr, Jacob, Concord, N.H., 62,
#8780

Carr, James, Ill., 62, #8705

Carr, James, Nashville, Tenn.,
41, #3467

Carr, James, g/o c/o, Cincinnati,
Ohio, 130, #7708

Carr, John, c/o, Private Bill, 14,
#2350

Carr, John, c/o, Va., 4, #460

Carr, Joshua, c/o, Philadelphia,
Pa., 143, #7274

Carr, Samuel, Ind., 85, #16395

Carr, Samuel, New Albany, Ind.,
106, #8632

Carr, Sarah, c/o, N.C., 99,
#3666

Carr, William, a/o, Albany,
N.Y., 117, #4455

Carrick (or Garrick), Adam, c/o,
S.C., 118, #4601

Carrigan, Gilbert, a/o, New York
City, 108, #9989

Carrington, Clement, e/o,
Richmond, Va., 106, #8887

Carrington, Hannah, N.J., 97,
#1897

Carroll, Charles, g/o c/o,
Cleveland, Ohio, 131,
#8189

Carroll, Dempsey, Mobile, Ala.,
54, #6698

Carroll, Edy, Ga., 129, #6980

Carroll, Edy, Ga., 132, #9300

Carroll, James, N.Y., 86,
#16977

Carroll, Naoma, Cincinnati,
Ohio, 138, #6677

Carroll, Naomi, Cincinnati,
Ohio, 137, #4415

Carroll, Naomi, c/o, Cincinnati,
Ohio, 141, #2983

Carrouthers, John, c/o, N.C., 43,
#4100

Carskadden, Sareptay,
Philadelphia, Pa., 141,
#2016

Carson, James, Ky., 72, #12681

Carson, James, a/o, Ky., 117,
  #3861
Carson, Mary, —, 91, #19189,
  card
Carson, Mary, Ga., 135, #1745
Carson, Rufus, Albany, N.Y.,
  45, #4591
Carson, Thomas, Ky., 120,
  #6323, card
Carson, Thomas, c/o, Ky., 4,
  #6323
Carson, Walter, Ind., 89,
  #18345, slip
Carson, Walter, w/o, Ga. Militia,
  4, #19189
Carson, William, Ky., 52,
  #6220
Carter, Charles, Ga., 40, #3256
Carter, Charles, Ga., 55, #7129
Carter, Elisha, Jacksonville,
  Fla., 133, #603
Carter, Ephraim, N.C., 62,
  #8851
Carter, Ephraim, N.C., 84,
  #15967
Carter, Henry, N.C., 80, #14755
Carter, James, a/o, Fayetteville,
  N.C., 108, #9751
Carter, James M., w/o,
  Richmond, Va., 76, #13851
Carter, John, Va., 75, #13650
Carter, Joseph, Ky., 99, #3665,
  card
Carter, Landon, c/o, N.C., 51,
  #6068
Carter, Lucy, e/o, Richmond,
  Va., 36A, #F6 V8
Carter, Margaret, Philadelphia,
  Pa., 127, #4775
Carter, Margaret, Philadelphia,
  Pa., 129, #6735

Carter, Martha, a/o, Richmond,
  Va., 107, #9478
Carter, Mary, S.C., 116, #3338
Carter, Mary, S.C., 125, #2385
Carter, Phebe, a/o, Albany,
  N.Y., 111, #783
Carter, Sarah, Ky., 134, #927
Carter, Sarah, Richmond, Va.,
  72, #12628
Carter Sr., Samuel, Knoxville,
  Tenn., 50, #5565
Carter, Solomon, g/o c/o, Ga.,
  130, #7628
Carter, Thomas, a/o, Knoxville,
  Tenn., 102, #5691
Carter, William, Nashville,
  Tenn., 94, #536
Carter, William, Richmond, Va.,
  42, #3704
Carter, William, Richmond, Va.,
  51, #5960
Carter, William, Va., 47, #4893
Carter, William, w/o, Ky., 134,
  #868
Carter, William, w/o, Mass.,
  106, #8411
Carter, William M., w/o, S.C.,
  95, #1129
Cartter, William, c/o, Albany,
  N.Y., 134, #955
Cartwright, Justitian, a/o, Ky.,
  103, #6486
Cartwright, Mary, c/o,
  Pittsburgh, Pa., 80, #14977
Carty, Dennis, New York City,
  140, #306
Carty, Dennis, New York City,
  140, #1220
Caruthers, John, Ark., 53,
  #6465
Caruthers, John, Ark., 61,
  #8488

Carver, Phebe, c/o, Boston,
Mass., 55, #7127
Carver, Philip, w/o, Albany,
N.Y., 81, #15148
Cary, Anson, e/o, Albany, N.Y.,
92, #19842
Cary, Joseph, —, 88, #17971,
card
Cary, Joseph, w/o, Albany,
N.Y., 4, #17971
Casbolt, Polly, Ill., 113, #1893
Casbolt, Polly, Ill., 114, #2075
Casbury (or Carbey), Peter, c/o,
Md., 115, #2708
Case, Asahel, Conn., 4, #18163
Case, Asanel, Conn., 89,
#18163, card
Case, George, Ohio, 46, #4667,
card
Case, Ichabod, c/o, Albany,
N.Y., 117, #4549
Case, Nathan, a/o, Poultney, Vt.,
102, #5407
Case, Timothy, Ill., 79, #14560
Case, Timothy, Ill., 80, #14891
Casey, Andrew J., Mo., 141,
#2541
Casey, Andrew J., St. Louis,
Mo., 140, #9795
Casey, Diadema (or Sally), g/o,
Maine, 131, #8106
Casey, Hezekiah, Mobile, Ala.,
51, #6021
Casey, Hugh, g/o c/o, Conn.,
37, #F1825
Casey, John, a/o, Ky., 84,
#16038
Casey, Lewis F., —, 113, #1738
Casey, Martha, Miss., 128,
#5706
Casey, William, Mobile, Ala.,
51, #6018

Casey, William, Mobile, Ala.,
64, #9225
Casey, William, Tuscaloosa,
Ala., 72, #12716
Casey, William, w/o, N.C., 41,
#3530
Cash, William, Wheeling, Va.,
45, #4434
Cash, William, Wheeling, Va.,
56, #7293
Cashwell, William, Richmond,
Va., 71, #12418
Casin, Cannon, S.C., 56,
#7407, card
Casler, Maria, a/o, Albany,
N.Y., 112, #994
Casnor, Margaret, Ill., 108,
#10112
Cason, Cannon, S.C., 63, #9104
Cason, William, Ga., 66,
#10090
Cason, William, Ga., 133, #398,
card
Cason, William, Richmond, Va.,
108, #9804
Cason, William, comm/o,
Richmond, Va., 108,
#10257
Cassady, George, a/o,
Cincinnati, Ohio, 136,
#3195
Cassel, Thomas, c/o, N.C., 4,
#4393
Cassell, Thomas, —, 44, #4393,
card
Cassels, Thomas, Fayetteville,
N.C., 45, #4605, card
Castar, Isaac, Philadelphia, Pa.,
69, #10909
Castle, Abigail, c/o, Albany,
N.Y., 89, #18446

Castle, Bazle, c/o, Ky., 107,
#9162

Castle, Lydia, Albany, N.Y., 77,
#13993

Castleberry, Paul, S.C., 128,
#5670

Caswell, Ezra, a/o, Boston,
Mass., 114, #2260

Caswell, Lemuel, g/o c/o, Conn.,
37, #F1820

Caswell, Saml., Ind., 53, #6415

Caswell, William, w/o, Boston,
Mass., 59, #8007

Cathcart, Joseph, c/o,
Knoxville, Tenn., 98,
#2782

Catheral, Joseph, Ohio, 88,
#17832

Catherel, Joseph, Ohio, 56,
#7418

Catherel, Joseph, Ohio, 75,
#13656

Catherell, Joseph, Ohio, 98,
#2950

Cathey, George, a/o, Mo., 96,
#1649

Catlin, Putnam, e/o,
Philadelphia, Pa., 118,
#4800

Catlin, Simeon, c/o, Albany,
N.Y., 75, #13551

Cauffiel, John, w/o, Pittsburgh,
Pa., 132, #9722

Caughman, Bernard, S.C., 130,
#7832

Caughron, Joseph, Ind., 47,
#4909

Caulder, John, Ga., 62, #8847

Cavarly, Caroline, Hartford,
Conn., 31, #69

Cavarly, Caroline, N.Y., 39,
#2954

Caveeno, Charles, Iowa, 110,
#11212

Cavenee, Joseph, Philadelphia,
Pa., 62, #8736

Caviller, John, c/o, N.J., 122,
#8726

Cawlkins, Joel, Ind., 52, #6267

Cawood, Berry, Ky., 47, #4887

Caycaux, Joseph, w/o, Albany,
N.Y., 65, #9985

Caywood, Catherine, Albany,
N.Y., 50, #5563

Ceosepy, Charles C., San
Francisco, Calif., 140,
#730

Chabert, Leon, late PA, La., 127,
#4485

Chabert, Leon, PA, New Orleans,
La., 117, #3844

Chabert, Leon, PA, New Orleans,
La., 118, #5075

Chadbourne, Timothy, c/o,
Maine, 112, #1114

Chadsey, Benjamin, w/o,
Albany, N.Y., 114, #2412

Chadwick, Elias, g/o c/o, Conn.,
37, #F1820

Chadwick, John, Ky., 61, #8612

Chadwick, John, Ky., 78,
#14288

Chadwick, John, Ky., 107,
#9321

Chadwick, John, w/o, Ky., 110,
#11075

Chadwick, Lucinda, Ky., 141,
#2556

Chadwick, Lucinda, Louisville,
Ky., 138, #4746

Chaffee, Live, c/o, Boston,
Mass., 121, #7212

Chaffin, Ellis, Ill., 43, #4098

Chaffin, Ellis, w/o, Ill., 4,
#4098
Chainey, John, Madison, Ind.,
74, #13140
Chalkers, Demaras, c/o,
Poultney, Vt., 96, #1823
Chamberlain, Charles, a/o,
Albany, N.Y., 110, #282
Chamberlain, John, w/o, Maine,
81, #15156
Chamberlain, Milly,
Fayetteville, N.C., 105,
#7762 V#14
Chamberlain, Phineas, w/o,
Albany, N.Y., 103, #6561
Chamberlin, Abigail, c/o,
Philadelphia, Pa., 4,
#13185
Chamberlin, Judah, Ohio, 53,
#6381
Chamberlin, Judah, Ohio, 65,
#9762
Chamberlin, Molly, Boston,
Mass., 64, #9271
Chamberlin, Moses, w/o, Pa.,
74, #13185, card
Chamberlin, Nathaniel, Mass.,
88, #17907, card
Chamberlin, Nathaniel, w/o,
Mass., 4, #17907
Chambers, Edward, c/o, Md.,
127, #4898
Chambers, James, —, 83,
#15672, card
Chambers, James, a/o, Va., 86,
#16982
Chambers, James, w/o, Md., 4,
#15672
Chambers, John, Albany, N.Y.,
39, #2956
Chambers, John, Ohio, 59,
#8132

Chambers, Joseph, —, 82,
#15375, slip
Chambers, Joseph, Wheeling,
Va., 43, #4026
Chambers, Robert, e/o, Va., 83,
#15574
Chambers, Sally, Albany, N.Y.,
127, #4159
Champers, Joseph, w/o,
Wheeling, Va., 4, #15375
Champlin, Jonathan, N.Y., 89,
#18385, card
Champlin, Jonathan, c/o,
Albany, N.Y., 4, #18385
Champlin, Mary, c/o, Hartford,
Conn., 31, #5902
Chandler, Ballard, a/o, Albany,
N.Y., 59, #7959
Chandler, Isaac, w/o, Albany,
N.Y., 80, #14872
Chandler, John, Ky., 54, #6649
Chandler, John, Ky., 75,
#13713
Chandler, John, c/o, Ky., 85,
#16653
Chandler, Joseph, Ohio, 53,
#6417
Chandler, Josiah, w/o, Vt., 54,
#6886
Chandler, Modecai, S.C., 39,
#3059
Chandler, Modicai, Charleston,
S.C., 104, #7657
Chandler, Nathan, w/o, Albany,
N.Y., 49, #5341
Chandler, Samuel, w/o, Concord,
N.H., 103, #6576
Chandoin, John, Ill., 53, #6355
Chaney, John, a/o, Pittsburgh,
Pa., 4, #17781
Chaney, John, c/o, Madison,
Ind., 102, #5472

Chapam, Mary, Albany, N.Y.,
75, #13699

Chapel, Polly, Fayetteville,
N.C., 105, #7762 V#12

Chapin, Abigail, c/o, Mass., 53,
#6353

Chapin, Asa, Conn., 31, #43

Chapin, Huldah, a/o, Vt., 78,
#14363

Chapin, Joseph, c/o, Boston,
Mass., 70, #11047

Chapin, Levi, —, 138, #4865,
slip

Chapin, Levi, c/o, Mass., 4,
#4865

Chapin, Levi, c/o, Mass., 4,
#4135

Chapin, Nathan, w/o, Mass., 86,
#16840

Chapin, Peter, Mass., 46, #4748

Chaplin, John, c/o, Maine, 41,
#3466

Chapman, Ebenezer, Albany,
N.Y., 62, #8821

Chapman, Eleanor, Ga., 130,
#7214

Chapman, Eleanor, Ga., 132,
#8942

Chapman, Eleanor, Ga., 135,
#2098

Chapman, Jerusha, c/o, Albany,
N.Y., 61, #8442

Chapman, Joseph, a/o, S.C., 92,
#19759

Chapman, Leanna, a/o, N.C.,
103, #6636

Chapman, Lydia, a/o, Albany,
N.Y., 94, #501

Chapman, Michael, —, 96,
#1668, slip

Chapman, Michael, Pittsburgh,
Pa., 4, #1668

Chapman, Nathum, Conn., 31,
#322

Chapman, Samuel, c/o, Hartford,
Conn., 56, #7240

Chapman, Samuel, c/o, Ind.,
121, #6978

Chapman, Smith, e/o,
Portsmouth, N.H., 68,
#10748

Chapman, T. F., —, 110,
#11021, slip

Chapman, William, a/o, N.C.,
113, #1671

Chapman, William, a/o,
Nashville, Tenn., 84,
#16297

Chappel, Eunice, c/o, Conn.,
100, #3897

Chappell, Sarah, Jackson,
Tenn., 132, #8944

Chappell, Thomas, w/o,
Philadelphia, Pa., 112,
#1084

Charles, Andrew, g/o c/o, Ky.,
140, #598 (alias Andrew
Chalis)

Charley, Christiana, Ind., 121,
#6938

Charlton, Francis, Richmond,
Va., 42, #3714

Charnock, John, Richmond, Va.,
64, #9458

Charnock, John, c/o, Va., 91,
#19222

Charrock, John, Va., 76,
#13785

Chart (formerly Beard),
Susannah, Ky., 116, #3062

Chart (formerly Beard),
Susannah, g/o c/o, Ky.,
116, #3403

Chase, Alice, c/o, Mass., 110,
#249

Chase, Amariah, —, 85,
#16697f1

Chase, Emily, Mich., 123,
#9881

Chase, Ezra, c/o, Mass., 77,
#14088

Chase, George, c/o, Ohio, 4,
#4667

Chase, Parker, N.H., 65, #9761

Chase, Sarah, Conn., 30, #38,
card

Chasmen, Caleb, w/o, Albany,
N.Y., 53, #6585

Chauncey, John, Ind., 83,
#15733

Cheeks, Delila, Knoxville,
Tenn., 120, #6061

Cheeks, Delila, Knoxville,
Tenn., 127, #4471

Cheeves, Bartholomew, Mass.,
43, #3930

Chelton, Stephen, a/o, Ky., 119,
#5726

Cheney, Betsey, c/o, Concord,
N.H., 139, #8356

Cheney, Mary, Vt., 64, #9424

Cheney, William, Albany, N.Y.,
59, #8106

Cherry, Joshua, —, 46, #4658,
card

Cherry, Joshua, Nashville,
Tenn., 4, #4658

Cherry, Joshua, Nashville,
Tenn., 4, #4921

Chesley, John, w/o, Albany,
N.Y., 116, #3313

Chesnut, Benjamin, Pittsburgh,
Pa., 52, #6343

Chesnut, Benjamin, Pittsburgh,
Pa., 75, #13472

Chesnut, Benjamin, Pittsburgh,
Pa., 82, #15421

Chester, John, w/o, Knoxville,
Tenn., 78, #14387

Chichester, Mary, Conn., 31,
#15

Chickering, Nathaniel, w/o, —,
39, #3113

Chieves, Joel, Richmond, Va.,
50, #5683

Chilcot, Lydia, —, 96, #1821,
slip

Chilcot, Lydia, a/o, Richmond,
Va., 4, #1821

Chilcot, Lydia, a/o, Richmond,
Va., 4, #12477

Child, Zachariah, Mass., 48,
#5099

Childers, Henry, Ky., 113,
#1428

Childers, Isom, Ill., 4, #5648

Childers, Isom, Ill., 68, #10783

Childers, James, w/o, Ga.
Militia, 101, #5265

Childress, Isom, Ill., 39, #3154

Childress, James, c/o, Ga.
Militia, 103, #6823

Childs, Ann, c/o, Vt., 67,
#10478

Childs, Charles, Philadelphia,
Pa., 128, #5664

Childs, Charles, Philadelphia,
Pa., 129, #6782

Childs, Charles, Philadelphia,
Pa., 133, #498

Childs, Robert, D.C., 143,
#6826

China, John, c/o, S.C., 118,
#4706

China, John, c/o, S.C., 118,
#5000

Chinn, Elizabeth, a/o, N.C.,
126, #3190
Chipman, Jesse, w/o, Albany,
N.Y., 89, #18539
Chips, Sarah, —, 85, #16697f4
Chisham, Catherine, c/o, Ky.,
98, #2806
Chitty, Elizabeth, Richmond,
Va., 95, #1289
Choat, Greenberry, Ill., 47,
#4978
Choat, Jonathan, c/o,
Portsmouth, N.H., 113,
#1646
Choate, Miriam, a/o c/o, Mass.,
137, #4588
Choice, William, c/o, S.C., 113,
#1641
Chouteau, Pierre, —, 124, #889,
card
Christey, Isaac, c/o, Albany,
N.Y., 52, #6264
Christeyonce, Isaac, c/o,
Albany, N.Y., 67, #10361
Christian, Daniel, Baltimore,
Md., 91, #19391
Christian, Daniel, Md., 84,
#16145
Christian, Elizabeth, c/o, Va.,
68, #10602
Christian, Elizabeth, c/o, Va.,
73, #12879
Christian, Ferrier V., Boston,
Mass., 143, #7330
Christian, Robert, Richmond,
Va., 58, #7712
Christian, Robert, Richmond,
Va., 65, #9851
Christian, Robert, Richmond,
Va., 47, #4928
Christian, Robert, Va., 77,
#14031

Christian, Thomas, w/o, Va.,
122, #8370
Christmas, Richard, Ga., 52,
#6132
Christmas, Richard, Ga., 58,
#7879
Christmas, Richard, Ga., 74,
#13275
Christmas, Richard, Ga., 75,
#13572
Christmon, Jacob, Albany,
N.Y., 66, #10128
Christopher, William,
Cincinnati, Ohio, 143,
#6580
Christy, William A., g/o c/o,
Wheeling, Va., 135, #2207
Chubbick, Simeon, c/o, Albany,
N.Y., 90, #18646
Church, Joel W., c/o, Albany,
N.Y., 117, #4252
Church, Joel W., c/o, Albany,
N.Y., 119, #5419
Church, Joshua, —, 118, #4860,
card
Church, Joshua, w/o, Detroit,
Mich., 4, #4860
Church, Priscilla, c/o, Conn.,
113, #1720
Church, Willard, Albany, N.Y.,
86, #16751
Churche, Alexander, Albany,
N.Y., 39, #3077
Churchhill, James, Maine, 53,
#6357
Churchill, Elizabeth,
Philadelphia, Pa., 83,
#15621
Churchill, Isaac, Albany, N.Y.,
55, #7067
Churchill, Oliver, Albany, N.Y.,
66, #10231

Cimonton, Lucy, a/o, Maine, 59, #8094

Cinlin, Matthew, New York City, 141, #2282

Claborne, Howard, North Agency, 102, #5849, card

Claffin, Hennrietta, c/o, Albany, N.Y., 100, #4259

Clafflin, Henrietta, c/o, Albany, N.Y., 103, #6728

Claiborn, Thomas, Albany, N.Y., 97, #2051

Claiborn, Thomas, Albany, N.Y., 98, #2848

Claiborne, Leonard, w/o, Richmond, Va., 4, #16527

Claiborne, Leonard, w/o, Va., 85, #16527, card

Clakin, Nathaniel, w/o, Albany, N.Y., 89, #18464

Clancy, John, Pittsburgh, Pa., 88, #17781, card

Clapp, Adam, Ill., 99, #3441, card

Clapp, Adam, c/o, Ill., 4, #3441

Clapp, Elizabeth W., Maine, 114, #2178

Clardy, Thomas, a/o, Richmond, Va., 128, #5637

Claridge, Francis A., Ill., 138, #4764

Claridge, Francis A., Spingfield, Ill., 141, #2557

Clark, Adrew, Conn., 31, #17

Clark, Amos, Conn., 72, #12692

Clark, Benjamin, Albany, N.Y., 89, #18534

Clark, Benjamin, c/o, Albany, N.Y., 98, #2913

Clark, Betsey, Mass., 72, #12595

Clark, Catherine, Philadelphia, Pa., 135, #2340

Clark, Corp. Iasher, c/o, N.Y. Milita, 117, #4044

Clark, Corp. Iasher, c/o, N.Y. Milita, 117, #4043

Clark, Daniel, −, 48, #5119, card

Clark, Daniel, c/o, Albany, N.Y., 112, #974

Clark, David, Conn., 31, #25

Clark, Eleazer, R.I., 72, #12626

Clark, Elias, Conn., 31, #108

Clark, Eliza, Portsmouth, Maine, 142, #5934

Clark, Elizabeth, Boston, Mass., 95, #1057

Clark, Elizabeth, c/o, Mass., 123, #9792

Clark, Hannah, New York City, 71, #12359

Clark, Hannah, a/o, Albany, N.Y., 74, #13245

Clark, Henry, c/o, N.J., 120, #6476

Clark, Ira, Conn., 31, #8

Clark, Isaac, c/o, New York City, 4, #5052

Clark, Israel, g/o w/o, Mass., 49, #5359

Clark, James, Philadelphia, Pa., 52, #6215

Clark, James, Richmond, Va., 4, #7137

Clark, James, Va., 96, #1549, card

Clark, James, c/o, Richmond, Va., 4, #1549

Clark, Jane, Ky., 108, #10157

Clark, Jane, Ky., 96, #1493

Clark, John, Calif., 131, #8342

Clark, John, Nashville, Tenn.,
75, #13629

Clark, John, a/o, Ohio, 98,
#2835

Clark, John, w/o, Madison, Ind.,
133, #475

Clark, John C., Philadelphia,
Pa., 83, #15694

Clark, Joshua, w/o, Albany,
N.Y., 90, #18624

Clark, Keziah, a/o, Va., 122,
#8520

Clark, Lavina, a/o, Vt., 78,
#14362

Clark, Lewis, Huntsville, Ala.,
52, #6281

Clark, Margaret, c/o, Albany,
N.Y., 113, #1613

Clark, Margaret, c/o, Albany,
N.Y., 114, #2161

Clark, Mattiah, w/o, Mass., 109,
#10401

Clark, Mehitable, c/o, Mass.,
81, #15048

Clark, Micajah, c/o, Ky., 69,
#10908

Clark, Nathan, Conn., 31, #16

Clark, Norman, a/o, Concord,
N.H., 89, #18265

Clark, Rachel, Madison, Ind.,
106, #8751

Clark, Rachel, Madison, Ind.,
97, #1952

Clark, Rhoda, c/o, Albany, N.Y.,
87, #17305

Clark, Richard, w/o, N.J., 89,
#18181

Clark, Roger, w/o, Albany,
N.Y., 64, #9434

Clark, Ruth, Iowa, 116, #3132

Clark, Samuel, Mo., 141, #3018

Clark, Samuel, Va., 75, #13677

Clark, Samuel, c/o, Albany,
N.Y., 68, #10668

Clark, Samuel, e/o, Richmond,
Va., 36A, #F1 V1

Clark, Samuel, w/o,
Philadelphia, Pa., 68,
#10785

Clark, William, Ga., 124,
#1162, card

Clark, William, S.C., 40, #3246

Clark, William, S.C., 46, #4662

Clark, William, Wheeling, Va.,
83, #15806

Clark, William, w/o,
Philadelphia, Pa., 76,
#13764

Clark, William R., New York
City, 94, #520

Clark, James, Pittsburgh, Pa.,
127, bet. #4382 & #4407),
card

Clarke, Eliza, Ill., 111, #369

Clarke, Francis, Albany, N.Y.,
56, #7254

Clarke, John, N.C., 42, #3677

Clarke, John, e/o, N.H., 107,
#8943

Clarke, Matthew, Mass., 73,
#12922

Clarke, Robert, a/o, Jackson,
Tenn., 128, #5638

Clarke, Tamar, c/o, Fayetteville,
N.C., 132, #9209

Clarke, William, c/o, Ga., 4,
#1162

Clarkson, Phebe, Mo., 102,
#5642

Clarkson, Phebe, Mo., 102,
#5944

Clarkson, Phebe, Mo., 106,
#8871

Clavert, Spencer, Ky., 41,
#3451
Clawson, Ezra, a/o, Albany,
N.Y., 65, #9854
Clay, Samuel, c/o, Burlington,
Vt., 116, #3452
Clay, William, w/o, Jonesboro,
Tenn., 55, #7205
Clay, William, w/o, Knoxville,
Tenn., 85, #16728
Clayton, Elizabeth, Richmond,
Va., 36A, #F6, card
Clayton, John, w/o,
Philadelphia, Pa., 57,
#7456
Clayton, Leah, Pittsburgh, Pa.,
4, #304
Clayton, Leah, c/o, Pittsburgh,
Pa., 4, #10246
Clearwater, Matthew, New York
City, 65, #9913
Cleaveland, Hannah, c/o,
Albany, N.Y., 141, #2774
Cleaveland, Nehemiah, w/o,
Mass., 48, #5187
Cleaves, Abraham, w/o, Maine,
116, #3446
Cleavor (now Geabhart),
Eleanor, c/o, Ky., 113,
#1383
Cleborn, William, Richmond,
Va., 47, #4944
Clem, Jesse R., c/o, Ill., 131,
#8660
Clem, Jesse R., g/o c/o, Ill.,
134, #745
Clement, Isaac, c/o, Montpelier,
Vt., 124, #1511
Clement, Timothy, a/o, N.H.,
98, #2894
Clements, Abrm., Ky., 53,
#6406

Clements, Benjamin, c/o,
Fayetteville, N.C., 130,
#7742
Clements, Cornelius, N.C., 42,
#3778
Clements, David, Ind., 63,
#9116
Clements, David, Madison, Ind.,
44, #4392
Clements, Edmond, —, 103,
#6974, card
Clements, John, w/o, Richmond,
Va., 61, #8395
Clements, Mildred, a/o,
Fayetteville, N.C., 127,
#4285
Clemmons, John, N.C., 43,
#3936
Clendenin, George, e/o,
Philadelphia, Pa., 104,
#7328
Clendenin, Rebecca,
Philadelphia, Pa., 83,
#15671
Cleveland, Aremas B., Albany,
N.Y., 138, #4812
Cleveland, Isaac, w/o, Albany,
N.Y., 51, #5947
Cliboura, William, Richmond,
Va., 44, #4214
Click, Henry, e/o, Jonesboro,
Tenn., 131, #8864
Clifford, Miachael, w/o, Ill., 63,
#8966
Clifford, William, N.H., 88,
#17862, card
Clifford, William, N.H., 4,
#17862
Clifton, George, N.Y., 143,
#7482
Clifton, Job, c/o, Ill., 121,
#7611

Clifton, William, w/o, N.C., 45, #4573

Cline, Jonas, Pittsburgh, Pa., 43, #4148

Cline, Jonas, w/o, Ill., 76, #13949

Clinger (now Breiner), Catharine, Philadelphia, Pa., 114, #2004

Clinkinbeard, Isaac, Ky., 61, #8609

Clinton, James, c/o, N.J., 125, #1684

Clinton, Richard, Nashville, Tenn., 41, #3387

Clinton, Thomas, —, 135, #2199, card

Clinton, Thomas, c/o, Md., 4, #2199

Clonant, Israel, Albany, N.Y., 67, #10486

Clontz, Jeremiah, N.C., 40, #3174

Close, Henry, Pa., 62, #8801, card

Close, Henry, w/o, Philadelphia, Pa., 5, #8801

Cloud Sr., Noah, w/o, S.C., 59, #8061

Cloud, Unity, c/o, S.C., 96, #1742

Cloud, William, Va., 71, #12403

Clough, Gilman, Bellows Falls, Vt., 50, #5561

Clough, Gilman, Vt., 55, #6983

Clough, Gilman, Vt., 73, #12880

Cloutz, Chloe, c/o, N.C., 103, #6744

Clute, Garret D., Albany, N.Y., 64, #9499

Clute, Garrit D., Albany, N.Y., 52, #6152

Clute, Helen, c/o, Albany, N.Y., 112, #872

Coan, John, a/o, Conn., 96, #1498

Coates, William, Richmond, Va., 56, #7292

Coats, William, St. Augustine, Fla., 51, #5986

Cobb, Amey, c/o, R.I., 54, #6671

Cobb, Arthur, w/o, 3rd Artillery, 49, #5420

Cobb, Franics, Concord, N.H., 41, #3428

Cobb, John, w/o, S.C., 95, #854

Cobb, Mallakiah, w/o, Maine, 133, #265, cancelled

Cobb, Pharaoh, Jonesboro, Tenn., 112, #1128, card

Cobb, Pharaoh, Jonesboro, Tenn., 45, #4505

Cobb, Pharoah, Jonesboro, Tenn., 56, #7257

Cobb, Pharoah, c/o, Jonesboro, Tenn., 5, #1128

Cobb, Roland, Maine, 105, #7869

Cobb, Sylverster, Burlington, Vt., 54, #6679

Cobb, Sylvester, Albany, N.Y., 64, #9254

Cobbs, Ann G., c/o, Richmond, Va., 110, #172

Cobbs, Ann G., c/o, Richmond, Va., 111, #378

Cobbs, John, Richmond, Va., 100, #3932

Cobbs, John, Richmond, Va., 55, #7073

Cobbs, John, Va., 85, #16672

Cobbs, Thomas, a/o, Knoxville, Tenn., 12, #7702

Cobleigh, Reuben, w/o, Ohio, 108, #10087

Coburn, Moses B., c/o, Mass., 89, #18268

Cochran, Elizabeth, Pittsburgh, Pa., 96, #1404

Cochran, James, e/o, Mass., 79, #14688

Cochran, John, h/o, Nashville, Tenn., 41, #3435

Cochran, John C., PA, Charleston, S.C., 116, #3796

Cochran, John C., PA, Charleston, S.C., 118, #5062

Cochrane, Lt. Richard E., w/o, —, 100, #3822

Cochrane, Lt. Richard E., w/o, 4th Inf., 102, #5737

Cochrane, Lt. Richard E., w/o, 4th Inf., 103, #6783

Cochrane, Lt. Richard E., w/o, 4th Inf., 104, #7638

Cochrane, Lt. Richard E., w/o, 4th Inf., 106, #8546

Cochrane, Lt. Richard E., w/o, 4th Inf., 107, #9532

Cochrane, Lt. Richard E., w/o, 4th Inf., 99, #3240

Cochrane, Lt. Richard E., w/o, 4th Inf., 101, #5057

Cock, Jacob, c/o, Albany, N.Y., 106, #8386

Cockenbaugh, John, Philadelphia, Pa., 72, #12486

Coddington, Benjamin, Md., 54, #6728

Codgden, Mary, c/o, Philadelphia, Pa., 116, #3609

Codrington, Margaret, c/o, N.J., 5, #592

Cody, Elizabeth, a/o, Vt., 78, #14364

Coe, Ebenezer, e/o, Conn., 38, #F1820

Coff, William, Va., 69, #10850

Coffee, George, Ore., 139, #8268

Coffee, George, Ore., 141, #1363

Coffee, George, Ore., 114, #2052

Coffee, Mary, a/o, Ky., 5, #8171

Coffee, Osborne, w/o, Ky., 105, #8171, card

Coffer, Reuben, w/o, Ky., 72, #12676

Coffey, Mary, Ky., 112, #993, card

Coffey, Mary, Nashville, Tenn., 5, #993

Coffey, Osborne, Ky., 72, #12682, card

Coffin, Petu, w/o, Maine, 95, #787

Coffman, Chloe, a/o, Ky., 142, #4029

Coger, Peter, Wheeling, Va., 70, #12080

Coger, Peter, Wheeling, Va., 71, #12236

Coger, Pvt. William, w/o, 25th Inf., 112, #1011

Coghill, Thomas, Richmond, Va., 47, #5036

Cogswell, Rufus, Mass., 72, #12539

Cogswell, Rufus, Mass., 104, #7458

Cogswell, Ruth, e/o, N.H., 74, #13129

Cohick, Daniel, c/o, Philadelphia, Pa., 117, #4097

Coker, Catherine, Ill., 128, #5989

Colbourn, Theoda, c/o, Poultney, Vt., 101, #4970

Colburn, James, c/o, N.H., 68, #10627

Colburn, Sarah, c/o, Conn., 84, #16187

Colburn, Theodo, c/o, Vt., 61, #8393

Colburn, Lt. A. V., 1st Cav., 133, #495, special

Colby, Benjamin, Concord, N.H., 61, #8494

Colby, Christopher, a/o, Philadelphia, Pa., 138, #4713

Cole, Capt. —, Albany, N.Y., 55, #7226

Cole, Abijah, Maine, 67, #10469

Cole Sr., Abraham, w/o, Richmond, Va., 54, #6610

Cole, Andrew, e/o, Boston, Mass., 82, #15271

Cole, Daniel, Richmond, Va., 110, #10945

Cole, Daniel, e/o, Richmond, Va., 5, #7445

Cole, Gideon, Philadelphia, Pa., 102, #5791

Cole, Jacob, w/o, New York City, 66, #10079

Cole, James, a/o, Albany, N.Y., 69, #10903

Cole, Joseph, N.C., 41, #3442

Cole, Joseph, N.C., 46, #4761

Cole, Joseph, c/o, N.C., 118, #4893

Cole, Levi, Albany, N.Y., 45, #4543

Cole, Mary Catherine, c/o, Maine, 138, #5380

Cole, Mourning, Richmond, Va., 98, #2832

Cole, Royal, Philadelphia, Pa., 65, #10020

Cole, Royal, Philadelphia, Pa., 46, #4753

Cole, Rufus, Albany, N.Y., 122, #8405

Cole (formerly Avery), Sarah, Bradford, Vt., 129, #6499

Cole, William, w/o, Albany, N.Y., 58, #7730

Coleman, Catharine, a/o, Ky., 119, #5332

Coleman, Charles, Miss., 88, #17918

Coleman, Charles P., Tuscaloosa, Ala., 69, #10874

Coleman, Charles P., Tuscaloosa, Ala., 76, #13855

Coleman, Elias T., Spingfield, Ill., 143, #7343

Coleman, Hawes, Richmond, Va., 47, #4949

Coleman, Hawes, Va., 41, #3405

Coleman, Jacob, c/o, Madison, Ind., 123, #265

Coleman, John, Pittsburgh, Pa., 102, #5943, card

Coleman, John, w/o, Pittsburgh, Pa., 5, #5943

Coleman, Leonard, Wheeling,
Va., 39, #3139

Coleman, Richard, c/o, R.I., 77,
#14078

Coleman, Robert, Richmond,
Va., 72, #12634

Coleman, Robert, Va., 90,
#18596

Coleman, Solomon, c/o,
Montpelier, Vt., 121,
#6977

Coleman, Theophilis, N.C., 45,
#4529

Coleman, William, Knoxville,
Tenn., 83, #15657

Coleman, William, La., 123,
#324

Coleman, William, La., 125,
#2035

Coleman, William, New Orleans,
La., 119, #5556

Colfax, Elizabeth, Albany, N.Y.,
103, #6446

Colgan, John, D.C., 111, #459

Colgan, William, a/o,
Cincinnati, Ohio, 138,
#5077

Coll, Levi, Albany, N.Y., 44,
#4328

Collard, Abraham, w/o, Albany,
N.Y., 80, #14798

Colleston, Abigail, Albany,
N.Y., 70, #12096

Collett, Elizabeth, Ky., 84,
#16070

Colley, George, Conn., 31,
#112

Collier, Mary, Cincinnati, Ohio,
131, #8305

Collings, James W., g/o c/o,
Pittsburgh, Pa., 135, #2425

Collingsworth, John, Ill., 85,
#16483

Collins, Benjamin, c/o, Ohio,
83, #15724

Collins, Daneil, a/o, Maine,
116, #3274

Collins, David, Nashville,
Tenn., 104, #7225

Collins, Ebenezer, Pittsburgh,
Pa., 75, #13407

Collins, Eli, Ark., 41, #3452

Collins, John, c/o, S.C., 81,
#15186

Collins, Louisa, Nashville,
Tenn., 117, #4081

Collins, Mary, N.Y., 137,
#4498, card

Collins, Mary, N.Y., 137,
#4516, card

Collins, Samuel, Utica, N.Y.,
58, #7865

Collins, Solomon, Wheeling,
Va., 84, #15968, card

Collins, Solomon, a/o, Va., 5,
#15968

Collins, Stephen, Ky., 52,
#6237

Collins, William, Ind., 44,
#4313

Collins, William, Ohio, 61,
#8431

Colquett, Ransom, c/o, N.C.,
120, #6307

Colson, Christopher, w/o, Ohio,
103, #6743

Colson, Patty, a/o, Cleveland,
Ohio, 130, #7423

Colver, David, Ohio, 104,
#7620

Colville, James, c/o, Ohio, 59,
#8070

Colvin, Henry, a/o, Ky., 134, #999

Colvin, John, New York City, 134, #710

Colvin, John, New York City, 138, #6062

Colvin, Lydia, c/o, Burlington, Vt., 112, #808

Colvin, Mason, a/o, Richmond, Va., 127, #4269

Colyer, John, Ind., 101, #5261, card

Colyer, John, Mo., 96, #1647

Colyer, John, St. Louis, Mo., 92, #19929

Colyer, John, w/o, Mo., 5, #5261

Combs, John, Ky., 40, #3301

Combs, Nancy, Va., 121, #6958

Combs (or Combes), William, Ky., 68, #10642, card

Commet, Martha, Concord, N.H., 62, #8861

Comming, Thomas, Albany, N.Y., 66, #10126

Compton, Mary, c/o, N.J., 72, #12476

Comstock, Aaron, Conn., 31, #26

Comstock, Amy, Conn., 31, #67

Comstock, Anson, Albany, N.Y., 84, #16058

Comstock, Anson, c/o, Albany, N.Y., 84, #16308

Comstock, Elihu, g/o c/o, Conn., 37, #F1820

Comstock, John, Conn., 31, #305

Comstock, Martin S., w/o, Albany, N.Y., 109, #10580

Conant, Charles O., Concord, N.H., 116, #3480

Conaway, Mahala, Ga., 127, #4544

Condor, Adam, Mo., 128, #5069

Cone, Henry, a/o, Conn., 38, #F1828

Congdon, Elisha, g/o c/o, Conn., 37, #F1820

Congdon, John, c/o, Providence, R.I., 91, #19336

Conger, Benjamin, c/o, Ga., 108, #9803

Conger, Stephen M., w/o, N.J., 123, #60

Conger, Zach. S., Iowa, 90, #18953

Conger, Zachariah S., Iowa, 92, #19603

Conger, Zachariah S., Iowa, 94, #239

Conine, Andrew, w/o, Ky., 72, #12713

Conkey, Joshua, Albany, N.Y., 5, #15966

Conkey, Joshua (or John), N.Y., 84, #15966, card

Conkeys, Richard, Albany, N.Y., 40, #3203

Conklin, Hannah, c/o, Albany, N.Y., 125, #1602

Conklin, John, c/o, N.J., 120, #6342

Conklin, William G., −, 129, #7059, card

Conklin, William G., Ill., 5, #7059

Conklin, William G., Ill., 128, #6063

Conn, George, a/o, Charleston, S.C., 101, #5250

Connaway, John, Philadelphia, Pa., 56, #7285

Connaway, John, Philadelphia, Pa., 80, #14831

Connell, Christopher, Philadelphia, Pa., 45, #4497

Connelly, Hugh, c/o, Albany, N.Y., 124, #449

Connelly, John, Ky., 88, #17936

Connelly, Rice, Mo., 137, #4339

Connelly, Tempy, Ky., 141, #3019

Conner, James, w/o, S.C., 55, #6992

Conner, John, Albany, N.Y., 113, #1596

Conner, John, St. Louis, Mo., 134, #1366

Conner, Lawrence, a/o, Va., 75, #13462

Conner, Mary, Richmond, Va., 36A, #F6, card

Conner, Rosanna, Ind., 78, #14512

Conner, Rosanna, c/o, Ill., 98, #2772

Connor, Francis, N.Y., 121, #7602

Connoway, John, Philadelphia, Pa., 65, #10022

Conrad, John, c/o, Philadelphia, Pa., 81, #15053

Conroy, James, D.C., 130, #7712

Constable, Garnet, New York City, 64, #9689

Constantinan, Nicholas, w/o, Albany, N.Y., 75, #13455

Converse, Zurvah, a/o, Conn., 132, #9450

Conway, Arthur, a/o, Md., 104, #7188

Conway, Thomas, Madison, Ind., 135, #2065

Conyers, Sarah, N.C., 115, #2660

Conyers, Straugham, c/o, S.C., 127, #4730

Conyne, Peter, e/o, Albany, N.Y., 85, #16429

Coodner, Conrod, a/o, Ill., 75, #13414

Cook, Ambrose, a/o, Albany, N.Y., 87, #17342

Cook, Ann, Richmond, Va., 128, #5337

Cook, Ann, Fayetteville, N.C., 105, #7762 V#20

Cook, Ann, e/o, Richmond, Va., 36A, #F5 V1

Cook, Atwater, Albany, N.Y., 40, #3245

Cook, Benjamin, Mobile, Ala., 79, #14709

Cook, Elijah, Mich., 49, #5326

Cook, Eliza, Cincinnati, Ohio, 141, #2014

Cook, Enos, a/o, Philadelphia, Pa., 121, #7513

Cook, James M., Detroit, Mich., 142, #3442

Cook, Jonah, a/o, Conn., 38, #F1825

Cook, Jonathan, w/o, Albany, N.Y., 72, #12564

Cook, Lucy, a/o, Albany, N.Y., 100, #3893

Cook, Moses B., c/o, —, 64, #9425

Cook, Moses B., c/o, Detroit, Mich., 58, #7676

Cook, Oliver, w/o, Albany,
N.Y., 70, #12122
Cook, Peter, c/o, Philadelphia,
Pa., 81, #15052
Cook, Randolph, —, 45, #4631
Cook, Pvt. Samuel, w/o, Sea
Fencibles, 61, #8500
Cook, Silas, Mass., 87, #17438
Cook, Stephen, c/o, N.Y., 143,
#6569
Cook, Thomas, Cincinnati,
Ohio, 127, #4232
Cook, Zachariah, c/o, Ohio,
107, #9365
Coolbaugh, John, Philadelphia,
Pa., 57, #7446
Coolbaugh, John, Philadelphia,
Pa., 41, #3481
Coolbaugh, John, w/o,
Philadelphia, Pa., 92, #36
Cooledge, Daniel, w/o, Mass.,
85, #16415
Cooley, Betsy, Albany, N.Y.,
131, #8726
Cooley, Dorothy, a/o, N.H., 78,
#14353
Cooley, Electa, c/o, Mass., 141,
#1493
Cooley, Justin, Albany, N.Y.,
42, #3625
Cooley, Roger, w/o, Mass., 117,
#3908
Cooley, Thomas, w/o, Albany,
N.Y., 104, #7224
Coombs, Dorothy, c/o,
Portsmouth, Maine, 133,
#186
Cooms, Samuel C., w/o, Maine,
51, #5972
Coon, Bridget, c/o,
Philadelphia, Pa., 134,
#1406

Coone, Dennis, w/o, Pittsburgh,
Pa., 124, #838
Coonwell, Stephen L., g/o c/o,
La., 127, #4609
Cooper, Ambrose, Jacksonville,
Fla., 58, #7719
Cooper, Benjamin A., Mo., 5,
#523
Cooper, Benjamin A., Mo., 111,
#523, card
Cooper, Catherine, Knoxville,
Tenn., 132, #9103
Cooper, Charles S., New York
City, 111, #702
Cooper, Dorothy, a/o, Ky., 114,
#2100
Cooper, Eiles, Va., 77, #13967
Cooper, Giles, Richmond, Va.,
63, #8909
Cooper, Hannah, a/o,
Cincinnati, Ohio, 113,
#1599
Cooper, Isaac, Albany, N.Y., 60,
#8177
Cooper, James, Knoxville,
Tenn., 40, #3326
Cooper, James, Knoxville,
Tenn., 49, #5438
Cooper, Laban, Albany, N.Y.,
137, #4352
Cooper, Laber, Albany, N.Y.,
77, #14186
Cooper, Lydia, Albany, N.Y.,
61, #8535
Cooper, Obediah, a/o,
Cleveland, Ohio, 114,
#2250
Cooper, Richard, c/o,
Pittsburgh, Pa., 44, #4312
Cooper, Samuel, —, 107,
#9333, card

Cooper, Samuel, Fort Wash.,
    108, #10347, card
Cooper, Sarah, Ill., 105, #7757
Cooper, Sarah, Richmond, Va.,
    104, #7186
Cooper, Sterling, w/o, N.C.,
    104, #7234
Cooper, William, a/o, Albany,
    N.Y., 81, #15135
Coovent, James, New York City,
    65, #9963
Coovert, Daniel, N.J., 5, #1913,
    card
Cope, Henry, c/o, Md., 130,
    #7889
Copeland, Jesse, c/o, 10th Inf.,
    96, #1717
Copeland, Jesse, w/o, 10th Inf.,
    96, #1715
Copeland, John, a/o, W. Tenn.,
    59, #8142
Copeland, Ripley, w/o, S.C., 95,
    #971
Copeland, Zacheus, Knoxville,
    Tenn., 101, #5292, card
Copes, Parker, Richmond, Va.,
    67, #10544
Copes, Parker, Richmond, Va.,
    104, #7627
Copes, Parker, Richmond, Va.,
    95, #1019
Copley, Benjamin, Mass., 76,
    #13727
Copley, Benjamin, w/o, Mass.,
    87, #17319
Copley, Mathew, a/o w/o,
    Boston, Mass., 62, #8804
Coppedge, Thomas, a/o,
    Richmond, Va., 134, #1276
Copps, Josiah, Philadelphia,
    Pa., 44, #4242

Coppupe (or Covington),
    Higgins, c/o, Knoxville,
    Tenn., 123, #120, card
Corbet, Jacob, c/o, Ky., 89,
    #18136
Corbett, John, w/o, N.C., 63,
    #8998
Corbin, Anderson, Wheeling,
    Va., 70, #11190
Corbin, Joseph, Albany, N.Y.,
    45, #4512
Corbin, Patience, a/o, Albany,
    N.Y., 107, #8961
Corbin, Stephen, New York
    City, 107, #8962
Corbit Sr., Samuel, Richmond,
    Va., 47, #5022
Corbit Sr., Samuel, Richmond,
    Va., 61, #8638
Corbit Sr., Samuel, a/o,
    Richmond, Va., 107, #9476
Cordes, John, Richmond, Va.,
    48, #5211
Corey, David, Ohio, 64, #9165
Corey, Isaac, Burlington, Vt.,
    40, #3179
Corey, Martha, c/o, Burlington,
    Vt., 131, #8540
Corey, Moller, c/o, Boston,
    Mass., 54, #6783
Corey, Nancy, Ohio, 98, #2579
Corey, Sarah, Conn., 31, #64
Corgan, John N., D.C., 143,
    #6878
Corgan (formerly Penrod),
    Louisa, c/o, Ill., 113,
    #1458
Corks Sr., Benjamin, Ga., 55,
    #7212
Corley, Abner, c/o, Charleston,
    S.C., 104, #7113

Corley, Elizabeth, a/o,
Richmond, Va., 36A, #F2
12
Corley, George, Philadelphia,
Pa., 42, #3726
Corley, George, Philadelphia,
Pa., 51, #6001
Corley, Zacheus, Tuscaloosa,
Ala., 80, #14968
Corliss, Bliss, w/o, Montpelier,
Vt., 64, #9680
Corn, Elizabeth, a/o,
Morganton, N.C., 122,
#8567
Cornelison, John, Ill., 52,
#6146
Cornelius, Henry, Philadelphia,
Pa., 65, #9721
Cornell, William, Pittsburgh,
Pa., 41, #3560
Cornell, William, Pittsburgh,
Pa., 45, #4604
Cornett, William, a/o, Ky., 120,
#6322
Corning, David, g/o c/o, Conn.,
37, #F1824
Cornish, Gabriel, w/o, Albany,
N.Y., 92, #19601
Cornish, George, e/o, Conn.,
85, #16596
Cornish, Tempy, N.C., 117,
#3976
Cornue, Wessel, w/o, Albany,
N.Y., 72, #12601
Corrington, Benjamin, w/o,
N.J., 49, #5310
Corson, James, Ky., 103, #6362
Corss, Thomas J., Spingfield,
Ill., 140, #599
Corwin, Richard, a/o, New York
City, 106, #8770

Cory, Gabriel, Philadelphia, Pa.,
58, #7763
Cory, Gabriel, Philadelphia, Pa.,
41, #3516
Cosby, Garland, c/o, Ky., 102,
#6136
Cosby, Garland, c/o, Ky., 101,
#5083
Cosby, John, Ky., 56, #7376
Cosley, Mary, a/o, Richmond,
Va., 136, #2842
Cosper, David, New Albany,
Ind., 79, #14687
Cosper, John, a/o, Philadelphia,
Pa., 120, #6317
Cotner, George W., Mo., 106,
#8873
Cotton, Charles F., w/o, Miss.,
129, #6756
Cotton, William, c/o, Concord,
N.H., 111, #394
Couch, Jane, c/o, Maine, 120,
#6439
Couch, William D., Richmond,
Va., 56, #7329
Couch, William J., Richmond,
Va., 70, #12213
Couch, William J., Richmond,
Va., 45, #4541
Couch, William J., w/o,
Richmond, Va., 91, #19409
Cougleton, Pvt. David, w/o, 9th
Inf., 114, #2254
Couillard, John, a/o, Augusta,
Maine, 142, #6026
Coulter, Martin, e/o, N.C., 115,
#2918
Couney, Mehitable, c/o, Albany,
N.Y., 70, #11175
Countryman, Applonia, Albany,
N.Y., 108, #10151

Courser, Simeon, Albany, N.Y.,
125, #1720
Courtright, Joseph,
Philadelphia, Pa., 139,
#9322
Covell, Judah, Maine, 39, #2959
Covenhoven, Robert,
Philadelphia, Pa., 46,
#4760
Covert, Daniel, Ky., 114,
#1913, card
Covert, Ellison, N.J., 92,
#19900
Covington, Winney, Nashville,
Tenn., 130, #7305
Covvinton, Hannah, N.J., 143,
#6750
Cowan, David, Ind., 58, #7803
Cowardin, George M., g/o c/o,
Ill., 137, #3906
Cowden, James, N.J., 51,
#5896, card
Cowden, James, a/o, N.Y., 5,
#5896
Cowles, Isaac, c/o, Conn., 31,
#4814
Cowles, Phineas, c/o, Vt., 57,
#7450
Cox, Bartlett, Richmond, Va.,
91, #19349
Cox, Benjamin, Ohio, 45,
#4620
Cox, Betsey Ann, g/o,
Tallahassee, Fla., 90,
#18678
Cox, Irena, a/o, Montpelier, Vt.,
123, #296
Cox, James, N.C., 5, #7440
Cox, James, a/o, N.C., 5, #4625
Cox, John, Ky., 109, #10463,
slip
Cox, John, a/o, Ky., 5, #10463

Cox, Joseph, Tenn., 48, #5114,
card
Cox, Martha, Ga., 136, #2779
Cox, Martha, Ga., 137, #4581
Cox, Mary, Jackson, Tenn.,
127, #4121
Cox, Mary, Jackson, Tenn.,
129, #6956
Cox, Michael, Ohio, 63, #8959
Cox, Nancy, La., 121, #7968
Cox, Richard, Ga., 45, #4601
Cox, Richard, Ga., 56, #7379
Cox, Robert J., Ky., 123, #9878
Cox, Sarah, Mo., 110, #45
Cox, Sarah, e/o, Richmond, Va.,
132, #9153
Cox, Solomon, w/o, S.C., 60,
#8230
Cox, Thomas, w/o, Ga., 127,
#4849
Cox, Zachariah, Ga., 132, #9891
Coxe, Partlette, c/o, Richmond,
Va., 99, #3229
Coy, Ephraim, Conn., 31, #272
Coyle, Isabella, Philadelphia,
Pa., 70, #12214
Coyle, Mark, w/o, Md., 85,
#16406
Coyle, Patrick, Ky., 5, #7205
Coyle, Patrick, Ky., 104, #7205
Cozer, John, c/o, Pittsburgh,
Pa., 120, #6574
Crab, Jeremiah, Ohio, 109,
#10767
Crabtree, Dicey, N.C., 115,
#2505
Crabtree, Isaac, Nashville,
Tenn., 109, #10839
Crabtree, Isaac, a/o, Ky., 5,
#10839
Crabtree, Jacob, Richmond, Va.,
47, #4950

Crabtree, James, Mo., 123,
#9675
Crabtree, James, Mo., 123, #326
Crabtree, Newman, Albany,
N.Y., 72, #12603
Crabtree, Newman, Albany,
N.Y., 81, #15173
Craft, Achillis, Ky., 96, #1674
Craft, Archilles, Ky., 109,
#10455
Craft, Archilles, Ky., 112,
#1013
Craft, Archilles, Ky., 117,
#4229
Craft, Archillis, Ky., 79,
#14640
Craft, Archillis, Ky., 89,
#18329
Craft, Archillis, Ky., 124,
#1416, card
Craft (formerly Van O'linda),
Jane, Albany, N.Y., 113,
#1430
Crafts, Achillis, a/o, Ky., 5,
#1416
Crafts, Samuel, Maine, 54,
#6597
Craig, Alexander, Jackson,
Tenn., 48, #5208
Craig, Elizabeth, Pittsburgh,
Pa., 110, #276
Craig, Emeline, —, 39, #2946
Craig, Frazee, w/o, N.J., 82,
#15485
Craig, John, Ohio, 76, #13853
Craig, Lewis S., g/o c/o, D.C.,
142, #3716
Craig, Mary, c/o, Ky., 98,
#2985
Craig, Robert, w/o, Ky., 56,
#7400

Craig, William, Des Moines,
Iowa, 143, #6947
Craig, William, Wheeling, Va.,
95, #1133
Craig, William, Wheeling, Va.,
52, #6205
Craighead, Thomas B., g/o,
Nashville, Tenn., 135,
#2255
Crain, Daniel, Conn., 72,
#12487
Crain, Rhoda, Montpelier, Vt.,
112, #838
Cram, Samuel, w/o, N.H., 55,
#7126
Cram, Zebulon, a/o, Burlington,
Vt., 118, #4780
Cramer, Jacob, g/o c/o,
Cleveland, Ohio, 130,
#7726
Crampton, Thomas, —, 126,
#3469, slip
Crampton, Thomas, c/o, Md., 5,
#3469
Crance, Michael, Nashville,
Tenn., 113, #1264
Crandall, Abner, w/o, Albany,
N.Y., 75, #13532
Crandall, Amiriah, c/o,
Cleveland, Ohio, 141,
#2051
Crandall, Gideon, e/o, Albany,
N.Y., 96, #1414
Crandall, Levi, c/o, Mass., 76,
#13726
Crandall, Peter, w/o, Albany,
N.Y., 75, #13454
Crandall, Simeon, Conn., 31,
#360
Crane, Abijah, w/o, Maine, 115,
#2915

Crane, Catherine, Albany, N.Y.,
71, #12438
Crane, David D., w/o, N.J., 53,
#6477
Crane, John, Nashville, Tenn.,
120, #6344, card
Crane, John, c/o, N.J. or N.Y.,
5, #6344
Crane, Mayfield, a/o, Miss., 5,
#19479
Crane, Tryphana, —, 135,
#2341, slip
Crane, Tryphena, a/o, Albany,
N.Y., 5, #2341
Crane, William, S.C., 62, #8766
Crane, William, S.C., 72,
#12480
Crane, William, S.C., 75,
#13526
Crane, William, e/o, S.C., 95,
#852
Cranson, Asa, w/o, Albany,
N.Y., 76, #13806
Cranston, Elizabeth, Albany,
N.Y., 72, #12612
Cranston, Gustavus, c/o, Va.,
77, #14025
Cranston, James, g/o c/o,
Conn., 37, #F1820
Cranston, Zulpha, a/o, Albany,
N.Y., 95, #1159
Cranz, Theodore, Cincinnati,
Ohio, 117, #4285
Crase, Philip, Ind., 5, #6780,
card
Cratrot, Bgen. Charles, U.S.
Army, 117, #4181, slip
Crauce, Michale, Mo., 138,
#4945
Crawford, Hannah, Fayetteville,
N.C., 125, #2599

Crawford, John, Knoxville,
Tenn., 81, #15051, card
Crawford, John, Knoxville,
Tenn., 42, #3598
Crawford, John, Ohio, 85,
#16735
Crawford, John, c/o, Ill., 131,
#8661
Crawford, John, c/o, Ill., 133,
#550
Crawford, John, c/o, Knoxville,
Tenn., 5, #15051
Crawford, Joseph, Mass., 40,
#3288
Crawford, Josias, New Albany,
Ind., 134, #1055
Crawford, Robert, Philadelphia,
Pa., 76, #13948
Crawford, Robert, c/o,
Nashville, Tenn., 75,
#13400
Crawford, Spencer, Albany,
N.Y., 104, #7613
Crawford, William, w/o,
Concord, N.H., 44, #4237
Crawley, William, w/o, N.C.,
122, #8321
Creamer, Charles M., Calif.,
128, #6104
Creamer, Daniel, c/o, Jonesboro,
Tenn., 114, #2399
Creamer, Eleanor, c/o,
Philadelphia, Pa., 122,
#8087
Cresey, Manuel, La., 43, #4068
Cress, George, Ohio, 5, #5287
Creswell, Andrew, E. Tenn., 77,
#14044, card
Creswell, Andrew, e/o, Tenn., 5,
#14044
Creswell, Samuel, Ky., 42,
#3586

Cresy, Manuel, La., 51, #5906

Crew, James, E. Tenn., 84, #15993, card

Crews, James, e/o, Knoxville, Tenn., 7, #15993

Crews, Polly, Richmond, Va., 36A, #F5 V2

Crippen, Bulah, e/o, Conn., 31, #4314

Crippen, Mary, a/o, Albany, N.Y., 114, #2390

Crippen, Phebe, c/o, Albany, N.Y., 65, #9788

Crise, Barnet, Albany, N.Y., 65, #10012

Crise, Barnet, Albany, N.Y., 80, #14893

Crise, Barnet, Albany, N.Y., 92, #180

Crise, Barnet, Albany, N.Y., 100, #3965

Crise, Barnet, Albany, N.Y., 51, #5916

Crise, Barnet, e/o, Albany, N.Y., 105, #8086

Crisp, John, Jackson, Tenn., 53, #6490

Crissey, Moses, a/o, Pittsburgh, Pa., 107, #9662

Critchlow, —, Pittsburgh, Pa., 111, #778

Critchlow, Mary, c/o, Pittsburgh, Pa., 5, #778

Crittenden, William S., Mass., 89, #18279, card

Crittenden, William S., w/o, Mass., 5, #18279

Critz, Nancy, Richmond, Va., 95, #1335

Crizbe, Joseph, Albany, N.Y., 101, #5084

Crocker, David, c/o, Pa., 109, #10781

Crocker, Hannah, Albany, N.Y., 96, #1391

Crocker, Jesse, Richmond, Va., 47, #5022

Crocker, Jesse W., c/o, Ill., 118, #4883

Crocker, John H., San Francisco, Calif., 142, #5770

Crocker, Leonard, New York City, 74, #13339

Crocker, Noah, Montpelier, Vt., 101, #5006 V#24

Crocker, Oliver, Albany, N.Y., 105, #7996

Crocker, Rolon, c/o, N.H., 58, #7743

Crocker, Zipha, a/o, Fayetteville, N.C., 138, #4819

Crockett, Anthony, —, 92, #19749, slip

Crockett, Anthony, e/o, Ky., 84, #16166

Crockett, Joseph, —, 92, #19545, slip

Crockett, Robert, c/o, Ky., 55, #7211

Croel, Elizabeth, e/o, N.J., 127, #4470

Croel, Joel, w/o, N.J., 96, #1544

Crofford, Stephen, Pittsburgh, Pa., 76, #13746

Croft, James, w/o, N.Y., 85, #16446

Cromer, John, g/o, Ind., 49, #5347

Cromlow, Ann, Philadelphia, Pa., 113, #1790

Crondus, Dorothy, a/o, Ky.,
121, #6923
Cronk, John, —, 124, #963,
card
Cronk, John, Pittsburgh, Pa., 5,
#963, card
Crook, Charles, Albany, N.Y.,
54, #6663
Crook, James, c/o, Ky., 106,
#8840
Crook, John, Ky., 55, #7037
Crook, William A., Miss., 124,
#478
Crook (formerly Stephens),
Mary B., Portsmouth, N.H.,
126, #3744
Crooker, Priscilla, c/o, Mass.,
64, #9500
Croomes, Emily, g/o c/o, Ill.,
116, #3287
Crosby, John, Ky., 68, #10600
Crosby, Orris, Ill., 113, #1522
Crose, Philip, Ind., 54, #6780,
card
Crosland, Lavinia, c/o, S.C.,
110, #11069
Crosland, Lavinia, g/o c/o, S.C.,
109, #10428
Cross, Abijah, Mass., 42, #3729
Cross, Abijah, Mass., 105,
#7982
Cross, George, Ohio, 119,
#5287, card
Cross, John, Vt., 63, #9007
Cross, John, Vt., 67, #10556
Cross, Joseph, Maine, 51,
#6037
Cross, Mordicai, Indianapolis,
Ind., 143, #7032
Cross, Mordicai, g/o c/o,
Indianapolis, Ind., 139,
#9339

Cross, Samuel, Ohio, 48, #5148
Cross, Thomas J., Ill., 116,
#3133
Cross, Col. Truman, w/o, Asst.
QM General, 105, #8318
Cross, Col. Truman, w/o, Asst.
QM, 107, #9142, #General
Cross, Col. Truman, w/o, Asst.
QM General, 102, #5433
Cross, Col. Truman, w/o, Asst.
QM General, 104, #7395
Cross, Col. Truman, w/o, Asst.
QM General, 108, #10101
Cross, Col. Truman, w/o, Asst.
QM General, 109, #10875
Cross, Col. Truman, w/o, Asst.
QM General, 99, #3652
Cross, Zachariah, lr/o, Mo., 91,
#19224
Crossman, Elijah, w/o, Albany,
N.Y., 97, #2168
Crossman, George, g/o c/o, Ill.,
132, #8911
Crossman, Noah, Mass., 87,
#17380, card
Crossman, Noah, c/o, Mass., 5,
#17380
Crosson, Achsah, a/o, Ga., 119,
#5538
Crosson, John, w/o, Ga., 73,
#12831
Crouch, John, c/o, Va., 85,
#16373
Crouch, Polly, Ky., 140, #453
Crouch, Samuel G., g/o c/o, Ill.,
129, #6955
Crouch, William, w/o, Va., 120,
#6276
Croul, John, w/o, 29th Inf., 138,
#6615
Crouts, Micheal, Ind., 47, #5027

Crow, Abraham, Ga., 81,
#15098
Crow, Abraham, Ga., 83,
#15580
Crow, Abraham, S.C., 53, #6436
Crow, Maria, Ga., 134, #1363
Crow, Wilson, c/o, Mo., 131,
#8184
Crowell, Jerusha, Philadelphia,
Pa., 53, #6354
Crowell, Menia, Albany, N.Y.,
63, #8932
Crowley, James, Mo., 60, #8252
Crowley, James, Mo., 72,
#12703
Crowninshield, Benjamin, w/o,
Mass., 44, #4352
Crowninshield, Mary, Boston,
Mass., 102, #5802
Crowninshield, Mary, a/o,
Mass., 112, #1214
Crownover, Daniel, Ark., 78,
#14529
Crownover, Daniel, S.C., 40,
#3248
Crownover, Daniel, S.C., 45,
#4448
Croxall, Charles, c/o, Md., 100,
#4348
Croxton, Carter, Richmond, Va.,
43, #3877
Cruise, Michael, Mo., 139,
#7829
Crum, Jacob, c/o, —, 130,
#7327, slip
Crum, Richard, N.J., 40, #3199
Crumley, Thomas, c/o, Ga., 115,
#2647
Crump, Dorcas E., Ky., 114,
#2014
Crutcher, James, c/o, Va., 92,
#19745

Crutchfield, John, Ky., 87,
#17581
Crys, Sarah, Knoxville, Tenn.,
94, #601
Culberton, David, Ky., 128,
#5405
Culbertson, Lt. J., 4th Artillery,
122, #8976
Culp, John, S.C., 48, #5231
Culton, Joseph, Ind., 60, #8189
Culton, Joseph, Ind., 73,
#12848
Culton, Joseph, Ind., 73,
#12868
Culver, Aaron, w/o, Albany,
N.Y., 50, #5780
Culver, Christopher, c/o, Conn.,
96, #1485
Culver, Hannah, c/o, Burlington,
Vt., 133, #333
Culver, James, c/o, Vt., 142,
#3460
Cumby, Isaac A., g/o c/o, Miss.,
130, #7355
Cummings, Asa, Maine, 51,
#6020
Cummings, Elijah, Mass., 39,
#3029
Cummings, Elijah, Mass., 86,
#17176
Cummings, Elijah, e/o, Mass.,
87, #17598
Cummings, Thomas, Albany,
N.Y., 129, #7096
Cummings, Mathew, c/o, Ky.,
53, #6554
Cummins, Joseph, c/o,
Philadelphia, Pa., 133,
#162
Cunell, Nicholas, Mass., 42,
#3725

Cunning, Christopher, Ind., 41, #3374

Cunning, Robert, w/o, Pittsburgh, Pa., 138, #5397

Cunningham, Anna, Conn., 31, #67

Cunningham, Ansell, w/o, Savannah, Ga., 5, #18473

Cunningham, Charles, Albany, N.Y., 53, #6504

Cunningham, Edward, Mo., 125, #1650

Cunningham, Elizabeth, c/o, Conn., 31, #6883

Cunningham, Hannah, N.C., 118, #4573

Cunningham, James, —, 107, #9328, card

Cunningham, James, Mo., 49, #5464

Cunningham, James, Mo., 53, #6488

Cunningham, John, Nashville, Tenn., 5, #5984

Cunningham, John, Nashville, Tenn., 5, #7607

Cunningham, John, Tenn., 51, #5984, card

Cunningham, John, Tenn., 57, #7607, card

Cunningham, John, Tenn., 71, #12298, card

Cunningham, John S., —, 140, #9789, slip

Cunningham, Munell, Ky., 76, #13910

Cunningham, Murrell, Ky., 42, #3609

Cunningham, Murrell, Ky., 64, #9487

Cunningham, Phebe, Wheeling, Va., 75, #13566

Cunningham, Phebe, Wheeling, Va., 83, #15579

Cunningham, Phoebe, a/o, Wheeling, Va., 106, #8638

Cunningham, Richard, Ohio, 106, #8629, card

Cunningham, Richard, a/o, Ohio, 5, #8629

Cunningham, William, Wheeling, Va., 45, #4479

Cunningham, William, c/o, Nashville, Tenn., 99, #3657

Cunningham, William, c/o, Nashville, Tenn., 100, #4370

Currier, Ammi, w/o, Albany, N.Y., 101, #5304

Currier, Joseph, a/o, Albany, N.Y., 135, #1863

Curry, John, Ohio, 91, #19492, card

Curry, Polly, alias Mary P., Miss., 135, #2237

Curry, Rachel, Richmond, Va., 126, #3375

Curry, William, w/o, Albany, N.Y., 100, #4209

Curtis, Augustus, Conn., 31, #117

Curtis, Catharine, c/o, Albany, N.Y., 117, #4214

Curtis, James, comm/o, Ky., 81, #15180

Curtis, James, w/o, Ky., 85, #16461

Curtis, Joel, w/o, Albany, N.Y., 6, #5429

Curtis, John, Pittsburgh, Pa., 136, #3291

Curtis, John, Wheeling, W. Va., 40, #3191

Curtis, Jonathan, Vt., 79,
#14647
Curtis, Josiah, Ohio, 47, #4902
Curtis, Jotham, Mich., 78,
#14341
Curtis, Oliver, w/o, Mass., 50,
#5781
Curtis, Robert, Conn., 74,
#13219
Curtis, Samuel, a/o, N.H., 82,
#15235
Curtis, Silas, a/o, N.Y., 82,
#15252
Curtz, Thomas, c/o,
Philadelphia, Pa., 92,
#19814
Curvan, John, S.C., 83, #15802
Cusack (formerly Batton), Mary,
St. Louis, Mo., 128, #5860
Cushing, John W., c/o, Bellows
Falls, Vt., 47, #4943
Cushman, David, a/o, Albany,
N.Y., 70, #11143
Cushman, Hannah, Conn., 31,
#36
Cusick, Nicholas, c/o, Albany,
N.Y., 79, #14570
Cussard, Philip, c/o, Pittsburgh,
Pa., 41, #3518
Custar, Jame, Richmond, Va.,
95, #1058
Custar, Jane, Richmond, Va.,
104, #7612
Custer, Jane, Richmond, Va., 95,
#1256
Custer, John, g/o c/o,
Cincinnati, Ohio, 140, #17
Custis, Isaac W., Nashville,
Tenn., 137, #4169
Cutler, Joseph, c/o, Albany,
N.Y., 77, #14076

Cutler, Josiah, a/o, Mich., 79,
#14629
Cutright, Peter, Ill., 56, #7388
Cutter, Joseph, Concord, N.H.,
71, #12285
Cutts, William, w/o, Ind., 131,
#8797
Cylder, John, c/o, New York
City, 118, #4864
Cylder, Sally, c/o, New York
City, 118, #4863
Cypress, Andrew, Ohio, 75,
#13515
Cypress, Andrew, Ohio, 84,
#15986
Cyre, Nicholas, Richmond, Va.,
87, #17501

D

Dabney, Sarah, Ill., 134, #1492
Daboll, John, e/o, Conn., 38,
#F1826
Dacon, Jonathan, Richmond,
Va., 105, #7826
Dade, Bvt. Maj. Francis L., w/o,
—, 68, #10610
Dade, Bvt. Major Francis L.,
w/o, —, 64, #9279
Dade, F. L., w/o, —, 42, #3709
Dade, F. L., w/o, 4th Inf., 49,
#5327
Dade, Francis L., w/o, 4th Inf,
53, #6559
Daggett, Tristram, c/o, Portland,
Maine, 108, #9731
Dailey, James M., g/o c/o,
Madison, Ind., 139, #8753
Dailey, James M., w/o, New
Albany, Ind., 110, #11106
Dailey, Jane, c/o, Albany, N.Y.,
79, #14714

Dailey, Jesse, w/o, Richmond, Va., 100, #3777

Dailey, John, Trenton, N.J., 104, #7519

Daily, John, a/o, Richmond, Va., 137, #3806

Dale, Bvt. Maj. F. L., w/o, —, 58, #7809

Dale, Polly, Richmond, Va., 137, #4547

Daley, Silas, w/o, Albany, N.Y., 75, #13489

Dallas, Robert, Richmond, Va., 57, #7656

Dallen, William, w/o, Ill., 53, #6518

Dalton, John, Knoxville, Tenn., 50, #5822

Dalton, John, w/o, Knoxville, Tenn., 6, #5822

Dalton, Mary, —, 77, #14187, card

Damon, Lucy, Wisc., 107, #9278

Damon, Mercy, c/o, Mass., 113, #1472

Dan, Squire, Hartford, Conn., 31, #54

Dana, Daniel, Pittsburgh, Pa., 44, #4213

Dana, Joseph, a/o, Albany, N.Y., 125, #1988

Dandridge, Elizabeth, a/o, Richmond, Va., 133, #579

Danforth, Olive, a/o, N.H., 77, #14129

Danforth, Thomas, PA, New Albany, Ind., 116, #3789

Danforth, Thomas, PA, New Albany, Ind., 114, #2402

Daniel, Benjamin W., Nashville, Tenn., 73, #12834

Daniel, Benjamin W., Nashville, Tenn., 87, #17575

Daniel, Beverly, Ky., 78, #14402

Daniel, Bruckner, N.C., 54, #6643

Daniel, Buchner, N.C., 46, #4749

Daniel, Ezekeil, S.C., 68, #10592

Daniel, Henry, La., 129, #7042

Daniel, James, w/o, Richmond, Va., 127, #4846

Daniel, Jesse, La., 96, #1839

Daniel, John M., Ky., 139, #8133

Daniel, John M., Ky., 140, #9887

Daniel, Richard, Richmond, Va., 98, #3091

Daniel, Richard, Richmond, Va., 51, #5924

Daniel, Warner J., g/o c/o, Ill., 131, #8199

Daniel, William, Ind., 44, #4337

Daniel, William, Ind., 58, #7932

Daniel, William, Ind., 67, #10449

Daniel, William, Ind., 75, #13438

Daniels, Anna, c/o, Portsmouth, N.H., 115, #2755

Daniels, Eleazer, Albany, N.Y., 76, #13932

Daniels, Lucian, c/o, Pittsburgh, Pa., 6, #9666

Daniels, Lydia, Albany, N.Y., 115, #2958

Daniels, Nehimiah, w/o, N.Y., 109, #10785

Daniels, Sarah Ann, Augusta, Maine, 142, #5317

Daniels, Susannah, c/o, Wisc.,
   102, #6007
Daniels, Warner J., c/o, Ill.,
   117, #4128
Danielson, Abigail, a/o, Albany,
   N.Y., 124, #1353
Dankins, John, N.C., 132,
   #9004, card
Danton, Sally, a/o, Mass., 128,
   #5595
Darlin, David, w/o, Albany,
   N.Y., 65, #9770
Darling, Asenath, h/o, Detroit,
   Mich., 126, #3238
Darling, Benjamin, Albany,
   N.Y., 75, #13698
Darling, John, g/o c/o, Conn.,
   37, #F1825
Darling, Joseph, Detroit, Mich.,
   52, #6265
Darling, Joseph, Mich., 60,
   #8290
Darling, Joseph, Mich., 66,
   #10216
Darling, Leuice, Albany, N.Y.,
   72, #12607
Darlington, Elizabeth,
   Philadelphia, Pa., 77,
   #14005
Darlington, Elizabeth,
   Philadelphia, Pa., 91,
   #19076
Darrach, John, S.C., 40, #3173
Darrin, Daniel, w/o, Albany,
   N.Y., 91, #19223
Darris, Rhoda E., Spingfield,
   Ill., 142, #5971
Darrow, Danl., Albany, N.Y.,
   53, #6521
Darrow, George, Albany, N.Y.,
   138, #4937

Darrow, George, Ohio, 83,
   #15575
Darrow, Sarah, lr/o, New York
   City, 138, #4643
Darwin, John, a/o, S.C., 127,
   #4010
Dashiel, Levi, c/o, Md., 49,
   #5322
Daub, Dilman, w/o,
   Philadelphia, Pa., 124,
   #1303
Daugherty, William, Ind., 64,
   #9218
Davenport, Claibourne, Ky., 87,
   #1771-, card
Davenport, Henry, New York
   City, 61, #8528
Davenport, Jacobus, N.Y., 91,
   #19255
Davenport, Mary S., e/o, N.Y.,
   108, #9903
Davenport, Noah, Albany, N.Y.,
   74, #13308
Davenport, Richard, N.Y., 116,
   #3787, card
Davenport, Richard, c/o,
   Albany, N.Y., 6, #3787
Davenport, Squire, Ohio,
   Pittsburgh, Pa., 117,
   #4275, card
Davenport, Squire, a/o,
   Pittsburgh, Pa., 6, #4275
Davenport, Squire, c/o,
   Pittsburgh, Pa., 6, #18670
Davenport, Thomas, Maine,
   104, #7529
David, Enos, Ind., 54, #6635
David, Henry, Ind., 76, #13789
David, Henry, w/o, Madison,
   Ind., 97, #2166

Davidhiser, Elizabeth, a/o,
  Philadelphia, Pa., 113,
  #1844
Davidson, Catharine, a/o, Ohio,
  6, #2640
Davidson, Catherine,
  Cincinnati, Ohio, 115,
  #2644, card
Davidson, Eleanor, Pittsburgh,
  Pa., 115, #2886
Davidson, Isaac, Ind., 48, #5087
Davidson, James, Md., 107,
  #9323, card
Davidson, John, Ga., 46, #4805
Davidson, John, Nashville,
  Tenn., 39, #3007
Davidson, Judith, Va., 82,
  #15284
Davidson, Nathan, La., 78,
  #14238
Davidson, Lt. Col. William, Inf.,
  128, #—, card
Davidson, Lt. Col. William, Inf.,
  128, #5983, card
Davidson, William, Inf., 122,
  #8061, card
Davie, Solomon, w/o, Boston,
  Mass., 59, #8135
Davis, Aaron, w/o, N.C., 62,
  #8864
Davis, Abigail, c/o, Conn., 31,
  #5982
Davis, Abraham, w/o,
  Richmond, Va., 6, #7942
Davis, Alexander W., Detroit,
  Mich., 116, #3522
Davis, Andrew, Knoxville,
  Tenn., 92, #197
Davis, Benjamin, New York
  City, 60, #8174
Davis, Benjamin, New York
  City, 62, #8697

Davis, Benjamin, c/o, N.Y.,
  111, #444
Davis, Benjamin, c/o, New York
  City, 110, #5
Davis, Betsey, c/o, New York
  City, 124, #426
Davis, Betsey, c/o, New York
  City, 124, #902
Davis, Clement, w/o, N.C., 60,
  #8298
Davis, Daniel, Conn., 119,
  #5445
Davis, Daniel, Ohio, 99, #3371
Davis, David, over/o, Albany,
  N.Y., 58, #7855
Davis, Dorcas, c/o, Mass., 67,
  #10508
Davis, Edmund, R.I., 72, #12580
Davis, Edmund, R.I., 87, #17494
Davis, Emor M., Philadelphia,
  Pa., 134, #1577
Davis, Entire, Maine, 110,
  #11007, slip
Davis, Forrest, a/o, Ky., 102,
  #6137
Davis, Goldsmith, a/o, Albany,
  N.Y., 133, #9969
Davis, Hugh, Va., 97, #1978,
  card
Davis, Hugh, a/o, Richmond,
  Va., 6, #1978
Davis Jr., Isaac, e/o, Richmond,
  Va., 6, #10225
Davis, Jacob, w/o, Albany,
  N.Y., 78, #14347
Davis, James, Jacksonville,
  Fla., 95, #1099
Davis, James, Knoxville, Tenn.,
  39, #3046
Davis, James, Ky., 47, #4999
Davis Sr., James, N.C., 47,
  #4853

Davis, John, —, 70, #12169,
card
Davis, John, Ky., 82, #15528,
card
Davis, John, Va., 82, #15260
Davis, John, c/o, Philadelphia,
Pa., 117, #4256
Davis, John, w/o, Cincinnati,
Ohio, 6, #12169
Davis 2nd, John, Pittsburgh,
Pa., 90, #18831, card
Davis 2nd, John, a/o, Cleveland,
Ohio, 136, #2749
Davis 2nd, John, c/o,
Pittsburgh, Pa., 6, #18831
Davis, Joseph, Albany, N.Y., 6,
#5443
Davis, Joseph, Conn., 119,
#5444
Davis, Joshua, w/o, Ohio, 97,
#2473
Davis, Josiah, c/o, N.C., 43,
#3937
Davis, Ledowick, Ind., 52,
#6324
Davis, Leonard, Richmond, Va.,
42, #3582
Davis, Leonard, Richmond, Va.,
47, #4993
Davis, Leonard, Va., 66, #10173
Davis, Levi, c/o, Ohio, 107,
#9079
Davis, Lewis, Jonesboro, Tenn.,
123, #266
Davis, Lewis, e/o, Va., 119,
#5176
Davis, Nancy, N.C., 104, #7232
Davis, Nancy, a/o, S.C., 130,
#8065
Davis, Nathaniel, Mass., 43,
#3867

Davis, Peter, c/o, Albany, N.Y.,
109, #10625
Davis, Peter, c/o, Albany, N.Y.,
110, #11005
Davis, Philomon, Ind., 47,
#5027
Davis, Polly, a/o, Richmond,
Va., 36A, #F6 V12
Davis (late Blunt), Polly Ann,
Mo., 116, #3521
Davis, Rachel, Philadelphia, Pa.,
101, #4851 V#26
Davis, Richard, w/o, Ohio, 109,
#10468
Davis, Robert A., Ill., 131,
#8670
Davis, Samuel, Huntsville, Ala.,
57, #7532
Davis, Samuel, Ky., 54, #6600
Davis, Samuel, Ohio, 73,
#12783
Davis, Samuel, c/o, N.C., 117,
#3956
Davis, Samuel, c/o, N.C., 117,
#4374
Davis, Samuel, w/o, N.C., 68,
#10580
Davis, Spencer, Ohio, 61, #8388
Davis, Thomas, Knoxville,
Tenn., 40, #3329
Davis, Thomas, Philadelphia,
Pa., 56, #7409
Davis, Thomas, S.C., 68,
#10734
Davis, Thomas, w/o, Ky., 73,
#12849
Davis, Thomas, w/o, Mass., 88,
#17858
Davis, Thomas, S.C., 53, #6503
Davis, William, Ky., 135,
#2301
Davis, William, La., 73, #12816

Davis, William, Mobile, Ala.,
54, #6900
Davis, William, Richmond, Va.,
92, #19573
Davis, William, Richmond, Va.,
92, #19819
Davis, William, Va., 87, #17723
Davis, William, w/o, Richmond,
Va., 97, #2470
Davis 3rd, William, w/o,
Albany, N.Y., 54, #6808
Davis 4th, William, w/o, Maine,
43, #3846
Davis, William E., Mobile, Ala.,
131, #8416
Davis, William S., N.Y., 83,
#15778
Davis, Willie, c/o, Nashville,
Tenn., 121, #7593
Davis, Zachariah, E. Tenn., 76,
#13796, card
Davis, Zachariah, E. Tenn., 82,
#15486, card
Davis, Zachariah, Knoxville,
Tenn., 6, #15486
Davis, Zachariah, Knoxville,
Tenn., 6, #13796
Davis, Zebulon, Maine, 60,
#8322
Davison, Bracket, Mo., 64,
#9504
Davison, Brackett, Mo., 54,
#6878
Davison, Brackett, Mo., 139,
#9266
Dawens, Edward, N.J., 56, #7256
Dawes, Dolly, Mass., 111, #364
Dawes, Dolly, Mass., 123,
#9402
Dawson, Lt. S. K., Ft. Sullivan,
Maine, 85, #16407

Day, Amos, w/o, N.J., 112,
#947
Day, Anthony, Albany, N.Y.,
42, #3744
Day, Catherine B., Knoxville,
Tenn., 113, #1866
Day, Daniel, N.H. and Ill., 78,
#14523, card
Day, Daniel, c/o, N.H., 7,
#14523
Day, Joseph, w/o, Vt., 87,
#17413
Day, Mary, a/o, Nashville,
Tenn., 86, #17013
Day 2nd, Nathaniel, w/o, Maine,
87, #17711
Day, Noah, a/o, Albany, N.Y.,
74, #13284
Day, Solomon, c/o, Albany,
N.Y., 91, #19504
Day (formerly Gaines), Susan C.,
Ky., 118, #4729
Day (formerly Gaines), Susan C.,
c/o, Ky., 118, #4730
Dayton, Mary, c/o, Conn., 31,
#12921
Deake, Julia Ann, Ill., 139,
#7895
Deakins, Martha, Mo., 130,
#7498
Deal, George, c/o, Philadelphia,
Pa., 97, #1890
Deal, Jacob, N.C., 45, #4427
Deal, Jacob, N.C., 54, #6595
Deal, Samuel, Ind., 122, #8770
Deal, Samuel, Madison, Ind.,
112, #990
Deal, Samuel, Madison, Ind.,
117, #3959
Deal, Samuel, Madison, Ind.,
128, #5114
Deall, Daniel, Ind., 53, #6442

Dean, Anna, a/o, Albany, N.Y.,
103, #6963
Dean, Betsey, a/o, Va., 6,
#10771
Dean, Betsy, Va., 68, #10771,
card
Dean, Howell H., Richmond,
Va., 36A, #F4 V5
Dean, Jabex, w/o, Albany, N.Y.,
65, #9838
Dean, John, w/o, Ky., 89,
#18157
Dean, John, w/o, Va., 39, #3088
Dean, Joseph, Mass., 112,
#1220
Dean, Lemuel, N.H., 87,
#17678, card
Dean, Lemuel, a/o, N.H., 6,
#17678
Dean, Louisa, Ga., 135, #1797
Dean, Reuben, Conn., 43, #3810
Dean, Zebediah, lr/o, Mass., 64,
#9677
Deane, Solomon W., St.
Johnsbury, Vt., 140, #315
DeAngelis, Elizabeth, Albany,
N.Y., 97, #2445
Deathey, James, Richmond, Va.,
44, #4208
Deathey, James, Va., 84,
#16119
Deatley, James, Va., 68, #10768
Deatley, Joseph, Richmond, Va.,
57, #7516
DeAugelis, Elizabeth, Albany,
N.Y., 107, #8901
DeBerry, Benjamin, N.C., 6,
#2141
Debrill, Charles, Nashville,
Tenn., 40, #3342
Decker, Jacob, e/o, Philadelphia,
Pa., 94, #273

DeCoursey, William, w/o, Ohio,
81, #15016
Deer, James, Pittsburgh, Pa., 70,
#12115
Deer, Martin, Richmond, Va.,
110, #11029
Deer, Martin, e/o, Va., 122,
#8238
Defever, Nancy, Ky., 117,
#4380
Defever, Nancy, a/o, Ky., 137,
#4252
Defevers, John, w/o, Ky., 103,
#6712
Defnall, David, c/o, Ga., 107,
#9626
Deforest, Mary, New York City,
129, #6532
DeForrest, Abram, a/o,
Philadelphia, Pa., 119,
#5758
Defrance, John, w/o, Pittsburgh,
Pa., 6, #9436
Defrane, John, Pittsburgh, Pa.,
64, #9436, card
DeFreest, Rachael, Albany,
N.Y., 41, #3356
Defreest, Rachel, Albany, N.Y.,
81, #15171
DeGraffenreid, William, —, 117,
#3995, slip
DeGraft, John, c/o, Albany,
N.Y., 50, #5730
Degraw, Luke, New York City,
61, #8490
Degraw, Luke, New York City,
61, #8511
Deim, Jacob, c/o, Philadelphia,
Pa., 119, #5148
Delamater, Elizabeth, Albany,
N.Y., 89, #18536

Delaney, James, Mo., 128,
#5663
Delavan, Daniel, c/o, New York
City, 109, #10567
Delawater, Elizabeth, Albany,
N.Y., 80, #14752
Demmon, Huldah, c/o, Vt., 58,
#7903
Demott, William, Albany, N.Y.,
134, #951
Deneen, James, Ohio, 42, #3748
Denham, Harden, Ky., 39, #2997
Dennin, Charles, g/o c/o, New
York City, 126, #3297
Dennis, Anna, Albany, N.Y., 78,
#14346
Dennis, Philip, a/o, Albany,
N.Y., 134, #976
Dennis, William, Northampton
Co., Va., 80, #14770, card
Dennis, William, a/o, Va., 6,
#14770
Dennison, Joseph, g/o c/o,
Conn., 37, #F1820
Denny, Charles, Ill., 50, #5604
Dent, George, Md., 55, #7217
Dent, George, Md., 81, #15039
Dent, George, e/o, Md., 116,
#3671
Dent, John, Ky., 6, #14018
Denton, David, w/o, Ky., 55,
#6943
Denton, Elizabeth, Richmond,
Va., 36A, #F4 V6
Depew, David, —, 101, #5285,
card
Depew, David, —, 99, #3542,
card
Depew, John, Pittsburgh, Pa.,
41, #3371
Depoister, John, a/o, Ind., 85,
#16356

Depuy, Cornelius, c/o, New York
City, 108, #9967
Derby, Sarah, c/o, Albany, N.Y.,
88, #17943
Derby, Simeon, a/o, Concord,
N.H., 87, #17655
Dermon, Oliver, c/o, Concord,
N.H., 55, #6938
Derrick, Joseph A., Calif., 123,
#9400
Deshazo, William, w/o,
Richmond, Va., 64, #9361
Deshler, Charles, c/o,
Philadelphia, Pa., 115,
#2831
Deshow, Henry, w/o, Albany,
N.Y., 125, #1806
DeShuitzenbache, Louis,
Philadelphia, Pa., 117,
#3971
Desmukes, Paul, w/o, Nashville,
Tenn., 43, #3895
Despair, Benjamin, w/o, S.C.,
98, #2922
Deusler, Catherine, Albany,
N.Y., 70, #11177
Deusler, Catherine, c/o, Albany,
N.Y., 98, #2629
Deveney, Daniel, c/o,
Philadelphia, Pa., 127,
#4792
Deverick, Mary, Richmond, Va.,
107, #9080
Devericks, John, Va., 40, #3340
Devinney, James, —, 79,
#14696, card
Devins, Nancy, Va., 76, #13766
Devoe, John, c/o, Albany, N.Y.,
59, #8108
Dewalt, Ann, c/o, Albany, N.Y.,
111, #388

DeWaltz, Peter, w/o,
Philadelphia, Pa., 108,
#10158

Dewing, Elijah, Mass., 124,
#505

Dewitt, Egbert, Albany, N.Y.,
52, #6342

DeWitt, Paul, w/o, Philadelphia,
Pa., 117, #4402

DeWolf, Daniel, Conn., 31,
#352

DeWolf, Edward, Albany, N.Y.,
92, #209

DeWolf, Edward, c/o, Albany,
N.Y., 100, #4379

Dewolf, Joseph, Philadelphia,
Pa., 6, #5134

DeWolf, Peter, Pittsburgh, Pa.,
114, #2054, card

DeWolf, Peter, c/o, Ohio, 6,
#2054

Dexter, Abigal, c/o, Conn., 31,
#12037

Dexter, Elisha, w/o, New York
City, 48, #5067

Dexter, Mary, c/o, Mass., 123,
#29

Dey, Margaret, c/o, Trenton,
N.J., 104, #7536

Dey, Rebecca, Trenton, N.J.,
104, #7535

Diamond, Harvey N., a/o, Ill.,
108, #10176

Dibble, John, c/o, Windsor, Vt.,
42, #3685

Dibble, Lois, Albany, N.Y., 89,
#18433

Dibrell, Charles, a/o, Nashville,
Tenn., 114, #2099

Dick, John, La., 53, #6459

Dick, William, c/o,
Philadelphia, Pa., 124,
#671

Dicken, Elizabeth, Ga., 64,
#9495

Dicken, Elizabeth, Ga., 71,
#12278

Dicken, John, w/o, Ky., 109,
#10782

Dickens, Griffith, e/o,
Richmond, Va., 6, #3030

Dickens, John A., Ky., 143,
#6635

Dickens, Thomas, —, 118,
#4797, card

Dickerson, Polly, Richmond,
Va., 127, #4231

Dickerson, Polly, Richmond,
Va., 134, #1011

Dickerson, Walter, Ind., 62,
#8875

Dickey, Ebenezer, Ky., 40,
#3168

Dickey, Jesse, Ill., 132, #9208

Dickey, Mary, c/o, Concord,
N.H., 63, #9099

Dickey, Moses, Pittsburgh, Pa.,
51, #6054

Dickey, Robert, a/o, Cincinnati,
Ohio, 115, #2698

Dickinson, Ann, c/o, Richmond,
Va., 71, #12246

Dickinson, Jemima, a/o,
Richmond, Va., 136, #3485

Dickinson, Jesse, c/o,
Philadelphia, Pa., 90,
#18948

Dickinson, John, c/o, Albany,
N.Y., 99, #3217

Dickinson, Justin, Albany,
N.Y., 53, #6586

Dickinson, Justin, Mich., 112,
#1234
Dickinson, Philemon, PA,
Trenton, N.J., 118, #5009
Dickson, Abner, Huntsville,
Ala., 50, #5499
Dickson, Sarah, Albany, N.Y.,
73, #12994
Dickson, Sarah, Albany, N.Y.,
78, #14324
Dickson, Philemon, PA,
Trenton, N.J., 114, #2434
Dieterle, Christina M., D.C.,
132, #9411
Dieterle, Christina Marguretta,
D.C., 143, #7045
Dieterte, Christainna M., D.C.,
141, #2598
Dilday, Amos, N.C., 56, #7378
Dilday, Amos, c/o, N.C., 95,
#1024
Dilday, Joseph, w/o, N.C., 76,
#13902
Dildee, Amos, N.C., 42, #3676
Dildine, Jonathan, Knoxville,
Tenn., 48, #5127
Dill, George, Albany, N.Y., 51,
#5917
Dill, John, Albany, N.Y., 43,
#3938
Dill, Mary, Mass., 115, #2773
Dill, Thomas, c/o, Pittsburgh,
Pa., 6, #14504
Dill, Thomas, Pittsburgh, Pa.,
78, #14504, card
Dillard, John, Ga., 91, #19088,
card
Dille, David, Pa., 120, #6623
Dillen, Henry, Nashville, Tenn.,
68, #10657
Dilley, Ephraim, Wheeling, Va.,
54, #6681

Dilley, Ephriam, Pittsburgh,
Pa.., 115, #2921, card to
Wheeling, Va
Dilley, Ephriam, a/o, Wheeling,
Va., 6, #2921
Dilley Sr., Ephraim, Wheeling,
Va., 39, #2944
Dillon, —, N.C., 46, #4676,
card
Dillon, Arthur, La., 128, #5581
Dillon, Benjamin, N.C., 6,
#4676, card
Dillon, Thomas, Ga., 20, #4963
Dillon, Thomas, —, 6, #4963,
card see Isum Peacock
Dimmick, Shubel, Albany, N.Y.,
6, #9756
Dimmick, Shubel, N.Y., 65,
#9746, card
Dimond, Abigail, Portsmouth,
N.H., 105, #7825
Dingman, Andrew, Philadelphia,
Pa., 58, #7762
Dinguid, George, a/o, Va., 84,
#16153
Dinsmore, Abraham, Bellows
Falls, Vt., 43, #4012
Dishow, Lewis, N.C., 83,
#15550
Dishow, Lewis, N.C., 86,
#16803
Dix, Amy, a/o, Montpelier, Vt.,
102, #5722
Dixon, Alexander, Ohio, 55,
#7028
Dixon, Alexander, Ohio, 90,
#18695
Dixon, Ann, e/o, Nashville,
Tenn., 132, #9882
Dixon, Anna, Columbus, Ohio,
143, #6625

Dixon, Hannah, Philadelphia,
Pa., 115, #2780
Dixon, John, w/o, Albany, N.Y.,
114, #2002
Dixon, Nathaniel, Richmond,
Va., 47, #4987
Dixon, Nathaniel, c/o,
Richmond, Va., 65, #9961
Dixon, Robert, Albany, N.Y.,
44, #4336
Dixon, Thomas, Ky., 84,
#16167
Dixon, Thomas, N.Y., 85,
#16557
Dixon (formerly Johnson),
Susannah, c/o, Mo., 114,
#2110
Doane, Martha, Mass., 47,
#4868
Dobbins, Catherine, c/o, Maine,
132, #9158
Dobbins, David, c/o, Nashville,
Tenn., 123, #9618
Dobbins, John, w/o, Richmond,
Va., 96, #1880
Dobbs, Hannah, e/o, Knoxville,
Tenn., 90, #18958
Dobson, Joseph L., w/o, N.C.,
75, #13513
Dobson, Mary, a/o, N.C., 122,
#8264
Dockstader, John, c/o, Albany,
N.Y., 99, #3293
Dodd, Moses, c/o, N.J., 69,
#10957
Dodd, Susannah, c/o, Conn., 31,
#2064
Dodd, William, c/o, Knoxville,
Tenn., 102, #5500
Dodge, Charles, Philadelphia,
Pa., 143, #7085
Dodge, John, Mass., 40, #3321

Dodge, Nathaniel, Albany, N.Y.,
106, #8384
Dodge, Nelson A., Augusta,
Maine, 143, #6691
Dodge, Robert, c/o, N.H., 121,
#7214
Dodge, William, c/o, Albany,
N.Y., 137, #4305
Doe, James, Maine, 39, #3097
Doefler, Andrew, g/o c/o,
Philadelphia, Pa., 129,
#6823 (alias Andrew
Devlin)
Doing, Robert, Ill., 112, #1062
Doing, Robert, Ill., 113, #1647
Doll, John, Philadelphia, Pa.,
60, #8219
Dollerson, Esther, c/o, Albany,
N.Y., 96, #1458
Dolliver, Aligail, c/o, Albany,
N.Y., 86, #17260
Dolsbury, Lyles, Richmond, Va.,
52, #6339
Dolson, John, N.Y., 57, #7662,
card
Dolson, John, w/o, Albany,
N.Y., 7, #7662
Domming, Davis, w/o, Albany,
N.Y., 92, #19701
Donaldson, Margaret, Nashville,
Tenn., 130, #7237
Donaldson, William, Ga., 57,
#7592
Donnell, John, a/o, Va., 88,
#17938
Donner, John H., La., 74,
#13172
Doolin, Christopher, Albany,
N.Y., 130, #7921
Doolittle, Mary, Richmond, Va.,
132, #9548

Doolittle, Nathaniel, c/o,
Albany, N.Y., 87, #17696
Dooly (formerly Davis), Nancy,
Ga., 7, #2344
Dorgin, John, c/o, Md., 69,
#10948
Dorsey, Rachel, a/o, Md., 65,
#9865
Dorsey, Greenbury, PA, New
Orleans, La., 114, #2255
Doss, John, c/o, Knoxville,
Tenn., 134, #1344
Doss, John, e/o, Va., 85,
#16396
Doss, William, Knoxville,
Tenn., 56, #7365
Dossey, John, Ky., 83, #15594
Doty, Ellis, c/o, Albany, N.Y.,
136, #3041
Doty, Ezra, a/o, Philadelphia,
Pa., 69, #10921
Doty, John, a/o, N.J., 114,
#2074
Doty, John, w/o, Albany, N.Y.,
78, #14382
Doty, Jonathan, e/o, Pittsburgh,
Pa., 123, #9673
Doty Sr., Jonathan, Pittsburgh,
Pa., 98, #2951
Doty, Peter, Ohio, 64, #9630
Doty, Peter, Ohio, 75, #13655
Doty, Peter, c/o, Cincinnati,
Ohio, 133, #9913
Doty, Thomas T., Huntsville,
Ala., 64, #9196
Doty, Zebulon, Pittsburgh, Pa.,
79, #14706
Doubleday, Aschel, Bellows
Falls, Vt., 63, #8967
Doud, Benjamin, Albany, N.Y.,
89, #18463

Dougal, Henry, w/o, Pittsburgh,
Pa., 137, #4044
Dougan, James, Nashville,
Tenn., 42, #3693
Dougherty, James W., a/o, Ky.,
135, #1946
Dougherty, John, Philadelphia,
Pa., 79, #14737
Dougherty, John, Philadelphia,
Pa., 43, #3881
Dougherty, John, Philadelphia,
Pa., 47, #4851
Dougherty, John, Philadelphia,
Pa., 52, #6127
Dougherty, Mary, New York
City, 123, #198
Dougherty, Patrick,
Philadelphia, Pa., 63,
#8896
Dougherty, William, a/o,
Madison, Ind., 96, #1409
Doughty, Calvin, c/o, Ill., 118,
#4842
Doughty, Nathaniel, c/o, Maine,
142, #5222
Douglas, Jeremiah, −, 49,
#541-, card
Douglass, James H., Ill., 118,
#4574
Dove, William, Richmond, Va.,
104, #7475
Dow, Ruth, N.H., 81, #14999
Dow, Ruth, Portsmouth, N.H.,
72, #12570
Dowden, Thomas, w/o,
Richmond, Va., 48, #5123
Dowens, Edward, N.J., 74,
#13229
Dowler, Mary, a/o, −, 106,
#8609
Downer, Laura H., Ill., 113,
#1457

Downes, Thomas, w/o, Ohio,
105, #8191
Downing, George R., N.H., 60,
#8253
Downing, Phineas, c/o, Conn.,
57, #7500
Downing, Stephen, c/o, Mich.,
132, #9740
Downing, Stephen, c/o, Mich.,
133, #9919
Downing, Stephen, c/o, Mich.,
133, #97
Downs, David, Conn., 31, #56
Downs, John H., Cleveland,
Ohio, 141, #3044
Dows, Eleazer, Albany, N.Y.,
66, #10228
Dows, Elezer, Albany, N.Y., 88,
#17809
Doxey, Jeremiah, Jackson,
Tenn., 53, #6362
Doxtator, Peter, Albany, N.Y.,
88, #17888
Doyle, James, c/o, Maine, 110,
#11136
Doyle, John, Mo., 127, #4057
Doyle, John, Mo., 131, #8164
Doyle, John, Wisc., 138, #6579
Doyle, John, a/o, Knoxville,
Tenn., 90, #18787
Dozier, Peter, Ill., 128, #5055
Drake, Jacob, N.J., 41, #3547
Drake, Jeremiah, w/o, N.Y., 100,
#4520
Drake, Josiah, w/o, Albany,
N.Y., 101, #5162
Drake, Oliver, w/o, Mass., 47,
#4997
Drake, Phinehas, w/o, Conn.,
65, #9983
Drake, Richard, c/o, Albany,
N.Y., 103, #6647

Drake, Richard, c/o, Albany,
N.Y., 103, #7091
Drake, Richard, w/o, N.C., 84,
#16100
Draper, Jonathan, Pittsburgh,
Pa., 70, #12114
Draper, Sally, Richmond, Va.,
36A, #F4 V4
Dresser, Elizabeth, c/o, Maine,
110, #11081
Drew, Wethea, c/o, Boston,
Mass., 101, #5022
Drewry, Luther, w/o, Albany,
N.Y., 104, #7538
Driggs, Dudley, a/o, Va., 90,
#18754
Drinkwater, Hannah,
Philadelphia, Pa., 126,
#3462
Drown, Sarah, Mass., 94, #725
Drullinger, Frederick, c/o, Ohio,
90, #18546
Drum, Capt. Irwin H., w/o, 4th
Artillery, 102, #5442
Drum, Capt. S. H., w/o, 4th
Artillery, 112, #983
Drum, Capt. S. H., w/o, 4th
Artillery, 109, #10769
Drum, Capt. Simon, w/o, 4th
Inf., 113, #1711
Drum, Capt. Simon H., w/o, 4th
Artillery, 107, #8933
Drum, Capt. Simon H., w/o, 4th
Artillery, 104, #7226
Drum, Capt. Simon H., w/o, 4th
Artillery, 111, #343
Drum, Capt. Simon H., w/o, 4th
Artillery, 103, #6522
Drum, Capt. Simon H., w/o, 4th
Artillery, 105, #8123
Drum, Lt. S. H., special
payment, 92, #12

Drum, Parris, a/o w/o, Ohio,
111, #761, #militia
Drum, Philip, Pittsburgh, Pa.,
63, #9119
Drum, Philip, Pittsburgh, Pa.,
81, #15185
Drum, Philip, Pittsburgh, Pa.,
89, #18225
Drumheller, Leonard, w/o,
Richmond, Va., 117, #3828
Drummond, Grieve, Richmond,
Va., 61, #8604
Drummond, Grieve, Richmond,
Va., 51, #5909
Drummond, Grieve, Va., 80,
#14928
Drummond, Mary, Va., 70,
#12023
DuBois, Martin, Md., 82,
#15278
Dubose, Peter, e/o, S.C., 101,
#5270
Duboy, Basent, Albany, N.Y.,
40, #3189
Ducker, Enoch, Ky., 122, #8231
Ducker, Enoch, Ky., 127, #4409
Ducker, Enoch, Ky., 137, #4633
Dudley, Benjah, Bellows Falls,
Vt., 63, #8967
Dudley, John, Albany, N.Y., 67,
#10487
Dudley, John, Ill., 81, #15071
Dudley, Martha, —, 126, #3471,
slip
Dudley, Martha, c/o, New York
City, 137, #4119
Dudley, Nathan, Maine, 64,
#9143
Dudley, Thomas, c/o, Poultney,
Vt., 96, #1370
Dufan, Michael, w/o, Albany,
N.Y., 65, #9821

Duffer, James H., Mo., 102,
#5906
Duffer, James H., Mo., 138,
#5977
Duffer, James H., Mo., 101,
#4737
Duffil, Thomas, w/o, Ga., 108,
#10146
Duffin, Richard, Boston, Mass.,
143, #7264
Duffy, Edward, New York City,
55, #7223
Duffy, Felix, w/o, New York
City, 141, #3052
Duffy, John, c/o, Ga., 126,
#3144
Dufour, Angelina, Mo., 113,
#1897
Dugan, William, Ohio, 67,
#10468
Duggins, Mary, c/o, Maine, 98,
#2651
Dukes, Isaac, w/o, Ohio, 60,
#8179
Dull, Joseph, g/o c/o,
Philadelphia, Pa., 128,
#5218
Dunbar, Amos, a/o, Pittsburgh,
Pa., 131, #8767
Dunbar, Eunice, a/o, Mass., 132,
#9130
Dunbar, Miles, w/o, Albany,
N.Y., 68, #10638
Dunbar, Rachel, c/o, Mass., 63,
#8976
Dunbar, Thomas, Ky., 79,
#14575
Dunbar, Thomas, Ky., 82,
#15241
Dunbar, William, Cincinnati,
Ohio, 104, #7652

Dunbar, William, Ohio, 72,
#12620
Dunbar, William, Ohio, 106,
#8523
Dunbar, William, Ohio, 98,
#2658
Dunbar, William, c/o,
Cincinnati, Ohio, 124,
#616
Duncan, Charles, w/o, Va., 53,
#6360
Duncan, Daniel C., g/o c/o,
Springfield, Ill., 140, #1124
Duncan, E., —, 107, #9130, card
Duncan, Elijah, —, 97, #2257,
card
Duncan, Elizabeth, Madison,
Ind., 7, #9130
Duncan, Hannah, a/o, Ky., 114,
#2257
Duncan, James, Ga., 113,
#1600, card
Duncan, James, Ga., 113,
#1611, card
Duncan, James, Ga., 113, #60,
card
Duncan, Jared, w/o, Albany,
N.Y., 60, #8291
Duncan, John, Ind., 116, #3599
Duncan, Rhoda, c/o, Knoxville,
Tenn., 123, #9171
Duncan, Richardson, w/o,
Albany, N.Y., 99, #3261
Duncan, Robert, S.C., 59, #8000
Duncan, Robert, S.C., 83,
#15597
Dunham, Cersham, w/o, Bellows
Falls, Vt., 54, #6680
Dunham, Elizabeth, a/o, Boston,
Mass., 7, #6997
Dunham, Joseph, c/o, Albany,
N.Y., 82, #15507

Dunham, Lucy, c/o, Albany,
N.Y., 106, #8734
Dunham, Samuel, w/o, Albany,
N.Y., 89, #18327
Dunham, Stephen, w/o, Albany,
N.Y., 108, #10024
Dunkley, John, w/o, Richmond,
Va., 7, #17641
Dunkley, Moses, Richmond,
Va., 7, #4848
Dunkley, Moses, Va., 47,
#4948, card
Dunlap, Preston A., Albany,
N.Y., 142, #4501
Dunlap, Samuel, a/o, Wheeling,
Va., 82, #15494
Dunlay, Thomas H.,
Cananadaigua, N.Y., 7, #79
Dunlop, James M., g/o c/o, Ill.,
131, #8489
Dunn, Alexander, Calif., 131,
#8724
Dunn, Alexander, New York
City, 116, #3769
Dunn, Catharine, c/o, Knoxville,
Tenn., 7, #1864
Dunn, Catherine, Knoxville,
Tenn., 113, #1864, card
Dunn, Elizabeth, Albany, N.Y.,
103, #6833
Dunn, James, —, 41, #3523,
card
Dunn, James, —, 104, #7412,
card
Dunn, James, Va., 7, #3523
Dunn, James, w/o, Albany, N.Y.,
7, #7412
Dunn, Jane, a/o, Va., 113,
#1266
Dunn, Priscilla, c/o,
Philadelphia, Pa., 59,
#7946

Dunn, Thomas, Ga., 72, #12548
Dunn, Thomas, w/o, Va., 73,
   #12951
Dunning, David, Conn., 31,
   #152
Dunning, Hannah, a/o, Albany,
   N.Y., 78, #14322
Dunning, Maria, c/o, Albany,
   N.Y., 7, #4486
Dunsett, Cato, c/o, Mass., 133,
   #248 (alias Cato Nay)
Dunworth, George, Conn., 71,
   #12248
Dupee, John, w/o, Mass., 70,
   #11178
Dupuey, Daniel, w/o, Albany,
   N.Y., 134, #763
Dupuy, Mary, Richmond, Va.,
   63, #8924
Durand, Ebenezer, a/o, Conn.,
   38, #F1826
Durand, Elizabeth, c/o, Vt., 70,
   #11089
Durand, Isaac, a/o, Conn., 38,
   #F1826
Durden, Polly, N.C., 101, #4844
Durfey, Mary, a/o, Albany, N.Y.,
   98, #2660
Durham, John, Ky., 71, #12394
Durham, Mathew, c/o, Ga., 7,
   #9788
Durham, Mathew, c/o, Ga., 7,
   #9957
Durham, Mathew, c/o, Ga., 7,
   #10137
Durham, Matthew, Ga., 108,
   #9788, card
Durham, Matthew, Ga., 108,
   #10137, card
Durney, Philip, w/o,
   Philadelphia, Pa., 114,
   #2072

Durrand, Elizabeth, c/o, Vt., 59,
   #8141
Durrant, Joshua, c/o, Vt., 68,
   #10756
Durst, David, —, 92, #19645,
   card
Dusenberry, William, a/o,
   Albany, N.Y., 7, #7814
Dustin, Frances, St. Augustine,
   Fla., 51, #5987
Dustin, John, Concord, N.H.,
   46, #4703
Dustin, Moses, Philadelphia,
   Pa., 55, #7138
Dustin, Stephen, w/o,
   Portsmouth, N.H., 92,
   #19797
Dwelly, Joseph, w/o, Mass., 64,
   #9183
Dwelly, Pearce, w/o, Albany,
   N.Y., 76, #13765
Dwelly, Rose, c/o, Ala., 111,
   #694
Dwyer, Michael, Wisc., 136,
   #3622
Dyall, Margaret, Cincinnati,
   Ohio, 139, #8615
Dyche, Eva, Cincinnati, Ohio,
   141, #3045
Dye, Jairus, Albany, N.Y., 121,
   #7969
Dye, Jairus, Albany, N.Y., 122,
   #8864
Dygert, Severonus, Albany,
   N.Y., 70, #11057
Dyson, John, Va., 71, #12385

E

Eager, James, w/o, Albany,
   N.Y., 116, #3810

Eagglesone, Asa, w/o, Albany, N.Y., 70, #12035

Eaker, Margaret, Albany, N.Y., 70, #12131

Eakin, William, w/o, Nashville, Tenn., 107, #9654

Ealy, John, c/o, Jackson, Tenn., 89, #18177

Earle, Eunice, Mass., 62, #8813

Earle, Samuel, Tuscaloosa, Ala., 75, #13658

Early, Abraham, Jonesboro, Tenn., 137, #3896

Early, Abraham, Jonesboro, Tenn., 137, #4128

Early, James, Augusta, Maine, 143, #6335

Earp, Josiah, Ky., 7, #3714, card

Earp, Josiah, Ky., 116, #3714, card

Earp, Susannah, N.C., 126, #3974, card

Easley, Drury, Nashville, Tenn., 81, #15163

Easter, John, Richmond, Va., 47, #4954

Eastham, Thomas, Richmond, Va., 96, #1802

Eastis, Elisha, w/o, Ky., 59, #8052

Eastman, Anna, g/o, Portsmouth, N.H., 139, #7234

Eastman, Betsey, Albany, N.Y., 138, #6473

Eastman, Charles, Pittsburgh, Pa., 76, #13781

Eastman, Eli, Vt., 62, #8758

Eastman, Joanna, a/o, Portsmouth, N.H., 67, #10394

Eastman, Mary, Albany, N.Y., 98, #2909

Eastman, Samuel, Milwaukee, Wisc., 143, #7518

Easton, Giles, c/o, D.C., 7, #4080 1/2

Easton, Julian, c/o, Conn., 69, #10827

Eastwood, Daniel, w/o, Albany, N.Y., 46, #4729

Eastwood, John, w/o, Albany, N.Y., 64, #9627

Eaton, Abigail, c/o, Boston, Mass., 119, #5641

Eaton, Abijah, s/o, Bellows Falls, Vt., 74, #13296

Eaton, David, c/o, N.H., 123, #9130

Eaton, Ebenezer, w/o, Albany, N.Y., 67, #10524

Eaton, Ezra, c/o, Albany, N.Y., 51, #6045

Eaton, Josiah, Conn., 90, #18680

Eaton, Maverick, Bellows Falls, Vt., 63, #8967

Eaton, Sarah, c/o, Portsmouth, N.H., 123, #9085

Ebehart, Jacob, Ga., 72, #12680

Eberhart, Jacob, Ga., 62, #8683

Eberhart, Jacob, Ga., 80, #14923

Eberhart, Jacob, Savannah, Ga., 104, #7548

Eberling, William, Ohio, 110, #99

Eblin, Samuel, Ill., 44, #4378

Eccleston, Ichabod, g/o c/o, Conn., 37, #F1821

Eckhart, Elizabeth, c/o, Philadelphia, Pa., 129, #6883

Eddy, Abisha, Mass., 133, #335 1/2

Eddy, Phebe, c/o, R.I., 134, #1243

Eddy, Seth, c/o, Mass., 89, #18256

Eddy, William R., Ohio, 60, #8339

Eddy, William R., Ohio, 64, #9132

Edenfield, David, w/o, Ga., 130, #7421

Edgar, James, w/o, Md., 43, #3845

Edgar, Nathaniel T., w/o, Philadelphia, Pa., 133, #9968

Edgert, Stephen, N.Y., 39, #2950

Edgerton, Prudence, Philadelphia, Pa., 119, #5220

Edgerton, Roger, w/o, Albany, N.Y., 94, #373

Edleman, Leonard, Ky., 76, #13728

Edman, Andrew, w/o, Philadelphia, Pa., 96, #1770

Edman, Samuel, —, 115, #2974, card

Edmond, Samuel, Ohio, 94, #635

Edmonston, Thomas, D.C., 84, #15941

Edmundston, William, e/o, Fayetteville, N.C., 108, #10234

Edson Sr., James, S.C., 94, #722

Edward, Polley, —, 125, #2499, card

Edwards, Ann, D.C., 142, #4916

Edwards, Benjamin, Richmond, Va., 71, #12392

Edwards, Daniel, Albany, N.Y., 97, #2170

Edwards, George, e/o, Ky., 73, #12820

Edwards, Harvalin, Albany, N.Y., 75, #13694

Edwards, Henry, Fla., 59, #8058, card

Edwards, Henry, c/o, Fla., 7, #8058

Edwards, Hezekiah, c/o, Conn., 31, #2660

Edwards, James M., Ky., 134, #1482

Edwards, Olive, Albany, N.Y., 72, #12609

Edwards, Perry, w/o, R.I., 54, #6699

Edwards, Samuel M., Miss., 121, #7957

Edwards, Thomas, Ohio, 47, #4894

Edwards, Thomas, Ohio, 88, #17849

Edwards, Thomas, Ohio, 53, #6393

Edwards, William, Nashville, Tenn., 7, #4627, card

Edwards, William, Nashville, Tenn., 45, #4627, card

Edwards, William L., 5th Ga. regiment, 91, #19412, fodder

Eggart, John, e/o, Pittsburgh, Pa., 121, #7446

Eggleston, Jemima, Conn., 31, #155

Eichelber, Martin, w/o, Baltimore, Md., 76, #13773

Eidson, James, S.C., 96, #1408

Eidson Sr., James, —, 98,
#3058, card

Eidson Sr., James, a/o, S.C., 7,
#3058

Eldred, Columbus C., a/o,
Cleveland, Ohio, 7, #5748

Eldredge, William, c/o, Mass.,
134, #1142

Eldredge (formerly Wickerson),
Levina, Mass., 137, #4604

Eldridge, William, w/o, Albany,
N.Y., 7, #3419

Elkin, Joshua, Ky., 81, #15073

Elkin, Joshua, Ky., 86, #16802

Elkins, Gazaway, Spingfield,
Ill., 141, #3371

Elkins, James, w/o, Ky., 63,
#9025

Elkins, Richard, Nashville,
Tenn., 42, #3686

Ellam, Charles, c/o, N.C., 43,
#3909

Ellenwood, Hananiah, c/o,
Albany, N.Y., 7, #2932

Ellenwood, Hananiah, c/o,
Albany, N.Y., 7, #3112

Ellenwood, Samuel, w/o, Vt., 64,
#9401

Eller, Calvin, Ga., 120, #6201

Eller, John, g/o c/o, Madison,
Ind., 127, #4469

Ellidge, Jacob, c/o, Knoxville,
Tenn., 136, #3366

Ellington, David, Ky., 126,
#3372, slip

Ellington, David, c/o, Ky., 7,
#3372

Elliot, Richard, Mass., 46,
#4750

Elliot, Winifred, Richmond, Va.,
42, #3804

Elliott, Abigail, c/o, Ga., 119,
#5187

Elliott, Alexander, a/o, Ky.,
124, #1265

Elliott, Anlexander, Louisville,
Ky., 108, #9984 V#19

Elliott, Benjamin, Albany, N.Y.,
50, #5548, card

Elliott, Benjamin, c/o, Albany,
N.Y., 7, #5548

Elliott, Bradford W., Ill., 112,
#1225

Elliott, Bradford W., w/o, Ill.,
135, #2139

Elliott, Catharine, Ga., 7,
#10092

Elliott, Christopher, Cincinnati,
Ohio, 142, #3982

Elliott, Elizabeth, Richmond,
Va., 36A, #F1 V6

Elliott, George, w/o, Albany,
N.Y., 60, #8259

Elliott, Harman B., Mo., 131,
#8263

Elliott, Henry, c/o, Ind., 111,
#680

Elliott, John, a/o, Richmond,
Va., 94, #356

Elliott, Nathaniel, c/o, R.I., 91,
#19144

Elliott, Rebecca, Philadelphia,
Pa., 83, #15621

Elliott, Rebecca, c/o, Pittsburgh,
Pa., 117, #4077

Elliott, Reuben, Ohio, 81,
#15144

Elliott, Sarah, Md., 62, #8807

Elliott, William, Philadelphia,
Pa., 66, #10107

Elliott, William, c/o, Ind., 64,
#9640

Ellis, Asa, Albany, N.Y., 107,
#8899
Ellis, Charles, Burlington, Vt.,
44, #4314
Ellis, Charles, Burlington, Vt.,
46, #4722
Ellis, Charles, Ky., 64, #9457
Ellis, Desire, c/o, Providence,
R.I., 114, #2017
Ellis, Elias, Albany, N.Y., 122,
#8303
Ellis, Ezekiel, Mass., 70,
#12092, card
Ellis, Ezekiel, Mass., 8, #12092
Ellis, Jane, c/o, Ky., 126, #3431
Ellis, Jesse, Ohio, 83, #15588
Ellis, Joseh, Jonesboro, Tenn.,
102, #5883
Ellis, Joseph, Jonesboro, Tenn.,
89, #18164
Ellis, Lyman, w/o, Albany,
N.Y., 136, #3575, card
Ellis, Rebecca, a/o, Boston,
Mass., 94, #303
Ellis, Sally, g/o, Conn., 31, #1
Ellis, Samuel, Ky., 94, #676
Ellis, Shadrack, Ga., 51, #6004
Ellis, Sylvia, a/o, Albany, N.Y.,
7, #3575
Ellison, Charles, w/o, Nashville,
Tenn., 120, #6494
Ellison, David, —, 52, #6153,
card
Ellison, David, c/o, Albany,
N.Y., 7, #6153
Ellridge, Abraham, Huntsville,
Ala., 64, #9359
Ellsbury, Mary, a/o, Madison,
Ind., 133, #588
Ellsworth, Benjamin, c/o,
Mich., 84, #16169

Ellsworth, Eliphaet, w/o,
Albany, N.Y., 86, #17169
Ellsworth, John, Pittsburgh, Pa.,
52, #6125
Ellsworth, John, Pittsburgh, Pa.,
64, #9211
Ellsworth, Lucy, a/o, Mass., 75,
#13719
Elmer, Samuel, Conn., 31, #470
Elston, Jonathan, Mo., 56,
#7315
Elston, Jonathan, Mo., 74,
#13253
Elton, Grace, Conn., 81, #15034
Elwell, James, W. Tenn., 64,
#9520
Elwell, James, Wisc., 39, #2970
Elwell, James, Wisc., 74,
#13366
Elwell, James, Wisc., 76,
#13747
Elwell, James, Wisc., 81,
#15025
Elwell, James, Wisc., 139,
#8089
Elwell, Joshua, Conn., 31, #3
Elwood, Isaac, a/o, Albany,
N.Y., 115, #2604
Emerson, Charles N., Mass.,
124, #1394
Emerson, Joseph, c/o,
Pittsburgh, Pa., 116, #3302
Emerson, Samuel M., w/o,
Concord, N.H., 54, #6799
Emery, Lois, a/o, Albany, N.Y.,
99, #3478
Emery, Mary, c/o, Mass., 107,
#8906
Emery, Peter, w/o, Albany, N.Y.,
44, #4329
Emery, Ruth, Mass., 62, #8835

Emery, William, a/o, Concord,
N.H., 76, #13772

Emmerson, Thomas, PA,
Windsor, Vt., 64, #9249

Emmons, James, Mich., 110,
#11112

Emmons, James, w/o, Mich., 7,
#11112

Emmons, Lydia, Concord, N.H.,
103, #6336

Emory, Abigail, h/o, Portland,
Maine, 104, #7425

Engart, Benjamin, Ohio, 54,
#6764

England, John, Richmond, Va.,
52, #6111

England, Mary, Richmond, Va.,
72, #12578

Englehopt, Barbara, a/o,
Philadelphia, Pa., 95,
#1066

Engleman, Conrad, D.C., 113,
#1459

Ennis, Hannah, g/o, R.I., 77,
#14160

Enos, David, a/o, Poultney, Vt.,
95, #1208

Enos, Jerusha, c/o, Vt., 57,
#7442

Ensmore, Phebe D., Montpelier,
Vt., 101, #5006 V#8

Enswoth, Jesse, Conn., 31,
#159

Entrekin, Thomas, w/o, S.C.,
113, #1395

Entriken, Mary, c/o, Ga., 119,
#5424

Entrot, Henry, N.Y., 39, #3135

Epelstyne, Jacob, e/o, Albany,
N.Y., 131, #8907

Ephland, David, Terre Haute,
Ind., 43, #3990

Epley, John, Nashville, Tenn.,
84, #16170

Epley, John, Nashville, Tenn.,
43, #3806

Eply, John, Nashville, Tenn.,
70, #11102

Epperson, Thomas, Jonesboro,
Tenn., 71, #12463

Epperson, Thomas, Jonesboro,
Tenn., 97, #2080

Eppes, Henry W., a/o,
Richmond, Va., 7, #8908

Erb, Henry, c/o, Philadelphia,
Pa., 52, #6118

Erb, Jacob, e/o, Philadelphia,
Pa., 84, #15974

Ernest, George, Ga., 45, #4638

Erskine, Agatha, Richmond, Va.,
36A, #F4 V6

Erskine, Agatha, Richmond, Va.,
36A, #F5 V1

Erwin, David, w/o, Albany,
N.Y., 116, #3337

Erwin, David, w/o, Ind., 98,
#2537

Esen, James, g/o c/o,
Indianapolis, Ind., 135,
#2002

Eson, James, c/o, Ind., 123,
#9160

Eson, James, g/o c/o,
Indianapolis, Ind., 126,
#3760

Espey, Henry J., Ky., 129,
#6444

Espy, Henry J., Ky., 131, #8343

Esser, Jacob, Philadelphia, Pa.,
62, #8862

Esser, Jacob, Philadelphia, Pa.,
80, #14833

Esser, Mary A., e/o,
Philadelphia, Pa., 119,
#5462
Estell, John H., Nashville,
Tenn., 120, #6493
Estell, Samuel, Ky., 85, #16496
Estelle, John H., Nashville,
Tenn., 127, #4381
Estes, John, Richmond, Va., 60,
#8349
Estes, John, w/o, Knoxville,
Tenn., 7, #19312
Estes, Molly, c/o, Ky., 120,
#6444
Etheridge, Bartlett, La., 134,
#1082
Etler, John, —, 112, #870, card
Etter, John, a/o, Nashville,
Tenn., 7, #870
Ettick, George T., c/o, Albany,
N.Y., 53, #6520
Etting, Cornelia, c/o, Albany,
N.Y., 128, #5481
Eubauk, Achilles, w/o, Mo., 92,
#19763
Evans, Agness, Huntsville, Ala.,
101, #4817
Evans, Andrew, Knoxville,
Tenn., 7, #4325
Evans, Arden, Knoxville, Tenn.,
97, #2090, slip
Evans, George, a/o, Wheeling,
Va., 124, #840
Evans, George, c/o, Wheeling,
Va., 123, #61
Evans, Gilbert, w/o, Jonesboro,
Tenn., 115, #2539 (alias
Gettrel Evans)
Evans, Henry, c/o, N.Y. Milita,
104, #7368
Evans, Henry, c/o, N.Y. Milita,
104, #7369

Evans, Henry, c/o, N.Y. Milita,
104, #7370
Evans, Henry, w/o, N.Y. Milita,
104, #7367
Evans, Hezekiah, w/o,
Spingfield, Ill., 142, #4702
Evans, James, Richmond, Va.,
56, #7265
Evans, John, N.Y., 47, #4891,
card
Evans, John, c/o, N.H., 119,
#5127
Evans, John, e/o, Ky., 116,
#3710
Evans, John, w/o, Ky., 44,
#4317
Evans, Lydia, Indianapolis, Ind.,
141, #3330
Evans, Mary, Pittsburgh, Pa.,
126, #3432
Evans, Mary, a/o, Ky., 138,
#5001
Evans, Moses, Conn., 31, #48
Evans, Naomi, Albany, N.Y.,
55, #7057
Evans, Peny, S.C., 51, #5872
Evans, Philip, S.C., 98, #2807
Evans, Roba, Albany, N.Y.,
101, #5181
Evans, Sampson, Richmond,
Va., 58, #7742
Evans, Sampson, Richmond,
Va., 67, #10341
Evans, Sampson, Richmond,
Va., 76, #13908
Evans, Sampson, Va., 85,
#16693
Evans, Samuel, Albany, N.Y.,
41, #3474
Evans, Thankful, e/o, Maine,
127, #4277

Evans, Thomas S., c/o, Miss., 121, #7250

Evans Sr., William, Ga., 47, #5035

Evans, Willam, Richmond, Va., 45, #4559

Evans, William, Mo., 76, #13748

Evans, William, Nashville, Tenn., 64, #9653

Evans, William, Richmond, Va., 43, #3919

Evans, William, Richmond, Va., 51, #5908

Evans, William, w/o, Richmond, Va., 61, #8651

Evans, William C., Little Rock, Ark., 134, #928

Evans, William C., Little Rock, Ark., 136, #2896

Evans, William C., Nashville, Tenn., 50, #5511

Everett, George H., Albany, N.Y., 123, #9401

Everett, John, Richmond, Va., 7, #2684, card

Everett, William, E. Tenn., 83, #15568, card

Everett, William, w/o, Knoxville, Tenn., 8, #15273

Everett, William, w/o, Ky., 8, #15568

Everhard, John, Philadelphia, Pa., 90, #18773

Everhart, John, Philadelphia, Pa., 78, #14491

Everhart, John, Pittsburgh, Pa., 81, #15188

Evers, Andrew, c/o, Philadelphia, Pa., 7, #4847

Everson, Dorothy, Albany, N.Y., 63, #9011

Everson, Dorothy, Albany, N.Y., 100, #4577

Everts, Carl, g/o c/o, D.C., 133, #48

Everts, Carl (or Charles), D.C., 143, #6735

Evinger, Eve, Philadelphia, Pa., 113, #1375

Evinger, Eve, Philadelphia, Pa., 124, #1171

Evins, David, w/o, Ind., 8, #6321

Ewers, Rufus, c/o, Burlington, Vt., 132, #9318

Ewing, Sarah, Knoxville, Tenn., 114, #2224

Ewing, William, —, 55, #7188, card

Ewing, William, Pittsburgh, Pa., 42, #3594

Eyman, Henry, Ohio, 57, #7466

F

Fackenthall, Michael, Philadelphia, Pa., 43, #3906

Fackler, Francis, La., 105, #7844

Fagan, Henry, Pa., 120, #6232, card

Fagan, Henry, c/o, N.J., 8, #6232

Fagen, John, c/o, Philadelphia, Pa., 136, #3519

Fagg, Joel, Nashville, Tenn., 81, #15000

Fagg, Joel, w/o, Nashville, Tenn., 8, #2007

Failing, Philip, Albany, N.Y.,
88, #18128
Fain, Ebenezer, Ga., 45, #4599
Fairbank, Prudence, a/o,
Montpelier, Vt., 101,
#5300
Fairbanks, Eunice, c/o, Mass.,
117, #3870
Fairchild, Abend, Ky., 75,
#13637
Fairchild, Ephraim, w/o,
Philadelphia, Pa., 58,
#7840
Fairchild, Joseph, c/o, Albany,
N.Y., 89, #18142
Fairchild, William, St. Louis,
Mo., 129, #6534
Fairfax, Caroline, Richmond,
Va., 36A, #F2
Fairfax, Caroline A., D.C., 141,
#3405
Fairfield, Hannah, c/o, Maine,
72, #12708
Fairfield, Polly, Maine, 85,
#16427
Falconbury, Jacob, Ind., 99,
#3645
Falconbury, Jacob, w/o,
Madison, Ind., 8, #3645
Falkner, John, Pittsburgh, Pa.,
43, #4153, card
Fall, Aaron, Ohio, 62, #8703
Fall, Aaron, Ohio, 67, #10509
Fallen, Catharine, Montpelier,
Vt., 101, #5006 V#3
Falls, William, N.C., 50, #5535,
card
Falwell, James, w/o, Richmond,
Va., 97, #2054
Fannery, Joseph D., g/o c/o, Ill.,
128, #5146

Fanning, Jonathan, Albany,
N.Y., 64, #9663
Fanning, Lt. Col. Alexander C.
W., 2nd Artillery, 121,
#7691, slip
Fanning, Thomas, New York
City, 138, #6562
Farden, Mary, a/o, Va., 77,
#14081
Fargo, Charles O., Mass., 143,
#6521
Faris, Elijah, Ky., 56, #7430
Faris, Margaret, Richmond, Va.,
126, #3159
Faris, Martin, Richmond, Va.,
36A, #F6, card
Faris, Moses, Ky., 8, #15664
Faris, Rebecca, Indianapolis,
Ind., 139, #9105
Farler, Francis, Richmond, Va.,
102, #5399
Farley, Patsey, Richmond, Va.,
117, #4075, card
Farley, Patsey, a/o, Richmond,
Va., 8, #4075
Farley Sr., Thomas, w/o,
Richmond, Va., 8, #10437
Farmer, Benjamin, e/o c/o,
Portsmouth, N.H., 132,
#9700
Farmer, Charles, w/o, Concord,
N.H., 53, #6455
Farmer, Elizabeth, c/o, Va., 84,
#16084
Farmer, Ermine, Richmond, Va.,
72, #12589
Farmer, Ermine, Richmond, Va.,
103, #6651
Farmer, Eunice, Richmond, Va.,
106, #8460
Farmer, Ezekiel, Ohio, 59,
#8123

Faxon, Priscilla, R.I., 72,
#12529
Fay, Moses, c/o, Albany, N.Y.,
137, #4503
Fay, Patty, a/o, Mass., 134,
#1443
Fay, Thomas, a/o, Vt., 65,
#9853
Feagle, Adam, S.C., 120, #6521
Feagle, Adam, S.C., 122, #8657
Feagle, Adam, S.C., 126, #3922
Feagle, Adam, S.C., 135, #1980
Fearson, Elizabeth, c/o, D.C.,
124, #884
Feather, Mary, c/o, Pittsburgh,
Pa., 123, #9116
Feather, Mary, c/o, Pittsburgh,
Pa., 123, #9350
Feathers, Mary, a/o c/o,
Pittsburgh, Pa., 123, #214
Felkins, John, c/o, W. Tenn.,
60, #8220
Fellows, Josiah, N.H., 66,
#10267
Fellows, Willis, w/o, Ill., 8,
#12283
Felton, Willis, —, 71, #12283,
card
Fenebee, Samuel, Fayetteville,
N.C., 50, #5632
Fenn, Edward, Conn., 32, #485
Fenn, John, w/o, Pittsburgh,
Pa., 62, #8724
Fennel, Joseph, N.C., 42, #3564
Fenner, Mary, Albany, N.Y., 77,
#14092
Fenner, Mary, Albany, N.Y., 95,
#1048
Fenton, Adonijah, c/o, Utica,
N.Y., 99, #3482
Fenton, Samuel, w/o, Albany,
N.Y., 111, #490

Fentress, James, Nashville,
Tenn., 60, #8337
Fentress, James, Nashville,
Tenn., 79, #14690
Fentress, James, a/o, Nashville,
Tenn., 88, #17795
Ferduw, Charles, Cananadaigua,
N.Y., 143, #7542
Ferebee, Samuel, N.C., 43,
#4049
Fergason, William, w/o, Ky.,
76, #13886
Ferguson, Allen, w/o, Albany,
N.Y., 103, #6888
Ferguson, Elizabeth, La., 122,
#8445
Ferguson, Elizabeth, La., 125,
#2421
Ferguson, Jacob H., a/o,
Richmond, Va., 8, #6607
Ferguson, John, Pittsburgh, Pa.,
129, #6665
Ferguson, John, St. Louis, Mo.,
128, #5965
Ferguson, Lewis, a/o, Ill., 8,
#18538
Ferguson, Lewis, Ill., 89,
#18535, card
Ferguson, Moses, Mo., 71,
#12271
Ferguson, Richard, Mich., 66,
#10237
Ferguson, William, Richmond,
Va., 8, #3983
Ferguson, William, Richmond,
Va., 100, #3983, card
Fernsler, Henry, Wheeling, Va.,
73, #12768
Ferrell, Sarah, Nashville, Tenn.,
116, #3770
Ferris, Chaity, c/o, Albany,
N.Y., 77, #14158

Ferris, Charity, Albany, N.Y.,
78, #14427
Ferris, Charity, c/o, Albany,
N.Y., 77, #14128
Ferris, Henry B., w/o, Albany,
N.Y., 58, #7937
Ferris, Isaac, Tenn., 73, #12812,
card
Ferris, Joshua, Albany, N.Y.,
67, #10451
Ferris, Mary Ann, N.Y., 103,
#6975
Ferris, Mary Ann, N.Y., 109,
#10844
Ferris, Ransford A., a/o, Conn.,
38, #F1824
Ferry, Henry, D.C., 140, #245
Fetch, Hubbard, c/o, Mich., 140,
#484
Fetter, Sarah, New York City,
102, #6052 V#13
Fetterer, William, New York
City, 138, #6335
Fickle, Benjamin, Ohio, 53,
#6396
Fickle, Benjamin, w/o, Ohio,
85, #16334
Fickle, Benjamin, w/o, Ohio,
85, #16335
Field, Ann, Albany, N.Y., 58,
#7812
Field, Benjamin, c/o, N.J., 94,
#674
Field, Frances, c/o, Ky., 120,
#5834
Field, George, Fort Gibson,
Ark., 102, #5602
Field, George, Little Rock, Ark.,
94, #345
Field, George, Mass., 137,
#4074

Field, Capt. George P., w/o, 3rd
Inf., 103, #6525
Field, Capt. George P., w/o, 3rd
Inf., 105, #8291
Field, Capt. George P., w/o, 3rd
Inf., 100, #4516
Fields, Bartholomew, Mobile,
Ala., 78, #14337
Fields, Bartholomew, Mobile,
Ala., 62, #8832
Fields, Bartholomew, Mobile,
Ala., 69, #11003
Fields, Capt. George P., w/o, 3rd
Inf., 108, #10032
Fields, Capt. George P., w/o, 3rd
Inf., 111, #457
Fields, George, Ark., 82,
#15281
Fields, George, Ark., 91,
#19246
Fields, John, a/o, N.C., 8,
#4221
Fields, Joseph, Ky., 82, #15248
Fields, Joseph, Vt., 83, #15611
Fiers, William, Ky., 43, #3966
Fiers, William, w/o, Ky., 47,
#4866
Fifield, Beborah, a/o,
Portsmouth, N.H., 99,
#3172
Figeby, Peter, c/o, Md., 116,
#3563
Fight, Elizabeth, a/o, N.C., 121,
#6924
Filer, Hoace, g/o c/o, Conn., 37,
#F1820
Files, Adam J., Mobile, Ala., 58,
#7690
Files, Adam J., Mobile, Ala., 61,
#8614
Filley, Jemima, e/o, Conn., 95,
#1131

Fisher, Michael, Philadelphia,
Pa., 66, #10167
Fisher, Michael, Philadelphia,
Pa., 73, #12787
Fisher, Michael, Philadelphia,
Pa., 103, #6739
Fisher, Michael, Philadelphia,
Pa., 95, #988
Fisher, Michael, w/o,
Philadelphia, Pa., 112,
#1028
Fisher, Michal, Philadelphia,
Pa., 62, #8842
Fisher, Philip, c/o, Md., 115,
#2825
Fisher, Thomas, Nashville,
Tenn., 83, #15880, card
Fisher, Thomas, W. Tenn., 68,
#10730
Fisher, Thomas, e/o, Nashville,
Tenn., 8, #15880
Fisher, Pvt. Thomas, N.Y.
Milita, 115, #2716 pay due
Fisk, Betsy, Boston, Mass., 95,
#1339
Fisk, Eben, w/o, Bradford, Vt.,
136, #2879
Fisk, John, Albany, N.Y., 90,
#18878
Fisk, Orange, Albany, N.Y.,
111, #735
Fister, George, c/o,
Philadelphia, Pa., 65,
#9920
Fitch, Daniel, c/o, Conn., 131,
#8419
Fitch, Prentice, Albany, N.Y.,
77, #14118
Fithian, Isaac, a/o, Pittsburgh,
Pa., 88, #17824
Fitts, John, Va., 80, #14876

Fitz, Robert W., Richmond, Va.,
61, #8588
Fitzgerald, Aaron, Pittsburgh,
Pa., 115, #2804 V#30
Fitzgerald, Harvey, Va., 67,
#10348
Fitzgerald, Harvey, Va., 84,
#16295
Fitzgerald, Major E. H., Fort
Buchanan, N.M., 130,
#7517
Fitzgerald, Michael, c/o,
Albany, N.Y., 113, #1895
Fitzgerald, Michael, g/o c/o,
Albany, N.Y., 124, #406
Fitzgerald, William, Madison,
Ind., 104, #7683
Fitzgerald, William, a/o, Ky.,
117, #4204
Fitzhugh, Daniel, a/o,
Richmond, Va., 59, #8087
Fitzhugh, William, Albany,
N.Y., 71, #12379, card
Fitzhugh, William, e/o, Albany,
N.Y., 8, #12379
Fitzhugh (formerly Dusy), Jane,
Ill., 117, #4117
Fitzwater, Jonathan,
Philadelphia, Pa., 124,
#407
Flagg, Eugene E., Spingfield,
Ill., 143, #6820
Flagg, F. H., PA, Tallahassee,
Fla., 117, #3834
Flagg, George P., g/o, Mass.,
140, #9848
Flagg, Rachel, c/o, S.C., 89,
#18258
Flagg, William, w/o, Vt., 89,
#18194
Flagg, Samuel D., SpC, Madison
Barr, N.Y., 112, #1221

Flaherty, John, Pittsburgh, Pa.,
134, #1315
Flanders, Henry, c/o, N.Y., 109,
#10794
Flanders, Jacob, a/o, Ky., 103,
#6346
Flanders, John, a/o, Richmond,
Va., 59, #7948
Flanders, Sally, Concord, N.H.,
111, #367
Flanekin, Andrew, w/o,
Philadelphia, Pa., 127,
#4004
Flannegan, William, c/o, Ga.,
120, #5878
Flansburgh, William F., Albany,
N.Y., 64, #9153
Fleanor, Nicholas, Mo., 131,
#8335
Fleckner, Mary, Richmond, Va.,
36A, #F3 V8
Fleckner, Mary, e/o, Richmond,
Va., 36A, #F5 V10
Fleming, Catherine, Vt., 66,
#10246
Fleming, Mitchel, a/o, Mo.,
120, #6595
Fleming, Robert, Ga., 41, #3367
Fleming, William, Ga., 72,
#12652
Fleshman, Moses, —, 8, #6711,
card
Fleshman, Moses, Richmond,
Va., 56, #7334
Fleshman, Moses, Richmond,
Va., 50, #5798
Fleshman, Moses, Va., 66,
#10142
Fleshman, Moses, Va., 103,
#6711, card
Fletcher, James, Mo., 76,
#13827

Fletcher, John, a/o, Ky., 119,
#5557
Fletcher, Jonathon, w/o,
Bellows Falls, Vt., 74,
#13288
Fletcher, Mary, c/o, Richmond,
Va., 113, #1623
Fletcher, Mary, c/o, Richmond,
Va., 113, #1909
Fletcher, Sarah, Concord, N.H.,
65, #9904, card
Fletcher, Sarah, c/o, N.H., 8,
#9904
Fletcher, Susan, Richmond, Va.,
132, #9301
Fletcher, Thomas, e/o,
Knoxville, Tenn., 135,
#1759
Fliedner, Louisa, New York City,
112, #997
Fling, Richard, Ohio, 60, #8190
Flinn, John, c/o, N.C., 98,
#2817
Flint, Betty, e/o, Boston, Mass.,
117, #4555
Flint, Daniel, w/o, Boston,
Mass., 61, #8463
Flint, Jabez, New York City, 71,
#12355
Flint, Phebe, Mass., 87, #17317
Floid (now Lewzader), Lucinda,
Cincinnati, Ohio, 8, #5033
Flowers, Absalom, Richmond,
Va., 47, #4878
Flowers, Absalom, Va., 87,
#17622
Flowers, Ann, Nashville, Tenn.,
83, #15691
Flowers, Ann, Nashville, Tenn.,
105, #7858
Flowers, Ann, Nashville, Tenn.,
115, #2870

Flowers, Ann, a/o, Nashville, Tenn., 121, #7147

Flowers, Mary Ann, Richmond, Va., 36A, #F3 V14

Flowers, Thomas, a/o, New Albany, Ind., 8, #12260

Flowers, Zephon, a/o, Philadelphia, Pa., 135, #2043

Floyd, Benjamin, c/o, Mass., 137, #4414

Floyd, George, e/o, Ky., 103, #7048

Floyd, Henry, Ky., 8, #5647

Floyd, Luke, a/o, Pa., 110, #164

Floyd, Martha, c/o, Mass., 137, #4502

Flynn, Bridget, Philadelphia, Pa., 142, #3511

Flynn, Catherine, E. Fla., 70, #12104

Flynn, Charles E., g/o, E. Fla., 84, #15976

Flynn, Ord. Sgt.John, AAQM, 137, #3907

Fobes, Johhn, w/o, Albany, N.Y., 8, #17576

Fobes, John, Albany, N.Y., 87, #17576, card

Fobes, Nathan, c/o, Pittsburgh, Pa., 111, #377

Fogg, Elizabeth, c/o, Richmond, Va., 105, #8017

Fogg, Joel, —, 135, #2007, card

Fogge, Arthur R., w/o, Nashville, Tenn., 127, #4589

Foley, Caty, c/o, Nashville, Tenn., 79, #14627

Folk, Thomas M., D.C., 138, #4691

Folts, George, Albany, N.Y., 134, #1335, card

Fonda, Angelica, Ill., 73, #12977

Fonda, Eldred, Albany, N.Y., 50, #5823

Fondey, Vrooman, Mo., 60, #8342

Fondey, Vroooman, Philadelphia, Pa., 39, #3035

Fons, John, Ky., 70, #11126

Fontaine, Ann, Richmond, Va., 63, #8906

Foolmein, Capt. Harry, AQM, 118, #49--, card

Foot, James, Iowa, 126, #3982

Foot, James, Pittsburgh, Pa., 86, #16996

Foot, Joseph, Albany, N.Y., 116, #3784

Forbes, Judith, Richmond, Va., 36A, #F6, card

Forby, James, Albany, N.Y., 40, #3244

Ford, Alexander, Mo., 73, #12896, card

Ford, Alexander, w/o, Mo., 8, #12896

Ford, Amos, Conn., 32, #9

Ford, Ann, Nashville, Tenn., 109, #10404

Ford, Anne, Nashville, Tenn., 74, #13085

Ford, Hopeful, a/o, Philadelphia, Pa., 109, #10770

Ford, Isaac, w/o, Philadelphia, Pa., 81, #15005

Ford, James, Ky., 98, #2669

Ford, James, w/o, Ky., 8, #2669

Ford, John, a/o, Va., 77, #14064

Ford, Martha, Pittsburgh, Pa.,
105, #7747
Ford, William, Ky., 9, #3374
Ford, William, Ky., 99, #3374,
card
Ford, William, c/o, Richmond,
Va., 62, #8874
Ford Sr., John, E. Tenn., 62,
#8740
Ford Sr., John, Knoxville,
Tenn., 69, #10849
Ford Sr., John, w/o, Ky., 96,
#1867
Fordham, Nathan, New York
City, 53, #6440, card
Fordham, Nathan, c/o, N.Y., 9,
#6440
Foree, Jesse, Ky., 44, #4304
Foree, Jesse, Ky., 44, #4415
Forester, William, Richmond,
Va., 59, #7993
Forester, William, Richmond,
Va., 63, #9088
Forester, William, Richmond,
Va., 73, #12741
Forester, William, Richmond,
Va., 76, #13884
Forkner, Ezekiel, Jackson,
Tenn., 102, #5950
Forrest, Lucy, Richmond, Va.,
36A, #F3 V9
Forrest, William, N.C., 73,
#12744
Forrest, William, N.C., 81,
#15100
Forshey, Thomas, Ohio, 42,
#3679, card
Forshey, Thomas, c/o,
Wheeling, Va., 9, #3679
Forshey, Thomas, c/o,
Wheeling, Va., 9, #7128

Forster, Benjamin, a/o,
Philadelphia, Pa., 9,
#10108
Forsyth, John, Ohio, 47, #5021,
card
Fort, Tomlinson, Ga., 123,
#9087
Fortner, Emanuel F., Ind., 41,
#3384
Fortner, Emanuel F., Ind., 54,
#6672
Forward, Oliver, Madison, Ind.,
139, #7093
Forward, Oliver, Madison, Ind.,
139, #8088
Forward, Oliver, Madison, Ind.,
141, #1353
Forward, Oliver, Madison, Ind.,
141, #2451
Foshey, Thomas, Ohio, 89,
#18206, card
Foss, George, N.H., 41, #3519
Foster, Abner, Ill., 58, #7839
Foster, Anthony, N.C., 48,
#5185
Foster, Anthony, N.C., 62,
#8814
Foster, Anthony, N.C., 71,
#12462
Foster, Armstrong, Fayetteville,
N.C., 105, #7762 V#12
Foster, Benan, w/o, Portland,
Maine, 99, #3228
Foster, Benjamin, N.Y. &
Philadelphia, Pa., 108,
#10108
Foster, Elizabeth, c/o,
Richmond, Va., 98, #2539
Foster, George, a/o, N.C., 103,
#6637
Foster, Henry, w/o, Ky., 121,
#7418

Foster, Ira L., Ohio, 57, #7464

Foster, Jacob, w/o, Bellows
Falls, Vt., 50, #5815

Foster, Joel, La., 9, #4310

Foster, Joel, La., 9, #15769

Foster, John, Conn., 32, #134

Foster, John, a/o, Ky., 118,
#4858

Foster, Lankin, Richmond, Va.,
64, #9151

Foster, Larkin, Va., 74, #13335

Foster, Larkin, w/o, Richmond,
Va., 107, #8900

Foster, Nancy, a/o, Richmond,
Va., 100, #4355

Foster, Nathaniel, w/o, Ohio,
76, #13921

Foster, Parla, Albany, N.Y., 62,
#8820

Foster, Rufus, Montpelier, Vt.,
106, #8633

Foster, Tammy, c/o, Mass., 59,
#8033

Foster, Vincent, Albany, N.Y.,
44, #4246

Foster, William, w/o, Ill., 133,
#491

Foster, William, w/o, Richmond,
Va., 41, #3362

Fotts, George, c/o, Albany,
N.Y., 8, #1335

Foulder, Robert, New Orleans,
La., 114, #2109

Foulin, Henry, —, 116, #3251,
card

Fouye, Philip, w/o, Albany,
N.Y., 44, #4249

Fowle, John, w/o, 6th Inf, 46,
#4796

Fowle, John, w/o, 6th Inf, 52,
#6176

Fowle, Lt. Col. John, w/o, —,
56, #7279

Fowle, Lt. Col. John, w/o, —,
70, #12186

Fowle, Lt. Col. John, w/o, —,
77, #14133

Fowle, Lt. Col. John, w/o, —,
81, #15058

Fowle, Lt. Col. John, w/o, —,
84, #16002

Fowle, Lt. Col. John, w/o, —,
87, #17533

Fowler, Alexander, Ind., 109,
#10778

Fowler, Alexander, Madison,
Ind., 112, #984

Fowler, Anna, a/o, Conn., 114,
#2358

Fowler, Francis, Pittsburgh, Pa.,
143, #7034

Fowler, John, Conn., 32, #0

Fowler, Jonathan, c/o, Albany,
N.Y., 114, #2279

Fowler, Joseph, e/o, Wheeling,
Va., 64, #9660

Fowler, Reuben, Conn., 32,
#486

Fowler, Theodosius, c/o, N.Y.,
84, #16157

Fowlkes, Josiah, w/o, Va., 40,
#3306

Fox, Augustus C., comm/o, New
York City, 101, #4889

Fox, Augustus C., comm/o,
N.Y., 90, #18860

Fox, Augustus C., g/o, New York
City, 68, #10637

Fox, Barbara, Knoxville, Tenn.,
130, #7417

Fox, Chloe, Albany, N.Y., 9,
#7421

Fox, Chloe, Albany, N.Y., 119, #5390, card
Fox, Chloe, Albany, N.Y., 121, #7421, card
Fox, Chloe, c/o, Albany, N.Y., 9, #5390
Fox, Consider, Albany, N.Y., 70, #12002, card
Fox, Consider, c/o, Albany, N.Y., 9, #12002
Fox, Daniel, Ky., 56, #7385
Fox, Daniel, Lexington, Ky., 39, #3058
Fox, David, N.J., 119, #5763, card
Fox, David, c/o, Albany, N.Y., 9, #5763
Fox, David, e/o, Pa., 105, #8253
Fox, Edward, w/o, N.H., 87, #17292
Fox, Jabez, Conn., 32, #327
Fox, Jesse, Conn., 32, #382
Fox, John, —, 75, #13421, card
Fox, Joseph, w/o, Pittsburgh, Pa., 117, #4432
Fox, Mercy, Philadelphia, Pa., 83, #15621
Fox, Stepen, w/o, Ohio, 86, #17247
Fox, Stephen, Ohio, 72, #12600
Fox, Vaniah, Albany, N.Y., 64, #9362
Fox, William, c/o, Cincinnati, Ohio, 122, #8534
Fox, William H., g/o c/o, Cincinnati, Ohio, 126, #3379
Fox Sr., John, N.C., 9, #4010
Fox Sr., John, w/o, N.C., 9, #13421
Foxen, Benjamin, —, 121, #6967, slip

Foxworthy, William, w/o, Ky., 99, #3222
Foy, Patty, Mass., 74, #13202
Fraker, Philip, w/o, Albany, N.Y., 64, #9233
France, John, Ohio, 110, #123
Francisco, Cornelius, w/o, Albany, N.Y., 49, #5306
Francisco, Mary B., a/o, Richmond, Va., 137, #3840
Frank, Henry, w/o, Albany, N.Y., 9, #9835
Frank, Jacob, Pa., 39, #3138
Frank, Jacob, Pittsburgh, Pa., 60, #8350
Frank, Jacob, Pittsburgh, Pa., 73, #12810
Frank, Michael, w/o, Albany, N.Y., 89, #18501
Frank Sr., Henry, N.Y., 65, #9835
Franklin, Absolom, w/o, Ky., 68, #10599
Franklin, Addison, Philadelphia, Pa., 130, #7983
Franklin, Agness, Richmond, Va., 71, #12234
Franklin, Benjamin, w/o, Mass., 87, #17601
Franklin, John, w/o, Va., 83, #15595
Franklin, Lafayette, Richmond, Va., 130, #7429
Franklin, Reuben, e/o, Ky., 9, #19796
Franklin, Thomas, w/o, Richmond, Va., 77, #13969
Franks, Christiana, Philadelphia, Pa., 83, #15621
Franks, Henry, Ohio, 69, #10872

Franks, Henry, w/o, Pittsburgh, Pa., 45, #4456

Franks, Richard, c/o, Jonesboro, Tenn., 123, #9776 (alias Richard Barrett)

Fransworth, Anna, a/o, Montpelier, Vt., 92, #19906

Franum, Elisha, c/o, Pittsburgh, Pa., 130, #7966

Fraser, Daniel, Montpelier, Vt., 105, #8151

Fraser, Daniel, a/o, Vt., 120, #5995

Fraser, Susan, a/o, Richmond, Va., 9, #2098

Frazer, Daniel, Vt., 61, #8484

Frazer, Donald, New York City, 47, #4926

Frazeur, Micager, Ky., 98, #2683

Frazeur, Micager, w/o, Ky., 9, #2683

Frazeur, Susan, Va., 114, #2098, card

Frazier, Christian, w/o, N.J., 75, #13545

Frazier, Daniel, Vt., 83, #15587

Frazier, James, S.C., 59, #8093

Frazier, James, w/o, S.C., 94, #252

Frazier, Thomas, w/o, Jackson, Tenn., 102, #5917

Frazier, William, a/o, St. Louis, Mo., 138, #5157

Frederick, Mary, a/o, Pittsburgh, Pa., 129, #6544

Frederick, Michael, Philadelphia, Pa., 74, #13297

Freeman, Elijah, g/o c/o, D.C., 133, #578

Freeman, Elijah N., g/o c/o, D.C., 125, #1830

Freeman, Elizabeth, S.C., 113, #1400

Freeman, Elizabeth, S.C., 114, #2050

Freeman, Frances, S.C., 114, #2022

Freeman, Frances, S.C., 123, #9157

Freeman, John, Ky., 78, #14420, card

Freeman, John, Ky., 59, #8014

Freeman, John, w/o, Ky., 9, #14420

Freeman, John, w/o, Richmond, Va., 94, #398

Freeman, Mary, Mo., 114, #2189, card

Freeman, Michael, a/o, Ky., 121, #6790

Freeman, Nathan, Pittsburgh, Pa., 56, #7243

Freeman, Rufus, Ohio, 41, #3424

Freeman, Rufus, Ohio, 62, #8710

Freeman, Rufus, Ohio, 74, #13304

Freeman, Rufus, Ohio, 80, #14946

Freeman, Rufus, Ohio, 83, #15883

Freeman, Rufus, Ohio, 86, #16887

Freeman, Rufus, Ohio, 98, #3078

Freeman, Sally, Richmond, Va., 128, #5159

Freeman, Samuel, Pittsburgh, Pa., 116, #3811

Frieslain, Henry, Philadelphia, Pa., 132, #9478

Frisbee, Abigail, a/o, Albany, N.Y., 133, #105

Frisbee, Israil M., w/o, Cincinnati, Ohio, 114, #2267

Frisbee, Olive, e/o, Philadelphia, Pa., 117, #4041

Frisbee, Rachel, c/o, Conn., 58, #7815

Frisbee, Sarah, c/o, Albany, N.Y., 115, #2506

Frisbee, Thomas, w/o, Albany, N.Y., 116, #3672

Frisbie, Abraham, c/o, Pa., 121, #7838

Frisbie, Rachel, c/o, Hartford, Conn., 63, #8897

Frizzell, late Crow, Julia Ann, Mo., 116, #3491

Frolinger, Henry, N.C., 48, #5215

Frost, Hannah, c/o, Maine, 85, #16520

Frost, John, Burlington, Vt., 45, #4421

Frost, John, Maine, 78, #14285, card

Frost, John, c/o, Maine, 9, #14285

Frost, Joseph, Ill., 54, #6642

Frost, Joseph, w/o, Ill., 74, #13371

Frost, Mary, a/o, Richmond, Va., 117, #4358

Frost, Rachel, c/o, Boston, Mass., 118, #4940

Frost and Snow, a/o, Morganton, N.C., 121, #6957

Frouk, Jacob, Pittsburgh, Pa., 86, #17238

Fry, Joanna, Albany, N.Y., 104, #7537

Fry, Philip, w/o, Philadelphia, Pa., 49, #5312

Frye, Dolly, c/o, D.C., 61, #8581

Frye, Mary Ann, Portsmouth, Maine, 142, #5771

Fryer, John, a/o, Richmond, Va., 103, #6895

Fryer, Sevier, Knoxville, Tenn., 125, #2431

Fugate, James, Mo., 102, #5676

Fugate, James, Mo., 107, #9395

Fugate, John H., Ky., 45, #4485

Fuhr, William, Philadelphia, Pa., 109, #10529 V#65

Fulgham, John, e/o w/o, Va. Milita, 94, #602

Fulk, Theresa, Madison, Ind., 134, #1334

Fulkerson, John, Pittsburgh, Pa., 39, #2963

Fulkison, John, a/o, Jonesboro, Tenn., 101, #4707

Fuller, Abraham, a/o, Vt., 91, #19275

Fuller, Ambrose, Pittsburgh, Pa., 91, #18972

Fuller, Benjamin, Albany, N.Y., 61, #8598, card

Fuller, Daniel, w/o, Concord, N.H., 104, #7641

Fuller, David, Albany, N.Y., 61, #8622

Fuller, David, Albany, N.Y., 62, #8822

Fuller, Frederick, Montpelier, Vt., 101, #5006 V#9

Fuller, John, w/o, Albany, N.Y., 67, #10363

Fuller, John, w/o, Mass., 142, #4028

Fuller, Jonathan, Albany, N.Y., 51, #5971

Fuller, Joseph, Conn., 32, #563

Fuller, Joseph, w/o, Mass., 45, #4454

Fuller, Joshua, a/o, Albany, N.Y., 119, #5292

Fuller, Lydia, c/o, Albany, N.Y., 64, #9625

Fuller, Lydia, c/o, Maine, 113, #1545

Fuller, Mary, N.C., 117, #4221, slip

Fuller, Nathan, Conn., 88, #18021

Fuller, Polly, Conn., 32, #440

Fuller, Pvt. Samuel, c/o, N.Y. Milita, 114, #1920

Fuller, Sarah, Albany, N.Y., 130, #7771

Fuller, Sarah, Albany, N.Y., 132, #9002

Fuller, Sarah, c/o, Albany, N.Y., 114, #2053

Fuller, Nathanial, late PA, Bellows Falls, Vt., 63, #8967

Fuller, Edward N., PA, Portsmouth, N.H., 118, #5078

Fullerton, Charles, Mich., 126, #3517

Fullerton, Nathaniel, late PA, Vt., 86, #17024

Fullington, Ezekiel, w/o, Burlington, Vt., 45, #4562

Fulmer, Jabob, S.C., 40, #3188

Fulmer, Jacob, w/o, S.C., 65, #9747

Fulto (now Swartz), Frances, Cleveland, Ohio, 112, #896

Fulton, James, New Orleans, La., 115, #2538

Fulton, Robert, —, 125, #1845, card

Fultz, Francis, Pittsburgh, Pa., 114, #2119

Fultz, Francis, Pittsburgh, Pa., 140, #898

Funderburk, John, Ga., 63, #8997

Funderburk, John, Ga., 85, #16331

Fundirbrerk, John, Ga., 67, #10316

Funk, Clarissa, Albany, N.Y., 102, #5908

Funkhouser, Elizabeth, Ky., 136, #2531

Funston, John, cons/o, Ill., 127, #4088

Funston, John, cons/o, Ill., 129, #6623

Funston, John, g/o, Ill., 125, #1929

Funstone, John, cons/o, Chicago, Ill., 140, #792

Fuqua, Celia, Va., 76, #13792

Furgason, James, E. Tenn., 58, #7934

Furgason, James, Knoxville, Tenn., 69, #10904

Furgason, James, Knoxville, Tenn., 77, #14202

Furgeson, James, Knoxville, Tenn., 46, #4817

Furguson, Thomas, Ky., 45, #4486

Furr, Enoch, Richmond, Va., 57, #7542

Furr, Enoch, Richmond, Va., 67, #10404

Furr, Enoch, Richmond, Va., 47, #4960

Furr, Enoch, w/o, Richmond, Va., 95, #1231

Furr, Enock, Va., 87, #17385

Fussell, William, La., 115, #2592, card

Fyler, Polly, Conn., 94, #333

G

Gabbard, Jacob, Ky., 118, #4866

Gaddy, Martha, Richmond, Va., 72, #12533

Gaddy, Martha, Va., 75, #13557

Gafford, Mary, a/o, Richmond, Va., 102, #5713

Gage, Aaron, Jackson, Tenn., 64, #9385

Gage, Hannah, c/o, Albany, N.Y., 108, #10159

Gage, John, g/o, Ohio, 41, #3385

Gage, Phineas, e/o, Concord, N.H., 82, #15256

Gage, Thaddeus, Albany, N.Y., 60, #8361

Gahan, John, Boston, Mass., 141, #2277

Gailand, Humphrey, c/o, Knoxville, Tenn., 127, #4097

Gaines, Ambrose, Jonesboro, Tenn., 92, #19888

Gaines, Ambrose, w/o, Jonesboro, Tenn., 9, #19888

Gaines, James, N.C., 62, #8815

Gaines, Myra C., D.C., 142, #5060, card

Gaines, Myra Clark, D.C., 9, #5060

Gaines, Robert, c/o, Ky., 124, #384

Gaines, William, Albany, N.Y., 142, #3546, card

Gaines, Williams, Albany, N.Y., 9, #3546

Gaines Sr., James, N.C., 45, #4546

Galbreath, George M., c/o, Ill., 112, #1050

Galbreath, Phebe, Ill., 100, #4114

Galbreath, William, Ind., 65, #9740, card

Galbreath, William, Madison, Ind., 50, #5510

Galbreath, William, w/o, Madison, Ind., 9, #9740

Gale, Rhonda, a/o, N.H., 77, #13995

Gale, Richard, Mo., 54, #6788

Gale, Richard, Mo., 79, #14664

Gale, Richard, a/o, Mo., 90, #18894

Galisbury, William, Philadelphia, Pa., 67, #10479

Gall, George, Ohio, 66, #10296

Gallagher, John, Mo., 138, #6381

Gallagher, Peter, La., 103, #6556

Gallespie, James, c/o, Ohio, 67, #10336

Gallimore, Sally, Fayetteville, N.C., 133, #534

Galloway, Charles, Mo., 109, #10512

Galloway, Elizabeth, —, 114, #1955

Gallup, Robert, e/o, Albany, N.Y., 135, #2027

Gallup, Robert, e/o, Albany, N.Y., 135, #2128

Galt, Anna, a/o, Richmond, Va., 36A, #F1 V10

Galusha, Abigail, Chicago, Ill., 141, #2485

Galuska, Lemuel, Albany, N.Y., 88, #17811

Gamans, Nathan, Albany, N.Y., 9, #16918

Gamble, David, Ind., 106, #8846, slip

Gamble, David, Madison, Ind., 10, #8846

Gamble, James, Pittsburgh, Pa., 10, #15371

Gamblin, Joshua, w/o, Ky., 111, #656

Gamison, James, Ill., 67, #10547

Gammar, Pvt. Joshusa, w/o, Va. Milita, 110, #11118

Gammon, Jesse, Knoxville, Tenn., 97, #1945

Gammon, Joshua, c/o, Portland, Maine, 108, #9770

Ganey, William, N.C., 54, #6805

Gann, Thomas, a/o, Knoxville, Tenn., 77, #14136

Gann, William, La., 61, #8489

Gann, William, La., 92, #184

Gano, Daniel, w/o, Ky., 109, #10780

Gano, Jemima, a/o, Ky., 133, #679

Gapen, Stephen, Wheeling, Va., 46, #4669

Gapen, Stephen, w/o, Wheeling, Va., 58, #7693

Gardenier, Capt. J. R. B., Subsistence Claim, 82, #15477

Gardinen, Capt. George W., w/o, 2nd Artillery, 58, #7680

Gardiner, Capt. George W., w/o, —, 63, #9122

Gardiner, Capt. George W., w/o, —, 67, #10474

Gardiner, Caswell, w/o, Philadelphia, Pa., 114, #2415

Gardiner, Geo. W., w/o, 2nd Artillery, 53, #6352

Gardner, Betsey, c/o, Albany, N.Y., 107, #9276

Gardner, David, Hartford, Conn., 32, #117

Gardner, George, Richmond, Va., 61, #8571

Gardner, George, Va., 41, #3527

Gardner, George, Va., 80, #14897

Gardner, George, Va., 90, #18654

Gardner, George, Va., 90, #18705

Gardner, George M., N.J., 120, #6594

Gardner, George M., N.J., 133, #195

Gardner, John, a/o, N.C., 87, #17429

Gardner, John, w/o, New York City, 49, #5324

Gardner, Josiah, Albany, N.Y., 106, #8601, card

Gardner, Josiah, e/o, Albany,
N.Y., 10, #8601
Gardner, Jotham, Ill., 44, #4301
Gardner, Phebe, c/o, Albany,
N.Y., 135, #2174
Gardner, Sarah, c/o, Mass., 106,
#8810
Gardner, Seth, w/o, Albany,
N.Y., 44, #4353
Gardner, Thomas, w/o, Albany,
N.Y., 89, #18353
Gardner, Townsend S., w/o,
Albany, N.Y., 87, #17351
Gardner, William, a/o, Albany,
N.Y., 117, #4509
Garfield, Nathaniel, Albany,
N.Y., 63, #8879
Garfield, Nathaniel, w/o,
Albany, N.Y., 10, #8879
Garison, Abraham, w/o, Mich.,
51, #5963
Garland, Humphrey, c/o,
Knoxville, Tenn., 127,
#4288
Garland, Jacob, Montpelier, Vt.,
94, #439
Garland, Lucy, a/o, Nashville,
Tenn., 98, #3059
Garlington, Christopher, Miss.,
116, #3773
Garman, William, w/o,
Wheeling, Va., 46, #4724
Garner, Joseph, w/o, Mobile,
Ala., 79, #14695
Garner, Lucy, a/o, Richmond,
Va., 101, #5195
Garner, Lucy Ann, D.C., 140,
#9794
Garnet, John, w/o, New York
City, 47, #4903
Garnsey, Joel, Albany, N.Y., 75,
#13700

Garnsey, Joel, w/o, Albany,
N.Y., 10, #1926
Garrell, John, w/o, Richmond,
Va., 44, #4241
Garretson, Melicent, a/o, New
Albany, Ind., 134, #828
Garrett, Deborah, Mass., 43,
#3815, card
Garrett, Stasha, —, 95, #1264,
card
Garris, Thomas, a/o w/o, Ind.,
106, #8549, #militia
Garrish, Joseph, a/o, N.J., 117,
#4498
Garrison, Dennis, c/o, New York
City, 122, #8865
Garrison, James, Ill., 50, #5603
Garrison, James, Ill., 80,
#14782
Garrison, James, w/o, Ill., 97,
#2076
Garrity, James, Albany, N.Y.,
143, #6557
Garten, Nathanial, Richmond,
Va., 58, #7917
Garusey, Joel, Albany, N.Y., 97,
#19--, card
Gaskill, George, New York City,
112, #1091
Gaspenson, John, w/o,
Knoxville, Tenn., 10,
#9039
Gassaway, James, Mobile, Ala.,
55, #7056
Gassett, Vashti, Bellows Falls,
Vt., 50, #5757
Gaster, Jacob, Fayetteville,
N.C., 105, #7762 V#34
Gastine, Elisha, a/o, Albany,
N.Y., 76, #13870
Gaston, Daniel, Philadelphia,
Pa., 50, #5751

Gaston, Janet, a/o, Ill., 75,
#13433
Gaston, Joseph, w/o, S.C., 110,
#11167
Gaston, Nancy, c/o,
Philadelphia, Pa., 68,
#10618
Gaston, William, Ill., 75,
#13431, card
Gaston, William, a/o, Ill., 10,
#13431
Gates, Hannah, c/o, Boston,
Mass., 67, #10428
Gates, John, c/o, Vt., 10, #9194
Gates, Rachel, a/o, Conn., 32,
#559
Gates, Ruth, c/o, Conn., 32,
#936
Gates, Silas, a/o, Albany, N.Y.,
131, #8361
Gates, Sylvanus, c/o,
Philadelphia, Pa., 138,
#4634
Gates, William, Ill., 129, #6448
Gatewood, William, e/o,
Richmond, Va., 126, #2983
Gatliff, Charles, a/o, Ky., 105,
#8332
Gatlin, Stephen, Ga., 106,
#8823
Gatlin, Stephen, Ga., 112,
#1130
Gatman, Henry, Albany, N.Y.,
65, #9833, card
Gay, James, Albany, N.Y., 46,
#4816
Gay, William, E. Fla., 74,
#13187
Gaylord, Sylvia, Conn., 32, #70
Geabhart (formerly Cleaver),
Eleanor, Ky., 112, #1094

Geabheart (formerly Cleaver),
Eleanor, c/o, Ky., 113,
#1261
Gearhart, Jacob, Philadelphia,
Pa., 50, #5473
Gearhart, Jacob, c/o,
Philadelphia, Pa., 112,
#835
Geates, John, —, 90, #18851,
card
Gee, Belinda, c/o, Md., 94, #700
Gee, Mary, a/o, Ky., 133, #256
Geer, Amah, Mass., 95, #921
Geer, Nathan, e/o, Conn., 79,
#14653
Gent, Mary Ann, a/o, Nashville,
Tenn., 102, #5695
Gentry, David, Nashville, Tenn.,
117, #4421
Gentry, George, Richmond, Va.,
57, #7508
Gentry, George, Richmond, Va.,
110, #11107
Gentry, George, Va., 73, #12758
Gentry, George, Va., 86, #16782
Gentry, Gestin, a/o, Ky., 142,
#5318
Geoghegan, Thomas, w/o, Md.,
131, #8891
Geomans, John, e/o, E. Fla., 79,
#14598
George, Jesse, Pittsburgh, Pa.,
53, #6536
George, Jesse, Pittsburgh, Pa.,
120, #6099
George, John, Indianapolis,
Ind., 43, #3945
George, John, Madison, Ind.,
10, #7758
George, John, Madison, Ind.,
48, #5159

George, Jordan, w/o, Ky., 76, #13856

George, Joseph, w/o, Va., 40, #3314

George, Margaret, Maine, 64, #9538

George, Margaret, Maine, 71, #12419

George, Samuel, N.H., 88, #17859

George, William, La., 121, #6900

George, William, La., 123, #9131

George, William, Va., 91, #19188, card

Geren, Maryline, Nashville, Tenn., 115, #2830

German, Elizabeth, Cleveland, Ohio, 141, #3001

German, William, Wheeling, Va., 52, #6204

Gerolman, Henry, c/o, New York City, 64, #9298

Gertstenberger, Christian, w/o, La., 129, #6406

Getman, Maria, Albany, N.Y., 104, #7170

Geven, Solomon, Knoxville, Tenn., 76, #13770

Ghormeley, James S., c/o, La., 124, #913

Ghormley, James S., c/o, La., 122, #8449

Ghormley, Joseph, Ohio, 46, #4716

Gibbon, John, w/o, Cleveland, Ohio, 135, #1707, card

Gibboney, Alexander, c/o, Philadelphia, Pa., 136, #2886

Gibbons, Delia D., Jacksonville, Fla., 73, #12763

Gibbons, Delia D., St. Augustine, Fla., 54, #6711

Gibbs, Caty, Mo., 73, #12774

Gibbs, David, Conn., 32, #27

Gibbs, Jeremiah, Ga., 129, #6548

Gibbs, Joshua, c/o, Pittsburgh, Pa., 102, #5821

Gibbs, Luman, Va., 71, #12345

Gibbs, Luman, Va., 78, #14473

Gibbs, Lumon, Va., 79, #14694

Gibbs, Slyvanus, Conn., 32, #598

Gibbs, Suman, Richmond, Va., 56, #7429

Gibbs, Thomas, a/o, Burlington, Vt., 130, #7623

Gibson, Erasmus, S.C., 53, #6516

Gibson, George, Ky., 52, #6231

Gibson, George, Ky., 70, #11063

Gibson, Jacob, Huntsville, Ala., 57, #7545

Gibson, Joseph, N.C., 52, #6089

Gibson, Nicholas, Richmond, Va., 53, #6388

Gibson, Rhoda, c/o, Albany, N.Y., 110, #11025

Gibson, Roger, Mass., 81, #15062

Gibson, Roger, c/o, Mass., 79, #14584

Gibson, Thomas, a/o, Va., 118, #4970

Giddens, John, Conn., 32, #212

Giddings, Isaac, c/o, Mass., 41, #3415

Gideon, Peter, Ohio, 81, #15064

Gideon, Peter, Richmond, Va.,
  63, #9117
Gideon, Peter, Va., 92, #19948,
  card
Gideon, Peter, e/o, Richmond,
  Va., 10, #19948
Giffin, Stephen, Ohio, 54,
  #6628
Giffing, Elizabeth, a/o, Albany,
  N.Y., 129, #6586
Giffis, Reuben, w/o, N.C., 87,
  #17609
Giffis, William, Albany, N.Y.,
  100, #3987
Gifford, John, a/o, Albany,
  N.Y., 132, #8952
Gifford, Lot, c/o, Mass., 134,
  #823
Gifford, Stephen, Ill., 76,
  #13804
Gifford, William, a/o, Ohio, 74,
  #13087
Gilbert, Asahel, c/o, Ill., 118,
  #5002
Gilbert, Isaac, g/o c/o, Conn.,
  37, #F1824
Gilbert, James, Ga., 51, #6056
Gilbert, Jemima, a/o, Albany,
  N.Y., 105, #7689
Gilbert, Jonathan, w/o, Albany,
  N.Y., 96, #1687
Gilbert, Lemuel, Conn., 32,
  #227
Gilbert, Margaret, a/o, Albany,
  N.Y., 104, #7348
Gilbert, Miriam, a/o, Albany,
  N.Y., 116, #3354
Gilbert, Moses, Conn., 32, #192
Gilbert, Saml, Richmond, Va.,
  51, #6081
Gilbert, Sewel, Ohio, 80,
  #14841

Gilbert, Solomon, c/o, N.Y.,
  142, #4105
Gilbert, Thaddeus, Ohio, 74,
  #13263
Gilbert, Thankful, Albany, N.Y.,
  79, #14595
Gile, Nancy, Albany, N.Y., 125,
  #1742
Giles, Leanor, Richmond, Va.,
  36A, #F5 V5
Giles, Patsey, a/o, Richmond,
  Va., 138, #4860
Gill, James, Tuscaloosa, Ala.,
  65, #9742
Gill, John, w/o, Va., 121, #7629
Gill, Jones, Richmond, Va., 54,
  #6879
Gill, Thomas, c/o, Ill., 54,
  #6633
Gill, Thomas, c/o, Ill., 55,
  #7054
Gill, Thomas, w/o, S.C., 67,
  #10312
Gill, Thomas, S.C., 51, #6055
Gill, William, c/o, Burlington,
  Vt., 132, #9235
Gilleland, Ann A., N.C., 113,
  #1557
Gilleland, Nancy G., Richmond,
  Va., 36A, #F3 V12
Gillen, William, w/o, Albany,
  N.Y., 49, #5382
Gilles, Joseph, a/o, Albany,
  N.Y., 136, #2606
Gilles, Parcy, g/o, Cincinnati,
  Ohio, 131, #8100
Gillespie, Daniel, Ga., 80,
  #14806
Gillespie, Daniel, S.C., 59,
  #7992
Gillespie, Daniel, S.C., 64,
  #9248

Gillespie, James, Tuscaloosa, Ala., 88, #17857

Gillespie, James T., w/o, Tenn. Militia, 96, #1729

Gillet, Isaac, a/o, Conn., 68, #10747

Gillet, Jabez, Albany, N.Y., 86, #16915

Gillet, Joseph, Philadelphia, Pa., 118, #4704, card

Gillet, Luther, Albany, N.Y., 41, #337_

Gillett, Nathaniel, c/o, Pittsburgh, Pa., 111, #722

Gillett, Stephen, Albany, N.Y., 66, #10124

Gillett, Stephen, Albany, N.Y., 50, #5582

Gilley, Francis M., Nashville, Tenn., 134, #1180

Gilliam, John, w/o, Ky., 98, #2703

Gilliams, John, c/o, N.C., 10, #17746

Gillian, Elizabeth, Louisville, Ky., 108, #9984 V#32

Gillian, John, —, 88, #17746, card

Gillidand, Elizabeth, c/o, Springfield, Ill., 141, #1477

Gilliland, Mary, c/o, —, 116, #3467, card

Gills, John, Richmond, Va., 57, #7547

Gills, John, Richmond, Va., 44, #4234

Gills, Mary, Richmond, Va., 101, #5303

Gilman, Sarah, Maine, 107, #9123

Gilmon, Charles, N.Y., 80, #14850

Gilmore, Alexander, New Albany, Ind., 49, #5362

Gilmore, Elizabeth, a/o, Albany, N.Y., 139, #7162

Gilner, Henry, a/o, Conn., 38, #F1822

Gilpin, Benjamin, Mobile, Ala., 59, #8015

Gilson, Peter, a/o, Montpelier, Vt., 112, #1044

Ginger, Henry, Ill., 55, #7156

Ginnell, William, R.I., 113, #1385

Gist, Elizabeth, Ky., 121, #7067

Giswold, Simeon, e/o, Albany, N.Y., 95, #1306

Given, John, Jackson, Tenn., 52, #6211

Given, John, Jackson, Tenn., 63, #9075

Givens, James, Jackson, Tenn., 66, #10219

Givens, James, Jackson, Tenn., 76, #13893

Gladding, Monroe, —, 142, #4898, slip

Glantz, John, Philadelphia, Pa., 57, #7514

Glantz, John, Philadelphia, Pa., 79, #14635

Glantz, John, Philadelphia, Pa., 80, #14970

Glascock, Robert, Richmond, Va., 52, #6177

Glasgo, William, w/o, Ga., 103, #6684

Glasgow, James, Philadelphia, Pa., 52, #6092

Glasgow, James, w/o, Philadelphia, Pa., 125, #2432

Glasgow, Richard, S.C., 51, #6050

Glass, Cena, Ky., 112, #832

Glass, Cena, Ky., 127, #4201

Glasscock, Robert, Richmond, Va., 45, #4470

Glaze, Thomas, Tuscaloosa, Ala., 88, #17828

Glazier, Ebenezer, c/o, Albany, N.Y., 142, #5955

Glazier, Moses, Albany, N.Y., 72, #12605

Gleason, Hannah, c/o, Vt., 58, #7739

Gleason, John, c/o, Mass., 64, #9615

Glenn, James, S.C., 39, #3161

Glenn, William, La., 132, #9030

Glenson, James, Mich., 143, #6774

Glidden, Abigal, a/o, N.H., 84, #16205

Gliddon, Deborah, c/o, Maine, 108, #9747

Gliddon, Deborah, c/o, Maine, 108, #9748

Glontz, John, Pittsburgh, Pa., 54, #6876

Glover, Jonathan, Mo., 85, #16694

Glover, Jonathan, Mo., 94, #747

Glover, Joseph, Ky., 45, #4647

Glover, Richard, Jonesboro, Tenn., 137, #3630

Glozen, Phinehas, est/o, Concord, N.H., 76, #13941

Glyssen, Elizabeth, S.C., 61, #8600

Goad, William, Jonesboro, Tenn., 53, #6464

Goben, William, w/o, Albany, N.Y., 86, #17257

Goble, Aligail, Ohio, 85, #16537

Godard, Isaac, Hartford, Conn., 32, #335

Goddard, John, Ga., 51, #5946

Goddard, John, Ga., 62, #8682

Goddard, John, w/o, Ga., 131, #8442

Godfrey, Isaac, Conn., 32, #457

Godfrey, Zachariah, Ind., 97, #2322

Godwin, Abraham, e/o, N.J., 120, #6606

Godwin, Moses, Conn., 32, #378

Goens, David, E. Tenn., 73, #12891, card

Goens, David, Knoxville, Tenn., 49, #5381

Goens, David, Knoxville, Tenn., 51, #6041

Goff, Job, Wheeling, Va., 47, #5032

Going, Mary, Richmond, Va., 129, #6275

Going, William, Fayetteville, N.C., 50, #5672

Going, William, N.C., 94, #720

Going, William, Fayetteville, N.C., 105, #7762 V#14

Goins, Anner, c/o, Albany, N.Y., 66, #10127

Golden, Edward, Mo., 139, #9240

Golden, Edward, Mo., 142, #4161

Golden, Edward, St. Louis, Mo., 133, #516

Goldsborough, Catharine, New Albany, Ind., 137, #4227

Goldsbrough, Catharine,
Indianapolis, Ind., 141,
#2859
Goldsmith, James, a/o, Albany,
N.Y., 104, #7421
Goldsmith, John, Ga., 45,
#4610
Gon [torn], David, S.C., 41,
#3525, card
Gondelock, David, S.C., 10,
#3526
Good, Eli, w/o, New York City,
41, #3473
Good (or Goard), William, w/o,
Jonesboro, Tenn., 110,
#10920
Goodale, Isaac, w/o, Albany,
N.Y., 117, #4487
Goodale, Richard, a/o,
Richmond, Va., 98, #2620
Goodall, Richd., Richmond, Va.,
53, #6428
Goodard, Jesse, Albany, N.Y.,
106, #8608
Goode, Jane, Richmond, Va.,
124, #662
Goode, Jane, Richmond, Va.,
133, #9977
Goode, John, Ky., 72, #12683,
card
Goode, John, w/o, Ky., 10,
#12683
Goodenow, William, Mass., 47,
#5037
Gooderl, John, —, 119, #5674,
slip
Gooding, Thaddeus, a/o,
Concord, N.H., 101, #5152
Goodman Sr., John, Va., 77,
#14047
Goodnight, Christoper, Va., 73,
#12995

Goodnight, Christopher,
Richmond, Va., 61, #8637
Goodnight, Christopher, w/o,
Wheeling, Va., 119, #5638
Goodnow, Eber, Albany, N.Y.,
75, #13696
Goodnum Sr., John, Richmond,
Va., 54, #6648
Goodown, Jacob, Ga., 45, #4612
Goodrich, Batsy, c/o, Concord,
N.H., 112, #1051
Goodrich, Francis, a/o,
Burlington, Vt., 51, #5957
Goodrich, Phebe, a/o, Albany,
N.Y., 10, #9383
Goodrum, John, Richmond, Va.,
47, #4959
Goodson, Benjamin, La., 107,
#9471
Goodson, Benjamin, Miss., 91,
#19205
Goodson, Benjamin, w/o, La.,
129, #6245
Goodson, Thomas, S.C., 46,
#4765
Goodson, Thomas, S.C., 57,
#7588
Goodson, Thomas, Va., 49,
#5418, card
Goodson, Thomas, c/o,
Richmond, Va., 10, #5418
Goodson, Thomas, c/o,
Richmond, Va., 50, #5587
Goodspeed, Esther, a/o, Mass.,
142, #5125
Goodwin, Albert L., New
Albany, Ind., 133, #300
Goodwin, Benjamin, Maine, 88,
#17772
Goodwin, Daniel, w/o, Ky., 125,
#2033

Goodwin, Lemuel, N.C., 43,
#3996
Goodwin, Lemuel, N.C., 64,
#9700
Goodwin, Lemuel, N.C., 87,
#17538
Goodwin, Pierce, N.C., 99,
#3484
Goodwin, Ruth, Maine, 67,
#10378
Goodwin, Seth, w/o, Albany,
N.Y., 116, #3389
Goodwin, Thomas, Boston,
Mass., 64, #9238
Goodyear, Edward, a/o, N.Y.,
123, #9119
Goold, Abigail, Albany, N.Y.,
106, #8570
Goolsberry, Mack, a/o, Ky., 71,
#12249
Goolsberry, Mack, g/o c/o, Ky.,
57, #7647
Goone, Elizabeth, Nashville,
Tenn., 84, #16029
Gordon, Abner, w/o, Jonesboro,
Tenn., 92, #94
Gordon, Charles, w/o, Nashville,
Tenn., 87, #17564
Gordon, Elizabeth, Miss., 98,
#2783
Gordon, Frederick, c/o, Tenn.
Militia, 105, #7793
Gordon, George W., w/o, 2nd
Artillery, 49, #5316
Gordon, Isaac, S.C., 47, #4862
Gordon, James, Albany, N.Y.,
58, #7827
Gordon, James, w/o, Albany,
N.Y., 10, #4465
Gordon, Mary, Ky., 100, #3827
Gordon, Moses, w/o, —, 137,
#4244, card

Gordon, Nancy, a/o, Albany,
N.Y., 122, #8371
Gordon, Robert, Ind., 54, #6644
Gordon, Robert, w/o, Ind., 95,
#1322
Gordon, Samuel, w/o, Albany,
N.Y., 10, #10913
Gordon, Timothy, c/o, Mass.,
136, #3527
Gore, Elizabeth, Nashville,
Tenn., 69, #10852
Gorham, Nathan, Conn., 32,
#395
Gorham, Seth, —, 52, #6135,
card
Goring, William, N.C., 73,
#12789
Gorman, W. A., D.C., 115,
#2554
Gorman, Willis A., D.C., 130,
#7849
Goss, Catharine, c/o, Windsor,
Vt., 42, #3585
Goss, Mark, Windsor, Vt., 54,
#6782
Gossett, William, S.C., 73,
#12717
Gossler, Mary, Philadelphia,
Pa., 97, #2283
Gott, John, w/o, Albany, N.Y.,
62, #8691
Gott, Sarah, a/o, Albany, N.Y.,
136, #3215
Gott, Story, w/o, Albany, N.Y.,
84, #16309
Gould, Charles C., Augusta,
Maine, 143, #6336
Gould, Eusebid, a/o, N.H., 118,
#4598
Gould, Isaac, a/o, Albany, N.Y.,
116, #3713

Gould, Mille, Boston, Mass.,
96, #1838
Gould, Noah, c/o, Albany, N.Y.,
134, #750
Gould, Timothy, w/o, N.J., 124,
#503
Goulsby, Isaac, Mo., 76,
#13791
Gowen, Jacob, w/o, Ind., 52,
#6276
Grace, John, Ga., 52, #6334
Grace, John, c/o, N.J., 118,
#4802
Grace, John, w/o, Ga., 66,
#10292
Grace, Nancy, Ga., 108, #10156
Grace, William, c/o, Ind., 119,
#5504
Graff, Samuel, Philadelphia, Pa.,
52, #6093
Graffam, Eleanor, c/o, Portland,
Maine, 108, #10280
Graft, Philip, Philadelphia, Pa.,
59, #8156
Graft, Philip, Philadelphia, Pa.,
43, #3892
Gragg, Hannah, a/o, Vt., 89,
#18202
Gragg, Henry, Tuscaloosa, Ala.,
88, #17789
Gragg, William, N.C., 106,
#8743, card
Gragg, William, N.C., 61,
#8386
Graham, Benjamin G., g/o c/o,
Conn., 37, #F1825
Graham, Esther, Boston, Mass.,
84, #16005, card
Graham, John, Cincinnati, Ohio,
142, #5956
Graham, Pvt. John, a/o w/o,
Ohio, 112, #1254, #militia

Graham, Joseph, c/o, N.C., 60,
#8178
Graham, Michael, Va., 78,
#14450, card
Graham, Michael, e/o,
Richmond, Va., 10, #14450
Graham, Robert, Boston, Mass.,
134, #1054
Graham, Robert T., Mass., 123,
#230
Graham, Thomas, Huntsville,
Ala., 84, #15982
Graham, William, Ohio, 62,
#8704
Graham, William, Ohio, 76,
#13754
Granger, Rececca, a/o, Mass.,
70, #12017
Granger, Thomas, c/o,
Pittsburgh, Pa., 109,
#10543
Grannis, David, Albany, N.Y.,
42, #3565
Grant, Asenath, Mass., 71,
#12341
Grant, Beriah, w/o, Mass., 110,
#11192
Grant, Elizabeth, c/o, Maine,
103, #6361
Grant, Elizabeth, c/o, Portland,
Maine, 104, #7221
Grant, Elizabeth, c/o, R.I., 120,
#6218
Grant, Elizabeth, g/o, Maine,
68, #10719
Grant, Hamilton, a/o, Conn., 38,
#F1822
Grant, Hiram, Albany, N.Y.,
126, #3983
Grant, Hiram, Albany, N.Y.,
129, #6273
Grant, John, Ky., 52, #6249

Grant, Joseph, Ga., 56, #7304
Grant, Joshua, Portland, Maine,
104, #7542
Grant, Joshua, g/o, Maine, 100,
#4357
Grant, Joshua, g/o, Maine, 59,
#8133
Grant, Joshua, g/o, Maine, 79,
#14608
Grant, Polly, c/o, New York
City, 109, #10569
Grant, William, Mo., 132,
#9721
Granville, James, Pittsburgh,
Pa., 82, #15371, card
Grass, George, a/o, Vt., 83,
#15610
Grass, Peter, Richmond, Va., 48,
#5047
Grass, Peter, Va., 77, #14032
Grass, Samuel, w/o, Mass., 49,
#5276
Grass, William, w/o, N.C., 10,
#8743
Gratton, Crary, w/o, Albany,
N.Y., 109, #10480
Gratton, Thomas, Albany, N.Y.,
74, #13201
Graves, Hannah, Philadelphia,
Pa., 83, #15840
Graves, James, Ky., 42, #3573
Graves, James, Ky., 74, #13334
Graves, Jedediah, Ind., 50,
#5558
Graves, Jedediah, New Albany,
Ind., 48, #5155
Graves, Josiah, c/o, Mass., 43,
#4033
Graves, Thomas, Ky., 68,
#10699
Graves, William, c/o, Albany,
N.Y., 78, #14348

Gravitt, John, a/o, Ky., 124,
#1347
Gray, Alexander M., w/o,
Richmond, Va., 36A, #F4
V21
Gray, Daniel, c/o, Cincinnati,
Ohio, 119, #5759
Gray, Daniel, c/o, Cincinnati,
Ohio, 122, #8322
Gray, Edward M., Philadelphia,
Pa., 10, #2092
Gray, Eleanor, e/o, Va., 65,
#9987
Gray, Elliot, —, 61, #8447, card
Gray, Frazier, w/o, Ohio, 108,
#9730
Gray Sr., Gabriel, Richmond,
Va., 57, #7553
Gray, Isaac, Ky., 54, #6885
Gray, James, Richmond, Va., 44,
#4236
Gray, James, Va., 45, #4597
Gray, Jeremiah, La., 127, #4708
Gray, Jeremiah, New Orleans,
La., 119, #5291
Gray, Joseph, Jonesboro, Tenn.,
52, #6288
Gray, Joseph, Jonesboro, Tenn.,
68, #10388
Gray, Mary, Philadelphia, Pa.,
138, #6053
Gray, Morton, Knoxville, Tenn.,
84, #15953
Gray, Nathaniel, Ohio, 62,
#8709
Gray, Nathaniel, Ohio, 78,
#14409
Gray, Rachel, e/o, Pulaski,
Tenn., 114, #2259
Gray, William, Ky., 82, #15249
Gray, William, Md., 128, #4995

Gray, Lt. William H., 11th Inf., 103, #6729

Greeley, Joseph, e/o, N.H., 84, #15944

Greeley, Joseph, e/o, N.Y., 84, #15945

Green, Abel, c/o, Albany, N.Y., 82, #15341

Green, Anna, Burlington, Vt., 50, #5490

Green, Anna, Ky., 71, #12427

Green, Anna, a/o, N.J., 135, #2338

Green, Benjamin, Wisc., 128, #6069

Green, Charles, w/o, Albany, N.Y., 84, #16238

Green, Clark H., R.I., 124, #946

Green, Cleophas, c/o, Mass., 49, #5342

Green, David, N.C., 39, #3143

Green, Duty, Ohio, 67, #10349

Green, Duty, Ohio, 74, #13311

Green, Duty, Ohio, 75, #13595

Green, Elisabeth, Richmond, Va., 36A, #F1 V20

Green, George, Albany, N.Y., 104, #7586

Green, Jane, a/o, New York City, 134, #1402

Green, Jeremiah, w/o, Mass., 87, #17602

Green, Joel, w/o, Albany, N.Y., 45, #4457

Green, Joel C., Cincinnati, Ohio, 119, #5182

Green, John, Albany, N.Y., 62, #8666

Green, John, Albany, N.Y., 79, #14556

Green, John, Huntsville, Ala., 51, #6074

Green, Joseph, e/o, N.J., 135, #2342

Green, Kennon J., e/o w/o, Va. Milita, 72, #12645

Green, Michael, Mo., 132, #9491

Green, Oliver, c/o, Albany, N.Y., 117, #4228

Green, Reuben, Albany, N.Y., 40, #3295

Green, Richard, Nashville, Tenn., 87, #17614

Green, Rufus, Albany, N.Y., 54, #6709

Green, Ruth, c/o, Albany, N.Y., 68, #10811

Green, Samuel, Albany, N.Y., 106, #8430, card

Green, Samuel, a/o, Albany, N.Y., 10, #8430

Green, Sarah, a/o, R.I., 10, #3196

Green, Sarah Ann, c/o, Ill., 102, #6233

Green, Sarah Anne, c/o, Ill., 101, #4670

Green, Sarah Anne, c/o, Ill., 101, #5014

Green, Sherwood, La., 97, #1953

Green, Thomas, Ga., 57, #7529

Green, Thomas, Ga., 70, #11165

Green, Thomas, Va., 103, #6565, card

Green, Timothy, c/o, Albany, N.Y., 51, #5925

Green, Tobias, Philadelphia, Pa., 143, #6258

Green, William, —, 65, #9885, card

Green, William, a/o, Nashville, Tenn., 10, #19228

Green, Zacharriah, New York
City, 102, #6052 V#46

Green 2nd, John, w/o, Ohio, 40,
#3349

Greenbugh, Manuel, g/o, Maine,
92, #172

Greene, John, w/o, Mass., 73,
#12801

Greene, William, —, 91,
#19228, card

Greene, William, w/o,
Richmond, Va., 10, #9885

Greenhut, Joseph, Ill., 10,
#3189

Greenhut, Joseph, Spingfield,
Ill., 141, #3189, card

Greening, Nehemiah, Richmond,
Va., 45, #4495

Greenman, John, Albany, N.Y.,
71, #12437

Greenwald, Jacob, Philadelphia,
Pa., 41, #3462

Greenway, William, c/o,
Jonesboro, Tenn., 66,
#10252

Greenwell, Ignatius, Mo., 40,
#3310

Greenwell, Ignatius, Mo., 62,
#8836

Greenwell, Ignatius, a/o, Mo.,
102, #5803

Greenwood, Ignatius, Mo., 56,
#7351

Greer, John, Huntsville, Ala.,
116, #3135

Greer, John, Little Rock, Ark.,
134, #1222

Greer, Meshack, w/o, Knoxville,
Tenn., 113, #1447

Greer, Richard, Nashville, Tenn.,
66, #10268

Greer, Richard, Nashville, Tenn.,
94, #314

Greer, Samuel, —, 119, #5175,
slip

Greer, Samuel, Knoxville, Tenn.,
10, #5175

Greers, Richard, Nashville,
Tenn., 71, #12408

Gregg, James, w/o, Albany,
N.Y., 117, #4276

Gregg, Mary, Albany, N.Y., 10,
#4276

Gregg, William, N.C., 82,
#15264

Gregory, Abraham, w/o, N.C.,
121, #6876

Gregory, Bry, Nashville, Tenn.,
10, #5711

Gregory, Bry, Nashville, Tenn.,
102, #5711, card

Gregory, George, Knoxville,
Tenn., 104, #7677

Gregory, George, w/o,
Knoxville, Tenn., 90,
#18752

Gregory, James, Ohio, 45,
#4544

Gregory, Mathew, a/o, Albany,
N.Y., 108, #9756

Gregory, Stephen, Philadelphia,
Pa., 46, #4731

Gregory, Thomas W., g/o c/o,
La., 125, #2813

Greiner, Christian, D.C., 143,
#6948

Greiner, Christiana, D.C., 129,
#6625

Gresham, Robert, Jackson,
Tenn., 110, #11048

Grete, Christian, New York City,
115, #2981

Grete, Christian, New York City,
125, #2857
Grewell, Michael, Philadelphia,
Pa., 80, #14878
Gribbon, Margaret, a/o,
Cleveland, Ohio, 10, #1707
Grider, Henry, Ky., 89, #18180,
card
Grider, Henry, w/o, Ky., 10,
#18180
Grider, John, Ky., 73, #12805
Gridley, Silas, Conn., 32, #—
Gridstaff, Henry H., Jonesboro,
Tenn., 132, #9347
Grier, George, Pittsburgh, Pa.,
101, #4754
Griffen, William, S.C., 56,
#7416
Griffen, Zachariah, Va., 77,
#14101
Griffin, Anna, Albany, N.Y., 79,
#14715
Griffin, Clara, Richmond, Va.,
130, #7234
Griffin, Daniel, c/o, Albany,
N.Y., 112, #1016
Griffin, James, w/o, Ga., 49,
#5281
Griffin, John, —, 112, #1043,
card
Griffin, John, Old Peace
Establishment, 10, #1043
Griffin, Joseph, S.C., 55, #6920
Griffin, Joseph, S.C., 69,
#11014
Griffin, Joseph, S.C., 103,
#6809
Griffin, Joseph, a/o, Vt., 83,
#15811
Griffin, Nancy, Fayetteville,
N.C., 132, #9201

Griffin, Nancy, New Albany,
Ind., 108, #9986
Griffin, Nathaniel, c/o, Concord,
N.H., 117, #4485
Griffin, Sarah, Ga., 113, #1601
Griffin, William, Oregon City,
O.T., 127, #4608
Griffin, Zachariah, Va., 64,
#9621
Griffis, Wiliam, N.J., 107,
#9565+
Griffith, Elisha, —, 39, #3158,
card
Griffith, Elisha, Pittsburgh, Pa.,
10, #3150
Griffith, Eunice, —, 71, #12417,
card
Griffith, Eunice, Ohio, 10,
#12417
Griffith, Isaac, N.C., 78, #14489
Griffith, Isaac, N.C., 80, #14882
Griffith, Orlando B.,
Philadelphia, Pa., 142,
#5066
Griffith, Philemon, c/o, Md., 10,
#7783
Griffith, Samuel, Pittsburgh, Pa.,
77, #14029, card
Griffith, Samuel, a/o, Richmond,
Va., 92, #19598
Griffith, Samuel, c/o, Pittsburgh,
Pa., 10, #14029
Grigg, Josiah, Richmond, Va.,
57, #7507
Grigg, Josiah, Richmond, Va.,
72, #12635
Grigg, Josiah, Va., 45, #4594
Griggs, Benjamin, c/o, N.J., 86,
#16886
Grigory, Read, g/o c/o, Conn.,
37, #F1820

Grigsby, Moses, w/o, Ind., 52, #6273

Grigsby, William, Madison, Ind., 135, #1819

Grill, William, Richmond, Va., 59, #8140

Grimes, Isaac, g/o c/o, Cincinnati, Ohio, 131, #8087

Grimes, Isaac, g/o c/o, Cincinnati, Ohio, 141, #2040

Grimes, John, c/o, Md., 132, #9206

Grimmit, Josiah, Nashville, Tenn., 78, #14380

Grindstaff, Abraham, Mo., 106, #8566

Grindstaff, Abraham, Mo., 111, #639

Grindstaff, Abraham, Mo., 127, #4742

Grindstaff, Henry H., Jonesboro, Tenn., 137, #4194

Grinke, Mary, c/o, S.C., 69, #11013

Grinmet, Josiah, Nashville, Tenn., 39, #3160

Grinonean (formerly Preston), Mary M., Pittsburgh, Pa., 132, #9547

Grinsteade, William, a/o, Richmond, Va., 91, #19521

Grist, Benjamin, w/o, Ga., 113, #1788

Grist, Catherine, Ga., 130, #7304

Griswell, William, w/o, Philadelphia, Pa., 135, #2093

Griswold, Andrew, w/o, Hartford, Conn., 60, #8183

Griswold, Asenath, a/o, Albany, N.Y., 118, #5098

Griswold, Benjamin, Vt., 123, #9560, card

Griswold, Benjamin, c/o, Burlington, Vt., 10, #9560

Griswold, Edward, Albany, N.Y., 138, #5096

Griswold, Eunice, c/o, Conn., 98, #2727

Griswold, John, Philadelphia, Pa., 80, #14883

Griswold, Simeon, e/o, Albany, N.Y., 94, #633

Groat, Isaac, Albany, N.Y., 89, #18393

Grooms, Abraham, Ohio, 64, #9289

Grooms, John, g/o c/o, Mo., 126, #3314

Grooms, Jonathan, Va., 69, #10942

Groover, Peter, Ga., 123, #142, card

Grosee, Chauncey R., Mass., 132, #9613

Gross, David, c/o, Ky., 65, #9841

Groton, Benjamin, Albany, N.Y., 39, #3105

Grout, Hilkiah, c/o, Burlington, Vt., 131, #8463

Grove, Jacob, Richmond, Va., 36A, #F2 -

Grove, Philip, Philadelphia, Pa., 98, #3077

Grove, Wendell, w/o, Pittsburgh, Pa., 122, #8293

Grover, Peter, Ga., 10, #142

Groves, Sarah, Fayetteville, N.C., 131, #8186

Groves, Sarah, Richmond, Va.,
36A, #F3 V10

Growney, Michael, New York
City, 116, #3598

Growney, Michael, New York
City, 126, #3834

Gruber, Philip, a/o, S.C., 73,
#12871

Gryder, Martin, Ky., 68, #10700

Guartney, Michael, Richmond,
Va., 58, #7703

Gudger, William, a/o w/o, N.C.,
92, #19985

Guest, William, S.C., 67,
#10314

Guest, William, w/o, S.C., 95,
#851

Guffy, Alexander, w/o, Ky., 103,
#6954

Guice, John, w/o, Ga., 82,
#15240

Guice Sr., John, Ga., 65, #9760

Guida (or Gryder), Martin, Ky.,
110, #59, card

Guild, Mittee, a/o, Boston,
Mass., 103, #6577

Guild, Mittee, a/o, Boston,
Mass., 104, #7199

Guilder, Mary, Cincinnati, Ohio,
126, #3675

Guill, William, Pa., 76, #13774,
card

Guill, William, Richmond, Va.,
55, #6925

Guill, William, w/o, Va., 11,
#13774

Guill, William, w/o, Va., 74,
#13353

Guinan, William, St. Johnsbury,
Vt., 141, #2037

Gulick, Elizabeth, e/o, Albany,
N.Y., 126, #3592

Gulka, Louise, D.C., 124, #837

Gunn, Abel, New York City, 87,
#17379

Gunn, Gabriel, w/o, Ga., 123,
#340

Gunter, Elizabeth, Md., 143,
#6592

Gurganus, Reuben, N.C., 45,
#4568

Gurmison, John W.,
Topographical Engineers,
137, #4458, slip

Gurney, George, N.Y., 50,
#5797

Gurney, Jacob, c/o, Portland,
Maine, 108, #10174

Gustene, Joel, w/o, D.C., 11,
#16027

Gustin, Eleanor, Ohio, 100,
#4401

Gustin, Eleanor, Ohio, 101,
#4969

Gustin, Eleanor, e/o, Cincinnati,
Ohio, 135, #2019

Gustius, Joel, D.C., 84, #16027,
card

Guthrie, Elizabeth, c/o,
Pittsburgh, Pa., 110,
#11108

Guthrie, Mary, a/o, Jackson,
Tenn., 100, #3892

Guthrie, John B., late PA,
Pittsburgh, Pa., 115, #2804

Guy, James, c/o, N.C., 121,
#7637

Guyal, Perrie A., New Orleans,
La., 134, #1272

Guyton, Aaron, w/o, S.C., 92,
#19751

H

Haag, Joseph, Ore., 136, #3008

Haag, Joseph, —, 140, #9930
V#1

Haas, Christian, Richmond, Va.,
56, #7344

Hack, William, w/o, Richmond,
Va., 54, #6877

Hackathorn, David,
Philadelphia, Pa., 42,
#3760

Hackathorn, David, Pittsburgh,
Pa., 67, #10499

Hackenberry, Samuel, g/o c/o,
Philadelphia, Pa., 135,
#1862

Hackendron, David, —, 117,
#4365, card

Hackett, Zelpha, Mass., 113,
#1707

Hackney, Jane V., Richmond,
Va., 106, #8412

Hackney, John, Richmond, Va.,
67, #10403

Hackney, Joseph, c/o, N.C., 59,
#7961

Hackney, Joseph, c/o, N.C., 70,
#12095

Hackney, Thomas, Nashville,
Tenn., 70, #12051

Hackwood, Thomas, Va., 80,
#14812

Hackworth, Dorothy, Va., 68,
#10601

Hadden, William, La., 104,
#7334

Haddleson, William, Ohio, 64,
#9228

Haddon, William, La., 106,
#8614

Haddon, William, La., 97, #2251

Haddon, William, La., 98, #2893

Haddon, William, a/o, La., 118,
#4652

Hadky, Isaac, c/o, Albany, N.Y.,
84, #16068

Hadnall, Frances M., Richmond,
Va., 130, #7648

Hafley, Nancy J., Knoxville,
Tenn., 116, #3412

Hagan, Arthur, Ill., 48, #5089

Hagan, Henry, D.C., 128, #5280

Hagen, Charles, c/o, Madison,
Ind., 57, #7610

Hagen, Solomon, Bellows Falls,
Vt., 63, #8967

Hagenbuck, Stephen, Mo., 107,
#9078

Hagerty, Saloma, Pittsburgh,
Pa., 112, #1027

Hagerty, Saloma, Pittsburgh,
Pa., 121, #7462

Haggard, James, a/o, Ill., 92,
#19909

Haggard, John, N.C., 64, #9699

Haggard, William, Ky., 55,
#7107

Haggins, Henry, Pa., 40, #3283

Hailes, Silas, w/o, S.C., 116,
#3702

Hailey, Anthony, Ohio, 100,
#3764, card

Hailey, Anthony, c/o, Ohio, 11,
#3764

Hailey, Barnabas, w/o, Ky., 113,
#1896

Hain, David, Fayetteville, N.C.,
105, #7762 V#28

Haines, Charity, Ky., 74,
#13399

Haines, John, Philadelphia, Pa.,
41, #3463

Haines, John, c/o, Albany, N.Y.,
91, #18974

Haines, Nancy, Richmond, Va.,
137, #3645

Hainsford, Charles, Ky., 47,
#4906

Hair, Private James, e/o w/o,
28th Inf., 79, #14730

Hair 1st, John, Boston, Mass.,
39, #2940

Hakes, John, c/o, Albany, N.Y.,
96, #1419

Hale, Amos, N.H., 89, #18531

Hale, Daniel, w/o, Albany, N.Y.,
45, #4628

Hale, Hannah, c/o, Albany,
N.Y., 64, #9568

Hale, Hannah, c/o, Albany,
N.Y., 64, #9569

Hale, Leonard, w/o, Va., 42,
#3696

Hale, Nicholas, W. Tenn., 64,
#9486

Hale, Thomas, Richmond, Va.,
44, #4238

Haley, James, Nashville, Tenn.,
11, #15076, card

Haley, James, W. Tenn., 81,
#15076, card

Halfpenny, John, a/o, Ky., 132,
#9884

Hall, Anna, c/o, Maine, 62,
#8843

Hall, Anthony, w/o, Pittsburgh,
Pa., 108, #9765

Hall, Benjamin, c/o, Albany,
N.Y., 115, #2489

Hall, Carlos, Cleveland, Ohio,
128, #5986

Hall, Cyrus, Albany, N.Y., 102,
#6002

Hall, Cyrus, Albany, N.Y., 50,
#5546

Hall, Cyrus, Albany, N.Y., 51,
#5921

Hall, Cyrus, Montpelier, Vt.,
101, #5006 V#14

Hall, Danl., c/o, Mass., 53,
#6543

Hall, Edward, Ill., 48, #5241

Hall, Eleanor, c/o, Mass., 106,
#8537

Hall, Isham, Richmond, Va., 64,
#9391

Hall, Jacob, Bellows Falls, Vt.,
44, #4272

Hall, James, D.C., 140, #307

Hall, James, w/o, St. Augustine,
Fla., 51, #5998

Hall, John, —, 99, #3577, card

Hall, John, Albany, N.Y., 113,
#1789

Hall, John, Richmond, Va., 11,
#5009

Hall, John, Va., 41, #3522

Hall, John, a/o, Richmond, Va.,
11, #3577

Hall, John, w/o, Ky., 44, #4373

Hall, John, w/o, Philadelphia,
Pa., 69, #10823

Hall, Joseph, Baltimore, Md.,
142, #4850

Hall, Levi, Vt., 83, #15793

Hall, Levi, e/o, Richmond, Va.,
11, #17275

Hall, Levi, Concord, NH, 86,
#1727-, card

Hall, Luther, w/o, Maine, 57,
#7571

Hall, Mary, Mass., 118, #4798

Hall, Mildred, Richmond, Va.,
126, #3313

Hall, Nathan, Richmond, Va.,
54, #6603

Hall, Peter, c/o, New Albany,
Ind., 56, #7383

Hall, Rhodes, c/o, Mich., 117,
#4507

Hall, Ruth, Ky., 120, #6419

Hall, Ruth, Louisville, Ky., 122,
#8727

Hall, Samuel, w/o, Burlington,
Vt., 104, #7423

Hall, Sarah, Albany, N.Y., 80,
#14787

Hall, Stephen, Mass., 42, #3753

Hall, Susan, Ky., 121, #7240

Hall, William, a/o, N.C., 118,
#4756

Hall, James, late PA, Cincinnati,
Ohio, 121, #7990

Hall (now Flanders), Almira,
N.H., 109, #10655

Hall Sr., Moses, Madison, Ind.,
57, #7605

Hall Sr., Solomon, S.C., 52,
#6144

Hallack, Joshua, w/o, N.Y., 52,
#6253

Hallam, John, Conn., 32, #635

Hallett, Benjamin, e/o, Boston,
Mass., 121, #7479

Hallett, Thomas, Conn., 32,
#565

Halley, Charlotte, Richmond,
Va., 124, #663

Halley, John, Richmond, Va.,
45, #4504

Halsey, Henry, N.C., 70,
#12038

Halsey, Malachi, a/o,
Fayetteville, N.C., 96,
#1776

Halsey, Silas, —, 108, #9974,
card

Halsey, Major Silas, 32nd Inf.,
122, #8141, card

Halstead, John, c/o, Cincinnati,
Ohio, 123, #9879

Halstead, John, c/o, Cincinnati,
Ohio, 123, #74

Ham, Benjamin, N.H., 40,
#3223

Hamblet, Phineas, lr/o, Concord,
N.H., 90, #18832

Hambridge, Sarah, Philadelphia,
Pa., 127, #4847

Hambright, Sarah, Philadelphia,
Pa., 128, #5266

Hambright, Sarah, Philadelphia,
Pa., 139, #7150

Hamersly, John, w/o, Madison,
Ind., 83, #15916

Hamil, Isaac, w/o, Albany, N.Y.,
87, #17417

Hamiliton, John, c/o, Ga., 116,
#3174

Hamilton, Alexander, Richmond,
Va., 64, #9507

Hamilton, Alexander, Richmond,
Va., 54, #6613

Hamilton, Alexander, Va., 85,
#16688

Hamilton, Barton, Huntsville,
Ala., 60, #8285

Hamilton, Barton, Huntsville,
Ala., 69, #11030

Hamilton, Benjamin, Louisville,
Ky., 108, #9984 V#38

Hamilton, Catherine,
Philadelphia, Pa., 74,
#13221

Hamilton, David, Jackson,
Tenn., 43, #4011

Hamilton, David, Jackson,
Tenn., 51, #6029

Hamilton, David, e/o, S.C., 59,
#8086
Hamilton, David, w/o, Jackson,
Tenn., 11, #16085
Hamilton, Elizabeth,
Philadelphia, Pa., 117,
#4526
Hamilton, James, Knoxville,
Tenn., 48, #5156
Hamilton, James, Knoxville,
Tenn., 73, #12815
Hamilton, James, w/o, N.C., 96,
#1840
Hamilton, James, w/o,
Richmond, Va., 108,
#10241
Hamilton, Jane, D.C., 113,
#1511
Hamilton, John, Ind., 66,
#10183, card
Hamilton, John, Mo., 78,
#14276
Hamilton, John, c/o, Ga., 116,
#3404
Hamilton, John, c/o, Ind., 11,
#10185
Hamilton, John, c/o, Ind., 11,
#10183
Hamilton, John, w/o, Ill., 89,
#18493
Hamilton, Mary, Albany, N.Y.,
79, #14669
Hamilton, Richard, Philadelphia,
Pa., 42, #3581
Hamilton, Richard, w/o,
Philadelphia, Pa., 88,
#18050
Hamilton, Robert, w/o, Ohio,
77, #13998
Hamilton, Samuel C.,
Cincinnati, Ohio, 138,
#6643

Hamilton, Schuyler, New York
City, 127, #4257
Hamilton, Thomas, N.C., 43,
#3935
Hamilton, Thomas, N.C., 54,
#6902
Hamilton, Thomas, N.C., 65,
#10031
Hamilton, Thomas, N.C., 76,
#13745
Hamlet, Chesley, c/o,
Louisville, Ky., 117, #4222
Hamlin, America, w/o, Maine,
46, #4668
Hamlin, Caroline, Conn., 32,
#28
Hamlin, Mark, w/o, Conn., 88,
#18122
Hamm, Happy, Ky., 11, #4923
Hamm, Happy, Ky., 127, #4923,
card
Hammel, Hugh, w/o, Pittsburgh,
Pa., 110, #11173
Hammer, Henry, Ky., 94, #261
Hammer, Henry, Richmond, Va.,
42, #3588
Hammer, Henry, Richmond, Va.,
47, #4989
Hammer, Henry, w/o, Va., 76,
#13797
Hammet, Caleb, e/o, Albany,
N.Y., 99, #3444
Hammond, Hensdale, c/o,
Albany, N.Y., 135, #2180
Hammond, Joshua, S.C., 64,
#9662
Hammond, Joshua, S.C., 82,
#15495
Hammond, Joshua, S.C., 106,
#8381
Hammond, Joshua, S.C., 112,
#1212

Hammond, Joshua, a/o, S.C.,
120, #5937
Hammond, Lucy, a/o, Albany,
N.Y., 108, #10364
Hammond, Obadiah, Ky., 102,
#6171
Hammond, Sarah, a/o, Ohio,
119, #5447
Hammond, Thomas C., g/o c/o,
Mo., 129, #6909
Hammond, Titus, w/o, N.Y.,
109, #10889
Hammons, George, Ill., 125,
#2518
Hammons, George, Ky., 140,
#891
Hammons, George, Ky., 142,
#5319
Hampton, John, w/o, Ga., 88,
#18049
Hampton, Joyce, c/o, Ga., 133,
#264
Hanald, Winnefred, a/o, Ky.,
135, #2353
Hancock, Benjamin, w/o,
Richmond, Va., 44, #4244
Hancock, John, Ga., 136, #2527
Hancock, Mary, Madison, Ind.,
120, #5957
Hancock, Samuel, c/o, N.C.,
123, #9246
Hand, Jane A., a/o, Ky., 134,
#998
Handcock, John, w/o, N.C., 49,
#5380
Handerson, Abigail, a/o,
Concord, N.H., 98, #3081
Handford, Ebenezer, Conn., 32,
#624
Handley, Charles, —, 100,
#4395, card

Handley, Charles, Boston,
Mass., 11, #4395
Handley, James H., Richmond,
Va., 62, #8738
Handley, James H., Richmond,
Va., 43, #3882
Handlin, Mathias, Ohio, 57,
#7485
Handlin, Mathias, w/o, Ohio,
71, #12459
Handlin, Mathias, w/o, Ohio,
78, #14261
Handricks, George, w/o, Ind.,
66, #10182
Handy, Ruth, a/o, Mass., 139,
#7533
Handy, Samuel, a/o, Albany,
N.Y., 127, #4483
Hankinson, Joseph, N.J., 83,
#15753, card
Hankinson, Joseph, N.J., 45,
#4513
Hankinson, Joseph, w/o, N.J.,
11, #15753
Hankley, Moses, Va., 87,
#17641, card
Hanks, Chloe, Burlington, Vt.,
135, #1895
Hanks, Ebenezer, w/o, Mass.,
11, #10582
Hanna, Robert, Pittsburgh, Pa.,
49, #5350
Hanna, Robert, Pittsburgh, Pa.,
72, #12583
Hannaman, Christopher, c/o,
Ind., 11, #8650
Hannaman, William, —, 52,
#6293, card
Hannaman, William, —, 61,
#8650, card
Hannaman, William, Ind., 11,
#6293

Hannan, Esom, Va., 94, #343, card

Hannan, Esom, w/o, Richmond, Va., 11, #343

Hannick, Lettice, a/o, Cincinnati, Ohio, 125, #2154

Hannon, Elizabeth, e/o, S.C., 127, #4052

Hannon, Esom (or Asom), Richmond, Va., 61, #8621

Hannum, Anna, c/o, Boston, Mass., 103, #6726

Hanpher, Eleanor, c/o, Baltimore, Md., 113, #1638

Hansbrough, Sarah, Richmond, Va., 36A, #F6, card

Hanscom, Mary, a/o, Portsmouth, Maine, 135, #1901

Hansford, Charles, Ky., 58, #7801

Hansford, Charles, Ky., 62, #8767

Hansford, Charles, Ky., 73, #12920

Hansford, Charles, Ky., 79, #14686

Hansford, Charles, Ky., 81, #14998

Hansford, Charles, Ky., 87, #17478

Hanson, Eliza, Albany, N.Y., 126, #3352

Hapham, Jeremiah, D.C., 109, #10647

Happas, Michael, a/o, Philadelphia, Pa., 73, #12955

Happy, Barbara, New York City, 89, #18518

Haptain, Abraham, Ohio, 53, #6394

Harber, Adam, w/o, Nashville, Tenn., 106, #8379

Harbison, James, Ind., 58, #7778

Harbison, James, w/o, Ind., 91, #18973

Harbour, Noah, Richmond, Va., 72, #12629

Harbour, Noah, Richmond, Va., 48, #5223

Harbst, Peter, a/o, Philadelphia, Pa., 105, #8174

Hardee, Nancy, S.C., 95, #1010

Hardenbergh, Thomas H., Albany, N.Y., 62, #8700

Hardenbrook, Lodwick, Ohio, 83, #15614

Hardenburgh, Thomas H., Albany, N.Y., 60, #8357

Hardick, Christina, New York City, 138, #6608

Hardin, Benjamin, Ark., 65, #9812

Hardin, George, w/o, Albany, N.Y., 65, #9769

Hardin, James, c/o, New York City, 117, #3907

Hardin, Lewis, S.C., 105, #8337

Hardin, Pleuright, g/o c/o, Ky., 127, #4145

Hardin, Polly, Ky., 120, #5873

Hardin, Susannah, a/o, Ky., 11, #5552

Hardin, Thomas, Ky., 56, #7361

Hardin, Thomas, Ky., 62, #8872

Harding, Cloez, e/o, Albany, N.Y., 116, #3336

Harding, Jemima, Mass., 68, #10709

Harding, Jeremiah, Conn., 32,
#437
Harding, Thomas, Ind., 42,
#3697
Hardion, James, —, 91, bet.
#19007 & #19054, card
Hardison, James, Nashville,
Tenn., 11, #19014
Hardman, Sarah, Cincinnati,
Ohio, 141, #2860
Hardy, -, Ashville, N.C., 131,
#8301, slip
Hardy, Sarah Ann, Ky., 109,
#10619
Hardy, William, w/o, Maine, 99,
#3578
Hardy, J. F. E., PA, Ashville,
N.C., 114, #2407
Hare, Richard, e/o, Richmond,
Va., 103, #6786
Hare Sr., Richard, Richmond,
Va., 101, #4686
Hare Sr., Richard, Va., 80,
#14942
Hargis, Elizabeth, a/o, N.C.,
114, #2314
Hargon, Michael, w/o, Ky., 86,
#17026
Hargrave, John, c/o, Ill., 85,
#16365
Harkerider, John, a/o, Va., 119,
#5145
Harkness, Elizabeth, e/o, Ill.,
113, #1549
Harlander, Goerge, w/o, Ky., 45,
#4614
Harlow, James, w/o, Boston,
Mass., 101, #4864
Harman, Charles, w/o,
Nashville, Tenn., 116,
#3437

Harman, Gideon, Miss., 62,
#8806
Harman, John, c/o, Philadelphia,
Pa., 51, #5952
Harman, Samuel, c/o, Maine, 11,
#4766
Harmon, Gideon, Miss., 55,
#6946
Harmon, Henry, c/o, 28th Inf,
53, #6581
Harmon, Henry, c/o, 28th Inf,
53, #6582
Harmon, Henry, w/o, 28th Inf,
53, #6583
Harmon, Jehiel, Conn., 32,
#460
Harmon, John, a/o, Albany,
N.Y., 86, #16752
Harmon, Rebecca Jane Eastin,
c/o, Ill., 123, #9816
Harmon, Samuel, Maine, 46,
#4766, card
Harp, Samuel, Spingfield, Ill.,
141, #1915
Harper, Adam, Ky., 115, #2807
Harper, Adam, Ky., 121, #7191
Harper, Daniel, w/o, Ohio, 64,
#9251
Harper, Richard, Mich., 140,
#1157
Harper, Richard, New York City,
111, #673
Harper, Richard, New York City,
121, #7140
Harper, Richard, a/o, Knoxville,
Tenn., 121, #7297
Harper, Sarah, N.C., 103, #6480
Harras, Mary, N.Y., 143, #7033
Harrel, Simon, Va., 121, #6895,
card
Harrell, George, Ohio, 65,
#9786

Harrell, George, Ohio, 71,
#12456
Harrell, George, w/o, Ohio, 86,
#16936
Harrell, Lydia, Richmond, Va.,
36A, #F6, card
Harrington, Asenath, a/o,
Concord, N.H., 66, #10270
Harrington, Drury, S.C., 97,
#2185, card
Harrington, Drury, e/o, S.C., 11,
#6895
Harrington, Uriah, w/o, Vt., 60,
#8216
Harris, Andrew, w/o, Albany,
N.Y., 43, #4095
Harris, Benjamin, Ga., 54,
#6723
Harris, James, New York City,
87, #17290
Harris, James, Richmond, Va.,
56, #7350
Harris, James, Va., 78, #14331
Harris, James, w/o, Richmond,
Va., 99, #3156
Harris, John, a/o, Montpelier,
Vt., 123, #9620
Harris, John, w/o, 2nd Artillery,
84, #16303
Harris, John, w/o, Concord,
N.H., 118, #4801
Harris, John W., Cincinnati,
Ohio, 135, #1876
Harris, John W., Ore., 138,
#5771
Harris, Jonathan, w/o, N.H., 46,
#4739
Harris, Joseph, w/o, Ga., 88,
#18071
Harris, Joshua, Albany, N.Y.,
94, #298

Harris, Keziah, Cincinnati,
Ohio, 136, #2849
Harris, Keziah, c/o, Cincinnati,
Ohio, 140, #1126
Harris, Lavinia, a/o, Knoxville,
Tenn., 113, #1258
Harris, Lydia, a/o, Ky., 95,
#1065
Harris, Mary, a/o, Richmond,
Va., 97, #2134
Harris, Mary P., Ga., 110, #216
Harris, Mary P., Ga., 133, #5
Harris, Mathew, Ga., 85, #16364
Harris, Moses, Albany, N.Y.,
105, #7824
Harris, Moses, Ohio, 103,
#6964
Harris, Rachel, a/o, Albany,
N.Y., 114, #2361
Harris, Rebecca, a/o, Richmond,
Va., 36A, #F2 V4
Harris, Relief, Mass., 73,
#12970
Harris, Richmond, Ky., 64,
#9430
Harris, Richmond, Ky., 91,
#19090
Harris, Richmond, Ky., 115,
#2449
Harris, Richmond, Ky., 99,
#3595
Harris, Robin, N.C., 51, #5926
Harris, Robin, w/o, N.C., 98,
#2961
Harris, Temperance, Montpelier,
Vt., 101, #5006 V#94
Harris, Thomas, Philadelphia,
Pa., 124, #894
Harris, Thomas, Philadelphia,
Pa., 138, #5025
Harris, Thomas, w/o, Ky., 107,
#9005

Harris, Walter, w/o, N.H., 96,
#1510
Harris, William, w/o, Richmond,
Va., 11, #18642
Harrison, Anthony A., w/o, Ill.,
87, #17668
Harrison, Ezekiel, Ill., 81,
#15049
Harrison, George, N.J., 57,
#7609
Harrison, James, —, 64, #9512,
card
Harrison, James, Nashville,
Tenn., 60, #8371
Harrison, James, Richmond, Va.,
59, #7991
Harrison, James, Richmond, Va.,
48, #5152
Harrison, James, Va., 74,
#13158
Harrison, James, w/o, Nashville,
Tenn., 11, #9512
Harrison, Mary, Richmond, Va.,
100, #3779
Harrison, Mary, e/o, Ky., 130,
#7888
Harrison, Nathan, c/o, Conn.,
82, #15459
Harrison, Reuben, Richmond,
Va., 56, #7264
Harrison, Reuben, Richmond,
Va., 47, #4876
Harrison, Reuben, Va., 68,
#10613
Harrison, Richard, Va. half pay,
92, #19702, slip
Harrison, Richard, w/o,
Richmond, Va., 108,
#10000
Harrison, Rosanna, a/o, N.C.,
109, #10850

Harrison, Simon, w/o, Maine,
72, #12687
Harrison, Thomas, Nashville,
Tenn., 54, #6806
Harrison, Thomas, w/o, W.
Tenn., 63, #8934
Harriss, Lemuel, D.C., 121,
#8033
Harriss, Richmond, Ky., 115,
#2916
Harross, Joseph, a/o, Conn., 38,
#F1820
Harsin, Garret, w/o, Ind., 74,
#13067
Hart, Adam, c/o, Madison, Ind.,
124, #991
Hart, Anthony, w/o, Richmond,
Va., 106, #8515
Hart, Elias, Conn., 32, #279
Hart, George, c/o, Albany, N.Y.,
11, #6543
Hart, Ithurel, Conn., 32, #484
Hart, Mary, c/o, Va., 66, #10065
Hart, Munsn, Conn., 32, #196
Hart, Nancy, Wheeling, Va., 40,
#3317
Hart, Polly, c/o, Boston, Mass.,
97, #2139
Hart, Sally, Concord, N.H., 127,
#4012
Hart, Samuel, a/o, Richmond,
Va., 114, #2040
Hart, Selah, —, 40, #3175, card
Hart, Selah, c/o, Conn., 32,
#3175
Hart, Benjamin S., PA, New York
City, 109, #10629
Hart Sr., Thomas, Albany, N.Y.,
91, #19362
Hartley, Emily, Mo., 139,
#8398

Hartley, Laban, Nashville,
Tenn., 39, #3060

Hartman, Adam, Philadelphia,
Pa., 42, #3600

Hartman, Adam, c/o, Albany,
N.Y., 111, #384

Hartman, Christopher, w/o,
Ohio, 58, #7866

Hartman, John, Wheeling, Va.,
43, #3931

Hartman, John, Wheeling, Va.,
46, #4813

Hartman, John, Wheeling, Va.,
53, #6542

Hartman, John, Wheeling, Va.,
63, #8971

Hartman, John, w/o, Wheeling,
Va., 100, #3871

Hartman, Mary, Ohio, 40, #3196

Harton, Elizabeth, a/o,
Morganton, N.C., 137,
#4468

Hartshoon, William, e/o w/o,
37th Inf., 116, #3240

Hartshorn, Hannah, Albany,
N.Y., 77, #14090

Hartwick, William, w/o, N.J.
Militia, 100, #3875

Harvey, Edward, c/o, R.I., 76,
#13944

Harvey, Jane, a/o, Ohio, 70,
#12102

Harvey, John, Huntsville, Ala.,
53, #6403

Harvey, Nathan, c/o, Conn., 69,
#10836

Harvey, Sarah, c/o, Maine, 110,
#71

Harwood, Osborn S., Md., 44,
#4291

Harwood, Osborne S., Md., 59,
#8129

Harwood, Peter, w/o, Mass., 48,
#5242

Hashfield, Elizabeth, a/o, Ky.,
140, #991

Haskell, Ebenezer, w/o, Mass.
Militia, 141, #3188

Haskell, Rebecca, c/o, Maine,
94, #627

Haskell, Susannah, Maine, 124,
#431

Haskell, Susannah, Maine, 129,
#6388

Haskew, John, S.C., 66, #10047

Haskins, Ann, e/o, N.C., 89,
#18211

Hasse, Alexander, g/o c/o, D.C.,
130, #7651

Hast, George, —, 120, #6543,
card

Hastings, Benjamin, e/o, N.H.,
119, #5637

Hastings, Nancy, Mass., 70,
#12024

Hastings, E. P., PA, Detroit,
Mich., 119, #5606

Hasty Sr., James, N.C., 75,
#13636

Hasty, Rebecca, a/o, Ky., 100,
#4279

Hatch, Alexander, N.C., 11,
#1008

Hatch, Alexandria, N.C., 113,
#1668, card

Hatch, Bethiah, Boston, Mass.,
99, #3465

Hatch, Jane, Augusta, Maine,
139, #8956

Hatch, Jeremiah, Ill., 105,
#8060

Hatch, Jeremiah, Ill., 106,
#8597

Hatch, Jeremiah, Ill., 108,
#10150
Hatch, Jeremiah, Ill., 108,
#10279
Hatch, Lewis, Albany, N.Y., 75,
#13691
Hatch, Lewis, c/o, Albany, N.Y.,
103, #7081
Hatch, Silvanus, Maine, 74,
#13037
Hatcher, Amasa, w/o, Albany,
N.Y., 104, #7625
Hatcher, Henry, Ky., 122,
#8774, slip
Hatcher, Henry, a/o, Ky., 11,
#8774
Hatcher, John, w/o, Richmond,
Va., 11, #5313
Hatchett, Edward, Richmond,
Va., 57, #7439
Hatchett, Edward, Va., 47, #4904
Hatchett, Edward, Va., 73,
#12759
Hatfield, Ann, Philadelphia, Pa.,
103, #6948
Hatfield, Lydia C., Philadelphia,
Pa., 114, #1994
Hatfield, William H., a/o,
Philadelphia, Pa., 129,
#6525
Hathaway, Ann, a/o, Vt., 120,
#6628
Hathaway, Charlotte, a/o, R.I.,
132, #9369
Hathaway, Richard, w/o,
Pittsburgh, Pa., 43, #3849
Hathaway, Tryphena, c/o, Mass.,
74, #13173
Hathaway, Typhena, Mass., 75,
#13628
Hathway, Zenas, e/o, Albany,
N.Y., 87, #17415

Hatton, Basil, Md., 78, #14270
Hauck, George M., Richmond,
Va., 64, #9258
Hauck, George W., Richmond,
Va., 51, #5927
Hause, Private George, w/o, 17th
Inf, 68, #10694
Haven, Joel, Cincinnati, Ohio,
105, #7851
Havens, Nathaniel, Albany,
N.Y., 107, #9247
Havens, Peter, a/o, Mich., 82,
#15346
Havis, Elizabeth, S.C., 114,
#2318
Hawes, David, Mass., 43, #3823
Hawes, Ezekiel, Miss., 69,
#10906
Hawes, Ezekiel, w/o, Miss., 115,
#2920
Hawes, Zenas, Conn., 32, #214
Hawk, Isaac, Va., 97, #2070,
card
Hawk, Isaac, c/o, Richmond,
Va., 11, #2070
Hawkes, Elijah, w/o, Pittsburgh,
Pa., 124, #839
Hawkins, Christopher, Albany,
N.Y., 100, #4308
Hawkins, David, Albany, N.Y.,
53, #6358
Hawkins, Ebenezer, Mich., 42,
#3568
Hawkins, Hamilton S., c/o,
Baltimore, Md., 118, #5038
Hawkins, Henry, Ky., 62, #8768
Hawkins, Henry, Ky., 80,
#14984
Hawkins, Isaac, Conn., 32, #622
Hawkins, James, Knoxville,
Tenn., 11, #1843

Hawkins, James, Knoxville,
Tenn., 53, #6413
Hawkins, Nancy, Philadelphia,
Pa., 95, #1134
Hawkins, Robert, Ill., 138,
#4761
Hawkins, Robert, Richmond,
Va., 106, #8693
Hawkins, Robert, Va., 123,
#9319
Hawkins, Sarah, N.Y., 90,
#18881
Hawkins, Thomas, Philadelphia,
Pa., 75, #13715
Hawkins, Uriah, c/o, Albany,
N.Y., 73, #12959
Hawkins, William, Richmond,
Va., 56, #7428
Hawkins, William, Richmond,
Va., 47, #4990
Hawkins (now Draper), Anna A.,
Baltimore, Md., 113, #1535
Hawks, Reuben, w/o, Vt., 88,
#17750
Hawley, Anna, Conn., 32, #14
Hawley, Chapman, Mich., 75,
#13501, card
Hawley, Chapman, w/o, Mich.,
11, #13501
Hawley, Daniel, Miss., 91,
#18985
Hawley, Mary E., Conn., 32,
#294
Haws, Benjamin, w/o, Mass.,
97, #1997
Hay, Thomas, —, 102, #6172,
slip
Hay, Thomas, Ky., 65, #9872
Hay, Thomas, e/o, Ky., 12,
#6172
Hayden, George W., Albany,
N.Y., 110, #43

Hayden, George W., Albany,
N.Y., 122, #8346
Hayden, Samuel, w/o,
Pittsburgh, Pa., 74, #13307
Haydon, John, w/o, Pittsburgh,
Pa., 46, #4801
Hayes, Benajah, Albany, N.Y.,
41, #3359
Hayes, Ezekiel, Conn., 32, #777
Hayes, James, c/o, Concord,
N.H., 47, #4908
Hayes, John, S.C., 77, #13963
Hayes, John, S.C., 80, #14800
Hayes, Sarah, a/o, Ga., 127,
#4170
Hayes, Seth, Conn., 32, #92
Hayes, Thomas, —, 80, #14788,
card
Hayes, Thomas, —, 82, #15277,
slip
Hayman, Pvt. Stephen, w/o, Va.
Milita, 115, #2811
Haynes, James, e/o, Knoxville,
Tenn., 111, #393
Haynes, John, w/o, Ky., 98,
#2892
Haynes, Margire, e/o, Albany,
N.Y., 117, #4083
Haynes, Rueben, c/o, Boston,
Mass., 89, #18363
Haynes, Sophia, Philadelphia,
Pa., 83, #15746
Haynes, Sophia, Philadelphia,
Pa., 54, #6678
Haynie, Ann, a/o, Tenn., 109,
#10668
Hays, David, c/o, N.C., 88,
#17906
Hays, Elizabeth, Ill., 133, #122
Hays, John H., w/o, Md., 54,
#6850

Hays, Peter, Indianapolis, Ind., 136, #3344
Hays, Samuel, Richmond, Va., 57, #7505
Hays, Samuel, Richmond, Va., 47, #4990
Hays, Samuel, Va., 67, #10420
Hays, Samuel, Va., 82, #15322
Hays, Samuel, Va., 84, #16077
Hays, Samuel, w/o, Richmond, Va., 101, #5122
Hays, Teresa, a/o, Md., 134, #1504
Hays, William, c/o, Knoxville, Tenn., 49, #5440
Hays, William N., g/o c/o, Little Rock, Ark., 128, #5302
Hayward, Margaret, Albany, N.Y., 122, #8448
Hayward, Ruth, Bellows Falls, Vt., 44, #4268
Hayward, Ruth, a/o, Vt., 90, #18626
Hayward, Samuel, w/o, Montpelier, Vt., 103, #6481
Hayward, Simeon, e/o, Albany, N.Y., 133, #323
Haywood, Amity, c/o, Vt., 60, #8218
Haywood, George C., c/o, Tuscaloosa, Ala., 123, #9388
Haywood, Josiah, w/o, New York City, 98, #2973
Haywood, Margaret, Albany, N.Y., 122, #8335
Haywood, Susannah, e/o, Maine, 110, #11183
Haywood, Thomas H., Ohio, 122, #8406

Hazeltine, Abigail, Boston, Mass., 122, #8830
Hazelton, Solomon, Albany, N.Y., 72, #12611
Hazen, Jacob, c/o, Maine, 95, #1234
Hazlegrove, Tabitha, Richmond, Va., 133, #580
Hazlegrove, Tabitha, Richmond, Va., 133, #581
Hazlewood, Nancy, Ky., 141, #3020
Head, Druzilla, c/o, Portsmouth, N.H., 134, #785
Head, Elizabeth, Miss., 117, #4238
Head, Mehatable, Albany, N.Y., 127, #4040
Headman, Maria R., Philadelphia, Pa., 131, #8260
Heal, R. P., Ky., 142, #5628
Heal, Robert P., Ky., 87, #17477
Heal, Robert P., Ky., 130, #7398
Heal, Robert P., La., 81, #15077
Heald, Oliver, w/o, Maine, 84, #16313
Healey, Mary, a/o, R.I., 108, #10179
Healey, Thomas, St. Louis, Mo., 138, #6282
Healy, mary, R.I., 43, #3853
Hearsey, William, a/o, Boston, Mass., 65, #9784
Heath, Benjamin, w/o, N.H., 111, #616, card
Heath, Benjamin W., Richmond, Va., 135, #1842
Heath, Daniel, w/o, Concord, N.H., 115, #2753

Heath, David, Md., 116, #3619
Heath, David, Mich., 142, #3565
Heath, Dolly, c/o, Portsmouth, N.H., 12, #616
Heath, Isaac, Maine, 46, #4653
Heath, Maria M., a/o, Augusta, Maine, 142, #5637
Heath, Patience, e/o, Albany, N.Y., 121, #6698
Heath, Samuel C., w/o, Albany, N.Y., 45, #4618
Heatherly, James, Rouge River War, 137, #4012, #forage
Heaton, Nathaniel, a/o, Conn., 38, #F1826
Hebard, Bushnell, Conn., 32, #457
Hebard, Jabez, Conn., 32, #224
Hebbard, Mary, Cincinnati, Ohio, 137, #4416
Hebbard, Mary, c/o, Cincinnati, Ohio, 139, #7161
Hebbard, Ozias, w/o, Cincinnati, Ohio, 118, #4616
Hebert, Angelique, Albany, N.Y., 95, #1235
Hechar, Massy, Pittsburgh, Pa., 80, #14908
Hecock, Aaron, a/o, Conn., 83, #15596
Heddleson, William, Cincinnati, Ohio, 116, #3687
Hedger, Thomas, Ky., 68, #10617
Hedger, William, w/o, New York City, 40, #3290
Hedrick, James, w/o, Madison, Ind., 137, #4511
Heer, Alexander, New York City, 98, #2628

Hefflebower, Jacob, Pa., 68, #10644
Hefflebower, Jacob, Philadelphia, Pa., 81, #15209
Hefflebower, Jacob, Philadelphia, Pa., 39, #2983
Heileman, Julius F., w/o, —, 42, #3803
Heileman, Lt. Col. Julius F., w/o, —, 64, #9564
Heileman, Lt. Col. Julius F., w/o, —, 75, #13661
Heimberger, Gustavus, La., 114, #2243
Helm, Lina T., a/o, Ill., 75, #13544
Helm, Peleg, a/o, Albany, N.Y., 114, #2180
Helmbrighs, Henry, w/o, Albany, N.Y., 127, #4407
Helme, Niles, a/o, Albany, N.Y., 79, #14569
Helmer, John G., a/o, Albany, N.Y., 110, #61
Hemenway, Hepzibah, c/o, Boston, Mass., 102, #5834
Hendee, Caleb, a/o, Conn., 32, #10496
Henderson, Anna M., a/o, D.C., 136, #2740
Henderson, Daniel, c/o, N.H., 87, #17731
Henderson, David, e/o, Richmond, Va., 116, #3421
Henderson, Jemima, Ind., 12, #7321
Henderson, Jemima, Ind., 127, #4732, slip

Henderson, Jemima, c/o,
Indianapolis, Ind., 12,
#4732
Henderson, John, Ind., 52,
#6322
Henderson, John, Ind., 64,
#9215
Henderson, John, w/o, Ind., 104,
#7321, card
Henderson, Meshack, Knoxville,
Tenn., 42, #3700
Henderson, Nancy, Ky., 140,
#213
Henderson, Robert, Ga., 58,
#7825, card
Henderson, Robert, w/o, Ga., 12,
#7825
Hendley, E. J. C., c/o,
Cincinnati, Ohio, 123,
#9027
Hendley, Penite, Mo., 133, #318
Hendrick, Abijah, c/o, Mass.,
77, #14077
Hendrick, Coe, Conn., 32, #434
Hendricks, Abijah, c/o, Mass.,
74, #13285
Hendricks, Hillary, Natchez,
Miss., 78, #14486
Hendricks, Hillory, Huntsville,
Ala., 64, #9156
Hendricks, Hillory, Mich., 87,
#17719
Hendricks, Hillory, Miss., 84,
#16132
Hendrickson, William,
Pittsburgh, Pa., 40, #3281
Hendrix, Nathaniel, Ill., 44,
#4277
Hendry, Nathaniel, Ill., 49,
#5390
Hennis, Benjamin, Ky., 112,
#1064

Henry, Elizabeth, a/o,
Knoxville, Tenn., 12,
#4679
Henry, Hugh, Nashville, Tenn.,
120, #5907, card
Henry, Hugh, e/o, Nashville,
Tenn., 12, #5907
Henry, John, Pittsburgh, Pa.,
82, #15370, card
Henry, John, Pittsburgh, Pa.,
72, #12670
Henry, John, w/o, Pittsburgh,
Pa., 12, #15370
Henry, Malcolm, Mo., 81,
#15197
Henry, Mary, New Albany, Ind.,
105, #8076
Henry, Moses, Va., 75, #13558
Henry, Peter, w/o, Philadelphia,
Pa., 79, #14748
Henry, William, Richmond, Va.,
12, #12579
Henry, William, Richmond, Va.,
56, #7301
Henson, Elizabeth, Ky., 143,
#6160
Henson Sr., Jesse, w/o, Ky., 99,
#3285
Heradnicks, Hillory, Huntsville,
Ala., 59, #8172
Herbert, Josiah, c/o, Ky., 124,
#624
Herbert, Josiah, c/o, Ky., 124,
#625
Herbert, Thomas, a/o, Va. State
Navy, 119, #5249
Hereford, John, Richmond, Va.,
71, #12432
Hereford, John, Richmond, Va.,
52, #6156
Herick, Betsey, a/o, Mass., 139,
#8351

Herndon, William, Richmond,
Va., 98, #2798
Herod, William, Nashville,
Tenn., 45, #4565, card
Herod, William, c/o, Nashville,
Tenn., 12, #4565
Heron, William, Richmond, Va.,
47, #4901
Herrick, Alice, a/o, Albany,
N.Y., 107, #9559
Herrick, Ephraim, —, 101,
#5235, card
Herrick, Ephraim, Albany, N.Y.,
12, #5235
Herrick, Jonathan, Albany,
N.Y., 78, #14349
Herring, Christian, Philadelphia,
Pa., 44, #4230
Herring, James, a/o, Va., 111,
#784
Herring, Jesse, w/o, Ga., 79,
#14588
Herring, Judy, Va., 111, #785
Herring, Katherine, c/o, Conn.,
32, #5325
Herrington, John, Philadelphia,
Pa., 113, #1716
Herron, John, Philadelphia, Pa.,
140, #447
Herth, Catherine, D.C., 127,
#4786
Herth, Catherine, D.C., 133,
#161
Hess, Barbara, c/o, Philadelphia,
Pa., 114, #1995
Hess, Daneil, a/o, Albany, N.Y.,
89, #18250
Hesse (now Selgecke), Anna C.,
D.C., 122, #8598
Hester, Abraham, c/o, S.C., 98,
#2921

Hester, Thomas J., Ky., 127,
#4946
Hetfield, Stephen, w/o,
Philadelphia, Pa., 113,
#1817
Hewes, William, Ill., 103,
#7086
Hewes, William, Vt., 54, #6842
Hewes, William, Vt., 62, #8741
Hewes, William G., PA, New
Orleans, La., 61, #8402
Hewett, Andrew, e/o, Vt., 118,
#4896
Hewit, Hannah, c/o, Albany,
N.Y., 64, #9426
Hewit, Hannah, c/o, Albany,
N.Y., 64, #9586
Hewitt, Experience, c/o, Albany,
N.Y., 59, #8066
Hewitt, John, Richmond, Va.,
96, #1423
Hewitt, Margaret, c/o,
Richmond, Va., 129, #6697
Hewitt, Robert A., Mo., 111,
#329
Heyshaw, David, w/o, Wheeling,
Va., 46, #4724
Hibbard, Mary, Cincinnati,
Ohio, 135, #2066
Hibbard, William, Conn., 32, #-
Hickman, —, —, 92, #19871,
slip
Hickman, Edwin, N.C., 60,
#8243
Hickman, Edwin, N.C., 81,
#15099
Hickman, Elizabeth, Mo., 111,
#718
Hickman, Elizabeth, Mo., 129,
#7097
Hickman, James, Ky., 56, #7380

Hickman, Joel, e/o, Ky., 118,
  #4939
Hickman, Judith, Nashville,
  Tenn., 111, #683
Hickman, Samuel, N.C., 94,
  #721, card
Hickman, Samuel, N.C., 12,
  #721
Hickman, William, Mo., 77,
  #14182, card
Hickock, Amos, g/o c/o, Conn.,
  37, #F1820
Hickox, James, Conn., 32, #538
Hicks, Abraham, w/o, R.I., 60,
  #8331
Hicks, Jesse, S.C., 51, #6046
Hicks, Jesse, S.C., 99, #3616
Hicks, Jesse, w/o, S.C., 127,
  #4727
Hicks, John, a/o, Miss., 88,
  #18046
Hicks, John, w/o, Wheeling,
  Va., 58, #7869
Hicks, Mary, Fayetteville, N.C.,
  131, #8187
Hicks, Mary, a/o, Fayetteville,
  N.C., 137, #4526
Hicks, Solomon, Ky., 42, #3613
Hicks, Theodore E., Ill., 132,
  #9032
Hicks, Theodore E., Ill., 132,
  #9742
Hicks, U. E., W.T. Vols., 139,
  #8063
Hiem, John, c/o, Philadelphia,
  Pa., 121, #7239
Hiem, John, g/o c/o,
  Philadelphia, Pa., 132,
  #9616
Higbee, Abigail, a/o,
  Burlington, Vt., 124,
  #1035

Higdon, Philip, Ga., 56, #7305
Higdon, Philip, Huntsville, Ala.,
  64, #9398
Higer, Sarah, a/o, Ky., 123,
  #9114
Higgins, Hannah, New York
  City, 113, #1342
Higgins, Hannah, New York
  City, 123, #9592
Higgins, James, New York City,
  124, #1510
Higgins, Jane, c/o, Albany,
  N.Y., 86, #17166
Higgins, Lt. Thaddeus, w/o, 4th
  Inf., 101, #4704
Higgins, Lt. Thaddeus, w/o, 4th
  Inf. Peace Estab., 96, #1868
Higgins, Lt. Thadeus, w/o, 4th
  Inf., 102, #5394
Higgins, Thaddeus, w/o, 4th Inf.,
  100, #3864
Higgins, William, Cincinnati,
  Ohio, 118, #4809
Higgins, William, Cincinnati,
  Ohio, 130, #7328
Higgs, Moore, w/o, N.C.
  Militia, 95, #1238
High, Gardner, w/o, N.C., 51,
  #5884
High, Rachel, —, 98, #2841,
  card
High, Rachel, c/o, N.C., 12,
  #2841
Highey, Brewster, Ohio, 54,
  #6809
Highley, Brewster, Ohio, 80,
  #14840
Highsmith, Moses, N.C., 108,
  bet. #10204 & #10220, card
Hight, George, w/o, Richmond,
  Va., 43, #3964

Hight, Lovia, c/o, Richmond, Va., 97, #2126
Hight, Mathew, Richmond, Va., 12, #5682
Hight, Mathew, Va., 78, #14455
Hight, Thomas, Ind., 54, #6645
Hight, Thomas, Ind., 71, #12371
Hightower, Joshua, Ky., 140, #1090
Hilburn, John, Ga., 91, #19319
Hilburn, Margaret, N.C., 127, #4543
Hilburn Sr., John, Ga., 74, #13056
Hildebrand, Jacobine, D.C., 138, #6433
Hildebrand, Jacobine, D.C., 140, #896
Hildebrand, Jacobine, New York City, 122, #8269
Hildebrand, Jacobine, New York City, 126, #3873
Hildebrand, Jacobine, New York City, 131, #8279
Hildebrandt, Jacobine, New York City, 115, #2985
Hildreth, Sarah, a/o, New York City, 142, #4730
Hiles, Amos, La., 104, #7322
Hiles, Amos, La., 106, #8353
Hiles, Amos, La., 113, #1778
Hiles, Amos, La., 124, #432
Hiles, John, Ky., 55, #6996
Hiles, John, Ky., 116, #3620
Hill, Abner, Conn., 32, #608
Hill, Abram, Mo., 64, #9180
Hill, Abram, Mo., 71, #12270
Hill, Abram, Mo., 79, #14571
Hill, Alpheus, Albany, N.Y., 43, #3858
Hill, Ann, a/o, Ky., 123, #339

Hill, Daniel, a/o, Albany, N.Y., 120, #6689
Hill, Ebenezer, Conn., 32, #570
Hill, Elizabeth, Mo., 128, #5783
Hill, Elizabeth, c/o, Mo., 137, #3666
Hill, Ephraim P., Boston, Mass., 140, #9840
Hill, Esther, a/o, Boston, Mass., 99, #3334
Hill, Frederick, a/o, Ky., 12, #6578
Hill, Jonas, s/o, Nashville, Tenn., 74, #13286
Hill, Joseph, Ohio, 78, #14535
Hill, Joseph, Ohio, 81, #15072
Hill, Lewis, R.I., 85, #16371
Hill, Nancy, a/o, Ga., 99, #3294
Hill, Priscilla, c/o, Fayetteville, N.C., 131, #8282
Hill, Reuben, N.C., 46, #4808
Hill, Rhoda, e/o, Philadelphia, Pa., 64, #9393
Hill, Robt., c/o, Albany, N.Y., 53, #6561
Hill, Rosilla, Concord, N.H., 71, #12282
Hill, Sarah, c/o, Boston, Mass., 104, #7233
Hill, Thomas, w/o, Mo., 116, #3086
Hill, William, Richmond, Va., 86, #16883, card
Hill, William, c/o, Richmond, Va., 12, #16883
Hill, Paris, PA, Providence, R.I., 118, #4992
Hillan, James, e/o, Richmond, Va., 100, #3964
Hillard, David, c/o, Albany, N.Y., 110, #215

Hoagland, Richard, c/o, N.J., 12, #3521

Hoak, Margaret, c/o, Albany, N.Y., 94, #660

Hoar, Charity, c/o, Mass., 114, #2103

Hoavenburg, E. J. H. V., New York City, 55, #7066

Hoban, Joseph, D.C., 111, #607

Hobart, Jeremiah, N.H., 87, #17291

Hobbs, Susannah, Richmond, Va., 36A, #F6 V7

Hobbs, Thomas, Knoxville, Tenn., 121, #7702, card

Hock, John H., Ind., 122, #8596

Hodge, Nancy, c/o, S.C., 109, #10398

Hodgeman, Sibel, c/o, Mass., 95, #838

Hodges, Christopher, w/o, Albany, N.Y., 87, #17449

Hodges, Daniel, w/o, Albany, N.Y., 132, #9033

Hodges, Marcus A., Nashville, Tenn., 137, #4612

Hodges, Nathaniel, Mass., 82, #15290

Hodges, Philemon, a/o, Ga., 125, #1953

Hodges, William, Mass., 74, #13177

Hodges, William, S.C., 62, #8694

Hodgins, Lucius, w/o, Ill., 123, #286

Hodgkins, Nathaniel, Conn., 33, #458

Hodgman, Eunice, a/o, Montpelier, Vt., 109, #10414

Hodgskins, John, a/o, Concord, N.H., 119, #5374

Hoeranbrough, Eggo T. H. V., New York City, 76, #13887

Hoff, George, Cincinnati, Ohio, 143, #6154

Hoffman, Martin, N.C., 52, #6261

Hoffmine, Samuel, c/o, Ohio, 55, #7061

Hoffner, Martin, N.C., 70, #11152

Hoffner, Martin, N.C., 71, #12425

Hofman, Henry, w/o, Md., 54, #6797

Hofstaler, George, Huntsville, Ala., 57, #7555

Hogan, James, w/o, D.C., 125, #1624

Hogan, John B., Mobile, Ala., 75, #13593

Hogan, William, c/o, S.C., 111, #356

Hogan, William, g/o c/o, Ill., 128, #5281

Hogeboom, John, Albany, N.Y., 68, #10703

Hogeland, James, Richmond, Va., 110, #279, card

Hogg, James, g/o c/o, Richmond, Va., 125, #1705

Hogg, Patty, N.C., 103, #6720

Hogue, Samuel A., Ill., 12, #946

Holbrook, Abigail, a/o, N.H., 108, #10011

Holbrook, John, c/o, Mass., 83, #15911

Holbrook, Sarah, c/o, Mass., 48, #5049

Holcomb, Apollus, w/o, Albany, N.Y., 107, #9226

Holcomb, Elizabeth, Albany,
N.Y., 73, #12773
Holcomb, Ezekiel, w/o, Albany,
N.Y., 44, #4322
Holcomb, Peter, c/o, Conn., 53,
#6448
Holcomb, Sarah, c/o, Cleveland,
Ohio, 132, #9081
Holcomb, Sherwood, Ga., 79,
#14619
Holcomb, Sherwood, w/o, Ga.,
97, #1956
Holcomb, Timothy, Conn., 33,
#10507
Holden, Jemima, Montpelier,
Vt., 101, #5006 V#15
Holden, John, Maine, 109,
#10746, card
Holden, John, c/o, Maine, 12,
#10746
Holder, Daniel, w/o, S.C., 94,
#249
Holiday, Horace S., Ill., 55,
#6997
Holland, Charles, Mobile, Ala.,
59, #7956
Holland, Charles, Tuscaloosa,
Ala., 85, #16521
Holland, Henry, c/o, Ga., 119,
#5534
Holland, Jacob, Tuscaloosa,
Ala., 88, #17791
Holland, Mary, c/o, Md., 95,
#995
Holland, Meredith, a/o w/o, Va.
Milita, 94, #515
Holland, Park, c/o, Maine, 111,
#781
Holland, Theodocia, Ky., 64,
#9184
Holland, William, E. Tenn., 62,
#8760

Hollenbeck, Jacob, w/o, New
York City, 43, #3955
Holley, Nathan, c/o, Albany,
N.Y., 46, #4712
Holliday, Benjamin, c/o, Tenn.,
54, #6666
Holliday, Benjamin, c/o, Tenn.,
54, #6667
Holliday, Benjamin, c/o, Tenn.,
54, #6668
Holliday, George, Ky., 12,
#5819, card
Hollingshead, Sarah, e/o,
Pittsburgh, Pa., 124, #489
Hollingsworth, Henry, N.C., 52,
#6344
Hollis, William, Mobile, Ala.,
79, #14661
Hollister, Hope, Albany, N.Y.,
77, #14091
Holloway, George, Ky., 50,
#5819, card
Holloway, Mary, Maine, 115,
#2922, card
Holloway, Mary, c/o, Maine, 11,
#2922
Hollowell, Miles, w/o, Ky., 101,
#5010
Holly, Osborn, w/o, N.C., 103,
#6812
Holman, Isaac, Ind., 70, #12170
Holman, Isaac, Ind., 103,
#6758, card
Holman, Isaac, New Albany,
Ind., 69, #10873
Holman, Isaac, w/o, New
Albany, Ind., 12, #6758
Holman, John, Albany, N.Y.,
43, #3861
Holman, Lilles, Ind., 12, #3157
Holman, Lilles, Indianapolis,
Ind., 139, #8260

Holman, Lilles, New Albany,
Ind., 128, #5113
Holman, Lilles, New Albany,
Ind., 134, #1407
Holman, Lt. J. H., Exp. & Topl.
Recon., 137, #4019
Holme, William, R.I., 142,
#5168
Holmes, Abigail, Conn., 33,
#100
Holmes, Abijah, c/o, N.Y., 86,
#16783
Holmes, Betsy, c/o, Albany,
N.Y., 104, #7160
Holmes, Ebenezer, Conn., 33,
#233
Holmes, Edward F., c/o, Albany,
N.Y., 56, #7340
Holmes, Elias M., Ill., 138,
#6125
Holmes, Jedediah, w/o,
Pittsburgh, Pa., 74, #13273
Holmes, John, w/o, New York
City, 64, #9596
Holmes, Louisa J., Ga., 118,
#4934
Holmes, Asst. Surg. R. S.,
special payment, 92,
#19869
Holmes, Samuel, w/o, Albany,
N.Y., 50, #5597
Holmes, Seth, w/o, Albany,
N.Y., 120, #6413
Holms, Robert, e/o, Mass., 125,
#2803
Holsonbake, Mary, c/o, S.C.,
132, #9104, card
Holt, Anna, c/o, Conn., 94,
#563
Holt, Charles, Huntsville, Ala.,
57, #7557

Holt, Claiborn, c/o, S.C., 110,
#292
Holt, Elizabeth, Montpelier, Vt.,
101, #5006 V#14
Holt, George, N.C., 54, #6861
Holt, George, N.C., 85, #16695
Holt, Lydia, c/o, Mass., 44,
#4324
Holt, Mary, Mass., 83, #15618
Holt, Mary Ann, Indianapolis,
Ind., 143, #7345
Holt, Shadrach, c/o, Tenn., 116,
#3686
Holt, Thomas, Pittsburgh, Pa.,
58, #7826
Holts, Catherine, Cincinnati,
Ohio, 139, #6827
Holzmuler, Ottilia, Philadelphia,
Pa., 116, #3385 [in
German]
Hombeck, Abraham, w/o, Ind.,
84, #15960
Homsher, Adam, c/o,
Philadelphia, Pa., 141,
#3087
Honea, Tobias, w/o, Ga., 73,
#12839
Honeywell, Eratus, c/o,
Cleveland, Ohio, 141,
#3021
Hood, Enoch, w/o, Albany,
N.Y., 104, #7357
Hood, John, Ky., 57, #7589
Hood, John, a/o, Albany, N.Y.,
104, #7422
Hood, Thomas, w/o, Nashville,
Tenn., 110, #299
Hook, Mary, Richmond, Va., 72,
#12567
Hook, Mary, Richmond, Va.,
114, #2393, card

Hook, Mary, Richmond, Va., 95, #1049

Hook, Mary, Richmond, Va., 100, #4390

Hook, Mary, a/o, Richmond, Va., 12, #2393

Hook, William, Va., 72, #12563, card

Hook, William, w/o, Richmond, Va., 12, #12563

Hooker, Israel, c/o, Albany, N.Y., 102, #5935

Hooker, James G., Jackson, Tenn., 67, #10442

Hooker, Jurusha, g/o, N.C., 72, #12714

Hooker, William, Mass., 133, #656

Hooper, Elizabeth, a/o, Ga., 72, #12519

Hooper, James, w/o, Savannah, Ga., 12, #5460

Hooper, Jesse, c/o, W. Tenn., 63, #9038

Hooten, Elijah, a/o, Nashville, Tenn., 94, #272

Hooton, Elijah, W. Tenn., 68, #10746

Hoover, Ann Barbara, Nashville, Tenn., 124, #815

Hoover, Henry, Nashville, Tenn., 73, #12870

Hoover, John M., w/o, Nashville, Tenn., 112, #871

Hoover, Michael, Richmond, Va., 48, #5138

Hoover, Michael, Va., 57, #7644

Hoover, William P., Ohio, 44, #4348

Hoover, William P., Ohio, 49, #5265

Hoover, William P., Ohio, 100, #4058

Hope, John, Richmond, Va., 60, #8340

Hope, John, Richmond, Va., 64, #9446

Hope, John, Va., 86, #16799

Hopkins, Isaac, Ga., 120, #6412, card

Hopkins, Isaac, Ga., 96, #1884

Hopkins, Isaac, c/o, Ga., 12, #6412

Hopkins, Joseph, New York City, 125, #2128

Hopkins, Joseph, New York City, 127, #4961

Hopkins, Joseph, New York City, 138, #6591

Hopkins, Joseph, w/o, New York City, 141, #1483

Hopkins, Phebe, c/o, Ohio, 73, #12889

Hopkins, Richard, R.I., 60, #8191, card

Hopkins, Richard, c/o, Providence, R.I., 12, #8191

Hopkins, Robert, w/o, Albany, N.Y., 52, #6259

Hopkins, Theophilus, w/o, Maine, 60, #8283

Hopkins, Thomas, S.C., 76, #13756

Hopping, Harriett D., a/o, Albany, N.Y., 120, #6332

Hopps, Adam, N.C., 64, #9441

Horkinson, Josiah, a/o, Ohio, 113, #1556

Hormam, Gideon, Mich., 57, #7628

Horn, Amanda, D.C., 126, #3076
Horn, Edward, Nashville, Tenn., 115, #2455
Horn, Joseph, Ohio, 69, #10998
Horn, Joseph, e/o, Ohio, 77, #14127
Horn, William, Ky., 141, #2910
Horn (or Horan), Eleanor, Richmond, Va., 138, #4811
Horn (or Horan), Eleanor, Md., 125, #2823
Hornbeck, Peter, c/o, N.Y., 79, #14610
Hornbeck, Samuel, Ky., 47, #5003
Hornbeck, Samuel, c/o, Albany, N.Y., 110, #11041
Hornell, John, w/o, Va., 86, #16821
Horrell, Martha, Richmond, Va., 66, #10136
Horsham, Joel, w/o, Boston, Mass., 119, #5421
Hortman, Christiana, a/o, Wheeling, Va., 12, #1129
Horton, Abigail, Maine, 117, #3948
Horton, Daniel, c/o, Jonesboro, Tenn., 64, #9400
Horton, George, w/o, 24th Inf, 49, #5358
Horton, Hepsibeth, a/o, Albany, N.Y., 95, #1225
Horton, John, w/o, Jonesboro, Tenn., 92, #19966
Horton, Thomas, —, 80, #14966, card
Horton, Thomas, w/o, Decatur, Ind., 12, #16966
Hortwick, Dorotha, N.J., 83, #15919

Hosford, Joseph, Albany, N.Y., 116, #3070
Hosier, John, Albany, N.Y., 115, #2957, card
Hosier, John, c/o, Albany, N.Y., 12, #2957
Hoskins, Charles, subsistance, 110, #10950, slip
Hoskins, Lt. Charles, w/o, 4th Inf., 103, #6523
Hoskins, Lt. Charles, w/o, 4th Inf., 104, #7275
Hoskins, Lt. Charles, w/o, 4th Inf., 105, #8201
Hoskins, Lt. Charles, w/o, 4th Inf., 107, #9027
Hoskins, Lt. Charles, w/o, 4th Inf., 108, #10060
Hoskins, Lt. Charles, w/o, 4th Inf., 109, #10885
Hoskins, Lt. Charles, w/o, 4th Inf., 111, #486
Hoskins, Lt. Charles, w/o, 4th Inf., 100, #4392
Hoskins, Lt. Charles, w/o, 4th Inf., 100, #4540
Hoskins, Kesiah, cons/o, Conn., 103, #6570
Hosley, Sampson, a/o, Albany, N.Y., 136, #3229
Hostetter, Urich, —, 69, #10916, card
Hosty Sr., James, N.C., 67, #10450
Hotchkiss, Lydia, g/o c/o, Conn., 37, #F1820
Hotchkiss, Ruth, Conn., 33, #223
Hotchkiss, Ruth, c/o, Conn., 68, #10720
Houck, George M., Richmond, Va., 48, #5211

Hough, John, N.C., 90, #18855
Hough, John, w/o, Fayetteville,
    N.C., 100, #4107
Hough, Martin, N.C., 45, #4540
Hough, William, Ohio, 43,
    #3909
Houghey, William, w/o, —, 45,
    #4473
Houghton, Abijah, N.H., 46,
    #4656, card
Houghton, Abijah, Portsmouth,
    N.H., 12, #4656
Houghton, Annah, a/o,
    Pittsburgh, Pa., 120, #6060
Houghton, Mary, Albany, N.Y.,
    12, #2069
Houghton, Mary, Albany, N.Y.,
    135, #2069, card
Houghton, Mary, c/o, Albany,
    N.Y., 135, #2176
Houghton, Polly, N.Y., 131,
    #8759, card
Houghton, Polly, h/o, Mass.,
    12, #8759
Houghton, Sibbell, Bellows
    Falls, Vt., 75, #13647
Houghton, Simeon, w/o,
    Albany, N.Y., 44, #4243
Hourick, David, w/o, Ohio, 90,
    #18839
House, Anna, comm/o, Albany,
    N.Y., 131, #8165
House, Catharine, c/o, Albany,
    N.Y., 13, #803
House, Nicholas, w/o, Albany,
    N.Y., 112, #803, card
Houser, Andrew, S.C., 64, #9318
Houser, Andrew, S.C., 70,
    #12171
Houser, Andrew, S.C., 79,
    #14680

Houser, Ludwick, Pittsburgh,
    Pa., 41, #3438
Houston, Asenath, e/o,
    Fayetteville, N.C., 115,
    #2474
Houston, Conrad, Ind., 142,
    #4199, card
Houston, James, N.C., 40,
    #3318
Houston, John, c/o, Cincinnati,
    Ohio, 13, #2628
Houston, Leonard, Ind., 57,
    #7614
Houston, Leonard, w/o, Ind., 13,
    #4199
Houston, Mary, Ga., 96, #1629
Houston, Purnell, a/o,
    Richmond, Va., 135, #1919
Houston, Samuel, Nashville,
    Tenn., 88, #17818
Houston, Samuel, Nashville,
    Tenn., 94, #391
Houston, Wiliam, Jonesboro,
    Tenn., 63, #8877
Houston, William, Jonesboro,
    Tenn., 47, #5023
Hovey, William, w/o, Ohio, 51,
    #6079
Howard, Adam, c/o, Bellows
    Falls, Vt., 13, #5183
Howard, Bathsheba, a/o, Albany,
    N.Y., 66, #10306
Howard, Benjamin, Conn., 33,
    #240
Howard, Brooks, Mich., 56,
    #7244
Howard, Claiborn, N.C., 94,
    #518
Howard, Clarissa, a/o, Iowa,
    122, #8088
Howard, Edward, Albany, N.Y.,
    60, #8217

Howard, Edward, Albany, N.Y.,
79, #14705
Howard, Edward, Albany, N.Y.,
52, #6145
Howard, Eunice, Mass., 95, #946
Howard, G. T., claim, 132,
#9808
Howard, George F., a/o, Ga.,
131, #8862
Howard, Hardy, N.C., 57, #7590
Howard, Isabella, Ky., 102,
#5805
Howard, James, Ky., 13, #3386
Howard, James, Va., 67, #10443
Howard, James, Va., 86, #16822
Howard, Jeremiah, Concord,
N.H., 47, #5033
Howard, John, c/o, Ky., 117,
#4118
Howard, John, w/o, Knoxville,
Tenn., 113, #1478
Howard, John D., w/o, Mass.,
85, #16532
Howard, Jonathan, c/o, 9th Inf.,
59, #8115
Howard, Jonathan, c/o, 9th Inf.,
59, #8116
Howard, Jonathan, w/o, 9th Inf.,
56, #7326
Howard, Joseph, Albany, N.Y.,
51, #6013
Howard, Joshua, c/o, Concord,
N.H., 61, #8448
Howard, Oliver, Burlington, Vt.,
47, #4940
Howard, Oliver, Madison, Ind.,
137, #4477
Howard, Samuel, Maine, 87,
#17293, card
Howard, Samuel, a/o, Maine, 13,
#17293

Howard, Thomas, w/o, Ky., 117,
#3883
Howard, William, N.C., 56,
#7282
Howe, Daniel, Pittsburgh, Pa.,
41, #3357
Howe, George, Ore., 140, #446
Howe, Noah, Detroit, Mich.,
143, #6074
Howe, Peter, Ohio, 71, #12450
Howe, Solomon, a/o,
Burlington, Vt., 110,
#11026
Howe, Thomas M., PA,
Pittsburgh, Pa., 104, #7469
Howell, Charles, c/o, Richmond,
Va., 123, #267
Howell, Edward, Conn., 33,
#733
Howell, Hopkins, a/o, Ga., 87,
#17435
Howell, Hopkins, c/o, Ga., 73,
#12829
Howell, John, N.C., 53, #6414
Howell, Martha, Va., 85,
#16588
Howell, Samuel, Ohio, 43,
#3967
Howell, Samuel, Ohio, 62,
#8687
Howell (formerly Lockwood),
Phebe G., Ind., 112, #1108
Howland, Abraham, Maine, 96,
#1836
Howland, Isaac, w/o, Albany,
N.Y., 79, #14597
Howland, Joseph, Albany, N.Y.,
59, #8017
Howland, Lydia, c/o, Boston,
Mass., 53, #6525
Howry, John, w/o, —, 131,
#8778

Howser, George W., Mo., 127,
#4812
Hoyer, Jacob, c/o, Philadelphia,
Pa., 137, #3988
Hoyer, Maria A., Cincinnati,
Ohio, 113, #1637
Hoyer, Maria A., Ohio, 112,
#865
Hoyt, Eleazer, Conn., 47, #4857
Hoyt, Elijah, Conn., 33, #110
Hoyt, Elizabeth, c/o, —, 107,
#8968
Hoyt, Jesse, Conn., 33, #623
Hoyt, John, Conn., 33, #487
Hoyt, Jonathan, Bellows Falls,
Vt., 50, #5562
Hoyt, Jonathan, Vt., 55, #6981
Hoyt, Jonathan, Vt., 73, #12881
Hoyt, Merriam, c/o, Concord,
N.H., 102, #5984
Hoyt, Richard, a/o, Portsmouth,
N.H., 115, #3016
Hoyt, Thomas, Bellows Falls,
Vt., 63, #8967
Hubbard, Abner, Albany, N.Y.,
111, #571
Hubbard, George, c/o, N.H., 79,
#14621
Hubbard, Henry, New York City,
69, #10883
Hubbard, Israel, Pittsburgh, Pa.,
56, #7229
Hubbard, Jonathan, Maine, 98,
#3144
Hubbard, Joseph, Richmond,
Va., 44, #4356
Hubbard, Joseph, Richmond,
Va., 45, #4554
Hubbard, Joseph, Va., 65,
#10011
Hubbard, Joseph, Va., 90,
#18563

Hubbard, Mary, Vt., 78, #14330
Hubbard, Peter, Ill., 62, #8698
Hubbard, Sarah, a/o, Maine, 136,
#3419
Hubbark, Roswell, g/o c/o,
Conn., 37, #F1824
Hubbell, Abijah, Ohio, 71,
#12454
Hubbell, Abijah, Ohio, 72,
#12618
Hubbell, Abijah, w/o, Ohio, 82,
#15524
Hubbell, Betsy, Cincinnati,
Ohio, 131, #8721
Hubbell, David, a/o, Conn., 38,
#F1820
Hubbell, Lucy, c/o, Conn., 85,
#16711
Hubbs, John, Ky., 13, #4899
Hubbs, John, Ky., 13, #14340
Hubbs, John, Ky., 71, #12471
Huber, Christian, Philadelphia,
Pa., 75, #13483
Huber, Christian, Philadelphia,
Pa., 54, #6907
Huber, Comfort, c/o,
Philadelphia, Pa., 75,
#13487
Huddleston, Bethia L.,
Nashville, Tenn., 112,
#1236
Huddleston, Creed I., c/o,
Nashville, Tenn., 130,
#7235
Hudgins, Elizabeth, Ky., 13,
#3813
Hudgins, H. H., c/o, Mo., 13,
#2700
Hudnall, Frances M., Richmond,
Va., 136, #2866
Hudnall, John, Richmond, Va.,
60, #8319

Hudnall, John, Va., 80, #14849
Hudnall, John, w/o, Richmond,
    Va., 97, #1936
Hudson, Brooks, Vt., 60, #8330
Hudson, Charles, Va., 72,
    #12574
Hudson, Charles, a/o, Richmond,
    Va., 99, #3544
Hudson, Merit W., c/o, Ill., 130,
    #7813
Hudson, Thomas, Va., 75,
    #13679
Huey, Jefferson, w/o, Ill., 123,
    #9240
Huey, Lewis, Ky., 53, #6505
Huff, Ann, Albany, N.Y., 123,
    #9880
Huff, Isaac, w/o, N.J., 77,
    #14082
Huff, Jacob, c/o, Philadelphia,
    Pa., 130, #7611
Huff, Peter, Kans., 139, #8560
Huff, Stephen, S.C., 85, #16519
Huffman, Daniel, c/o, Albany,
    N.Y., 60, #8274
Huffman, Lucretia, S.C., 98,
    #2546
Huffman, William, w/o, Albany,
    N.Y., 87, #17656
Hufstutler (formerly Croomes),
    Emily, Ill., 113, #1525
Hugget, Mildred, Richmond, Va.,
    42, #3634
Huggins, Robert, Albany, N.Y.,
    42, #3669
Huggins, Samuel, c/o, S.C., 129,
    #6869
Hughes, Benjamin, w/o,
    Nashville, Tenn., 55,
    #7149
Hughes, Esther, Ky., 84, #16319

Hughes, Francis, Jonesboro,
    Tenn., 60, #8173
Hughes, Francis, Jonesboro,
    Tenn., 63, #9001
Hughes, Francis, c/o, Jonesboro,
    Tenn., 78, #14487
Hughes, George W., Ark., 111,
    #516
Hughes, George W., Ark., 112,
    #1240
Hughes, Hannha, a/o, N.C., 118,
    #5108
Hughes, Jessee, c/o, Va., 46,
    #4747
Hughes, John, Ky., 77, #14215
Hughes, Margaret, c/o,
    Philadelphia, Pa., 60,
    #8209
Hughes, Spotswood H., g/o c/o,
    Richmond, Va., 130, #8048
Hughey, Asst. Surg. William,
    w/o, —, 79, #14701
Hughey, Asst. Surg. William,
    w/o, —, 85, #16509
Hughey, Asst. Surg. Willison,
    w/o, —, 83, #15701
Hughey, Asst. Surg. Willison,
    w/o, —, 56, #7312
Hughey, Asst. Surg. Willison,
    w/o, —, 70, #12196
Hughey, Asst. Surg. Willison,
    w/o, —, 75, #13553
Hughey, Asst. Surgeon William,
    w/o, —, 65, #10035
Hughey, Asst. Surgeon Willison,
    w/o, —, 61, #8505
Hughy, Wilson, w/o, —, 51,
    #5995
Hulbert, Daniel, c/o, N.H., 51,
    #5961
Hule (formerly Wimp), Mary,
    Ky., 126, #2939

Hulet, Set, c/o, Albany, N.Y.,
44, #4288
Hulett, Charles, c/o, Richmond,
Va., 106, #8834
Hulett, Nehemiah, Albany, N.Y.,
70, #12175
Hulett, Nehemiah, Albany, N.Y.,
52, #6208
Hulick, Mary, a/o, Ohio, 13,
#595
Huling, Andrew, Va., 85,
#16342
Huling, Andrew, a/o, Richmond,
Va., 91, #19516
Huling, John, a/o, Burlington,
Vt., 137, #4144
Hull, George, Richmond, Va.,
39, #3014
Hull, George, Richmond, Va.,
51, #5955
Hull, Isham, Richmond, Va., 54,
#6701
Hull, James, c/o, N.J., 60,
#8228
Hull, John, 19th Inf., 88,
#17966
Hull, Zephaniah, w/o, Conn.,
101, #4750
Hulse, Mathias, N.J., 104,
#7462
Hulse, Matthias, w/o, N.J., 13,
#7462
Hummele, John George,
Philadelphia, Pa., 45,
#4607
Humphrey, Abraham, Hartford,
Conn., 54, #6804
Humphrey, Amos, w/o, Albany,
N.Y., 61, #8462
Humphrey, David, w/o, —, 61,
#8526, card

Humphrey, David, w/o, S.C., 13,
#8526
Humphrey, Ebenezer, a/o, Ind.,
86, #16806
Humphrey, Edwin C., Albany,
N.Y., 114, #2020
Humphrey, George, c/o, Ind., 13,
#5689
Humphrey, James, c/o, Albany,
N.Y., 78, #14443
Humphrey, Merrit, Ky., 129,
#6822, card
Humphrey, Merrit, a/o, Ky., 13,
#6822
Humphrey, Prudence, c/o, Conn.,
63, #8958
Humphrey, Sally, Albany, N.Y.,
89, #18255
Humphreys, John, Jonesboro,
Tenn., 135, #2449
Humphreys, Richard, g/o c/o,
Cincinnati, Ohio, 132,
#9771
Humphreys, AAQM, MSK F. C.,
Charleston Arsenal, S.C.,
137, #4020
Humphries, George, —, 119,
#5689, card
Humphries, John, Jonesboro,
Tenn., 126, #3692
Humphries, Joseph, c/o, Ohio,
109, #10412
Hundley, Joseph, Va., 80,
#14930
Hungerford, John P., e/o, Va.,
108, #9868
Hunsucker, Ann, Mo., 124, #779
Hunt, Abijah, —, 94, #562, card
Hunt, Abijah, —, 112, #1014,
card
Hunt, Abijah, Albany, N.Y., 13,
#1014

Hunt, Abijah, Albany, N.Y., 13,
#562
Hunt, Abraham, Ky., 98, #2885
Hunt, Ann, Philadelphia, Pa.,
56, #7319
Hunt, Anna, Concord, N.H., 83,
#15566
Hunt, Ebenezer, w/o, Mass., 58,
#7914
Hunt, Esli, S.C., 41, #3556
Hunt, Hannah, a/o, Albany,
N.Y., 124, #1206
Hunt, Hannah, a/o, Ohio, 113,
#1726
Hunt, Jedediah, Albany, N.Y.,
51, #5914
Hunt, Jedediah, Detroit, Mich.,
50, #5775
Hunt, John, c/o, Mass., 125,
#2264
Hunt, Richard, w/o, Ky., 49,
#5259
Hunt, Russell, Conn., 33, #499
Hunt, Seth, w/o, Vt., 88, #17920
Hunt, Wheeler D., La., 119,
#5222
Hunt, William, g/o c/o, Iowa,
127, #4184
Hunt, William, g/o c/o, Iowa,
127, #4185
Hunt, William, g/o c/o, Iowa,
133, #331
Hunt, Winnefred, a/o, Ky., 103,
#6797
Hunter, Ann, a/o, Ky., 98,
#2984
Hunter, Franics, Richmond, Va.,
67, #10360
Hunter, Hannah, Ky., 116,
#3061
Hunter, Jacob, w/o, Ky., 129,
#6549

Hunter, John, Philadelphia, Pa.,
58, #7749
Hunter, John, Philadelphia, Pa.,
73, #12761
Hunter, John, w/o, Ky., 45,
#4639
Hunter, Mary, e/o, Montpelier,
Vt., 101, #5194
Hunter, Ruth, a/o, Ky., 137,
#3839
Hunter, Samuel, w/o, Nashville,
Tenn., 43, #3859
Hunter, Sarah, Albany, N.Y.,
126, #3560
Huntington, Andrew, w/o,
Albany, N.Y., 98, #2557
Huntington, Azariah, Conn., 33,
#252
Huntington, Christopher, w/o,
Philadelphia, Pa., 122,
#8522
Huntington, Hezekiah, a/o,
Conn., 134, #1124
Huntington, John, w/o, Albany,
N.Y., 69, #11023
Huntington, Susannah, c/o,
Albany, N.Y., 98, #2859
Huntley, Ezekial, Conn., 33,
#433
Huntley, George W., a/o, Mich.,
109, #10645
Huntley, Hoel, c/o, Conn., 33,
#17684
Huntley, Reuben, Albany, N.Y.,
46, #4730
Huntoon, Susannah, Concord,
N.H., 91, #19137
Huntoon, William, Mich., 105,
#8349
Hunully, Robert, Ky., 116,
#3045

Hurd, David, a/o, Conn., 38,
#F1829
Hurdle, Lawrence, w/o, D.C.,
107, #9689
Hurlbert, Elizabeth, Albany,
N.Y., 68, #10635
Hurlburt, Eunice, Conn., 33, #23
Hurlburt, Eunice, c/o, Hartford,
Conn., 60, #8320
Hurst, Henry, Ky., 107, #9560,
card
Hurst, Henry, a/o, Ky., 13,
#9560
Huse, Louisa, Montpelier, Vt.,
117, #3893
Huske, John, PA, Fayetteville,
N.C., 105, #7762
Huske, John, PA, Fayetteville,
N.C., 105, #7796
Hustead, Robert, w/o,
Philadelphia, Pa., 50,
#5793
Husted, Ruth, a/o, N.J., 111,
#621
Huston, Daniel, Pittsburgh, Pa.,
39, #3090
Hutchins, Mary, Cleveland,
Ohio, 133, #422
Hutchins, Moses, —, 117,
#4076, card
Hutchinson, Cornelius,
Pittsburgh, Pa., 107,
#9692, card
Hutchinson, Cornelius, a/o,
Pittsburgh, Pa., 13, #9692
Hutchinson, Eleazer, Conn., 33,
#463
Hutchinson, Israel, c/o, Mass.,
41, #3517
Hutchinson, Joseph, Ky., 60,
#8343

Hutchinson, Joseph, w/o, Ky.,
80, #14993
Hutchinson, Mary, Philadelphia,
Pa., 71, #12253
Hutchinson, Philip, Ill., 127,
#4717
Hutchinson, Thompson, Act of 3
Feb 1853, 114, #2341
Hutchinson, William, a/o,
Philadelphia, Pa., 89,
#18383
Hutchison, David, Mo., 77,
#14062
Hutchison, David, Mo., 80,
#14964
Hutchison (formerly Fortner),
Anne, Philadelphia, Pa.,
130, #7332
Hutton, James, a/o,
Philadelphia, Pa., 131,
#8298
Huyek, William, Philadelphia,
Pa., 81, #15032
Hyatt, Josinah, Cincinnati,
Ohio, 125, #1871
Hyde, Catharine, a/o, Mass., 95,
#920
Hyde, Irvin, Nashville, Tenn.,
39, #2987
Hyde, Joel, Conn., 33, #459
Hyde, Joshua, w/o, Boston,
Mass., 13, #9102
Hylton, William, La., 126,
#3434
Hyre, Elizabeth, a/o, Wheeling,
Va., 114, #2149

I

Iams, John Frederick, w/o,
Knoxville, Tenn., 13,
#9448

Ice, Andrew, Madison, Ind., 57, #7616

Ice, Andrew, e/o, Ind., 13, #9972

Ice, Andrew, Madison, Ind., 108, between #9967 and #9974, card

Ichle, Conrad, Philadelphia, Pa., 136, #3007

Ide, Joseph, a/o, R.I., 67, #10342

Iden, John, Ohio, 87, #17591

Idol, Jacob, N.C., 66, #10311

Imlay, Isaac, c/o, N.J., 85, #16397

Ingalls, Abigail, a/o, Albany, N.Y., 122, #8928

Ingalls, Caleb, a/o, Albany, N.Y., 121, #7805

Ingalls, Joseph H., Windsor, Vt., 41, #3511

Inge, Lt. Zebulon M. P., w/o, 2nd Dragoons, 103, #6656

Inge, Lt. Zebulon M. P., w/o, 2nd Dragoons, 101, #4874

Inge, Lt. Zebulon P., w/o, 2nd Dragoons, 106, #8391

Inge, Lt. Zeubelon M. P., w/o, 2nd Inf., 110, #11044

Inge, Zebulon M. P., w/o, 2nd Dragoons, 99, #3437

Ingersoll, Justis, w/o, Mich., 123, #9138

Inglett, John, g/o c/o, Ill., 130, #7584

Ingraham, Amos, c/o, Albany, N.Y., 67, #10536

Ingraham, James, w/o, Conn., 33, #324

Ingram, Andrew, Ind., 103, #6691, card

Ingram, Edwin, —, 92, #19973, card

Ingram, Edwin, Fayetteville, N.C., 13, #19975

Ingram, Nancy, Richmond, Va., 36A, #F6, card

Ingram, Seth, Burlington, Vt., 106, #8420

Ingram, Seth, Burlington, Vt., 73, #12913

Ingram, Seth, Portsmouth, Vt., 102, #5820

Ingram, Seth, Vt., 82, #15471

Inglis, William, c/o, Md., 135, #____

Inman, Rufus, Ohio, 13, #8531

Inscoe, William, Va., 46, #4699

Inscoe, William, Va., 66, #10172

Inscole, William, Va., 75, #13598

Iran, William, w/o, Fayetteville, N.C., 92, #19535

Irby, David, Richmond, Va., 98, #2540

Irby, Douglas, Richmond, Va., 67, #10359

Irby, Douglas, Va., 77, #14148

Irby, Douglas, Va., 77, #14200

Irby, Douglas, c/o, Richmond, Va., 131, #8755

Irby, Douglas, c/o, Richmond, Va., 132, #9490

Irwin, Ann, Ga., 127, #4408

Irwin, Ann, Ga., 128, #5966

Irwin, James, Ohio, 60, #8351

Irwin, 1st Lt. Douglas, w/o, 3rd Inf., 100, #4425

Irvin, Lt. Douglas S., w/o, 3rd Inf., 104, #7264

Irwin, Lt. Douglas S., w/o, 3rd Inf., 105, #8190

Irwin, Lt. Douglas S., w/o, 3rd Inf., 99, #3641

Irwin, Lt. Douglas S., w/o, 3rd
Inf., 101, #5366
Irwin, Lt. Douglas S., w/o, 3rd
Inf., 103, #6496
Irwin, Lt. Douglas S., w/o, 3rd
Inf., 111, #401
Irwin, Lt. Douglas S., w/o, 3rd
Inf., 109, #10884
Irwin, Lt. Douglas S., w/o, 3rd
Inf., 107, #9032
Irwin, Lt. Durglass S., w/o, 3rd
Inf., 108, #10038
Irvin, James, N.C., 73, #12790
Irvin, James, w/o, N.C., 104,
#7218
Irvin (formerly McConnell),
Mary, Pittsburgh, Pa., 124,
#1191
Irvine (or Irwin), John,
Richmond, Va., 45, #4488
Irving, P. M., New York City,
115, #2495
Isabel, Polly, Ky., 142, #3832
Isaman, Michael, Pittsburgh,
Pa., 41, #3508
Isbel, Joel, w/o, Mich., 55,
#7088
Iseman, Christian, a/o,
Pittsburgh, Pa., 106, #8622
Isenhart, Margaret, Cleveland,
Ohio, 143, #6971
Isham, George I., c/o, Ohio, 99,
#3158
Isick, Abraham, N.C., 43, #3960
Israel, John, c/o, New York City,
105, #8262
Ives, Amos, Albany, N.Y., 83,
#15723, card
Ives, Amos, c/o, Albany, N.Y.,
13, #15727
Ives, John P., N.C., 44, #4381

J

Jack, James, Philadelphia, Pa.,
78, #14537
Jack, James, Pittsburgh, Pa., 55,
#7147
Jack, Matthews, c/o, Pittsburgh,
Pa., 97, #2132
Jack, Nancy, Pittsburgh, Pa.,
111, #363
Jackson, Alexander, Ohio, 82,
#15517
Jackson, Catherine, Richmond,
Va., 36A, #F6, card
Jackson, Churchwell, Knoxville,
Tenn., 40, #3227
Jackson, Daniel, Conn., 33, #8
Jackson, Elizabeth, Jackson,
Tenn., 127, #4286
Jackson, Elizabeth, Jackson,
Tenn., 128, #5709
Jackson, Elizabeth, c/o, Ky., 13,
#945
Jackson, Isaac, Pittsburgh, Pa. &
Ohio, 117, #4406
Jackson, Isaac, c/o, Pittsburgh,
Pa., 13, #4406
Jackson, James, Richmond, Va.,
107, #8944
Jackson, John, Cincinnati,
Ohio, 138, #5024
Jackson, Joseph, e/o,
Portsmouth, Maine, 134,
#973
Jackson, Joseph, w/o, Albany,
N.Y., 44, #4380
Jackson, Judith, Fayetteville,
N.C., 105, #7762 V#3
Jackson, Martha, a/o,
Portsmouth, N.H., 74,
#13340

Jackson, Martha A., Ga., 130, #7356

Jackson, Martha Ann, Ga., 126, #3077

Jackson, Rebecca, c/o, Mass., 68, #10661

Jackson, Robert, a/o, New York City, 142, #3903

Jackson, Samuel, w/o, Knoxville, Tenn., 95, #945, card

Jackson, Thomas, La., 59, #7985

Jackson, Thomas, La., 69, #10946

Jackson, William, Nashville, Tenn., 69, #10888

Jackson, William, Nashville, Tenn., 72, #12571

Jackson, William, Va., 68, #10663

Jackson, William, w/o, Richmond, Va., 52, #6179

Jackson (now Diggers), Mary, Ga., 120, #5876

Jacob, Lewis, Mich., 113, #1521

Jacobs, David, Mo., 126, #2918

Jacobs, Elizabeth, Philadelphia, Pa., 95, #947

Jacobs, Ezekiel, Conn., 33, #312

Jacobs, Zachariah, N.C., 58, #7769

Jacobson, Isaac, Albany, N.Y., 134, #1654

Jacques, Hope, c/o, Albany, N.Y., 103, #6571

James, David, Mo., 128, #5470

James, Elizabeth, c/o, R.I., 65, #9818

James, Henry, g/o c/o, Nashville, Tenn., 131, #8414

James, Henry, g/o c/o, Nashville, Tenn., 133, #645

James, Isaac, Va., 70, #12082

James, Jesse, g/o c/o, Madison, Ind., 139, #8506

James, John, w/o, New York City, 13, #4488

James, Jonathen, Mo., 53, #6416

James, Martha, Ga., 136, #2867

James, Mary, Richmond, Va., 137, #4573

James, Mary, a/o, Richmond, Va., 36A, #F5 V4

James, Rhoda, a/o, Albany, N.Y., 95, #989

James, Thomas, Ind., 55, #6923

James, William, Philadelphia, Pa., 39, #2924

Jameson, John, Md., 53, #6359

Jameson, John, Knoxville, Tenn., 48, #5229

Jameson, John, Ky., 96, #1497, card

Jameson, John, a/o, Ky., 13, #1497

Jameson, John, w/o, Knoxville, Tenn., 62, #8845

Jameson, Margaret, Albany, N.Y., 96, #1720

Jameson, Margaret, Albany, N.Y., 96, #1851

Jameson, Robert, Mo., 81, #15027

Jamieson, Joseph, S.C., 41, #3397

Jamieson, Joseph, S.C., 56, #7275

Jamieson, Margaret, Richmond, Va., 98, #2969

Jamieson, Margaret, a/o, Richmond, Va., 111, #629

Jamieson, Nancy, a/o, Albany, N.Y., 109, #10683

Jamison, John, c/o, Pittsburgh, Pa., 73, #12917

Jamison, Margaret, Albany, N.Y., 76, #13903

Jamison, Robert, Mo., 58, #7850

Jamsen, Matthew H., w/o, Albany, N.Y., 44, #4400

Janes, Lonson, Albany, N.Y., 129, #6538

Jared, Joseph, Nashville, Tenn., 80, #14890

Jared, Joseph, Nashville, Tenn., 95, #1050

Jarman, Betsey, Conn., 114, #2222

Jarrell, Nancy, a/o, Richmond, Va., 107, #9397

Jarvis, Drusilla, a/o, S.C., 13, #466

Ja[rvis], Elisha, w/o, S.C., 111, #466, card

Jarvis, Mary, a/o, Ky., 139, #9327

Jean, Philip, N.C., 46, #4694

Jee, Andrew, Ind., 66, #10180

Jefferies, William, Ky., 92, #19658

Jeffers, Allen, Knoxville, Tenn., 50, #5777

Jeffers, Allen, Knoxville, Tenn., 44, #4316

Jeffers, Allen, c/o, Knoxville, Tenn., 63, #8892

Jeffers, Jacob, w/o, Md., 99, #3328

Jefferson, William, e/o, 15th Inf., 83, #15738

Jeffres, William, w/o, Ky., 116, #3809

Jeffries, Alexander, Richmond, Va., 72, #12482

Jeffries, Gowin, Ind., 80, #14909, card

Jeffries, Gowin, c/o, Ind., 13, #14909

Jeffries, Paul C., PA, Ottumwa, Iowa, 118, #5102

Jemson, Judith, Bellows Falls, Vt., 75, #13647

Jencks, Susannah, Albany, N.Y., 74, #13244

Jencks, Susannah, Albany, N.Y., 98, #3076

Jenison, Joseph B., c/o, Albany, N.Y., 59, #8096

Jenison, Levi, Concord, N.H., 58, #7741

Jenkins, Charles, a/o, N.C., 111, #644

Jenkins, Jiney, Madison, Ind., 114, #2056

Jenkins, John, Ga., 72, #12544

Jenkins, Joseph, c/o, Albany, N.Y., 100, #3934

Jenkins, Nathaniel, c/o, Albany, N.Y., 88, #17810

Jenkins, Samuel, Albany, N.Y., 70, #11115, card

Jenkins, Thomas, Wisc., 113, #1341

Jenkins (or John Tinker), Lemuel, —, 81, #15091, card

Jenks, Jacob, Pittsburgh, Pa., 115, #2872, card

Jenks, Jacob, c/o, Pittsburgh, Pa., 13, #2872

Jenks, Thomas, c/o, N.C., 41,
#3558
Jenness, Temperance, a/o,
Montpelier, Vt., 104,
#7594
Jennings, Aaron, Conn., 62,
#8695
Jennings, Edmond, w/o,
Nashville, Tenn., 13,
#17952
Jennings, Edmund, W. Tenn.,
88, #17952, card
Jennings, Epiphalet, Conn., 33,
#515
Jennings, James, N.C., 79,
#14631
Jennings, Justus, a/o, Albany,
N.Y., 107, #9195
Jennings, Noah, Albany, N.Y.,
64, #9300
Jennings, Royal, E. Tenn., 85,
#16430, card
Jepherson, Mary, a/o, Boston,
Mass., 142, #3522
Jerry, Josiah, Ky., 40, #3169
Jessup, George, Albany, N.Y.,
133, #64
Jeter, James, S.C., 50, #5634
Jeter, James, w/o, S.C., 63,
#9021
Jewell, Elisha, w/o, D.C., 50,
#5489
Jewell, Ephriam, Pittsburgh, Pa.,
39, #2929
Jewell, Mildred, Richmond, Va.,
61, #8635
Jewell, Mildred, c/o, Richmond,
Va., 99, #3344
Jewell, William, c/o, Jonesboro,
Tenn., 125, #2480
Jewett, Caleb, a/o, Conn., 38,
#F1820

Jewett, Ezekiel, Albany, N.Y.,
107, #9688
Jewett, Joseph M., Pittsburgh,
Pa., 96, #1523
Jewett, Samuel, w/o,
Portsmouth, N.H., 69,
#10841
Jewitt, Joseph, w/o, Mass., 105,
#7769
Jewts, William, g/o c/o, Albany,
N.Y., 124, #1004
Job, Robert, Pa., 40, #3289
Jobe, Ira B., Springfield, Ill.,
116, #3195
Jobe, Sarah, Mo., 131, #8079
John, Elizabeth, c/o, Pittsburgh,
Pa., 128, #5679
John, Lt. Thomas, 2d U.S. Inf.,
123, #1--, card, Col. 7th
Mass. Inf.
Johns, William, w/o, Md., 143,
#7865
Johns (formerly Tierney),
Catharine, Albany, N.Y.,
115, #2887
Johnson, Abner, Nashville,
Tenn., 78, #14292
Johnson, Abner, Nashville,
Tenn., 40, #3268
Johnson, Abraham, c/o, Ga.,
120, #5996
Johnson, Abraham, c/o, Ga.,
120, #6219
Johnson, Absalom, a/o, Ky.,
123, #295
Johnson, Benjamin, c/o, N.J.,
90, #18947
Johnson, Benjamin, w/o,
Richmond, Va., 57, #7472
Johnson, Caleb, Mich., 61,
#8487

Johnson, Caleb, Mich., 64,
#9595
Johnson, Caleb, Miss., 87,
#17412
Johnson, Calvin, Bellows Falls,
Vt., 63, #8967
Johnson, Dalmath, w/o, Ky., 70,
#11125
Johnson, Dianah, Albany, N.Y.,
13, #7767
Johnson, Dianah, Albany, N.Y.,
105, #7767, slip
Johnson, Drusilla, Burlington,
Vt., 126, #3348
Johnson, Elijah, e/o, S.C., 119,
#5361
Johnson, Elisha, Bellows Falls,
Vt., 63, #8967
Johnson, Eliza, Philadelphia,
Pa., 126, #3441
Johnson, Eliza, Philadelphia,
Pa., 142, #3833
Johnson, Elizabeth, c/o,
Albany, N.Y., 53, #6454
Johnson, Elizabeth, c/o, New
York City, 118, #4856
Johnson, Ellis, w/o, S.C., 112,
#1120
Johnson, Enos, h/o, Conn., 33,
#328
Johnson, Esther, Richmond,
Va., 95, #1360
Johnson, Esther, Richmond,
Va., 96, #1801
Johnson, Evi, Conn., 33, #799
Johnson, Franklin, Mo., 110,
#10992
Johnson, Franklin, Mo., 113,
#1305
Johnson, Franklin, Mo., 137,
#4120

Johnson, George W., Mo., 131,
#8417
Johnson, Grace, a/o, Albany,
N.Y., 87, #17733
Johnson, Hannah, c/o, Augusta,
Maine, 106, #8730
Johnson, Harvey, Burlington,
Vt., 42, #3764
Johnson, Henry, Albany, N.Y.,
39, #3078
Johnson, Hezekiah, Albany,
N.Y., 106, #8388
Johnson, Howell, S.C., 68,
#10667
Johnson, Howell, w/o, S.C.,
116, #3466
Johnson, Isaac, w/o, Conn., 33,
#782
Johnson, Isaiah, c/o, Albany,
N.Y., 79, #14620
Johnson, James, c/o, N.J., 114,
#2051
Johnson, James, w/o, Ashville,
N.C., 116, #3788
Johnson, James H., Albany,
N.Y., 142, #3971, card
Johnson, James H., w/o,
Albany, N.Y., 13, #3971
Johnson, Jesse, a/o, Nashville,
Tenn., 87, #17442
Johnson, Jesse, w/o, Iowa, 129,
#6539
Johnson, Pvt. John, N.Y.
Milita, 114, #2347 pay due
Johnson, Johnson, w/o, Albany,
N.Y., 100, #3813
Johnson, Joseph, Ga., 66,
#10092
Johnson, Joseph, c/o, Ga., 104,
#7350
Johnson, Joseph, c/o, Ga., 105,
#7954

Johnson, Joseph, c/o, Ga., 107, #9564

Johnson, Joseph, c/o, Ga., 97, #2339

Johnson, Joseph, c/o, Ga., 98, #2963

Johnson, Joseph, c/o, Philadelphia, Pa., 13, #19426

Johnson, Justus, Albany, N.Y., 40, #3271

Johnson, Justus, Albany, N.Y., 49, #5311

Johnson, Lucney, c/o, Albany, N.Y., 83, #15779

Johnson, Luther, c/o, Albany, N.Y., 64, #9287

Johnson, Morris S., Evansville, Ind., 114, #2438

Johnson, Moses, w/o, Concord, N.H., 46, #4651

Johnson, Nancy, a/o, S.C., 112, #973

Johnson, Obadiah, Richmond, Va., 46, #4719

Johnson, Obadiah, w/o, Va., 85, #16589

Johnson, Peter, N.J., 51, #5896

Johnson, Peter, w/o, Richmond, Va., 101, #5109

Johnson, Polly, Concord, N.H., 109, #10519

Johnson, Rebecca, a/o, Mass., 130, #7898

Johnson, Richard, w/o, Mass., 50, #5639

Johnson, Richard M., D.C., 57, #7649

Johnson, Robert, Cananadaigua, N.Y., 143, #7324

Johnson, Robert, w/o, Jonesboro, Tenn., 90, #18753

Johnson, Sally, c/o, Portsmouth, N.H., 116, #3353

Johnson, Samuel, −, 13, #17813, card

Johnson, Samuel, Montpelier, Vt., 88, #17813, card

Johnson, Sarah, a/o, Ga., 65, #9794

Johnson, Solomon, Miss., 45, #4588

Johnson, Solomon, Miss., 55, #6955

Johnson, Solomon, Miss., 59, #7975

Johnson, Stephen, c/o, Mass., 106, #8457

Johnson, Thomas, Knoxville, Tenn., 121, #7398

Johnson, Timothy, N.H., 86, #16981

Johnson, Timothy, c/o, Albany, N.Y., 54, #6662

Johnson, Uriah, Ohio, 46, #4826

Johnson, Uriah, Ohio, 75, #13502

Johnson, William, E. Fla., 83, #15670

Johnson, William, Ga., 42, #3688

Johnson, William, Pa., 87, #17428, card

Johnson, William, Philadelphia, Pa., 66, #10096

Johnson, William, a/o, Albany, N.Y., 91, #19259

Johnson, William, a/o w/o, Ky., 103, #6667

Johnson, William, c/o, Albany, N.Y., 118, #4897

Johnson, William, c/o, N.J., 115, #2701

Johnson, William, c/o, S.C., 13, #12614

Johnson, William, w/o, Philadelphia, Pa., 13, #17428

Johnson, William, w/o, Philadelphia, Pa., 74, #13049

Johnson, William, w/o, Philadelphia, Pa., 80, #14768

Johnson Sr., William, a/o, Ky., 95, #1089

Johnston, Archibald, Ky., 47, #4879

Johnston, Archibald, Ky., 65, #9745

Johnston, Clabourn, Mo., 57, #7504

Johnston, Clabourn, w/o, Mo., 72, #12514

Johnston, James, a/o, Ky., 128, #4983

Johnston, Solomon, Miss., 49, #5340

Johnston, Solomon, Miss., 61, #8663

Johnston, Samuel, SpC, (Rations), 99, #3311

Jomes, Susanna, Tenn., 119, #5216

Jones, Aaron, Md., 102, #6086, card

Jones, Aaron, a/o, Md., 14, #6086

Jones, Abigal, Concord, N.H., 61, #8512

Jones, Abner, N.C., 60, #8275

Jones, Amorella, Richmond, Va., 112, #1237

Jones, Amos, w/o, Mass., 44, #4217

Jones, Azubak, Mass., 95, #960

Jones, Benjamin, Albany, N.Y., 73, #12772, card

Jones, Benjamin, c/o, Philadelphia, Pa., 134, #1274

Jones, Benjamin, w/o, Albany, N.Y., 14, #12772

Jones, Catharine, Va., 99, #3721, card

Jones, Catherine, Richmond, Va., 66, #10251

Jones, Catherine, Richmond, Va., 79, #14566

Jones, Catherine, a/o, Richmond, Va., 14, #3721

Jones, Charlotte, Ga., 131, #8898

Jones, Cornelius, New York City, 77, #14037, card

Jones, Cornelius, w/o, Richmond, Va., 14, #14037

Jones, Cracker, c/o, Ohio, 65, #9884

Jones, Daniel, Jonesboro, Tenn., 128, #5498, card

Jones, Daniel, Knoxville, Tenn., 14, #5498

Jones, Darling, w/o, Jonesboro, Tenn., 114, #2360

Jones, Elisha, c/o, N.C., 70, #11145

Jones, Elizabeth, Richmond, Va., 124, #1195

Jones, Fances, c/o, Richmond, Va., 97, #2141

Jones, Frances, Richmond, Va., 63, #9994

Jones, Gray, Richmond, Va.,
103, #7063
Jones, Gray, Richmond, Va., 98,
#2949
Jones, Gray, Richmond, Va., 51,
#5919
Jones, Gray, Va., 75, #13618
Jones, Harrison, Ga., 59, #7974
Jones, Harrison, Ga., 67,
#10372
Jones, Harrison, Ga., 76,
#13821
Jones, Harrison, w/o, Ga., 13,
#13821
Jones, Henry, w/o, Richmond,
Va., 54, #6724
Jones, Isaac, Ga., 49, #5274
Jones, Jacob, S.C., 126, #3039,
card
Jones, James, Ky., 80, #14888
Jones, James, Richmond, Va.,
55, #7198
Jones, James, Richmond, Va.,
51, #5927
Jones, James, Va., 84, #16078
Jones, James, e/o, Richmond,
Va., 108, #10244
Jones, Jason, w/o, Md., 49,
#5320
Jones, Jeremiah, S.C., 54,
#6599
Jones, Jesse, a/o, N.C., 102,
#5862
Jones, John, Albany, N.Y., 39,
#3061
Jones, John, Huntsville, Ala.,
86, #17014
Jones, John, Ky., 46, #4746,
card
Jones, John, Maine, 39, #3126
Jones, John, N.C., 80, #14889

Jones, John, Philadelphia, Pa.,
134, #1340
Jones, John, Richmond, Va., 66,
#10271
Jones, John, S.C., 48, #5081
Jones, John, S.C., 48, #5160
Jones, John, S.C., 54, #6847
Jones, John, S.C., 77, #14145
Jones, John, a/o, Nashville,
Tenn., 80, #14799
Jones, John, c/o, Richmond,
Va., 46, #4737
Jones, John, w/o, Nashville,
Tenn., 137, #4384
Jones, Jonathan, Philadelphia,
Pa., 89, #18257
Jones, Joseph, Conn., 33, #784
Jones, Joshua, Wheeling, Va.,
82, #15504
Jones, Josiah, Fla., 91, #19500
Jones, Lavina, Richmond, Va.,
14, #3220
Jones, Magdalina, Spingfield,
Ill., 141, #1895
Jones, Mary, Knoxville, Tenn.,
96, #1630
Jones, Mary, Knoxville, Tenn.,
98, #2692
Jones, Milly, Richmond, Va.,
60, #8210
Jones, Milly, a/o, Ga., 14,
#9038
Jones, Richard, w/o, Pulaski,
Tenn., 58, #7936
Jones, Sally, Mo., 128, #5147
Jones, Sally, Mo., 133, #9967
Jones, Samuel, S.C., 61, #8508
Jones, Samuel, c/o, Albany,
N.Y., 65, #9836
Jones, Samuel, w/o, Albany,
N.Y., 119, #5135

Jones, Samuel, w/o, New York
City, 116, #3272
Jones, Sarah, Wheeling, Va.,
128, #5488
Jones, Sarah, a/o, Wheeling,
Va., 137, #4508
Jones, Silas, w/o, Pittsburgh,
Pa., 83, #15565
Jones, Simeon, g/o c/o,
Cleveland, Ohio, 135,
#1988
Jones, Stephen, Ky., 47, #4887
Jones, Stephen, g/o c/o, Miss.,
129, #6757
Jones, Stephen F., Mass., 143,
#6751
Jones, Susannah, Jonesboro,
Tenn., 111, #561
Jones, Susannah, Knoxville,
Tenn., 14, #361
Jones, Tavenner, w/o, Va., 77,
#14054
Jones, Taverner, Richmond, Va.,
66, #10272
Jones, Taverner, Richmond, Va.,
51, #5955
Jones, Thomas, Va., 96, #1541,
card
Jones, Thomas, a/o, Richmond,
Va., 14, #1541
Jones, Thomas, g/o c/o, Ill.,
116, #3527
Jones, Thomas, w/o, Ky., 107,
#9469
Jones, Thomas, w/o, Va., 99,
#3220, card
Jones, Vincent, Ala., 51, #6047,
card
Jones, William, —, 63, #9018,
card
Jones, William, Ky., 50, #5742

Jones, William, c/o, Nashville,
Tenn., 14, #9018
Jones Jr., Joseph, w/o,
Pittsburgh, Pa., 88, #17847
Jordan, Catherine, e/o,
Richmond, Va., 128, #5862
Jordan, Elizabeth, c/o, R.I., 69,
#11031
Jordan, Garrett, w/o, La., 119,
#5376
Jordan, Philip, Concord, N.H.,
73, #12905
Jordan, Susannah, Ky., 66,
#10249
Jordan, T., —, 136, #3553, slip
Jordan, William, Richmond, Va.,
51, #5955
Jorden, Philip, c/o, Concord,
N.H., 73, #12813
Jorden, Sarah, Ky., 116, #3072
Jordon, John, N.Y., 85, #16447
Jordon, John, w/o, Pa., 86,
#16900
Jordon, Nancy, Albany, N.Y.,
66, #10129
Jordon, Sarah, Ky., 136, #3012
Jourdan (formerly Stone), Nancy,
Madison, Ind., 136, #2547
Joy, Bennet, Mich., 117, #4190
Joy, Mathew, La., 133, #159
Joyner, Joshua, Richmond, Va.,
47, #5022
Joyner, Sarah, Richmond, Va.,
36A, #F6, card
Joyner, William R., Va., 122,
#8802
Joynes, William R., Richmond,
Va., 36A, #F1 V8
Juckett, Elijah, Conn., 33, #534
Judd, Anthony, Albany, N.Y.,
79, #14626

Judd, Deborah, a/o, Albany, N.Y., 99, #3301
Judd, Demas, c/o, Albany, N.Y., 122, #8267
Judd, Sarah, Ohio, 67, #10444
Judkins, Philip, c/o, Maine, 116, #3591
Judson, Lemuel, Conn., 33, #535
Judson, Nathaniel, c/o, Albany, N.Y., 108, #9762
Judson, Phineas, c/o, Albany, N.Y., 63, #9073
Judson, T. Herbert, Miss., 128, #5758
Judson, T. Herbert, Miss., 137, #4582
Jumper, Daniel, w/o, Maine, 92, #81
June, Benjamin, c/o, Albany, N.Y., 110, #42
June, Reuben, Conn., 33, #517
Justice, Elizabeth, c/o, Pittsburgh, Pa., 73, #12833
Justin, Walcut, N.Y., 110, #11076, card

K

Kaene, Robert, Albany, N.Y., 40, #3229
Kahn, Michael, Philadelphia, Pa., 80, #14971
Kahn, Michael, Philadelphia, Pa., 105, #7864
Karacker, George, w/o, Ga., 130, #7401
Kearney, Daniel, Mo., 64, #9392
Kearney, Daniel, Mo., 75, #13412

Kearney, Daniel, Wisc., 88, #18100
Kearney, James, N.J., 126, #3450
Kearney, William H., g/o, Albany, N.Y., 137, #4311
Kearney, William H., g/o c/o, Albany, N.Y., 138, #5919
Keasley, Elizabeth, g/o, Pittsburgh, Pa., 138, #5070
Keber, Conrad, Philadelphia, Pa., 101, #4851 V#40
Kebling, John, a/o, Bradford, Vt., 138, #4662
Kee-wai-pai, Mo., 119, #5420
Keeblinger, Adam, w/o, Richmond, Va., 95, #892
Keeffer, John, w/o, Philadelphia, Pa., 138, #5794
Keegan, Catherine, Cleveland, Ohio, 136, #3494
Keel, Simon, N.C., 59, #8053
Keeler, Deborah, Conn., 33, #137
Keeler, Hezekiah, a/o w/o, Burlington, Vt., 107, #9139
Keeler, John, Philadelphia, Pa., 43, #3971
Keeler, Mercy, Montpelier, Vt., 123, #9650
Keeler, Nathaniel, w/o, Albany, N.Y., 125, #1712
Keen, John, Ill., 127, #4848
Keen, John, g/o c/o, New Albany, Ind., 136, #3495
Keen, Mary R., Nashville, Tenn., 84, #16037
Keene, William R., w/o, Ky., 138, #6295
Keep, James, c/o, Pittsburgh, Pa., 126, #2903

Keep, Lydia, c/o, Portland,
Maine, 104, #7127

Keepers, William R., Mo., 103,
#6713

Kees, Pvt. James, w/o, 15th Inf.,
113, #1875

Keese, William, g/o c/o,
Philadelphia, Pa., 139,
#8594

Keeton, David, Ohio, 53, #6395

Kehas, Paul, New York City,
120, #6115

Kehela, Christopher, w/o, Ga.,
49, #5383

Kehl, Catharine, c/o, Pittsburgh,
Pa., 72, #12550

Kehoe, Paul, Mo., 143, #7087

Keifer, Anna M., Philadelphia,
Pa., 68, #10672

Keiley, John, Mass., 136,
#3443

Keily, John, sisters of, Mass.,
142, #5444

Kein, Alfred, N.Y., 143, #6954

Keinecke, Henry, Mo., 126,
#3146

Keischer, Charles, Cincinnati,
Ohio, 138, #5033

Keiser, Michael, Cleveland,
Ohio, 141, #3145

Keisling, John, Ind., 41, #3542

Keith, James, Albany, N.Y., 59,
#8138

Keith, John, Ga., 42, #3794

Keith, John, w/o, Ga., 132,
#9005

Keith, Judith, a/o, Richmond,
Va., 36A, #F2 V1

Keitrich, Jacob, w/o, Pittsburgh,
Pa., 14, #4962

Kelch, John, Albany, N.Y., 81,
#15044

Kell, James, Savannah, Ga.,
104, #7585

Keller, Anna Barbara, D.C., 132,
#8977

Keller, Conrad, Philadelphia,
Pa., 138, #5654

Keller, John, Mo., 102, #5675

Keller, John, w/o, Albany, N.Y.,
48, #5066

Keller (formerly Huff), Martha,
Indianapolis, Ind., 136,
#3193

Kelley, Elizabeth, Nashville,
Tenn., 104, #7457

Kelley, William, Maine, 43,
#3901

Kelley, Israel W., PA, Concord,
N.H., 114, #2377

Kellicut, Thomas, Albany, N.Y.,
83, #15803

Kellley, George B., Cleveland,
Ohio, 132, #9845

Kellogg, Betsey, Albany, N.Y.,
133, #9966

Kellogg, Daniel, c/o, Conn.,
117, #4079

Kellogg, Enoch, a/o, Albany,
N.Y., 99, #3497

Kellogg, Enos, Burlington, Vt.,
42, #3795

Kellogg, Helmont, Conn., 33,
#3927

Kellogg, Horace, c/o, Albany,
N.Y., 64, #9511

Kellogg, John, c/o, Mass., 137,
#4300

Kellogg, Lucritia, Bellows Falls,
Vt., 75, #13647

Kellogg, Phinehas, w/o, Va., 76,
#13832

Kellogg, Phiney, c/o,
Pittsburgh, Pa., 112, #949

Kelly, David, c/o, Mass., 134, #1324
Kelly, Elizabeth, c/o, W. Tenn., 63, #9036
Kelly, George B., Cleveland, Ohio, 131, #8720
Kelly, Giles, Ga., 45, #4636
Kelly, Giles, Ga., 80, #14987
Kelly, James, Nashville, Tenn., 67, #10483
Kelly, James, Philadelphia, Pa., 135, #1843
Kelly, James, Philadelphia, Pa., 142, #5067
Kelly, James C., Boston, Mass., 143, #6247
Kelly, John, Iowa, 106, #8890
Kelly, John, Iowa, 114, #2177
Kelly, John, Iowa, 115, #2488
Kelly, John, Iowa, 115, #2912
Kelly, John, Ohio, 64, #9205
Kelly, John U. S., a/o, Ky., 134, #779
Kelly, Jonaphan, —, 76, #13874, card
Kelly, Jonathan, e/o, N.H., 14, #13874
Kelly, Patrick, New York City, 128, #5320
Kelly, Uriah D., Springfield, Ill., 14, #3383
Kelly, Uriah D., Springfield, Ill., 141, #3383, card
Kelly, William, Ga., 62, #8701
Kelly, William, Ky., 66, #10253
Kelly, William, Ky., 97, #2298
Kelly, John, PA, Portsmouth, N.H., 115, #2514
Kelsey, Stephen, w/o, Conn., 33, #341
Kelsy, Samuel, Albany, N.Y., 61, #8445

Kelton, Hannah, Boston, Mass., 95, #1279
Kelton, Joseph H., SpC, Provisions, 98, #2739
Kemp, Abigail, a/o, Mass., 130, #7757
Kemp, Ebenezer, c/o, Maine, 126, #3145
Kemp, Jonas, w/o, Boston, Mass., 122, #8576
Kemp, Molly, Boston, Mass., 67, #10427
Kemper, Charles, Richmond, Va., 45, #4469
Kemper, Charles, w/o, Va., 84, #16143
Kenady, David, Ky., 70, #11100
Kendall, Aaron, Ky., 58, #7666
Kendall, Aaron, Richmond, Va., 92, #19910
Kendall, Aaron, Va., 39, #3151
Kendall, Aaron, Va., 85, #16689
Kendall, Clayton, N.J., 45, #4426, card
Kendall, Clayton, c/o, Trenton, N.J., 14, #4426
Kendall, Elizabeth, c/o, Mass., 64, #9578
Kendall, John, Albany, N.Y., 44, #4338
Kendall, John, Albany, N.Y., 48, #5158
Kendall, Nathan, Mass., 71, #12273
Kendall, Nathan, Mass., 110, #11102
Kendall, Noah, w/o, Boston, Mass., 101, #5116
Kendall, Timothy, Vt., 89, #18189
Kendelsperger, Jacob, Ohio, 54, #6745

Kendelspeyer, Jacob, w/o, Ohio, 109, #10445

Keneda, William, a/o, Nashville, Tenn., 121, #7178

Keneday, Joseph, Lexington, Ky., 50, #5559

Keniston, David D., Mass., 128, #5587

Kenmoure, John, S.C., 40, #3291

Kennard, Stephen D., w/o, Spingfield, Ill., 140, #1089

Kenneday, Thomas, N.C., 52, #6096

Kennedy, David, Ky., 76, #13839

Kennedy, Jane, Ky., 116, #3046

Kennedy, Samuel, Va., 96, #1413, card

Kennedy, Sherwood, w/o, Conn., 97, #2140

Kennedy, Thomas, Mo., 142, #3837

Kennedy, Thomas, a/o, Ky., 103, #6899

Kennedy, William, a/o, Nashville, Tenn., 14, #5909

Kennedy, Wm. A., Cincinnati, Ohio, 143, #7325

Kennerly, William, Richmond, Va., 62, #8678

Kennerty, Samuel, c/o, Richmond, Va., 14, #1413

Kenney, Elizabeth, a/o, Maine, 125, #2178

Kenniff, Dennis, Indianapolis, Ind., 140, #1125

Kenniff, Dennis, Ky., 123, #231

Kennon, Oreashy, a/o, Nashville, Tenn., 91, #19229

Kenny, John, Ore., 132, #9743

Kent, Absalom, Wheeling, Va., 14, #7823

Kent, Absolom, Wheeling, Va., 58, #7823, card

Kent, Alexander, c/o, Va., 84, #16198

Kent, Andrew J., Mich., 136, #2532

Kent, B. C., Albany, N.Y., 119, #5138

Kent, Charles, Albany, N.Y., 56, #7363

Kent, Emanuel, c/o, Md., 67, #10407

Kent, Ezekiel, c/o, Albany, N.Y., 116, #3629

Kent, Joseph H., Boston, Mass., 142, #5873

Kent, Richard, c/o, Boston, Mass., 64, #9270

Kent, Samuel, a/o w/o, Ohio, 108, #10220

Kent, Thomas, Pittsburgh, Pa., 50, #5500

Kent, Thomas, Pittsburgh, Pa., 56, #7299

Kent, Thomas, Pittsburgh, Pa., 62, #8711

Kent, Thomas, Pittsburgh, Pa., 70, #12203

Kent, William, Ohio, 57, #7447

Kenyon, Moses, R.I., 74, #13145

Keough, William, c/o, Md., 126, #3388

Kephart, Jacob, w/o, Ky., 123, #9079

Kepler, George P., Philadelphia, Pa., 61, #8474

Kepler, Samuel, w/o,
    Philadelphia, Pa., 74,
    #13301
Kepps, Jacob, Richmond, Va.,
    48, #5068
Kerby, Archibald, S.C., 75,
    #13441
Kerby, Leonard T., a/o, Ky., 94,
    #600
Kerby, William, Nashville,
    Tenn., 73, #12940
Kerby, William, Nashville,
    Tenn., 77, #14016
Kerney, Daniel, w/o, Spingfield,
    Ill., 139, #8970
Kerns, Lydia, c/o, Mass., 105,
    #8200
Kerns (formerly Noal),
    Elizabeth, Richmond, Va.,
    36A, #F4 V14
Kerr, Andrew, S.C., 49, #5361
Kerr, Andrew, S.C., 57, #7528
Kerr, Andrew, S.C., 65, #9994
Kerr, Elizabeth, N.C., 97, #2482
Kerr, Leah, Philadelphia, Pa.,
    129, #6784
Kerr, William, c/o, Albany,
    N.Y., 110, #10954
Kershner, William, Fla., 95,
    #1093, slip
Kessinger, Adam, Pa., 69,
    #10905
Kessler, John, Pa., 68, #10698,
    card
Kessler, John, Philadelphia, Pa.,
    14, #10698
Kesten, Joseph, w/o, Ohio, 77,
    #13964
Kester, Joseph, Ohio, 41, #3555
Kesterson, John, Jonesboro,
    Tenn., 53, #6463

Kesterson, John, Jonesboro,
    Tenn., 63, #8878
Kesterson Sr., John, Jonesboro,
    Tenn., 44, #4283
Ketcham, Samuel, New York
    City, 63, #9015
Ketchans, Polly, c/o, Albany,
    N.Y., 83, #15730
Ketchum, Polly, c/o, New York
    City, 99, #3299
Ketchum, Polly, c/o, New York
    City, 99, #3479
Ketchum, Sarah, Albany, N.Y.,
    133, #226
Ketler, Joseph, Pa., 71, #12416
Kettel, Jonathan, Mass., 107,
    #8964
Ketterman, Daniel, Richmond,
    Va., 102, #6149
Ketterman, Daniel, Richmond,
    Va., 95, #1033
Ketterman, Daniel, Richmond,
    Va., 95, #1202
Ketterman, Daniel, Va., 66,
    #10159
Ketterman, Daniel, Va., 77,
    #14156
Ketterman, Daniel, Va., 90,
    #18594
Ketterman, Daniel, w/o,
    Richmond, Va., 14, #6149
Ketterman, Daniels, Va., 80,
    #14941
Key, Henry, Richmond, Va., 53,
    #6481
Key, John, w/o, Va., 65, #9763
Key, Sarah, Ky., 128, #5672,
    card
Key, Sarah, a/o, Ky., 14, #5672
Keyes, Elias, w/o, Pittsburgh,
    Pa., 109, #10444

Keyes, John, c/o, New York
City, 14, #3675
Keyes, Peter, Albany, N.Y., 80,
#14963
Keys, John, New York City,
116, #3675
Keys, Jonathan, w/o, Albany,
N.Y., 118, #4824
Kezer, David, w/o, Maine, 76,
#13892
Khett, Capt. S. G., Mt. Rifles,
103, #6686, claim
Kibbe, David, a/o, Albany, N.Y.,
117, #4464
Kidd, James, Richmond, Va., 72,
#12542, card
Kidd, James H., Ga., 14, #9090
Kidd, William, Ga., 56, #7306
Kidwell, James E., Cleveland,
Ohio, 140, #164
Kidwell, Ruth, Mo., 141, #1753
Kidwell, Ruth, Mo., 141, #1754
Kiesel, Regina, c/o, D.C., 132,
#9410
Kiker, George, N.C., 105, #7739
Kilby, John, Conn., 57, #7457
Kilgore, James, c/o,
Philadelphia, Pa., 113,
#1645
Killin, John, Ohio, 63, #9112
Kilpatrick, Jackson, Pittsburgh,
Pa., 142, #4840
Kimball, Caleb, Concord, N.H.,
137, #3761
Kimball, Charles B., Mich.,
141, #3005
Kimball, Jemima, Wheeling,
Va., 70, #11056
Kimball, Lucy, c/o, Maine, 122,
#8347
Kimbro (formerly Grigg),
Martha, Ill., 135, #1664

Kincaid, Alice, Richmond, Va.,
126, #2979
Kincaid, James, —, 64, #9432,
card
Kincaid, James, —, 92, #183,
card
Kincaid, James, w/o, Richmond,
Va., 98, #2966
Kincaid, John, Tuscaloosa, Ala.,
88, #17850
Kincaid, Rebecca, Louisville,
Ky., 142, #4170
Kincaid, Robert, Ky., 39, #3153
Kincaid, Robert, Ky., 57, #7494
Kincaid, Robert, Ky., 68,
#10717
Kincaid, Robert, w/o, Ky., 99,
#3547
Kincaid, Robert, w/o, N.C., 62,
#8707
Kincaid, Thomas, Va., 66,
#10151
Kindelsperger, Jacob, Ohio, 72,
#12523
Kindelsperyer, Jacob, Ohio, 75,
#13568
Kindle, William, Jackson,
Tenn., 52, #6167
King, Abigail, c/o, Mass., 64,
#9690
King, Alesander, h/o, N.J., 48,
#5064
King, Andrew, w/o, Knoxville,
Tenn., 72, #12572
King, Ann, Philadelphia, Pa.,
64, #9602
King, Asaph, a/o, Boston,
Mass., 92, #33
King, Charles, w/o, Richmond,
Va., 64, #9326
King, Ebenezer, Albany, N.Y.,
44, #4350

King, Elizabeth, Philadelphia,
Pa., 66, #10105
King, Elizabeth, e/o,
Philadelphia, Pa., 77,
#14116
King, James, Ga., 84, #16199
King, Jane, c/o, Conn., 59,
#7988
King, Jesse, —, 99, #3543, card
King, Jessie, c/o, Richmond,
Va., 14, #3543
King, John, Ky., 43, #3920,
card
King, John, N.C., 71, #12424
King, John, Pittsburgh, Pa., 81,
#15024
King, John, S.C., 63, #9022
King, John, c/o, Va., 91,
#19256
King, John, e/o, Albany, N.Y.,
80, #14962
King, John, w/o, Ga., 87,
#17623
King, John, w/o, Ky., 14, #3920
King, John, w/o, N.C., 94, #313
King, Jonah, Conn., 33, #340
King, Jonathan, c/o, Pittsburgh,
Pa., 50, #5803
King, Joshua, Conn., 33, #2
King, Lemuel, e/o, Conn., 38,
#F1828
King, Nancy, Va., 122, #8585
King, Nathaniel, Richmond, Va.,
48, #5104
King, Nathaniel, a/o, Va., 65,
#9804
King, Olive, e/o, Maine, 110,
#258
King, Rachel, Ga., 125, #2129
King, Reuben, Albany, N.Y.,
106, #8403
King, Richard, Ga., 48, #5090

King, Silence, a/o, Mass., 126,
#3078
King, Sylvester M., Spingfield,
Ill., 142, #3983
King, Thomas, a/o w/o,
Fayetteville, N.C., 133,
#9911
King, Ursuala, Mobile, Ala.,
125, #2501
King, Ursula, Mobile, Ala., 130,
#7430
King, Ursula, Mobile, Ala., 130,
#7530
King, William, Ky., 54, #6863
King, William, Ky., 78, #14468
King, Robert, late PA,
Knoxville, Tenn., 129,
#6148
Kingery, Joseph, Mo., 53,
#6486
Kingery, Joseph, Mo., 82,
#15269
Kingman, Thomas, c/o, N.J.,
119, #5491
Kingsberry, Asa, c/o, Albany,
N.Y., 54, #6707
Kingsbury, Harriet N., New York
City, 127, #4255
Kingsbury, Thomas, w/o,
Albany, N.Y., 60, #8309
Kingsbury, William, Pittsburgh,
Pa., 69, #10886
Kingsley, Elias, w/o,
Burlington, Vt., 136,
#2702
Kingsley, Elijah, c/o, Mass., 68,
#10636
Kingsley, Zephaniah, c/o,
Philadelphia, Pa., 102,
#5574
Kinkead, Thomas, Richmond,
Va., 59, #8005

Kinkead, Thomas, Va., 76,
#13759
Kinlin, Elizabeth, Philadelphia,
Pa., 143, #7543
Kinnard, John, Mobile, Ala., 64,
#9247
Kinnard, John, Mobile, Ala., 63,
#8956
Kinney, Anne, a/o, Albany,
N.Y., 137, #4187
Kinney, John, Ohio, 67, #10408
Kinney, Marion M., Ky., 125,
#1880
Kinney, Peter, e/o, Pittsburgh,
Pa., 118, #5082
Kinney, Stephen, Ohio, 55,
#6922
Kinnison, Jacob, —, 69,
#10821, card
Kinnison, Jacob, Richmond,
Va., 14, #10821
Kinser, Elizabeth, Richmond,
Va., 100, #3780
Kinsman, Loomis, g/o c/o,
Philadelphia, Pa., 137,
#4510
Kinyon, Alexander, w/o,
Albany, N.Y., 90, #18712
Kinyon, Elizabeth, a/o, R.I., 78,
#14439
Kipps, Elizabeth, Richmond,
Va., 124, #546
Kipps, Jacob, Richmond, Va.,
56, #7413
Kipps, Jacobs, Richmond, Va.,
66, #10210
Kips, Jacob, Richmond, Va., 76,
#13883
Kipton, Thomas, Ohio, 69,
#10860
Kirby, Archibald, S.C., 39,
#3074

Kirby, Elizabeth, a/o,
Richmond, Va., 136, #2874
Kirby, Tarrance, Ky., 140,
#1189
Kirckwood, David, w/o, Ohio,
111, #357
Kirkendall, Margaret, Columbus,
Ohio, 142, #5634
Kirkpatrick, Isaac, w/o,
Philadelphia, Pa., 56,
#7318
Kirsner, Wenfil, D.C., 138,
#5491
Kirsner, Wenfil, D.C., 138,
#5605
Kirsner, Winfel, a/o, D.C., 142,
#4561
Kirtland, Charles, a/o, Albany,
N.Y., 51, #5949
Kissinger, Adam, Philadelphia,
Pa., 81, #15145
Kitchen, James, Ill., 76, #13800
Kitchen, James, Ind., 81,
#15167
Kitchen, John, Miss., 40, #3252
Kitchen (formerly Custer),
Nancy, Cincinnati, Ohio,
129, #6476
Kitchens, John, Knoxville,
Tenn., 76, #13763
Kittle, Jacob, Wheeling, Va.,
40, #3316
Kitts, George, New York City,
142, #5397
Klaner, Frederick, c/o, New York
City, 124, #895
Klaus (now Homer), Josephine,
La., 118, #4651
Klauss, Jacob, g/o c/o, La., 125,
#2479
Klaver, Frederick, New York
City, 128, #5722

Klaver, Frederick, c/o, New York
City, 117, #3849
Klay (or Clay), Henry,
Jacksonville, Fla., 71,
#12414
Klein, Auguste, New York City,
140, #29
Kline, John, w/o, Albany, N.Y.,
92, #19891
Kline, John N., c/o, Richmond,
Va., 14, #19746
Klinederst, Christian, e/o,
Philadelphia, Pa., 89,
#18286
Knap, Ephraim, Albany, N.Y.,
53, #6501
Knapp, Ephraim, Albany, N.Y.,
56, #7419
Knapp, Ephraim, a/o, Albany,
N.Y., 77, #14094
Knapp, George W., c/o,
Madison, Ind., 113, #1429
Knapp, Jacob, Conn., 33, #846
Knapp, John, Albany, N.Y., 55,
#7154
Knapp, John, Albany, N.Y., 59,
#8072
Knapp, Josiah, c/o, Albany,
N.Y., 45, #4450
Knapp, Lodema, a/o, Ohio, 99,
#3221
Knapp, Samuel B., Wisc. Terr.,
14, #13510
Knapp, Samuel B., Wisc. Terr.,
14, #13575
Knapp, William, Albany, N.Y.,
39, #3024
Kniffin, Rachel, a/o, New York
City, 138, #4873
Knigh, William, e/o, Ohio, 110,
#305

Knight, Artermus, c/o, Concord,
N.H., 53, #6519
Knight, Elizabeth, Richmond,
Va., 36A, #F5 V1
Knight, Elizabeth, Richmond,
Va., 126, #3380
Knight, Elizabeth, a/o, Ky.,
133, #240
Knight, Hannah, c/o, Maine,
123, #166
Knight, Jacob, Ind., 50, #5744
Knight, James, c/o, Albany,
N.Y., 86, #17167
Knight, John, a/o, Conn., 116,
#3703
Knight, Mary, a/o, Richmond,
Va., 36A, #F5 V33
Knight, Night, Ill., 66, #10260
Knight, Peter, Wheeling, Va.,
44, #4207
Knight, Peter, Wheeling, Va.,
47, #5032
Knight, Sally, Albany, N.Y., 80,
#14859
Knight, Thomas, w/o, N.Y.,
109, #10755
Knight, William, w/o, Va., 75,
#13422
Knighten, Margaret, Richmond,
Va., 127, #4981
Knote (or Nott), William,
Richmond, Va., 36A, #F1
V21
Knott, Leonard A., g/o c/o, Ill.,
125, #2155
Knowles, Martha, c/o, Ohio, 58,
#7675
Knowlton, John, Albany, N.Y.,
14, #10691
Knox, Benjamin, N.C., 52,
#6234

Landers, John, Ga., 74, #13068
Landers, John, w/o, Ga., 15, #13068
Landers, Mahittabel, c/o, N.Y., 96, #1777
Landers, Olive, c/o, Albany, N.Y., 115, #2944
Landers, Thomas, Va., 73, #12941
Landon, Ebenezer, Ohio, 53, #6382
Landon, Ebenezer, c/o, Albany, N.Y., 124, #901
Landon, James, Jonesboro, Tenn., 69, #10884, card
Landon Jr., John, g/o c/o, Conn., 37, #F1820
Landon, Nathaniel, Detroit, Mich., 44, #4257
Landres, Nancy, e/o, Richmond, Va., 36A, #F3 V12
Landrum, James, w/o, Jonesboro, Tenn., 15, #10884
Landrum, Sarah S., Richmond, Va., 36A, #F1 V24
Landrum, Thomas, c/o, Ky., 95, #876
Landsdale, Isaac, Mobile, Ala., 59, #7957
Lane, Aaron G., Concord, N.H., 111, #736
Lane, Abraham, N.J., 58, #7915, card
Lane, Abraham, c/o, N.J., 74, #13306
Lane, Alexander, Philadelphia, Pa., 71, #12387
Lane, Alexander, w/o, Philadelphia, Pa., 100, #4258

Lane, Derrick, e/o, Albany, N.Y., 115, #2914
Lane, Elizabeth, c/o, New York City, 99, #3548
Lane, Henry S., Ky., 76, #13777, card
Lane, Jacob, Philadelphia, Pa., 114, #2330
Lane, John, N.C., 105, #7751
Lane, John, a/o, Pittsburgh, Pa., 126, #3504
Lane, John W., Philadelphia, Pa., 124, #429
Lane, John W., Philadelphia, Pa., 130, #7802
Lane, Joseph, w/o, Knoxville, Tenn., 107, #9417
Lane, Rebecca, c/o, Tenn., 114, #2145
Lane, Ruth, a/o, Concord, N.H., 132, #9718
Lane, Samuel, Concord, N.H., 15, #10419
Lane, Samuel, c/o, Concord, N.H., 15, #4292
Lane, Tidence, w/o, Knoxville, Tenn., 87, #17669
Lane, Turner, Tenn., 89, #18328, card
Lane, Turner, e/o, Nashville, Tenn., 15, #18328
Lane, William, Mo., 100, #3763
Lane (formerly McLouth), Clarissa, Mich., 128, #5710, #MI
Lane, Newton, late PA, Louisville, Ky., 108, #9984
Lane, Newton, late PA, Louisville, Ky., 110, #11010
Lanehart, Adam, Miss., 124, #487

Lang, Francis, Madison, Ind.,
136, #2485

Lang, John, w/o, Concord, N.H.,
116, #3390

Langdon, Submit, Pittsburgh,
Pa., 88, #18022

Langford, Martha, Tallahassee,
Fla., 90, #18597

Langsdon, James V., Ky., 50,
#5828, card

Langstaff, Hannah, N.J., 96,
#1509

Langwell, William, Albany,
N.Y., 134, #1455

Lanham, Abel, w/o, E. Tenn.,
64, #9370

Lanham, Sarah, Louisville, Ky.,
136, #3442

Lanier, J. F. D., PA, Madison,
Ind., 115, #2512

Lanman, James, Ill., 52, #6087

Lanman, James, Ind., 75,
#13657

Lanman, James, Ind., 53, #6480

Lanman, Naomi, Mass., 75,
#13620

Lanning, John, N.C., 65, #9996

Lanning, Rebecca, N.J., 96,
#1589

Lanning, Sarah, N.C., 99, #3650

Lanning, Sarah, N.C., 100,
#4037

Lansdale, Isaac, Tuscaloosa,
Ala., 65, #9738

Lantham, Christopher, Conn.,
38, #F1825

Lantz, George, Wheeling, Va.,
103, #7075

Larabee, Anna, c/o, Burlington,
Vt., 106, #8401

Laraway, Isaac, c/o, Albany,
N.Y., 134, #1337

LaRew, James, N.J., 86,
#17226, card

Larew, James, N.J., 15, #17226

Larimore, Hugh, Mo., 65, #9800

Larkin, Elizabeth, Mo., 131,
#8400

Larkin, Michael, Mass., 124,
#1205

Larkin, Michael, Mass., 127,
#4230

Larkin, Michael, Mass., 127,
#4851

Larkin, Thomas, w/o, Albany,
N.Y., 100, #4521

Larkin, Charles H., PA,
Milwaukee, Wisc., 118,
#5117

Larkin, Pardelete, PA,
Milwaukee, Wisc., 116,
#3799

Larose, Jacob, c/o, Cincinnati,
Ohio, 117, #3957

Larrabec, Lebbeus, Mich., 50,
#5547

Larrabee, Ann, c/o, Boston,
Mass., 99, #3563

Larrabee, Lebbeus, Mich., 80,
#14978

Larrabee, Lebbeus, w/o, Mich.,
99, #3354

Larrimore, James, Fayetteville,
N.C., 129, #7112

Lary, John, Richmond, Va., 41,
#3407

Laselton, Ferman, Albany, N.Y.,
55, #6985

Lash, Peter, w/o, Pittsburgh, Pa.,
128, #5148

Lashley, Edmund, Ga., 45,
#4600

Lasser, Benjamin, N.C., 55,
#6919

Layman, Jacob, c/o, Knoxville, Tenn., 125, #2263

Layton, Thomas, Ill., 82, #15381

Lazarus, Elizabeth, a/o, Philadelphia, Pa., 136, #3061

Lazarus, Rachel, S.C., 100, #3812

Lea, James A., g/o c/o, Knoxville, Tenn., 132, #9368

Leabo, Isaac S., Indianapolis, Ind., 143, #6581

Leabo, Isaac S., Madison, Ind., 115, #2707

Leach, Abner, Pittsburgh, Pa., 80, #14869

Leach, Abner, Pittsburgh, Pa., 122, #8966, card

Leach, Abner, a/o, Pittsburgh, Pa., 15, #8728

Leach, Abner, a/o, Pittsburgh, Pa., 15, #8966

Leach, John, c/o, Maine, 130, #7649

Leach, Samuel, a/o, Albany, N.Y., 116, #3451

Leach, William, a/o, Jackson, Tenn., 118, #5081

Leache, Thomas, Wheeling, Va., 39, #3083

Leak, James, Ga., 40, #3287

Leake, William, Richmond, Va., 15, #7515

Leake, William, Va., 57, #7515, card

Leant, Moses, c/o, Albany, N.Y., 100, #3757

Learned, Abel, Bellows Falls, Vt., 47, #5008

Leavens, Noah, c/o, Albany, N.Y., 81, #15204

Lebeck, Jacob, Philadelphia, Pa., 95, #1368

Lebkecker, Michael, Philadelphia, Pa., 41, #3377

Lebleecher, Michael, Philadelphia, Pa., 52, #6107

Ledbitter, Richard, w/o, N.C., 87, #17507

Lee, Burwell, w/o, Ga., 131, #8262

Lee, David, Conn., 87, #17569

Lee, Ezra, Conn., 33, #670

Lee, Israel, a/o, Albany, N.Y., 107, #9634

Lee, James, N.C., 99, #3213, card

Lee, Noah, Burlington, Vt., 82, #15377, card

Lee, Noah, Vt., 15, #15377

Lee, Phebe, Albany, N.Y., 114, #2152

Lee, Rhoda, Mich., 79, #14573

Lee, Richard, c/o, N.J., 121, #6934

Lee, Samuel, Ky., 61, #8415

Lee, Samuel, Ky., 64, #9594

Lee, Westbrook, N.C., 62, #8708

Lee, William, N.Y., 85, #16501

Lee, William, c/o, Conn., 58, #7910

Lee, William, w/o, N.J., 89, #18502

Lee, Zebulon, Ohio, 64, #9166

Lee, Zebulon, Ohio, 80, #14839

Lee, Zebulon, w/o, Ohio, 105, #8346

Leech, William, Jackson, Tenn., 80, #14814

Leeds, Jeremiah, w/o, N.J., 55, #7204

Leeds, Thomas, a/o, Mass., 87, #17599

Leeker, Sarah, New York City, 102, #6052 V#8

Leeper, John, Mo., 60, #8258

Leet, Allen, w/o, Vt., 99, #3338

Leffar, John, Pa., 39, #3072

Leftwich, Joel, a/o, Richmond, Va., 102, #6245

Leggett, Lewis, Albany, N.Y., 112, #1075

Leggitt, William, w/o, Ill., 129, #6595

Legit, John, Ark., 76, #13771

Legro, Betty, Maine, 88, #18121

Legue, Edmund, w/o, Nashville, Tenn., 53, #6363

Lehr, Philip, Philadelphia, Pa., 54, #6702

Lehr (or Leaher), Peter, w/o, Maine, 46, #4689

Leib, Ann Christina, N.C., 135, #2272

Leibley, Andrew, w/o, Philadelphia, Pa., 86, #16873

Leibrick, Nancy, Richmond, Va., 36A, #F2 V27

Leidey, Samuel, Philadelphia, Pa., 46, #4812

Leidley, Samuel, Philadelphia, Pa., 86, #16899

Leiers, James, N.C., 54, #6664

Leighton, Hannah, a/o, Boston, Mass., 86, #16882

Leighton, Hannah, a/o, Mass., 86, #17045

Leiphert, Cecelia, a/o, New York City, 124, #507

Lejoy, Abraham, c/o, N.Y., 59, #7947

Leland, Lydia, a/o, Vt., 120, #6343

Lemaster, George, Va., 68, #10813

Lemaster, George, Va., 76, #13762

Lemasters, George, Richmond, Va., 57, #7436

Lemasters, George, Richmond, Va., 48, #5136

Leming, Frederick, Mo., 113, #1284

Leminoff, Nicholas, New York City, 109, #10397

Lemon, Jacob, Richmond, Va., 64, #9694

Lemon, Jacob, Va., 84, #16296

Lemon, Jane G., Richmond, Va., 36A, #F6, card

Lemonds, Robert, a/o, Fayetteville, N.C., 128, #5201

Lemore, Thomas, Jackson, Tenn., 48, #5149

Lenning, Frederick, D.C., 136, #3003

Lenning, Frederick, D.C., 140, #366

Lenning, Frederick, Mo., 109, #10750

Lenning (or Lemway), Rederick, Mo., 123, #190

Lenoir, William, e/o, N.C., 88, #18091

Lenox, James, c/o, Md., 134, #1149

Lent, James W., c/o, Albany, N.Y., 50, #5578

Leonard, Ephraim, c/o, Mass.,
137, #4260
Leonard, Esther, Pittsburgh, Pa.,
62, #8713
Leonard, Esther, c/o, D.C., 111,
#660
Leonard, Hannah, c/o, Albany,
N.Y., 120, #6696
Leonard, John, Mo., 139, #6748
Leonard, John, N.J., 142, #3894
Leonard, Lot, w/o, Philadelphia,
Pa., 119, #5653
Leonard, Michael, c/o, Ky., 64,
#9358
Leonard, Susannha, Richmond,
Va., 100, #3853
Leonardson, John T., Albany,
N.Y., 85, #16606
Lepper, Jacob, w/o, Albany,
N.Y., 47, #4919
Lepper, Mary, Albany, N.Y., 79,
#14552
Leray, John, Conn., 33, #875
Leroux, Paul, Ga., 101, #4845
Lesser, Simon, D.C., 143,
#6281
Lessig, David, Philadelphia, Pa.,
52, #6174
Lester, Asa, e/o, Conn., 66,
#10063
Lettice, James, a/o, Albany,
N.Y., 15, #3345
Letts, Abigail, New York City,
70, #12190
Leuning, Frederick, Mo., 120,
#6200
Levalley, Took, c/o, Albany,
N.Y., 76, #13933
Levasey, George, Jonesboro,
Tenn., 127, #4530

Levenston, Anne, c/o,
Philadelphia, Pa., 100,
#4280
Levi, Henry, g/o c/o, Conn., 37,
#F1820
Levi, Mary, Ohio, 73, #12743
Levinus, Thomas, Tenn., 69,
#10972, card
Levinus, Thomas, w/o, New York
City, 15, #10972
Lewis Sr., Aaron, Mobile, Ala.,
74, #13032
Lewis, Andrew, Richmond, Va.,
71, #12346
Lewis, Angustus, c/o, Conn., 33,
#848
Lewis, Catherine, Cincinnati,
Ohio, 126, #3603
Lewis, Daniel B., Miss., 111,
#687
Lewis, Daniel B., Miss., 120,
#6541
Lewis, Daniel B., Miss., 123,
#9280
Lewis, Daniel R., Miss., 124,
#918
Lewis, Darius, c/o, Mass., 108,
#10326
Lewis, Eleazer, w/o, Conn., 58,
#7685
Lewis, Ezekiel, —, 83, #15747
Lewis, George, c/o, Mass., 134,
#1286
Lewis, Gilbert, New York City,
73, #12808
Lewis, Hayden, w/o, Mo., 118,
#4711
Lewis, Herbert, a/o, N.C., 75,
#13573
Lewis, Isaac E., Madison, Ind.,
117, #3970

Lewis, Isaac P., Madison, Ind.,
139, #7467
Lewis, Jabez, a/o, Albany, N.Y.,
99, #3614
Lewis, Jacob, w/o, Richmond,
Va., 15, #10950
Lewis, James, Nashville, Tenn.,
81, #15018
Lewis, James, Nashville, Tenn.,
41, #3437
Lewis, James R., New Orleans,
La., 113, #1461
Lewis, James R., —, 140, #9930
Lewis, John, Ga., 40, #3165
Lewis, John, Richmond, Va., 51,
#6025
Lewis, John, Va. to Ohio, 68,
#10560, card
Lewis, Joseph, c/o, Mass., 137,
#4149
Lewis, Morgan, e/o, New York
City, 99, #3223
Lewis, Nancy, c/o, N.J., 51,
#6030
Lewis, Nancy, c/o, N.J., 58,
#7829
Lewis, Robert, w/o, Va., 43,
#3941
Lewis, Solomon, Conn., 33,
#570
Lewis, Solomon, Knoxville,
Tenn., 47, #4861
Lewis, Solomon, Knoxville,
Tenn., 49, #5279
Lewis, Stephen, Conn., 33, #43
Lewis, Thomas, a/o, Richmond,
Va., 15, #6589
Lewis, Thomas, g/o c/o, Md.,
138, #6594
Lewis, TImothy, Albany, N.Y.,
65, #9988

Lewis, William, Richmond, Va.,
61, #8654
Ley, Michael, Pa., 122, #8036
Libbey, Hannah, c/o, Maine, 78,
#14421
Libby, Abigail, c/o, Maine, 131,
#8639
Libengoods, Jacob, w/o,
Pittsburgh, Pa., 15, #8888
Libingood, Jacob, w/o,
Pittsburgh, Pa., 106,
#8888, card
Libley, Moses, Mass., 94, #235
Libscomb, Winny, Wheeling,
Va., 109, #10846, card
Liddell, Ruth, Ga., 73, #12997
Lifford, Elizabeth, Richmond,
Va., 137, #4326
Light, John, Jonesboro, Tenn.,
72, #12597
Light, Vachel, Jonesboro,
Tenn., 87, #17524
Light, Vachol, Jonesboro,
Tenn., 66, #10097
Ligon, Wiliam, Ky., 80, #14895
Ligon, William, Ky., 64, #9402
Ligon, William, Ky., 78,
#14493
Lilly, Leonard, Albany, N.Y.,
127, #4188
Lilvar, Aaron, Jonesboro, Tenn.,
71, #12464
Limonds, Alexander, N.C., 79,
#14746
Lincoln, Abiather, —, 78,
#14528, card
Lincoln, Abiather, Mich., 15,
#14528
Lincoln, Abierther, Md., 89,
#18377
Lincoln, Abigail, Burlington,
Vt., 92, #129

Linsley, Golding, S.C., 47,
#4863
Linsley, Hannah, a/o, Albany,
N.Y., 99, #3615
Linsly, Simeon, Ohio, 64,
#9418
Lint, Jacob, Philadelphia, Pa.,
72, #12688
Linter, Peter, e/o, Ohio, 122,
#8580
Linton, Jane, a/o, Md., 65,
#9819
Linton, John, Mobile, Ala., 90,
#18805
Linton, John, c/o, Mobile, Ala.,
122, #8240
Linton, Joseph, Mass., 116,
#3173, card
Linton, Joseph, c/o, Boston,
Mass., 15, #3173
Linvill, William, Ga., 64, #9232
Linville, William, Ga., 66,
#10089
Linville, William, Ga., 72,
#12562
Linville, William, w/o, Ga., 94,
#550
Lipford, Anthony P., Va., 116,
#3558, card
Lipford, Anthony P., w/o,
Richmond, Va., 15, #3558
Lipford, Elizabeth, Richmond,
Va., 125, #2221
Lipford, Henry, Richmond, Va.,
63, #9010
Lipford, Henry, Richmond, Va.,
51, #6010
Lipford, Henry, Va., 125, #1791
Lippard, Mary, Madison, Ind.,
106, #8413
Lippard, Mary, Madison, Ind.,
99, #3644

Lippard, Mary, Madison, Ind.,
122, #8775
Lippencott, Amelia, N.J., 56,
#7272
Lippencott, Charles, g/o c/o,
Cincinnati, Ohio, 141,
#2452
Lippett, Moses, c/o, Conn.,
102, #6162
Lippford, Elizabeth, Richmond,
Va., 134, #1049
Lipscomb, Ambrose, Wheeling,
Va., 15, #9489
Lipscomb, Richard, Richmond,
Va., 42, #3678
Lipscomb, Richard, Richmond,
Va., 45, #4432
Lipscomb, Richard, w/o,
Richmond, Va., 54, #6725
Lipscomb, Winny, a/o,
Wheeling, Va., 15, #10846
Lisenby, Susan, Ky., 139,
#8090
Lisenby, Susan, Ky., 141,
#2454
List, Jacob, Ky., 45, #4545
List, Jacob, Ky., 78, #14408
Lister, William, S.C., 73,
#12907
Litch, William, c/o, Portsmouth,
N.H., 98, #3007
Litchford, Arthur, Richmond,
Va., 52, #6219
Litchford, Arthur, Va., 82,
#15449
Lithgow, Arthur, Mass., 83,
#15551
Littlefield, Benjamin, w/o,
Maine, 63, #8898
Littlefield, David, w/o, Maine,
41, #3383

Logan, Richard R., New York
City, 102, #6052 V#48
Logan, Samuel, c/o, N.Y., 42,
#3670
Logsden, James V., w/o, Ky.,
15, #5828
Logwood, Peggy, a/o,
Richmond, Va., 101, #5193
Lohr, Peter, Richmond, Va., 39,
#3062
Lomax, Tabita, Fayetteville,
N.C., 129, #7141
Lomay, Tabillea, Fayetteville,
N.C., 105, #7762 V#48
Lomoy, William, a/o,
Fayetteville, N.C., 130,
#7238
London, Archibald, c/o,
Philadelphia, Pa., 131,
#8561
Long, Anderson, Mo., 41,
#3475
Long, Anderson, Mo., 49,
#5337
Long, Anderson, Mo., 56,
#7355
Long, Anderson, Mo., 57,
#7639
Long, Anderson, Mo., 74,
#13086
Long, Andrew, w/o,
Philadelphia, Pa., 86,
#16871
Long, Anthony, Ky., 60, #8363
Long, Anthony, Ky., 63, #8996
Long, George, Jonesboro,
Tenn., 46, #4721
Long, George, Jonesboro,
Tenn., 52, #6317
Long, George, Jonesboro,
Tenn., 43, #3957
Long, Henry, Md., 55, #7115

Long, Henry, c/o, Richmond,
Va., 108, #9914
Long, Henry, w/o, Jonesboro,
Tenn., 47, #4923
Long, John, Ill., 57, #7643, card
Long, John, w/o, Ill., 15, #7643
Long, Margaret, a/o, Md., 121,
#7241
Long, Nicholas, a/o, Ky., 119,
#5358
Long, Nicholas, w/o, Knoxville,
Tenn., 79, #14718
Long, Richard, a/o, Nashville,
Tenn., 15, #9329
Long, Robert, S.C., 92, #139,
card
Long, Robert, S.C., 61, #8471
Long, Robert, e/o, S.C., 15,
#139
Long, Stephen, a/o, Poultney,
Vt., 102, #6088
Longfellow, Mary, c/o, Maine,
113, #1314
Longley, Ezekiel, c/o,
Burlington, Vt., 130,
#7931
Loofbourrow, David, Pittsburgh,
Pa., 80, #14862
Look, Jarre, c/o, Boston, Mass.,
91, #19416
Lookebee, David, N.C., 40,
#3328
Looker, John, Burlington, Vt.,
105, #7752
Loomis, Ezra, Albany, N.Y., 78,
#14534
Loomis, Ezra, Albany, N.Y., 82,
#15218
Loomis, Ezra, Vt., 55, #6908
Loomis, Israel, Conn., 33, #351
Loomis, Jacob, Conn., 33, #13

Loomis, Jacob, e/o, Boston, Mass., 96, #1492

Loomis, Jerome, Albany, N.Y., 49, #5391

Loomis, Jerome, w/o, Albany, N.Y., 70, #11142

Loomis, Samuel, a/o, Conn., 38, #F1825

Loomis, Simon, w/o, Albany, N.Y., 92, #19846

Loomis 2nd, Isaiah, Conn., 80, #14921

Looney, John, S.C., 84, #15988

Lord, Asa, Mich., 121, #6723

Lord, Frederick, c/o, Conn., 95, #937

Lord, Ichabod, c/o, Maine, 99, #3545

Lord, Joseph, Conn., 33, #299

Lord, Robert, alias William, g/o c/o, Maine, 132, #8946

Lord, Robert, alias William, g/o c/o, Maine, 139, #7292

Lord, Tryhena, c/o, Conn., 91, #18964

Lord, Tryphena, Conn., 33, #14

Lord, William, a/o, Bellows Falls, Vt., 71, #12272

Loring, Ann, c/o, Boston, Mass., 103, #7074

Loring, Benjemin, a/o, New York City, 95, #877

Loring, Samuel, N.Y., 73, #12727

Loring, Samuel, w/o, New York City, 15, #12727

Lorinsburg, Nathan M., Burlington, Vt., 125, #2595

Losee, John, N.Y., 82, #15533, card

Losee, John, e/o, Albany, N.Y., 15, #15533

Losey, Moses, c/o, Madison, Ind., 15, #869

Lothrop, Daniel, c/o, Maine, 46, #4762

Lott, Jacob, Philadelphia, Pa., 70, #12219

Lott, John, Albany, N.Y., 55, #6916

Loud, Benjamin, c/o, Maine, 69, #10826

Loud, David, a/o, Mass., 135, #1672

Loud, Mary Ann, Philadelphia, Pa., 143, #7545

Loud, Silvanus, Mass., 71, #12380

Loudon, Archibald, c/o, Philadelphia, Pa., 70, #12189

Loudon, Eunice, Ill., 64, #9192

Loudon, Nathaniel, Mich., 89, #18176

Loudon, Thomas C., Ill., 139, #7788

Loudon, Thomas E., Ill., 128, #5318

Loudon, Thomas E., Ill., 136, #3623

Loughton, David, a/o, Albany, N.Y., 135, #2288

Lounsberry, Sarah, New York City, 99, #3481

Love, Edmund, w/o, Knoxville, Tenn., 15, #4201

Love, Edward, —, 44, #4201, card

Love, Elias, c/o, Richmond, Va., 62, #8873

Love, Elias, c/o, Richmond, Va., 67, #10315

Love, Joseph T., Mo., 141,
#2050
Love, Robert, Richmond, Va.,
104, #7640
Love, Robert, Richmond, Va.,
95, #1083
Love, Samuel, Knoxville, Tenn.,
86, #16956
Love, Samuel M., Knoxville,
Tenn., 76, #13911
Love, Samuel M., Knoxville,
Tenn., 84, #15992
Love, Thomas, Ill., 128, #5833
Love, Thomas, N.Y., 78,
#14527
Love, Thomas B., w/o, New York
City, 118, #4634
Lovelace, Anne, a/o, Ky., 82,
#15460
Lovelady, Thomas, Richmond,
Va., 52, #6110
Loveland, Amos, Pittsburgh,
Pa., 76, #13780
Loveland, Amos, Pittsburgh,
Pa., 81, #15141
Loveland, Amos, w/o,
Cleveland, Ohio, 116,
#3541
Loveland, Isaac, Pittsburgh, Pa.,
43, #4018
Lovell, Elizabeth S., c/o, Maine,
89, #18192
Lovell, Mary, Mass., 66,
#10198
Lovering, Isaac, w/o, Boston,
Mass., 54, #6845
Lovern, Frances, Va., 65, #9792
Lovern, Frances, Va., 83,
#15759
Lovern, Richd., w/o, Richmond,
Va., 53, #6466

Lovet, John, w/o, N.Y., 83,
#15581
Loving, Mary, a/o, Richmond,
Va., 16, #19777
Low, Bezalul, c/o, Maine, 46,
#4843
Low, Elisha, Madison, Ind., 129,
#6518
Low, Jane, c/o, New York City,
61, #8649
Low, John, w/o, Maine, 112,
#806
Low, Mary, c/o, Albany, N.Y.,
116, #3355
Low, Remember, c/o, Maine,
115, #2693
Lowden, Thomas E., Ill., 125,
#2376
Lowdry, Nathaniel, w/o, Mass.,
87, #17600
Lowe, Robert, Va., 71, #12344
Lowe, Thomas, Ill., 125, #2759
Lowe, Thomas, Ill., 137, #4628
Lowe, Thomas, Spingfield, Ill.,
138, #5198
Lowe, Thomas, a/o, N.C., 113,
#1552
Lowe, Trecy, S.C., 127, #4679,
card
Lowe, Trecy, c/o, S.C., 16,
#4679
Lowe (formerly Archer), Martha
D., Madison, Wisc., 143,
#6465
Lowell, John, Utica, N.Y., 104,
#7541
Lowell, Timothy, —, 121,
#7669, card
Lowell, Timothy, c/o, Albany,
N.Y., 16, #7669
Lowes, Bella, w/o, Mass., 44,
#4215

Lown, Peter, w/o, Mich., 87,
#17425
Lowrey, John, W. Tenn., 49,
#5271
Lowrey, Levi, w/o, Ga., 112,
#1008
Lowrey, Simeon, e/o, Ga., 58,
#7901
Lowrey, Thomas, w/o, Ky., 102,
#5425
Lowry, Ann, a/o, Richmond,
Va., 115, #2456
Lowry, Susan, a/o, Richmond,
Va., 36A, #F3 V13
Lowry, Herman, PA, Bellows
Falls, Vt., 75, #13647
Loxey, Moses, Ind., 112, #869,
card
Lozier, Abraham, w/o, Albany,
N.Y., 65, #9894
Lozier, Elizabeth, New York
City, 73, #12809
Lozier, Helebrant, w/o, New
York City, 64, #9226
Lubar, Daniel, Philadelphia, Pa.,
120, #6197, card
Lucas, Basil, Va., 78, #14464,
card
Lucas, Basil, w/o, Richmond,
Va., 16, #14464
Lucas, Basil, w/o, Va., 75,
#13423
Lucas, Basil, w/o, Va., 75,
#13525
Lucas, George, c/o, Philadelphia,
Pa., 125, #1722
Lucas, Mary, Mobile, Ala., 71,
#12352
Lucas, Mary, Mobile, Ala., 79,
#14616
Lucas, William, Albany, N.Y.,
89, #18338

Lucas, William, Albany, N.Y.,
89, #18339
Lucas, William, Ky., 43, #3943
Lucas, William, Ky., 48, #5232
Lucas, William, Louisville, Ky.,
104, #7515
Luce, Damaris, Mass., 80,
#14826
Luce, John, Albany, N.Y., 86,
#17242
Luce, Malachi, c/o, Mass., 86,
#16736
Luce, Parnal, c/o, Conn., 59,
#8050
Luckett, Royall, c/o, Va., 91,
#19095
Luckey, Hugh, Jackson, Tenn.,
48, #5245
Luckey, Hugh, w/o, Jackson,
Tenn., 74, #13302
Luddington, Lemuel, c/o,
Pittsburgh, Pa., 56, #7316
Lufberry, Abraham, N.J., 97,
#2241
Lugar, Margaret, a/o, Richmond,
Va., 92, #19967
Lugg, Elizabeth, a/o, Va., 85,
#16337
Luke, John, —, 136, #2826, slip
Luks, John, c/o, Pittsburgh, Pa.,
137, #3695
Lull, Abigail, a/o, Montpelier,
Vt., 108, #10184
Lumbard, Daniel, Vt., 57,
#7565, card
Lumbard, Mercy, Mass., 70,
#11189
Lumbley, William, w/o, Ark.,
90, #18550
Lumm, Jesse, Pittsburgh, Pa.,
40, #3284

Lumsden, Patty, Richmond, Va.,
95, #1009
Lusk, Elizabeth, Miss., 119,
#5508
Lusk, Elizabeth, Miss., 122,
#8252
Lusk, Elizabeth, Miss., 124,
#821
Lusk, John, Pittsburgh, Pa., 51,
#5969
Lusk, Joseph, —, 58, #7740,
card
Lusk, Joseph, Knoxville, Tenn.,
40, #3315
Lusk, Joseph, c/o, Knoxville,
Tenn., 16, #7740
Lusk, Joseph, c/o, Knoxville,
Tenn., 16, #12952
Lusk, Michael, N.Y., 88,
#17865
Lusky, Juno, Morganton, N.C.,
123, #333
Lutes, Elijah, —, 137, #4614,
card
Lutes, Elijah, Cincinnati, Ohio,
16, #1148
Lutes, Elijah, Cincinnati, Ohio,
16, #4614
Lutes, Elijah, Cincinnati, Ohio,
136, #3367
Luther, Elizabeth, N.C., 88,
#17745
Luther, George, w/o, N.C., 66,
#10224
Luther, John, La., 41, #3400
Luther, Levi, a/o, Conn., 79,
#14738
Luther, Michael, Fayetteville,
N.C., 127, #4945
Luther, Lt. R. A., AAQM, 88,
#17890, slip

Luther, Lt. R. A., AAQM, 88,
#17955, slip
Luther, R. A., 2nd Artillery, 122,
#8886, slip
Luther, Rachel, a/o, R.I., 122,
#8116
Luther, Stephen, w/o, Boston,
Mass., 94, #305
Luther, Thomas, c/o, R.I., 123,
#9562
Lyles, Susan E., Miss., 137,
#3895
Lyman, John, a/o, Albany, N.Y.,
103, #6848
Lyman, Mary, Conn., 99, #3635
Lynam, Betsy, Ky., 115, #2808
Lynch, Amelia C., Richmond,
Va., 36A, #F2 V26
Lynch, Bartholomew,
Philadelphia, Pa., 112,
#1074
Lynch, Elijah, w/o, N.C., 72,
#12706
Lynch, Henry, Mo., 41, #3425
Lynch, Henry, Mo., 48, #5116
Lynch, Henry, Mo., 57, #7512
Lynch, Henry, Mo., 68, #10749
Lynch, Henry, Mo., 76, #13802
Lynch, James, La., 119, #5460
Lynch, Peter, Mo., 140, #182
Lynch, Peter, Mo., 142, #5936
Lynde, Hannah, a/o, Vt., 78,
#14413
Lyndes, David, g/o c/o, Conn.,
37, #F1820
Lynes, John, a/o, Conn., 38,
#F1825
Lynn, Sebey, Knoxville, Tenn.,
130, #7938
Lynn, William F., Ky., 39,
#3057

Lynn, William F., a/o, Ky., 88, #18113

Lynton, John, Mobile, Ala., 69, #10953

Lyon, Catherine, c/o, Albany, N.Y., 78, #14386

Lyon, Hezekiah, g/o c/o, Jonesboro, Tenn., 133, #116

Lyon, James, c/o, Va., 68, #10812

Lyon, Joshua, Conn., 33, #—

Lyon, Joshua, Conn., 61, #8387

Lyon, Joshua, Conn., 74, #13317

Lyon, Moses, Albany, N.Y., 73, #12762

Lyon, Moses, Albany, N.Y., 78, #14524

Lyon, Naomi, N.J., 90, #18826

Lyon, Sarah, c/o, Conn., 68, #10686

Lyon, Thomas, Wisc., 84, #16301

Lyon, William, Ky., 53, #6405

Lyth, William, Philadelphia, Pa., 109, #10575

M

Maag, Henry, e/o, Philadelphia, Pa., 98, #3093

Mabray, John, Ga., 111, #573

Mabray, John, Ga., 112, #1211

Mabry, David, w/o, N.J., 74, #13055

Mabry, John, c/o, Ky., 121, #7806

Mabry (or Mabrey), John, Ga., 136, #2932

MacDill, David, Ohio, 57, #7463

Mace, Henry, Nashville, Tenn., 132, #9792

Mack, Betty, Madison, Ind., 105, #8019

Mack, Hezekiah, c/o, Conn., 63, #9095

MacKay, Alexander, w/o, 1st Artillery, 52, #6244

MacKay, Alexander D., w/o, —, 42, #3654

MacKay, Lt. Alexander D., w/o, —, 63, #8961

MacKay, Lt. Alexander D., w/o, —, 72, #12696

Mackay, Lt. Alexander D., w/o, —, 77, #13974

MacKay, Lt. Alexander D., w/o, 1st Artillery, 57, #7597

Mackey, Thomas, S.C., 53, #6404

Macky, Ann E., Jackson, Tenn., 129, #6503

Macomber, Henry, Concord, N.H., 121, #7839

Macomber, Henry, Concord, N.H., 122, #8424

Macomber, Henry, Concord, N.H., 120, #6275

MacRae, John, N.C., 44, #4297, card

Madden, David, Albany, N.Y., 40, #3351

Madden, Jane, Madison, Ind., 132, #9276

Madden, John, Cincinnati, Ohio, 129, #6262

Madden, John, Ohio, 123, #9279

Maddox, Jacob, c/o, Knoxville, Tenn., 120, #5958

Maddox, John, Richmond, Va., 104, #7447

Malick, John, Va., 77, #14214
Mallary, Aaron, Burlington, Vt.,
    41, #3552
Mallicoat, James, Mo., 128,
    #5707
Mallory, Catharine, Richmond,
    Va., 36A, #F6, card
Mallory, Catharine L.,
    Richmond, Va., 120, #5897
Mallory, James, Albany, N.Y.,
    58, #7828
Mallory, John, Huntsville, Ala.,
    52, #6297
Mallory, Lemuel, w/o, Ind., 114,
    #2150
Mallory, Samuel, Conn., 33,
    #948
Mallory, William, W. Tenn., 82,
    #15445, card
Maloney, Archibald, w/o,
    Richmond, Va., 101, #4691
Maloney, Patrick, Mo., 130,
    #7359
Malony, Archibald, Richmond,
    Va., 57, #7544
Malony, Archibald, Richmond,
    Va., 52, #6340
Maltbie, Zacheus, c/o, Albany,
    N.Y., 17, #18449
Manard, James, Richmond, Va.,
    106, #8436
Manard, James, Va., 77, #14033
Manchester, Joseph, —, 91,
    #19363, slip
Manchester, Mary, a/o, R.I.,
    129, #7061
Manchester, Nabby, —, 90,
    #18876, card
Mancriff, Sarah, Boston, Mass.,
    139, #7419
Mangum, John, Mobile, Ala.,
    60, #8374

Manier, David, Richmond, Va.,
    137, #4517, card
Manley, Isaac, Pittsburgh, Pa.,
    142, #4841
Manley, Isaac, Pittsburgh, Pa.,
    142, #4985
Manley, Susanna, Ohio, 98,
    #2998
Manley, Thomas, a/o, Albany,
    N.Y., 96, #1686
Manly, James M., Nashville,
    Tenn., 138, #4847
Mann, Abraham, c/o, N.J., 83,
    #15640
Mann, Amos, w/o, Maine, 86,
    #16747
Mann, Andrew, w/o, Albany,
    N.Y., 97, #2082
Mann, Hannah, Mass., 60,
    #8276
Mann, Hannah, a/o, Mass., 91,
    #19366
Mann, James, Mich., 47, #4982
Mann, Joseph, Richmond, Va.,
    45, #4467
Mann, Mary, Richmond, Va.,
    97, #2069
Manning, Isaac, w/o, N.J., 99,
    #3688
Manning, James, e/o c/o, N.C.
    Militia, 94, #752
Manning, James, w/o & c/o,
    N.C. Militia, 94, #751
Manning, Joshua, w/o, S.C., 91,
    #19498
Manning, Sarah, c/o, Conn., 34,
    #589
Manning, Thomas, a/o,
    Cincinnati, Ohio, 17, #241
Mannon, Henry, w/o,
    Burlington, Vt., 51, #5920

Mansell, Joseph, a/o, Maine,
110, #171
Mapel, Mary, a/o, Philadelphia,
Pa., 17, #4731
Maple, Stephen, Pittsburgh, Pa.,
96, #1779
Maple, Stephen, w/o,
Philadelphia, Pa., 101,
#4731, card
Marble, Phebe, c/o, Vt., 64,
#9142
Marcurn, Thomas, w/o, N.C., 61,
#8449
Marden, Lawrence, S.C., 71,
#12280
Mareh, Sally, c/o, Maine, 142,
#5223
Margeon, Thomas Gibbez, PA,
New Orleans, La., 87,
#17284
Margh, Stephen, w/o, Boston,
Mass., 97, #2098
Marick Sr., John, Mobile, Ala.,
62, #8833
Marion, Samuel, Jonesboro,
Tenn., 87, #17694
Mariquart, Jacob, New York
City, 62, #8692
Markell, Elizabeth, c/o,
Cleveland, Ohio, 128,
#5282
Markham, Jeremiah, e/o, Conn.,
38, #F1828
Markham, Nelly, Richmond,
Va., 97, #1959
Markham, Nelly, Richmond,
Va., 101, #4846
Markham Sr., Thomas, Va., 90,
#18755
Markhom, Elizabeth, Boston,
Mass., 62, #8778

Markley, Catharine, e/o,
Philadelphia, Pa., 97,
#2109
Markley, Philip, D.C., 56,
#7404
Markley, Philip, D.C., 74,
#13332
Marks, Lucy, c/o, Va., 88,
#17777
Marks, Samuel, w/o, Albany,
N.Y., 87, #17352
Markwood, Ellen, Richmond,
Va., 36A, #F4 V14
Marowzkis, Paul, Mo., 125,
#1799
Marquant, Christian, Ohio, 106,
#8394
Marr, Aurey, c/o, Md., 126,
#3444
Marr, James, a/o, Maine, 137,
#4304
Marsden, John, Philadelphia,
Pa., 54, #6798
Marsdeu, John, Philadelphia,
Pa., 71, #12421
Marsh, Allyn, Conn., 38,
#F1825
Marsh, Deliverance, Mass., 68,
#10622
Marsh, Eleazer, c/o, Pittsburgh,
Pa., 134, #1403
Marsh, Elizabeth, Indianapolis,
Ind., 17, #12647
Marsh, Elizabeth C., —, 39,
#2945
Marsh, Jasper, w/o, Albany,
N.Y., 85, #16340
Marsh, Lucy, a/o, Mass., 139,
#6960
Marsh, Reuben, a/o, Albany,
N.Y., 97, #1913

Marsh, Roswell, Conn., 51,
#5913

Marsh, Seymour, Albany, N.Y.,
51, #5988

Marsh, Stephen, Boston, Mass.,
70, #11122

Marsh, Stephen, Mass., 80,
#14898

Marsh, Thomas, a/o, Richmond,
Va., 124, #816

Marsh, William, w/o, Ind., 72,
#12647, card

Marshall, Benjamin, —, 80,
#14973, card

Marshall, Benjamin, c/o, N.C.,
17, #14973

Marshall, Daniel, Albany, N.Y.,
90, #18850

Marshall, Elizabeth, Va., 85,
#16637

Marshall, Hezekiah, Pa., 67,
#10376

Marshall, Jesse, Ga., 56, #7307

Marshall, John, —, 113, #1664,
slip

Marshall, John, e/o, Ky., 104,
#7161

Marshall, Keziah, Wheeling,
Va., 128, #6056

Marshall, Lucy, N.C., 46, #4672

Marshall, Robert, Md., 17,
#19161

Marshall, Samuel, Concord,
N.H., 115, #2653

Marshall, Thomas, Richmond,
Va., 77, #13966

Marshall, Thomas, Va., 66,
#10285

Marshall, Thomas, c/o,
Richmond, Va., 17, #1664

Marston, Joseph P., c/o, Maine,
120, #6029

Marston, Rhoda, a/o,
Portsmouth, N.H., 125,
#2234

Martin, Calvin, g/o c/o, N.C.,
128, #5338

Martin, Charles, Ind., 121,
#7013

Martin, Charles, Miss., 111,
#609

Martin, Charles, Miss., 118,
#4813

Martin, Charles, Miss., 128,
#6103

Martin, Elizabeth, N.C., 111,
#693

Martin, Elizabeth, R.I., 121,
#6955

Martin, Elizabeth, a/o,
Fayetteville, N.C., 124,
#664

Martin, George, N.C., 89,
#18462

Martin, Henry, Pittsburgh, Pa.,
70, #12201

Martin, Henry, Pittsburgh, Pa.,
81, #15131

Martin, Isaac, Vt., 85, #16405

Martin, J. Baptiste, c/o, Albany,
N.Y., 113, #1636

Martin, J. Baptiste, c/o, Albany,
N.Y., 114, #2086

Martin, Jacob, c/o, Pittsburgh,
Pa., 43, #4063

Martin, James, e/o, Ky., 115,
#2553

Martin, John, w/o, Nashville,
Tenn., 40, #3235

Martin, John D., Richmond, Va.,
131, #8402

Martin, John D., Richmond, Va.,
99, #3534

Martin, John D., Va., 82,
#15232
Martin, John D., Va., 120,
#6675
Martin, John M., Mo., 114,
#2055
Martin, John W., Mo., 131,
#8901
Martin, Joseph, c/o, Albany,
N.Y., 123, #9564
Martin, Joseph, c/o, Albany,
N.Y., 114, #2414
Martin, Joshua, w/o, Bellows
Falls, Vt., 52, #6217
Martin, Kinchen, N.C., 82,
#15233
Martin, Laticia, a/o, Ky., 17,
#1969
Martin, Lititia, Ky., 125,
#1969, slip
Martin, Mary, Ky., 126, #3374
Martin, Nancy, c/o, N.C., 82,
#15231
Martin, Nancy, c/o, N.C., 84,
#16099
Martin, Patsy, N.C., 75, #13571
Martin, Pleasant, e/o, Nashville,
Tenn., 125, #2801
Martin, Private John, w/o, 30th
Inf., 107, #9372
Martin, Reuben, —, 121, #6956,
slip
Martin, Reuben, a/o, Ohio, 17,
#6956
Martin, Robert, Knoxville,
Tenn., 39, #3045
Martin, Robert, a/o, Knoxville,
Tenn., 77, #14020
Martin, Samuel, N.C., 43, #----,
card
Martin, Samuel, c/o, N.C., 17,
#4146

Martin, William, —, 103,
#6762, card
Martin, William, Ky., 125,
#1968, card
Martin, William, Wheeling, Va.,
47, #5032
Martin, William, a/o, Ky., 17,
#1968
Martin, William, a/o, Wheeling,
Va., 17, #6262
Martin, William, c/o, Albany,
N.Y., 110, #54
Martin, William, w/o,
Richmond, Va., 112, #880
Martin (formerly Smith),
Rosanna, La., 127, #4932
Martindale, Uriah, e/o, Mass.,
89, #18352
Martindale, Samuel, N.C., 8,
#364, in file of J.
Falconbury
Martinsen, Adolph, Des Moines,
Iowa, 142, #4725
Martinson, Adolph, Iowa, 142,
#5224
Martz, George, Pittsburgh, Pa.,
72, #12538
Martz, George, Pittsburgh, Pa.,
72, #12689
Martz, John B., Mich., 143,
#6693
Marvin, Jonathan, w/o, Vt., 54,
#6790
Mason, Alexander L.,
Indianapolis, Ind., 125,
#2478
Mason, Alexander L., Madison,
Ind., 124, #1368
Mason, Ebenezer, Maine, 39,
#3094
Mason, Elijah, w/o, Albany,
N.Y., 44, #4211

Mason, John, Mo., 109, #10797
Mason, John, St. Louis, Mo.,
    104, #7656
Mason, Joseph, Ky., 123,
    #9404, card
Mason, Peter, Ind., 61, #8439
Mason, Peter, Va., 54, #6607,
    card
Mason, Phebe, New York City,
    98, #2797
Mason, Phebe, c/o, Mass., 136,
    #3620
Mason, R. B., g/o c/o, Mo.,
    128, #6017
Mason, Simeon, Mass., 40,
    #3186
Mason, Simeon, Mass., 45,
    #4587
Mason, Simeon, c/o, Mass., 86,
    #16804
Mason, Smith, Richmond, Va.,
    86, #17219
Mason, William, N.C., 52,
    #6097
Mason, William H.,
    Philadelphia, Pa., 104,
    #7214
Mason, Peter, Va., 8, #6607, in
    file of J. Ferguson
Massey, Elizabeth, Fayetteville,
    N.C., 133, #653
Massey, John, Va., 40, #3324
Massie, Sally, e/o, Va., 79,
    #14652
Massy, Charles, w/o, Ind., 82,
    #15311
Masters, Enoch, w/o, N.C., 120,
    #6114
Masterson, Margaret, a/o, Ky.,
    109, #10613
Masterson, Patrick, w/o, Ky.,
    126, #3147

Matheney, William, Jackson,
    Tenn., 44, #4212
Matheney, William, Jackson,
    Tenn., 45, #4556
Matheny, Sarah, S.C., 113,
    #1388
Mather, Elihu, w/o, Ill., 83,
    #15726
Mather, Hepzibah, Conn., 45,
    #4451
Mather, Huldah, Bellows Falls,
    Vt., 75, #13647
Mather, Joseph, Conn., 34,
    #314
Mather, Mathaniel, Conn., 66,
    #10166
Mather, Nathaniel, e/o, Conn.,
    114, #2191
Mather, Samuel, c/o, Conn., 98,
    #3009
Mathers, William, Mo., 73,
    #12859
Matheson, Thomas, Maine, 110,
    #55
Matheson, Thomas, Maine, 119,
    #5289
Matheson, Thomas, Portland,
    Maine, 143, #7519
Mathew, Elizabeth, c/o, Albany,
    N.Y., 72, #12664
Mathew, Isaac, Wheeling, Va.,
    71, #12237
Mathews, Benjamin, Huntsville,
    Ala., 52, #6308
Mathews, Desire, Maine, 72,
    #12665
Mathews, Francis M.,
    Spingfield, Ill., 140, #658
Mathews, James, w/o, N.J., 71,
    #12356
Mathews, Peter H., w/o, Ky.,
    125, #2383

Mathews, Rebecca, Mo., 132,
#9477
Mathews, Rebecca, St. Louis,
Mo., 138, #5140
Mathews, William, Ky., 86,
#16870
Mathewson, Betty, R.I., 86,
#17116
Mathia, Philip, Cleveland, Ohio,
143, #6644
Mathis, William J., Madison,
Ind., 130, #8016
Mathison, Jacob, Mo., 126,
#3290
Mathison, Jacob, Mo., 133,
#158
Matkins, John, w/o, N.C., 97,
#2015
Matlbie, Zacheus, Albany, N.Y.,
89, #18449, card
Matlock, Nathaniel, Ky., 46,
#4802
Matlock, Nathaniel, w/o,
Lexington, Ky., 17, #4802
Matteson, Hezakiah, w/o,
Albany, N.Y., 50, #5620
Matteson, Sally, c/o, Albany,
N.Y., 130, #7429
Matteson, Sally, c/o, Albany,
N.Y., 130, #7529
Matthews, James, a/o, N.C.,
102, #5864
Matthews, Jesse, w/o, Va., 84,
#16117
Matthews, Miranda, New
Orleans, La., 138, #4661
Matthews, Thankful, Mass., 72,
#12663
Matthewson, Sgt. Gardner, c/o,
25th Inf., 100, #4104
Mattingly, Dicander, c/o,
Richmond, Va., 126, #3141

Maugnum, John, Tuscaloosa,
Ala., 86, #17224
Maupin, Margaert, Ky., 129,
#6520
Maupin, Margaret, Ky., 140,
#892
Maupin, Thomas, w/o, Ky., 127,
#4169
Maupin, William, Va., 81,
#15008
Maury, Thomas, —, 123, #241,
card
Maut, William, —, 97, #190-,
card
Maxcy, Betsey Ann, a/o, Ill.,
128, #5785
Maxcy, Joel, Ill., 74, #13203
Maxey, Joel, Ill., 61, #8594
Maxfield, David, a/o, R.I., 75,
#13481
Maxfield, Robert, c/o, Maine,
125, #2354
Maxson, Stephen, —, 112,
#887, card
Maxson, Stephen, c/o, Albany,
N.Y., 17, #887
Maxwell, Adam, Pittsburgh, Pa.,
39, #----
Maxwell, Elizabeth, Pittsburgh,
Pa., 17, #2930
Maxwell, James, e/o, Pittsburgh,
Pa., 107, #9280
May, Abram, w/o, Madison,
Ind., 98, #2912
May, Carpemone, a/o,
Jonesboro, Tenn., 123,
#213
May, John, N.C., 99, #3239,
slip
May, John, e/o, Concord, N.H.,
130, #7455

May, John, w/o, N.C., 17,
#3239

May, Rhoda, Knoxville, Tenn.,
105, #7989

May, Thomas, Jackson, Tenn.,
64, #9656

May, Thomas, N.C., 61, #8450

May, Thomas, a/o, Tenn., 123,
#9498

Mayes, Elisha C., c/o, Ill., 134,
#1002

Mayfield, Elijah, Nashville,
Tenn., 39, #3159

Mayhew, David, w/o,
Philadelphia, Pa., 51,
#6022

Mayhew, John, w/o, N.C., 74,
#13175

Mayner, Henry, w/o, S.C., 110,
#10967

Mayo, Benjamin, Va., 118,
#4814, card

Mayo, Benjamin, w/o,
Richmond, Va., 17, #4814

Mayo, Isaac, w/o, Maine, 98,
#2861

Mayo, John, Ga., 43, #3977

Mayo, John, Ga., 72, #12546

Mayo Sr., John, Ga., 64, #9195

Mayo Sr., John, Ga., 52, #6166

Mays, Leity, a/o, Richmond,
Va., 125, #2386

McAdams, Joannah, a/o,
Pittsburgh, Pa., 112, #1127

McAfee, Benajmin,
Philadelphia, Pa., 42,
#3647

McaGalthery, Rachael,
Philadelphia, Pa., 71,
#12391

McAleer, Matthew, Madison,
Ind., 126, #3203

McAllister, Herrictta, a/o,
Knoxville, Tenn., 136,
#2658

McAllister, John, w/o, N.C.,
113, #1548

McAllister, Joseph, —, 59,
#8105, card

McAllister, Joseph, c/o, Ky.,
16, #8105

McArthur, Duncan, t/o, Albany,
N.Y., 62, #8805

McAuley, Daniel, a/o, N.C.,
108, #9717

McAuley, John, N.J., 128,
#5963

McBee, —, Miss., 84, #16028,
card

McBee, Elijah, c/o, S.C. Militia,
137, #4007

McBee, Elijah, c/o, S.C. Militia,
137, #4008

McBee, Elijah, c/o, S.C. Militia,
137, #4009

McBee, Silas, Mass., 16,
#16038, card

McBee, Silas, Natchez, Miss.,
68, #10620

McBird, Alexander, Pa., 108,
#10262, card

McBride, Bridget, New York
City, 126, #3373

McBride, Daniel, w/o,
Philadelphia, Pa., 110,
#10997

McBride, John, w/o, 27th Inf.,
138, #4840

McCabe, Peter, Mo., 105, #8136

McCalester, Daniel, c/o, Ky.,
129, #6587

McCall, David, a/o c/o, S.C.,
137, #4208

McCall, Thomas, Wheeling, Va., 47, #4930

McCallester, John A., Oregon Volunteers, 129, #6759

McCance, David, Ga., 40, #3303

McCane, James, w/o, S.C., 61, #8599, card

McCargo, Radford, Mo., 59, #8051

McCarter, Isabella, c/o, N.C., 101, #4753

McCarter, James, Mobile, Ala., 57, #7482

McCarter, James, Tuscaloosa, Ala., 73, #12819

McCarter, James, Va., 66, #10075

McCartney, Henry, w/o, Philadelphia, Pa., 62, #8739

McCarty, Daniel, c/o, Ill., 118, #4985

McCarty, Daniel, g/o c/o, Ill., 123, #323

McCarty, Daniel, g/o c/o, Ill., 125, #1711

McCarty, Daniel, g/o c/o, Ill., 135, #2300

McCarty, James, La., 137, #4444

McCarty, Mary, Ky., 135, #2198, card

McCarty, Mary, a/o, Ky., 16, #2198

McCarty, Sarah, Philadelphia, Pa., 115, #2727

McCaskill, Kenneth, Miss., 69, #10840

McCauley, John, c/o, Richmond, Va., 72, #12577

McCauley, John W., La., 112, #895

McCauley, Martha, e/o, N.C., 16, #5640

McCauley, Matthew, w/o, N.C., 102, #5640, card

McCausland, Mary, c/o, Maine, 141, #3294

McCaw, James, S.C., 40, #3285

McCaw, James, w/o, S.C., 16, #8599

McCerger, Radford, Mo., 53, #6564

McChellan, James, —, 83, #15785

McChesney, Abigal, c/o, Albany, N.Y., 79, #14554

McClain, Abijah, w/o, Philadelphia, Pa., 119, #5634

McClain, Alexander, Pittsburgh, Pa., 71, #12466, card

McClain, John, Ga., 51, #5990

McClain, John, c/o, Philadelphia, Pa., 61, #8586

McClanahan, William, w/o, Va., 90, #18696

McClarey, Benjamin, w/o, Albany, N.Y., 110, #11179

McClarran, Sarah, Pittsburgh, Pa., 114, #2003

McClean, Alexander, Pittsburgh, Pa., 98, #297-, card

McClean, Alexander, a/o, Pittsburgh, Pa., 16, #2762

McClean, Sarah, New York City, 102, #6023, card

McCleary, William, Baltimore, Md., 49, #5321

McClellan, James, Pittsburgh, Pa., 50, #5743

McClellan, James, Pittsburgh, Pa., 70, #12202

McClellan, James, Pittsburgh, Pa., 95, #967

McClellan, James, Pittsburgh, Pa., 97, #2110

McClellan, Joseph, c/o, Ky., 117, #4438

McClenden, Sarah, c/o, Miss., 16, #6023

McClendon, Shadrack, Miss., 97, #2155, card

McClintock, Hugh, Ky., 82, #15378

McCluer, Newton H., Mo., 120, #6113

McClune, Samuel, Ill., 59, #7976

McClung, Alex K., Miss., 111, #713

McClung, Joseph, Ohio, 57, #7533

McClung, Joseph, Ohio, 64, #9264

McClung, Robert, Ohio, 65, #9710

McClure, Andrew, Del., 44, #4228

McClure, Newton H., Mo., 121, #6894

McClure, Newton H., Mo., 140, #585

McCluren (formerly Slade), Eloise, c/o, Ill., 114, #2246

McClurken, Thomas, w/o, Ill., 100, #4544

McClurlein, Mathew, Ind., 57, #7619

McCluskain, Thomas, Ill., 42, #3743

McCollum, Patrick, N.J., 48, #5214

McComas, John, Va., 42, #3690

McConnel, James, Huntsville, Ala., 64, #9206

McConnell, James, Mobile, Ala., 54, #6622

McConnell, Mary, N.C., 120, #5997

McConnell, Noah, Oregon City, O.T., 142, #5978

McConnell, Susannah, Cincinnati, Ohio, 121, #7767

McCord, John, N.Y., 86, #17010

McCord, William, Ind., 54, #6895

McCord, William, Ind., 57, #7618

McCorkle, William A. L., Ore., 140, #681

McCorkle, William A. L., Vancouver, W.T., 142, #3609

McCormack, Andrew, w/o, Springfield, Ill., 107, #9326

McCormick, Elizabeth, Springfield, Ill., 142, #4903

McCormick, Grissil, c/o, Philadelphia, Pa., 16, #1349

McCormick, Joseph, Ala., 44, #4161

McCormick, Joseph, a/o, Richmond, Va., 138, #4688

McCormick, Mathew, Ore., 133, #4

McCormick, Mathew, Oregon City, O.T., 128, #5327

McCormick, Sarah, Albany, N.Y., 64, #9552

McCormick, Stephen, New York City, 126, #3559

McCory, John, w/o, Nashville,
Tenn., 89, #18340
McCosky, John, Knoxville,
Tenn., 98, #2957, card
McCoy, Alexander, c/o, Ky.,
135, #2070
McCoy, Daniel, Nashville,
Tenn., 81, #15002
McCoy, David, g/o c/o, Conn.,
37, #F1820
McCoy, Hugh, Pittsburgh, Pa.,
139, #9267
McCoy, John, c/o, Md., 107,
#9270
McCoy, Nancy, c/o, Pittsburgh,
Pa., 115, #2775
McCoy, Redden, S.C., 118,
#4707, slip
McCoy, Reddin, c/o, S.C., 16,
#4707
McCoy, Reddin, e/o, S.C., 16,
#5316
McCoy, Reddon, S.C., 119,
#5316, slip
McCoy, Robert, Ind., 70,
#11073
McCoy, William, Albany, N.Y.,
66, #10125
McCracken, James, w/o, Md.,
79, #14591
McCrady, Robert, Pittsburgh,
Pa., 95, #935
McCrary, John, Huntsville, Ala.,
65, #9813
McCrary, John, Nashville,
Tenn., 53, #6412
McCrary, John, Nashville,
Tenn., 55, #6990
McCraw, Francis, w/o,
Richmond, Va., 58, #7835

McCraw, Mary H., e/o,
Richmond, Va., 108,
#10023
McCray, James, Va., 70, #12180
McCray, James, w/o, Va., 70,
#12081
McCray, William, Philadelphia,
Pa., 71, #12358
McCreary, George, Ohio, 41,
#3443
McCreary, James, c/o, Madison,
Ind., 117, #4302
McCreary, William,
Philadelphia, Pa., 104,
#7349
McCreight, Robert, S.C., 46,
#4725
McCreight, Robert, t/o, S.C.,
56, #7406
McCreight, Robert, t/o, S.C.,
66, #10202
McCrery, James, g/o c/o,
Indianapolis, Ind., 134,
#1655
McCrevy, Archibald, a/o w/o,
S.C., 124, #1562
McCrillis, Ruth, Portsmouth,
Maine, 132, #9719
McCrosky, James, a/o, Ky.,
122, #8151
McCrury, Margaret, Md., 116,
#3275
McCubbin, Nicholas, c/o, —,
118, #4861, card
McCullough, William, Ky., 42,
#3742
McCumber, John, Ill., 48,
#5216
McCumber, John, Ill., 63,
#9118
McCune, Thomas, Wheeling,
Va., 89, #18448, card

McCune, Thomas, a/o,
Wheeling, Va., 16, #2957
McCune (or McCowen), John,
w/o, Ga. Militia, 97, #2097
McCurdy, Alexander, c/o,
Pittsburgh, Pa., 65, #9748
McCurdy, Archibald, N.C., 117,
#4176, card
McCurdy, Archibald, w/o, N.C.,
16, #4176
McCutchan, William, Richmond,
Va., 52, #6159
McCutchan, William, Va., 42,
#3665
McCutchan, William, w/o,
Richmond, Va., 106, #8521
McDaniel, Benjamin, W. Tenn.,
46, #4704
McDaniel, Elizabeth, c/o,
Nashville, Tenn., 80,
#14927
McDaniel, Jane, Mo., 130,
#7770
McDaniel, John, w/o,
Philadelphia, Pa., 16,
#12537
McDeed, John, w/o, Ill., 134,
#764
McDeerman, Thomas, c/o,
Richmond, Va., 54, #6882
McDerment, Joseph, Ala., 83,
#15780
McDerment, Joseph, Huntsville,
Ala., 52, #6290
McDermit, James, Cananadaigua,
N.Y., 143, #6459
McDill, John, S.C., 16, #9200
McDonald, Archibald, a/o, Va.,
70, #12052
McDonald, Benjamin, Ill., 79,
#14725

McDonald, Benjamin, c/o, Ill.,
73, #12751
McDonald, Benjamin, g/o c/o,
Ill., 83, #15658
McDonald, Benjamin, g/o c/o,
Ill., 61, #8391
McDonald, Dorcas, c/o, Maine,
103, #6795
McDonald, Doreas, c/o, Maine,
102, #5714
McDonald, Hannah, a/o, Ohio,
112, #1187
McDonald, Hugh, Mo., 73,
#12998
McDonald, Hugh, Mo., 76,
#13937
McDonald, James, w/o, S.C., 64,
#9145
McDonald, John, Iowa, 92,
#19991
McDonald, John, Savannah, Ga.,
104, #7521
McDonald, John, S.C., 55,
#6817
McDonald, John, S.C., 81,
#15184
McDonald, John, Wisc., 81,
#15006
McDonald, John A. J., w/o,
Cincinnati, Ohio, 141,
#1352
McDonald, Mary S.,
Philadelphia, Pa., 114,
#2302
McDonald, Thomas, —, 121,
#6824, slip
McDonough, France, —, 118,
#4885, slip
McDonough, Francis, Ind., 119,
#5438
McDonough, Francis, c/o,
Madison, Ind., 140, #325

McDonugh, Rodgers, La., 118,
#5021
McDougal, Alexander, Ky., 80,
#14926
McDowell, James, Pa., 136,
#3107, card
McDowell, James, c/o,
Philadelphia, Pa., 16,
#3109
McDowell, James, w/o,
Morganton, N.C., 123,
#341
McDowell, Thomas, w/o,
Philadelphia, Pa., 88,
#17780
McElhannon, John, Ga., 91,
#19000, card
McElhannon, John, c/o, Ga., 16,
#19000
McElroy, Alexander, Mo., 137,
#3997
McElveen, William, w/o, S.C.,
58, #7710
McElyea, Patrick, Nashville,
Tenn., 82, #15549
McElyea, Patrick, Nashville,
Tenn., 83, #15887
McEnnis, Michael T. M., D.C.,
143, #6600
McEver, Catherine, c/o,
Richmond, Va., 102, #5930
McEwing, Patrick, c/o, Va., 69,
#10979
McFadden, Edward, Nashville,
Tenn., 64, #943-, card
McFadden, John, c/o,
Philadelphia, Pa., 71,
#12393
McFadden, Manapha, Pittsburgh,
Pa., 138, #4944
McFalls, Arthur, w/o, N.C., 61,
#8625

McFarland, James, c/o, 31st Inf,
49, #5355
McFarland, James, w/o, 31st Inf,
49, #5357
McFarland, Sarah, c/o, Maine,
88, #17919
McFarland, William, Mass., 48,
#5194
McFarlin, Andrew, c/o, Albany,
N.Y., 70, #12144
McFemin, Saml., Jackson,
Tenn., 53, #6441
McFeren, William, Jackson,
Tenn., 40, #3218
McFerrin, William, Jackson,
Tenn., 78, #14431
McGartine, Joseph, Ohio, 119,
#5290
McGartline, Joseph, Cincinnati,
Ohio, 135, #2005
McGartlne, Joseph, Cincinnati,
Ohio, 142, #5017
McGarvey, Robert, Madison,
Ind., 131, #8744
McGee, Joseph, Iowa, 111, #701
McGee, Joseph, Iowa, 130,
#7349
McGee, Joseph, Iowa, 123,
#9829
McGee, Joseph, Iowa, 142,
#5250
McGee, Margaret, Philadelphia,
Pa., 69, #10925
McGee, Ralph, h/o, Ky., 98,
#2863
McGehy, William, Ala., 75,
#13444, card
McGeorge, William, w/o,
Richmond, Va., 16, #19188
McGill, James, a/o, Ky., 118,
#4668

McGill, Sarah, a/o, Ky., 118,
#4666
McGinnis, Andrew, w/o, Ky.,
56, #7375
McGinnis, Anna, a/o, Ky., 103,
#6779
McGinnis, James, e/o,
Philadelphia, Pa., 112,
#1218
McGirk, Andrew S., c/o, Mo.,
48, #5115
McGoraghey, Margaert, Albany,
N.Y., 100, #4375
McGoraghey, Margaret, Albany,
N.Y., 111, #424
McGoraghey, Morgan, Albany,
N.Y., 65, #9984
McGrady, Edward, Boston,
Mass., 142, #6022
McGriger, James, Philadelphia,
Pa., 86, #16898
McGrigger, James, Philadelphia,
Pa., 49, #5277
McGuire, Susan, S.C., 135,
#2095
McGuire, William, Richmond,
Va., 74, #13144, card
McGuirt, Washington, g/o c/o,
Ga., 130, #8038
McHaney (or McHenry), Terry,
c/o, Richmond, Va., 16,
#6178
McHenry, James, Ky., 75,
#13714
McHenry, James, w/o, Ky., 87,
#17716
McHenry, Terry, Richmond, Va.,
52, #6178
McHingly, John, w/o,
Richmond, Va., 64, #9445
McIlhany, Felix, Ohio, 107,
#9113

McIlroy, William, N.J., 16,
#5095
McIlvar, John, Ill., 116, #3775
McIlvar, John, a/o, Ill., 126,
#3087
McIlwain, Ebenezer, Bellows
Falls, Vt., 63, #8967
McIlwaine, Ebenezer, Bellows
Falls, Vt., 63, #8967
McIntire, William, w/o, New
York City, 68, #10715
McIntosh, Candace, a/o,
Nashville, Tenn., 121,
#7298
McIntosh, John, c/o, Maine,
100, #4587
McIntosh, William, w/o, S.C.,
109, #10602
McIntosh, Williams, Miss., 74,
#13054
McInturff, Mary, c/o, Jonesboro,
Tenn., 131, #8662
McIntyre, Catherine, Pittsburgh,
Pa., 110, #324
McIroy, William, N.J., 48,
#5095, card
McJunkin, Joseph, a/o, S.C.,
101, #5153
McJunkin, Joseph, a/o, S.C.,
101, #5158
McKarney, James, Knoxville,
Tenn., 41, #3395
McKay, Alexander, w/o, 1st
Artillery, 46, #4727
Mckay, Lt. Alexander, w/o, —,
67, #10416
McKay, Nancy, a/o, Va., 69,
#10922
McKean, Alexander, a/o,
Concord, N.H., 49, #5385
McKee, Andrew, a/o, Albany,
N.Y., 85, #16338

McKee, Daniel, w/o, Nashville, Tenn., 79, #14617

McKee, Elizabeth, E. Fla., 64, #9399

Mckee, James H., Ky., 143, #6161

McKee, Mary, c/o, Pittsburgh, Pa., 115, #2930

McKellup, Samuel, a/o, Vt., 66, #10265

McKenna, Mary Ann, Pa., 128, #6105

McKenna, Mary Ann, Philadelphia, Pa., 138, #5251

McKenna, Mary Ann, Philadelphia, Pa., 143, #6582

McKennan, Elizabth, c/o, Pittsburgh, Pa., 67, #10406

McKenney, John, Ga., 87, #17433, card

McKiddy, Thomas, Knoxville, Tenn., 51, #6033

McKinley, David, Pittsburgh, Pa., 76, #137-, card

McKinley, Robert, —, 133, #590, slip

McKinley, Robert, c/o, Nashville, Tenn., 16, #590

McKinney, Edmond, w/o, N.C., 114, #2315

McKinney, Margaret, c/o, Maine, 110, #217

McKinney, William, N.C., 51, #5905

McKleroy, Mary, a/o, Ga., 127, #4076

McKnight, Julianna K., e/o, Jackson, Tenn., 133, #9985

McKnight, Samuel, Ky., 140, #920

McKnight, William, Ark., 65, #10036

McKnight, William, Ark., 82, #15325

McKown, James, Ohio, 65, #9744

McKown, James, Ohio, 70, #11045

McKown, James, w/o, Ohio, 109, #10568

Mclain, John, Ga., 96, #1424

McLanahan, Elizabeth, a/o, Philadelphia, Pa., 116, #3688

McLane, Capt. George, w/o, Mounted Rifles, 138, #6251

McLane, Capt. George, w/o, Mounted Rifles, 139, #9165

McLane, Capt. George, w/o, U.S. Mounted Rifles, 141, #2075

McLane, Capt. George, w/o, U.S. Mounted Rifles, 142, #4909

McLane, George, w/o, —, 143, #6512

McLane, George, w/o, U.S. Mounted Rifles, 142, #3363

McLaughlin, Catherine, Albany, N.Y., 139, #6816

McLaughlin, Israel, w/o, Concord, N.H., 80, #14860, card

McLaughlin, John, Philadelphia, Pa., 114, #1996

McLaughlin, John, g/o c/o, Spingfield, Ill., 140, #9437

McLaughlin, Judith, Richmond, Va., 36A, #F4 V1

McLaughlin, William, w/o, Cleveland, Ohio, 141, #3203

McLean, Arthur, Md., 128, #5571

McLean, John, Albany, N.Y.,
16, #15125

McLean, John, N.Y., 81,
#15125, card

McLean, Nancy, Ind., 63, #8995

McLellan, Daniel, Fayetteville,
N.C., 105, #7762 V#32

McLellan, Daniel, a/o,
Fayetteville, N.C., 107,
#9994

McLenahan, Charles, w/o,
Philadelphia, Pa., 61,
#8460

McLeod, William, a/o, Ga., 128,
#5489

McLin, Frederick, Ky., 39,
#3152

McLin, Frederick, w/o, Ky., 101,
#5215

McLough, William, Va., 76,
#13943

McLoughlin, Lydia, N.H., 16,
#14860

McLouth, Nathan, g/o c/o,
Mich., 134, #1331

McMahan, David, g/o c/o,
Indianapolis, Ind., 127,
#4791

McMahon, Archibald, S.C., 92,
#19758

McMahon, Barbara, c/o, Md.,
112, #1184

McMahon, Mary, New York
City, 138, #6103

McMannis, John, Ind., 60,
#8272

McMannis, John, Ind., 71,
#12372

McManus, John, Ind., 89,
#18454

McMenaway, Alexander, a/o,
Nashville, Tenn., 91,
#19230

McMickell, Peter, Ill., 64,
#9652

McMillan, Hugh, Miss., 137,
#4337

McMillan, James, Albany, N.Y.,
17, #8273

McMillan, Jane, Madison, Ind.,
128, #5750, card

McMillan, Robt., Ohio, 53,
#6372

McMillan, William, —, 60,
#8240, card

McMillan, William, w/o,
Philadelphia, Pa., 17,
#8240

McMillen, Hugh, Mo., 140,
#217

McMillen, Jane, c/o, Madison,
Ind., 17, #5750

McMillen, Thomas, w/o,
Pittsburgh, Pa., 102, #6022

McMillion, Smith, Ill., 120,
#6284

McMinn, Joseph, Mo., 128,
#5678

McMinn, Joseph, Mo., 130,
#7453

McMinn, Robert, Jonesboro,
Tenn., 79, #14582

McMinn, Robert, Jonesboro,
Tenn., 88, #17848

McMullen, James, c/o, Maine,
120, #6423

McMullen, John, g/o c/o,
Cincinnati, Ohio, 140,
#170

McMullen, Sarah, Albany, N.Y.,
78, #14381

McMurray, John, Charleston, S.C., 51, #5901

McMurry, John, Charleston, S.C., 50, #5821

McNair, Archibald, c/o, Philadelphia, Pa., 77, #14089

McNair, David, e/o, Fort Gibson, Ark., 112, #904

McNair, Robert, c/o, Albany, N.Y., 89, #18213

McNatt, John, W. Tenn., 59, #8130

McNeal, Anna, Jonesboro, Tenn., 130, #7991

McNeal, Anna, Mo., 135, #1846

McNeese, Robert, S.C., 53, #6517

McNeil, Gen. John, w/o, Act of 20 Jan 1853, 114, #2223

McNeil (formerly Fowler), Fanny, Nashville, Tenn., 125, #2399

McNeill, Hector, N.C., 50, #5533

McNeill, John C., Albany, N.Y., 56, #7348

McNelly, Henry, a/o, Vt., 67, #10322

McNickle, Robert, Mo., 105, #8020

McNish, Sarah, Albany, N.Y., 76, #13934

McPeaters, David, Ill., 76, #13915

McPheeters, Andrew, Mo., 107, #9261

McPheeters, Andrew, a/o, Mo., 17, #1093

McPherson, Rebecca, Ky., 103, #6363

McPollan, James, New York City, 70, #12173

McPollan, James, New York City, 122, #8968

McQuire, John, Ky., 117, #4002, card

McSwine, George, c/o, Philadelphia, Pa., 136, #2613

McTune, John, N.Y., 108, #9700

McVay, Benjamin, Wheeling, Va., 45, #4616

McVey, Eli, w/o, Knoxville, Tenn., 57, #7530

McWain, Andrew, c/o, Bellows Falls, Vt., 50, #5838

McWilliams, James, Ky., 102, #5846

McWilliams, John, Richmond, Va., 92, #181

McWilliams, John, Va., 86, #16998

Meacham, Benjamin, g/o c/o, Conn., 37, #F1824

Meacham, Chloe, a/o, Albany, N.Y., 118, #4941

Meachem, Simeon, w/o, Albany, N.Y., 50, #5512

Mead, Elizabeth, c/o, Albany, N.Y., 96, #1883

Mead, Jeremiah, Conn., 34, #92

Mead, Jotham, Albany, N.Y., 67, #10440

Mead, Lewis, w/o, New York City, 94, #304

Mead, Silas, Albany, N.Y., 75, #13453

Mead, Silas, Albany, N.Y., 53, #6486

Mead, Susannah, Ohio, 99, #3687

Meade, Abigail, a/o, Conn.,
115, #2809
Meade, Abigail, a/o, Conn.,
115, #2810
Meade, Alfred, Ohio, 107, #9034
Meade, William, Va., 65,
#10010
Meade, William, a/o, Va., 75,
#13460
Meaden, Anderw, Knoxville,
Tenn., 50, #5468
Meaden, Andrew, E. Tenn., 55,
#7134
Meaden, Andrew, E. Tenn., 58,
#7896
Meaden, Andrew, c/o, Knoxville,
Tenn., 92, #19889
Meadow, Josiah, Va., 75,
#13570
Meadows, Jacob, Richmond,
Va., 52, #6173
Meadows, James, Richmond,
Va., 42, #3597
Meadows, James, Richmond,
Va., 47, #4993
Meadows, James, w/o, Ill., 53,
#6401
Meads, Washington, g/o c/o,
Philadelphia, Pa., 135,
#2212
Mealer, Sally, N.C., 106, #8762
Means, Robert, Ohio, 43, #4058
Mear, John, Mo., 112, #1251
Mear, John, Mo., 139, #8905
Mearsden, John, Philadelphia,
Pa., 40, #3343
Mebane, 1st Lt. John A., 2nd
Artillery, 121, #7694, card
Mebane, John, e/o, N.C., 54,
#6732
Mechling, William T., 8th Inf.,
133, #9971

Meckel, Samuel, New York City,
141, #2302
Mecks, Alexander, Pulaski,
Tenn., 47, #4922
Medideth, Jesse, Ala., 136,
#3336, card
Medlock, Mary, Indianapolis,
Ind., 141, #1916
Meech, Desine, c/o, Vt., 68,
#10726
Meech, Joshua, g/o c/o, Conn.,
37, #F1820
Meeds, Cato, Pittsburgh, Pa.,
52, #6143
Meeds, Cato, Pittsburgh, Pa.,
71, #12373
Meek, Alexander, Pulaski,
Tenn., 64, #9230
Meek, Jacob, Ind., 61, #8608
Meeker, Jonathan, a/o, Albany,
N.Y., 97, #2100
Meeks, Britain, Ga., 45, #4641
Meeks, Britain, Ga., 63, #9000
Meese, Baltzer, a/o,
Philadelphia, Pa., 76,
#13873
Megguier, Job H., Maine, 133,
#123
Mehoy, Bartholomew,
Pittsburgh, Pa., 40, #3170
Meins, John, Cincinnati, Ohio,
143, #6973
Meipner, Hulda R., New York
City, 115, #2446
Melick, Elizabeth, Philadelphia,
Pa., 124, #1232
Mellen, Rebecca, c/o, Boston,
Mass., 58, #7804
Mellen, Rebecca, c/o, Mass., 58,
#7678
Mellin, Thomas, Philadelphia,
Pa., 101, #4724

Mellon, Capt. Charles, w/o, —,
59, #8003

Mellon, Capt. Charles, w/o, —,
74, #13022

Mellon, Capt. Charles, w/o, —,
64, #9459

Mellon, Capt. Charles, w/o, —,
79, #14586

Mellon, Charles, w/o, —, 43,
#3814

Mellon, Charles, w/o, 2nd
Artillery, 49, #5328

Mellon, Charles, w/o, 2nd
Artillery, 54, #6760

Mellott, Benjamin, c/o,
Pittsburgh, Pa., 136, #3386

Melson, Polly, Richmond, Va.,
36A, #F4 V12

Melton, William, w/o, Ga., 122,
#8331

Melvin, Mary E., Md., 142,
#4851

Memfield, Ithamar, a/o, Boston,
Mass., 64, #9280

Menefee, Mary, Richmond, Va.,
71, #12452

Meperoll, Charles, Albany,
N.Y., 51, #5923

Mercer, David, c/o, Pittsburgh,
Pa., 122, #8128

Mercer, Jacob, Ga., 17, #3793

Mercer, Thomas, La., 69,
#10947

Mercer, Thomas, La., 90,
#18592

Merchant, Joseph, a/o, Boston,
Mass., 122, #8429

Meredith, Samuel, w/o, Ind., 84,
#15977

Meriam, David, a/o, Burlington,
Vt., 108, #9942

Meriwether, William, a/o, Ky.,
81, #15087

Merriam, Isaac, Concord, N.H.,
43, #4020

Merriam, Timothy, w/o, Mass.,
43, #3950

Merrick Sr., John, Mobile, Ala.,
69, #11004

Merril, Daniel, N.C., 95, #1350,
card

Merril, Daniel, N.C., 17, #1350

Merrill, Asa, c/o, Albany, N.Y.,
99, #3535

Merrill, Jacob, Maine, 104,
#7512

Merrill, Mary S., c/o, Mass.,
124, #635

Merrill, Sally, Albany, N.Y., 71,
#12235

Merrill, Sally, Albany, N.Y., 90,
#18582

Merrills, Nathaniel, Conn., 34,
#200

Merrit, Ezekiel, w/o, N.Y., 112,
#1010, card

Merrit, Sarah, a/o, Albany, N.Y.,
17, #1010

Merritt, Edward, N.Y., 143,
#6427

Merritt, Major, a/o, Richmond,
Va., 116, #3143

Merritt, William, a/o, Maine,
116, #3542

Merritt, William, w/o, N.C., 87,
#17308

Merrow, Esther, c/o,
Portsmouth, N.H., 128,
#5421

Merry, Philip, w/o, Richmond,
Va., 45, #4564

Merry, Rose, a/o, Richmond,
Va., 92, #123

Merryman, Elizabeth H., Richmond, Va., 36A, #F4 V13

Mersereau, Joshua, Philadelphia, Pa., 17, #8244

Meserall, Charles, Albany, N.Y., 92, #177, card

Messer, Christian, Ohio, 41, #3423

Messer, Christian, Ohio, 57, #7476

Messeroll, Charles, c/o, Albany, N.Y., 17, #177

Metcalf, Benjamin, Bellows Falls, Vt., 63, #8967

Metcalf, Elizabeth, c/o, Fayetteville, N.C., 128, #5684

Metcalf, William H., Mass., 96, #1550

Metcalf, Frank, Teamster, 137, #4021

Methous, Nancy, Richmond, Va., 54, #6601

Mickel, Samuel, Philadelphia, Pa., 108, #9949

Mickle, Robert, Mo., 75, #13476

Middlebrook, Lucy, a/o, Richmond, Va., 36A, #F2 V9

Middleton, John, Ohio, 17, #9632

Middleton, John, Ohio, 17, #12615

Midkiff, Mary, a/o, Richmond, Va., 117, #4253

Midriff, John, Va., 41, #3393

Miers, Daniel, New York City, 42, #3662

Miers, Daniel, c/o, New York City, 17, #3662

Mifflin, Jonathan, Philadelphia, Pa., 74, #13393

Mikesell, Jacob, Ind., 52, #6319

Milbourn, Andrew, Pittsburgh, Pa., 81, #15117

Milburn, Andrew, Pittsburgh, Pa., 60, #8317

Miles, Jesse, a/o, Ky., 91, #19210

Miles, Jesse A., Cincinnati, Ohio, 124, #430

Miles, John, Bellows Falls, Vt., 63, #8967

Miles, Mary, a/o, Ky., 126, #3947

Miles, Mary, e/o, Cincinnati, Ohio, 131, #8405

Miles, Patty, Ky., 105, #7959

Miles, Patty, Va., 80, #14773

Miles, Patty, a/o, Ky., 122, #8221

Miles, Polly, Madison, Ind., 133, #536, card

Miles, Polly, a/o, Indianapolis, Ind., 17, #536

Miles, Simon, Conn., 34, #382

Miles, Thomas, Va., 83, #15768

Miles, William, Philadelphia, Pa., 65, #9871

Miles, William, c/o, Philadelphia, Pa., 97, #2440

Milk, Morgan, Mobile, Ala., 73, #12908

Mill, George M., PA, Fayetteville, N.C., 107, #9533

Millard, James, Evansville, Ind., 117, #4286

Millard, Mary, Albany, N.Y., 71, #12441

Millard, Samuel, w/o, Albany, N.Y., 90, #18713
Miller, Aaron J., c/o, Mass., 59, #8030
Miller, Adah, Albany, N.Y., 79, #14713
Miller, Amos, a/o, Albany, N.Y., 106, #8596
Miller, Ann, e/o, Richmond, Va., 96, #1542
Miller, Anna, Albany, N.Y., 128, #5680
Miller, Asa, c/o, Maine, 111, #681
Miller, Barney, Ind., 61, #8417
Miller, Betsey, c/o, Vt., 64, #9606
Miller, Caleb, c/o, Conn., 30, #4900
Miller, Calvin J., Mo., 140, #20
Miller, Catherine, a/o, Va., 17, #19053
Miller, Christiana, Philadelphia, Pa., 140, #9438
Miller, Conrad, Philadelphia, Pa., 41, #3553
Miller, Daniel, w/o, Va., 73, #12760
Miller, Elas, Philadelphia, Pa., 67, #10410
Miller, Elizabeth, Albany, N.Y., 102, #5916
Miller, Elizabeth, e/o, Albany, N.Y., 118, #4823
Miller, Elizabeth, e/o, Ky., 97, #2197
Miller, Emanuel, Philadelphia, Pa., 17, #7544
Miller, Francis, Ill., 55, #6995
Miller, Francis, Ky., 57, #7458
Miller, Frederick, w/o, Jackson, Tenn., 120, #6341

Miller, George, Ky., 67, #10377
Miller, George, Ky., 77, #14213
Miller, George, Mo., 139, #8880
Miller, Henry, Ind., 48, #5071
Miller, Henry, Ind., 101, #4871, card
Miller, Henry, Nashville, Tenn., 46, #4839
Miller, Henry, Nashville, Tenn., 49, #5262
Miller, Henry, Ohio, 53, #6373
Miller, Henry, c/o, Philadelphia, Pa., 92, #19761
Miller, Henry, w/o, Pittsburgh, Pa., 43, #3907
Miller, Hiram F., a/o, Knoxville, Tenn., 116, #3490
Miller, Jacob, N.C., 45, #4539
Miller, Jacob, w/o, Philadelphia, Pa., 97, #2081, card
Miller, James, E. Tenn., 79, #14611, card
Miller, James, Knoxville, Tenn., 17, #14611
Miller, James, Knoxville, Tenn., 63, #8993
Miller, James, Knoxville, Tenn., 71, #12423
Miller, James, Knoxville, Tenn., 39, #3022
Miller, James, Knoxville, Tenn., 49, #5439
Miller, James, c/o, Md., 119, #5331
Miller, James, g/o c/o, Md., 130, #7426
Miller, James M., Mo., 136, #3242
Miller, James M., Mo., 140, #1017

Miller, Jemima, a/o, Pittsburgh, Pa., 136, #3076

Miller, Joanna, c/o, Cincinnati, Ohio, 139, #8840

Miller, John, 19th Inf., 79, #14742

Miller, John, 19th Inf., 79, #14743

Miller, John, Ky., 106, #8358

Miller, John, a/o, Philadelphia, Pa., 101, #5127

Miller, John, c/o, 19th Inf., 78, #14280

Miller, John, c/o, Mo., 124, #972

Miller, John, g/o c/o, Mo., 138, #4740

Miller, John, w/o, Philadelphia, Pa., 89, #18296

Miller, John A., Mo., 96, #1410

Miller, John P., w/o, Pittsburgh, Pa., 66, #10109

Miller, John V., w/o, Vt., 58, #7852

Miller, Levi, c/o, Albany, N.Y., 92, #224

Miller, Mark, Jackson, Tenn., 102, #5572

Miller, Martin, c/o, Philadelphia, Pa., 111, #447

Miller, Martin, w/o, E. Tenn., 55, #7218

Miller, Mary A., a/o, Philadelphia, Pa., 110, #140

Miller, Mordecai, Indianapolis, Ind., 42, #3563

Miller, Nancy, c/o, Philadelphia, Pa., 17, #2081

Miller, Nelson, R.I., 70, #11156

Miller, Noah, c/o, Ind., 92, #19928

Miller, Peter, Albany, N.Y., 88, #18095

Miller, Private George, w/o, 14th Inf., 101, #4783

Miller, Richard, Pittsburgh, Pa., 39, #3049

Miller, Valentine, Philadelphia, Pa., 64, #9449

Miller, William, Jackson, Miss., 94, #547

Miller, William, Mich., 65, #9799

Miller, William, Miss., 54, #6697

Miller, William, Miss., 55, #6993

Miller, William, Natchez, Miss., 83, #15602

Miller, William, Richmond, Va., 51, #5918

Miller, William, Louisville, Ky., 108, #9984 V#48

Miller, William H., Ky., 142, #5593

Miller, William W., N.Y., 143, #6460

Miller Sr., Joseph, a/o, Ky., 105, #8110

Milligan, Cookson, Albany, N.Y., 54, #6744

Milliken, Joel, w/o, Maine, 73, #12903

Milliken, Samuel, Albany, N.Y., 62, #8818

Mills, George, a/o, Richmond, Va., 116, #3453

Mills, Hardy, Ind., 55, #6915

Mills, Hardy, c/o, Madison, Ind., 129, #6882

Mills, Morgan, Mobile, Ala.,
79, #14660
Mills, Morgan, w/o, Mobile,
Ala., 81, #15211
Mills, Philip, w/o, Maine, 49,
#5348
Mills, Ruth, g/o, Wheeling, Va.,
98, #2809
Mills, Sally, a/o, Richmond,
Va., 96, #1579
Mills, Stephen, New York City,
42, #3684
Mills, Thomas, Wheeling, Va.,
63, #8989
Mills, Valentine K., a/o c/o,
Philadelphia, Pa., 130,
#7325
Mills, Valentine K., g/o c/o,
Philadelphia, Pa., 139,
#9092
Mills, John, a/o, Ohio, 122,
#8544 (alias John Ripley)
Millwee, William, w/o, S.C., 73,
#12784
Milsaps, William, w/o, 28th
Inf., 84, #16147
Milton, Edward, New York City,
132, #9509
Milton, Edward, New York City,
138, #5640
Milton, Elijah, e/o, Ky., 138,
#6681
Minard, Imanna, c/o, Rutland,
Vt., 141, #1500
Minear, David, c/o, Richmond,
Va., 18, #4517
Miner, Anderson, Vt., 62,
#8834, card
Miner, Anderson, c/o, Windsor,
Vt., 18, #8834
Miner, Chauncey, Philadelphia,
Pa., 92, #138

Miner, David, Albany, N.Y., 67,
#10438
Miner, James, c/o, New York
City, 116, #3160
Miner, William, w/o, Conn., 95,
#1343
Miniar, Elizabeth, Wheeling,
Va., 129, #6576
Minot, George, PA, Concord,
N.H., 118, #5064
Miracle, Polly, Albany, N.Y.,
82, #15396
Mirvard, Lorenzo D., Springfield,
Ill., 143, #6886
Mise, Mary, c/o, Conn., 34,
#5062
Mitchel, William, Mo., 49,
#5360
Mitchell, Alexander M., D.C.,
124, #1059
Mitchell, Alies, a/o, Concord,
N.H., 18, #8945
Mitchell, Amasa, Ohio, 40,
#3322
Mitchell, Ann, c/o, N.C., 113,
#1851
Mitchell, Charles, Ky., 44,
#4403
Mitchell, Charles, Ky., 46,
#4736
Mitchell, David, c/o, Albany,
N.Y., 135, #2399
Mitchell, Elijah, Ohio, 95,
#1082
Mitchell, Elizah, a/o, Ohio, 106,
#8773
Mitchell, George, Albany, N.Y.,
58, #7716
Mitchell, George, Albany, N.Y.,
58, #7838
Mitchell, George, S.C., 48,
#5086

Mitchell, George, e/o, S.C., 98, #2929

Mitchell, George, w/o, Albany, N.Y., 100, #4356

Mitchell, George, w/o, N.C., 49, #5302

Mitchell, Jesse, Miss., 95, #1047

Mitchell, Jesse, Miss., 84, #15975

Mitchell, John, Maine, 18, #15589

Mitchell, John, Maine, 83, #15589, card

Mitchell, John, Nashville, Tenn., 60, #8346

Mitchell, John, Philadelphia, Pa., 39, #2984

Mitchell, John, W. Tenn., 64, #9263, card

Mitchell, John, c/o, Ky., 83, #15709

Mitchell, John, c/o, Philadelphia, Pa., 18, #19163

Mitchell, John, w/o, Wheeling, Va., 18, #15374

Mitchell, Joshua, Portland, Maine, 141, #3408

Mitchell, Margaret C., Richmond, Va., 72, #12617

Mitchell, Margaret C., a/o, Richmond, Va., 106, #8744

Mitchell, Nancy, Ohio, 62, #8831

Mitchell, Nancy, Ohio, 78, #14525

Mitchell, Nathaniel, w/o, —, 132, #8945, card

Mitchell, Nicholas, Md., 132, #9409

Mitchell, Samuel, e/o, Conn., 38, #F1819

Mitchell, Sarah, c/o, R.I., 127, #4295

Mitchell, Thomas, Albany, N.Y., 81, #15119

Mitchell, William, Albany, N.Y., 51, #6053

Mitchell, William, Ohio, 62, #8667

Mitchell, William, a/o, Nashville, Tenn., 119, #5737

Mitchell, William, a/o, Va., 81, #15118

Mitchell (formerly Walker), Elizabeth, Mo., 118, #4650

Mix, Esther, c/o, Albany, N.Y., 64, #9229

Mix, Levi, w/o, New York City, 70, #11162

Mix, Polly, c/o, Albany, N.Y., 104, #7539

Mix, Timothy, a/o, Conn., 113, #1703

Mizer, Hannah, a/o, N.J., 116, #3048

Mizner, Henry, Ind., 69, #11005

Moast, John, w/o, Philadelphia, Pa., 122, #8425

Moe, John, Albany, N.Y., 140, #9873

Moffett, Elizabeth, Va., 85, #16673

Moffett, Jesse, w/o, Richmond, Va., 18, #5137

Mola, Gasper, Pittsburgh, Pa., 122, #8568, card

Moler, Casper, c/o, Pittsburgh, Pa., 18, #8568

Molly, Richard, R.I., 119, #5423

Momma, Bernhard, g/o c/o, D.C., 142, #3454

Monaghan, Martin, Albany, N.Y., 120, #6075

Monier, John, c/o, Albany, N.Y., 82, #15257

Monks, Rachel, c/o, Pittsburgh, Pa., 119, #5645

Monroe, Amasa, g/o c/o, Conn., 37, #F1825

Monroe, John, —, 102, #6251, card

Monroe, John, c/o, Ky., 81, #15177

Monroe, Lt. Col. John, Special, 19, #4726

Montague, Thomas, w/o, Va., 69, #10892

Monteath, Margaret, —, 122, #8986, card

Montgomery, Alexander, Ky., 18, #4044

Montgomery, Alexander, Ky., 48, #5050

Montgomery, Alexander, Ky., 54, #6621

Montgomery, John, Ind. to Ill., 53, #6351

Montgomery, John, Ky., 61, #8582

Montgomery, John, Pittsburgh, Pa., 78, #14272

Montgomery, Michael L. K., Ohio, 101, #4841, card

Montgomery, Michael L. K., Pittsburgh, Pa., 101, #4841, card

Montgomery, Michael L. K., Wheeling, Va., 101, #4841, card

Montgomery, Mitchell R., w/o, Wheeling, Va., 18, #4841

Montgomery, Rhoda A., Madison, Ind., 115, #2996

Montgomery, Richard, w/o, Va., 121, #7704

Montgomery, Thomas, Ky., 97, #1885, card

Montgomery, Thomas, e/o, Ky., 18, #1885

Montgomery, William, Mo., 86, #16798, card

Montgomery, William, a/o, Mo., 18, #16798

Montindale, Samuel, Fayetteville, N.C., 50, #5537

Moody, Clement, a/o, N.H., 88, #17999

Moody, Edmond, Ill., 56, #7389

Moody, Martha, Portsmouth, N.H., 72, #12616

Moody, Thomas, Ga., 41, #3392

Moody, Thomas, w/o, Savannah, Ga., 18, #3392

Moody, William, Mich., 67, #10557

Moody, William, Richmond, Va., 45, #4496

Moon, James, Philadelphia, Pa., 46, #4732

Moon, Paul, c/o, Albany, N.Y., 127, #4313

Mooney, James, Pittsburgh, Pa., 139, #8350

Mooney, William, a/o, N.C., 119, #5536

Mooney, William, c/o, Md., 127, #4716

Moor, Perez, w/o, Albany, N.Y., 85, #16556

Moor, William, c/o, Albany, N.Y., 55, #7135

Moore, —, Mobile, Ala., 66,
#10235, card
Moore, Alexander, c/o,
Fayetteville, N.C., 125,
#1681
Moore, Benjamin D., a/o c/o,
Mo., 129, #6653
Moore, Benjamin D., c/o, Mo.,
111, #634
Moore, Benjamin D., c/o, Mo.,
117, #4372
Moore, Chalres, D.C., 140,
#386
Moore, Charles, Ill., 69,
#10926, card
Moore, Charles, w/o, Ill., 18,
#10926
Moore, David, a/o, Ky., 72,
#12473
Moore, David, a/o, Mo., 18,
#935
Moore, Duncan, Mobile, Ala.,
59, #7958
Moore, Ebenezer, Wisc., 109,
#10454
Moore, Ebenezer, a/o, Albany,
N.Y., 85, #16438
Moore, Eleanor, Nashville,
Tenn., 104, #7215
Moore, Eleanor, Nashville,
Tenn., 98, #3008
Moore, Elizabeth, e/o, Concord,
N.H., 120, #5892
Moore, Isaac, —, 70, #11076,
card
Moore, Isaac, c/o, Mass., 91,
#19272
Moore, Isaac, w/o, Ga., 18,
#11076
Moore, James, —, 128, #5921,
card

Moore, James, Philadelphia, Pa.,
40, #3197, card
Moore, James, Pittsburgh, Pa.,
97, #2428, card
Moore, James, c/o, Knoxville,
Tenn., 18, #5291
Moore, James, w/o,
Philadelphia, Pa., 18,
#3197
Moore, James, w/o,
Philadelphia, Pa., 18,
#2428
Moore, James L., w/o, Ohio, 77,
#13979
Moore, Jesse, N.J., 44, #4286
Moore, John, w/o, —, 103,
#7019, card
Moore, John, w/o, Albany,
N.Y., 101, #5389
Moore, John, w/o, Albany,
N.Y., 110, #323
Moore 2nd, John, a/o, Chicago,
Ill., 142, #4923
Moore, Joseph, Madison, Wisc.,
143, #7331
Moore, Joseph, Pittsburgh, Pa.,
106, #8895
Moore, Joseph, a/o, Madison,
Ind., 142, #5935
Moore, Joseph, c/o, N.J., 50,
#5509
Moore, Joseph, g/o, Madison,
Ind., 141, #1413
Moore, Joseph, g/o, Madison,
Ind., 138, #6675
Moore, Lt. J. C., AAQM, 116,
#3820
Moore, Martha, Richmond, Va.,
18, #1060, card
Moore, Martha, Richmond, Va.,
112, #1060, card
Moore, Mary, Ga., 105, #7845

Moore, Milton S., c/o, Mo.,
118, #4755
Moore, Obadiah, Mobile, Ala.,
60, #8287
Moore, Reuben, a/o, Albany,
N.Y., 125, #2574
Moore, Ruth, a/o, Rutland, Vt.,
139, #8183
Moore, Sally, c/o, Ky., 18,
#7019
Moore, Sarah, a/o, Richmond,
Va., 101, #5225
Moore, Stephen H., w/o, Md.,
82, #15410
Moore, Susannah, a/o, Albany,
N.Y., 130, #8017
Moore, Thomas, Nashville,
Tenn., 101, #4816
Moore, William, —, 104,
#7353, card
Moore, William, Ind., 52, #6294
Moore, William, Mo., 128,
#5536
Moore, William, Mo., 130,
#7568
Moore, William, Mo., 132,
#9075
Moore, William, Mo., 133, #81
Moore, William, w/o, N.C., 18,
#7353
Moore, William, w/o, Pa., 110,
#166
Moore, William P., New York
City, 141, #2304
Moore, Wilson, c/o, Ky., 18,
#4582
Moore, Wm., Ky., 45, #4582,
card
Moore (now Cochran), Semira,
Mo., 110, #287

Moore, William H., PA,
Huntsville, Ala., 116,
#3792
Moore, William H., PA,
Huntsville, Ala., 118,
#5046
Moore Sr., Daniel, N.C., 112,
#935, card
Moore Sr., Daniel, c/o, N.C., 18,
#698
Moore Sr., Isaac, Ga., 40, #3251
Moorehead, William, S.C., 58,
#7837
Moores, David, a/o, Portsmouth,
Maine, 18, #5939
Mooring, John, c/o,
Fayetteville, N.C., 18,
#8111
Moors, Relief, Portland, Maine,
98, #2995
Moran, Delialia, N.C., 95,
#1026
Moran, Michael, w/o, R.I., 137,
#3801
More, David, w/o, Conn., 65,
#9997
Morecy, Patrick, Mass., 125,
#1651
Morecy, Patrick, Mass., 142,
#3958
Morehead, John, Ky., 136,
#3492, card
Morehead, John H., Mo., 96,
#1508
Morehouse, Gersham, Albany,
N.Y., 85, #16632
Morehouse, Gershom, Albany,
N.Y., 75, #13531
Morehouse, Gershom, Albany,
N.Y., 55, #7180
Morehouse, Isaac, e/o, Albany,
N.Y., 108, #10078

Morel, James S., PA, Ga., 119,
#5196
Morel, James S., PA, Savanah,
GA, 117, #3845
Moreland, Alfred, w/o,
Richmond, Va., 101, #4744
Morelock, Catherine, Mo., 139,
#8614
Moretz, Henry, Mo., 134, #1486
Morey, Ruth, Albany, N.Y.,
117, #4393
Morey, Ruth, Albany, N.Y.,
118, #4614
Morgan, Benjamin, W. Tenn.,
88, #17961, card
Morgan, Benjamin, w/o, Va.,
82, #15253
Morgan, Daniel, New York City,
48, #5048
Morgan, Daniel, c/o, New York
City, 44, #4326
Morgan, Ebenezer, Conn., 34,
#222
Morgan, Hannah, c/o, Albany,
N.Y., 101, #5026
Morgan, Jackquill, Va., 110,
#147, card
Morgan, Jackquill, w/o,
Richmond, Va., 19, #147
Morgan, James, Knoxville,
Tenn., 78, #14438
Morgan, James, N.C., 64, #9654
Morgan, James, N.C., 66,
#10214
Morgan, James, Tuscaloosa,
Ala., 69, #10862
Morgan, James, c/o, Ill., 18,
#2252
Morgan, Jesse, —, 120, #6421,
card

Morgan, Jesse, c/o,
Philadelphia, Pa., 18,
#6421
Morgan, John, Ky., 56, #7391
Morgan, John, Ky., 129, #7098
Morgan, John, Miss., 53, #6398
Morgan, John, w/o, Jackson,
Miss., 18, #1359
Morgan, Joseph, c/o, Albany,
N.Y., 101, #5025
Morgan, Major Edwin H., 11th
Inf., 121, #68--, card
Morgan, Mary, e/o, S.C., 71,
#12286
Morgan, Rhoda, a/o, Mass.,
131, #8415
Morgan, Sally, Ohio, 73,
#12731
Morgan, Skiff, Vt., 106, #8884,
slip
Morgan, Skiff, c/o, Burlington,
Vt., 18, #8884
Morgan, Susannah, Richmond,
Va., 99, #3182
Morgan, T. G., PA, New Orleans,
La., 84, #16221
Morgan, Thomas, Jonesboro,
Tenn., 57, #7562
Morgan, Thomas, Jonesboro,
Tenn., 41, #3538
Morgan, William, Ind. to Ky.,
87, #17516, card
Morgan, William, Richmond,
Va., 61, #8613
Morgan, William, a/o, Ky., 19,
#17516
Morin, Edward, Ky., 119,
#5362, card
Morin, Edward, a/o, Ky., 19,
#5362
Moring, John, N.C., 131, #8111
Moring, John, N.C., 61, #8626

Moriquart, Jacob, c/o, New York City, 121, #7515

Moritz, Henry, St. Louis, Mo., 126, #3349

Morose, Elijah, w/o, Conn., 72, #12526

Morrell, Jeremiah, Bellows Falls, Vt., 63, #8967

Morrick Sr., John, Mobile, Ala., 78, #14336

Morrill, Nathaniel, N.H., 84, #15963

Morris, Benjamin, Ohio, 57, #7539

Morris, Capt. Lewis, w/o, 3rd Inf., 101, #4644

Morris, Capt. Lewis N., w/o, 3rd Inf., 107, #9052

Morris, Capt. Lewis N., w/o, 3rd Inf., 111, #463

Morris, Capt. Lewis N., w/o, 3rd Inf., 103, #6469

Morris, Capt. Lewis N., w/o, 3rd Inf., 104, #7567

Morris, Capt. Lewis N., w/o, 3rd Inf., 105, #8166

Morris, Capt. Lewis N., w/o, 3rd Inf., 108, #10315

Morris, Capt. Lewis N., w/o, 3rd Inf., 109, #10882

Morris, Claiborne, h/o, Richmond, Va., 98, #2833

Morris, Daniel, Ky., 122, #8866

Morris, Daniel, c/o, Albany, N.Y., 42, #3680

Morris, Daniel, w/o, Philadelphia, Pa., 96, #1743

Morris, Deborah, c/o, Philadelphia, Pa., 134, #1179

Morris, Dennis, a/o, N.J., 117, #4295

Morris, George, c/o, Philadelphia, Pa., 69, #10923

Morris, Henry, Albany, N.Y., 141, #1617

Morris, John, Ala., 44, #4161

Morris, Jonathan, c/o, Pittsburgh, Pa., 102, #5672

Morris, R. M., −, 111, #526, card

Morris, Seth, Jonesboro, Tenn., 56, #7387

Morris, Travis, Ill., 59, #8031

Morris, Travis, c/o, Ill., 80, #14801

Morris, William, Ark., 66, #10098

Morris, William, Nashville, Tenn., 108, #10089

Morris, William, w/o, Cincinnati, Ohio, 122, #8450

Morrison, David, Cincinnati, Ohio, 140, #901

Morrison, Ezra, Ky., 126, #3023, card

Morrison, Ezra, c/o, Ky., 19, #3023

Morrison, Jame, Albany, N.Y., 49, #5289, card

Morrison, James, Philadelphia, Pa., 44, #4270

Morrison, James, Philadelphia, Pa., 46, #4693

Morrison, James, c/o, Albany, N.Y., 19, #5289

Morrison, John, Richmond, Va., 71, #12266

Morrison, John, Richmond, Va., 97, #2481

Morrison, John, Va., 41, #3373
Morrison, John, e/o, Jonesboro, Tenn., 92, #20001
Morrison, Morris, c/o, N.C., 100, #4263
Morrison, Sarah, e/o, N.C., 102, #5786
Morrow, Albert G., c/o, S.C., 130, #7672
Morrow, Albert G., g/o c/o, S.C., 123, #284
Morrow, David, Mich., 61, #8618
Morrow, David, Natchez, Miss., 68, #10819
Morrow, Janet, a/o, S.C., 124, #1527
Morrow, John, Nashville, Tenn., 42, #3603
Morse, Danl., Maine, 52, #6148
Morse, Elihu, Albany, N.Y., 67, #10485
Morse, Elihu, c/o, Albany, N.Y., 124, #725
Morse, Enos, w/o, Albany, N.Y., 81, #15157
Morse, Josiah, w/o, Albany, N.Y., 19, #19114
Morse, Micah, Albany, N.Y., 94, #241
Morton, Edward, Richmond, Va., 108, #10195
Morton, Edward, Richmond, Va., 47, #4852
Morton, James, Richmond, Va., 102, #6001, card
Morton, James, e/o, Richmond, Va., 19, #6001
Morton, Joel, Albany, N.Y., 43, #3850
Morton, Josiah, Fayetteville, N.C., 41, #3441

Morton, Josiah, N.C., 52, #6108
Morton, Josiah, N.C., 70, #11164
Morton, Josiah, c/o, Fayetteville, N.C., 94, #267
Morton, Oliver, Ga., 51, #5954
Morton, Oliver, Ga., 64, #9185
Morton, Oliver, w/o, Ga., 116, #3159
Mory, Ruth, Albany, N.Y., 112, #954
Mosby, Diana, Ky., 108, #9707
Mosby, Joseph, Ky., 92, #178
Mosby, Joseph, Ky., 95, #1369
Mosby, Joseph, Ky., 100, #4528
Mosby, Susannah, a/o, Richmond, Va., 95, #1352
Moseley, Mary, Va., 65, #9772
Moser, Christian, e/o, Pa., 57, #7513
Moseror (or Musser), John, Richmond, Va., 58, #7889
Moses, Eunice, c/o, Cincinnati, Ohio, 139, #8395
Moses, John, Vt., 90, #18556
Moses, Joshua, Ky., 48, #5178, card
Moses, Joshua, Ky., 19, #5178
Mosher, Jabez, Albany, N.Y., 106, #8383
Mosher, Josiah, c/o, Albany, N.Y., 104, #7222
Mosier, Daniel, w/o, Ohio, 82, #15274
Mosley, Joseph, Albany, N.Y., 76, #13920
Mosley Sr., James, S.C., 59, #8060

Muller (or Miller), Frederica,
New York City, 117, #3955
Muller (or Miller), Frederica,
D.C., 128, #5407
Muller (or Miller), Frederick,
D.C., 133, #164
Mullins, Joshua, Ky., 119,
#5509, card
Mullins, Joshua, w/o, Ky., 19,
#5509
Mullins, Malone, Ga., 78,
#14345
Mumford, James H., w/o, Va.,
84, #16242
Munday, Benjamin H.,
Richmond, Va., 47, #4875
Munday, Benjamin H., Va., 39,
#3006
Mundy, William, w/o,
Knoxville, Tenn., 132,
#9029
Munger, Jonathan, w/o, Ohio,
45, #4557
Munger, William H., Mo., 142,
#5929
Munks, William, w/o,
Philadelphia, Pa., 91,
#19005
Munks, William, Philadelphia,
Pa., 90, #18862
Munn, Calvin, w/o, Mass., 110,
#6
Munn, James, a/o w/o, Ohio, 98,
#3145
Munro, Nathaniel, c/o, R.I., 69,
#10936
Munroe, John, —, 127, #4726,
card
Munrow, John, w/o, Maine, 19,
#6251
Munsell, Levi, Ohio, 57, #7475

Munsh, Robert, w/o, S.C., 82,
#15542
Munson, Moses, Fla., 58, #7807
Munson, Moses, a/o, E. Fla., 87,
#17665
Murdock, Lucretia, Albany,
N.Y., 74, #13047
Murdock, William, Mich., 134,
#1080
Murdock, William Q., Detroit,
Mich., 139, #8925
Murphey, Charles, c/o,
Richmond, Va., 19, #6258
Murphey, John, E. Tenn., 55,
#7125
Murphey, John, a/o, Richmond,
Va., 18, #5137
Murphey, John, w/o, Knoxville,
Tenn., 73, #12799
Murphy, Charles, c/o,
Richmond, Va., 52, #6258,
card
Murphy, Edward, Boston, Mass.,
143, #7496
Murphy, Frances, a/o, Ky., 141,
#2020
Murphy, Hugh, N.C., 50, #5581,
card
Murphy, Hugh, c/o, N.C., 19,
#5581
Murphy, Michael M., Mo., 111,
#376
Murphy, Michael W., La., 132,
#9179
Murphy, Patrick, New York City,
121, #7875
Murphy, Smith, a/o, R.I., 89,
#18508
Murphy, William, g/o, Mo., 85,
#16375
Murphy, William C., Ill., 46,
#4715

N

Nadeau, Basil, c/o, Albany,
N.Y., 122, #8896
Nagel, Caspar, Detroit, Mich.,
143, #6874
Nail, Reuben, Ga., 43, #4085
Nail, Reuben, Ga., 52, #6335
Nail, Reuben, Ga., 68, #10685
Nail, Reuben, Ga., 75, #13581
Nail, Reuben, Ga., 90, #18802
Nail, Reuben, Savannah, Ga.,
100, #4290, card
Nall, Richard, w/o, Nashville,
Tenn., 101, #5013
Nanness, John P., PA, D.C., 91,
#19156
Napier, William P., e/o,
Richmond, Va., 98, #3092
Narremore, John, c/o, —, 119,
#5359, card
Nash, Benajmin, Mass., 73,
#12725, card
Nash, Benjamin, lr/o, Boston,
Mass., 19, #12925
Nash, Hollis, c/o, Albany, N.Y.,
115, #2690
Nash, Noah, Conn., 34, #1013
Nash, S. K., —, 123, #9460,
slip
Nash, Skippard K., N.C. Vols.,
121, #6927, slip
Nash, William, Nashville,
Tenn., 116, #3136, card
Nash, William, c/o, Jackson,
Tenn., 19, #3136
Nason, Benjamin, N.H., 85,
#16729
Nason, Willaby, Mass., 88,
#17984
Naughton, Solomon, Vt., 63,
#8886
Naylor, Charles, Pittsburgh, Pa.,
121, #7514

Neal, Benjamin, w/o, Madison,
Ind., 120, #6568
Neal, Elizabeth, Richmond, Va.,
135, #1886
Neal, James, w/o, S.C., 127,
#4850
Neal, John, w/o, Richmond, Va.,
94, #310
Neal, Rebecca, Ga., 136, #3040
Neal, William, Richmond, Va.,
66, #10212
Neale, Delilah, D.C., 138,
#6630
Neale, Delilah, D.C., 143,
#6974
Nease, Martin, a/o, Jackson,
Tenn., 111, #387
Needham, Daniel, Mass., 95,
#836, card
Needham, Daniel, c/o, Mass.,
19, #836
Needles, John, c/o, Cincinnati,
Ohio, 142, #3523
Neel, William, Richmond, Va.,
48, #5109
Neels, John, w/o, Albany, N.Y.,
43, #3956
Neely, Nicholas, Huntsville,
Ala., 101, #5374
Negus, Lydia, Albany, N.Y.,
108, #9956
Negus, Noles, w/o, Albany,
N.Y., 88, #17860
Neighman, A. Franklin, g/o,
Philadelphia, Pa., 140,
#652
Neill, James, Ky., 42, #3612
Nelson, Benjamin, Albany,
N.Y., 46, #4785
Nelson, Benjamin, c/o, Albany,
N.Y., 133, #49

Nelson, Deliala, Knoxville,
Tenn., 130, #7456
Nelson, John, Albany, N.Y., 63,
#9045
Nelson, John, Va., 19, #2131
Nelson, Moses, Ohio, 62, #8764
Nelson, Moses, Ohio, 81,
#14994
Nelson, Moses, w/o, Ky., 123,
#141
Nelson, Paul, c/o, Albany, N.Y.,
110, #11207
Nelson, Paul, w/o, Albany, N.Y.,
41, #3471
Nelson, Peter, Nashville, Tenn.,
126, #3928
Nelson, Robert K., Ind., 123,
#9571
Nelson, William, w/o,
Knoxville, Tenn., 115,
#2740
Nelson, William R., Charleston,
S.C., 108, #10273
Nelson, William R., S.C., 115,
#2569
Nelson, William R., S.C., 125,
#1928
Nelson, William R., S.C., 137,
#3717
Nesbitt, John, e/o, Nashville,
Tenn., 19, #19750
Nestell, Catharine, c/o, Albany,
N.Y., 94, #634
Netherton, Rebecca, a/o,
Indianapolis, Ind., 141,
#1722
Nettle, Mary, Richmond, Va.,
95, #1224
Nettles, William, a/o, S.C., 110,
#10925
Neville, Jesse, e/o, S.C., 94,
#250

Neville, John, Wheeling, Va.,
64, #9488
Neville, John, Wheeling, Va.,
81, #15096
Neville, John, Wheeling, Va.,
88, #17807
Neville, John, Wheeling, Va.,
71, #12386
New, George W., Ky., 67,
#10481
New, Jacob, w/o, Ky., 64, #9633
New, William, N.C., 47, #4956
Newberry, Sarah, a/o,
Philadelphia, Pa., 110,
#265
Newby, Levi, Va., 123, #282,
card
Newby, Levi, e/o, Richmond,
Va., 19, #282
Newby, Thomas, a/o, Richmond,
Va., 99, #3508
Newcomb, Lemuel, w/o, Mass.,
94, #237
Newcomb, Lucy, Boston, Mass.,
101, #5321
Newell, Daniel, c/o, N.H., 70,
#11136
Newell, Joseph, a/o, Vt., 65,
#9793
Newell, Reverius, Burlington,
Vt., 143, #6949
Newell, Samuel, Ky., 73,
#12726
Newell, Samuel, lr/o, Ind., 91,
#19141
Newell, Samuel, lr/o, Ky., 91,
#19140
Newhall, Elizabeth, c/o, Mass.,
59, #7938
Newland, David, c/o, Albany,
N.Y., 84, #15978

Newland, Herod, g/o c/o,
Madison, Ind., 134, #735
Newman, Daniel, Nashville,
Tenn., 92, #207
Newman, Deborah, a/o, Albany,
N.Y., 19, #593
Newman, Edmund, Ky., 42,
#3657
Newman, Jacob, —, 138, #5572,
slip
Newman, Sally, a/o, Maine, 116,
#3273
Newman, M. D., PA, Richmond,
Va., 116, #3819
Newsom, Tabitha, Miss., 128,
#5420
Newson, Tabitha, Miss., 124,
#1401
Newton, Abigail, c/o, Madison,
Ind., 116, #3088
Newton, Abraham, Jackson,
Tenn., 66, #10099
Newton, Abraham, Jackson,
Tenn., 75, #13437
Newton, Abraham, Jackson,
Tenn., 82, #15261
Newton, Abraham, w/o, Jackson,
Tenn., 103, #6666
Newton, Alice, c/o, Cincinnati,
Ohio, 115, #2595
Newton, Henry, Richmond, Va.,
91, #19494, card
Newton, Henry, c/o, Richmond,
Va., 19, #19494
Newton, Jeremiah, w/o, Mass.,
72, #12483
Newton, John, Ind., 52, #6318
Newton, Lydia, Bellows Falls,
Vt., 63, #8967
Newton, Nabby, Albany, N.Y.,
98, #2558

Newton, Samuel, w/o, Vt., 62,
#8840
Nibarger, Christian, Ohio, 72,
#12619
Nicholas, William, w/o,
Pittsburgh, Pa., 90, #18540
Nichols, Abiah, Conn., 34, #40
Nichols, Charles, Knoxville,
Tenn., 39, #3012
Nichols, Isaac B., Ga., 129,
#7039
Nichols, John, w/o, Hartford,
Conn., 92, #19947
Nichols, Rosina, comm/o,
Philadelphia, Pa., 127,
#4545
Nichols, Sarah, a/o, Portsmouth,
N.H., 141, #2280
Nichols, Thomas, c/o, Mass.,
68, #10789
Nichols, Willibe, Ind., 57,
#7617
Nicholson, Anastasia L.,
Richmond, Va., 36A, #F3
V16
Nicholson, Caty, c/o, N.C., 92,
#19605
Nickell, Isabell, Ky., 143,
#6731
Nickells, Richard, e/o,
Nashville, Tenn., 119,
#5185
Nickerson, Deborah, Boston,
Mass., 102, #5907
Nickerson, Stephen, Mass., 39,
#2988
Nickle (now Moore), Elizabeth,
Madison, Ind., 119, #5507
Nicklisson, Israel, w/o, Albany,
N.Y., 65, #9774
Nicolas, George, Philadelphia,
Pa., 59, #8006

Nicolet, J. N., —, 82, #15246, card

Nigh, Michale M., g/o c/o, Spingfield, Ill., 141, #2382

Nighberger, Christian, Ohio, 64, #9269

Niles, Jehiel, c/o, Albany, N.Y., 122, #8965

Niles, John, w/o, Concord, N.H., 96, #1553

Niles, Sarah J., Cincinnati, Ohio, 117, #4572

Nimmro, Lt. William A., 4th Artillery, 119, #5194

Nix, James, Ga., 67, #10375

Nix, James, Ga., 77, #13984

Nix, James, Savannah, Ga., 44, #4231

Nix, John, Ky., 19, #9576

Nixon, Richard, w/o, New York City, 95, #977

Noble, James, Mo., 41, #3426

Noble, James, Mo., 49, #5339

Noble, James, Mo., 56, #7357

Noble, James, Mo., 56, #7358

Noble, Lyman, w/o, Albany, N.Y., 75, #13693

Noble, Mark, a/o, Conn., 38, #F1824

Nobles, Zilpha, S.C., 63, #8929

Noel, Taylor, e/o, Ky., 112, #918

Noestel, Elizabeth, Albany, N.Y., 42, #3716

Noestel, Elizabeth, c/o, Albany, N.Y., 70, #11179

Noestell, Elizabeth, Albany, N.Y., 51, #5922

Nolen, Shadrack, Jackson, Tenn., 84, #15952

Nolton, Nathan, a/o, Albany, N.Y., 108, #10286

Norey, Ruth, a/o, Albany, N.Y., 129, #6654

Norman, John, Ind., 58, #7779

Norman, Lydia, N.C., 117, #4431

Norman, Thomas, w/o, Richmond, Va., 100, #4253

Norman, William, N.C., 79, #14601

Norris, Desire, Conn., 34, #306

Norris, Desire, c/o, Conn., 34, #10558

Norris, Edward, Albany, N.Y., 40, #3267

Norris, Huldah, c/o, Cleveland, Ohio, 130, #8078

Norris, John, c/o, Va. Milita, 95, #941

Norris, John, w/o, Wheeling, Va., 39, #3073

Norris, Joseph, c/o, Madison, Ind., 122, #8409

Norris, Lucy, Mass., 76, #13725

Norris, William, a/o, Knoxville, Tenn., 91, #19084

Norten, Giles, Mich., 50, #5806

North, Eliza, e/o, Richmond, Va., 36A, #F5 V9

North, Martha, Va., 77, #14189

North, Martha, a/o, Richmond, Va., 99, #3596

Northcraft, Edward, Md., 41, #3427

Northern, Joseph, N.C., 83, #15754

Northrop, Isaac, c/o, Conn., 81, #15166

Northrop, Martin V. B., Albany, N.Y., 143, #7615

Northum, Asa, Albany, N.Y., 108, #10346

Northum, Asa, g/o, Albany, N.Y., 54, #6659

Norton, Elias, w/o, Boston, Mass., 19, #7676

Norton, Elijah, w/o, Albany, N.Y., 88, #17915

Norton, Giles, Mich., 59, #7998

Norton, Hannah, c/o, Portsmouth, Maine, 138, #6061

Norton, Jane, Mich., 116, #3089

Norton, Joseph, c/o, Albany, N.Y., 111, #578

Norton, Noah W., a/o, Pittsburgh, Pa., 139, #7042

Norton, Obed, c/o, Mass., 90, #18781

Norton, Ozias, c/o, Conn., 89, #18312

Norton, Ozias, c/o, Pittsburgh, Pa., 85, #16414

Norton, Seba, Albany, N.Y., 52, #6139

Norton, Ulysses, Mo., 122, #8615

Norwood, George, Ga., 44, #4172

Norwood, John, w/o, N.C., 69, #10941

Nothern, Joseph, N.C., 66, #10144

Nott (or Knott), Abraham, w/o, Albany, N.Y., 98, #2640

Nowell, Henry H., c/o, Richmond, Va., 123, #31

Nowels, John, g/o c/o, Ill., 130, #7904

Nowels, John, g/o c/o, Ill., 135, #2013

Noyes, Alonzo B., Fla., 79, #14558

Noyes, Alonzo B., Tallahassee, Fla., 89, #18507

Noyes, Dudley, Albany, N.Y., 80, #14877

Noyes, Silas, g/o, Boston, Mass., 97, #2099

Nulowsky, Terese, La., 129, #6446

Nunn, Mary G., Pulaski, Tenn., 115, #2610

Nunn, Wharton, w/o, Knoxville, Tenn., 90, #18893

Nutter, Rebecca, Richmond, Va., 133, #515

Nutter, Rebecca, Va., 120, #6285

Nutting, Molly, w/o, Boston, Mass., 67, #10429

Nye, Daniel, Bellows Falls, Vt., 63, #8967

Nye, Ichobad, w/o, Ohio, 83, #15735

O

O'Brian, Ichabed, Philadelphia, Pa., 41, #3432

O'Brien, Daniel, a/o, Pittsburgh, Pa., 121, #7630

O'Brien, Justin, D.C., 110, #105

O'Daniel, Sarah, Ky., 115, #2919

O'Donaghy, Agnes, Albany, N.Y., 102, #5427

O'Hara, Elizabeth, N.J., 80, #14829

O'Leary, Elizabeth, New York City, 141, #2012

O'Mohondra, Emily, Nashville, Tenn., 117, #4420

O'Neal, Elizabeth, e/o, Ky., 133, #242

Oliver, John, Richmond, Va.,
    62, #882-, card
Oliver, Rhesa, Fla., 46, #4807
Oliver, Richard, Ky., 59, #8016
Oliver, Richard, Ky., 63, #9014
Oliver, Richard, Ky., 103,
    #6654, card
Oliver, Richard, a/o, Ky., 19,
    #6654
Oliver, Susannah, Fayetteville,
    N.C., 123, #9444
Oliver, Susannah, N.C., 119,
    #5219
Oliver, Susannah, a/o,
    Fayetteville, N.C., 132,
    #9319
Olmstead, Alden, g/o c/o, Conn.,
    37, #F1820
Olmstead, Esther, Mo., 62,
    #8783
Olmstead, James, Albany, N.Y.,
    19, #15663
Olmstead, James, New York
    City, 83, #15663, card
Olmsted, Content, Conn., 34,
    #164
Olney, Tabitha, c/o, Albany,
    N.Y., 104, #7216
Onderkink, John, c/o, Albany,
    N.Y., 53, #6512
Oney, William, Richmond, Va.,
    44, #4318
Oney, William, Richmond, Va.,
    48, #5221
Oney, William, e/o, Richmond,
    Va., 137, #4328
Opic, Major Leroy, w/o, —, 60,
    #8187
Oram, Darby, e/o, N.J., 120,
    #6487
Orchard, Thomas, Ohio, 58,
    #7841

Orcutt, Abiah, a/o, N.H., 74,
    #13036
Orcutt, David, e/o, Conn., 38,
    #F1819
Orear, Daniel, Ga., 65, #9708
Orear, Daniel, Ga., 69, #11001
Orenan (formerly Huffman),
    Joanna, Madison, Ind., 117,
    #4082
Orme, Charles, a/o, Ind., 71,
    #12374
Orme, Moses, Md., 43, #3898,
    card
Orme, Moses, Mo., 19, #3898
Ormsby, Joseph, Albany, N.Y.,
    49, #5367
Ormsley, Elisha, a/o, Utica,
    N.Y., 110, #11086
Orndorff, Christian, c/o, Va., 19,
    #19472
Orndorff, Mary, Richmond, Va.,
    36A, #F3 V17
Orr, Saviours, w/o, New York
    City, 138, #5291
Orser, Jonas, c/o, New York
    City, 51, #6015
Orvis, Ambrose, Albany, N.Y.,
    65, #9949
Osborn, Abraham, Mich., 50,
    #5753
Osborn, Betsey, c/o, Mass., 48,
    #5207
Osborn, Daniel, Albany, N.Y.,
    118, #4767, card
Osborn, Daniel, c/o, Albany,
    N.Y., 19, #4767
Osborn, Ethan, e/o, N.J., 136,
    #2492
Osborn, Grizzle, c/o, Conn., 65,
    #9709
Osborn, James H., Mo., 42,
    #3787

Osborn, Jerusha, a/o, Conn., 34,
#8875
Osborn, John, c/o, Boston,
Mass., 19, #32
Osborn, Louisa, Hartford, Conn.,
64, #9567
Osborn, Rhoda, Conn., 34, #414
Osborn, William S., Albany,
N.Y., 118, #4765
Osborne, John, —, 92, #32, card
Osborne, Joseph, c/o, Albany,
N.Y., 19, #1615
Osborne, Thomas, w/o, Mass.,
50, #5638
Osbourn, Hugh, w/o, Pittsburgh,
Pa., 106, #8745
Osgood, Lemuel H., Mass., 50,
#5795
Osgood, Lemuel H., Mass., 51,
#5989
Oshead, Jethro, S.C., 56, #7372
Osmun, John, N.J., 88, #18012
Osteen, Argent, g/o c/o,
Jacksonville, Fla., 108,
#9944
Osteen, David, Nashville, Tenn.,
52, #6131
Osteen, nancy, Miss., 134,
#1091
Osteen, Nancy, Miss., 136,
#2512
Oster, John, D.C., 141, #1874
Oster, John, D.C., 143, #7344
Ostrander, Patty, c/o, Albany,
N.Y., 84, #16307
Otis, John, Albany, N.Y., 80,
#14870
Ott, Beulah, Maine, 98, #2836
Ott, Bulah, Portland, Maine,
104, #7187
Ott, John, Charleston, S.C., 54,
#6598

Ott, John, S.C., 71, #12251
Ott, William M., Philadelphia,
Pa., 133, #627
Ottis (or Otto), Daniel, c/o,
Philadelphia, Pa., 123, #64
Ottis (or Otto), Daniel, g/o c/o,
Philadelphia, Pa., 129,
#6814
Otto, Francis, Cincinnati, Ohio,
126, #3676
Our, Searchman, Richmond, Va.,
60, #8358
Our, Searchman, Richmond, Va.,
46, #4709
Our, Searchman, Va., 74,
#13204
Our, Searchman, w/o, Richmond,
Va., 92, #179
Outhouse, Peter, Ill., 83, #1561-
, card
Outhoutt, Richard, a/o, D.C.,
141, #2317
Overly, Henry, c/o, Mo., 102,
#6113
Overstreet, Thomas, Ky., 92,
#20
Overstreet, Thomas, Richmond,
Va., 64, #9664
Overton, Jonathan, c/o,
Fayetteville, N.C., 124,
#1367
Owen, Bailey, w/o, Nashville,
Tenn., 78, #14392
Owen, Elizabeth, a/o, Richmond,
Va., 106, #8449
Owen, Harraway, Ind., 70,
#11151
Owen, John R., c/o, Mo., 128,
#5410
Owen, Susanna, Ohio, 104,
#7622

Owen, William, c/o, Albany,
N.Y., 114, #2303
Owens, Joseph, Mo., 131,
#8861
Owens, Joseph, Mo., 133, #80
Owens, Nancy, e/o, Ky., 114,
#2127
Owens, Stephen, w/o,
Pittsburgh, Pa., 43, #3946

P

Pace, John, Mo., 107, #9279,
card
Pace, John, w/o, St. Louis, Mo.,
19, #9279
Pace, Mary, Richmond, Va.,
113, #1908
Pace, Newson, w/o, Richmond,
Va., 98, #3031
Pacham, Sarah, Ky., 140, #893
Packard, Josiah B., Mo., 82,
#15379
Packard, Josiah B., Mo., 86,
#16819
Packer, Charles B., g/o c/o,
Philadelphia, Pa., 128,
#5694
Packer, Jacob, c/o, N.J., 121,
#6902
Packer, Joseph, g/o,
Philadelphia, Pa., 113,
#1555
Padget, Frederick, Richmond,
Va., 92, #19562
Padget, Frederick, Richmond,
Va., 55, #6935
Padget, Frederick, Va., 78,
#14320
Padgett, Elbert, w/o, Charleston,
S.C., 134, #1001

Page, Benjamin, a/o c/o,
Cleveland, Ohio, 140,
#9904
Page, Capt. John, w/o, 4th Inf.,
110, #124
Page, Capt. John, w/o, 4th Inf.,
103, #6338
Page, Capt. John, w/o, 4th Inf.,
105, #7802
Page, Capt. John, w/o, 4th Inf.,
106, #8653
Page, Capt. John, w/o, 4th Inf.,
108, #10025
Page, Capt. John, w/o, 4th Inf.,
109, #10552
Page, Capt. John, w/o, 4th Inf.,
99, #3663
Page, Capt. John, w/o, 4th Inf.,
100, #4497
Page, Capt. John, w/o, 4th Inf.,
101, #5216
Page, Ebenezer, g/o c/o, Conn.,
37, #F1820
Page, Eliza, Montpelier, Vt.,
101, #5006 V#12
Page, Elizabeth M., Ill., 125,
#2838
Page, Elizabeth M., Ill., 127,
#4287
Page, Foster, Vt., 57, #7498
Page, George A., Cleveland,
Ohio, 120, #6382
Page (or Paige), George A.,
Cleveland, Ohio, 135,
#1965
Page, James L., Vt., 78, #14370
Page, John, c/o, Mass., 70,
#12220
Page, Lucy, Richmond, Va.,
36A, #F6, card
Page, Titus, w/o, Albany, N.Y.,
55, #6960

Page, Zeruiah, a/o, Poultney,
Vt., 100, #4399
Paige, Capt. George H., AQM,
137, #3879, slip
Pain, John, Ohio, 83, #15817
Pain, John, w/o, Ohio, 89,
#18362
Pain (now Ledbetter), Huldy C.,
Nashville, Tenn., 110,
#11082
Paine, David, g/o c/o, Conn.,
37, #F1820
Paine, John, Ohio, 57, #7563
Paine, John, Ohio, 63, #9113
Painter, George, N.C., 56,
#7345
Painter, Sarah, Richmond, Va.,
96, #1580
Palmateer, Abraham, c/o, New
York City, 65, #9962
Palmer, Catharine, Cincinnati,
Ohio, 116, #3177
Palmer, Daniel, Philadelphia,
Pa., 72, #12566
Palmer, Daniel, Philadelphia,
Pa., 82, #15458
Palmer, Daniel, Philadelphia,
Pa., 110, #3
Palmer, Daniel, Philadelphia,
Pa., 101, #4824
Palmer, Daniel, Philadelphia,
Pa., 39, #3125
Palmer, Elisha, Va., 80, #14983
Palmer, Fores, e/o, R.I., 73,
#12953
Palmer, J. N., —, 128, #5824,
card
Palmer, J. N., —, 129, #6370,
card
Palmer, J. N., —, 129, #6605,
card
Palmer, James, Va., 67, #10448

Palmer, Jared, c/o, Albany, N.Y.,
127, #4680
Palmer, Jared, w/o, Albany,
N.Y., 64, #9697
Palmer, Ozias, Albany, N.Y.,
106, #8825
Palmer, Susannah, a/o,
Nashville, Tenn., 101,
#4875
Palmer, Thomas, Knoxville,
Tenn., 108, #10185
Palmer, Thomas, Tenn., 110,
#100
Palmerton, Elizabeth, Albany,
N.Y., 108, #10307
Palmerton, Elizabeth, Albany,
N.Y., 124, #484
Pane, David, c/o, N.C., 62,
#8853
Pano, Loran, w/o, Burlington,
Vt., 124, #1352
Pape, Maria A. E., New York
City, 116, #3460
Papste, Christian, La., 122,
#8685
Papste, Christian, La., 128,
#5210
Parke, Zebulon, —, 104, #7463,
slip
Parkenson, Jacob, Ga., 84,
#16087
Parker, Abraham, c/o, Ky., 96,
#1760
Parker, Alexander, Va., 109,
#10900
Parker, Alexander, e/o,
Richmond, Va., 20, #10900
Parker, Amanda, Des Moines,
Iowa, 143, #7369
Parker, Anna, c/o, Albany, N.Y.,
98, #2738

Parker, Barnabus, e/o, Maine, 122, #8241
Parker, Benjamin, a/o, Ky., 126, #3387
Parker, Elizabeth, Conn., 34, #22
Parker, Ezra, a/o, Mich., 91, #19184
Parker, James, Ill., 120, #6076
Parker, James, Ill., 127, #4428
Parker, James, Ohio, 115, #2995
Parker, James, w/o, Va., 87, #17615
Parker, John, e/o, Ky., 132, #9275
Parker, John, w/o, Wheeling, Va., 103, #6912
Parker, Kedar, N.C., 41, #3453
Parker, Nahum, c/o, N.H., 66, #10213
Parker, Nancy, Richmond, Va., 95, #996
Parker, Private Josiah, w/o, 4th Inf., 69, #10978
Parker, Rebecca, Maine, 60, #8245
Parker, Rebecca, Maine, 62, #8848
Parker, Richard, c/o, Albany, N.Y., 95, #1140
Parker, Richard, w/o, Knoxville, Tenn., 133, #481
Parker, Silas, a/o, Vt., 78, #14414
Parker, Thankful, Mass., 126, #3627
Parker, William, Albany, N.Y., 64, #9155, card
Parker, William, Albany, N.Y., 66, #10225
Parker, William, a/o, Albany, N.Y., 20, #18326

Parker, Zebulon, a/o, Pittsburgh, Pa., 20, #7463
Parker 2nd, William, Albany, N.Y., 20, #9155
Parker 2nd, William, w/o, Albany, N.Y., 20, #15179
Parkerson, Jacob, Ga., 48, #5197
Parkerson, Joseph, Richmond, Va., 49, #5349
Parkes, Nancy, Richmond, Va., 59, #8160
Parkes, Nancy, Richmond, Va., 64, #9371
Parkes, Nancy, Va., 65, #10008
Parkes, Nancy, Va., 71, #12225
Parkes, Nancy, Va., 75, #13575
Parkes 2nd, William, Albany, N.Y., 81, #15179, card
Parkhurst, Azel, c/o, Vt., 90, #18840
Parkhurst, Pierce, Conn., 34, #344
Parkinson, Ezekiel, w/o, Va., 82, #15369
Parkinson, Thomas, w/o, Wheeling, Va., 57, #7626
Parks, Catherine, La., 127, #4003
Parks, George, w/o, Bedford, Ind., 20, #17537
Parks, Henry, c/o, Ga., 98, #3100
Parks, Josiah, Mass., 85, #16531
Parks, Luther, Louisville, Ky., 39, #3079
Parks, Malinda, Ill., 133, #9974
Parks, Nancy, Richmond, Va., 97, #1983
Parks Sr., Benjamin, Ga., 51, #5997

Parlin, Eleazer, a/o, Maine, 110, #11113

Parmly, John, Ky., 45, #4613

Parr, Martha D., c/o, Ga., 124, #1230

Parr, Moses, c/o, Albany, N.Y., 74, #13252

Parris, John B., Mo., 112, #988

Parrish, Ebenezer, Philadelphia, Pa., 78, #14344

Parrish, Levi H., Albany, N.Y., 66, #10230

Parrish, N., R., Ga., 112, #1213

Parrish, Nathan, a/o, Philadelphia, Pa., 108, #10173

Parrish, Robert, w/o, Nashville, Tenn., 71, #12401

Parrish, Robert N., Ga., 112, #883

Parrish, Robert N., Savannah, Ga., 126, #3011

Parrot, William, Richmond, Va., 46, #4829

Parrott, John, Conn., 34, #436

Parrott, Marilda, Ga., 122, #8353

Parrott, Wiliam, Richmond, Va., 106, #8516

Parrott, William, Richmond, Va., 58, #7909

Parrott, William, Richmond, Va., 53, #6487

Parrott, William, Va., 80, #14795

Parshall, James, c/o, Albany, N.Y., 114, #2126

Parson, Walter, c/o, Iowa, 20, #18345

Parsons, Amos, Boston, Mass., 65, #9719

Parsons, Amos, Montpelier, Vt., 108, #10235

Parsons, Gideon, Albany, N.Y., 96, #1780

Parsons, Jabez, Pittsburgh, Pa., 105, #7806

Parsons, James, c/o, Boston, Mass., 54, #6751

Parsons, James, g/o c/o, Richmond, Va., 125, #2721

Parsons, John, N.H., 86, #16792

Parsons, Joseph, w/o, N.C., 48, #5061

Parsons, Justin, Pittsburgh, Pa., 82, #15543

Parsons, Nancy, N.C., 100, #3924

Parsons, Nancy, N.C., 66, #10143

Parsons, Nancy, N.C., 77, #14108

Parsons, Nancy, e/o, N.C., 107, #9639

Partridge, Amos, w/o, Albany, N.Y., 100, #4309

Partridge, Martha, Albany, N.Y., 126, #3591

Partridge, Mary, c/o, Maine, 105, #8029

Pask, Ruth, c/o, Portland, Maine, 99, #3262

Pasko, John, w/o, Albany, N.Y., 46, #4815

Pasmore, Lucy, Conn., 34, #336

Patch, Ephraim, w/o, Albany, N.Y., 62, #8757

Patch, Joseph, Mass., 70, #12218

Patchim, Isaac, Conn., 34, #175

Patchin, Squire, c/o, Albany, N.Y., 118, #5093

Patchin, Squire, c/o, Albany,
N.Y., 98, #3082
Patchin, Squire, c/o, Albany,
N.Y., 98, #3143
Patchin, Squire, c/o, Albany,
N.Y., 99, #3215
Patchin, Squire, c/o, Albany,
N.Y., 99, #3250
Patching, Talcutt, La., 60,
#8247
Patching, Talcutt, La., 94, #626
Patching, Talcutt, La., 96,
#1675
Pate, Prisilla, Richmond, Va.,
76, #13824
Paterson, William, c/o, Ill., 76,
#13803
Patrick, Hiram, Madison, Ind.,
137, #4572
Patrick, Isabella, c/o, S.C., 124,
#847
Patrick, Reuben, c/o, Albany,
N.Y., 118, #4779
Pattee, James P., a/o, Concord,
N.H., 111, #715
Pattee, Phebe, a/o, Concord,
N.H., 111, #643
Patten, 2Lt. George, 3rd
Artillery, 123, #9759, card
Patten, Joseph, Knoxville,
Tenn., 50, #5592
Patten, Lt. George, 3rd Artillery,
121, #6951, slip
Patten, Mary, a/o, Portsmouth,
N.H., 110, #194
Patterson, Alex., Maine, 48,
#5120
Patterson, Alexander, S.C., 20,
#14314, card
Patterson, Alexander, c/o,
Maine, 20, #5120

Patterson, James, Tenn., 109,
#10867
Patterson, James, c/o,
Philadelphia, Pa., 88,
#17870
Patterson, James, w/o, Ill., 125,
#1913
Patterson, John, Ky., 105,
#8071
Patterson, John, Ky., 139,
#6721
Patterson, John, Ky., 96, #1486
Patterson, John, Ky., 97, #2402
Patterson, John, w/o, Ky., 139,
#6722
Patterson, William, Ill., 49,
#5269
Patterson, William, Maine, 127,
#4922
Patterson Sr., Alexander, S.C.,
49, #5363
Pattison, Chloe, c/o,
Burlington, Vt., 115,
#2509
Patton, John, w/o, Nashville,
Tenn., 96, #1781
Patton, Matthew, S.C., 106,
#8456, card
Patton, Matthews, w/o, S.C., 20,
#8456
Patton, Samuel, a/o, Ky., 96,
#1827
Patton, William, Mo., 99,
#3634
Patton, William, Philadelphia,
Pa., 79, #14734
Patton, William, Philadelphia,
Pa., 137, #4522, card
Patton, William, s/o,
Philadelphia, Pa., 119,
#5186

Pearson, Samuel, Ohio, 122,
#8251, card
Pearson, Sarah, Vt., 65, #9820
Pearson, Thomas, e/o, Madison,
Ind., 130, #7488
Pearson, William C., g/o c/o,
Pulaski, Tenn., 127, #4340
Pease, Abner, c/o, Pittsburgh,
Pa., 44, #4206
Pease, Charles, w/o, Conn., 88,
#17805
Peasely, Mary, a/o, Albany,
N.Y., 101, #5320
Peck, Abel, w/o, Knoxville,
Tenn., 115, #2776
Peck, Christian, c/o, Concord,
N.H., 97, #2410
Peck, Elizabeth, a/o, Albany,
N.Y., 141, #1521
Peck, Gaius, a/o, Vt., 109,
#10721
Peck, Hannah, Conn., 34, #171
Peck, Henry, Ga., 60, #8372
Peck, John, Philadelphia, Pa.,
53, #6562
Peck, John B., a/o, Richmond,
Va., 129, #6986
Peck, Joseph, Conn., 34, #1029
Peck, Lewis, Pittsburgh, Pa.,
143, #6029
Peck, Loving, a/o, Albany,
N.Y., 134, #1162
Peck, Lydia, a/o, Nashville,
Tenn., 122, #8831
Peck, Olive, c/o, Vt., 64, #9623
Peck, Peter, Richmond, Va., 56,
#7426
Peck, Solomon, Albany, N.Y.,
41, #3531
Peck, William, w/o, N.Y., 53,
#6526

Peck, John, late PA, Burlington,
Vt., 95, #1031
Peckham, Lucy, Conn., 34, #450
Peckham, Lucy, a/o, Conn., 107,
#9663
Peden, Alexander, e/o, S.C., 94,
#247
Pednick, Benjamin,
Philadelphia, Pa., 79,
#14733
Pednik, Benjamin, Philadelphia,
Pa., 72, #12651
Pedrick, Benjamin, c/o,
Philadelphia, Pa., 120,
#6100
Peers, Elizabeth, a/o, Ky., 124,
#386
Peet, Sally, Conn., 34, #324
Pegg, Benjamin, Ohio, 20,
#3433
Pegg, Elias, Ohio, 59, #8109,
card
Pegg, Ellis, c/o, Ohio, 20,
#8109
Peirce, Bowen, c/o, R.I., 123,
#9795
Peirce, John, N.C., 61, #8390
Pelham, Abijah, c/o, Cincinnati,
Ohio, 136, #2558
Pell, Henry, New York City,
137, #4548
Pell, Josiah, Philadelphia, Pa.,
80, #14910
Pell, Josiah, w/o, Philadelphia,
Pa., 117, #3895
Pell, William, Ind., 65, #9969,
card
Pell, William, w/o, Ind., 20,
#9969
Pellett, Samuel, w/o, Albany,
N.Y., 137, #4571

Pelton, Albert, g/o c/o,
Cleveland, Ohio, 133, #648
Pelton, Joseph, c/o, Concord,
N.H., 115, #2959
Pember, Clarissa, a/o,
Cleveland, Ohio, 20, #6294
Pemberton, Julia F., Chicago,
Ill., 143, #7265
Penber, Eli, w/o, Ohio, 138,
#6294
Penby, John, N.C., 80, #14911
Pence, Nancy, Richmond, Va.,
71, #12361
Pendleton, David, e/o, Conn.,
38, #F1826
Pendleton, Micajah, Richmond,
Va., 48, #5129
Pendleton, Michajah, Richmond,
Va., 44, #4235
Pendleton, Philip, Va., 96,
#1826, slip
Pendleton, Philip, e/o,
Richmond, Va., 20, #1826
Penfield, Isaac, N.Y., 105,
#8080, card
Penfield, Isaac, c/o, Albany,
N.Y., 20, #8080
Pennell, Bathsheba, Portsmouth,
Maine, 130, #7727
Pennington, Henry, E. Fla., 89,
#18205
Pennington, Henry, Fla., 69,
#10837
Pennington, Henry,
Jacksonville, Fla., 65,
#9903
Pennington, Henry, Tallahassee,
Fla., 132, #9451
Pennington, John, w/o, N.J.,
75, #13543
Pennington, Kinchin, N.C., 45,
#4608

Penticost, William, w/o, Ga.,
89, #18309
Peonix, Overton, w/o, N.C., 57,
#7577
Perine, William, e/o, Albany,
N.Y., 118, #4615
Perkins, Abner, e/o, Albany,
N.Y., 114, #2182
Perkins, Archelaus, Mo., 76,
#13828
Perkins, Christian, e/o, Ky.,
103, #7053
Perkins, Cote, e/o, Albany,
N.Y., 65, #9883
Perkins, Eliab, a/o, Albany,
N.Y., 88, #17808
Perkins, Elias, Richmond, Va.,
61, #8605
Perkins, Elizabeth, Portsmouth,
N.H., 84, #16206, card
Perkins, Elizabeth, a/o, N.H.,
20, #16206
Perkins, Enoch, Maine, 58,
#7873
Perkins, George, Iowa, 65,
#9918
Perkins, George, Iowa, 73,
#12999
Perkins, George, tr/o, Ky., 140,
#9450
Perkins, George, tr/o, Ky., 139,
#8878
Perkins, Jane, Richmond, Va.,
36A, #F3 V21
Perkins, Lyman, g/o c/o, Conn.,
37, #F1820
Perkins, Mark, e/o, Mass., 139,
#7894
Perkins, Rufus, w/o, Albany,
N.Y., 20, #8280
Perkins, Thomas, S.C., 39,
#3018

Perkins, William, c/o, Albany, N.Y., 129, #6526
Perkins, John, w/o, Nashville, Tenn., 75, #13442 (alias Thomas Carson)
Permout, Godfrey, New York City, 120, #6141
Perril, John, a/o, Cincinnati, Ohio, 117, #3918
Perrill, John, c/o, Cincinnati, Ohio, 116, #3610
Perrin, Nathan, Jonesboro, Tenn., 64, #9212
Perrine, William, Philadelphia, Pa., 47, #4992
Perrine, William, w/o, Philadelphia, Pa., 64, #9187
Perry, Abraham, Mobile, Ala., 120, #5891, card
Perry, Anna, a/o, Albany, N.Y., 123, #9115
Perry, Benjamin, c/o, Ky., 120, #6411
Perry, Daniel, Huntsville, Ala., 54, #6616
Perry, Daniel, Huntsville, Ala., 90, #18555
Perry, Danl, Huntsville, Ala., 51, #6026
Perry, David, g/o c/o, New Albany, Ind., 129, #7110
Perry, Eli, Conn., 34, #1053
Perry, James, c/o, Maine, 80, #14881
Perry, Jeremiah, w/o, Albany, N.Y., 103, #6727
Perry, Jonathan, a/o, Albany, N.Y., 91, #19130
Perry, Mary, c/o, Albany, N.Y., 91, #18963

Perry, Thomas, Ohio, 68, #10590
Perry, Thomas, w/o, Ohio, 87, #17679
Perryman, John, w/o, W. Tenn., 88, #17953, card
Peters, Adrian, N.H., 64, #9126
Peters, Comfort, a/o, Portsmouth, N.H., 130, #7842
Peters, Elizabeth, Richmond, Va., 63, #8928
Peters, Elizabeth, Richmond, Va., 101, #4894
Peters, Jacob, Philadelphia, Pa., 61, #8406
Peters, Jacob, Philadelphia, Pa., 47, #4870
Peters, Jesse, Ga., 52, #6149
Peters, John, Richmond, Va., 102, #6008
Peters, John, Va., 69, #10924
Peters, John, Va., 85, #16550
Peters, John, c/o, Va., 46, #4818
Peters, Martha, a/o, Mass., 108, #10327
Peters, William, E. Tenn., 60, #8347
Peters, William, Ga., 108, #9728
Peters, William, Ga., 114, #2015
Peters, William, Ga., 122, #8447
Peters, William, Ga., 129, #6575
Peters, William, Ga., 136, #3228
Peterson, Abigail, New York City, 103, #6648

Peterson, Elijah, h/o, —, 86,
#17004
Peterson, Isaac, Albany, N.Y.,
44, #4245, card
Peterson, Isaac, w/o, Albany,
N.Y., 20, #4245
Peterson, John, Boston, Mass.,
143, #7036
Peterson, Matsen, Pittsburgh,
Pa., 51, #5883
Peterson, Matson, Pittsburgh,
Pa., 55, #7210
Peterson, Matson, Pittsburgh,
Pa., 111, #410
Petir (or Peters), Jacob, w/o,
D.C., 129, #6522
Petlee, Andrew, a/o, Albany,
N.Y., 121, #7512
Petrea, George, g/o c/o,
Spingfield, Ill., 141, #3235
Petred, Catharine, Ill., 116,
#3772
Pettiford, George, w/o,
Fayetteville, N.C., 124,
#996
Pettigrew, James, Tuscaloosa,
Ala., 70, #11101
Pettigrew, James, Tuscaloosa,
Ala., 74, #13033
Pettigrew, Judith, Philadelphia,
Pa., 115, #2447
Pettingal, Obediah, Maine, 74,
#13333
Pettit, Elisha, Springfield, Ill.,
142, #4936
Pettit, John, Albany, N.Y., 70,
#12157, card
Pettit, John, c/o, Albany, N.Y.,
20, #12157
Petts, James, a/o, N.H., 79,
#14697

Petty, Lucretia, New York City,
129, #6781
Petty, Samuel, Albany, N.Y., 66,
#10229
Petty, Samuel, a/o, Albany,
N.Y., 106, #8700
Petty, Sarah, Ky., 140, #9650
Petty, Sarah, a/o, Ky., 20,
#9650
Peurson, William C., g/o c/o,
Pulaski, Tenn., 125, #2266
Pfannernschmidt, Agatha, D.C.,
138, #6463
Pfannernschmidt, Agatha, D.C.,
141, #2396
Phaglee, John, Philadelphia,
Pa., 140, #774
Phares, Andrew, Albany, N.Y.,
63, #8893
Pharis, Cyrus, g/o c/o, Ky., 133,
#9997
Phelps, Alexander, Philadelphia,
Pa., 45, #4558
Phelps, Deborah, Conn., 34,
#169
Phelps, Deborah, Conn., 34,
#32
Phelps, Giles, c/o, Albany,
N.Y., 51, #6069
Phelps, Israel, w/o, Albany,
N.Y., 77, #14159
Phelps, John, c/o, Albany, N.Y.,
118, #5094
Phelps, John, c/o, Albany, N.Y.,
119, #5690
Phelps, John, c/o, Albany, N.Y.,
121, #7703
Phelps, Jonathan, Albany, N.Y.,
59, #8127
Phelps, Levina, Philadelphia,
Pa., 83, #15621

Phelps, Mary, a/o, Albany,
N.Y., 111, #723
Phelps, Norman, c/o, Mich.,
129, #6397
Phelps, Oliver, Philadelphia,
Pa., 78, #14428
Phelps, Oliver, Philadelphia,
Pa., 102, #5677
Phelps, Oliver, Philadelphia,
Pa., 96, #1708
Phelps, Oliver, Philadelphia,
Pa., 39, #2958
Phelps, Oliver, Philadelphia,
Pa., 47, #4920
Phelps, Oliver, c/o, Albany,
N.Y., 121, #7701
Phifer, Martin, c/o, N.C., 20,
#5656
Philips, Elizabeth, Philadelphia,
Pa., 83, #15621
Philips, Gideon, Conn., 34,
#149
Philips, James, g/o c/o,
Indianapolis, Ind., 124,
#1415
Philips, John, Fayetteville,
N.C., 50, #5591
Philips, John, N.C., 43, #3969
Philips, Naomi, c/o, Boston,
Mass., 20, #8670
Philips, Norton, w/o, Portland,
Maine, 50, #5527
Philips, Philip, w/o, D.C., 54,
#6608
Philips, William, W. Tenn., 62,
#8839
Phillips, A. B., g/o, Madison,
Ind., 112, #933
Phillips, Charles, Albany, N.Y.,
108, #10152

Phillips, Comfort, e/o,
Richmond, Va., 36A, #F5
V9
Phillips, James, g/o c/o,
Indianapolis, Ind., 126,
#3759
Phillips, James, g/o c/o,
Indianapolis, Ind., 129,
#6588
Phillips, Job, Conn., 34, #427
Phillips, Levi, Ga., 46, #4755
Phillips, Lodoiska L., New
Orleans, La., 133, #165
Phillips, Naomi, — , 122,
#8670, slip
Phillips, Polly, Fayetteville,
N.C., 127, #4369
Phillips, William, Nashville,
Tenn., 44, #4229
Phillips, William, Nashville,
Tenn., 54, #6687
Phillips, William, w/o,
Philadelphia, Pa., 124,
#820
Phillips, Zechariah, a/o, Ky.,
122, #8326
Philps, Abigail, a/o, Conn.,
116, #3196
Phinnex, John, Maine, 99,
#3510
Phipps, Jean, Richmond, Va.,
101, #5117
Phipps, Ragena, Jackson, Tenn.,
130, #7905
Phipps, Samuel, c/o, Albany,
N.Y., 85, #16341
Phipps, Samuel, c/o, Albany,
N.Y., 92, #37
Pickard, John, c/o, Albany,
N.Y., 97, #2516
Pickart, Tabitha, a/o, Boston,
Mass., 121, #7595

Pitman, Ambrose, a/o, Ky., 124,
#830
Pitt, Joseph, w/o, Va. Milita,
94, #503
Pittman, George, Va., 43, #3839
Pitts, Henry, S.C., 41, #3515
Pitts, Henry, S.C., 64, #9210
Pitts, Major, Richmond, Va., 47,
#4977
Pitts, Robert G., g/o c/o, Iowa,
130, #7647
Pittsburgh, John Lusk, —, 41,
#3368
Place, Ann, Ohio, 62, #8869
Place, George, g/o c/o, Conn.,
37, #F1824
Place, Griffin, Albany, N.Y.,
120, #—, card
Place, Jeremiah, R.I., 68,
#10718
Plaisted, Roger, Maine, 104,
#7496
Plakard, Christian, a/o,
Cincinnati, Ohio, 111,
#714
Plakerd, Christian, g/o, Ohio,
55, #6958
Platt, Lydia, Conn., 78, #14518
Pleasant, William, N.C., 63,
#9003, card
Pleasant, William, c/o, N.C., 20,
#9003, card
Plimpton, Mary, Mass., 83,
#15913
Plumb, Isaac, w/o, Albany, N.Y.,
126, #3197
Plummer, Richard, w/o, N.C.,
41, #3536
Plunkett, Peter, w/o, 30th Inf.,
133, #665
Plylmpton, Tabitha, c/o, Mass.,
105, #8113

Plymel, William, w/o, Mo., 114,
#2018
Pock, Mary, Ky., 128, #5532
Pogue, Sarah P., Ill., 115, #2984
Poindexter, Chapman, w/o, Ky.,
120, #6569
Poindexter, Sally, Richmond,
Va., 105, #8295
Poindexter, Thomas, Richmond,
Va., 51, #6003
Poindexter, Thomas, Va., 75,
#13651
Poindexter, Thomas, Va., 90,
#18618
Pointer, Sarah, Richmond, Va.,
94, #440
Pokley, John, Albany, N.Y., 65,
#9989
Polhemus, John, c/o,
Philadelphia, Pa., 90,
#18641
Polhemus, John, h/o,
Philadelphia, Pa., 39,
#2972
Polland, Jas, Ind., 53, #6478
Pollard, Chattian, Knoxville,
Tenn., 89, #18219
Pollard, Chattin, E. Tenn., 65,
#9862
Pollard, Chattin, Knoxville,
Tenn., 69, #10893
Pollard, Chattin, Knoxville,
Tenn., 75, #13493
Pollard, Chattin, Knoxville,
Tenn., 89, #18505
Pollard, Chattin, w/o,
Knoxville, Tenn., 92,
#19778
Pollard, James, Ind., 134,
#1280, card
Pollard, James, c/o, Madison,
Ind., 20, #1280

Pollard, Leonor, a/o, Ky., 97,
#1898
Polloard, Braxton, Ky., 76,
#13755
Pollock, David, Philadelphia,
Pa., 62, #8802
Polly, Mary, Ky., 116, #3635
Pomeroy, Ichabod, e/o,
Pittsburgh, Pa., 102, #5409
Pomroy, Ira, w/o, Albany, N.Y.,
86, #17168
Pond, Barnabas, w/o, Albany,
N.Y., 117, #4298
Pond, Beriah, Albany, N.Y., 43,
#4093
Pond, Dan, Vt., 60, #8226, card
Pond, Dan, c/o, Vt., 20, #8226
Pond, Jabez, w/o, Boston,
Mass., 108, #9985
Pond, Josiah, c/o, Burlington,
Vt., 135, #2391
Pond, Oliver, c/o, Mass., 90,
#18872
Ponds, John H., e/o, Va., 87,
#17589
Pool, Abigal, Conn., 82,
#15545
Pool, Allen P., w/o, Ky., 140,
#800
Pool, John, N.C., 61, #8627
Pool, John, c/o, N.J., 85,
#16458
Pool, Samuel, Ga., 58, #7891
Pool, Samuel, Ga., 64, #9128
Pool, Samule, Ga., 113, #1588,
card
Poor, Jane, Ky., 63, #8913
Poorman, Christain,
Philadelphia, Pa., 46,
#4848
Pope, Elender, Ky., 139, #7855
Pope, Harwood, N.C., 51, #5856

Pope, Harwood, N.C., 60, #8379
Pope, Harwood, N.C., 62, #8753
Pope, Harwood, w/o, N.C., 87,
#17546
Pope, Maria A. E., N.Y., 111,
#608
Pope, Maria A. E., New York
City, 124, #877
Pope, Maria A. E., New York
City, 132, #9106
Pope, Seth, Mass., 44, #4216
Pope, special, Capt. John, —,
131, #8600
Popham, Benjamin, Md., 56,
#7314
Poplin, Lucy, N.C., 97, #2299
Poplin, Lucy, a/o, N.C., 113,
#1841
Porch, Henry, Ky., 55, #7072
Porter, 2nd Lt. Theodeni H., w/o,
—, 98, #3117
Porter, Charles, w/o, Jonesboro,
Tenn., 55, #7090
Porter, D. D., —, 125, #2066,
card
Porter, D. D., —, 127, #4490,
card
Porter, D. D., —, 127, #4863,
card
Porter, David, a/o, Albany, N.Y.,
92, #19976
Porter, David V., 4th Inf., 109,
#10869
Porter, Dudley, Mass., 39,
#3111
Porter, Eli, Ohio, 119, #5537,
card
Porter, Eli, w/o, Cincinnati,
Ohio, 21, #5537
Porter, Elizabeth, Morganton,
N.C., 136, #2627

Porter, Ezekiel, w/o, Albany, N.Y., 70, #11118

Porter, Ezra, g/o c/o, Conn., 37, #F1820

Porter, George, Bellows Falls, Vt., 63, #8967

Porter, Hancock, S.C., 94, #246

Porter, Ira G., Mo., 49, #5397

Porter, Ira G., Mo., 64, #9585

Porter, James, Mobile, Ala., 54, #6602

Porter, John, Ky., 73, #12745

Porter, John, Ky., 80, #14792

Porter, John, w/o, Ky., 88, #17886

Porter, Joseph, a/o, Philadelphia, Pa., 21, #12893

Porter, Lt. Theoderic H., c/o, 4th Inf., 102, #6259

Porter, Lt. Theoderic H., c/o, 4th Inf., 105, #8274

Porter, Lt. Theoderic H., c/o, 4th Inf., 108, #10084

Porter, Lt. Theoderic H., w/o, 4th Inf., 102, #5764

Porter, Lt. Theoderick H., c/o, 4th Inf., 106, #8739

Porter, Lt. Theodoric H., c/o, 4th Inf., 110, #32

Porter, Lt. Theodoric H., c/o, 4th Inf., 103, #7066

Porter, Lt. Theodoric H., w/o, —, 100, #3914

Porter, Lt. Theodorick H., w/o, 4th Inf., 101, #4675

Porter, Lucy, a/o, Hartford, Conn., 100, #3973

Porter, Martha, Ky., 140, #460

Porter, Martha, Louisville, Ky., 108, #9984 V#55

Porter, Moses, c/o, Maine, 120, #6627

Porter, Moses, c/o, Maine, 121, #7860

Porter, Moses, c/o, Maine, 121, #7862

Porter, Nathaniel, w/o, N.H., 88, #17972

Porter, Rebecca, Albany, N.Y., 112, #809

Porter, Rebecca, a/o, Albany, N.Y., 133, #208

Porter, Robert, Wheeling, Va., 70, #12079

Porter, Robert, Wheeling, Va., 57, #7564

Porter, Rosaman, c/o, Ky., 126, #3988

Porter, Sally, Ky., 66, #10062

Porter, Samuel, a/o, Pittsburgh, Pa., 115, #2689

Porter, Stephen, w/o, Albany, N.Y., 103, #6560

Porter, Theoderick H., g/o c/o, Mo., 128, #5340

Porter, Trueman, Conn., 60, #8256, card

Porter, Truman, c/o, Albany, N.Y., 21, #8256

Porter, William S. S., Knoxville, Tenn., 132, #9846

Porterfield, Robert, Richmond, Va., 60, #8356

Portlock, John, c/o, Madison, Ind., 132, #9847

Posey, F. H., S.C., 109, #10465

Posey, Francis H., S.C., 135, #2483

Poss, Nicholas, c/o, Albany, N.Y., 99, #3593

Post, David, a/o, Pittsburgh, Pa., 111, #332

Post, John C., N.J., 84, #16237

Post, John H., w/o, N.J., 125, #1894

Potter, Abjah, a/o, Concord, N.H., 90, #18946

Potter, David, Albany, N.Y., 70, #12003

Potter, Elizabeth, c/o, Albany, N.Y., 104, #7579

Potter, Ezra, c/o, Conn., 85, #16554

Potter, Joseph, Pa., 73, #12893, card

Potter, Martha, Conn., 34, #45

Potter, Rachel, Conn., 115, #2772

Potter, Rachel, a/o, Conn., 115, #2774

Potter, Silas, w/o, Albany, N.Y., 65, #9811

Potts, David, Ohio, 39, #3032

Potts, James, Nashville, Tenn., 80, #14790

Potts, Jesse, w/o, Fla., 58, #7767

Potts, Jonathan, a/o, Ohio, 110, #89

Powell, Ann, Ky., 52, #6191

Powell, Asahel, Boston, Mass., 55, #7035

Powell, Ashel, Mass., 79, #14716

Powell, Charles, e/o, N.C., 95, #1088

Powell, Elizabeth, Richmond, Va., 117, #4230, card

Powell, Elizabeth, Va., 105, #773-

Powell, Felix, c/o, Albany, N.Y., 122, #8369

Powell, Levin H., w/o, Richmond, Va., 98, #2770

Powell, Lewis, Ga., 134, #1341, card

Powell, Lewis, Savannah, Ga., 44, #4270

Powell, Sarah, c/o, N.C., 98, #2962

Powell, Tomas, N.J., 120, #6626

Powell, William, Richmond, Va., 66, #10273

Powell, Young, c/o, Ill., 120, #6094

Powell, Young, c/o, Ill., 120, #6147

Powell, Young, g/o c/o, Ill., 132, #9236

Power, Joseph, comm/o, Ky., 103, #6885

Power, Joshua, Louisville, Ky., 108, #9984 V#57

Powers, Elizabeth, c/o, Mass., 83, #15912

Powers, Jeremiah, c/o, Ky., 42, #3695

Powers, Jesse, —, 111, #630, card

Powers, Jesse, c/o, Md., 21, #630

Powers, Jesse, w/o, Ky., 21, #12495

Powers, John, w/o, N.J., 118, #4766

Powers, Lydia, Burlington, Vt., 65, #9765

Powers, Nicholas, c/o, S.C., 120, #6544

Powers, Sybel, a/o, Albany, N.Y., 135, #2259

Pratt, Abel, Albany, N.Y., 42, #3701

Pratt, Ephraim, Albany, N.Y., 121, #6903

Pratt, Ephraim, c/o, Albany,
N.Y., 117, #4042
Pratt, Hannah, a/o, Vt., 63,
#9065
Pratt, James, Louisville, Ky.,
104, #7658
Pratt, James, w/o, Ky., 125,
#2742
Pratt, James, w/o, Philadelphia,
Pa., 57, #7543
Pratt, Jonathan, Va., 82, #15272
Pratt, Lydia, c/o, Albany, N.Y.,
94, #699
Pratt, Mary, a/o, Mass., 88,
#17762
Pratt, Noah, Albany, N.Y., 21,
#4532
Pratt, Noah, Albany, N.Y., 137,
#45--, card
Pratt, Paul, Albany, N.Y., 40,
#3247
Pratt, Seth, w/o, Maine, 85,
#16522
Pratt 2nd, Joseph, c/o, Mass.,
135, #2441
Pratt, Army Contractors, Benoni
P., Ft. Moultrie, Ga., 112,
#881
Prentice, Nathaniel, Ind., 47,
#4911
Presbury, Meredith, a/o,
Burlington, Vt., 126,
#3579
Prescott, Abel, Mass., 58,
#7679
Pressley, David, w/o, S.C., 92,
#19972
Preston, Chauncey H., g/o c/o,
Detroit, Mich., 140, #9984
Preston, Elizabeth, Ky., 90,
#18838

Preston, Fanny, c/o, Ky., 96,
#1545
Preston, James P., Richmond,
Va., 51, #6032
Preston, Solomon, w/o,
Philadelphia, Pa., 138,
#4724, card
Prettyman, Mary, D.C., 141,
#2039
Prewett, John, Richmond, Va.,
45, #4526
Prewett, John, w/o, Ky., 72,
#12624
Prewit, Zachariah, e/o,
Richmond, Va., 99, #3291
Prewitt, Solomon, —, 118,
#4753, card
Price, Abner, Albany, N.Y., 46,
#4767
Price, Daniel, Richmond, Va.,
56, #7336
Price, Daniel, Richmond, Va.,
67, #10340
Price, Daniel, Richmond, Va.,
77, #13983
Price, Daniel, Richmond, Va.,
48, #5181
Price, Ephraim, Ga., 40, #3286
Price, Ephraim, Ga., 51, #5953
Price, Ephraim, Ga., 77, #14146
Price, Henry, g/o, Philadelphia,
Pa., 81, #15143
Price, Jacob, Ohio, 94, #357,
card
Price, Jacob, Richmond, Va.,
36A, #F1 V14
Price, Jacob, Richmond, Va., 94,
#358, card
Price, Jacob, a/o, Ohio, 21,
#357
Price, Jacob, a/o, Richmond,
Va., 21, #358

Proud, Zebulon, a/o, Vt., 112, #867

Proudfoot, James, Pittsburgh, Pa., 67, #10327

Provance, Joseph Y., Pittsburgh, Pa., 74, #13188

Provandie, Louis, c/o, Albany, N.Y., 117, #4296

Provence, Joseph Y., Pittsburgh, Pa., 50, #5794

Provost, Thomas, Conn., 34, #454

Pruett, John, —, 78, #14296, card

Puckett, John B., Ga., 137, #3762

Puckett, Josiah, c/o, Nashville, Tenn., 117, #4227

Puckett, Nathaniel, Richmond, Va., 49, #5442

Puffer, Sarah, a/o, Albany, N.Y., 99, #3455

Puffer, Simeon, c/o, Albany, N.Y., 100, #4452

Pugh, James, w/o, Richmond, Va., 62, #8819

Pullen, Catharine, Richmond, Va., 104, #7126

Pullen, Catharine, Richmond, Va., 105, #7733

Pullen, Catharine, a/o, Richmond, Va., 111, #759

Pullen, Robert, Ga., 40, #3100

Pullen, Thomas, Va., 80, #14848

Pullen, Thomas, Va., 87, #17565

Pullen, Thomas, Va., 94, #517, card

Pullen, Thomas, a/o, Richmond, Va., 21, #517

Pulley, William, w/o, Nashville, Tenn., 48, #5103

Pulliam, Mosby, a/o, Richmond, Va., 128, #5156

Pullingen, Doras, Trenton, N.J., 143, #7497

Pully, Joseph, c/o, N.C. Militia, 92, #11

Pully, Joseph, e/o, N.C. Militia, 92, #10

Purcell, Edward, Madison, Ind., 92, #19694

Purcell, William D., a/o, Ky., 134, #789

Purdy, Josiah, Albany, N.Y., 122, #8829, card

Purdy, Josiah, c/o, Albany, N.Y., 21, #8829

Purham, Peter, c/o, Maine, 81, #15101

Purse, William, c/o, S.C., 98, #2547

Purvis, George, w/o, Richmond, Va., 113, #1490

Purvis, Jane, a/o, Ky., 118, #5097

Puryear, Jane, Richmond, Va., 72, #12636

Puryear, Jane, Richmond, Va., 98, #2815

Puryear, Reuben, w/o, Va., 87, #17473

Putnam, Daniel, g/o c/o, Conn., 37, #F1826

Putnam, John, c/o, Philadelphia, Pa., 98, #3090

Putnam, John, w/o, Bellows Falls, Vt., 69, #10842

Putnam, Sarah, Albany, N.Y., 71, #12434

Putnum, David L., Bellows Falls, Vt., 63, #8967

Pyatt, Robert, Wheeling, Va.,
45, #4624
Pygall, Thomas, c/o, —, 114,
#2176, slip
Pygall, Thomas, c/o, Wisc.,
117, #4080
Pyron, Allen, w/o, Mich., 78,
#14287
Pytts, Jonathan, Ky., 57, #7615

Q

Quantrill, Thomas, Md., 50,
#5556
Quarry, Elisha, w/o, Richmond,
Va., 51, #6082
Queen, William L., a/o, N.C.,
113, #1867
Quick, Ann, c/o, New York City,
141, #3360
Quick, Elizabeth, Richmond,
Va., 61, #8596
Quick, John, w/o, New York
City, 77, #14048
Quigley, Robert, Iowa, 111,
#628
Quigley, Samuel, Pittsburgh,
Pa., 75, #13406
Quigley, Samuel, Pittsburgh,
Pa., 77, #14083
Quin, John, Pittsburgh, Pa., 58,
#7912, card
Quin, John, New York City, 111,
#862
Quin, John, New York City, 117,
#3966
Quin, John, w/o, Pittsburgh, Pa.,
21, #7912
Quinn, Joseph, Trenton, N.J.,
143, #7266

Quinnby, Jonathan, c/o,
Portsmouth, N.H., 68,
#10708
Quont, Frederick, c/o, Albany,
N.Y., 60, #8321

R

Rackley, Micajah, w/o, E. Tenn.,
63, #8912
Rader, Henry, Va., 41, #3459
Rader, Michael, w/o, Richmond,
Va., 56, #7425
Rader, Richard, Richmond, Va.,
47, #4990
Rafferty, Margaret, La., 123,
#327
Rager, James N., Philadelphia,
Pa., 114, #1998
Ragin, Thomas, w/o, Madison,
Ind., 55, #7027
Ragland, Margaret, c/o,
Richmond, Va., 96, #1546
Ragsdale, Benjamin, Nashville,
Tenn., 71, #12250
Ragsdale, Benjamin, W. Tenn.,
64, #9518
Railsten, Mitchel, Knoxville,
Tenn., 51, #5885
Raines, Letisha, Knoxville,
Tenn., 73, #12767
Rainey, Isaac, Nashville, Tenn.,
43, #4050
Rains, Elizabeth, Mo., 110,
#11080
Rains, James, Ky., 113, #1843,
card
Rains, James, e/o, Ky., 21,
#1843
Rains, Martha, Miss., 129,
#7054

Rains, Nancy, Jackson, Tenn.,
126, #3301

Rains, Nancy, Jackson, Tenn.,
117, #4274

Rainsburg, John, Ohio, 59,
#8067

Rainsburg, John, Ohio, 71,
#12404

Rainsburg, John, Ohio, 73,
#12730

Rainsburg, John, a/o, Ohio,
110, #90

Raird, Z. M. P., Philadelphia,
Pa., 142, #5578

Raley, Sarah, Huntsville, Ala.,
101, #4852

Ralls, Kenaz, a/o, Richmond,
Va., 99, #3177

Ralston, Maragret, c/o,
Pittsburgh, Pa., 126, #3435

Ralya, David, a/o, Philadelphia,
Pa., 117, #4288

Ramage, John, Philadelphia,
Pa., 52, #6100

Ramsen, William, Wheeling,
Va., 91, #19418, card

Ramsey, Allen, Ill., 53, #6576

Ramsey, Joel, Richmond, Va.,
49, #5285

Ramsey, Marcey, R.I., 73,
#12927

Ramsey, Samuel, S.C., 39,
#3082

Ramsey, Samuel, S.C., 66,
#10150

Ramstead, James, Ind., 65,
#9743, card

Rand, Artemos, w/o, Vt., 89,
#18190

Rand, Henry, Ky., 67, #10338

Rand, Israel, c/o, Albany, N.Y.,
109, #10622

Rand, Israel, c/o, Albany, N.Y.,
119, #5669

Randal, Oliver, c/o, Portland,
Maine, 104, #7231

Randall, Amos, Conn., 34, #751

Randall, Deborah, e/o, Md., 121,
#7066

Randall, Elizabeth, a/o,
Wheeling, Va., 137, #4261

Randall, Hope, a/o, N.Y., 107,
#8927

Randall, Jacob, Richmond, Va.,
57, #7506

Randall, Jacob, Va., 66, #10158

Randall, Jacob, Va., 75, #13710

Randall, John, S.C., 63, #8974

Randall, Lydia, N.H., 73,
#12892

Randall, Mark, Portsmouth,
N.H., 43, #4105

Randall, Oliver, c/o, Portland,
Maine, 104, #7230

Randall, Phebe, S.C., 111, #368

Randall, Thomas, D.C., 73,
#12971

Randall, Thomas, D.C., 87,
#17277

Randall, Thomas, D.C., 94,
#624

Randle, Isham, Ill., 42, #3589,
card

Randle, Isham, Ill., 21, #3589

Randolph, Daniel F., c/o, N.J.,
60, #8227

Randolph, Elizabeth, a/o, Ky.,
124, #1081

Randolph, Henry, Mo., 140,
#900

Randolph, Hugh, Huntsville,
Ala., 75, #13415

Randolph, Hugh, Huntsville,
Ala., 82, #15516

Randolph, Hugh, Mich., 68, #10612

Randolph, Nancy, c/o, Madison, Ind., 109, #10396

Randolph, T. D., Miss., 120, #6199

Randolph, Thaddeus D., Jackson, Miss., 130, #8077

Randolph, Thaddeus D., Miss., 113, #1704

Randolph, Thaddeus D., Miss., 125, #1821

Randolph, Zedh F., w/o, Albany, N.Y., 51, #5845

Randoph, Thaddeus D., Miss., 136, #2748

Raney, John, Nashville, Tenn., 21, #14410

Raney, Nathaniel, Richmond, Va., 21, #972

Raney, Nathaniel, Richmond, Va., 95, #972, card

Rankin, John, Pittsburgh, Pa., 73, #12918

Rankin, Peggy, D.C., 104, #7142

Rankin, Peggy, D.C., 111, #782

Rankin, Peggy, a/o, D.C., 124, #506

Rankin, Robert, La., 58, #7674, card

Rankin, Robert, w/o, La., 21, #7674

Rankin, William, Ky., 74, #13094, card

Rankin, William, c/o, Ky., 21, #13094

Ransford, Rachel, a/o, Evansville, Ind., 118, #4575

Ransier, Fred W., c/o, N.J., 121, #6722

Ransier, John, N.Y., 43, #4101, card

Ransom, Elizabeth, a/o, Philadelphia, Pa., 138, #5540

Ransom, Ezekiel, w/o, Mich., 58, #7692

Ransom, Israel, w/o, Ind., 63, #8887

Ransom, James, Conn., 34, #1985

Ransom, James, Conn., 34, #3060

Ranson, Israel, Ind., 52, #6137

Ranstead, James, w/o, Ohio, 21, #9743

Rape, Gustavus, Nashville, Tenn., 111, #623

Raphael, Robert A., Mo., 101, #4870

Rardin (formerly Parks), Mary Jane, Indianapolis, Ind., 124, #1302

Rardon, Daniel, Ohio, 73, #12838

Rase, James, Richmond, Va., 58, #7748

Rasner (Resiceay), John, c/o, Ky., 123, #9565

Ratcliffe, Harper, c/o, Ky., 85, #16445

Rathbone, Joseph, c/o, Cleveland, Ohio, 21, #8403

Rathbone, Margaret, a/o, Cleveland, Ohio, 139, #6855

Rathburn, Joseph, Ohio, 122, #8403, card

Ratten, Thomas, Ind., 21, #6296

Raux, Lewis, w/o, S.C., 64, #9310

Rawley, Joseph, Ohio, 51,
#5868
Rawson, Abner, Mich., 82,
#15265
Rawson, Enoch, Ky., 75,
#13413
Ray, Benajmin, Va., 115,
#2969, card
Ray, Benjamin, Richmond, Va.,
53, #6584
Ray, Benjamin, Richmond, Va.,
56, #7328
Ray, Benjamin, Richmond, Va.,
61, #8583
Ray, Benjamin, Richmond, Va.,
44, #4303
Ray, Benjamin, Va., 68, #10630
Ray, Benjamin, Va., 103,
#7026, card
Ray, Benjamin, w/o, Richmond,
Va., 21, #2969
Ray, Benjamin, w/o, Richmond,
Va., 21, #7026
Ray, George, D.C., 140, #9410
Ray, George, D.C., 141, #2486
Ray, Jesse, N.C., 49, #5280
Ray, Nancy, Richmond, Va.,
36A, #F6, card
Ray, Thomas, w/o, R.I., 59,
#7987
Ray, William, e/o, Madison,
Ind., 21, #60
Raymond, Amos, Albany, N.Y.,
50, #5557
Raymond, Amos, Philadelphia,
Pa., 46, #4678
Raymond, John, Albany, N.Y.,
86, #16769
Raymond, John, c/o, Albany,
N.Y., 102, #5484
Raymond, Sands, w/o, N.Y., 81,
#15140

Raymond, William, Boston,
Mass., 64, #9691
Rayner, Amos, N.C., 74,
#13312
Raynes, Lawrence, Richmond,
Va., 42, #3763
Raynor, Joshua L., E. Fla., 80,
#14925
Rayson, Pamelia, c/o, Wheeling,
Va., 97, #1977
Rea, David, e/o, N.C., 79,
#14729
Rea, Henry, S.C., 56, #7273
Rea, Henry, S.C., 79, #14720
Read, James, w/o, 1st Artillery,
49, #5334
Read, William, c/o, S.C., 98,
#2545
Reading, George, Mo., 61,
#8482
Reading, Joseph, g/o c/o,
Indianapolis, Ind., 136,
#3309
Reading, Saml., c/o, Ky., 52,
#6246
Reafsnider, Henry, g/o c/o,
Philadelphia, Pa., 131,
#8261
Reagan, Michael, a/o, Ky., 116,
#3711
Reagan, William, Richmond,
Va., 57, #7661
Reagan, William, e/o,
Richmond, Va., 123, #9619
Reager, Conrad, c/o, Pittsburgh,
Pa., 95, #1233
Reamer, David, w/o, Ind., 97,
#2367
Reamer, Nancy, a/o, Madison,
Ind., 122, #8115
Reams, John, Ky., 73, #12925

Reams, John, Levenworth City, Kans., 139, #8613

Reams, John, Mo., 79, #14667

Reamy, Joseph, Madison, Ind., 125, #2802

Reardon, John W., Va., 122, #8847

Reardon, Margaret, Mass., 125, #2001

Reaves, Ashur, c/o, Cincinnati, Ohio, 135, #2045, card

Reaves, John, Mo., 84, #15965

Reavis, John, N.C., 65, #10029

Reavis, John, w/o, N.C., 84, #16224

Reddin, Christopher, c/o, Pittsburgh, Pa., 68, #10780

Redding, John, c/o, N.C., 101, #5286

Redeffer, William W., w/o, Madison, Ind., 131, #8278

Redin, Timothy, Albany, N.Y., 81, #14997, card

Redin, Timothy, Albany, N.Y., 21, #997

Redinger, Samuel, Huntsville, Ala., 60, #8176

Redman, John, w/o, Va., 66, #10157

Reed, Amos, c/o, Albany, N.Y., 133, #589

Reed, Elihu, c/o, Mass., 82, #15324

Reed, Elizabeth, Knoxville, Tenn., 85, #16481

Reed, Esther, La., 129, #6498

Reed, Frederick, Philadelphia, Pa., 74, #13118

Reed, Frederick, w/o, Poultney, Vt., 98, #2844

Reed, Garret L., Knoxville, Tenn., 127, #4189

Reed, George, w/o, S.C., 92, #19779

Reed, Isaac, Mass., 51, #5904

Reed, James, —, 47, #4991, card

Reed, James, Pittsburgh, Pa., 21, #4991

Reed, John, Albany, N.Y., 86, #17177

Reed, John, Ohio, 68, #10758

Reed, John, Ohio, 76, #13955

Reed, John, a/o, Ky., 120, #6381

Reed, John, w/o, Nashville, Tenn., 74, #13220

Reed, John, w/o, Philadelphia, Pa., 110, #226

Reed, Joseph, w/o, Albany, N.Y., 83, #15801

Reed, Justus, Conn., 34, #759

Reed, Lavina, g/o, N.C., 114, #2218

Reed, Leonard, w/o, Albany, N.Y., 40, #3323

Reed, Lovett, w/o, E. Tenn., 55, #7143

Reed, Mary B., N.C., 111, #484

Reed, Mathew, La., 135, #2265

Reed, Mathew, Mo., 124, #1017

Reed, Miliscent, Conn., 34, #181

Reed, Nathan, Tuscaloosa, Ala., 70, #11159

Reed, Nathan, Tuscaloosa, Ala., 74, #13309

Reed, Nathan, Tuscaloosa, Ala., 78, #14224

Reed, Samuel, Albany, N.Y., 56, #7362

Reed, Sibbey, Knoxville, Tenn., 83, #15851

Reed, Sibby, Knoxville, Tenn., 86, #16757

Reed, Solomon, g/o c/o, Conn., 37, #F1825
Reed, William, Ohio, 39, #3155
Reed, William, Ohio, 39, #3156
Reed, William, Ohio, 39, #3157
Reed, William, Ohio, 60, #8284
Reed, William, Ohio, 62, #8876
Reed, William, c/o, Boston, Mass., 120, #6559
Reed, William, w/o, Philadelphia, Pa., 106, #8586
Reed, William M., Philadelphia, Pa., 90, #18593
Reed 2nd, David, w/o, Maine, 21, #14198
Reed, Thomas, PA, Burlington, Vt., 123, #9068
Reed, A. M., PA, Jacksonville, Fla., 117, #3857
Reed, A. M., PA, Jacksonville, Fla., 118, #5014
Reed, Arthur, PA, Jacksonville, Fla., 127, #4227
Reed, Thomas, PA, Montpielier, Vt., 103, #7061
Reed, Thomas, PA, Montpielier, Vt., 101, #5006
Reese, Jonathan, w/o, Cincinnati, Ohio, 110, #11109
Reese, Polly, Knoxville, Tenn., 69, #10927
Reese, Polly, Knoxville, Tenn., 89, #18245
Reese, Polly, Knoxville, Tenn., 104, #7486
Reese, William, c/o, Philadelphia, Pa., 140, #80
Reese, William, Md. Militia, 112, #1031, arears pay

Reeve, David, a/o, N.J., 115, #2874
Reeve, William, S.C., 51, #5959
Reeves, James R., Little Rock, Ark., 136, #2875
Reeves, Joseph, a/o, Pittsburgh, Pa., 109, #10511
Reeves, Luther, Philadelphia, Pa., 83, #15621
Reeves, William, Ohio, 59, #8143
Reeves, William, Ohio, 69, #10907
Reeves, William, Ohio, 81, #15132
Regan, Darby, Knoxville, Tenn., 88, #17962
Regan, Darby, S.C., 90, #18689
Regel, Lewis, D.C., 143, #6759
Regen, Darby, Knoxville, Tenn., 85, #16724
Register, Edith, a/o, N.C., 100, #3748
Regnier, John B., Md., 136, #3400
Regua, Joseph, c/o, Albany, N.Y., 63, #8988
Reid, Alexr., Ind., 52, #6295
Reid, Catharine, c/o, N.J., 95, #1069
Reid, James B., c/o, N.C., 122, #8407
Reid, James B., g/o c/o, Fayetteville, N.C., 126, #3912
Reid, John, c/o, Va., 74, #13278
Reid, William, Philadelphia, Pa., 80, #14818
Reidinger, Saml., Huntsville, Ala., 52, #6260
Reiley, Christiana, a/o, Richmond, Va., 72, #12581

Reiley, John, c/o, Albany, N.Y., 57, #7448

Reilly, John E., Philadelphia, Pa., 142, #5023

Reilly, Philip, c/o, Tallahassee, Fla., 115, #2454

Reily, John, w/o, Ohio, 120, #6365

Reily, William, c/o, D.C., 115, #2625

Reimer, Jacob, Philadelphia, Pa., 104, #7302

Reiner, Jacob, Philadelphia, Pa., 108, #10378

Reiner, Jacob, Philadelphia, Pa., 113, #1520

Reiner, Jacob, a/o, Philadelphia, Pa., 135, #1671

Reizer, John, S.C., 51, #5965, card

Reizer, John, S.C., 68, #10727, card

Reizer, John, S.C., 21, #5965

Reizer, John, S.C., 39, #3036

Reizer, John, a/o, S.C., 21, #10727

Remington, Benedict, e/o, R.I., 116, #3308

Remington, Joshua, a/o, Burlington, Vt., 130, #7499

Rencan, Thomas, Ind., 55, #6984

Reneau, Thomas, New Albany, Ind., 56, #7384

Rennolds, Nancy H., Mo., 129, #6582

Reno, Mary, Ky., 66, #10239

Rent, May, c/o, Cleveland, Ohio, 129, #6533

Renz, John G., c/o, New York City, 114, #1936

Rescrode, Zachariah, Richmond, Va., 91, #19410

Resequire, John, w/o, Albany, N.Y., 70, #12123

Revell, Holiday, Richmond, Va., 105, #8340

Revis, Henry, e/o w/o, Ill., 21, #15615

Rewalt, Ann, c/o, Albany, N.Y., 105, #8183

Rex, Daniel, a/o, Philadelphia, Pa., 114, #2220

Rexford, Benjamin, w/o, Vt., 86, #16805

Rexrode, Zachariah, Richmond, Va., 99, #3190

Rexrode, Zachariah, Va., 67, #10436

Reynolds, Benedict, e/o, Pittsburgh, Pa., 108, #10022

Reynolds, Ezra, w/o, Albany, N.Y., 123, #9794

Reynolds, Isaac, Albany, N.Y., 79, #14710

Reynolds, Jonathan, Albany, N.Y., 21, #15255

Reynolds, Mary, Albany, N.Y., 65, #9834

Reynolds, Mary, a/o, Albany, N.Y., 113, #1806

Reynolds, Nathanial, Ohio, 58, #7691

Reynolds, Samuel, w/o, Nashville, Tenn., 99, #3507

Reynolds, William, g/o c/o, Conn., 37, #F1824

Rhoad, Daniel F., Wisc., 113, #1852

Rhoad, Daniel F., Wisc., 115, #2494

Rhodes, Elizabeth, a/o, Ill., 135, #2400

Rhodes, George, c/o, Richmond, Va., 64, #9692

Rhodes, Thomas, Wheeling, Va., 78, #14326

Rhodes, Thomas, Wheeling, Va., 86, #17115

Rhods, Daniel, w/o, Madison, Ind., 75, #13408

Rials, Eliza, S.C., 108, #10145

Rice, Ashbel, c/o, Maine, 57, #7631

Rice, Elizabeth, a/o, Fayetteville, N.C., 133, #307

Rice, Elizabeth M., a/o, Fayetteville, N.C., 136, #3077

Rice, Holmon, Ky., 61, #8646

Rice, Isaac, c/o, Pittsburgh, Pa., 84, #16305

Rice, Jesse, Albany, N.Y., 55, #7074

Rice, Jessie, Richmond, Va., 79, #14567

Rice, John, Maine, 43, #3820

Rice, Jonas, w/o, Mass., 88, #17983

Rice, Joseph, e/o, R.I., 99, #3445

Rice, Leonard, Ga., 87, #17710

Rice, Martha, Richmond, Va., 36A, #F5 V8

Rice, Martin, Mass., 42, #3751

Rice, Mary, Albany, N.Y., 98, #2882

Rice, Nathan, w/o, Ohio, 79, #14612

Rice, Sarah, a/o, Albany, N.Y., 103, #6719

Rice, William, Albany, N.Y., 48, #5230

Rich, Elijah, w/o, Ind., 60, #8329

Rich, Elizabeth, a/o, Maine, 119, #5827

Rich, Private Samuel, c/o, 37th Inf., 107, #9486

Rich, Thaddeus, Conn., 34, #1109

Rich, Thankful, c/o, Mich., 134, #744

Richard, John, N.C., 45, #4510

Richard, John, N.C., 56, #7408

Richards, Ambrose, Richmond, Va., 59, #8045

Richards, Ambrose, Va., 66, #10291

Richards, Amos, Mich., 53, #6364

Richards, Boswell, Va., 109, #10751

Richards, James, Mass., 72, #12527

Richards, James, Mass., 77, #14100

Richards, James, w/o, Ill., 103, #6487

Richards, John, Va., 75, #13552

Richards, John, Va., 90, #18613

Richards, Joseph, Mass., 126, #3743

Richards, Joshua, w/o, S.C., 133, #646

Richards, Mark, c/o, Montpelier, Vt., 106, #8784

Richards, Peter, Conn., 34, #31

Richards, Philemon, Va., 70, #12113

Richards, Stephen, Jackson, Tenn., 76, #13894

Richards, William, w/o,
Philadelphia, Pa., 85,
#16706
Richardson, Amos, Ga., 21,
#266
Richardson, Amos, Ga., 133,
#266, card
Richardson, David, Albany,
N.Y., 64, #9234
Richardson, David, Albany,
N.Y., 42, #3598 1/2
Richardson, David, Ky., 90,
#18699, card
Richardson, David, w/o, Ky., 22,
#18699
Richardson, Hannah, New York
City, 71, #12274
Richardson, James, Boston,
Mass., 52, #6216
Richardson, Jesse, Ky., 73,
#12841, card
Richardson, Jesse, w/o, Ky., 22,
#12841
Richardson, John, —, 60,
#8193, card
Richardson, John, c/o, Mass.,
90, #18873
Richardson, John, c/o,
Richmond, Va., 22, #8193
Richardson, John, w/o, W.
Tenn., 56, #7411
Richardson, Joseph,
Philadelphia, Pa., 75,
#13709
Richardson, Joseph, c/o,
Philadelphia, Pa., 98,
#3141
Richardson, Joshua, Ill., 47,
#4979
Richardson, Martha, Albany,
N.Y., 103, #6965

Richardson, Martha, Richmond,
Va., 36A, #F6 V10
Richardson, Mary Ann,
Philadelphia, Pa., 143,
#6692
Richardson, Richard, Richmond,
Va., 66, #10289
Richardson, Richard, Va., 77,
#13968
Richardson, Sally, a/o, Ky.,
137, #3678
Richardson, Sally, e/o, N.C.,
102, #5863
Richardson, Pvt. Samuel, w/o,
13th Inf., 110, #240
Richardson, Samuel, c/o, Mo.,
118, #4647
Richardson, Thomas, Ind., 52,
#6292
Richardson, William, Albany,
N.Y., 67, #10523
Richardson, William, Mass., 79,
#14594
Richardson, William, c/o,
Boston, Mass., 56, #7230
Richardson, William, w/o,
Boston, Mass., 85, #16602
Richardson, Winney, S.C., 112,
#884
Richey, Peter, W. Tenn., 57,
#7479
Richie, James, a/o, Tenn., 120,
#6340
Richie, John, S.C., 41, #3398
Richie, William, Cincinnati,
Ohio, 22, #5052
Richman (formerly Clinton),
Hannah, Philadelphia, Pa.,
114, #2073
Richmond, Anthony, g/o c/o,
Conn., 37, #F1820

Richmond, James, Ill., 67, #10476

Richmond, Thomas, a/o, Conn., 34, #12942

Rickard, Abner, a/o, Albany, N.Y., 107, #9035

Rickard, John, N.C., 54, #6763

Ricketts, Nathan, Ind., 54, #6609

Ricketts, Nathan, Ind., 81, #15112

Ricketts, Robert, Ind., 49, #5270

Ricketts, Robert, Ind., 120, #5945, card

Riddick, Edward, Richmond, Va., 22, #6445, card

Riddle, John, Fayetteville, N.C., 50, #5588

Riddle, John, Ga., 74, #13000

Ridean, James, a/o, Ga., 134, #743

Riden, John, Philadelphia, Pa., 42, #3643

Rider, Benjamin, c/o, New York City, 76, #13957

Rider, Moses, c/o, N.H., 67, #10439

Rider, Seneca, Albany, N.Y., 103, #6391

Rider, Seneca, Albany, N.Y., 107, #9274

Rider, Seneca, Albany, N.Y., 124, #488

Ridgeley, Lt. Henderson, w/o & c/o, 4th Inf., 114, #2032

Ridgely, 1st Lt. Henderson, w/o, 4th Inf., 102, #5998

Ridgely, Lt. Henderson, w/o, 4th Inf., 110, #11111

Ridgely, Lt. Henderson, w/o, 4th Inf., 103, #6725

Ridgely, Lt. Henderson, w/o, 4th Inf., 104, #7632

Ridgely, Lt. Henderson, w/o, 4th Inf., 106, #8477

Ridgely, Lt. Henderson, w/o, 4th Inf., 107, #9407

Ridgely, Lt. Henderson, w/o, 4th Inf., 108, #10293

Ridgely, Lt. Henderson, w/o, 4th Inf., 111, #645

Ridgely, Lt. Henderson, w/o, 4th Inf., 112, #1253

Ridgway, Isaac, w/o, New York City, 66, #10227

Ridout, Giles, c/o, Richmond, Va., 102, #5837

Riegelman, Conrad, w/o, Philadelphia, Pa., 58, #7933

Rieley, Christiana, a/o, Richmond, Va., 77, #14221

Rife, Peter, Richmond, Va., 102, #5774

Riggan, Richard D., a/o w/o, Va. Milita, 94, #505

Riggans, William P., N.C., 74, #13184

Riggs, Charles, c/o, Ill., 61, #8481

Riggs, Samuel, Jonesboro, Tenn., 97, #2012

Right, George W., Nashville, Tenn., 78, #14422

Riley, Alfred, Mo., 117, #4287

Riley, Alfred, Mo., 134, #1367

Riley, Jacob H., Del., 54, #6800

Riley, James, Albany, N.Y., 115, #2583

Riley, James, Albany, N.Y., 115, #2759

Riley, James, Miss., 103, #6923

Riley, James, Miss., 88, #17863

Riley, James, Miss., 89, #18321
Riley, Gen. Bennett, Gov. of
California, 122, #8876,
card
Rindress, James, w/o, Albany,
N.Y., 44, #4331
Rinehart, George, c/o,
Cincinnati, Ohio, 138,
#4648
Rineheart, George S., w/o,
Philadelphia, Pa., 80,
#14967
Ringo, Burtis, Ky., 107, #9033
Ringsthorp, Philip, Albany,
N.Y., 39, #3089
Ripley, Asa, w/o, Albany, N.Y.,
87, #17732
Ripley, Eleazer W., w/o, Ga., 61,
#8437
Ripley, Hezekiah, c/o, Conn.,
87, #17695
Ripley, Mary P., a/o, Albany,
N.Y., 134, #1312
Ripley, William, c/o, Boston,
Mass., 50, #5820
Rippy, Edward, N.C., 72,
#12705
Risdon, Daniel, Albany, N.Y.,
132, #8951
Rising, Samuel, g/o c/o, Conn.,
37, #F1824
Ritcher, Sarah, c/o, Mass., 124,
#906
Ritchie, William, —, 142,
#5052, card
Ritter, Frederick, w/o, Albany,
N.Y., 65, #9892
Ritter, Jacob, c/o, Philadelphia,
Pa., 113, #1901
Rixford, Saml., w/o, Albany,
N.Y., 52, #6192

Roach, Absalom, c/o, Va., 82,
#15442
Roach, Jonathan, w/o, Va., 69,
#10938
Roach, Mary, Richmond, Va.,
127, #4203
Roach, Ruth, Richmond, Va.,
108, #10377
Roach, Isaac, PA, Philadelphia,
Pa., 101, #4851
Roane, James K., Huntsville,
Ala., 51, #5991
Roark, John A., a/o, Ga., 124,
#891
Roark, William, a/o, Ill., 77,
#14212
Robb, Hugh, w/o, D.C., 44,
#4273
Robbins, Asa, Ill., 78, #14451
Robbins, Asa, c/o, Maine, 76,
#13807
Robbins, Bethia, Ind., 107,
#9659, card
Robbins, Bethiah, Madison,
Ind., 22, #9659
Robbins, Daniel, Maine, 41,
#3421
Robbins, Elizabeth, c/o, Mass.,
126, #3300
Robbins, Hannah, c/o, Conn.,
76, #13912
Robbins, Joseph, w/o, Mass.,
81, #15115
Robbins, Lorrin, c/o, Albany,
N.Y., 128, #5462
Robbins, Samuel, Maine, 22,
#3552
Robbins, William, w/o,
Wheeling, Va., 41, #3430
Roberson, John, Mobile, Ala.,
80, #14985

Roberson, William, c/o,
Knoxville, Tenn., 113,
#1772
Roberts, Alice, Richmond, Va.,
95, #855
Roberts, Alice, Va., 87, #17506
Roberts, Ambrose, c/o, Va., 46,
#4747
Roberts, Amos, Columbus,
Ohio, 143, #6306
Roberts, Ashbel, Conn., 34, #64
Roberts, David, Ill., 91, #19337
Roberts, Elizabeth, c/o, N.C.,
78, #14223
Roberts, Isaac, Huntsville, Ala.,
57, #7570
Roberts, Isaac, Va., 42, #3691
Roberts, John, Burlington, Vt.,
123, #9648
Roberts, John, Calif., 132,
#9230
Roberts, John, Vt., 81, #15200
Roberts, John, c/o, S.C., 49,
#5463
Roberts, John, c/o, S.C., 65,
#9801
Roberts, John, g/o, N.H., 91,
#19098
Roberts, John, w/o, Albany,
N.Y., 88, #17914
Roberts, Joseph, a/o, N.H., 89,
#18207
Roberts, Joshua, Mo., 78,
#14495
Roberts, Mark R., Jackson,
Tenn., 62, #8781
Roberts, Mark R., Jackson,
Tenn., 102, #5492
Roberts, Mary, Richmond, Va.,
106, #8355
Roberts, Mary, Richmond, Va.,
95, #1032

Roberts, Mary, Richmond, Va.,
101, #4931
Roberts, Namon, Ky., 42, #3574
Roberts, Namon, Ky., 81,
#15065
Roberts, Peter, S.C., 49, #5260
Roberts, Peter, S.C., 51, #5903
Roberts, Samuel, S.C., 51,
#6073
Roberts, Samuel, e/o, S.C., 95,
#853
Roberts, Simon, c/o, Maine,
139, #7676
Roberts, Zachariah, c/o, Md.,
108, #9904
Roberts 3d, John, N.H., 53,
#6458
Robertson, Catherine, S.C.,
132, #9615
Robertson, Daniel, La., 138,
#4755
Robertson, Estelle, c/o, Albany,
N.Y., 84, #16003
Robertson, George, w/o,
Richmond, Va., 104, #7324
Robertson, Mary, Richmond,
Va., 95, #820
Robertson, Mathew, Ky., 64,
#9532
Robertson, Matthew, Ky., 40,
#3225
Robertson, Matthew, Ky., 45,
#4632
Robertson, William, Nashville,
Tenn., 77, #14183
Robertson, William, w/o,
Nashville, Tenn., 95, #994
Robeson, James, N.C., 40,
#3162
Robeson, William, N.C., 40,
#3190

Robins, Elizabeth, Philadelphia, Pa., 83, #15621

Robinson, Benjamim, Ky., 22, #7382

Robinson, Benjamin, Richmond, Va., 100, #4527

Robinson, Bulah, Madison, Ind., 96, #1673

Robinson, Caleb, Albany, N.Y., 66, #10123

Robinson, Chloe D., Vt., 78, #14361

Robinson, Edmund, Ohio, 54, #6854

Robinson, Esther, c/o, Albany, N.Y., 22, #5652

Robinson, Frederick B., Mass., 143, #6752

Robinson, James, c/o, Ky., 44, #4187

Robinson, Jane, Wheeling, Va., 140, #9888

Robinson, Jeremiah, Mo., 69, #10971, card

Robinson, Jeremiah, a/o, Mo., 22, #10971

Robinson, John, c/o, Ill., 113, #1259

Robinson, John W., Spingfield, Ill., 141, #2667

Robinson, John W., c/o, Md., 118, #4754

Robinson, Joshua, Conn., 34, #1108

Robinson, Kun, w/o, Albany, N.Y., 92, #19657

Robinson, Lewis, Ohio, 63, #9061

Robinson, Louisa, Miss., 111, #670

Robinson, Margaret, Boston, Mass., 100, #4373

Robinson, Mary, —, 77, #14117, card

Robinson, Mary, Albany, N.Y., 22, #14117

Robinson, Mathw., Huntsville, Ala., 53, #6555

Robinson, Moses, —, 77, #14075, card

Robinson, Moses, w/o, Mass., 22, #14075

Robinson, Naomi, Mass., 71, #12469

Robinson, Noah, Montpelier, Vt., 22, #62

Robinson, Noah, a/o, —, 110, #62, card

Robinson, Oliver, w/o, Pittsburgh, Pa., 84, #16253

Robinson, Phebe, a/o, Maine, 136, #3308

Robinson, Robert, w/o, N.C., 61, #8495

Robinson, Thomas, Md., 54, #6781

Robinson, William, W. Tenn., 60, #8242

Robinson, William, w/o, S.C., 22, #5497

Robinson, Zephaniah, c/o, Mass., 134, #822

Robison, Benjamin, c/o, N.J., 121, #7583

Robuck, George, S.C., 47, #4946

Robuck, George, S.C., 48, #5247

Robuck, George, S.C., 51, #5873

Robuck, George, S.C., 64, #9384

Roby, Louisa, Richmond, Va., 36A, #F2 V30

Rochester, Ann, S.C., 70,
#12200
Rock, Michael, w/o, E. Tenn.,
68, #10679
Rockinstier, Joseph, a/o,
Albany, N.Y., 125, #1652
Rockwood, Hezekia, w/o,
Boston, Mass., 52, #6172
Rockwood, Samuel, N.H., 66,
#10215
Rodgers, Ahaz, S.C., 53, #6502
Rodgers, Daniel, N.C., 40,
#3163
Rodgers, Hugh, w/o, N.C., 79,
#14727
Rodgers, Jackson, w/o, Ill., 139,
#8476
Rodgers, John, D.C., 85,
#16636
Rodgers, John A., Knoxville,
Tenn., 69, #10857
Rodgers, Ralph, Nashville,
Tenn., 118, #4994
Rodgers, Robert A., a/o,
Philadelphia, Pa., 111,
#750
Roe, Joseph A., w/o, Ga., 125,
#1682
Roebuck, George, a/o, S.C.,
135, #1741
Roebuck, Raleigh, N.C., 53,
#6528, card
Rogers, Adonijah, Bellows
Falls, Vt., 46, #4692
Rogers, Asa, c/o, Mass., 50,
#5614
Rogers, Charles B., Mo., 102,
#6067
Rogers, Ebenezer, e/o, Conn.,
98, #2652

Rogers, Elizabeth, c/o,
Richmond, Va., 36A, #F2
V37
Rogers, Francis, w/o, Albany,
N.Y., 139, #8792
Rogers, Giudon, Conn., 34,
#761
Rogers, Hosea, Va., 48, #5106,
card
Rogers, Hosea, c/o, Richmond,
Va., 22, #5106
Rogers, Jedediah, w/o, N.Y., 43,
#3833
Rogers, John, w/o, Boston,
Mass., 71, #12467
Rogers, John A., D.C., 102,
#5739
Rogers, John A., Philadelphia,
Pa., 128, #5354
Rogers, John A., a/o,
Philadelphia, Pa., 138,
#4873
Rogers, John P., New York City,
134, #1150
Rogers, Joseph, a/o, Vt., 83,
#15676
Rogers, Leonard, Conn., 34,
#760
Rogers, Lucy, a/o, Mass., 125,
#2523
Rogers, Nathaniel, a/o, S.C.,
130, #7650
Rogers, Sarah, Philadelphia, Pa.,
106, #8482
Rogers, Thomas, a/o,
Burlington, Vt., 124, #727
Rogers, Thomas, a/o, Conn., 87,
#17430
Rogers, Thomas, c/o,
Portsmouth, N.H., 138,
#5076

Rogers, William, a/o, Maine,
64, #9472
Roland, Deborah, c/o, Boston,
Mass., 63, #9009
Rolfe, Lucy, a/o, Maine, 98,
#3047
Rollins, Moses, Wheeling, Va.,
63, #8986
Rollins, Moses, Wheeling, Va.,
70, #11090
Rollins, Robert, a/o, Concord,
N.H., 102, #6003
Rollins, Sarah, e/o, Montpelier,
Vt., 95, #1336
Rolston, David, Richmond, Va.,
98, #3028
Ronlston, Mitchell, Knoxville,
Tenn., 78, #14242
Ronneberg, Frederich,
Spingfield, Ill., 129, #6543
Ronneberg, Frederick, Ill., 124,
#548
Ronneberg, Frederick, Ill., 134,
#1663
Rood, Clark, Albany, N.Y., 104,
#7337
Rood, Clark, Albany, N.Y., 45,
#4640
Rooker, John, S.C., 62, #8742
Rooker, John, w/o, S.C., 70,
#12156
Rooks, Daniel, Philadelphia,
Pa., 44, #4388
Rooks, Daniel, Philadelphia,
Pa., 48, #5077
Rooney, Peter, Trenton, N.J.,
143, #7293
Root, Azariah, —, 85, #16697f3
Root, Ebenezer, w/o, Albany,
N.Y., 114, #2413
Root, Lemmuel, Philadelphia,
Pa., 89, #18435

Root, Lemuel, Philadelphia, Pa.,
79, #14651
Root, Lemuel, Philadelphia, Pa.,
84, #16142
Root, Lemuel, Philadelphia, Pa.,
117, #3949, card
Root, Lemuel, c/o, Philadelphia,
Pa., 22, #3949
Root, Lemuel, c/o, Philadelphia,
Pa., 115, #2980
Root, Nathan, c/o, Conn., 92,
#19847
Root, Sarah, c/o, Albany, N.Y.,
102, #6258
Root, Thomas, Albany, N.Y.,
68, #10666
Roots, Michael, Richmond, Va.,
57, #7552
Roots, Michael, Richmond, Va.,
55, #6959
Roots, Michael, Va., 70,
#12112
Rope, Howard, N.C., 70, #12215
Roper, Dorcas, Boston, Mass.,
79, #14671
Roper, Elizabeth, Richmond,
Va., 124, #722
Roper, Elizabeth, c/o, Mass.,
95, #1081
Roper, John, Ga., 46, #4804
Roper, Robert, c/o, N.C., 84,
#16315
Rose, Achsah, c/o, Ohio, 120,
#6000
Rose, Benjamin, La., 122,
#8806
Rose, Charles, w/o, Ky., 47,
#5001
Rose, Deriah, a/o, Concord,
N.H., 125, #1797
Rose, Elizabeth, Ky., 60, #8381

Rose, Elizabeth, N.J., 82,
#15457
Rose, John, a/o, N.C., 92, #131
Rose, Lydia, Ky., 126, #3851
Rose, Margaret, Pa., 111, #699,
card
Rose, Margaret, Philadelphia,
Pa., 22, #699
Rose, Mary, Spingfield, Ill.,
140, #685
Rose, Mary, Spingfield, Ill.,
141, #1249
Rose, Militty, Richmond, Va.,
36A, #F4 V5
Rose, Samuel, w/o, N.C., 44,
#4298
Rose, Sarah, a/o, Nashville,
Tenn., 98, #2580
Roseboom, Garrett, w/o, N.J.,
83, #15728
Rosebrough, John, w/o, Va., 75,
#13711
Rosebud, Lydia, c/o,
Philadelphia, Pa., 134,
#1141
Rosengrout, Mary, Albany,
N.Y., 62, #8844
Ross, Christopher, Albany,
N.Y., 58, #7875
Ross, David, N.C., 49, #5386
Ross, David, a/o, N.C., 120,
#6424
Ross, Ezekial, c/o, Ohio, 99,
#3298
Ross, Ezra, Albany, N.Y., 75,
#13697
Ross, John, Ky., 88, #17871,
card
Ross, John, W. Tenn., 46,
#4704
Ross, John, e/o, Ky., 22,
#17871

Ross, John, e/o, Ky., 22,
#15649
Ross, Sally, c/o, Ky., 111, #373
Ross, Sarah, Louisville, Ky.,
108, #9984 V#1
Ross, Thomas, w/o, N.C., 79,
#14648
Ross, William, D.C., 84,
#15949
Ross, Zephaniah, c/o, —, 102,
#6085
Rossen, Archeleus, Nashville,
Tenn., 41, #3446
Rossiter, Samuel, a/o, Conn.,
38, #F1824
Rosson, Archibald, W. Tenn.,
64, #9216
Roulston, Mitchell, Knoxville,
Tenn., 44, #4280
Round, Simeon, R.I., 87,
#17509
Roundtree, Mary, Nashville,
Tenn., 127, #4089, card
Rousa, John, w/o, N.Y., 86,
#17113
Rouse, Lewis, Ky., 99, #3443,
card
Rouse, Lewis, w/o, Ky., 22,
#3443
Rouse, Lewis, w/o, Ky., 22,
#3286
Roush, George, Ohio, 53, #6383
Routon, James, Richmond, Va.,
57, #7583
Routon, James, Va., 67, #10335
Rowe, Ebenezer, Mass. to
Maine, 108, #10236, card
Rowe, Ebenezer, c/o, Maine, 22,
#10236
Rowe, James, —, 84, #15924,
card

Rowe, James, a/o, Ky., 22,
    #15926
Rowe, Joseph, a/o, Albany,
    N.Y., 87, #17670
Rowe, Joshua, Ga., 56, #7311
Rowe, Joshua, Mobile, Ala., 68,
    #10678
Rowell, Thomas, c/o, N.H., 77,
    #14024
Rowland, Hampton H., g/o c/o,
    Ill., 127, #4146
Rowlet, Rebecca, c/o,
    Richmond, Va., 36A, #F2
    V42
Rowlett, William, Richmond,
    Va., 22, #9863
Rowlett, William, Va., 65,
    #9863, card
Rowley, Abigail, Ohio, 64,
    #9506
Rowley, Abijah, Ill., 68,
    #10670
Rowley, Joseph, w/o, Albany,
    N.Y., 47, #5016
Rowley, Nathaniel, Pittsburgh,
    Pa., 119, #5313
Rowley, Silas, Conn., 34,
    #4160
Rowley, Susannah, c/o,
    Philadelphia, Pa., 69,
    #10981
Royall, Jincey, a/o, Va., 85,
    #16553
Royaltree, John, Ky., 72,
    #12684
Royster, David, Richmond, Va.,
    39, #3017
Royster, David, e/o, Richmond,
    Va., 102, #5882
Rozar Sr., Robert, Ga., 62,
    #8699

Rozer Sr., Robert, Ga., 59,
    #8144
Rubble, John, Ohio, 131,
    #8742, card
Rubble, John, c/o, Cincinnati,
    Ohio, 22, #8742
Rucker, Elizaphen, w/o, Va.
    Milita, 120, #6229
Rucker, Fanny, Richmond, Va.,
    36A, #F3 V19
Ruckman, Elizabeth, Pittsburgh,
    Pa., 104, #7470
Ruckman, John, w/o, Pittsburgh,
    Pa., 83, #15841
Rudd, Daniel, Conn., 34, #26
Rudder, Jane, Va., 79, #14574,
    card
Rudder, John, Richmond, Va.,
    22, #14574
Ruddy, Patrick, Mass., 131,
    #8562
Ruddy, Patrick J., Mass., 141,
    #1883
Rude, Isaac, Conn., 86, #17225
Rudy, Jacob, Philadelphia, Pa.,
    88, #18129, card
Rudy, Jacob, Philadelphia, Pa.,
    22, #18129
Rue, Margaret, c/o, Pittsburgh,
    Pa., 137, #3688
Ruffcorn, Simon, a/o,
    Philadelphia, Pa., 75,
    #13567
Ruffner, Simon, w/o, Pittsburgh,
    Pa., 116, #3352
Rugg, Isaac, a/o, Albany, N.Y.,
    121, #7145
Ruggles, Benjamin, a/o, Conn.,
    38, #F1829
Rumery, Dominicus, w/o, Maine,
    56, #7332

Rumery, Dominicus, w/o, Maine,
60, #8241
Rumery, Dominicus, w/o, Maine,
60, #8261
Rumsey, William M., La., 134,
#1244
Rumsey, William M., New
Orleans, La., 122, #8516
Rundleman, George W., e/o,
Mo., 112, #1092
Runk, Samuel, Philadelphia, Pa.,
22, #12334
Runnals, Sarah, a/o, Richmond,
Va., 95, #1177
Runnels, Enoch, Burlington,
Vt., 107, #9642
Runnels, Samuel, Portsmouth,
N.H., 116, #3175
Runnels, Sarah, a/o, Mass., 127,
#4005
Runy, John, Philadelphia, Pa.,
109, #10462
Runyon, Mary, Ohio, 72,
#12690
Rupert, Adam, Pittsburgh, Pa.,
40, #3309
Rupert, Adam, Pittsburgh, Pa.,
60, #8341
Rupp, Andrew, Philadelphia, Pa.,
56, #7420
Rupp, Andrew, Philadelphia, Pa.,
75, #13556
Ruse, Aaron, e/o, Ohio, 118,
#5057
Rush, Jacob, Pa., 39, #3133
Rush, Jacob, Philadelphia, Pa.,
63, #9023
Rush, Jacob, w/o, Philadelphia,
Pa., 113, #1705
Rush, Jocob, Philadelphia, Pa.,
52, #6133

Rush, William, Pittsburgh, Pa.,
57, #7640, card
Rush, William, w/o, Pittsburgh,
Pa., 22, #7640, card
Rushburger, George, Pittsburgh,
Pa., 111, #697
Rushburger, George, Pittsburgh,
Pa., 134, #967
Rushing, Philip, Jackson,
Tenn., 47, #4924
Rushing, Richard, Jackson,
Tenn., 47, #4924
Rusk, Phebe, Richmond, Va.,
36A, #F3 V23
Russel, Philip, Ill., 54, #6841
Russel, Thomas, Huntsville,
Ala., 100, #4451
Russell, Abigail, Mass., 141,
#1917
Russell, Amanda M., Mich.,
114, #2120
Russell, Benjamin, Maine, 54,
#6727
Russell, Capt. Samuel L., w/o, —
, 59, #8117
Russell, Capt. Samuel S., w/o, —
, 58, #7859
Russell, Capt. Samuel L., —, 74,
#13078
Russell, Capt. Samuel L., w/o, —
, 78, #14429
Russell, Capt. Samuel L., w/o, —
, 82, #15511
Russell, Capt. Samuel L., w/o, —
, 69, #10932
Russell, Capt. Samuel L., w/o, —
, 85, #16410
Russell, Capt. Samuel L., w/o, —
, 86, #17271
Russell, Capt. Samuel L., w/o, —
, 89, #18263

Russell, Capt. Samuel S., w/o, —
, 64, #9557
Russell, Comfort, Richmond,
Va., 64, #9671
Russell, Comfort, Va., 65,
#10009
Russell, Comfort, Va., 71,
#12225
Russell, Comfort, Va., 75,
#13574
Russell, Comfort, a/o,
Richmond, Va., 95, #987
Russell, Comfort, a/o,
Richmond, Va., 95, #1158
Russell, Enoch, Ohio, 41, #3431
Russell, Enoch, Ohio, 61, #8592
Russell, Isaac, Albany, N.Y., 83,
#15881
Russell, John, R.I., 89, #18394
Russell, John, c/o, Albany,
N.Y., 123, #9192
Russell, John, c/o, Madison,
Ind., 118, #4898
Russell, Nabby, Concord, N.H.,
119, #5439
Russell, Nancy, Ga., 114, #2016
Russell, Nancy, Ga., 128, #6530
Russell, Robert, c/o, Richmond,
Va., 95, #910
Russell, Robert, w/o, Va., 40,
#3240
Russell, Robert S., Ky., 65,
#10040
Russell, Robert S., e/o, Ky.,
109, #10747
Russell, Robt. S., Ky., 52,
#6236
Russey Sr., James, w/o,
Nashville, Tenn., 117,
#3964
Rust, J. M., 4th Iowa Cav., 141,
#2762, slip

Rust, John, Ky., 124, #1016,
card
Rust, John, c/o, Ky., 22, #1016
Rust, Lucy, —, 92, #19693
Rust, Mary Ann, Fayetteville,
N.C., 115, #2662
Rust, Quarles E., Indianapolis,
Ind., 125, #2083
Ruter, Thomas, c/o, Richmond,
Va., 36A, #F2 V2
Ruth, Moses, Ill., 139, #8173
Rutherford, Elizabeth, Ky., 141,
#1876
Rutherford, John, w/o, Va., 66,
#10174
Rutherford, Mary, c/o, Mo., 136,
#2573
Rutz, -, —, 139, #7383, slip
Ryan, Harris, E. Tenn., 58,
#7744
Ryan, Harris, E. Tenn., 62,
#8850
Ryan, James, Ill., 56, #7401
Ryan, John, Mo., 142, #3959
Ryan, John, Mo., 142, #5320
Ryan, John, Wheeling, Va., 46,
#4830
Ryan, William, Vancouver,
W.T., 139, #8170
Ryan, William, Vancouver,
W.T., 140, #9930 V#3
Ryan, William, Vancouver,
W.T., 140, #9930 V#4
Ryburn, Elizabeth, c/o,
Pittsburgh, Pa., 134, #1029
Rye, David, c/o, 12th Inf, 49,
#5364
Ryfenburg, Adam, New York
City, 77, #14036
Ryhearson, Minney, Cincinnati,
Ohio, 129, #6414

Ryland, John, w/o, Richmond,
Va., 64, #9452
Rymer, George, Richmond, Va.,
92, #20002
Rymer, George, Va., 70, #12091
Rymer, George, Va., 86, #16781
Rymer, George, w/o, Richmond,
Va., 102, #5568
Rynearson, Minney, Ohio, 42,
#3605
Rynearson, Minney, Ohio, 54,
#6594
Rynearson, Minney, Ohio, 80,
#14758
Rynehart, Henry, w/o, N.J., 114,
#2280
Rynerson, Minney, Ohio, 96,
#1507

S

Sabin, Jonathan, c/o, Conn., 92,
#19674
Sabins, John, c/o, N.Y., 123,
#9446
Sackett, David, a/o, Pittsburgh,
Pa., 113, #1614
Safell, Charles, c/o, Md., 119,
#5128
Saffell, Charles, c/o, Md., 23,
#5128
Safford, Abigail, Albany, N.Y.,
78, #14401
Sage, David, w/o, Albany, N.Y.,
70, #11058
Sage, Enos, Conn., 34, #69
Sage, Simeon, c/o, Mass., 125,
#1931
Sage, Stephen, Mass., 77,
#13970
Sage, Stephen, Mass., 87,
#17318

Sailor, Philip, Pittsburgh, Pa.,
60, #8336
Sailor, Philip, c/o, Pittsburgh,
Pa., 99, #3488
Sale, Alice, Richmond, Va.,
36A, #F6 V26
Sale, Alice, Richmond, Va., 127,
#4264
Sales, John, R.I., 64, #9587,
card
Sales, John, c/o, R.I., 23, #9587
Salifield, Elizabeth, Pa., 121,
#7610
Salisbury, Andrew, Ohio, 85,
#16603
Salisbury, Andrew, a/o, Ohio,
113, #1426
Salisbury, Rachel, a/o, Albany,
N.Y., 101, #5214
Salisbury, William, w/o, R.I.,
118, #4894
Salmon, Asahel, Conn., 34,
#146
Salmon, George, S.C., 41,
#3554
Salnave, Peter, c/o, Albany,
N.Y., 110, #10966
Salsberry, Andrew, Mo., 48,
#5116
Salsberry, Andrew, Mo., 77,
#14154
Salsbury, Andrew, Mo., 58,
#7764
Salyers, Frances, c/o, Ky., 141,
#2909
Sample, Samuel, Knoxville,
Tenn., 49, #5419
Sampson, Elizabeth, Ky., 78,
#14289
Sampson, Henry, Philadelphia,
Pa., 82, #15323

Sampson, Joseph, Va., 70,
#12222

Sampson, Lucy, Richmond, Va.,
126, #3430

Sampson, Lucy, Richmond, Va.,
132, #9555

Samson, Samuel, Ohio, 64,
#9593

Samuel, William, Albany, N.Y.,
53, #6439

Samuels, William, New Albany,
Ind., 57, #7580

Sanborn, Elizabeth, Vt., 78,
#14371

Sanborn, Jeremiah, w/o,
Portsmouth, N.H., 69,
#10845

Sanborn, Sarah, c/o, Albany,
N.Y., 101, #5336

Sanborn, Sarah, c/o, Albany,
N.Y., 98, #2850

Sanborne, Josiah, N.H., 78,
#14321

Sanders, Elizabeth, Va., 70,
#12223

Sanders, Irene, g/o, Madison,
Ind., 113, #1622

Sanders, Jesse, — , 82, #15491,
card

Sanders, Jesse, Richmond, Va.,
22, #15491, card

Sanders, Mary, Philadelphia,
Pa., 127, #4982

Sanders, Nancy A., Mich., 113,
#1900

Sanders, Philip, h/o, N.C., 22,
#17749

Sanders, Richard, a/o, Nashville,
Tenn., 129, #6510

Sanders, Solomon, w/o,
Nashville, Tenn., 114,
#2162

Sanders, William, w/o,
Pittsburgh, Pa., 66, #10307

Sanders (formerly Smith), Sarah,
Ill., 124, #486

Sanders (now Livesay), Elizabeth
M., c/o, Ill., 110, #11022

Sanderson, David, g/o c/o,
Wisc., 126, #3981

Sanderson, Henry, Mass., 137,
#3885

Sandiford, Samuel, w/o, N.C.,
47, #4916

Sandiforth, Danield W., Albany,
N.Y., 52, #6106

Sanford, Rahamah, a/o, Albany,
N.Y., 140, #717

Sapp, Mary, N.C., 110, #11155

Sappington, Hartly, w/o, Mo.,
22, #12330

Sargent, James, Ohio, 105,
#7809

Sargent, Phineas, w/o, Concord,
N.H., 92, #19606

Sartell, John, Maine, 82,
#15326, card

Sartell, John, Portsmouth,
Maine, 22, #15326

Sasser, William, Miss. Militia,
23, #3186

Saterlee, Elisha, w/o,
Philadelphia, Pa., 58,
#7904

Satterlee, James, Philadelphia,
Pa., 80, #14753

Satterwhite, Robert, Va., 112,
#931, slip

Satterwhite, Robert, a/o,
Richmond, Va., 23, #931

Sattinger, David R., g/o c/o,
Philadelphia, Pa., 129,
#7099

Sauders, Pvt. Green, w/o, U.S. Volunteers, 115, #2929
Sauders, John, w/o, Ohio, 86, #16997
Saunders, David, Richmond, Va., 67, #10525
Saunders, David, Richmond, Va., 76, #13882
Saunders, David, w/o, Va., 87, #17547
Saunders, George, Richmond, Va., 47, #5036
Saunders, George, Va., 40, #3231
Saunders, George, w/o, Richmond, Va., 104, #7623
Saunders, James, w/o, Ind., 44, #4248
Saunders, Joseph, c/o, Ky., 56, #7386
Saunders, Phillips, N.C., 88, #17749
Saunders, Robert H., Va., 69, #10958
Savage, John, Albany, N.Y., 61, #8664
Savage, Sarah, Maine, 75, #13488
Savedge, Hartwell, c/o, Richmond, Va., 58, #7868
Sawel, John, Knoxville, Tenn., 49, #5438
Sawell, John, a/o, Knoxville, Tenn., 111, #341
Sawin, Abner, c/o, Mass., 88, #17825
Sawyer, Ebenezer, Bellows Falls, Vt., 75, #13647
Sawyer, Esther, Bellows Falls, Vt., 75, #13647
Sawyer, Israel, w/o, Albany, N.Y., 105, #8282

Sawyer, John, c/o, Albany, N.Y., 109, #10752
Sawyer, Mary, c/o, N.H., 109, #10616
Sawyer, William, c/o, Maine, 52, #6190
Saxton, John, Madison, Ind., 72, #12517
Sayne, Nathan, w/o, Albany, N.Y., 23, #14832
Sayre, Nathan, Albany, N.Y., 80, #14832, card
Scales, Peter, g/o c/o, Miss., 126, #3338
Scanlon, Patrick, N.Y., 88, #18130
Scanter, Elias, Ill., 59, #7981
Scarborough, John, Ill., 119, #5692, card
Scarborough, John, c/o, Ill., 23, #5692
Scay, Joseph, Richmond, Va., 55, #7076
Schackleford, Henry, Ky., 80, #14992
Schacklett, Elizabeth, e/o, Va., 86, #16820
Schafer, Sophia, Albany, N.Y., 74, #13370
Scheck, Sarah, c/o, New York City, 111, #579
Scheeham, William, c/o, Pittsburgh, Pa., 120, #6064
Scheer, John, a/o, La., 121, #6901
Schenck, Garret G., a/o, Cincinnati, Ohio, 23, #6652
Schenk, Ralph, w/o, Albany, N.Y., 44, #4385
Schermerhorn, Anna, a/o, Albany, N.Y., 117, #4525

Schilden, Martin, SpC,
Chillicotte, Ohio, 103,
#6950
Schlott, Catherine, Philadelphia,
Pa., 70, #11099
Schmid, Felix, a/o, Wisc., 141,
#3326
Schnattener, Elizabeth, D.C.,
143, #7046
Schneyer, Adolph, Pa., 109,
#10851
Schnurrer, Albert, g/o c/o, D.C.,
131, #8093
Schockley (now Wise), Mary,
Miss., 110, #11000
Schofield, Seely, c/o, Albany,
N.Y., 102, #5641
Schokley, James, c/o, Miss.,
115, #2982
Schoonever, James, Ohio, 41,
#3482
Schoonhover, Christopher, w/o,
Philadelphia, Pa., 116,
#3674
Schoonover, James, Ohio, 61,
#8617
Schott, Louis, La., 107, #9330
Schreider, Henry, Mo., 129,
#6292
Schrier, Abraham, Cincinnati,
Ohio, 112, #1235
Schuatterer, Elizabeth, D.C.,
141, #1378
Schupp, Maria, D.C., 140,
#9467
Schupp, Maria, D.C., 142,
#4588
Schuyler, Catherine, c/o,
Albany, N.Y., 129, #6387
Schwartz, Joseph, D.C., 140,
#55

Schwartz, Sophia P., Albany,
N.Y., 110, #11168
Schwartze, Sophia P., Albany,
N.Y., 139, #7466
Schwartze, Sophia P., Albany,
N.Y., 143, #6466
Scisson, Robert, c/o, Richmond,
Va., 115, #2460
Scivilly, Martin, w/o, Mo., 141,
#3204
Scofield, Susanna, c/o, Albany,
N.Y., 115, #2492
Scoggins, Jonah, Ind., 68,
#10598
Scoggins, Jonah, w/o, Ill., 103,
#6851
Scoggins, Willis, S.C., 50,
#5635
Scott, Abraham, w/o, Pittsburgh,
Pa., 23, #1635
Scott, Abraham, w/o, Pittsburgh,
Pa., 96, #1635, card
Scott, Alexander, Ind., 68,
#10615
Scott, Alexander, Ind., 81,
#15113
Scott, Ann, Richmond, Va., 101,
#4840
Scott, Benjamin, Ind., 48,
#5053
Scott, Bvt. Lt. Col. Martin, w/o,
5th Inf., 110, #10974
Scott, Bvt. Lt. Col. Martin, w/o,
5th Inf., 105, #8131
Scott, Bvt. Lt. Col. Martin, w/o,
5th Inf., 103, #6555
Scott, Bvt. Lt. Col. Martin, w/o,
5th Inf., 107, #8955
Scott, Bvt. Lt. Col. Martin, w/o,
5th Inf., 108, #10007
Scott, Bvt. Lt. Col. Martin, w/o,
5th Inf., 111, #370

Scott, Bvt. Lt. Col. Martin, w/o, 5th Inf., 112, #1023
Scott, Dennis, S.C., 40, #3339
Scott, Eleazer, c/o, Albany, N.Y., 137, #4287
Scott, Esther, a/o, Albany, N.Y., 139, #8026
Scott, Gen. W., —, 123, #70, card
Scott, Gen. W., —, 123, #262, card
Scott, Gen. W., —, 126, #3326, card
Scott, George, Ill., 44, #4227
Scott, George, Ill., 75, #13456
Scott, Henry, Ark., 81, #15191
Scott, Hines, g/o c/o, Miss., 128, #5727
Scott, Isaac, e/o, Pittsburgh, Pa., 104, #7361
Scott, James, E. Tenn., 59, #8004
Scott, James, Ind., 57, #7620
Scott, James, c/o, S.C., 136, #2864
Scott, James, w/o, New York City, 55, #7136
Scott, John, Ill., 42, #3730
Scott, John, Ill., 74, #13189
Scott, John, Philadelphia, Pa., 23, #11095
Scott, John, Philadelphia, Pa., 64, #9603
Scott, John, Philadelphia, Pa., 110, #11095, card
Scott, John, Philadelphia, Pa., 94, #597
Scott, John, Philadelphia, Pa., 47, #4854
Scott, John, a/o, Ohio, 110, #73
Scott, John, c/o, Cincinnati, Ohio, 137, #4494

Scott, John, g/o c/o, Conn., 37, #F1824
Scott, Joseph, Richmond, Va., 50, #5598
Scott, Joseph, Richmond, Va., 51, #6062
Scott, Joseph, Va., 39, #3150
Scott, Joseph, w/o, Burlington, Vt., 91, #19348
Scott, Lemuel, Burlington, Vt., 91, #19530
Scott, Lemuel, Vt., 87, #17742
Scott, Lemuel, Vt., 90, #18775
Scott, Lt. Col. Martin, w/o, 5th Inf., 101, #5293
Scott, Neil, D.C., 131, #8672
Scott, Priscella, e/o, Richmond, Va., 96, #1584
Scott, Thomas, Nashville, Tenn., 102, #5674
Scott, William, w/o, New York City, 61, #8403
Scott, Zerah, Philadelphia, Pa., 105, #7863
Scouton, Elias, Ill., 43, #3912
Scouton, Elias, Ill., 73, #12900
Scouton, Elias, w/o, Ill., 136, #3010
Scovel, Rachel, c/o, Cincinnati, Ohio, 121, #7179
Scovell, Rachel, c/o, Cincinnati, Ohio, 23, #9320
Scovil, Samuel, c/o, Albany, N.Y., 130, #7400
Scranton, John, Conn., 34, #1182
Scranton, Thomas, Conn., 34, #1072
Scribner, Sarah, a/o, Md., 113, #1475
Scriver, William, w/o, Albany, N.Y., 91, #19054

Scrivner, Mary, Nashville, Tenn., 81, #15041

Scroggins, Unity, S.C., 116, #3525

Scruggs, Elizabeth, Ky., 104, #7502

Scruggs, Timothy, c/o, Mo., 130, #7624

Scudder, Elizabeth, e/o, Madison, Ind., 114, #2245

Scudder, John H., e/o, Madison, Ind., 114, #2245

Seago, Lucinda, La., 132, #9583

Seagraves, Jacob, a/o, Ill., 129, #6214

Seaman, Henry, New York City, 40, #3215

Seaman, Stephen, Albany, N.Y., 43, #4060

Seamster, John, a/o, Richmond, Va., 94, #533

Seamster, John, a/o, Richmond, Va., 94, #534

Seapple, August, Mo., 117, #3832

Searcy, John, w/o, N.C., 79, #14728

Sears, Francis, c/o, N.Y., 86, #16995

Sears, Hannah, c/o, Albany, N.Y., 124, #724

Sears, Henry, g/o c/o, New York City, 130, #7318

Seat, James, N.C., 44, #4367

Seat, James, N.C., 46, #4761

Seat, James, N.C., 61, #8438

Seat, James, N.C., 61, #8628

Seaton, George, —, 23, #7242, card

Seaton Tyler, Private, —, 66, #10217

Seay, Joseph, Va., 79, #14739

Sebor, Jacob, g/o c/o, Conn., 37, #F1820

Sedgwick, Timothy, Conn., 34, #403

Sedore, Isaac, a/o, Albany, N.Y., 120, #6061

Seefield, Charles A., La., 114, #2362

Seely, Ebenezer, c/o, Philadelphia, Pa., 112, #804

Seely, John, Mo., 65, #9725, card

Seely, John, Mo., 23, #9725

Seely, Samuel, Philadelphia, Pa., 118, #4740

Seelye, Abigail, Conn., 34, #24

Seeper, John, Mo., 43, #3950

Seger, Catharine, a/o, Albany, N.Y., 130, #7497

Seherr, John, La., 116, #3054

Selcer, Frederick, Pittsburgh, Pa., 83, #15886

Self, Oney, c/o, Richmond, Va., 110, #114

Selfridge, John, Albany, N.Y., 48, #5063

Selfridge, Sarah, c/o, Detroit, Mich., 141, #2043

Selkrig, Jeremiah, Mich., 65, #10039

Selkrig, Jeremiah, Mich., 83, #15818

Sell, Dorothy, a/o, N.C., 104, #7668

Sellers, Benjamin E., w/o, Springfield, Ill., 134, #962

Sellers, Isaac, c/o, New Orleans, La., 113, #1612

Sellick, Elizabeth, New York City, 62, #8668

Semora, Thomas, Jackson, Tenn., 92, #61

Semple, Saml., Knoxville, Tenn., 53, #6579

Seneca Indian, Thomas, Albany, N.Y., 48, #5240

Senewell, James, Mo., 41, #3472

Sennett, Patrick, Wheeling, Va., 60, #8221

Sennett, Patrick, w/o, Wheeling, Va., 117, #4231

Sentell, Nancy, Ga., 124, #890

Sentell, Samuel, w/o, Ga., 98, #2668

Sephton, Sally, R.I., 42, #3775

Seres, Henry, g/o c/o, New York City, 139, #7163

Sergeant, Elijah, Ohio, 56, #7417

Servard, John, Carmi, Ill., 47, #4905

Serviss, William G., Ohio, 67, #10464

Sessions, John, a/o, Savannah, Ga., 104, #7587

Setson (or Letson), William, Albany, N.Y., 23, #4815

Sevan, John, Albany, N.Y., 54, #6657

Sevan, John, Conn., 35, #858

Sevan, John, Philadelphia, Pa., 64, #9319

Severson, Richard, c/o, Albany, N.Y., 116, #3193

Severy, John, c/o, Mass., 49, #5437

Sevier, Catherine, c/o, Knoxville, Tenn., 23, #8937

Seward, George, Portsmouth, N.H., 23, #4642

Sewell, James, Mo., 67, #10323

Sewell, John, Knoxville, Tenn., 40, #3325

Sewell, John, Md., 126, #3702, card

Sewell, John, c/o, Md., 23, #3702

Sewell, Thomas, Ohio, 136, #----, card

Sexton, Elijah, w/o, Albany, N.Y., 92, #19934

Sexton, James, Albany, N.Y., 135, #1848

Sexton, James, Albany, N.Y., 137, #4342

Sexton, John, N.C., 39, #2989

Sexton, Timothy, w/o, Knoxville, Tenn., 40, #3330

Seyke, William, w/o, Albany, N.Y., 116, #3227

Seymour, William B., Mich., 123, #9969

Seymour, William B., Mich., 131, #8516

Shackelford, Mary, c/o, Ga., 101, #4687

Shackleford, Henry, Ky., 47, #4887

Shackleford, Nancy, Ky., 134, #1457

Shackley, Barbara Ann, a/o, Pittsburgh, Pa., 95, #1018

Shafelt, William, w/o, Philadelphia, Pa., 141, #1727

Shaff, Henry, Albany, N.Y., 84, #16020

Shaffer, Adam, Philadelphia, Pa., 72, #12697, card

Shaffer, Adam, Philadelphia, Pa., 23, #12697

Shaffer, Adam, Philadelphia, Pa.,
59, #8073
Shaffer, Danl., w/o, N.C., 53,
#6556
Shall, Henry, w/o, Albany, N.Y.,
56, #7338
Shands, William, Richmond,
Va., 47, #4945
Shannon, Archibald B., Jackson,
Tenn., 80, #14757
Shannon, John, Ky., 136,
#3368
Shantz, Henry, w/o,
Philadelphia, Pa., 113,
#1868
Sharp, Andrew, Philadelphia,
Pa., 52, #6099
Sharp, Benjamin, Mo., 62,
#8715
Sharp, George, w/o, Mo., 126,
#3378
Sharp, John, w/o, Richmond,
Va., 24, #15898
Sharp, Samuel, w/o, Ky., 55,
#6934
Sharp, William, w/o, Knoxville,
Tenn., 92, #19692
Shaver, Anne, c/o, Madison,
Ind., 112, #1188
Shaver, Henry, Albany, N.Y.,
84, #16239
Shaver, Henry, Albany, N.Y.,
106, #8847
Shaver, Henry, Albany, N.Y.,
40, #3249
Shaver, Jacob, c/o, Albany,
N.Y., 23, #782
Shaver, John, Albany, N.Y., 58,
#7777
Shaver, Nancy, a/o, Madison,
Ind., 122, #8117

Shaw, Abigail, c/o, Portsmouth,
N.H., 137, #4084
Shaw, Benjamin, Pulaski, Tenn.,
39, #2941
Shaw, David, c/o, Albany, N.Y.,
64, #9127
Shaw, Eli, a/o, Pittsburgh, Pa.,
135, #2258
Shaw, Gilbert, w/o, Ga., 83,
#15884
Shaw, Icabod, —, 107, #9322,
card
Shaw, Ichabod, Philadelphia,
Pa., 23, #9322
Shaw, John, Ga., 66, #10088
Shaw, Joseph, Ill., 48, #5058
Shaw, Joseph, c/o, Albany,
N.Y., 102, #5673
Shaw, Martha R., Fayetteville,
N.C., 129, #7053
Shaw, Mary, Philadelphia, Pa.,
109, #10529 V#84
Shaw, Michael, a/o, N.C., 121,
#7676
Shaw, Phebe, a/o, Pittsburgh,
Pa., 96, #1632
Shaw, Richard, Pittsburgh, Pa.,
51, #5970
Shaw, William, c/o, New York
City, 69, #10839
Shaw, Zerviah, c/o, Albany,
N.Y., 46, #4679
Shay, Michael, Cincinnati,
Ohio, 123, #9796
Shay, Michael, Cincinnati,
Ohio, 130, #7992
Shay, Michael, Cincinnati,
Ohio, 139, #7124
Shay, Michael, N.Y., 122,
#8477
Shay, Seers, Philadelphia, Pa.,
132, #9635

Shay, Timothy, w/o, New York
  City, 55, #7123
Shea, Patrick, S.C., 90, #18837
Shea, Stephen, a/o,
  Philadelphia, Pa., 106,
  #8488
Shearer, Jeramiah, Philadelphia,
  Pa., 56, #7294
Shearman, George, Richmond,
  Va., 53, #6485
Shearman, George, Richmond,
  Va., 46, #4829
Shearman, Mary M., Richmond,
  Va., 105, #8072
Sheaver, Mary, a/o, New York
  City, 96, #1763
Shed, David, w/o, Albany, N.Y.,
  86, #17248
Shedd, Thomas M. D., Mass.,
  133, #299
Sheerman, Mary M., Richmond,
  Va., 99, #3722
Sheets, John, Wheeling, Va.,
  84, #16071
Sheets, John, Wheeling, Va.,
  87, #17324
Sheffer, Trunis, c/o, Albany,
  N.Y., 44, #4335
Sheffield, Mary, Ky., 127,
  #4930
Sheldon, Phebe, Conn., 34, #26
Shellenx, Jane, a/o, Albany,
  N.Y., 99, #3362
Shelton, James, c/o, Va., 83,
  #15710
Shelton, Mary, Richmond, Va.,
  36A, #F6 V27
Shelton, Wilson, Ind., 48,
  #5071
Shelty, Christopher, Albany,
  N.Y., 52, #6147

Shenault, Benjamin, w/o,
  Fayetteville, N.C., 124,
  #1034
Shener, Theodosia, Ga., 49,
  #5274
Shepard, Lt. O. L., special
  payment, 92, #19868
Shepard, Mary, a/o, Richmond,
  Va., 36A, #F4 V15
Shepard, Samuel, w/o,
  Montpelier, Vt., 86,
  #17249
Sheperd, Sally, c/o, Mass., 79,
  #14719
Shephard, Whitmore, a/o,
  Conn., 34, #5555
Shepherd, Charles, Albany,
  N.Y., 65, #9891
Shepherd, Charles, Albany,
  N.Y., 70, #12181
Shepherd, Charles, Ohio, 74,
  #13381
Shepherd, Eleanor, Richmond,
  Va., 45, #4574
Shepherd, James, w/o, Maine,
  46, #4690
Shepherd, Joseph, c/o, Mass.,
  76, #13724
Shepherd, Mary A. W., Ga., 112,
  #786
Shepherd, Mary Ann W., Ga.,
  102, #5793
Shepherd, Mary Ann W., Ga.,
  129, #6475
Shepherd, Rebecca, c/o, N.J.,
  90, #18640
Shepherd, Samuel, w/o,
  Nashville, Tenn., 85,
  #16649
Sheppard, Charles J., Ky., 125,
  #2253

Sheppard, Charles J., Ky., 130,
#7583

Sheppard, Charles J., Ky., 140,
#897

Sheppard, William, S.C., 129,
#6921

Sheridan, James, Mass., 137,
#4454

Sherman, Dennis, w/o, Albany,
N.Y., 89, #18513

Sherman, George, Richmond,
Va., 58, #7908

Sherman, George, Va., 66,
#10175

Sherman, George, w/o,
Richmond, Va., 57, #7566

Sherman, George, w/o,
Richmond, Va., 54, #6726

Sherman, Jeremiah, w/o,
Boston, Mass., 50, #5842

Sherman, John, Mass., 47,
#4958

Sherman, Martha, e/o, Albany,
N.Y., 113, #1262

Sherman, Mary M., Richmond,
Va., 23, #7351

Sherman, Nathaniel, Conn., 34,
#153

Sherman, Reuben, w/o, Concord,
N.H., 139, #6891

Sherman, Ruth, Albany, N.Y.,
89, #18238

Sherrer, George, w/o, Ga., 76,
#13842

Sherrills, Abraham, N.Y., 80,
#14816

Sherry, William, child of, Ky.,
45, #4583

Sherwin, Eunice, Vt., 109,
#10576

Sherwood, Luch, a/o, Albany,
N.Y., 107, #9138

Sherwood, Polly, Conn., 35,
#49

Sherwood, Thomas, Conn., 35,
#149

Shever, Frederick, Knoxville,
Tenn., 86, #16738

Shew, Stephen, c/o, Albany,
N.Y., 78, #14400, card

Shew, Stephen, w/o, Albany,
N.Y., 23, #14400

Shields, David, Cincinnati,
Ohio, 77, #14111, card

Shields, David, Ohio, 104,
#7144, card

Shields, David, e/o, Ohio, 23,
#7144

Shields, David, e/o, Ohio, 23,
#14111

Shields, Hector, Pittsburgh, Pa.,
68, #10629

Shields, James, Pa., 103, #6738,
card

Shields, James, a/o, Pittsburgh,
Pa., 23, #6738

Shields, John, w/o,
Philadelphia, Pa., 75,
#13440

Shields, Joshua, Ind., 52, #6306

Shields, Joshua, Ind., 81,
#15210

Shields, Mary, e/o, Philadelphia,
Pa., 115, #2923

Shinnick, Jacob, w/o, Md., 127,
#4144

Shipe, Philip, w/o, N.C., 44,
#4363

Shipee, Hannah, c/o, Albany,
N.Y., 59, #7980

Shipley, Elizabeth Ann, Ky.,
126, #3253

Shipley, Samuel, —, 69,
#10820, card

Shuck, Jacob, c/o, D.C., 24, #6390

Shucks, Jacob, D.C., 103, #6282, card

Shucks, Jacob, D.C., 103, #6390, card

Shufett, John, w/o, Albany, N.Y., 61, #8430

Shults, Didiamah, Ky., 61, #8587

Shultz (formerly Clem), Altetha R., Ill., 114, #2021

Shumaker, Nearmon, Ala., 136, #2885, card

Shumate, Karenhappock, alias Caty, Richmond, Va., 130, #7840

Shumway, Chloe, Albany, N.Y., 85, #16320

Shurts, Michael, w/o, N.J., 86, #17075

Shute, William, c/o, Albany, N.Y., 85, #16436

Shutis, Jacob, a/o, Albany, N.Y., 119, #5217

Shutto, Dadamah, Ky., 77, #14022

Sibley, Ann, a/o, Mass., 130, #7639

Sibley, Charles, Mass., 131, #8822

Sibley, John, Natchez, Miss., 78, #14373

Sickels, Zacharias, Albany, N.Y., 24, #18267, card

Sickels, Zacharias, Albany, N.Y., 89, #18267, card

Sickles, Mary, c/o, Albany, N.Y., 67, #10534

Sickles, Oliver B., Ga., 66, #10308

Siddell, Stephen, w/o, Ga., 116, #3774

Sigmond, Karl, Philadelphia, Pa., 110, #11003

Sigmond, Karl, Pittsburgh, Pa., 122, #8412

Sigourney, Andrew, c/o, Mass., 49, #5388

Sikes, Lucy, Conn., 115, #2733

Siles, John, W. Fla., 59, #8043

Sill, Samuel, Conn., 35, #758

Sillyman, Nancy, c/o, Philadelphia, Pa., 102, #6253

Sillyman, Thomas, c/o, Philadelphia, Pa., 102, #6066

Silver, Daniel, c/o, Mass., 113, #1694

Silverthorn, Ann, c/o, N.C., 97, #2306

Simerman, Simon, Mo., 112, #964

Simerman, Simon, Mo., 120, #6674

Siminton, Robert, Philadelphia, Pa., 82, #15518

Simmerman, Simon, Mo., 118, #4680

Simmingston, Joseph, Albany, N.Y., 86, #17200

Simmons, Arad, Concord, N.H., 42, #3652

Simmons, Frederick, Philadelphia, Pa., 62, #8824

Simmons, Hannah, New York City, 106, #8787

Simmons, Ivory, c/o, Albany, N.Y., 88, #18013

Simmons, Jehu, Va., 80, #14793

Simmons, Lt. Brice, w/o, Ga.
Militia, 103, #6922
Simmons, Margaret, Cincinnati,
Ohio, 130, #7487
Simmons, Samuel, w/o, N.H.,
88, #17995
Simmons, William, c/o, Albany,
N.Y., 24, #325
Simms, Maurice K., La., 137,
#4598
Simon, Cummy, Conn., 35,
#5618
Simonds, Ashney, c/o, Conn.,
116, #3781
Simons, Asa, Va., 82, #15343,
card
Simons, Asa, w/o, Richmond,
Va., 24, #15343
Simons, Deborah, a/o, Albany,
N.Y., 130, #7791
Simons, Elijah, c/o, Conn., 35,
#18361
Simons, Eliza, Montpelier, Vt.,
101, #5006 V#95
Simons, Maurice K., La., 125,
#1724
Simonton, Robert, Philadelphia,
Pa., 68, #10760
Simonton, Robert, Philadelphia,
Pa., 72, #12673
Simonton, Walter, w/o, Maine,
47, #4873
Simpkins, Charles, Wheeling,
Va., 74, #13298
Simpkins, John G., Ind., 64,
#9505
Simpson, Andrew, w/o, Albany,
N.Y., 98, #2653
Simpson, James, Mobile, Ala.,
59, #7962
Simpson, James, Mobile, Ala.,
79, #14704

Simpson, James, Va., 40, #3171
Simpson, Lawrence, c/o, Md.,
120, #6345
Simpson, Martha A., Nashville,
Tenn., 120, #6239
Simpson, Mary, Albany, N.Y.,
98, #3048
Simpson, Peter, c/o, Albany,
N.Y., 113, #1911
Simpson, William, c/o, Ill., 83,
#15725
Simpson, William, w/o, Ky., 83,
#15889
Sims, Augustine, Mo., 95,
#1025
Sims, Augustus, Ill., 65, #9705
Sims, Cuthbert, a/o, N.J., 120,
#6575
Sims, Edward, a/o, S.C., 119,
#5178
Sims, Jeremiah, Ohio, 67,
#10330
Sims, Martha, Richmond, Va.,
36A, #F2 V43
Sims, Rhodam, Mo., 78, #14536
Simsson, Caleb, Burlington,
Vt., 40, #3216
Sinck, Ann, a/o, Philadelphia,
Pa., 112, #1101
Sinclair, Robert, Mo., 61,
#8428
Sinclair, Robert, Mo., 62,
#8721
Sinclair, Robert, Mo., 66,
#10240
Singer, John, w/o, Mo., 119,
#5391
Singletary, Joseph, Fla., 46,
#4807
Singletary, Sarah P., a/o,
Fayetteville, N.C., 135,
#1897

Singleton, James, Mich., 44,
#4258
Singleton, James, Mich., 47,
#4867
Singleton, Lucy, Richmond, Va.,
36A, #F3 21
Singley, George, —, 98, #3101,
card
Sipe, Leonard, Ill., 46, #4715
Sisson, Seberry, c/o, R.I., 124,
#1115
Sisson, Sebery, c/o, R.I., 124,
#564
Sisson, Sophia, R.I., 53, #6426
Sisson, Sophia, c/o, R.I., 110,
#11114
Sithine (or Siffen), John, e/o,
N.J., 24, #4640
Sittell, Nathaniel, c/o, N.J.,
114, #2388
Six, Conrad, Cleveland, Ohio,
115, #2596
Sizer, Elizabeth, —, 126,
#3970, slip
Sizer, Elizabeth, c/o, Albany,
N.Y., 128, #5267
Skeele, John, a/o, Montpelier,
Vt., 97, #2068
Skein, Adam, Mobile, Ala., 86,
#16770
Skein, Adam, Mobile, Ala., 112,
#821
Skiff, John, Albany, N.Y., 50,
#5564
Skiff, Stephen, w/o, Albany,
N.Y., 62, #8756
Skillman, Lucretia, N.J., 101,
#4642
Skinner, Adie, D.C., 142, #3922
Skinner, Adie, Richmond, Va.,
36A, #F6 V28

Skinner, Adie, Richmond, Va.,
124, #502
Skinner, Albert, Ill., 44, #4220
Skinner, Benjamin, w/o, Mass.,
81, #15014
Skinner, Daniel, New York City,
67, #10535
Skinner, Elizabeth, c/o, Albany,
N.Y., 82, #15368
Skinner, Hannah, Pittsburgh,
Pa., 76, #13779
Skinner, Henry, Detroit, Mich.,
141, #1875
Skinner, Henry, Mich., 142,
#3610
Skinner, Isaac, Ky., 77, #14174
Skinner, Micah, c/o, Pittsburgh,
Pa., 88, #17839
Skinner, Uriah, Albany, N.Y.,
55, #6921
Skipton, Nancy, c/o,
Philadelphia, Pa., 101,
#4606
Skirven, Leonida, g/o c/o,
Madison, Ind., 127, #4468
Slack, George D., Albany, N.Y.,
141, #2796
Slack, Margaret, —, 96, #1617,
slip
Slack, Margaret, a/o,
Fayetteville, N.C., 24,
#1617
Slack, Rachel, e/o, N.J., 135,
#2333
Slade, Nathan, w/o, N.C., 118,
#4995
Slaughter, 1st Lt. William A.,
w/o, 4th Inf., 134, #912
Slaughter, George, Ga., 51,
#5956
Slaughter, Isaac, w/o, New York
City, 55, #6975

Slaughter, John, c/o, N.C., 84, #15985
Slaughter, Lt. W. A., w/o, 4th Inf., 136, #3181
Slaughter, Lt. William A., w/o, 4th Inf., 131, #8429
Slaughter, Lt. William A., w/o, 4th Inf., 135, #2082
Slaughter, William, Jonesboro, Tenn., 115, #2728, card
Slaughter, William, w/o, Richmond, Va., 77, #13990, card
Slauter, Ephraim, Pittsburgh, Pa., 24, #1211
Slaven, John, Va., 52, #6333
Slavens, Isaiah, Ind., 58, #7780
Slavens, Isaiah, Ind., 63, #9017
Slavens, Isaiah, Madison, Ind., 48, #5151
Slavin, John, Ky., 76, #13838
Slayback, William, c/o, Ohio, 50, #5804
Slayton, Ebenezer, a/o, Philadelphia, Pa., 104, #7355
Sledd, John, Va., 65, #10027
Sledd (or Slade), William, c/o, Va. Milita, 100, #4270
Sledd (or Slade), William, c/o, Va. Milita, 101, #4802
Sledd (or Slade), William, c/o, Va. Milita, 101, #4803
Slick, William, Philadelphia, Pa., 80, #14810
Slimp, John, a/o, Jonesboro, Tenn., 131, #8885
Sloan, John, S.C., 40, #3269
Sloan, John, S.C., 55, #7213
Sloan, Rachel, e/o, Albany, N.Y., 128, #5596
Sloan, Robert, N.C., 42, #3720

Sloan, Saml., Nashville, Tenn., 52, #6151
Sloan, Thomas, w/o, Ill., 86, #16851
Sloane, Robert, N.C., 45, #4538
Sloat (formerly Petrea), Catherine, Ill., 132, #9277
Slocomb, Charles J., c/o, Ga., 24, #7037
Slocumb, John Charles, Ga., 76, #13918
Slocumb, John Charles, Ga., 43, #4027
Slocumb, John Charles, Savannah, Ga., 64, #9701
Slone, William, Va., 67, #10318
Slossom, Deliverance, Albany, N.Y., 89, #18215
Slout, Philip, w/o, Albany, N.Y., 88, #17831
Slup, James B., Springfield, Ill., 143, #7326
Slye, Willam, c/o, Ohio, 80, #14961
Slye, William, —, 84, #16232, card
Slye, William, c/o, Ohio, 80, #14959
Small, Andrea, c/o, Ohio, 92, #19762
Small, Elizabeth, Jackson, Miss., 116, #3351
Smalley, David, Ohio, 41, #3411
Smart, Caleb, N.H., 24, #18574
Smart, Eunice, a/o, Concord, N.H., 137, #3812
Smart, Thomas, c/o, Richmond, Va., 135, #2220
Smedley, Lemuel, w/o, Philadelphia, Pa., 69, #10911

Smee, Isaac, Philadelphia, Pa.,
59, #8152
Smiley, Hannah, Boston, Mass.,
64, #9554
Smiley, Penelope, g/o c/o, E.
Fla., 83, #15791
Smith, —, —, 74, #13374, card
Smith, —, —, 86, #16893, card
Smith, Aaron, Wisc., 76,
#13805
Smith 2nd, Aaron, Wisc., 43,
#3947
Smith, Aaron, w/o, Ark., 85,
#16708
Smith, Abiah, Conn., 99, #3617
Smith, Abner, c/o, Montpelier,
Vt., 103, #6813
Smith Jr., Alpheus, Wisc., 128,
#6053
Smith, Alexander, Ga., 45,
#4637
Smith, America, Ky., 143,
#6471
Smith, Ann, a/o, Ky., 134,
#1125
Smith, Anthony, w/o, Conn.,
35, #3404
Smith, Austin, a/o, Albany,
N.Y., 113, #1639
Smith, Austin, a/o, Albany,
N.Y., 113, #1665
Smith, Austin, c/o, Ga., 121,
#7478
Smith, Basha, Richmond, Va.,
131, #8896
Smith, Benjamin, w/o, Maine,
53, #6537
Smith, Benjamin, Albany, N.Y.,
125, #2125
Smith, Benjamin, N.C., 66,
#10310, card

Smith, Benjamin, N.C., 24,
#10310
Smith, Benjamin M., New York
City, 40, #3348
Smith, Bernard, E. Tenn., 59,
#8032
Smith, Capt. Ephraim K., w/o,
5th Inf., 101, #5356
Smith, Capt. Ephraim K., w/o,
5th Inf., 103, #6447
Smith, Capt. Ephraim K., w/o,
5th Inf., 104, #7227
Smith, Capt. Ephraim K., w/o,
5th Inf., 105, #8186
Smith, Capt. Ephraim K., w/o,
5th Inf., 107, #8974
Smith, Capt. Ephraim K., w/o,
5th Inf., 108, #9959
Smith, Capt. Ephraim K., w/o,
5th Inf., 109, #10812
Smith, Capt. Ephraim K., w/o,
5th Inf., 111, #467
Smith, Capt. Ephraim K., w/o,
5th Inf., 112, #991
Smith, Capt. Ephraim K., w/o,
5th Inf., 113, #1708
Smith, Catharine, Richmond,
Va., 122, #8772
Smith, Charles, Richmond, Va.,
24, #7814
Smith, Charles, Richmond, Va.,
24, #14196
Smith, Charles, Va., 102,
#5838, card
Smith, Charles, w/o, Richmond,
Va., 24, #5838
Smith, Pvt. Daniel, w/o, S.C.
militia, 131, #8237
Smith, Darby, Ky., 52, #6235
Smith, Deborah A., Conn., 101,
#4626

Smith, Deborah Ann, Conn., 35,
#8769
Smith, Deborah Ann, Hartford,
Conn., 92, #19542
Smith, Elijah, w/o, Nashville,
Tenn., 140, #454
Smith, Elisha, —, 126, #3025,
card
Smith, Elisha, a/o, N.C., 24,
#3025
Smith, Elizabeth, Ga., 127,
#4787
Smith, Elizabeth, Ga., 128,
#5158
Smith, Elizabeth, Ga., 135,
#2339
Smith, Elizabeth, Ga., 137,
#4201
Smith, Elizabeth, N.C., 76,
#13872
Smith, Elizabeth, Richmond,
Va., 99, #3339
Smith, Elizabeth, a/o, N.C.,
120, #6613
Smith, Elizabeth, c/o, N.J., 133,
#621
Smith, Elizabeth, c/o,
Richmond, Va., 125, #1601
Smith, Enoch, Ga., 66, #10087
Smith, Enoch, Ga., 76, #13917
Smith, Enoch, Ga., 87, #17484
Smith, Enoch, h/o, Conn., 35,
#543
Smith, Esck, a/o, Vt., 84,
#15989
Smith, Ezekial, Conn., 35, #774
Smith, Ezekiel, Ga., 47, #4925
Smith, Fanny, New York City,
112, #1189
Smith, Fanny, New York City,
129, #6622

Smith, Flora, c/o, Va., 85,
#16613
Smith, Garrett, w/o, Albany,
N.Y., 120, #5998
Smith, George, a/o, Va., 120,
#6528
Smith Sr., George, Nashville,
Tenn., 42, #3682
Smith, George, c/o, Ill., 118,
#4739
Smith, Gideon, Pa., 40, #3239
Smith, Gideon, Philadelphia,
Pa., 43, #3856
Smith, Godfrey, a/o, Ky., 132,
#9525
Smith, Gregory, New York City,
70, #11071
Smith, Hannah, a/o, Portsmouth,
N.H., 126, #3948
Smith, Hannah, c/o, New York
City, 137, #4186
Smith, Hardy, w/o, Ga., 88,
#18005
Smith, Heber, a/o, Conn., 38,
#F1820
Smith, Henry, c/o, N.C., 105,
#8063
Smith, Hezikiah, c/o, Ind., 113,
#1272
Smith, Huldah, c/o, Boston,
Mass., 119, #5221
Smith, Isaac, Va., 40, #3320
Smith, Israel, w/o, Albany,
N.Y., 118, #5037
Smith, Israel, w/o, N.Y. Inf.,
134, #997
Smith, Jacob, Maine, 86,
#16860
Smith, Jacob, w/o, Boston,
Mass., 54, #6733
Smith, James, Albany, N.Y.,
104, #7675

Smith, James, S.C., 48, #5217
Smith, James, e/o, Albany,
    N.Y., 24, #1377
Smith, James, w/o, Cleveland,
    Ohio, 142, #4924
Smith, James, w/o, Ind., 69,
    #11009
Smith, James T., Maine, 82,
    #15276
Smith, James W., w/o,
    Philadelphia, Pa., 115,
    #2758
Smith, Jane, Charleston, S.C.,
    112, #837
Smith, Jane, N.Y., 96, #1377,
    card
Smith, Jedidiah, —, 134, #1495,
    card
Smith, Jeremiah, w/o, Albany,
    N.Y., 55, #7118
Smith, Jesse, w/o, Maine, 115,
    #2661
Smith, Joel, c/o, Mass., 74,
    #13183
Smith, John, —, 43, #3915, card
Smith, John, —, 97, #2430, card
Smith, John, a/o, Conn., 68,
    #10735
Smith, John, Ga., 81, #15164
Smith, John, Jonesboro, Tenn.,
    66, #10247
Smith, John, Ohio, 24, #588
Smith, John, Ohio, 77, #14219
Smith, John, Richmond, Va.,
    56, #7368, card
Smith, John, Richmond, Va.,
    43, #3904, card
Smith, John, Richmond, Va.,
    46, #4829
Smith, John, c/o, Richmond,
    Va., 24, #3904

Smith, John, c/o, Richmond,
    Va., 24, #7368
Smith 1st, John, Maine, 101,
    #4820
Smith 1st, John, c/o, Maine,
    101, #5043
Smith, John, a/o, Va., 88,
    #17944
Smith, John, c/o, Mass., 40,
    #3299
Smith, John, w/o, Bellows Falls,
    Vt., 73, #12828
Smith, John, w/o, Conn., 105,
    #7770
Smith, John, w/o, Ky., 24,
    #3915
Smith, John, w/o, Va., 40,
    #3217
Smith, John E., New York City,
    102, #6052 V#42
Smith, John M., S.C., 131,
    #8902
Smith, John O. C., Ohio, 76,
    #13923
Smith, John W., w/o, Conn.,
    140, #9361
Smith, Jonathan, c/o,
    Pittsburgh, Pa., 121, #7481
Smith, Joseph, Ky., 55, #6947
Smith, Joseph, Ky., 102, #5985
Smith, Joseph, Philadelphia,
    Pa., 52, #6113
Smith, Joseph, St. Louis, Mo.,
    129, #6497
Smith, Joseph, Louisville, Ky.,
    108, #9984 V#77
Smith, Joseph, w/o, Richmond,
    Va., 99, #3636
Smith, Josiah, N.Y., 85, #16482
Smith, Josiah, c/o, Conn., 115,
    #2523

Smith, Katurah, a/o, Hartford,
Conn., 134, #1300
Smith, Laton, E. Tenn., 80,
#14871, card
Smith, Leander, Mo., 135,
#2256
Smith, Lebedee, Ohio, 66,
#10297
Smith, Lemuel, a/o, Conn., 60,
#8318
Smith, Leonard, w/o, Pittsburgh,
Pa., 52, #6165
Smith, Levi, Albany, N.Y., 74,
#13337
Smith, Lewis, Albany, N.Y., 39,
#2955
Smith, Lindsey, c/o, Richmond,
Va., 96, #1833
Smith, Louisa, Jonesboro,
Tenn., 117, #3904
Smith, Lucy, Philadelphia, Pa.,
104, #7493
Smith, Lucy, Philadelphia, Pa.,
101, #4851 V#112
Smith, Lucy, Philadelphia, Pa.,
101, #4851 V#5
Smith, Lucy, Philadelphia, Pa.,
101, #4851 #6
Smith, Luther, Conn., 35, #71
Smith, Lydia, Albany, N.Y., 73,
#12956
Smith, Lydia, Richmond, Va.,
135, #1755
Smith, Margaret, Albany, N.Y.,
98, #2983
Smith, Margaret V., g/o,
Richmond, Va., 36A, #F3
V41
Smith (now Parrish), Maria E.,
Mich., 119, #5558
Smith, Martin, N.J., 70, #12204

Smith, Martin, Pittsburgh, Pa.,
83, #15792
Smith (nee Clark), Mary,
Detroit, Mich., 24, #7156
Smith, Mary, N.J., 24, #15017
Smith, Mary, Richmond, Va.,
131, #8663
Smith, Mary, a/o, Albany, N.Y.,
136, #3078
Smith, Mary, a/o, Conn., 134,
#1110
Smith, Mary, a/o, D.C., 24,
#5684
Smith, Matthew, c/o, Ill., 128,
#5473
Smith, Nicholas, N.Y. Militia,
136, #3176
Smith, Orange, g/o c/o, Conn.,
37, #F1820
Smith, Peter, Pittsburgh, Pa.,
46, #4708
Smith, Pvt. Peter, w/o, Sea
Fencibles, 113, #1440
Smith, Phebe, Richmond, Va.,
36A, #F3 V25
Smith, Philip, Richmond, Va.,
45, #4423
Smith, Phinehas, Conn., 45,
#4443
Smith, Polly, c/o, Albany, N.Y.,
138, #6432
Smith, Rachel, c/o, Albany,
N.Y., 83, #15656
Smith, Rebecca, Huntsville,
Ala., 51, #5874
Smith, Rebecca, a/o, Cincinnati,
Ohio, 138, #5097
Smith, Rebecca, a/o, Ky., 99,
#3592
Smith, Reuben, w/o, N.Y., 55,
#7040

Smith, Reuben, w/o, Richmond, Va., 91, #19419

Smith, Richard, w/o, Ind., 72, #12604

Smith, Robert, Pa., 117, #3894, slip

Smith, Robert, e/o, Philadelphia, Pa., 24, #3894

Smith, Samuel, Albany, N.Y., 64, #9144

Smith, Samuel, Conn., 35, #417

Smith, Samuel, La., 122, #8894

Smith, Samuel, Ohio, 60, #8338

Smith, Samuel, Ohio, 64, #9268

Smith, Samuel, Ohio, 66, #10294

Smith, Samuel, Ohio, 72, #12650

Smith, Samuel, Ohio, 76, #13942

Smith, Samuel, Ohio, 86, #17217

Smith, Samuel C., Conn., 35, #8772

Smith, Samuel F., PA, Philadelphia, Pa., 102, #5723

Smith, Sarah, Burlington, Vt., 47, #4937

Smith, Sarah, Mass., 67, #10324

Smith, Sarah A., Cincinnati, Ohio, 127, #4610

Smith, Sarah Ann, Cincinnati, Ohio, 131, #8575

Smith, Sarah Ann, Cincinnati, Ohio, 139, #7831

Smith, Sarah Ann, Cincinnati, Ohio, 143, #6075

Smith, Sherwood, W. Tenn., 46, #4706

Smith, Silas, a/o, Ohio, 64, #9646

Smith, Silas, a/o, Ohio, 65, #9787

Smith, Simeon, e/o, Mass., 90, #18772

Smith, Stephen, Conn., 35, #1325

Smith, Stephen, a/o, Albany, N.Y., 102, #5570

Smith, Susan, a/o, Va., 68, #10775

Smith, Susannah, e/o, S.C., 130, #7758

Smith, Temperance, a/o, Conn., 100, #3933

Smith, Thaddeus, Ohio, 48, #5180, card

Smith, Thaddeus, Ohio, 56, #7284, card

Smith, Thaddeus, Ohio, 24, #5180

Smith, Thaddeus, w/o, Ohio, 24, #7284

Smith, Thankful, c/o, R.I., 69, #10878

Smith, Thomas, Albany, N.Y., 138, #5436

Smith, Thomas, Cincinnati, Ohio, 138, #5158

Smith, Thomas, Richmond, Va., 57, #7437

Smith, Thomas, Richmond, Va., 66, #10274

Smith, Thomas, Richmond, Va., 47, #4976

Smith, Thomas, Va., 77, #14055

Smith, Thomas, Va., 107, #9396, card

Smith, Thomas, a/o, Richmond, Va., 24, #9396

Smith, Thomas, c/o, S.C., 123, #165

Smith, Thomas N., Nashville, Tenn., 126, #3246

Smith, Thomas N., Nashville, Tenn., 137, #3718

Smith, Timothy, c/o, Pittsburgh, Pa., 47, #5031

Smith, Wililams, Ga., 123, #1--, card

Smith, William, Conn., 35, #816

Smith, William, New York City, 111, #362

Smith, William, c/o, Knoxville, Tenn., 121, #6875

Smith, William, c/o, Knoxville, Tenn., 128, #5406

Smith, William, c/o, Knoxville, Tenn., 134, #1439

Smith, William, c/o, Knoxville, Tenn., 136, #3110

Smith, William, e/o, Va., 119, #5330

Smith, William, w/o, Ga., 24, #135

Smith, William, w/o, Ga. Militia, 99, #3337

Smith, William, w/o, Richmond, Va., 98, #2967

Smith, William H., w/o, Pa. Militia, 90, #18547

Smith, William J., Ohio, 56, #7347

Smith, Winna, Va., 77, #14155

Smithhart, Darby, Knoxville, Tenn., 82, #15348

Smithharth, Dorcas, Ky., 126, #3455

Smithson, Darby, Ky., 64, #9442

Smithson, Sarah B., Richmond, Va., 36A, #F4 V22

Smock, Lt. Henry, account, Tex. Mtd. Vols., 109, #10570

Smoot, James, c/o, Va. Milita, 119, #5525

Smoot, James, w/o, Va. Milita, 119, #5525

Smord, Michael, Richmond, Va., 66, #10286

Smuck, Christian, w/o, Philadelphia, Pa., 99, #3329

Snavely, Jacob, c/o, Md., 117, #4016

Snead, Philip, a/o, Richmond, Va., 24, #9573

Snead, Samuel, c/o, Pittsburgh, Pa., 79, #14689

Snead, Susan, Richmond, Va., 115, #2487

Snead, Susan A., Richmond, Va., 36A, #F6 V29

Snell, Henry, N.J., 74, #13228

Snelson, Sarah, a/o, Richmond, Va., 102, #6122

Snelson, Thomas, Mo., 44, #4239

Snelson, Thomas, Mo., 45, #4506

Snider, Catherine, Philadelphia, Pa., 62, #8706

Snider, Catherine, c/o, Philadelphia, Pa., 78, #14369

Snider, Elizabeth, a/o, Ga., 132, #9730

Snider, Eme, a/o, N.Y., 86, #16784

Snider, William D., c/o, Ky., 121, #7779

Snider, William D., g/o c/o, Ky.,
125, #1887
Snodgrass, William, —, 115,
#2453, card
Snodgrass, William, Jonesboro,
Tenn., 44, #4282
Snodgrass, William, a/o,
Jonesboro, Tenn., 24,
#2453
Snofford, John L., g/o c/o, Ill.,
126, #3949
Snow, Eleazer, a/o, Albany,
N.Y., 97, #2480
Snow, Frost and, N.C., 62,
#8812
Snow, Frost and, N.C., 72,
#12590
Snow, Frost and, N.C., 79,
#14747
Snow, John, Richmond, Va., 95,
#1148
Snow, Joshua, c/o, Maine, 74,
#13208
Snow, Mary, c/o, Boston,
Mass., 71, #12265
Snow, Samuel, c/o, R.I., 55,
#7099
Snow, William, w/o, Mass.
Militia, 141, #2274
Snowden, Aaron, Jacksonville,
Fla., 69, #10912
Snowden, Aaron, Tallahassee,
Fla., 84, #16141
Snowden, Aaron, w/o,
Jacksonville, Fla., 131,
#8535
Snowden, Ross, J., Philadelphia,
Pa., 109, #10529
Snukstar, Herril, Ore., 139,
#9033
Snyder, Elizabeth, c/o, Md., 79,
#14580

Snyder, Henry, w/o,
Philadelphia, Pa., 134,
#793
Snyder, John, e/o, —, 101,
#5217
Snyder, Peter, Pittsburgh, Pa.,
65, #9970
Snyder, Peter, c/o, Pittsburgh,
Pa., 100, #4450
Snyder, William, Cleveland,
Ohio, 127, #4382
Snyder, William, w/o, Albany,
N.Y., 98, #3035
Soap, Elizabeth, Nashville,
Tenn., 74, #13355
Soap, Elizabeth, Nashville,
Tenn., 80, #14955
Soap, Elizabeth, Nashville,
Tenn., 85, #16722
Soape, Elizabeth, La., 126,
#3369
Sockett, Sally, Richmond, Va.,
117, #4299
Sockett, Sally, Va., 117, #4443
Soesby, Danl., Ind., 52, #6303
Solerans, Maiano, Fremont's
Expedition, 121, #7726,
slip
Solms, Joseph, late PA,
Philadelphia, Pa., 123,
#9827
Soms, Joseph, PA, Philadelphia,
Pa., 83, #15747
Sonday, Adam, Philadelphia,
Pa., 41, #3447
Soper, Elias, Albany, N.Y., 142,
#3479
Soper, Jesse, Albany, N.Y., 54,
#6706
Sorrell, John, —, 95, #1207,
slip

Sorrell, Thomas, a/o, Richmond,
Va., 113, #1503

Sorrill, Hannah, Savannah, Ga.,
95, #1100

Souther (or Louther), Mary,
Mass., 24, #603

Southern, Gibson, c/o, S.C.,
118, #4938

Southern, Gipson, c/o, S.C.,
118, #4645

Southgate, Elijah, a/o, Mass.,
50, #5621

Southward, Andrew, a/o,
Hartford, Conn., 59, #8044

Southworth, George, Va., 41,
#3366

Southworth, Lucy, c/o,
Richmond, Va., 96, #1585

Sovern, Christopher, Va., 41,
#3526

Sowards, Rosanna, Cincinnati,
Ohio, 142, #5874

Sowell, Zadock, Ga., 132, #9806

Sowers, Mary, Richmond, Va.,
66, #10057

Soyars, James, w/o, Richmond,
Va., 69, #10879

Soyars, James, w/o, Richmond,
Va., 69, #10880

Soyars, Jane, e/o, Richmond,
Va., 136, #2548

Spafford, James W., g/o, Iowa,
116, #3611

Spain, Claiborn, c/o,
Fayetteville, N.C., 135,
#1945

Spain, Thomas, a/o, N.C., 92,
#127

Spain, William, w/o, N.C., 92,
#130

Spainhour, Elizabeth, a/o, N.C.,
100, #3982

Spalding, Abel, Ohio, 78,
#14515

Spalding, Samuel, w/o, Albany,
N.Y., 43, #3928

Spann, Charles, S.C., 119,
#5826, card

Spann, Charles, e/o, S.C., 24,
#5826

Sparks, James, a/o, Madison,
Ind., 125, #1914

Sparks, Leah, New York City,
64, #9223

Sparks, Lovina, Philadelphia,
Pa., 97, #2083

Sparks, Margaret, c/o, Albany,
N.Y., 140, #1121

Sparks, Mathew, Jackson,
Tenn., 24, #7556

Sparks, Mathew, a/o, Ill., 24,
#16105

Sparks, Solomon, c/o,
Philadelphia, Pa., 134,
#1102

Spaulding, Joseph, Vt., 70,
#12016

Spaulding, Samuel, Bellows
Falls, Vt., 63, #8967

Spear, Abigail, c/o, Mass., 88,
#17986

Spear, Abigail, e/o, Montpelier,
Vt., 117, #4154

Spear, Abraham, w/o, N.Y., 53,
#6540

Spear, John, Jacksonville, Fla.,
104, #7200

Spear, John, Jacksonville, Fla.,
97, #1935

Spear, John, La., 122, #8927

Spear, John, La., 127, #4228

Spear, John, La., 136, #2701

Spear, John, La., 133, #652

Spear, William, Pittsburgh, Pa.,
68, #10578, card
Spear, William, c/o, Pittsburgh,
Pa., 24, #10578
Spears, Samuel, w/o, Knoxville,
Tenn., 48, #5124
Spears, William C., Ohio, 111,
#464
Spedden, Ann, c/o, Md., 127,
#4312
Speer, Stewart, w/o, Pittsburgh,
Pa., 128, #5368
Spelts, John, Huntsville, Ala.,
90, #18645
Spence, Nancy, Richmond, Va.,
36A, #F6, card
Spence, Nancy, Richmond, Va.,
136, #2770
Spence, Nancy, Va., 122, #8265
Spencer, Ancel, Conn., 35,
#3177
Spencer, Anne, Albany, N.Y.,
122, #8801
Spencer, Daniel, Vt., 58, #7694
Spencer, Daniel, Vt., 66,
#10250
Spencer, David, Conn., 35, #408
Spencer, John, Mo., 115, #2452
Spencer, John, e/o, R.I., 111,
#719
Spencer, John, w/o, Pittsburgh,
Pa., 97, #2429
Spencer, John, w/o, Richmond,
Va., 99, #3157
Spencer, Mary, Richmond, Va.,
92, #19599
Spencer, Mfary, Va., 71, #12400
Spencer, Michael, w/o, Conn.,
100, #4291
Spencer, Molly, c/o, Richmond,
Va., 129, #6987

Spencer, Moses, Richmond, Va.,
24, #5448
Spencer, Moses, Richmond, Va.,
56, #7266
Spencer, Moses, Richmond, Va.,
119, #5448, slip
Spencer, Moses, Richmond, Va.,
45, #4483
Spencer, Orange, Philadelphia,
Pa., 48, #5133
Spencer, Reuben, w/o, N.H., 88,
#17929
Spencer, Samuel B., New York
City, 78, #14350
Spencer, Solomon, c/o, Maine,
63, #9097
Spencer, Thankful, c/o,
Pittsburgh, Pa., 76, #13936
Spencer, Timothy, w/o,
Richmond, Va., 42, #3575
Spencer, William, Morganton,
N.C., 129, #6246
Spencer, William W., Dubuque,
Iowa, 129, #7041
Spengeman, Henry, c/o, New
York City, 131, #8760
Sperry, Jacob, Conn., 35, #499
Sperry, Polly, c/o, Pittsburgh,
Pa., 115, #2597
Spicely, James, Va., 45, #4596
Spicer, Mary, Conn., 35, #192
Spiline, Thomas, N.H., 77,
#14204
Spiller, Louisa, Richmond, Va.,
36A, #F6, card
Spitfathom, John, w/o,
Richmond, Va., 60, #8277
Spitzer, John, Ill., 85, #16489
Spitzer, John, Ohio, 80, #14852
Spohn, John, a/o, Ohio, 110,
#11156

Spooner, Gardner, c/o,
    Montpelier, Vt., 102,
    #6065
Spraggins, William, Ga., 128,
    #6067
Spraggins, William, Ga., 129,
    #6688
Sprague, Frederick, w/o, Ohio,
    91, #19497
Sprague, James, Ohio, 67,
    #10452
Sprague, Lydia, a/o, Concord,
    N.H., 55, #6945
Sprague, Martha, a/o, Albany,
    N.Y., 112, #836
Spralding, James, Knoxville,
    Tenn., 74, #13243
Spring, John, La., 68, #10814
Springer, Benjamin, c/o,
    Pulaski, Tenn., 125, #1713
Springer, Bersheba, Albany,
    N.Y., 42, #3584
Springfield, Moses, N.C., 49,
    #5282
Springs, Micajah, N.C., 70,
    #12216
Squire, Noble, c/o, Albany,
    N.Y., 84, #16009
Squires, James, Pittsburgh, Pa.,
    105, #7748
St. George, Philip, —, 87,
    #17572, card
St. John, Jacob, w/o, Richmond,
    Va., 44, #4267
St. John, Louisiana, c/o, New
    York City, 135, #1746
Staats, John, c/o, Albany, N.Y.,
    67, #10426
Stacy, Abigail, Mass., 109,
    #10485
Stafford, Mary, Ky., 128, #5834
Stafford, Mary, Ky., 135, #1847

Stafford, Orpah, a/o, R.I., 118,
    #4841
Stagg, Daniel, Cincinnati, Ohio,
    125, #1583
Stahle, Barbara, Philadelphia,
    Pa., 96, #1389
Staley, George, w/o, Albany,
    N.Y., 75, #13506
Staley, Margaret, a/o,
    Richmond, Va., 24, #6148
Staley, Margaret, a/o,
    Richmond, Va., 103, #6369
Staley, Peter, Va., 39, #3031
Staley, Peter, w/o, Richmond,
    Va., 25, #3031
Stalker, Achsah, e/o, Albany,
    N.Y., 118, #5022
Stalker, John, Vt., 82, #15505
Stamp, Daniel, Albany, N.Y.,
    96, #1828
Stamp, Daniel, Albany, N.Y.,
    98, #2952
Stamp, Daniel, Albany, N.Y.,
    100, #3778
Stamps, Daniel, Nashville,
    Tenn., 72, #12528
Stanbury, H., —, 120, #6407,
    card
Standefer, Benjamin, w/o, E.
    Tenn., 55, #7144
Standridge, James, w/o, S.C.,
    61, #8533
Stanfield, James, c/o, Knoxville,
    Tenn., 107, #9416
Stank, Caleb, w/o, Pittsburgh,
    Pa., 51, #5892
Stanley, Page, Mo., 54, #6739
Stanley, Page, Mo., 59, #8153
Stanley, Page, Mo., 64, #9450
Stanley, Page, Mo., 103, #6782
Stannard, Eliaksim, c/o, Albany,
    N.Y., 79, #14712

Stedman, Hannah, a/o, Boston, Mass., 64, #9678

Stedman, Selah, e/o, Albany, N.Y., 99, #3454

Steed, John, c/o, N.C. Militia, 92, #19698

Steedman, Ansel G., g/o c/o, S.C., 136, #2619

Steel, Ceilia, a/o, Richmond, Va., 131, #8850

Steel, Levinia, Conn., 35, #408

Steel, Mary, c/o, Philadelphia, Pa., 25, #1151

Steel Sr., Francis, c/o, N.C., 25, #14579

Steele, Amon, w/o & c/o, 37th Inf., 86, #17104

Steele, Amon, w/o & c/o, 37th Inf., 86, #17105

Steele, Charles W., Cananadaigua, N.Y., 143, #7280

Steele, David, Richmond, Va., 45, #4462

Steele, Hannah, a/o, Knoxville, Tenn., 136, #2851

Steele, John, e/o, Albany, N.Y., 117, #4297

Steele, Ruth, e/o, Conn., 35, #5708

Steele, Samuel, E. Tenn., 64, #9622

Steele, Samuel, Knoxville, Tenn., 69, #10997

Steele, Samuel, Knoxville, Tenn., 100, #4038

Steele, Samuel, Mo., 78, #14494

Steele, Samuel, a/o, N.H., 69, #11006

Steele, Sarah, c/o, N.J., 84, #16163

Steenburgh, Katharine, c/o, Albany, N.Y., 91, #19361

Steerman, William W., w/o, Ky., 90, #18891

Steet (now Bray), Narcissa, Ind., 123, #9244

Steffey, Rosannah, Richmond, Va., 36A, #F6, card

Stegall, John, w/o, N.C., 41, #3477

Steigerwaldt, Frederick, c/o, N.C., 112, #953

Stephen, Jacob, w/o, Ohio, 54, #6612

Stephens, Jacob, Mo., 62, #8723

Stephens, Jane, e/o, N.C., 110, #4

Stephens, Joseph L., Ky., 43, #3921

Stephens, Joseph L., Ky., 52, #6239

Stephens, Joseph L., Ky., 100, #4003

Stephens, Mary, Ind., 77, #14203

Stephens, Moses, Albany, N.Y., 40, #3237

Stephens, James, w/o, Portsmouth, N.H., 126, bet. #3592 & #$3602

Stephens (or Stevens), Phineas, Pittsburgh, Pa., 98, #3098, card

Stephens Sr., John, c/o, Ky., 90, #18693

Stephensen, James, c/o, Philadelphia, Pa., 51, #5857

Stephenson, Abiather, a/o, Albany, N.Y., 116, #3094

Stevens, Thomas, w/o,
Philadelphia, Pa., 85,
#16721
Stevens, William, c/o, N.Y., 67,
#10500
Stevens, John A., PA, New York
City, 102, #6052
Stevenson, Charles, Ohio, 64,
#9288
Stevenson, Margaret, a/o,
Cincinnati, Ohio, 130,
#7411
Stevenson, Obadiah, c/o,
Pittsburgh, Pa., 124, #1113
Stevenson (now Bridwell), Sally,
S.C., 110, #11185
Steward, Martha, Richmond, Va.,
136, #2865
Steward, Marvin, Philadelphia,
Pa., 112, #1252
Steward, Marvin, Pittsburgh,
Pa., 136, #2848
Steward, Moses, Albany, N.Y.,
53, #6457
Stewart, Asa C., w/o, Mich., 63,
#9060
Stewart, Calvin, Vt., 63, #8888
Stewart 2nd, Charles, c/o,
Albany, N.Y., 97, #2085
Stewart, Elizabeth, Richmond,
Va., 134, #1301
Stewart, George, w/o, S.C., 109,
#10805
Stewart, Jacob, Mo., 48, #5227
Stewart, James, Ga., 67, #10537
Stewart, James, Richmond, Va.,
47, #4953
Stewart, John, Ark., 47, #4927
Stewart, John, Jackson, Tenn.,
48, #5193
Stewart, John, Richmond, Va.,
103, #7027

Stewart, John, Richmond, Va.,
98, #2924
Stewart, John, Va., 75, #13599
Stewart, Lucretia, a/o, Albany,
N.Y., 134, #1496
Stewart, Lucy, e/o, Richmond,
Va., 126, #3196
Stewart, Luzana, Knoxville,
Tenn., 131, #8804
Stewart, Margaert, e/o, N.J.,
112, #850
Stewart, Margaret, N.J., 45,
#4517
Stewart, Nathan E., Albany,
N.Y., 116, #3700
Stewart, Thomas, Philadelphia,
Pa., 62, #8841
Stewart, Thomas B., w/o,
Pittsburgh, Pa., 75, #13473
Stewart, William, Ga., 45,
#4611
Stewart, William, Ky., 66,
#10149
Stewart, William, Richmond,
Va., 68, #10779
Stewart, William, Richmond,
Va., 46, #4844
Stewart, William, Richmond,
Va., 47, #4877
Stewart, William, Savannah,
Ga., 39, #2942
Stewart, William, Va., 67,
#10317
Stewart, William, a/o, Va., 121,
#6827
Stewart (formerly Lewis), Sarah
A., Richmond, Va., 138,
#4742
Stichter, John W., Philadelphia,
Pa., 143, #6899
Stickland, Mary, c/o, Conn.,
130, #7353

Stickles, Jemima, c/o, Albany,
N.Y., 123, #9643
Stickney, Levi, a/o, Boston,
Mass., 71, #12465
Stiff, Molly, a/o, Va., 81,
#15183
Stiles, Candace, c/o, Albany,
N.Y., 102, #5721
Stiles, Hezekiah, Ohio, 64,
#9214
Stiles, Job, w/o, Philadelphia,
Pa., 85, #16614
Stiles, Lewis, a/o, Albany, N.Y.,
85, #16607
Stiles, Martin, Albany, N.Y.,
65, #9771
Stills, John, Mass., 64, #9157
Stillwagon, Jacob, w/o,
Philadelphia, Pa., 66,
#10256
Stillwell, Aaron, g/o c/o,
Madison, Ind., 125, #2473
Stilwell, Aaron, c/o, Ky., 120,
#6672
Stilwell, Joseph, c/o,
Philadelphia, Pa., 87,
#17374
Stimcipher, Joseph, Knoxville,
Tenn., 50, #5592
Stimpson, Thomas, w/o,
Boston, Mass., 113, #1769
Stinard, Oglesbery D., New York
City, 40, #3184
Stinson, David, Bellows Falls,
Vt., 63, #8967
Stinson, John, e/o, Fayetteville,
N.C., 124, #911
Stinson, Susana, a/o, Vt., 81,
#15190
Stith, Joseph, w/o, Ky., 62,
#8793

Stitzer, Henry, Philadelphia, Pa.,
91, #19241
Stober, Valentine, c/o,
Philadelphia, Pa., 87,
#17434
Stock, Judith, Albany, N.Y.,
106, #8408
Stockbridge, Mary, c/o, Maine,
73, #12769
Stocker, William, a/o, Albany,
N.Y., 132, #9152
Stocking, Elizabeth, c/o,
Boston, Mass., 121, #6791
Stockman, Jonathan, c/o,
Boston, Mass., 101, #4858
Stoddard, David, D.C., 92,
#19850
Stoddard, Lucy, c/o, Mass., 137,
#4017
Stoddard, Nathan, a/o, Conn.,
38, #F1825
Stoddard, Philo, w/o,
Burlington, Vt., 126,
#2902
Stoddard, Robert, c/o, Conn.,
92, #182
Stoel, David, a/o, Albany, N.Y.,
109, #10615
Stokely, Elizabeth, c/o,
Wheeling, Va., 130, #7843
Stokes, Jacob, g/o c/o,
Cleveland, Ohio, 129,
#6581
Stokes, Louisa, La., 118, #4667
Stokes, Massey, Ill., 130,
#7769
Stokes, Samuel, Richmond, Va.,
43, #3828
Stole, Charles P., W. Tenn., 84,
#15947, card
Stoll, Otto, Mass., 25, #3421

Stoll, Urban, w/o, New York
City, 134, #1499
Stone, Abigail, c/o, Maine, 116,
#3689
Stone, Abigail, c/o, Montpelier,
Vt., 107, #9136
Stone, Abner C., c/o, Boston,
Mass., 64, #9416
Stone, Alpheus, Mass., 133,
#246
Stone, Betsey, Philadelphia, Pa.,
125, #1649
Stone, Daniel, c/o, Conn., 107,
#9219
Stone, Ezekiel, a/o, N.H., 87,
#17677
Stone, Henry, w/o, N.Y. Militia,
136, #3187
Stone, Jacob, S.C., 59, #8171
Stone, Lucrecia, —, 136, #----,
slip
Stone, Nathaniel, —, 45, #4484
Stone, Richard, Philadelphia,
Pa., 25, #1554
Stone, Richard, Philadelphia,
Pa., 113, #1554, card
Stone, Rowland, Ky., 40, #3185
Stone, Rowland, Ky., 48, #5170
Stone, Solomon, Knoxville,
Tenn., 39, #3013
Stone, Timothy, Bellows Falls,
Vt., 50, #5771
Stone, Warren, Calif., 131,
#8798
Stonebraker, Sebastian, Ind.,
134, #1505, card
Stonebraker, Sebastian, e/o,
Madison, Ind., 25, #1505
Stoner, Philip, w/o, Ohio, 47,
#5024
Storer, Henry, Conn., 38,
#F1835

Storer, Henry, a/o, Conn., 35, #-
Storer, William, a/o, Conn.,
100, #3782
Storm, Isaac, Albany, N.Y., 61,
#8534
Storm, Rose Ann, Philadelphia,
Pa., 114, #2102
Story, John, Ky., 25, #9565
Story, John, Ky., 107, #9565,
card
Story, Molly, Ohio, 90, #18877
Story, William H., Mo., 115,
#2709
Story, William H., Mo., 126,
#3085
Stoudermire, William S.,
Mobile, Ala., 127, #4375
Stough, Martin, a/o, N.C., 122,
#8521
Stoughton, Flora, c/o, Conn.,
35, #1842
Stouseberger, Maria M., Va., 71,
#12227
Stout, Anne, Ky., 55, #6936
Stout, Elijah, Ky., 25, #8385
Stout, John, a/o, Philadelphia,
Pa., 82, #15432
Stover, Abraham, c/o, New
Albany, Ind., 136, #3034
Stow, Ichabod, w/o, Mass., 69,
#10870
Stow, John, Conn., 35, #806
Stow, Joshua, Conn., 70,
#12172
Stow, Mary, c/o, Mass., 120,
#6607
Stowe, Daniel, Albany, N.Y.,
63, #9042
Stowers, Lewis, Ga., 132,
#9667, card
Stowers, Lewis, e/o, Ga., 25,
#9667

Stoyer, John T., Baltimore, Md.,
113, #1830
Stoyer, John T., Md., 102,
#6079
Stoyer, John T., a/o, Md., 126,
#3442
Strader, John, N.C., 107, #9191
Strader, John, N.C., 59, #7986
Strader, John, N.C., 70, #11064
Stradley, John R., Morganton,
N.C., 137, #4193
Strahorn, David, w/o, Ill., 85,
#16725
Strain, Robert, c/o, Ohio, 64,
#9131
Strait, Nathan, a/o, R.I., 71,
#12402
Strange, Amos, w/o, S.C., 94,
#248
Strange, David, Richmond, Va.,
62, #8737
Strape, Susannah, a/o, N.C., 86,
#16957
Strattan, Hussey, a/o, Albany,
N.Y., 94, #334
Stratton, Joel, g/o, Cincinnati,
Ohio, 130, #7848
Stratton, Joel, g/o c/o,
Cincinnati, Ohio, 132,
#9572
Stratton, Joel, g/o c/o,
Cincinnati, Ohio, 139,
#6840
Stratton, Lois, Maine, 104,
#7667
Stratton, Samuel, Albany, N.Y.,
40, #3205
Stratton, Samuel, w/o, Mass.,
88, #18114
Stratton, Stephen, New York
City, 66, #10309

Strauss, Charles, Indianapolis,
Ind., 143, #6975
Strayhorn, John, c/o,
Fayetteville, N.C., 94,
#662
Streater, David, Calif., 126,
#3907
Street, David, Richmond, Va.,
61, #8636
Street, David, Va., 85, #16539
Streeter, Benjamin, N.Y., 97,
#2419
Streeter, Benjamin, a/o, Albany,
N.Y., 25, #2419
Streeter, David, New York City,
117, #4404
Streeter, Joel, c/o, Vt., 61,
#8502
Streeter, Joel, c/o, Vt., 69,
#10930
Stregel, Nicholas, w/o, Ga., 49,
#5459
Stregel, Sarah, a/o, Ga., 130,
#7303
Stribling, Mary, Miss., 133,
#59
Stribling, Samuel, a/o, Ky., 120,
#5934
Strickland, Anna, Conn., 96,
#1460
Strickland, Jesse, g/o c/o, Ill.,
127, #4591
Strickland, Joseph, a/o,
Pittsburgh, Pa., 114, #2293
Strickling, Alexander, Ohio, 63,
#9114
Striker, Abraham, w/o, N.Y., 78,
#14503
Strimback, John, Mo., 123,
#349
Strimback, John, Mo., 126,
#3905

Strimback, John, Ore., 141,
#2583
Stringers, William F., w/o & c/o,
Va. Milita, 75, #13716
Stringers, William F., w/o & c/o,
Va. Milita, 75, #13717
Stringers, William F., w/o & c/o,
Va. Milita, 75, #13718
Stringfellow, Nancy, Ga., 131,
#8296
Stringfellow, Nancy, Ga., 138,
#4745
Strobeck, Adam, N.Y., 99,
#3353, card
Strobeck, Adam, c/o, Albany,
N.Y., 25, #3353
Strobeck, Adam, c/o, Albany,
N.Y., 99, #3355
Strobridge, George, w/o,
Albany, N.Y., 64, #9316
Strolel, Albert, w/o, S.C., 69,
#10999
Strong, Charles, —, 101,
#4732, card
Strong, Charles, Ga., 44, #4399
Strong, Charles, Ga., 64, #9129
Strong, Charles, Ga., 75,
#13582
Strong, Charles, Ga., 82,
#15409
Strong, Elnathan, w/o, Albany,
N.Y., 132, #9741
Strong, Seth, Conn., 35, #727
Stropes, Adam, Ind., 52, #6304
Strother, Benjamin, Richmond,
Va., 97, #2439
Stroud, Delilah, c/o, N.C., 96,
#1648
Stroud, Hampton, La., 51, #5882
Stroud, Hampton, La., 70,
#12039
Stroud, William, Ga., 25, #6218

Stroud, Willilam, —, 52, #6218,
card
Strouse, Henry, Ill., 56, #7337
Strugis, Aaron, c/o, Ill., 25,
#18434
Stryker, Simeon, e/o, N.J., 110,
#314
Stuart, Alexander, Md., 105,
#8300
Stuart, Damaris, Boston, Mass.,
62, #8779
Stuart, Caleb, —, 90, between
#18563 & #18575, card
Stubbs, Lewis, S.C., 65, #9968
Stubbs, William, S.C., 48,
#5205
Stubbs, William, S.C., 51,
#5958
Studwell, Henry, a/o, Albany,
N.Y., 107, #9627
Sturgis, Aaron, Albany, N.Y.,
71, #12301
Sturgis, Aaron, Ill., 89, #18434,
card
Sturgis, Aaron, Ill., 75, #13649
Sturgis, Aaron, Ill., 83, #15601
Sturgis, Aaron, c/o, Ill., 88,
#17880
Sturgis, Jediadiah, w/o, Ohio,
82, #15262
Sturtevant, Sarah, a/o,
Portsmouth, Maine, 135,
#1773
Sturtivant, Hannah, Burlington,
Vt., 101, #4794
Sucher (formerly Armbuster),
Sophia, D.C., 133, #9935
Sucher (formerly Armbuster),
Sophia, D.C., 133, #9936
Suggs, George, c/o, Richmond,
Va., 134, #1277

Sullivan, Bridget, New York
City, 134, #1291
Sullivan, Mary, Ky., 135, #2064
Sullivan, Mary, Ky., 139, #8027
Sullivan, Mary, Ky., 140, #9474
Sullivan, Mary, Ky., 142, #5629
Sullivan, Milly, c/o, Ga., 120,
#6422
Sullivan, Peter, w/o, Ky., 75,
#13402
Sullivan (formerly Black), Ellen,
Fairfield, Iowa, 143, #6824
Sumerlin, Winburn, w/o, N.C.,
87, #17540
Summeford, William, S.C., 45,
#4645
Summerford, William, S.C., 64,
#9451
Summerford, William, S.C., 67,
#10313
Summers, John, w/o, Ky., 98,
#2624
Summers, Sarah, S.C., 119,
#5136
Summers, Sarah, S.C., 131,
#8761
Sumner, Adam, Philadelphia,
Pa., 80, #14954
Sunderland, George, D.C., 63,
#9086
Sunderland, Samuel,
Philadelphia, Pa., 75,
#13631
Sunderland, Samuel, c/o,
Burlington, Vt., 123,
#9037
Supler, Rachel, a/o, Pittsburgh,
Pa., 122, #8723
Surber, Jacob, Ohio, 116,
#3311, card
Surber, Jacob, c/o, Cincinnati,
Ohio, 25, #3311

Sutherland, Daniel, Ark., 62,
#8777
Sutherland, John, Philadelphia,
Pa., 25, #14030
Sutherland, John, Pittsburgh,
Pa., 77, #14030, card
Sutherland, Sarah, Ky., 119,
#5461
Sutherland, Sarah, Ky., 135,
#2357
Sutley, James, Ga., 48, #5092
Sutley, James, Ga., 57, #7613
Sutley, James, Ga., 66, #10091
Sutley, James, w/o, Ga., 111,
#543
Sutton, Benjamin, a/o, Ky., 25,
#3046
Sutton, John, Philadelphia, Pa.,
91, #19392
Sutton, John, w/o, Cincinnati,
Ohio, 117, #3969
Suydam, Hendrick, a/o, N.J.,
117, #4497
Swain, John, w/o, N.J., 55,
#7203
Swain, Mildred P., Mo., 133,
#47
Swallow, Andrew, Nashville,
Tenn., 45, #4464
Swallow, Andrew, Nashville,
Tenn., 95, #1141, card
Swallow, Andrew, w/o,
Nashville, Tenn., 25,
#1141
Swallow, Catharine, Nashville,
Tenn., 118, #4643, card
Swallow, Catherine, a/o,
Nashville, Tenn., 25,
#4643
Swan, Charles, Wheeling, Va.,
79, #14685, card

Swan, Charles, w/o, Wheeling, Va., 25, #14685

Swan, John, Albany, N.Y., 49, #5365

Swan, John, Albany, N.Y., 56, #7245

Swan, John, a/o, N.H., 25, #15990

Swan, Thomas, c/o, Nashville, Tenn., 117, #4226

Swan, William, Ga., 55, #6932

Swan, William, Ga., 66, #10106

Swan, William, Ga., 78, #14267

Swan, William, Ga., 86, #17276

Swan, James, PA, Baltimore, Md., 115, #2516

Swann, Elijah, Ga., 133, #538

Swann, Thomas, g/o c/o, Nashville, Tenn., 129, #6964

Swark, Margaret, Ky., 125, #1656

Swart, Cornelius, g/o c/o, Conn., 37, #F1820

Swart, Elizabeth, Albany, N.Y., 133, #702

Swartwood, Barnardus, Philadelphia, Pa., 68, #10697

Swartz, Sarah, Philadelphia, Pa., 129, #6805

Sweallow, Andrew, Nashville, Tenn., 42, #3789

Swearingen, Thomas, e/o, Miss., 109, #10872

Swearingen, Van, c/o, Ky., 58, #7890

Sweeney, John, Albany, N.Y., 135, #2459

Sweeney, John, w/o, Albany, N.Y., 124, #573

Sweeny, Joseph, Philadelphia, Pa., 64, #9501

Sweeny, Joseph, Philadelphia, Pa., 74, #13132

Sweeny, Joseph, Philadelphia, Pa., 81, #15056

Sweet, Priscilla, a/o, Portsmouth, N.H., 74, #13046

Sweeting, Nathaniel, c/o, Albany, N.Y., 85, #16339

Sweetland, Samuel, c/o, Burlington, Vt., 50, #5731

Swetland, Benjamin, c/o, Albany, N.Y., 114, #1938

Swett, John, w/o, Maine, 101, #5249

Swett, Stockman, Concord, N.H., 97, #1982

Swift, Ann, Philadelphia, Pa., 101, #5263

Swift, Lucy, Maine, 114, #1932, card

Swindle, John, w/o, Ky., 73, #12902

Swiney, Martha, Ky., 140, #907

Swingle, George, a/o, Ky., 125, #1603

Swingle Sr., George, Ky., 42, #3740

Swisshelm, John, w/o, Pittsburgh, Pa., 115, #2697

Sword, Michael, Richmond, Va., 77, #13982

Sword, Michael, Va., 46, #4733

Sword, Michael, Va., 71, #12413

Sword, Michael, e/o, Richmond, Va., 100, #3963

Sydars, Solomon, Va., 46, #4744, card

Sykes, Ashleel, a/o, Vt., 79,
#14628
Sykes, John, Albany, N.Y., 87,
#17495
Sykes, John, Richmond, Va.,
69, #10902
Sykes, John, Richmond, Va.,
45, #4590
Sykes, Lucy, Albany, N.Y., 121,
#6877
Sylvester, Esther, a/o, Maine,
98, #3018
Sylvester, Peter, c/o, Mass., 52,
#6230
Sylvester, Thomas, c/o, Maine,
54, #6731
Symonds, Jane B., Mass., 137,
#3644
Syms, John, Albany, N.Y., 105,
#7688

T

Tabor, Betsy, Vt., 71, #12264
Tabor, William, —, 125, #1726,
card
Tacum, John, Ind., 64, #9655
Taft, Ebener, w/o, Mass., 51,
#5866
Tager, Susannah, Philadelphia,
Pa., 96, #1390
Tainter, Stephen, Wisc., 79,
#14657
Taladay, Solomon, w/o,
Philadelphia, Pa., 61,
#8473
Talbert, Benjamin, Ga., 78,
#14293
Talbot, Isham, a/o, Ky., 92,
#19559
Talbot, John L., La., 44, #4321
Talbot, John L., La., 49, #5384

Talbot, Joseph, w/o, Maine, 95,
#785
Talcott, Phineas, c/o, Conn., 35,
#3873
Taliaferro, John, Va., 70,
#11153
Talley, John, Nashville, Tenn.,
96, #1771, card
Tallmadge, Rhobe, Albany,
N.Y., 64, #9297
Tallmadge, Rhobe, Albany,
N.Y., 69, #10875
Tallmidge, Rhobe, Albany,
N.Y., 50, #5673
Tallow, Thomas, w/o, N.C., 122,
#8746
Tally, John, w/o, Jackson,
Tenn., 25, #1771
Talmadge, Joel, w/o, Albany,
N.Y., 40, #3277
Talmage, Elisha, Conn., 35,
#1401
Tamer, Michael, c/o, Ga., 113,
#1523
Tankersly, Charles, c/o, Ga.,
132, #9466
Tanner, Abraham, Va., 80,
#14761
Tanner, Esther, Albany, N.Y.,
100, #4363
Tanner, Michael, Ga., 51, #5964
Tapp, Vincent, Va., 68, #10705
Tappan, John, New York City,
102, #6052 V#59
Tarlton, Eleanor, e/o, Ky., 95,
#961
Tarrant, Elisabeth, c/o,
Richmond, Va., 36A, #F3
V45
Tarrant, Osiller R., Jonesboro,
Tenn., 73, #12928

Tarry, Sarah C., Richmond, Va.,
130, #7486
Tart, Thomas, N.C., 47, #4961
Tate, Evan P., g/o c/o, Ga., 128,
#6068
Tatum, Mary, Nashville, Tenn.,
135, #1821
Tayler, Benjamin, w/o, Ky., 82,
#15236
Taylor, 1st Lt., w/o, 1st
Dragoons, 134, #714
Taylor, 1st Lt. O. H. P., w/o, 1st
Dragoons, 135, #2081
Taylor, Abraham, Philadelphia,
Pa., 44, #4319
Taylor, Abraham, Philadelphia,
Pa., 50, #5596
Taylor, Adam, w/o, Ky., 135,
#2456
Taylor, Anna, Richmond, Va.,
115, #2593
Taylor, Bartholomew, Ky., 41,
#3376
Taylor, Benjamin, Ky., 39,
#3098
Taylor, Benjamin, Ky., 57,
#7576
Taylor, Benjamin, Ky., 62,
#8769
Taylor, Benjamin, Ky., 67,
#10540
Taylor, Benjamin, Mo., 48,
#5192
Taylor, Benjamin, Mo., 57,
#7574
Taylor, Benjamin, Mo., 98,
#2933
Taylor, Benjamin, w/o, Ky., 94,
#259
Taylor, Capt. O. H. P., w/o, 1st
Dragoons, 132, #9517

Taylor, Chancey, w/o, 29th Inf.,
105, #7843
Taylor, Christopher, c/o, Md.,
61, #8469
Taylor, Christopher, c/o, Md.,
76, #13790
Taylor, Edmund, Ky., 45, #4647
Taylor, Edmund, Ky., 67,
#10539
Taylor, Eli, Conn., 35, #663
Taylor, Elias, Maine, 102,
#5712
Taylor, Elisha, g/o c/o, Conn.,
37, #F1826
Taylor, Eliud, Conn., 35, #21
Taylor, Elizabeth, c/o, Boston,
Mass., 103, #6768
Taylor, Gamabiel, Albany, N.Y.,
65, #9739
Taylor, Henry, Pittsburgh, Pa.,
61, #8443
Taylor, Isaaac, Conn., 35, #967
Taylor, Isaac, Knoxville, Tenn.,
136, #3011
Taylor, Isaac W., Ind., 54,
#6660
Taylor, Isaac W., Madison, Ind.,
101, #4619
Taylor, Isaac W., Madison, Ind.,
101, #4771
Taylor, James, Ohio, 123,
#9321
Taylor, James, a/o, Richmond,
Va., 103, #6943
Taylor, James, c/o, Ohio, 25,
#9321
Taylor, James, w/o, Ohio, 101,
#4620
Taylor, James, w/o, W. Tenn.,
64, #9379
Taylor, Jeremiah, S.C., 71,
#12259

Taylor, Job, Albany, N.Y., 90,
#18595
Taylor, John, Conn., 35, #1399
Taylor, John, Mo., 65, #9864
Taylor, John, Mo., 66, #10046
Taylor, John, a/o, Portsmouth,
N.H., 74, #13041
Taylor, John, a/o, Pittsburgh,
Pa., 136, #3250
Taylor, John, a/o, Portsmouth,
N.H., 74, #13042
Taylor, John M., w/o,
Philadelphia, Pa., 95,
#1043
Taylor, Joice, c/o, Mass., 134,
#820
Taylor, Jonathan, Conn., 35,
#1400
Taylor, Joseph, Ky., 48, #5098
Taylor, Joseph, Ky., 78, #14315
Taylor, Joseph, Ky., 86, #17268
Taylor, Joseph, Ky., 89, #18162
Taylor, Joseph, Ky., 90, #18949
Taylor, Joseph, c/o, Ky., 135,
#2289
Taylor, Josiah, w/o, Albany,
N.Y., 64, #9479
Taylor, Leonard, Vt., 64, #9327
Taylor, Leonard, w/o, Ky., 89,
#18351
Taylor, Lt./Bvt. Capt. O. H. P.,
w/o, 1st Dragoons, 136,
#3182
Taylor, Lydia, Albany, N.Y., 62,
#8675
Taylor, Mary, c/o, Boston,
Mass., 100, #4410
Taylor, Mary E. J., g/o, N.C.,
110, #11174
Taylor, Michael, Cincinnati,
Ohio, 141, #2283

Taylor, Nancy, Richmond, Va.,
36A, #F4 V24
Taylor, Nancy, Richmond, Va.,
36A, #F4 V13
Taylor, Nathan, c/o, Pittsburgh,
Pa., 131, #8719
Taylor, Nathan, g/o c/o,
Pittsburgh, Pa., 127, #4161
Taylor, Pheraby, Fayetteville,
N.C., 132, #9571
Taylor, Philip W., Ky., 81,
#15033
Taylor, Polly, alias Mary Ann,
Wheeling, Va., 131, #8722
Taylor, Pvt. William, w/o, Va.
Milita, 113, #1572
Taylor, Rhoda, h/o, Pittsburgh,
Pa., 102, #5408
Taylor, Richard, Richmond, Va.,
56, #7360
Taylor, Richard, Richmond, Va.,
54, #6647
Taylor, Richard, Va., 46, #4759
Taylor, Richard, Va., 80,
#14776
Taylor, Richard, Va., 85,
#16538
Taylor, Richard, a/o, Richmond,
Va., 97, #2368
Taylor, Sarah, Nashville, Tenn.,
132, #9636
Taylor, Sarah, Philadelphia, Pa.,
99, #3206
Taylor, Sarah, c/o, N.C., 99,
#3491
Taylor, Sibilla, Albany, N.Y.,
83, #15731
Taylor, Spencer, w/o, Conn.,
119, #5184
Taylor, Susan Ann, New York
City, 138, #5019

Taylor, Susannah, Richmond,
Va., 36A, #F6, card
Taylor, Thomas, Philadelphia,
Pa., 107, #9538
Taylor, Thomas, Richmond, Va.,
105, #8254
Taylor, Thomas, Va., 83,
#15882
Taylor, Thomas, Va., 100,
#4369
Taylor, Thomas, Wheeling, Va.,
78, #14327
Taylor, Thomas, a/o, Richmond,
Va., 113, #1546
Taylor, William, Richmond, Va.,
56, #7262
Taylor, William, Richmond, Va.,
66, #10055
Taylor, William, Richmond, Va.,
45, #4589
Taylor, William, a/o,
Fayetteville, N.C., 95,
#1337
Taylor, William, c/o, S.C., 112,
#1065
Taylor, William, w/o, Va., 74,
#13313
Taylor, Z., —, 123, #15, card
Taylor, Zachariah, —, 56,
#7263, card
Taylor, Zachariah, —, 77,
#14004, card
Taylor, Zachariah, Richmond,
Va., 25, #14004
Taylor, Zachariah, Richmond,
Va., 25, #7263
Taylor 2d, John, Albany, N.Y.,
60, #8297
Taylor Sr., John, e/o, N.C., 88,
#18090
Teal, Hannah, Conn., 35, #423

Teal, Nathan, w/o, Albany, N.Y.,
70, #11146
Teall, Joseph, w/o, Albany,
N.Y., 41, #3470
Teaney, Daniel, w/o, Va., 70,
#11074
Tearney, Elizabeth, N.C., 79,
#14745
Tearney, Elizabeth, a/o, N.C.,
88, #17887
Teater (now Barton), Elizabeth,
Ky., 110, #11087
Teeple, Jacob, w/o, Ind., 57,
#7452
Temple, John, g/o, Mass., 25,
#13156
Temple, Robert, —, 63, #9054
Temple, Robert, Vt., 64, #9241
Temple, Samuel, a/o, Va., 121,
#6749
Temple, Robert, Agent, Boston,
Mass., 86, #17228
Temple, Robert, late PA, Vt.,
127, #4027
Temple, Robert, PA, —, 87,
#17551
Temple, Robert, PA, Mass., 91,
#19143
Templeman, Samuel, —, 86,
#1685-, card
Templeton, Isaac, Philadelphia,
Pa., 72, #12531
Templeton, James, Philadelphia,
Pa., 77, #14053
Templeton, James, Philadelphia,
Pa., 87, #17437
Templeton, James, Philadelphia,
Pa., 87, #17483
Templeton, James, Philadelphia,
Pa., 94, #240
Templeton, Robert, Madison,
Ind., 48, #5169

Templeton, Samuel, c/o,
Richmond, Va., 25, #16855

Ten Eyck, Sarah, a/o, Trenton,
N.J., 92, #19907

Tench, William, w/o, Va., 78,
#14237

Tenmill, William A., Ga., 89,
#18506

Tennille, William A., Ga., 97,
#2401

Tenny, Temperance, Albany,
N.Y., 75, #13535

Tension, Philip, w/o, Albany,
N.Y., 43, #3997

Terett, Capt. Burdett A., w/o, 1st
Dragoons, 102, #5396

Terrell, Mary E., Richmond, Va.,
36A, #F2 V1

Terrett, Capt. Burdett A., c/o, 1st
Dragoons, 103, #6972

Terrett, Capt. Burdett A., c/o, 1st
Dragoons, 105, #8077

Terrett, Capt. Burdett A., c/o, 1st
Dragoons, 106, #8643

Terrett, Capt. Burdett A., w/o,
1st Dragoons, 103, #6596

Terrett, Capt. Burdett A., w/o,
1st Dragoons, 94, #684

Terrett, Capt. Burdett A., w/o,
1st Dragoons, 100, #4474

Terrett, Capt. Burdette A., w/o,
1st Dragoons, 98, #2654

Terrett, Capt. Burdette A., w/o,
1st Dragoons, 99, #3310

Terrett, Capt. Burtette A., w/o,
1st Dragoons, 96, #1575

Terrill, Dorothy, c/o, Ohio, 98,
#2573

Terrill, Mary E., Richmond, Va.,
36A, #F2 V38

Terrill, Thomas, c/o, Mass.,
136, #3311

Terrillager, James, Albany,
N.Y., 25, #6030

Terry, John, Richmond, Va.,
100, #4374

Terry, Joseph, Ga., 25, #10295

Terry, Nancy, Conn., 132,
#9467

Terry, Nathaniel, w/o, Ky., 41,
#3479

Terry, Sarah C., Richmond, Va.,
25, #9271

Terry, Sarah C., Richmond, Va.,
25, #1509

Terry, Thomas, c/o, N.C., 70,
#12094

Teters, Dicy M., Ill., 120, #6265

Tewilliger, James, Albany, N.Y.,
120, #6030, card

Thacher, Amasa, Albany, N.Y.,
55, #6974

Thacker, Joel, w/o, Nashville,
Tenn., 122, #8577

Thacker, Reuben, w/o, Ky., 138,
#4712

Thalchis, Samuel, Albany, N.Y.,
103, #6680, card

Tharp, Eliza Ann, Richmond,
Va., 102, #6078

Tharp, Hannah, c/o, Ohio, 110,
#11049

Tharp, John, a/o, Richmond,
Va., 99, #3183

Tharp, John, c/o, Ky., 62,
#8865

Tharp, Perry, w/o, Ky., 100,
#4494

Thatcher, John, Philadelphia,
Pa., 74, #13367

Thatcher, Obadiah, c/o,
Philadelphia, Pa., 52,
#6129

Thayer, Betsey, a/o, N.H., 91,
#19126
Thayer, Esther, c/o, Boston,
Mass., 57, #7630
Thayer, Hannah, a/o, Maine,
126, #3968
Thayer, Isaac, Bellows Falls,
Vt., 63, #8967
Thayer, Jane, c/o, Albany, N.Y.,
134, #1311
Thayer, John S., Boston, Mass.,
123, #9156
Thayer, Joseph, w/o, Pittsburgh,
Pa., 54, #6658
Thayer, Mary, Albany, N.Y.,
118, #5001
Thayer, Mary, Albany, N.Y.,
118, #5015
Thayer, Sarah, Mass., 77,
#14099
Thayer, Welthy, Vt., 67, #10350
Theobold, James, w/o, Ky., 77,
#14065
Theurman, Ernest L., New
Orleans, La., 133, #701,
card
Thomas, Abraham, w/o, N.Y.
Militia, 137, #4102
Thomas, Alex., Ky., 96, #1850
Thomas, Ann, c/o, Wisc., 88,
#18112
Thomas, Catlett, Richmond, Va.,
46, #4735
Thomas, Edward, Mo., 42,
#3569
Thomas, Edward, e/o, Mo., 25,
#7204
Thomas, Ezekiel, a/o,
Philadelphia, Pa., 137,
#4504
Thomas, Henry, Ind., 49, #5296,
card

Thomas, Henry, a/o, Ky., 69,
#10928
Thomas, Henry, w/o, Ind., 50,
#5637
Thomas, Henry, w/o, Ind., 25,
#5296
Thomas, James, Lexington, Ky.,
40, #3294
Thomas, James, Philadelphia,
Pa., 45, #4537
Thomas, James, Richmond, Va.,
45, #4575, card
Thomas, James, e/o,
Philadelphia, Pa., 25,
#7523
Thomas, James A., S.C., 125,
#1655
Thomas, John, Indianapolis,
Ind., 41, #3541
Thomas, John, N.C., 75,
#13482
Thomas, John, w/o, Pulaski,
Tenn., 25, #12337
Thomas, Jonathan, Knoxville,
Tenn., 25, #3436
Thomas, Joseph, Richmond,
Va., 48, #5139
Thomas, Joseph, w/o,
Richmond, Va., 64, #9551
Thomas, Noah, Pa., 98, #3115,
slip
Thomas, Noah, c/o, Mass., 26,
#3115
Thomas, Sally, N.C., 26,
#10405
Thomas, Simeon, Conn., 35,
#1384
Thomas, Temperance, e/o,
Knoxville, Tenn., 126,
#3863
Thomas, William S., Albany,
N.Y., 129, #6574

Thomason, Isaac, w/o, N.C., 52, #6095

Thommarson (formerly Coulter), Sarah, New Albany, Ind., 135, #2355

Thompson, Lt. Col. A. K., w/o, —, 63, #9108

Thompson, Lt. Col. A. R., w/o, —, 58, #7671

Thompson, Lt. Col. A. R., w/o, —, 68, #10648

Thompson, Lt. Col. A. R., w/o, —, 72, #12675

Thompson, Lt. Col. A. R., w/o, —, 81, #15074

Thompson, Lt. Col. A. R., w/o, 6th Inf, 50, #5624

Thompson, A. R., w/o, —, 52, #6348

Thompson, Absalom, e/o, S.C., 98, #2927

Thompson, Alexander, Philadelphia, Pa., 92, #19733, card

Thompson, Lt. Col. Alexander R., w/o, —, 77, #13994

Thompson, Lt. Col. Alexander R., w/o, —, 84, #15937

Thompson, Amos, Wisc., 89, #18485

Thompson, Amos, Wisc., 90, #18632

Thompson, Benjamin, Mass., 39, #2982

Thompson, Benjamin, c/o, Concord, N.H., 47, #4995

Thompson, Bethiah, Mass., 137, #3841

Thompson, Charles, w/o, Nashville, Tenn., 67, #10325

Thompson, Christina, c/o, Ga., 106, #8738

Thompson, Ebenezer, c/o, Mass., 72, #12584

Thompson, Evan, w/o, Ky., 107, #9470

Thompson, Hannah, c/o, Albany, N.Y., 104, #7560

Thompson, Isaiah W., S.C., 40, #3182

Thompson, James, Albany, N.Y., 122, #8924, card

Thompson, James, Ill., 60, #8305

Thompson, James, Mo., 84, #16072

Thompson, James, c/o, Philadelphia, Pa., 125, #2870

Thompson, Jane P., Nashville, Tenn., 117, #3829

Thompson, Jane P., Nashville, Tenn., 123, #9952

Thompson, Janell, N.C., 100, #4471

Thompson, Jared, a/o, N.C., 111, #342

Thompson, Jesse, c/o, Md., 110, #10921

Thompson, John, Ill., 44, #4371

Thompson, John, Ind., 63, #8975, card

Thompson, John, Ky., 77, #14197, card

Thompson, John, Mich., 69, #10914

Thompson, John, N.J., 127, #4202

Thompson, John, Ohio, 57, #7578

Thompson, John, Ohio, 63,
#8884
Thompson, John, Richmond,
Va., 61, #8606
Thompson, John, w/o, Madison,
Ind., 26, #8975
Thompson, John, w/o, New York
City, 26, #12121
Thompson, Joseph, Ky., 44,
#4404
Thompson, Joseph, Ky., 46,
#4736
Thompson, Mabel, c/o,
Philadelphia, Pa., 110,
#11033
Thompson, Martha, a/o,
Cincinnati, Ohio, 135,
#2133
Thompson, Mary W., e/o, New
York City, 136, #2935
Thompson, Phebe, c/o, Albany,
N.Y., 26, #8926
Thompson, Reuben, Albany,
N.Y., 60, #8360
Thompson, Rufus, w/o,
Pittsburgh, Pa., 78, #14297
Thompson, Sally, c/o, Maine,
133, #539
Thompson, Samuel, Pittsburgh,
Pa., 104, #7576
Thompson, Samuel, c/o, La.,
103, #6886
Thompson, Shadrack, Albany,
N.Y., 47, #4898
Thompson, Sherrod, Ga., 40,
#3293
Thompson, Thomas, w/o,
Albany, N.Y., 115, #2696
Thompson, Thomas, w/o,
Albany, N.Y., 99, #3218
Thompson 2d, John, N.Y., 70,
#12121, card

Thorla, Thomas, c/o, Pittsburgh,
Pa., 60, #8292
Thorn, Helen, N.Y., 84, #15923
Thorn, Helen, a/o, New York
City, 26, #2881
Thorn, Samuel, w/o, New York
City, 98, #2881, slip
Thorn, Zenia, Ind., 75, #13659
Thorn, Zenia, c/o, Ind., 60,
#8359
Thornhill, Thomas, a/o,
Richmond, Va., 133, #474
Thornhill, William, Ky., 83,
#15729
Thornhill, William, Richmond,
Va., 72, #12633
Thornton, George, Richmond,
Va., 102, #5613
Thornton, George, Richmond,
Va., 108, #10233
Thornton, Presley, Jackson,
Tenn., 108, #9994
Thornton, Presley, a/o, Jackson,
Tenn., 123, #9586
Thorp, James, w/o, Albany,
N.Y., 64, #9566
Thorp, Joel C., g/o c/o, Conn.,
37, #F1820
Thorp, John, Nashville, Tenn.,
70, #11062
Thorp, Nathan, w/o, Pittsburgh,
Pa., 99, #3546
Thorp, Reuben, Philadelphia,
Pa., 80, #14760
Thorp, Thomas, c/o, Va., 83,
#15675
Thrasher, George, Albany, N.Y.,
54, #6896
Thrasher, George, w/o, Ga., 110,
#11031
Thraw, Thomas, Albany, N.Y.,
143, #7520

Thrift, John, w/o, S.C., 91, #19279

Throop, Dan, c/o, Albany, N.Y., 113, #1912

Throop, Mary, c/o, Albany, N.Y., 113, #1910

Thrulow, Abaigail, c/o, Portland, Maine, 105, #7850

Thueman, Ernest L., La., 26, #701

Thurlo, Asa, w/o, Maine, 75, #13619

Thurman, Charles, Knoxville, Tenn., 40, #3234

Thurman, Molly M., a/o, Richmond, Va., 131, #8404

Thurman, William, Jonesboro, Tenn., 63, #8939

Thurman, William, Jonesboro, Tenn., 66, #10112

Thurston, John, c/o, Vt., 121, #6960

Thuss, Nicholas, Ore., 139, #8169

Thuston, John, Mass., 39, #3026

Thwing, Chloe, Albany, N.Y., 79, #14550

Thwing, Chloe, Philadelphia, Pa., 66, #10160

Tibbetts, Samuel, c/o, Portsmouth, N.H., 135, #2234

Tichenor, Joseph, a/o, Ky., 136, #3625

Ticker, Frances, N.C., 100, #4416

Tidwell, William L., S.C., 124, #726

Tidwell, William L., S.C., 127, #4910

Tidwell, William L., S.C., 133, #670

Tiernan, Michael, PA, Pittsburgh, Pa., 81, #15036

Tiernan, Michael, PA, Pittsburgh, Pa., 81, #15070

Tiffany, Ruthey, c/o, Albany, N.Y., 70, #11060

Tift, Amasa A., Albany, N.Y., 51, #6051

Tift, John, c/o, Albany, N.Y., 90, #18581

Tilden, John Bell, c/o, Richmond, Va., 53, #6510

Tileston, Cornelius, c/o, Mass., 96, #1721

Tiller, William, Va., 96, #1812, card

Tiller, William, Va., 97, #1906, card

Tilley, Bennet, Mo., 48, #5131

Tilley, Bennett, Mo., 59, #8049

Tilley, Franka, a/o, Mo., 103, #6935

Tilley, Lazarus, N.C., 88, #18072

Tillinghart, Daniel, a/o, Albany, N.Y., 112, #965

Tillinghast, Capt. Otis H., w/o, QM Dept., 139, #8657

Tillinghast, Capt. Otis H., w/o, QM USA, 141, #1511

Tillinghast, Capt. Otis H., w/o, QM USA, 141, #2837

Tillinghast, Capt. Otis H., w/o, QM USA, 142, #5701

Tillinghast, Otis H., w/o, QM USA, 142, #4106

Tillotson, Jacob, Albany, N.Y., 74, #13048

Tilly, Bennet, Mo., 68, #10684

Tilly, Bennet, Mo., 76, #13801

Tilson, Hester, New York City,
130, #7248
Tilton, John, c/o, N.J., 99,
#3633
Tindall, Wilie, N.C., 26, #2141,
#see Benj. De Berry
Tindall, Wilie, N.C., 6, #2141
Tiner, Demsey, Knoxville,
Tenn., 40, #3228
Tiney, Richard, Ohio, 121,
#7015
Tinker, Lucy, a/o, Conn., 116,
#3691
Tinker, Nathan, Conn., 35, #994
Tinsley, Golden, S.C., 120,
#6558, card
Tinsley, Golding, a/o, S.C., 26,
#6558
Tinsley, James, La., 90, #18789
Tinsley, James, S.C., 89,
#18212
Tinsley, Sarah, Ky., 115, #2643
Tinsley, William, w/o, Ky., 87,
#17325
Tipps, Jacob, w/o, N.C., 55,
#6924
Tipton, Luke, Jackson, Tenn.,
117, #3965
Tisdale, Barnabas, c/o, Concord,
N.H., 95, #1280
Titman, Philp, legal
representative of, N.C., 82,
#15506
Titus, Benjamin, w/o,
Pittsburgh, Pa., 119, #5652
Tobin, Lydia, —, 101, #5180,
card
Tobin, Lydia, e/o, Philadelphia,
Pa., 26, #5180
Todd, Lt. J. W., Washington
Arsenal, 133, #9949

Todd, Samuel B., Mo., 131,
#8307
Todd, Samuel B., Mo., 141,
#2119
Todd, Samuel B., Mo., 141,
#2668
Todd, Thomas, Ind., 62, #8693
Todd, Thomas, Ind., 81, #15110
Toler, Mary, Va., 120, #6168
Toler, Richard, w/o, Richmond,
Va., 92, #19578
Toliver, Frankey, a/o,
Morganton, N.C., 122,
#8863
Tolle, Charlotte, D.C., 120,
#6646
Tolman, Chloe, Boston, Mass.,
70, #11034
Tolman, Hannah, a/o, Albany,
N.Y., 84, #16114
Tolman, Hannah, c/o, Albany,
N.Y., 79, #14548
Tombs, Clifton, Richmond, Va.,
56, #7415
Tomer, Henry, Pittsburgh, Pa.,
26, #1385
Tomlinsen, Curtis, w/o, Conn.,
35, #5826
Tomlinson, Albert, Calif., 132,
#9401
Tomlinson, Lucy, Conn., 98,
#2860
Tompkins, Henry, New York
City, 41, #3369
Tompkins, James, Jonesboro,
Tenn., 135, #1896
Tompkins, James F., New York
City, 141, #3121
Tompkins, Silvanus, h/o, New
York City, 39, #2980
Toms, John, w/o, Albany, N.Y.,
26, #18662

Toney, Elizabeth, Fayetteville,
N.C., 128, #5199
Toney, Elizabeth, Fayetteville,
N.C., 132, #9412
Toney, William, E. Tenn., 62,
#8719
Tooker, Joseph, D.C., 91,
#19243, card
Tool Sr., James, w/o,
Charleston, S.C., 92,
#19824
Toolman, Harry, —, 138,
#6149, slip
Toombs, Elizabeth, Richmond,
Va., 64, #9250
Toombs, Elizabeth, Richmond,
Va., 71, #12241
Toombs, Emanuel, w/o, Va., 46,
#4701
Torrey, Abigal, Albany, N.Y.,
66, #10232
Torrey, Jesse, —, 87, #17651,
card
Torrey, Jonathan, c/o, Albany,
N.Y., 90, #18792
Tottingham, David, w/o,
Bellows Falls, Vt., 44,
#4310
Tower, Jerviah, a/o, Poultney,
Vt., 103, #7028
Towle, William, w/o, Maine, 56,
#7349
Towles, Henry, Ky., 71, #12458
Townes, Thomas, E. Tenn., 60,
#8181
Townley, Joshua, N.J., 71,
#12228
Townsend, Charles, w/o, New
York City, 64, #9224
Townsend, George, w/o,
Knoxville, Tenn., 121,
#7473

Townsend, Jeremiah, c/o,
Albany, N.Y., 87, #17448
Townsend, Meriam, c/o, Albany,
N.Y., 98, #2737
Townsend, Susannah, c/o, Ga.,
102, #5785
Toxel, Jacob, w/o, Knoxville,
Tenn., 26, #644
Tozer, Julius, Philadelphia, Pa.,
42, #3675
Tozer, Julius, w/o, Philadelphia,
Pa., 130, #7606
Tracey, Abigail, Conn., 35,
#151
Tracey, Mary, a/o, Conn., 101,
#4733
Tracy Sr., James, w/o, S.C., 66,
#10200
Trapp, Vincent, Richmond, Va.,
58, #7702
Trash, Ebenezer, Maine, 78,
#14291
Trask, Jesse, c/o, Mass., 101,
#4588
Trask, Retine, Pittsburgh, Pa.,
70, #12050
Trask, Retine, Pittsburgh, Pa.,
86, #17047
Tratrie, Daniel, a/o, Ky., 82,
#15289
Traverse, Mathias, c/o, Md., 45,
#4644
Travis, Arthur, Lexington, Ky.,
39, #3056
Travis, Slyvanius, Albany, N.Y.,
121, #7780, card
Travis, Sylvanus, c/o, Albany,
N.Y., 26, #7780
Treacle, Elizabeth, c/o,
Richmond, Va., 101, #5272

Trull, Elijah, Concord, N.H., 42,
#3759
Trull, Willard, c/o, Albany,
N.Y., 60, #8307
Truman, Solomon, w/o, Albany,
N.Y., 47, #4914
Trumbull, Robert, e/o, Vt., 78,
#14391
Truss, Thomas J., La., 135,
#2018
Tryman, William, Richmond,
Va., 71, #12243
Tryon, Elijah, Burlington, Vt.,
108, #10088
Tryon, Elizabeth, c/o, Conn.,
138, #5713
Tshu-ka-to, Fort Gibson, Ark.,
111, #475
Tshu-Ka-Tenorfod, Fort Gibson,
Ark., 102, #5731
Tubbs, John L., Little Rock,
Ark., 124, #848
Tubbs, John L., Little Rock,
Ark., 136, #3194
Tuck, Mary, a/o, Concord, N.H.,
120, #5890
Tucker, David, w/o, Nashville,
Tenn., 46, #4803
Tucker, Frances F., w/o,
Richmond, Va., 26, #940
Tucker, Francis, N.C., 121,
#6721
Tucker, George, Wheeling, Va.,
105, #7886, card
Tucker, Harburt, Ga., 45, #4634
Tucker, John, Nashville, Tenn.,
75, #13471
Tucker, Lucy, a/o, Richmond,
Va., 26, #4605
Tucker, Reuben, w/o, —, 101,
#4605, card

Tucker, Samuel, Boston, Mass.,
142, #5009
Tucker, Seth, Boston, Mass.,
120, #6437
Tucker, Thomas, —, 95, #948,
slip
Tucker, Thomas, Ind., 45, #4501
Tudee, Valentine, —, 114,
#2299, card
Tuder, Valentine, cur/o, Ky., 26,
#2299
Tudor, John, Ky., 47, #5002
Tuefo, native Cherokee, Fort
Gibson, Ark., 111, #476
Tufts, William, Ind., 81, #15111
Tuggle, Nancy, c/o, Richmond,
Va., 108, #10320
Tuggle, Thomas, c/o, Richmond,
Va., 108, #10319
Tuggs, William, Ind., 52, #6323
Tully, Chester R., Albany, N.Y.,
115, #2991
Tully, Sylvia, Albany, N.Y.,
107, #9361
Tuman, James, a/o w/o, N.C.
Militia, 94, #464
Tumey, Samuel, w/o, N.J., 70,
#12001
Tupper, Simeon, a/o, Pittsburgh,
Pa., 111, #423
Turk, Joseph, Mo., 130, #7961
Turley, James, w/o, Ill., 26,
#19490
Turley, Crasus, Ill., 91, #19490,
card
Turman, Joseph, Cincinnati,
Ohio, 124, #1060
Turman, Joseph, Cincinnati,
Ohio, 134, #1000
Turner, Andrew, Ill., 47, #4975
Turner, Asa, Albany, N.Y., 67,
#10522

Turner, Consider, c/o,
Portsmouth, N.H., 46,
#4655
Turner, Elisha, c/o, New York
City, 108, #9991
Turner, Elizabeth, Maine, 110,
#11213
Turner, Esther, Albany, N.Y.,
143, #6305
Turner, Jabez, Albany, N.Y., 68,
#10799
Turner, Jabez, Ill., 73, #12923
Turner, James, Ohio, 59, #8163,
card
Turner, Julius, Ill., 120, #6238
Turner, Lebdee, Albany, N.Y.,
41, #3532
Turner, Lebedee, Albany, N.Y.,
46, #4695
Turner, Lewis, e/o, Va., 79,
#14593
Turner, Samuel, La., 125, #1805
Turner, Samuel, Mo., 59, #8110
Turner, Samuel, Mo., 73,
#12852
Turner, Samuel, a/o, Mo., 26,
#2261
Turner, Sarah, Va., 65, #9795
Turner, William, — , 96, #1418,
card
Turner, William, Albany, N.Y.,
62, #8676
Turner, William, Albany, N.Y.,
117, #4508
Turner, William, a/o, Mich.,
111, #671
Turner, William, c/o, Albany,
N.Y., 116, #3561
Turner, William, c/o, Mich.,
110, #53
Turner, William, w/o, N.C., 26,
#1418

Turney, Hannah, a/o,
Philadelphia, Pa., 114,
#2188
Turnley, Franics, a/o, Va., 77,
#13991
Turpin, Obadiah, Conn., 35,
#4160
Tuttle, Abraham, Bellows Falls,
Vt., 63, #8967
Tuttle, Clement, Pittsburgh, Pa.,
76, #13833
Tuttle, John, a/o, Portsmouth,
N.H., 128, #5743
Tuttle, Lucy, c/o, Mass., 96,
#1491
Tuttle, Nicholas, Mo., 73,
#12894
Tuttle, Peletiah, Albany, N.Y.,
63, #9059
Tuttle, Roxanna, Albany, N.Y.,
100, #4106, card
Tuttle, Roxanna, a/o, Albany,
N.Y., 26, #4106
Twiford, George, N.C., 40,
#3260
Twigg, Daniel, Ky., 82, #153—
Tyler, Charles, Ky., 77, #14168
Tyler, Daniel, c/o, Mass., 73,
#12800
Tyler, Elizabeth, a/o, Richmond,
Va., 108, #10196
Tyler, Sarah, Montpelier, Vt.,
102, #5822
Tyler, Silas, c/o, Philadelphia,
Pa., 89, #18300
Tyler, William, Ky., 125,
#1930, card
Tyler, William, c/o, Albany,
N.Y., 80, #14960
Tyler, William, c/o, Albany,
N.Y., 82, #15234

Tyler, William, e/o, Jefferson,
Ky., 26, #1930

U

Uncle, Benjamin, c/o, Md., 127,
#4587
Underwood, John, w/o, Bellows
Falls, Vt., 51, #5847
Underwood, John, N.C., 8,
#3645, in file of J.
Falconbury
Underwood, John, Fayetteville,
N.C., 50, #5536
Underwood, Phineas, Ill., 46,
#4741
Underwood Sr., Phineas, Ill., 44,
#4240
Underwood, Silas, Albany, N.Y.,
58, #7715
Underwood, Susanna, c/o, Mass.,
95, #1187
Upham, Jonathan, w/o, Mass.,
68, #10623
Uptegraff, Mary, c/o,
Philadelphia, Pa., 62,
#8775
Uptegraff, Mary, c/o,
Philadelphia, Pa., 91,
#19194
Upton, George, Ga., 126,
#3802, card
Upton, George, w/o, Ga., 26,
#3802
Urlkinson, Hardin F., La., 124,
#1393
Utley, Alley, Ky., 122, #8281
Utley, Asa, c/o, Albany, N.Y.,
54, #6614
Utley, James, Fayetteville, N.C.,
136, #2684

Utter, Abraham, a/o, Madison,
Ind., 117, #4258
Utter, Jesse, w/o, Albany, N.Y.,
109, #10614
Utterback, Harman, Ky., 92,
#19672
Utterback, Harman, Ky., 113,
#1771
Utterback, Harmon, Ky., 104,
#7354

V

Vail, William, w/o, New York
City, 48, #5244
Vails, Samuel, a/o, Jackson,
Tenn., 121, #6917
Valentine, George, Ohio, 40,
#3282
Valentine, George, c/o,
Cincinnati, Ohio, 137,
#4069
Vallandingham, William, S.C.,
49, #5284
Van Alstine, Peter, c/o, Albany,
N.Y., 60, #8224
Van Benchoten, Elias, c/o, N.Y.,
80, #14783
Van Buskink, Rachael, Albany,
N.Y., 66, #10226
Van Cleaf, Mary A., Pittsburgh,
Pa., 118, #4859, card
Van Cusler, Henry, c/o, Albany,
N.Y., 48, #5153
Van Dike, David, w/o, Albany,
N.Y., 130, #7622
Van Dykes, Lydia, N.J., 65,
#10028
Van Eps, Garret, Albany, N.Y.,
105, #8102

Van Fleet, Cornelius,
Philadelphia, Pa., 57,
#7572
Van Fleet, Joshua, Ohio, 57,
#7474
Van Fleet, Joshua, Ohio, 64,
#9431
Van Fleet, Joshua, Ohio, 39,
#2943
Van Gordan, Elsie, a/o,
Philadelphia, Pa., 26,
#4244
Van Gordon, Abraham, Albany,
N.Y., 54, #6708
Van Horn, Matthias, w/o,
Albany, N.Y., 95, #899
Van Horne, Thomas, w/o,
Albany, N.Y., 75, #13534
Van Housen, Jacob, c/o, Albany,
N.Y., 124, #385
Van Mart, Hesny, New York
City, 55, #7097, card
Van Meter, Isaac, w/o, Ky., 105,
#7756
Van Meter (formerly Crouch),
Ruth P., Ill., 114, #2208
Van Northwick, Henry C., a/o,
N.J., 119, #5293
Van Patten, Adam, Albany, N.Y.,
61, #8405
Van Roe, James, Mo., 125,
#1861
Van Roe, James, Mo., 125,
#2444
Van Roe, James, Mo., 130,
#7249
Van Roe, James, Mo., 139,
#7033
Van Scoyk, Mary, Cincinnati,
Ohio, 127, #4931
Van Sickler, Mary, a/o, Albany,
N.Y., 115, #2756

Van Swidam, Esther, Albany,
N.Y., 60, #8324
Van Tapel, Elizabeth, New York
City, 40, #3183
Van Tranken, Evert, Albany,
N.Y., 44, #4327
Van Valkenbury, Catharine, a/o,
Albany, N.Y., 124, #553
Van Vlach, John B., Madison,
Ind., 143, #6259
Van Vleck, Catherine, c/o,
Albany, N.Y., 71, #12442
Van Vorst, Catherine, Albany,
N.Y., 61, #8576
Van Vorst, John W., Albany,
N.Y., 143, #7301
Van Vranken, Claus, c/o,
Albany, N.Y., 64, #9167
Van Vranken, Event, Albany,
N.Y., 64, #9168
Van Vranken, Rebecca, Albany,
N.Y., 83, #15617
Van Wagenen, Garret, c/o,
Albany, N.Y., 82, #15534
Van Winkle, Charlotte, a/o,
Boston, Mass., 122, #8720
Van Winkle, Elias, Philadelphia,
Pa., 105, #8096
Van Wormer, Catherine, Albany,
N.Y., 72, #12481
Van Wort, Henry, w/o, New York
City, 26, #7097
Vanansdall, Cornelius, Ohio, 79,
#14642
Vanarsdall, Cornelius, —, 87,
#17447, slip
Vanarsdall, Cornelius, Ky., 69,
#11010, card
Vanarsdall, Cornelius, Ohio, 26,
#17447
Vanarsdall, Cornelius, e/o, Ky.,
26, #11010

Vanasdall, Cornelius, Ohio, 81,
#15066
Vanater, John, Cincinnati, Ohio,
126, #3463
Vancamp, Daniel, g/o c/o, New
Albany, Ind., 137, #4480
Vance, John, Mo., 123, #9956
Vance, John, Mo., 136, #3484
Vance, John, Mo., 139, #8932
Vance, Nancy, a/o, Richmond,
Va., 95, #1255
Vance, Samuel, Jonesboro,
Tenn., 55, #6982, card
Vance, Samuel, w/o, Jonesboro,
Tenn., 26, #6982
Vance, William R., PA,
Louisville, Ky., 115, #2493
Vance, William R., PA,
Louisville, Ky., 116, #3780
Vancleaf, Mary Ann, e/o,
Pittsburgh, Pa., 26, #4859
Vandeman, John, w/o, Ohio, 64,
#9513
Vanderbill, Peter, c/o,
Philadelphia, Pa., 134,
#819
Vanderburgh, Henry, N.Y., 78,
#14481
Vanderburgh, Henry, c/o, New
York City, 100, #3866
Vanderburgh, James, Albany,
N.Y., 64, #9169
Vanderheyden, Elizabeth, a/o,
Albany, N.Y., 136, #3562
Vanderpool, Anthony, Pa., 84,
#16088, card
Vanderpool, Anthony, c/o, Pa.,
26, #16088
Vanderveer, Rachel, Albany,
N.Y., 85, #16437
Vanderworken, Martin, a/o,
Pittsburgh, Pa., 121, #7213

Vane, John, c/o, Md., 135,
#2286
Vanes, Jacob, g/o c/o,
Cleveland, Ohio, 125,
#1795
Vanfleet, Sarah, Philadelphia,
Pa., 103, #6740
Vanhorne, Samuel, c/o, Ky.,
118, #4703
Vanhoy, Barbara, Jackson,
Tenn., 129, #6758
Vankinle, David, N.J., 51,
#5893
Vanshoy, Abigail, Albany,
N.Y., 101, #4723
Vansices, Abraham, a/o, Albany,
N.Y., 98, #3111
Vansickler, Robert R., Chicago,
Ill., 143, #6821
Vanskiver, William, c/o,
Cleveland, Ohio, 123,
#9078
Vanslyke, Abigail, Albany,
N.Y., 46, #4711
Variel, Sarah, c/o, Maine, 129,
#6368
Varnee, Joseph, La., 109,
#10481
Varner, Joseph, La., 92, #70
Varner, Joseph, La., 106, #8845
Varner, Joseph, La., 110, #72
Varner, Joseph, La., 114, #2244
Varner, Joseph, New Orleans,
La., 81, #15042
Varner, Joseph, Richmond, Va.,
107, #9227
Varner Sr., David, S.C., 50,
#5619
Varnum, Molly, a/o, Vt., 83,
#15812
Vass, Vincent, w/o, Jackson,
Tenn., 110, #11182

Vaughan, Frederick, c/o, Ill., 99, #3485
Vaughan, Joel, Mobile, Ala., 98, #2911
Vaughan, John, Albany, N.Y., 120, #5935, card
Vaughan, John, S.C., 56, #7371
Vaughan, John, St. Augustine, Fla., 51, #6072
Vaughan, John, a/o, Albany, N.Y., 26, #5935
Vaughan, Martha, Richmond, Va., 105, #7884
Vaughan, William, c/o, Richmond, Va., 52, #6161
Vaughn, Almond, Va., 77, #14003
Vaughn, Almond, Va., 90, #18576
Vaughn, Joel, Mobile, Ala., 74, #13260
Vaughn, John, E. Fla., 80, #14892
Vaughn, John, Fla., 63, #9043
Vaughn, William, Richmond, Va., 42, #3755
Vaun, Daniel, Knoxville, Tenn., 119, #5825
Veale, James Carr, w/o, Ind., 68, #10628
Veatch, Jeremiah, w/o, Ky., 83, #15593
Veatch, Priscilla, Ky., 83, #15592
Veatch, Priscilla, c/o, Ky., 133, #239
Venable, William, w/o, Ill., 91, #19520
Venables, John, N.C., 45, #4530

Vendine, Francis, c/o, Philadelphia, Pa., 54, #6865
Verden, James, Ill., 46, #4822
Vermillian, Jesse, w/o, Va., 68, #10786
Vermillion, Jesse, Richmond, Va., 56, #7341
Vermillion, Jesse, Richmond, Va., 62, #8718
Vermillion, Jesse, w/o, Richmond, Va., 73, #12785
Vermillion, Mary, Richmond, Va., 105, #7922
Vermillion, Samuel, c/o, N.C., 26, #4297
Vermilyea, William, Albany, N.Y., 127, #4254
Verminet, Jane, a/o, Richmond, Va., 27, #5182
Verner, David, S.C., 39, #3102
Verner, John, c/o, Philadelphia, Pa., 139, #8588
Vernon, Richard, Tenn., 97, #2089, card
Vernon, Richard, a/o, Tenn., 27, #2089
Vernon, Thomas, Knoxville, Tenn., 50, #5782
Vernon, Thomas, Knoxville, Tenn., 68, #10594
Vernon, Thomas, Knoxville, Tenn., 57, #7582
Via, Mary, a/o, Richmond, Va., 100, #4264
Viall, John, R.I., 120, #6428
Vicars, William, c/o, N.C., 41, #3559
Vickers, William, Ga., 58, #7867, card
Vickery, Edward, Albany, N.Y., 53, #6399

Vickery, Polly, Albany, N.Y.,
97, #1947
Vickery, Polly, c/o, Albany,
N.Y., 106, #8615
Vickery, Polly, c/o, Albany,
N.Y., 112, #866
Vickory, William, Ga., 129,
#6934, card
Vickory, William, w/o, Ga., 27,
#6934
Videto, Joseph, c/o, Maine, 83,
#15758
Vincent, Jesse, S.C., 105,
#7979
Vincent, Jesse C., g/o c/o,
Madison, Ind., 141, #2669
Vincent, Mahala Ann, Ind., 120,
#6618
Vincent, Thomas, Jonesboro,
Tenn., 128, #5726
Vincent, Thomas, Ky., 67,
#10329
Vineyard, William, Madison,
Ind., 102, #5696
Vineyard, William, Ohio, 99,
#3555
Vining, John, Pulaski, Tenn.,
107, #9665
Vining, John, c/o, Maine, 97,
#2425
Vining, Mary, c/o, Maine, 97,
#2426
Vinson, Revecca, Mass., 63,
#8960
Vinton, Joseph, w/o, Mass., 63,
#9101
Vittilow, Samuel, Ky., 60,
#8208
Vleit, Mary, c/o, Philadelphia,
Pa., 114, #2433
Vliet, Daniel, N.J., 56, #7271

Vndever, George, c/o, S.C., 26,
#7838
Vogel, Ludwig, La., 123, #9970
Vogel, Ludwig, La., 127, #4529
Vogt, William, La., 126, #3632
Volunteers, Plattsburg, —, 105,
#7835, slip
Voores, Garret, Ind., 72, #12666
Vopeller, Luke, c/o, S.C., 91,
#19505
Vorhees, Margaret, Pittsburgh,
Pa., 62, #8867
Vorhees, Mary, c/o, N.J., 103,
#6574
Vorse, Jesse, Conn., 35, #805
Vosburg, Eliakim, w/o, Albany,
N.Y., 75, #13652
Vredenburgh, James, N.J., 63,
#8911
Vrooman, Elizabeth, Md., 133,
#334
Vrooman, Simon J., Albany,
N.Y., 77, #14181
Vrooman (now Sogsden),
Elizabeth, Iowa, 110,
#11004

W

Waddel, William, w/o, Albany,
N.Y., 70, #12072
Waddle, George, Mo., 108,
#9864
Waddle, George, Mo., 100,
#3768
Waddle, Martin, w/o, Jonesboro,
Tenn., 89, #18479
Waddle, Robert, c/o, Mo., 130,
#7431
Waddle, Robert, c/o, Mo., 130,
#7531

Waddle, Thomas, c/o, Va., 69,
#10935
Wade, Henry, g/o c/o, Conn.,
37, #F1820
Wadkins, Barbara, Ky., 143,
#7282
Wadkins, Darius, Pittsburgh,
Pa., 106, #8459
Wadkins, Darius, Pittsburgh,
Pa., 107, #9473
Wadkins, John, N.C., 62, #8854
Wadkins, John, N.C., 83,
#15915
Waggeman, G. G., —, 114,
#2163, slip
Waggoner, Isaac, c/o, Ill., 54,
#6692
Wagner, Charles, c/o, Ill., 119,
#5749
Wagner, Charles, g/o c/o, Ill.,
130, #7910
Wagner, Charles, g/o c/o, Ill.,
139, #7094
Wagner, Margaretta,
Philadelphia, Pa., 72,
#12704
Wagner, Margeretta,
Philadelphia, Pa., 57,
#7484
Wagstaff, Amelia, Charleston,
S.C., 125, #1952
Waid, Calvin, Huntsville, Ala.,
56, #7276
Waid, Harvey, g/o c/o, Concord,
N.H., 132, #9014
Wait, William C., g/o w/o, N.Y.,
74, #13053
Wait, William E. R., N.C., 115,
#2584
Waite, Lydia, Mass., 81, #15013
Wakefield, Henry, Nashville,
Tenn., 101, #4759

Wakefield, Henry, w/o,
Nashville, Tenn., 111,
#354
Wakefield, Polly, Concord,
N.H., 137, #4301
Wakefield, Thomas, w/o,
Nashville, Tenn., 114,
#2217
Wakelee, Mary, a/o,
Philadelphia, Pa., 110, #88
Walcot, Justin, c/o, Albany,
N.Y., 14, #11076
Walden, David, Huntsville, Ala.,
61, #8532
Walden, David, Tuscaloosa, Ala.,
76, #13950
Walden, Elizabeth, —, 123,
#283, card
Walden, Mary, a/o, Va., 82,
#15519
Walden, Mary, c/o, Conn., 60,
#8295
Wales, Beulah, c/o, Mass., 95,
#1186
Walker, Benjamin, w/o, Ill., 27,
#1150
Walker, Betsy, Wisc., 102,
#5784
Walker, Daniel, c/o, Richmond,
Va., 41, #3378
Walker Sr., Daniel, w/o, Ga., 99,
#3744
Walker, Edward, w/o, Maine, 46,
#4707
Walker, Eliakim, Concord, N.H.,
90, #18690, card
Walker, Eliakim, a/o, Concord,
N.H., 27, #18690
Walker, George, S.C., 59, #8103
Walker, George, S.C., 62, #8669
Walker, James, Jackson, Tenn.,
110, #11030

Walker, James, w/o, Ky., 74,
#13157
Walker, Jesse, Mo., 40, #3250
Walker, Jesse, Mo., 48, #5116
Walker, Jesse, Mo., 57, #7510
Walker, Jesse, Mo., 66, #10199
Walker, Jesse, Mo., 73, #12853
Walker, Jesse, g/o c/o, Ky., 135,
#1989
Walker, John, w/o, Knoxville,
Tenn., 91, #19276
Walker, John H., w/o, Ga., 129,
#6445
Walker, Joshua, w/o, Jonesboro,
Tenn., 125, #2262
Walker, Margaret, h/o, N.Y., 94,
#599
Walker, Mariah, Ga., 136,
#2685
Walker, Mary, Madison, Ind.,
134, #1362
Walker, Mashack, c/o, Ohio, 61,
#8611
Walker, Nancy, a/o, Maine, 82,
#15270
Walker, Richard, w/o, Nashville,
Tenn., 77, #14222
Walker, Richard, w/o, Nashville,
Tenn., 82, #15340
Walker, Sophia, Va., 88,
#17757
Walker (now Calhoon), Susan L.,
Ky., 126, #3163
Walker, Temperance, c/o, N.H.,
83, #15890
Walker, Thankful, Vt., 85,
#16321
Walker, Thomas, Richmond,
Va., 64, #9246
Walker, Timothy, w/o, Maine,
89, #18251

Walker, Velina, c/o, Milwaukee,
Wisc., 142, #5169
Walker, William, Huntsville,
Ala., 53, #6456
Walker, William, Richmond,
Va., 60, #8296
Walker, William, w/o,
Wheeling, Va., 27, #7958
Walker 2d, William, —, 110,
#139, slip
Walker 2nd, William, a/o,
Albany, N.Y., 27, #139
Walker, William D., g/o c/o,
Milwaukie, Wisc., 27,
#6558
Walker, William W., w/o,
Jackson, Tenn., 117, #4556
Walker, Zaccheus, N.H., 112,
#1090, card
Walker, Zacheus, a/o, Concord,
N.H., 27, #1090
Walkers, Ed. B., c/o, Ill., 114,
#1966
Walkins, Asa, N.Y., 28, #3878
Wall, Joseph, Fayetteville,
N.C., 134, #826
Wall, Peter, w/o, Richmond, Va.,
123, #9403
Wall, Willam, w/o, Md., 45,
#4606
Wallace, James, a/o, Pittsburgh,
Pa., 112, #873
Wallace, James, c/o, Va., 91,
#19125
Wallace, Ruth, a/o, S.C., 107,
#8988
Wallace, Samuel, Ill., 68,
#10784
Wallace, Samuel, w/o, Ill., 111,
#517
Wallace, William, —, 137,
#4518, card

Wallace, William, Pittsburgh,
Pa., 50, #5528
Wallace, William, c/o, —, 27,
#4518
Waller, Saral, Wheeling, Va.,
105, #7958, card
Wallis, David, Boston, Mass.,
97, #2169
Wallis, Mathew, w/o, W. Tenn.,
65, #9948
Walsworth, Elijah, Bellows
Falls, Vt., 63, #8967
Walter, Barbara, Philadelphia,
Pa., 106, #8620
Walter, Barbara, Philadelphia,
Pa., 124, #1092
Walter, Barbara, a/o,
Philadelphia, Pa., 125,
#1683
Walter, Daniel, Albany, N.Y.,
68, #10581
Walter, Jacob, Philadelphia, Pa.,
65, #10019
Walter, Jacob, Philadelphia, Pa.,
41, #3465
Walter, John, Albany, N.Y., 27,
#5649
Walter, Susannah, Pa., 141,
#2768, card
Walter, Susannah, c/o,
Philadelphia, Pa., 27,
#2768
Walters, Frederick, Wheeling,
Va., 67, #10352
Walters, Frederick, Wheeling,
Va., 76, #13952
Walters, Frederick, Wheeling,
Va., 84, #15994
Walters, Frederick, Wheeling,
Va., 48, #5117
Walters, Frederick, Wheeling,
Va., 57, #7627

Walters, Isaac, —, 92, #19772,
slip
Walters, Isabella, a/o,
Cleveland, Ohio, 122,
#8253
Walters, Jacob, Philadelphia,
Pa., 54, #6682
Walters, Jacob, Pittsburgh, Pa.,
61, #8634
Walters, James, w/o, Ohio, 52,
#6263
Walters, John, w/o, Pittsburgh,
Pa., 121, #7907
Walters, Paul, N.C., 43, #3813
Walton, Joel, —, 74, #13038,
card
Walton, Joel, e/o, Richmond,
Va., 27, #13038
Walton, Reuben, c/o, Maine,
116, #3312
Walton, Sarah, a/o, Nashville,
Tenn., 70, #12018
Walton, Tilmon, w/o, N.C., 86,
#16976
Walton, William, Philadelphia,
Pa., 69, #11026
Wamsley, William, Wheeling,
Va., 74, #13394
Wandell (now Perham), Louisa,
Albany, N.Y., 122, #8848
Wander, Andrew, Pittsburgh, Pa.,
89, #18465
Waner, George, w/o, Vt., 59,
#7997
Waples, Sabra P., e/o,
Richmond, Va., 36A, #F3
V37
Ward, Benjamin, Pittsburgh, Pa.,
124, #930, card
Ward, Benjamin, a/o, Pittsburgh,
Pa., 27, #930

Warner, Abigail, Conn., 35,
#618
Warner, Annis, e/o, Mass., 137,
#4072
Warner, Charles, w/o, Albany,
N.Y., 86, #17259
Warner, Elias, Mass., 92,
#19561, card
Warner, Elias, c/o, Mass., 27,
#19561
Warner, Moses, c/o,
Philadelphia, Pa., 133,
#103
Warner, Nathaniel, a/o, Mass.,
91, #18976
Warner, Rachel, c/o,
Philadelphia, Pa., 133,
#104
Warner, Solomon, c/o, Albany,
N.Y., 64, #9480
Warnock, John, S.C., 79,
#14600
Warnock, John, w/o, S.C., 94,
#682
Warnock, John P., Ga., 73,
#12840
Warnock, John P., Ga., 80,
#14808
Warnock, John P., Ga., 120,
#6137
Warnock (formerly Burch),
Barbara, Ill., 117, #4271
Warren, Elijah, Jackson, Tenn.,
59, #8059
Warren, Fife Major Isaac, w/o,
Va. Milita, 113, #1854
Warren, James, Ky., 92, #206
Warren, James, Madison, Ind.,
57, #7606
Warren, John, W. Tenn., 47,
#5006

Warren, Keziah, c/o, Maine,
106, #8565
Warren, Lydia, a/o, Maine, 136,
#2657
Warren, Mary, c/o, Albany,
N.Y., 44, #4292
Warren, Mary, c/o, Albany,
N.Y., 48, #5189
Warren, Nathan, Mass., 105,
#8347
Warren, Rachel, Conn., 35, #43
Warren, Samuel, S.C., 55, #7219
Warren, Samuel, a/o, S.C., 94,
#535
Warren, Stephen, Boston,
Mass., 64, #9390
Warren, Willam, w/o, Ky., 96,
#1866
Warren 3rd, John, c/o, Albany,
N.Y., 83, #15642
Washburn, Ebenezer, w/o,
Maine, 109, #10845
Washburn, James, Augusta,
Maine, 140, #622
Washington, Euphan M.,
Richmond, Va., 36A, #F5
V7
Washington, George W., a/o,
Cincinnati, Ohio, 123,
#9950
Wasson, Amea, a/o, Albany,
N.Y., 127, #4268
Wasson, Betshannah, Albany,
N.Y., 103, #7088
Wasson, Ellen, e/o, Richmond,
Va., 36A, #F6 V52
Wasson, John, w/o, Albany,
N.Y., 92, #19941
Waston, William, c/o, Madison,
Ind., 136, #2544
Water, Israel, Ill., 55, #7122

Waterberry, Nathaniel, c/o,
Conn., 72, #12496

Waterbury, Sally, Conn., 35,
#59

Waterhouse, Elizabeth, c/o,
Boston, Mass., 55, #7048

Waterman, Charles, w/o, Ohio,
27, #13854

Waterman, Clavin, w/o, Albany,
N.Y., 85, #16609

Waterman, Ignatius, —, 85,
#16697f2

Waterman, Zenos, Boston,
Mass., 65, #9764

Waters, Benjamin, Pittsburgh,
Pa., 54, #6901

Waters, Benjamin, c/o,
Pittsburgh, Pa., 111, #720

Waters, Daniel, w/o, Albany,
N.Y., 75, #13533

Waters, Jacob, w/o, Ohio, 66,
#10241

Waters, Richard, c/o, Conn.,
101, #4788

Watford, William, N.C., 59,
#8042

Watford, William, w/o, N.C.,
103, #6479

Watkins, Charles, D.C., 132,
#9889

Watkins, Charles, D.C., 139,
#7109

Watkins, Elizabeth, Ky., 143,
#6030

Watkins, John, a/o, Va., 85,
#16460

Watkins, Joshua, S.C., 128,
#6061

Watkins, Joshua, S.C., 134,
#1428

Watkins, Mary, Richmond, Va.,
36A, #F3 26

Watkins, Samuel, W. Tenn., 64,
#9419

Watkins, Sarha, Richmond, Va.,
126, #3385

Watkins, Spencer, E. Tenn., 64,
#9378

Watkins, Thomas, Ky., 70,
#11160

Watson, Barsha, N.C., 103,
#6428

Watson, Evan T., a/o, Ky., 64,
#9698

Watson, James, c/o,
Philadelphia, Pa., 69,
#10851

Watson, James A., Mobile, Ala.,
134, #1081

Watson, John, Ind., 63, #9019

Watson, John, Ind., 79, #14559

Watson, John, w/o, N.H., 59,
#8155

Watson, Joseph S., Little Rock,
Ark., 134, #825

Watson, Levi, w/o, N.C., 71,
#12297

Watson, Lydia, a/o, Fayetteville,
N.C., 135, #1796

Watson, Lydia, g/o, N.C., 120,
#6438

Watson, Mercy, c/o, Albany,
N.Y., 54, #6690

Watson, Peggy, Richmond, Va.,
36A, #F1 V45

Watson, Peggy, Richmond, Va.,
71, #12363

Watson, Richard, S.C., 121,
#7247

Watson, Richard, S.C., 130,
#7272

Watson, Sarah Ann, Md., 132,
#9013

Watson, Thomas, Mo., 62,
#8837, card
Watson, Thomas, Mo., 27,
#8837
Watson, Thomas, Hartford,
Conn., 51, #6028
Watson, William, Ky., 68,
#10589
Watson, William, S.C., 51,
#6050
Wattles, Cynthia, a/o,
Philadelphia, Pa., 107,
#9190
Wattles, Michael, N.Y., 106,
#8672, card
Wattles, William, e/o, Albany,
N.Y., 27, #8672
Watts, Ann, c/o, Richmond, Va.,
71, #12430
Watts, Jennett, Iowa, 142,
#3838
Watts, Johnson, Ky., 57, #7459
Watts, Johnson, Ky., 60, #8184
Watts, Mary, Maine, 121,
#6874, card
Watts, Mary, c/o, Maine, 27,
#6874
Watts, Peter, e/o, Ky., 96,
#1822
Watts, Philip, g/o c/o, Mo.,
135, #1931
Watts, Phillip, g/o c/o, St.
Louis, Mo., 128, #5859
Watts, Thomas, Detroit, Mich.,
49, #5414
Way, Durien, Conn., 35, #1076
Way, Mary, Conn., 68, #10770
Wayland, James, a/o, Conn., 38,
#F1828
Wayne, H. C., —, 127, #4830,
slip

Wayne, H. C., —, 125, #2250,
card
Wayne, H. C., —, 126, #3260,
card
Wayne, H. C., —, 126, #3885,
card
Wayne, H. C., —, 127, #4180,
card
Wayne, H. C., —, 128, #5512,
card
Wayne, H. C., —, 128, #6082,
card
Wayson, Margaert, c/o,
Wheeling, Va., 130, #7209
Wayt, William, Va., 66, #10283
Wayt, William, Va., 78, #14290
Weaver, Conrad, Philadelphia,
Pa., 106, #8598
Weaver, Constant, w/o, R.I., 60,
#8323
Weaver, Daniel, Philadelphia,
Pa., 105, #8322
Weaver, Dutee, R.I., 116,
#3309, card
Weaver, Feronica, Philadelphia,
Pa., 110, #11008
Weaver, Nancy, a/o, Richmond,
Va., 36A, #F1 V2
Weaver, Polly, a/o, Albany,
N.Y., 124, #1197
Weaver, Richard, c/o, Albany,
N.Y., 114, #2359
Weaver, Richard, c/o, Albany,
N.Y., 114, #2380
Weaver, Samuel, Ky., 82,
#15212
Weaver, Samuel, w/o, Ky., 88,
#18000
Weaver, Sarah, Mo., 135, #1941
Weaver, Silas, c/o, R.I., 27,
#3309

Weavers, Gertrude, Albany,
N.Y., 100, #3972
Webb, Albert, g/o c/o, Ill., 128,
#5626
Webb, Albert, g/o c/o,
Spingfield, Ill., 142, #3547
Webb, Austin, w/o, Ga., 91,
#19270
Webb, Benjamin F., w/o, Ky.,
142, #3904
Webb, Ebenezer, Conn., 36,
#1491
Webb, Elizabeth, a/o,
Jonesboro, Tenn., 133,
#117
Webb, George W., Mo., 106,
#8378
Webb, Isaac, Albany, N.Y., 65,
#9990
Webb, Isaac, c/o, Albany, N.Y.,
109, #10416
Webb, Isaac, w/o, Philadelphia,
Pa., 74, #13279
Webb, John, Ga., 40, #3257
Webb, John, c/o, Maine, 102,
#5571
Webb, Joshua, Conn., 36, #154
Webb, Martha Ann, Nashville,
Tenn., 80, #14828
Webb, Phebe, c/o, Conn., 133,
#586
Webb (formerly Dodge), Susan
E., Albany, N.Y., 133,
#118
Webber, John, c/o, Boston,
Mass., 102, #5881
Webber, William, c/o, Mich.,
132, #9660
Webber, William, g/o c/o,
Mich., 125, #2814
Weber, August N., St. Louis,
Mo., 27, #2238

Webster, Allen, —, 117, #3958,
card
Webster, Allen, w/o, Albany,
N.Y., 27, #3958
Webster, Lydia, Portsmouth,
N.H., 97, #1928
Webster, Lydia, c/o, Albany,
N.Y., 100, #4371
Webster, Lydia, c/o, Albany,
N.Y., 101, #4812
Webster, Mercy, c/o, Albany,
N.Y., 97, #2273
Webster, Nathaniel, w/o,
Bellows Falls, Vt., 47,
#5008
Webster, Sarah A., Ga., 120,
#6542
Webster, Wilbour, Louisville,
Ky., 108, #9984 V#82
Webster, William, Albany, N.Y.,
60, #8383
Webster, William, Albany, N.Y.,
105, #8348
Wedig, Charles, Md., 121,
#7905
Wedig, John, Mo., 113, #1624
Weed, Isaac, Conn., 36, #1306
Weed, Jehiel, c/o, Albany, N.Y.,
117, #4429
Weekley, Thomas, Wheeling,
Va., 63, #8990
Weeks, Ann, a/o, Jacksonville,
Fla., 96, #1666
Weeks, David P., Mass., 71,
#12451
Weeks, Esther, S.C., 67, #10435
Weeks, Esther, S.C., 82, #15544
Weeks, John, Nashville, Tenn.,
27, #10456
Weeks, John, Nashville, Tenn.,
109, #10456, card

Weeks, Joseph, a/o, Montpelier, Vt., 124, #893

Weeks, Joseph, e/o, Conn., 38, #F1824

Weeks, Theophilus, w/o, E. Fla., 86, #16797

Weidman, Mary, New York City, 112, #950

Weir, Lydia, c/o, Ill., 69, #10951

Weir, Lydia, c/o, Ill., 78, #14246

Weir, Lydia, c/o, Ill., 102, #6243

Weir, Lydia, c/o, Ill., 101, #4938

Weir (now Wright), Lucinda C., Savannah, Ga., 117, #4178, card

Weiss, Jacob, w/o, Philadelphia, Pa., 56, #7242

Weithkneeht, Martin, a/o, Philadelphia, Pa., 73, #12884

Welch, Isaac, c/o, Richmond, Va., 49, #5387

Welch, Isiah, Richmond, Va., 69, #10920

Welch, James, a/o, Ky., 83, #15612

Welch, John, Albany, N.Y., 84, #16044

Welch, John, Jackson, Tenn., 72, #12551

Welch, John, Jackson, Tenn., 92, #19760

Welch, John, w/o, Albany, N.Y., 55, #7142

Welch (formerly Taylor), Nancy, Philadelphia, Pa., 111, #331

Weldon, Peter, Mo., 132, #9844

Weldon, Peter, Mo., 137, #4303

Welker, Henry W., g/o c/o, Indianapolis, Ind., 140, #9455

Weller, Philip, N.J., 97, #1899

Weller, Philip, a/o, N.J., 27, #7219

Weller, Phillip, N.J., 104, #7219, card

Weller, Charles S., PA, San Francisco, Calif., 118, #5074

Wellington, Jeduthan, w/o, Mass., 58, #7747

Wellman, John, Albany, N.Y., 82, #15380, card

Wellman, John, w/o, Albany, N.Y., 27, #15380

Wellman, Rebecca, e/o, Philadelphia, Pa., 115, #2826

Wells, Agnes, a/o, Richmond, Va., 36A, #F5 V12

Wells, Asa, Albany, N.Y., 80, #14873

Wells, Bolling, Va., 42, #3692

Wells, Jacob, N.C., 54, #6620

Wells, Jacob, w/o, N.C., 127, #4897

Wells, John, Ind., 90, #18808

Wells, John, Ky., 80, #14944

Wells, Lucy, Mass., 105, #8045

Wells, Lucy, Richmond, Va., 36A, #F6 V32

Wells, Mordicai, Ky., 134, #1487

Wells, Nathaniel, c/o, Va., 121, #6954

Wells, Peter, c/o, Albany, N.Y., 27, #11115

Wells, Richard, w/o, Ky., 106, #8407

West, Timothy, a/o, N.H., 111,
#652
West, William, —, 77, #14166,
card
West, William, —, 89, #18478,
card
West, William, Ky., 27, #18478
West, William, Ky., 27, #14166
West, William, Nashville,
Tenn., 27, #12333
Westcoat, Joseph, Albany, N.Y.,
53, #6560, card
Westcoat, Joseph, c/o, Albany,
N.Y., 28, #6560
Westcott, Sarah, c/o, R.I., 81,
#15189
Westen, Charles T., g/o c/o,
Spingfield, Ill., 140, #775
Westfall, Massey, c/o, Madison,
Ind., 99, #3163
Westmoreland, Jesse, W. Tenn.,
53, #6511, card
Westmoreland, Jesse, c/o,
Nashville, Tenn., 28,
#6511
Weston, Betty, a/o, Vt., 121,
#7841
Weston, Charles T., g/o c/o, Ill.,
139, #7530
Weston, Charles T., g/o c/o,
Spingfield, Ill., 141, #2017
Weston, Henry, Spingfield, Ill.,
143, #6522
Weston, James, Fayetteville,
N.C., 41, #3391
Weston, James, e/o, N.C., 95,
#1087
Wetherbee, Abel, w/o, N.H., 70,
#11137
Wethered, Frances, e/o, Ky., 98,
#3012

Wetmore, Amelia S. C., Mo.,
126, #2926
Wetmore, Bela, w/o, Albany,
N.Y., 56, #7359
Wetzel, John, Ga., 53, #6427
Wever, Adma, c/o, Albany, N.Y.,
128, #5054
Weyson, Henry, Va., 94, #309,
card
Weysor, Henry, e/o, Va., 28,
#309
Whalen, Jeremiah, a/o, Albany,
N.Y., 113, #1379
Whaley, James, w/o, Ohio, 75,
#13569
Whaley, Jerusha, R.I., 52,
#6085
Whaley, Reynolds, Albany,
N.Y., 46, #4720
Wharton, Lelitia, Richmond,
Va., 36A, #F6, card
Whatley, Michael, Ga., 73,
#12901
Wheatley, Peggy, —, 122,
#8581, card
Wheatley, Peggy, a/o,
Nashville, Tenn., 28,
#8581
Wheaton, Betsey, c/o, R.I., 81,
#15146
Wheaton, Joseph, c/o, D.C.,
117, #4289
Wheaton, Roswell, over/o,
Conn., 82, #15280
Whedon, Edmund, w/o, Albany,
N.Y., 43, #3944
Whedow, Henry E.,
Cananadaigua, N.Y., 143,
#7088
Wheeler, Amos, w/o,
Montpelier, Vt., 86,
#17250

Wheeler, Benjamin, w/o,
Philadelphia, Pa., 104,
#7171
Wheeler, Edward, Albany, N.Y.,
43, #4103
Wheeler, Elizabeth, a/o,
Montpelier, Vt., 95, #968
Wheeler, Isaac, Ohio, 72,
#12588
Wheeler, John, w/o, Concord,
N.H., 98, #3057
Wheeler, Jonathan, Wheeling,
Va., 143, #6825
Wheeler, Julia, Conn., 36,
#13031
Wheeler, Loby, Philadelphia,
Pa., 66, #10168
Wheeler, Martha, c/o, Albany,
N.Y., 109, #10623
Wheeler, Micajah, Richmond,
Va., 102, #5865
Wheeler, Micajah, Richmond,
Va., 115, #2960
Wheeler, Micajah, Richmond,
Va., 44, #4184
Wheeler Sr., Macajah,
Richmond, Va., 45, #4480
Wheeler, Phinehas, c/o, Albany,
N.Y., 98, #2622
Wheeler, Samuel, Mo., 103,
#6618
Wheeler, Samuel, Mo., 107,
#9249
Wheeler, Samuel, Mo., 141,
#2013
Wheeler, Samuel, Mo., 142,
#6023
Wheeler, Samuel, St. Louis, Mo.,
142, #4697
Wheeler, Simeon, Ind., 72,
#12593

Wheeler, Solsberry, Concord,
N.H., 41, #3429
Wheeler, W. H. H., c/o, Maine,
131, #8709
Wheeler, William, c/o, Albany,
N.Y., 51, #5846
Whelock, Ralph, Albany, N.Y.,
104, #7577
Whetsell, Henry, Richmond,
Va., 63, #8940
Whetsell, Henry, a/o, Richmond,
Va., 28, #8940
Whight, Jonathan, w/o, Ky.,
100, #4207
Whipple, Olive, Concord, N.H.,
74, #13303
Whipple, Solomon, c/o, Boston,
Mass., 121, #6935
Whit, Elizabeth A., a/o,
Knoxville, Tenn., 121,
#7149
Whitaker, Abraham,
Philadelphia, Pa., 66,
#10245
Whitaker, Ann, c/o, Ky., 120,
#6283
Whitaker, Elizabeth, Richmond,
Va., 129, #6318
Whitaker, Elizabeth, Richmond,
Va., 101, #4885
Whitaker, Elizabeth, e/o,
Richmond, Va., 36A, #F4
V12
Whitaker, Elizabeth, e/o,
Richmond, Va., 134, #1364
Whitaker, Esau, g/o, c/o,
Indianapolis, Ind., 133,
#119
Whitaker, Jonathan, w/o, Ohio,
76, #13852
Whitaker, Mark, Ky., 41, #3528

Whitaker, Mary, c/o, Ohio, 112, #868
Whitaker, Susannah, c/o, N.H., 65, #9810
Whitcomb, John, w/o, Philadelphia, Pa., 69, #10838
Whitcomb, Rufus, w/o, Vt., 90, #18554
White, Abigail, c/o, Philadelphia, Pa., 134, #1441
White, Abraham, w/o, Indianapolis, Ind., 123, #294
White, Alexander A., c/o, La., 102, #5538
White, Andrew, Huntsville, Ala., 53, #6411
White, Anna, Vt., 64, #9239
White, Caty, e/o, Richmond, Va., 36A, #F5 V14
White, Charles, Ohio, 41, #3410
White, Christopher, Richmond, Va., 89, #18419
White, Christopher, Richmond, Va., 92, #19798
White, Christopher, Richmond, Va., 55, #7059
White, Christopher, Va., 90, #18614
White, David, Albany, N.Y., 104, #7514, card
White, David, N.Y., 28, #7514
White, David, Ohio, 57, #7567
White, David, w/o, 38th Inf., 137, #4134
White, David F., g/o c/o, Indianapolis, Ind., 137, #3838
White, Dorothy, c/o, Va., 78, #14446

White, Elijah, Va., 42, #3791, card
White, Elizabeth, c/o, Va., 77, #14170
White, Fortune C., Albany, N.Y., 135, #2008
White, Henry, c/o, N.Y., 84, #16262
White, Isaac, a/o w/o, Ind., 110, #110, #militia
White, Pvt. Isaac, c/o, Ind., 110, #109, #militia
White, Jemima, N.C., 111, #542
White, Jenkins, a/o, Albany, N.Y., 125, #1893
White, John, Mich., 67, #10333
White, John, Mo., 130, #7887
White, Joseph, Richmond, Va., 56, #7414
White, Joseph, Richmond, Va., 47, #5025
White, Joseph, Va., 67, #10334
White, Joseph, Va., 78, #14449
White, Joseph, a/o, Philadelphia, Pa., 134, #1409
White, Juliany, c/o, Albany, N.Y., 28, #10840
White, Juliany, c/o, Albany, N.Y., 28, #10691
White, Mary, Conn., 36, #1014
White, Nancy, Maine, 75, #13503
White, Nathaniel, La., 131, #8095
White, Nicholas, a/o, N.J., 137, #3701
White, Oliver, w/o, Albany, N.Y., 53, #6429
White, Penelope, Richmond, Va., 127, #4275

White, Rhodah, Philadelphia,
Pa., 68, #10702
White, Richard, Richmond, Va.,
44, #4224
White, Richard, Richmond, Va.,
45, #4455
White, Richard, e/o, Richmond,
Va., 114, #2013
White, Robert, c/o, Richmond,
Va., 116, #3242
White, Saml., w/o, Wheeling,
Va., 52, #6203
White, Sarah, Richmond, Va.,
36A, #F6 V31
White, Seth, c/o, Albany, N.Y.,
53, #6483
White, Seth, c/o, Boston, Mass.,
59, #8078
White, Solomon, Conn., 36,
#490
White, Thomas, Ohio to Ind.,
70, #12188, card
White, Thomas, Philadelphia,
Pa., 135, #2307, card
White, Thomas, a/o,
Philadelphia, Pa., 28,
#2307
White, Thomas, w/o, Ind., 28,
#12188
White, William, Ind., 52, #6316
White, William, c/o, Bellows
Falls, Vt., 51, #6034
White, William, w/o, Ind., 113,
#1551
White, William, c/o, Bellows
Falls, Vt., 52, #6164
White, Esther, Conn., 96, bet.
#1498 & #1502, card
Whitehead, Mark, c/o, Va.
Milita, 98, #2589
Whitehead, Mark, e/o w/o, Va.
Milita, 98, #2589

Whitehead, Thomas, Albany,
N.Y., 86, #16914
Whitehead, Thomas, Albany,
N.Y., 94, #432
Whitehurst, Simon, Ga., 96,
#1761
Whitententon, James H.,
Jackson, Tenn., 137, #4603
Whiteside, John, w/o, Albany,
N.Y., 96, #1547
Whiteside, William, Jackson,
Tenn., 107, #9238
Whitford, Sarah, Albany, N.Y.,
82, #15523
Whitford, Sarah, Albany, N.Y.,
90, #18611
Whitford, Sarah, e/o, Albany,
N.Y., 95, #1044
Whitford, Sarah, w/o, R.I., 95,
#976
Whiting, Pvt. David H., 13th
Inf., 114, #2386 pay due
Whiting, Joseph, Mass., 43,
#4031
Whiting, Nathan, Bellows Falls,
Vt., 46, #4795
Whitlock, James, Richmond,
Va., 61, #8641
Whitman, John, Conn., 36,
#429
Whitmarsh, Lot, c/o, Mass.,
126, #2936
Whitmarsh, Mary, c/o, Maine,
120, #5944
Whitmore, John, w/o,
Richmond, Va., 47, #4947
Whitney, Ezekiel, New York
City, 95, #1223, card
Whitney, Ezekiel, a/o, New York
City, 28, #1223
Whitney, Joshua, c/o,
Burlington, Vt., 28, #1972

Wilcox, Jared, c/o, Burlington, Vt., 116, #3526

Wilcox, John, a/o, Albany, N.Y., 84, #15956

Wilcox, John, a/o, Albany, N.Y., 115, #2450

Wilcox, John, c/o, Albany, N.Y., 80, #14976

Wilcox, Luther, w/o, Albany, N.Y., 121, #7776

Wilcox, Nathan B., Mo., 123, #9033

Wilcox, Rebecca, Conn., 64, #9616

Wild, Deborah, Mass., 117, #4259

Wild, Deborah, c/o, Boston, Mass., 103, #6846

Wild, Thomas, w/o, Albany, N.Y., 108, #9771

Wilden, John, c/o, Va. Milita, 64, #9278

Wilden, John, w/o, Va. Milita, 64, #9277

Wilder, Phineas, Mass., 68, #10790

Wildman, Polly, Albany, N.Y., 79, #14553

Wildman, Polly, c/o, Albany, N.Y., 111, #776

Wiles, Abraham, a/o, Fayetteville, N.C., 132, #9367

Wiley, Agnes, Richmond, Va., 102, #5931

Wiley, Alexander, Mich., 42, #3788

Wiley, Ebenezer, c/o, Mass., 56, #7402

Wiley, George W., g/o c/o, Ga., 137, #3807

Wiley, Isaac, Philadelphia, Pa., 74, #13341

Wiley, Isaac, Philadelphia, Pa., 87, #17402

Wiley, Isaac, w/o, Philadelphia, Pa., 135, #2044

Wiley, Jonathan, Pittsburgh, Pa., 82, #15443

Wiley, Keziah, c/o, Albany, N.Y., 129, #6881

Wiley, Rufus, N.C., 45, #4570

Wiley, Rufus, N.C., 70, #11135

Wiley, Rufus, N.C., 82, #15527

Wiley, William, Ind., 56, #7228, card

Wiley, William, w/o, Ind., 28, #7228

Wilford, John C., w/o, Albany, N.Y., 128, #5107

Wilford, Lewis, St. Augustine, Fla., 55, #7025

Wilheid, Frederick, a/o, Md., 102, #5601

Wilhite, John, Ky., 142, #3650, slip

Wilhite, John, c/o, Ky., 28, #3650

Wilkenson, Jonathan, w/o, Albany, N.Y., 54, #6848

Wilkerson, Benjamin, Miss., 106, #8783

Wilkerson, John, w/o, Cincinnati, Ohio, 87, #17508

Wilkerson, John, w/o, Fayetteville, N.C., 123, #9622

Wilkerson, Margaret, Fayetteville, N.C., 129, #6725

Wilkerson, Reuben, c/o, Albany, N.Y., 125, #2003

Wilkerson, William, Ind., 65,
#9737
Wilkin, John, Baltimore, Md.,
92, #19865
Wilkin, John, Md., 74, #13143
Wilkins, Catherine, c/o,
Pittsburgh, Pa., 28, #6347
Wilkins, Catherine, c/o,
Pittsburgh, Pa., 28, #6407
Wilkins, Catherine, c/o,
Pittsburgh, Pa., 28, #6723
Wilkins, George, Pittsburgh,
Pa., 44, #4262
Wilkins, John, c/o, N.J., 95,
#891
Wilkinson, Ann, Va., 74,
#13131
Wilkinson, Hardin F., La., 131,
#8772
Wilkinson, Samuel, a/o, Vt., 87,
#17505
Wilkinson, Stith, Ill., 126,
#3075
Wilkinson, Stith, Ill., 129,
#6707
Wilkinson, William, Richmond,
Va., 71, #12262
Wilkinson, William, w/o,
Albany, N.Y., 50, #5514
Wilks, Thomas, Miss., 86,
#17218
Wilks, Thomas, Miss., 89,
#18230
Wilks, Thomas, Natchez, Miss.,
81, #15208
Willam, Capt. William G., c/o,
Topographical Engineers,
99, #3351
Willard, Eli, w/o, Concord, N.H.,
102, #5983

Willard, Ephriam, w/o,
Philadelphia, Pa., 64,
#9693
Willard, Ezra, w/o, Maine, 115,
#2646
Willard, George C., w/o, Wisc.,
56, #7291
Willard, Jonathan, Concord,
N.H., 69, #10891
Willard, Longley, Burlington,
Vt., 44, #4305
Willard, Longley, Burlington,
Vt., 54, #6722
Willbanks, Mary, Ga., 130,
#7755
Willbanks, Richard, w/o, S.C.,
131, #8708
Willeford, Richard, S.C., 28,
#5252
Willes, Edward H., Md., 84,
#16261
Willes, John, c/o, Conn., 80,
#14920
Willett, Samuel, Albany, N.Y.,
75, #13695
Willey, Barzillia, Albany, N.Y.,
89, #18400
Willey, James, c/o, N.C., 60,
#8222
Willey, Josiah, w/o, N.H., 58,
#7790, card
Willey, Josiah, w/o,
Portsmouth, N.H., 28,
#7790
Willey, Nathan, Conn., 36,
#824
William, Edward, St. Louis, Mo.,
94, #455
William, Long, Mo., 55, #6910
Williams, Abiah, N.C., 28,
#15063

Williams, Anner, Conn., 99,
#3651
Williams, Bennett, c/o, Ky., 52,
#6207
Williams, Buckner, w/o, Ind.,
61, #8392
Williams, Caleb, w/o,
Philadelphia, Pa., 125,
#2500
Williams, Charles, c/o, Md., 59,
#8122
Williams, Daniel, Tenn., 88,
#17868, card
Williams, Daniel, e/o,
Nashville, Tenn., 28,
#17868
Williams, Darus, w/o, Albany,
N.Y., 43, #3951
Williams, David, a/o, Conn., 74,
#13138
Williams, Durell, Albany, N.Y.,
52, #6126
Williams, Ebenezer, w/o,
Philadelphia, Pa., 89,
#18447
Williams, Edward, Mo., 41,
#3445
Williams, Edward, Mo., 49,
#5338
Williams, Edward, Mo., 58,
#7793
Williams, Edward, Mo., 81,
#15181
Williams, Edward, w/o, Mo., 28,
#455
Williams, Eleann, a/o, Ky., 140,
#9649
Williams, Eli, Philadelphia, Pa.,
56, #7241
Williams, Eli, c/o, Philadelphia,
Pa., 136, #3111

Williams, Elisha, e/o, Conn.,
103, #6934
Williams, Elizabeth, N.C., 71,
#12407
Williams, Elizabeth, c/o,
Richmond, Va., 63, #9100
Williams, Emily, Conn., 36,
#65
Williams, Ezekial, Albany,
N.Y., 106, #8814
Williams, Hannah, c/o, Boston,
Mass., 123, #9617
Williams, Henry, Wheeling, Va.,
107, #9234
Williams, Isaac, Mobile, Ala.,
51, #6019
Williams, Isaac, Miss., 76,
#13875
Williams, Isaac, Natchez, Miss.,
69, #10940
Williams, Isaac, over/o,
Hartford, Conn., 61, #8461
Williams, Isaack, Natchez,
Miss., 81, #15162
Williams, J. C. D., Mich., 120,
#6028
Williams, James, Albany, N.Y.,
67, #10365
Williams, James, Richmond,
Va., 58, #7684
Williams, James, w/o, Va., 87,
#17647
Williams, James M., w/o,
Richmond, Va., 69, #10881
Williams, Janes, N.C., 123,
#9572
Williams, Jeremiah,
Philadelphia, Pa., 89,
#18386
Williams, Jeremiah, Wheeling,
Va., 44, #4202

Williams, Jesse, a/o, Ky., 28,
#17968
Williams, Jesse, a/o,
Montpelier, Vt., 28,
#19841
Williams, Jessee, Ky., 88,
#17968, card
Williams, John, Knoxville,
Tenn., 105, #7828
Williams, John, Ky., 133, #680
Williams, John, a/o, Albany,
N.Y., 119, #5177
Williams, Joseph V., La., 105,
#8321
Williams, Judith, Ky., 75,
#13653
Williams, Lew, Nashville,
Tenn., 44, #4387
Williams, Lewellin, c/o, Fla.,
90, #18633
Williams, Lewis, Ga., 28,
#10320
Williams, Longley, Vt., 50,
#5640
Williams, Lydia, Wisc., 80,
#14922
Williams, Margaret, Ill., 82,
#15548
Williams, Margaret, Ill., 83,
#15692
Williams, Margaret, Miss., 91,
#19491
Williams (formerly Ayres), Mary
A., Ga., 115, #2871
Williams, Molly, c/o, Ky., 98,
#2743
Williams, Nathaniel, c/o, New
York City, 28, #8244
Williams, Osborn, —, 118,
#5039, card
Williams, Osborn, c/o, Md., 28,
#5039

Williams, Pattey, comm/o,
Richmond, Va., 109,
#10522
Williams, Peter, Mobile, Ala.,
52, #6090
Williams, Peter, Tuscaloosa,
Ala., 75, #13420
Williams, Peter, Tuscaloosa,
Ala., 88, #17790
Williams, Phineas, Pittsburgh,
Pa., 51, #5867
Williams, Phineas, w/o,
Pittsburgh, Pa., 94, #384
Williams, Platt, Cincinnati,
Ohio, 108, #9947 (alias
William Patterson)
Williams, Reas, w/o, Knoxville,
Tenn., 108, #9958
Williams, Robert, Mo., 113,
#1818
Williams, Sally, Mass., 132,
#9204
Williams, Sarah, Concord, N.H.,
47, #4938
Williams, Sarah J., Knoxville,
Tenn., 122, #8292
Williams, Senak, Concord, N.H.,
53, #6587
Williams, Thanaky, Albany,
N.Y., 112, #863
Williams, Thomas, c/o, N.C.,
60, #8304
Williams, Thomas C., w/o,
Nashville, Tenn., 50,
#5467
Williams, William, Madison,
Ind., 45, #4446
Williams, William, c/o,
Topographical Engineers,
103, #6466
Williams, William, g/o c/o, Ky.,
127, #4894

Williams, Capt. William G., c/o,
—, 105, #8185
Williams, Capt. William G., c/o,
Topographical Engineers,
104, #7277
Williams, Capt. William G., c/o,
Topographical Engineers,
107, #9044
Williams, Capt. William G., c/o,
Topographical Engineers,
108, #10014
Williams, Capt. William G., c/o,
Topographical Engineers,
109, #10811
Williams, Capt. William G., c/o,
Topographical Engineers,
111, #434
Williams, Capt. William G., c/o,
Topographical Engineers,
100, #4419
Williams, William G., c/o, —,
101, #5305
Williams, Wilmoth, Richmond,
Va., 104, #7524
Williamson, Eleazer, c/o, Ohio,
63, #8957
Williamson, Jacob, w/o, N.J.,
125, #2177
Williamson, James, Albany,
N.Y., 53, #6434
Williamson, Thomas, Fayette,
Ind., 44, #4253
Williamson, Thomas, Ind., 49,
#5286
Williamson, Thomas, Ind., 70,
#11187
Williamson, Thomas, Madison,
Ind., 62, #8733
Williamson, Thomas, Ind., 52,
#6275
Williamson, William, w/o, S.C.,
117, #4237

Williamson, William F., Ill.,
122, #8563
Williamson, William F., a/o,
Ill., 124, #756
Williford, Richard, S.C., 53,
#6400, card
Williford, Richard, S.C., 28,
#6400
Willis, Alice, Montpelier, Vt.,
101, #5006 V#2
Willis, Edward, Ky., 90, #18694
Willis, Hezekiah, Albany, N.Y.,
108, #9726
Willis, James, Mo., 102, #5690
Willis, Jesse, Tallahassee, Fla.,
92, #19873
Willis, Jonathan, w/o, Vt., 28,
#18089
Willis, Joseph, Wheeling, Va.,
71, #12229
Willis, Otis W., Concord, N.H.,
113, #1589
Willis, Otis W., Concord, N.H.,
129, #6717
Willis, Otis W., Concord, N.H.,
136, #3227
Willis, Smith, w/o, Knoxville,
Tenn., 109, #10544
Willis, William, w/o, Wheeling,
Va., 124, #1351
Willis, William I., c/o, Ky.,
114, #2125
Williston, Ichabod, R.I., 69,
#10937
Williston, Lydia, Albany, N.Y.,
62, #8823
Willmore, Peggy, Richmond,
Va., 63, #8942
Willoford, Richard, S.C., 49,
#5252, card
Willouby, Salmon, Burlington,
Vt., 41, #3440

Willoughby, Sarah, Richmond, Va., 67, #10411
Wills, James, Mo., 87, #17563
Wills, James, Mo., 106, #8415
Wills, James, Mo., 107, #9472
Wills, James, Mo., 108, #10325
Wills, Leonard, Ga., 58, #7677
Wills, Leonard, Ga., 67, #10538
Wills, Leonard, Ga., 80, #14807
Wills, Nathaniel H., —, 116, #3712, slip
Wills, Otis W., Concord, N.H., 127, #4880
Willse, James, w/o, Mich., 109, #10620
Willson, Arthur, Pittsburgh, Pa., 115, #2804 V#37
Willson, Willam, Pittsburgh, Pa., 91, #19411
Willys, Thomas, Conn., 36, #170
Wilmott, Robert, c/o, Ky., 64, #9588
Wilson, Aaron, a/o, Concord, N.H., 113, #1471
Wilson, Agnes, c/o, N.J., 81, #15054
Wilson, Alexander, Philadelphia, Pa., 45, #4438
Wilson, Alexander, Philadelphia, Pa., 52, #6112
Wilson, Andrew, a/o, Cincinnati, Ohio, 138, #5680
Wilson, Asa, Wheeling, Va., 78, #14472
Wilson, Augustin, Ga., 45, #4598
Wilson, Augustine, S.C., 60, #8231

Wilson, Betsey, c/o, Maine, 131, #8297
Wilson, Betsey, c/o, Maine, 131, #8498
Wilson, Charles F., w/o, Mo., 137, #4189
Wilson, Eli B., w/o, Richmond, Va., 100, #3868
Wilson, Elizabeth, a/o, Ky., 128, #5339
Wilson, George C., w/o, Baltimore, Md., 123, #9182
Wilson, Isaac, w/o, Ohio, 81, #15155
Wilson, Israel, a/o, Pittsburgh, Pa., 116, #3144
Wilson, James, Ind., 73, #12770
Wilson, James, Indianapolis, Ind., 43, #4009
Wilson, James, Madison, Ind., 64, #9537
Wilson, James, Ind., 52, #6307
Wilson, Joab, c/o, Conn., 88, #17792
Wilson, John, a/o, Maine, 90, #18583
Wilson, John, w/o, Jonesboro, Tenn., 46, #4674
Wilson, John P., Ga., 125, #1862
Wilson, Joseph, Philadelphia, Pa., 60, #8380
Wilson, Joseph, w/o, Albany, N.Y., 106, #8365
Wilson, Joshua, Mobile, Ala., 53, #6497
Wilson, Joshua, Mobile, Ala., 56, #7432
Wilson, Joshua, Mobile, Ala., 73, #12788
Wilson, Martha, a/o, Albany, N.Y., 99, #3231

Wilson, Mary, Miss., 138,
#4664
Wilson, Nancy, Philadelphia,
Pa., 101, #4851 V#12
Wilson, Newman, S.C., 46,
#4792
Wilson, Newman, S.C., 49,
#5303
Wilson, Newman, S.C., 51,
#5907
Wilson, Noah, Philadelphia, Pa.,
118, #4895
Wilson, Obadiah, c/o,
Cincinnati, Ohio, 137,
#4073
Wilson, Philip, New York City,
119, #5157
Wilson, Rachel, a/o, Conn.,
101, #4784
Wilson, Robert, Ind., 60, #8299
Wilson, Robert, S.C., 41, #3396
Wilson, Samuel, e/o, N.C., 28,
#18503
Wilson, Sarah, Albany, N.Y.,
62, #8679
Wilson, Shuah, Concord, N.H.,
142, #4711
Wilson, Thomas, —, 106,
#8364, card
Wilson, Thomas, a/o, Albany,
N.Y., 28, #8364
Wilson, Thomas N., g/o c/o,
Pulaski, Tenn., 126, #3803
Wilson, Walter, a/o w/o,
Albany, N.Y., 106, #8885
Wilson, William, Pa., 44,
#4412, card
Wilson, William, Richmond,
Va., 63, #8907
Wilson, William, Wheeling,
Va., 39, #3084

Wilson, William, w/o,
Philadelphia, Pa., 28,
#4412
Wilson Sr., William, Richmond,
Va., 78, #14514
Wilt, Samuel, Philadelphia, Pa.,
139, #9115
Wilt, Thomas, Philadelphia, Pa.,
72, #12472
Wilt, Thomas, Philadelphia, Pa.,
80, #14811
Wilt, Thomas, w/o, Pa., 87,
#17616
Wiman, William, Pittsburgh,
Pa., 66, #10261
Wimbish, James, w/o,
Richmond, Va., 69, #10915
Winch, Jason, c/o, Vt., 59,
#7977
Winchel, James, e/o, New York
City, 70, #12128
Winchester, Daniel, Jackson,
Tenn., 46, #4756
Winchester, Daniel, w/o,
Jackson, Tenn., 89, #18229
Winchester, Richard, Ky., 105,
#7852
Winchester, Rosanna, g/o,
Jackson, Tenn., 134, #1550
Winchester, Rosannah, g/o,
Jackson, Tenn., 132, #9881
Winchester, Rosannah, g/o,
Jackson, Tenn., 134, #1378
Windham, Sarah, c/o, Md., 83,
#15752
Windhorst, Wilhelmina,
Louisville, Ky., 142, #4698
Winfield, Harris, Richmond, Va.,
44, #4408
Winfield, Harris, Va., 63,
#8908, card

Winfree, Francis W., Richmond,
   Va., 36A, #F4 V17
Wing, James, Mass., 81,
   #15015
Wingard, George, c/o,
   Cleveland, Ohio, 138,
   #5770
Winkler, Susanna, Ky., 96,
   #1653
Winkler, Susannah, Ky., 109,
   #10779, card
Winkler, Susannah, a/o,
   Louisville, Ky., 28, #10779
Winn, John, Va., 83, #15761
Winn, Susanna, Philadelphia,
   Pa., 72, #12494
Winn, Susanna, Philadelphia,
   Pa., 76, #13871
Winne, John D., c/o, Albany,
   N.Y., 50, #5580
Winne, William, w/o, Albany,
   N.Y., 115, #2645
Winneford, Judith, a/o, Ky.,
   130, #7446
Winneford, Judith, a/o, Ky.,
   130, #7546
Winslow, Asa, Pittsburgh, Pa.,
   57, #7451
Winslow, Asa, Pittsburgh, Pa.,
   68, #10643
Winslow, Charlotte, Mass., 131,
   #8130
Winslow, Deborah, c/o, Mass.,
   109, #10873
Winstead, Mandley, g/o, Ky.,
   96, #1719
Winters, Lewis, Detroit, Mich.,
   142, #5930
Winters, Lewis, Mich., 143,
   #6162
Winters, Lewis, Mich., 143,
   #7370

Winton, Nathan, Philadelphia,
   Pa., 43, #3812
Wise, Jacob, Philadelphia, Pa.,
   64, #9261
Wise, Jacob, Philadelphia, Pa.,
   87, #17685
Wise, Jacob, S.C., 64, #9130
Wise, Jacob, S.C., 70, #12111
Wise, Jacob, S.C., 73, #12978
Wise, Jacob, c/o, Philadelphia,
   Pa., 99, #3658
Wise, Peter, E. Tenn., 61, #8510
Wise, Peter, E. Tenn., 62, #8743
Wise, Peter, Knoxville, Tenn.,
   64, #9181
Wise, Peter, Knoxville, Tenn.,
   40, #3211
Wise, Peter, Knoxville, Tenn.,
   57, #7581
Wise, Peter, w/o, Ohio, 47,
   #4994
Wisecarver, George, Pittsburgh,
   Pa., 41, #3358
Wiser, George, Knoxville,
   Tenn., 39, #3023
Wisman, David, c/o, Mass., 49,
   #5352
Wisong, Fiatt, a/o, Va., 126,
   #3164
Wiswall, Sarah, Mass., 105,
   #8135
Wiswall, Sarah, Mass., 100,
   #3801
Witbeck, Lena, c/o, Albany,
   N.Y., 64, #9433
Witherall, Betsy, c/o, Albany,
   N.Y., 109, #10722
Witherow, James, Nashville,
   Tenn., 110, bet. #10974 &
   #10992, card
Withers, James, —, 91, #19214,
   slip

Withers, Jesse, c/o, Va., 65,
#9943
Withers, Capt. John, Special
Statement, 126, #3400
Withers, William R., c/o,
Richmond, Va., 64, #9256
Witherspoon, Mary, S.C., 132,
#9031
Witherspoon, Mary, c/o, S.C.,
126, #2978
Witherspoon, Mary, c/o, S.C.,
126, #3086
Withrow, James, Nashville,
Tenn., 83, #15770
Withrow, James, Nashville,
Tenn., 86, #16881
Withrow, James, Nashville,
Tenn., 90, #18849
Withrow, James, Nashville,
Tenn., 103, #6688
Withrow, James, Nashville,
Tenn., 95, #1017
Withrow, James, Nashville,
Tenn., 96, #1788
Withrow, James, Nashville,
Tenn., 92, #198
Withrow, James, a/o, Tenn.,
106, #8879
Witt, Burgess, w/o, Knoxville,
Tenn., 97, #2044
Witt, Eunice, c/o, N.H., 85,
#16526
Witt, Jacob, Philadelphia, Pa.,
47, #4851
Witt, Jesse, w/o, Va., 82,
#15419
Witt, Jesse, w/o, Va., 83,
#15809
Witt, Jesse, w/o, Va., 85,
#16384
Witt, Phebe, Ky., 96, #1654

Witt (or Wilt), Rebecca,
comm/o, Ky., 135, #2017
Witt, Thomas, Philadelphia, Pa.,
62, #8761
Witter, Gavan, Albany, N.Y.,
140, #9416
Witter, Gavin, Albany, N.Y.,
128, #5861
Wolcott, Elizabeth, Cleveland,
Ohio, 133, #263
Wolf, Andrew, c/o, Ga., 120,
#6420
Wolf, Henry, g/o c/o,
Philadelphia, Pa., 132,
#9515
Wolf, Michael, Pa., 120, #6198,
card
Wolf, Michael, a/o,
Philadelphia, Pa., 28,
#6198
Wolfe, Henry, w/o, Albany,
N.Y., 86, #16750
Wolfe, Jesse, Ind., 63, #8889
Wolford, John, Wheeling, Va.,
47, #4856
Wolford, John, Wheeling, Va.,
52, #6202
Womack, Abner, Ky., 42, #3694
Wonder, Andrew, Pittsburgh,
Pa., 66, #10056
Wood, Belfield, w/o, Nashville,
Tenn., 41, #3414
Wood, Charles, c/o,
Philadelphia, Pa., 122,
#8535, card
Wood, Charles, c/o, Pittsburgh,
Pa., 28, #8535
Wood, Daniel, a/o, Albany,
N.Y., 29, #8464
Wood, Daniel, c/o, Albany,
N.Y., 91, #19077

Wood, Daniel, e/o, Mass., 92, #19563

Wood, Ebenezer, w/o, N.H., 81, #15047

Wood, Eleazer, a/o, Montpelier, Vt., 110, #313

Wood, Ellit, Nashville, Tenn., 45, #4494

Wood, Emphriam, a/o, N.H., 65, #9919

Wood, Francis, Va., 81, #14995

Wood, Francis, Va., 89, #18223

Wood, James, c/o, Concord, N.H., 52, #6247

Wood, James, w/o, Ohio, 74, #13117

Wood, Joel, w/o, Albany, N.Y., 48, #5051

Wood, John, Ind., 91, #19089, card

Wood, John, Nashville, Tenn., 80, #14769

Wood, John, w/o, Richmond, Va., 94, #596

Wood, Joseph, e/o, Concord, N.H., 138, #5606

Wood, Joshua, w/o, Albany, N.Y., 100, #3910

Wood, Mary, Albany, N.Y., 121, #7248

Wood, Mary, Maine, 124, #778

Wood, Mary, Maine, 126, #3864

Wood, Mary, Richmond, Va., 97, #2497

Wood, Mary, c/o, Maine, 135, #2417

Wood, Nancy, Richmond, Va., 103, #6563

Wood, Obadiah, Ark., 66, #10248

Wood, Obadiah, Ark., 84, #16098

Wood, Phebe, Mass., 120, #6097, card

Wood, Phebe, a/o, Boston, Mass., 29, #6097

Wood, Samuel, Mich., 103, #7092

Wood, Sarah, c/o, New York City, 122, #8222

Wood, Thomas, Albany, N.Y., 77, #14026

Wood, William, w/o, N.C., 71, #12252

Woodall, Joseph, Ga., 40, #3255

Woodall, Samuel, N.C., 71, #12433

Woodard, Jesse, Albany, N.Y., 56, #7346

Woodard, Jesse, Albany, N.Y., 79, #14599

Woodard, Jesse, Albany, N.Y., 80, #14940

Woodard, Jesse, c/o, Albany, N.Y., 29, #7217

Woodberry, James H., c/o, Albany, N.Y., 80, #14813

Woodberry, Robert, w/o, Mass., 48, #5168

Woodbury, Rhoda, a/o, Maine, 120, #5936

Woodcock, Benjamin, w/o, Mass., 94, #238

Woodcock, Rhoda, Albany, N.Y., 47, #4907

Woodcock, Rhoda, a/o, Madison, Ind., 106, #8356

Woodel, Joseph, c/o, N.C., 122, #8929

Wooden, Daniel, New York City, 64, #9315

Woodford, Bissel, Albany, N.Y., 89, #18494

Woodford, Bissell, c/o, Albany, N.Y., 90, #18562

Woodhouse, Henry, Albany, N.Y., 80, #14825

Woodhouse, Henry, Albany, N.Y., 43, #3952

Woodhouse, Samuel, Conn., 36, #1483

Woodin, John, New York City, 116, #3176, card

Woodin, John, c/o, New York City, 29, #3176

Woodliff, Mary E. J., N.C., 119, #5651

Woodman, Benjamin, c/o, Maine, 88, #18094

Woodman, Edward, e/o, R.I., 64, #9641

Woodpin, Rebecca, Mo., 139, #7108

Woodruff, Caroline, Albany, N.Y., 101, #4910

Woodruff, Chloe, c/o, Conn., 36, #5970

Woodruff, Chloe, c/o, Conn., 36, #4233

Woodruff, John, c/o, Conn., 91, #18961

Woodruff, Robert, e/o, N.J., 97, #2484

Woodruff, Selah, w/o, Albany, N.Y., 101, #4909

Woods, Archibald, c/o, Ky., 47, #4897

Woods, Caldwell, Ky., 107, #9667, card

Woods, Joseph, c/o, Philadelphia, Pa., 29, #3337

Woods Sr., Joseph, Philadelphia, Pa., 136, #3337, card

Woods, Mary, Va., 75, #13596

Woods, Samuel, c/o, Richmond, Va., 133, #247

Woods Sr., William, Ky., 57, #7660

Woodson, Jacob, Richmond, Va., 44, #4389

Woodson, Wade N., Ky., 53, #6577

Woodsum, Samuel, Maine, 89, #18401

Woodward, Darius, c/o, Jacksonville, Fla., 108, #9729

Woodward, Jesse, N.Y., 104, #7217, card

Woodward, Jonathan, Concord, N.H., 97, #1999, card

Woodward, Jonathan, a/o, Concord, N.H., 29, #1999

Woodward, Jordan, N.C., 58, #7836

Woodward, Jordon, N.C., 80, #14778

Woodward, Josiah, Albany, N.Y., 85, #16551

Woodward, Nancy, Ga., 133, #671

Woodwell, Gideon, c/o, Mass., 29, #14880

Woodwell, Gidion, —, 80, #14880, card

Woodword, Benjamin, Richmond, Va., 56, #7261

Woodworth, Richard, Ohio, 90, #18774

Woodworth, Rosswell, w/o, Albany, N.Y., 107, #9196

Woodworth, Swift, a/o, Mich., 74, #13369

Woodworth, William, a/o, Albany, N.Y., 107, #8960

Woody, Martin, Richmond, Va.,
51, #5924

Wook, James E., Ky., 142,
#5236

Wooldridge, Josiah, w/o, Ky.,
56, #7381

Wooley, John, New York City,
133, #68

Woolsey, Alda, e/o, Albany,
N.Y., 92, #19695

Woolverton, Rachel, N.J., 73,
#12954

Woosley, Moses, Va., 80,
#14762

Wooster, Charles F., —, 131,
#8599, slip

Wooton, Silas P., Ohio, 99,
#3745

Word, Thomas, S.C., 46, #4827

Worden, Benjamin, c/o, Albany,
N.Y., 68, #10704

Worden, Benjamin, c/o,
Philadelphia, Pa., 121,
#7700

Worden, Billings, c/o, Albany,
N.Y., 116, #3277

Worden, Gilbert, Albany, N.Y.,
115, #2917, card

Workman, Peter, Knoxville,
Tenn., 70, #11124

Worley, William, w/o, N.C.
Militia, 86, #17097

Wormwood, Mathias, c/o,
Albany, N.Y., 55, #6948

Wormwood, Matthias, c/o,
Albany, N.Y., 100, #4408

Wornal, Charlotte, c/o,
Richmond, Va., 137, #3905

Wort, John, w/o, Philadelphia,
Pa., 79, #14630

Worthen, Judith, c/o, Maine, 98,
#2877

Wray, Henry, Richmond, Va.,
55, #7075

Wright, Aaron, c/o, Albany,
N.Y., 116, #3812

Wright, Ann, Md., 65, #10030

Wright, Asa, Albany, N.Y., 99,
#3553

Wright, Asa, Bellows Falls, Vt.,
29, #5319

Wright, Asa, S.C., 98, #2928

Wright, Asa, Windsor, Vt., 49,
#5319, card

Wright, Asa, a/o, Bellows Falls,
Vt., 50, #5827

Wright, Benjamin, Windsor, Vt.,
99, #3382

Wright, Benjamin, a/o,
Montpelier, Vt., 29, #3382

Wright, Betsey, Richmond, Va.,
71, #12377

Wright, Bolling, S.C., 59,
#8170

Wright, Bolling, S.C., 89,
#18158

Wright, Charity, e/o, New York
City, 109, #10406

Wright, Daniel, Huntsville, Ala.,
62, #8720

Wright, Elijah, c/o, Ky., 121,
#7148

Wright, Henry, Albany, N.Y.,
107, #9104

Wright, Henry, Albany, N.Y.,
96, #1837

Wright, Isaac, Mass., 131,
#8805

Wright, Isaiah, c/o, New York
City, 116, #3434

Wright, James, Ill., 45, #4550

Wright, James, Ill., 57, #7664

Wright, James, Ill., 73, #12771

Wright, James, Ill., 91, #19490, card

Wright, James H., g/o, Va., 117, #3833

Wright, Janet, Ky., 48, #5096

Wright, Jeremiah, Albany, N.Y., 63, #9041

Wright, John, New York City, 29, #600

Wright, John, Richmond, Va., 29, #13678

Wright, John, a/o, Richmond, Va., 95, #784

Wright, Jonathan, Ky., 45, #4621

Wright, Judah, g/o c/o, Conn., 37, #F1820

Wright, Mabel, c/o, Conn., 36, #1196

Wright, Mary, c/o, Concord, N.H., 58, #7708

Wright, Robert, Ohio, 89, #18231

Wright, Robert, Va., 88, #17748

Wright, Robt., Richmond, Va., 53, #6460

Wright, Silas, New York City, 52, #6142

Wright, Simeon, Conn., 36, #434

Wright, Thomas, a/o, Va., 86, #16768

Wright, William, Ind., 29, #4845

Wright, William, Ind., 48, #5042

Wright, William, Ind., 52, #6136

Wright, William, Ind., 46, #4845, card

Wright, Erastus, Ill., 89, #18535, card

Wrisley, Samuel, Conn., 36, #1024

Wyatt, John, Mo., 48, #5179

Wyatt, Mary, Richmond, Va., 71, #12233

Wyatt, Mary, Richmond, Va., 106, #8658

Wyatt, Mary, Richmond, Va., 99, #3300

Wyckoff, Samuel, Ohio, 64, #9605

Wylie, Francis, S.C., 40, #3292

Wylie, James, Boston, Mass., 117, #3982

Wyllis, Orren, Ind., 45, #442-

Wyllis, Orren, w/o, Ind., 122, #8266

Wyllis, Orren, Ind., 52, #6325

Wyllis, Owen, Ind., 58, #7911

Wyllys, Oliver St. John, Conn., 36, #59

Wyman, Dorcas, Bellows Falls, Vt., 63, #8967

Y

Yancey, Fanny, Va., 67, #10559

Yancey, Lewis, Ga., 50, #5590

Yancy, Lewis, w/o, Ga., 131, #8413

Yaple, John Nicholas, Albany, N.Y., 81, #15043

Yaple, John Nicholas, Albany, N.Y., 81, #15090

Yapple, John N., New York City, 107, #9625

Yarboro Sr., Henry, Jackson, Tenn., 78, #14479

Yarboro Sr., Henry, Jackson, Tenn., 39, #3145

Yarboro Sr., Henry, Jackson, Tenn., 48, #5150

Yarborough, Davis, Nashville,
Tenn., 75, #13443
Yarborough, Davis, Nashville,
Tenn., 100, #4113, card
Yarborough, Davis, W. Tenn.,
46, #4704
Yarbro, Henry, Jackson, Tenn.,
74, #13299
Yarden, John, e/o, Albany, N.Y.,
87, #17416
Yates, Jemima, N.C., 94, #344
Yates, Jemima, a/o, N.C., 122,
#8291
Yates, John, Va., 103, #6445,
card
Yeargan, Thomas, e/o,
Fayetteville, N.C., 127,
#4947
Yeates, John, a/o, Richmond,
Va., 29, #6445
Yeats, Benjamin, Ohio, 64,
#9290
Yerrington, John, Iowa, 141,
#3434
Yoho, Henry, Wheeling, Va.,
45, #4593
Yontz, Maria B., a/o, Richmond,
Va., 112, #820
Yorden, Nicholas, w/o, Albany,
N.Y., 80, #14809
York, Private Aaron, a/o w/o,
Tenn. Militia, 106, #8520
York, Allan, Conn., 36, #1535
York, Anna, Conn., 36, #622
York, Benjamin, N.H., 70,
#11117
York, Benjamin, a/o, N.H., 100,
#4017
York 2nd, Isaac, c/o, Maine,
109, #10467
York, Jeremiah, a/o, Ind., 92,
#19818

York, Matilda, Nashville, Tenn.,
110, #11032
Yorkshire, Thomas, a/o,
Richmond, Va., 29, #583
Youmans, Nathan, Albany, N.Y.,
86, #16918, card
Young, Charles, Pittsburgh, Pa.,
39, #2928
Young, Christian, —, 55,
#7036, card
Young, Clark, w/o, Vt., 91,
#19206
Young, Elia, R.I., 90, #18892
Young, Elias, a/o, R.I., 29,
#18912
Young, Elizabeth, c/o,
Philadelphia, Pa., 110,
#167
Young, Huldah, Richmond, Va.,
36A, #F1 V3
Young, Isaac, Pittsburgh, Pa.,
39, #3033
Young, Jacob W., a/o,
Nashville, Tenn., 105,
#8078
Young, James, N.J., 83,
#15891, card
Young, James, a/o, N.H., 68,
#10724
Young, James, a/o, S.C., 112,
#1186
Young, James, c/o, N.J., 29,
#15891
Young, John, Richmond, Va.,
56, #7320
Young, John, Va., 70, #12221
Young, John, c/o, Pittsburgh,
Pa., 113, #1317
Young, John, w/o, Richmond,
Va., 98, #2623
Young, John, w/o, Va., 123,
#9278

Young, Jonathan, c/o, N.Y.,
108, #9869
Young, Joseph, Mass., 106,
#8848
Young, Joseph R., Ill., 112,
#851
Young, Levi, w/o, S.C., 46,
#4783
Young, Lydia, a/o, New York
City, 64, #9643
Young, Mary, Ore., 141, #1362
Young, Mathias, w/o, Madison,
Ind., 55, #7026
Young, Morgan, Ind., 46, #4718
Young, Morgan, Ohio, 110,
#44, card
Young, Robert, w/o, N.H., 71,
#12422
Young, Samuel, c/o, Knoxville,
Tenn., 136, #2502
Young, Simon, Maine, 64,
#9577
Young, Stephen, Ill., 118,
#4906
Young, William, Ga., 131,
#8086
Young, William, Jackson,
Tenn., 91, #19213
Young 2d, William, c/o, Ky., 65,
#9873
Youngblood, Jacob, Ind., 54,
#6634
Youngblood, James, Mo., 140,
#922
Youngblood, John, Albany,
N.Y., 70, #11116, card
Yount, Polly, a/o, Ky., 29,
#4708
Youtz, Maria B., Richmond, Va.,
100, #3935
Yowell, William, w/o, Va., 109,
#10587

Yunt, Polly, —, 101, #4708,
slip

Z

Zachariah, Beers, Pittsburgh,
Pa., 55, #6909
Zachary, Griffin G., a/o, Tenn.,
109, #10897
Zanzinger, Willian C., Claim,
120, #6599
Zavedovski, Peter, Fla., 88,
#18135
Zea, Martin, w/o, Richmond,
Va., 55, #7038
Zeander, John C., Philadelphia,
Pa., 141, #2284
Zeigel, Henry, —, 140, #9930
V#5
Zeigler, Henry, —, 140, #9930
V#1
Zeigler, John, a/o, Md., 137,
#4256
Zimmerman, Elizabeth, Albany,
N.Y., 49, #5366
Zimmerman, Elizabeth, c/o,
Albany, N.Y., 111, #508
Zollinger, Peter, c/o, Md., 96,
#1378
Zornes, Andrew, Ky., 44, #4394
Zornes, Andrew, Ky., 45, #4493
Zumbro, Jacob, c/o,
Philadelphia, Pa., 116,
#3552
Zumwalt, Mary, Mo., 73,
#12729
Zurn, George, New York City,
140, #413

Other

Account of Monies Advanced
    Sundry Payers 20 Nov 1844,
    91, #19335
Accounts, Pension Agent,
    Cincinnati, Ohio, 94, #740
Accounts, Pension Agent,
    Philadelphia, Pa., 94, #756
Accounts, Pension Agent,
    Philadelphia, Pa., 95, #831
Bank of Burlington, Vermont, —
    , 58, #7882
Currys Co. of FL Militia at
    Mandairn, Florida in the
    year 1837, 44, #4203
Hartford, Conn, Branch Bank
    President, —, 30, #2054
Maggett's Co., S.C. soldiers, —,
    128, #4993, slip
Merchants & Manufacturers
    Bank, Pittsburgh, Pa., 81,
    #15037
Merchants & Manufacturers
    Bank, Pittsburgh, Pa., 81,
    #15068
Merchants & Manufacturers
    Bank, Pittsburgh, Pa., 83,
    #15621
Merchants & Manufacturers
    Bank, Pittsburgh, Pa., 83,
    #15647
Payrolls of Persons employed for
    the improvement of the
    Navigation of the Ohio
    River, —, 94, #20
Payrolls of Persons employed for
    the improvement of the
    Navigation of the Ohio
    River, —, 94, #17
State of Alabama, —, 98, #3080,
    slip

State of Illinois, Ill., 139,
    #8039, slip
State of New York, —, 121,
    #6834, slip
United States, Bank of the,
    Philadelphia, Pa., 100,
    #4405

Unknown with dates of death

—, d. 12Aug 1838, Ky., 91, #19368, card

—, d. 15 Apr 1842, D.C., 117, #4080, card

—, d. 15 Aug 1839, Knoxville, Tenn., 73, #12952

—, d. 16 Feb 1844, Nashville, Tenn., 94, #557, card

—, d. 17 Aug 1844, Albany, N.Y., 109, #10840

—, d. 18 Dec 1840, N.C., 79, #14579, card

—, d. 21 Jul 1837, Va., 49, #5313, card

—, d. 23 Mar 1821, Vt., 135, #1972, card

—, d. 24 Aug 1839, Ohio, 103, #6652, card

—, d. 25 Feb 1834, Va., 123, #9573, card

—, d. 27 Jun 1839, Pa., 95, #1349, card

—, d. 29 Aug 1849, N.Y., 111, #325, card

—, d. 29 May 1837, Va., 137, #3631, card

—, d. 29 Oct 1853, Va., 125, #2002, card

—, d. 5 Nov 1848, Ohio, 130, #8046, card

—, d. 6 Jan 1843, Miss., 96, #1415, card

—, d. 8 Jun 1839, S.C., 78, #14314, card

—, d. 8 Sept 1838, Mass., 63, #9102, card

—, d. 9 Feb 1840, —, 76, #13854, card

—, d. 9 Feb 1846, Pittsburgh, Pa., 122, #8728, card

—, Elizabeth, d. 11 May 1847, Knoxville, Tenn., 118, #4669, card

—, John, d. 18 Jan 1837, slip, 92, #19746

—, Joseph, d. 15 Aug 1846, Philadelphia, Pa., 119, #5134, card

—, Moses, d. 31 Aug 1833, N.J., 74, #13050, card

—, Robert, d. 26 Apr 1839, Pa., 89, #18495, card

—, Smith, 90, #18663, card

—, William, N.Y., 130, #7814, card

—, William, w/o, Albany, N.Y., 47, #5017, card